Cognitive Psychology
and Its Implications

Cognitive Psychology and Its Implications

Ninth Edition

John R. Anderson

Carnegie Mellon University

worth publishers
Macmillan Learning

New York

Senior Vice President, Content Strategy: Charles Linsmeier
Program Director, Social Sciences: Shani Fisher
Executive Program Manager: Christine Cardone
Program Editor: Sarah Berger
Developmental Editor: Len Neufeld
Assistant Editor: Dorothy Tomasini
Marketing Manager: Katherine Nurre
Marketing Assistant: Steven Huang
Media Editor: Stefani Wallace
Director, Content Management Enhancement: Tracey Kuehn
Senior Managing Editor: Lisa Kinne
Senior Content Project Manager: Kerry O'Shaughnessy
Production Supervisor: Robert Cherry
Lead Media Project Manager: Joseph Tomasso
Senior Workflow Project Manager: Paul Rohloff
Permissions Manager: Jennifer MacMillan
Photo Researcher: Brittani Morgan, Lumina Datamatics, Inc.
Permissions Associate: Michael McCarty
Director of Design, Content Management: Diana Blume
Design Services Manager: Natasha Wolfe
Cover Designer: John Callahan
Interior Design: Tamara Newnam
Art Manager: Matthew McAdams
Composition: Lumina Datamatics, Inc.
Printing and Binding: LSC Communications
Cover, Title Page, and Chapter Opener Photo: ImagesofIndia/Shutterstock

Library of Congress Control Number: 2019950029

ISBN-13: 978-1-319-06711-3
ISBN-10: 1-319-06711-5

1 2 3 4 5 6   24 23 22 21 20 19

Worth Publishers
One New York Plaza
Suite 4600
New York, NY 10004-1562
www.macmillanlearning.com

About the Author

JOHN ROBERT ANDERSON is Richard King Mellon Professor of Psychology and Computer Science at Carnegie Mellon University. He is known for developing ACT-R, the most widely used cognitive architecture in cognitive science. Anderson was also an early leader in research on intelligent tutoring systems: Computer systems based on his cognitive tutors currently teach mathematics to about 500,000 children in U.S. schools. He has served as president of the Cognitive Science Society and has been elected to the American Academy of Arts and Sciences, the National Academy of Sciences, and the American Philosophical Society. He has received numerous scientific awards, including the American Psychological Association's Distinguished Scientific Career Award, the David E. Rumelhart Prize for Contributions to the Formal Analysis of Human Cognition, the inaugural Dr. A. H. Heineken Prize for Cognitive Science, and the Atkinson Prize in Psychological and Cognitive Science from the National Academy of Sciences.

To Gordon Bower for 50 years of inspiration

Brief Contents

Contents

Preface

Writing this preface is an occasion to reflect on where the field of cognitive psychology has been, where it is, where it is going, and how all this is manifested in the ninth edition of *Cognitive Psychology and Its Implications*. The figure below provides one measure of how research over the years has served to shape my conception of cognitive psychology—a conception that I think is shared by many researchers in the field. The figure shows the number of works cited in this textbook that were published in each of the last 100 years. I have not felt the need to throw out references to classic studies that still serve their purpose, and so the figure partially reflects four periods in the evolution of cognitive psychology:

1. Before the end of World War II, behaviorism dominated psychology and there was relatively little interest in human cognition. The few citations to papers published in this period are mainly references to classic studies that still serve their purpose.

2. After 1950, the postwar generation of researchers broke the behaviorist grip on psychology and started the cognitive revolution. The growing number of citations during this time reflects the rise of a new way of studying and understanding the human mind.

3. At about the time when the first edition of this textbook was published, in 1980, the framework that the pioneers had established was there for

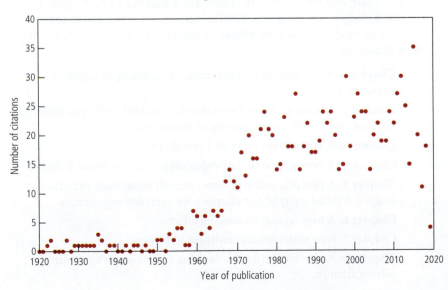

Citations to Works Published in Each Year, 1920–2019. Cognition-related research lay dormant until the middle of the twentieth century and then expanded enormously, with the coming of the cognitive revolution. The graph shows that this book contains a total of about 20 citations of works published in the years 1910–1949, compared with a total of about 1,000 citations of works published since 1950.

me to start with, and I was able to organize it into the coherent structure that appeared in the first edition. Starting in 1980 the number of citations basically levels off.

4. A major development in the field that really began to establish itself in the 1990s is hidden beneath the relatively stable level of citations in the figure. Early research had focused on behavioral measures because studying what was going on in the human brain seemed ethically impossible. However, new techniques in neural imaging arose in the 1990s that allowed us to relate early behavioral research to brain activity. This neuroscience research has been complemented by cognitive research on animals, particularly primates.

While it is easy to characterize how the field of cognitive psychology has gotten to where it is today, it is a challenge to see where it is going. There are a number of developments in the field (described in this new edition of the text) that make its future uncertain: The field is rethinking the question of whether it wants to be a science of the brain or a science of the mind and is trying to determine how these two goals relate to one another. New developments in artificial intelligence are changing both the framework in which we think about human intelligence and the tools for studying it. The field is debating what the best statistical and research methodologies are for uncovering reliable and important findings. While I am not sure what the future of cognitive psychology will be, the goal of this new edition is to capture the current state of the field.

New in the Ninth Edition

Writing a new edition always means making decisions about what to update, what to add, and what to delete. There are a number of new topics in this textbook, largely reflecting new developments in the field, but in some cases picking up on things that were missed in earlier editions. These are the major new additions:

Chapter 1: A new section on the increased centrality of cognitive neuroscience.

Chapter 2: New material on deep convolutional networks and their implications for our understanding of human vision.

Chapter 3: A new section on inattentional blindness.

Chapter 4: A new section on individual differences in visual imagery.

Chapter 5: A new discussion of how research using body cameras has enabled detailed study of our memory for everyday experiences.

Chapter 6: A new section on spacing effects.

Chapter 7: New material on eyewitness testimony.

Chapter 8: A new section on the decision to give up on a problem-solving attempt.

Chapter 9: A new section on the role of talent versus deliberate practice in the development of expertise.

Chapter 10: A new section on causal reasoning.

Chapter 11: A new section on choosing among multiple alternatives.

Chapter 14: New material on cognitive and neural correlates of intelligence.

In addition, the number of Implications boxes has nearly doubled, enabling me to place research in cognitive psychology in a larger context. These are the new Implications boxes:

Chapter 1: The Replicability Crisis

Chapter 2: Developments in Face-Recognition Software

Chapter 3: Cell Phones and Distraction

Chapter 4: Spatial Skills and STEM Education

Chapter 7: Is Forgetting Adaptive?

Chapter 8: When Humans Are Better at Solving Problems Than Computers

Chapter 11: What Can We Believe with High Confidence?

Chapter 12: Does Bilingualism Confer a Cognitive Advantage?

Chapter 13: Nonverbal Communication

Chapter 14: Is There a Relationship Between Age and Job Performance?

The Structure of This Book: A Note to Instructors

Instructors will use this textbook in their own ways, but when I teach from this book, I impose the following structure on it:

- The first chapter prepares students for understanding subsequent chapters, and the last chapter reflects on how all the pieces fit together in our picture of human cognition and intelligence.

- The meat of the textbook is the middle 12 chapters, which naturally organize themselves into 6 thematic pairs: perception and attention (Chapters 2 and 3), knowledge representation (Chapters 4 and 5), memory (Chapters 6 and 7), problem solving (Chapters 8 and 9), reasoning and decision making (Chapters 10 and 11), and language (Chapters 12 and 13).

- There is a major break between the first three pairs and the last three pairs. As I tell my class at that point: "Most of what we have discussed up to this point is true of all primates. Most of what we are going to talk about now is only true of humans."

Teaching and Learning Resources

Instructor resources accompanying this ninth edition of *Cognitive Psychology and Its Implications* include an instructor's resource manual, a computerized test bank, lecture slides, and illustration slides (all slides can be used as they are or customized to fit course needs).

- The **instructor's resource manual** features a chapter summary for each text chapter, highlighting key concepts and research studies; a list of learning objectives; online resources; and suggested readings, videos, and in-class discussion prompts. Resources are organized by topic, based on the chapter section headings.

- The **test bank** contains a mix of 100 essay, multiple choice, and short answer questions for each chapter. All questions are keyed to the American Psychological Association's goals for the undergraduate psychology major and Bloom's taxonomy. There are a wide variety of applied, conceptual, and factual questions, and each question is keyed to the topic and to the page in the text where the answer can be found.

- The **lecture slides** focus on key concepts and themes from the text and feature tables, graphs, and figures.

- The **illustration slides** include all the figures, photos, and tables featured in the text.

Acknowledgments

I appreciate the efforts of my editor Sarah Berger in organizing the reviews that provided much guidance on the needed revisions and her efforts in organizing the many aspects of ushering a new edition into publication. I appreciate the hard work of the developmental editor, Len Neufeld. This is the second edition he has worked on, and each time the book is again better in terms of getting the material across in an understandable and accurate form.

In addition to Sarah Berger and Len Neufeld, I also acknowledge the assistance of the following people from Worth Publishers: Kerry O'Shaughnessy, Senior Content Project Manager; Dorothy Tomasini, Assistant Editor; Matt McAdams, Art Manager; Paul Rohloff, Senior Workflow Project Manager; Bob Cherry, Production Supervisor; Sivaram Velayudham, Project Manager (at Lumina Datamatics); Jennifer MacMillan, Permissions Manager; Brittani Morgan Grimes, Photo Researcher; Michael McCarty, Permissions Associate; Stefani Wallace, Media Editor; Natasha Wolfe, Design Services Manager; and John Callahan and Tamara Newnam, who designed the cover and the interior, respectively.

I am grateful for the many comments and suggestions of the reviewers of this ninth edition: Patrick Carolan, Saint Mary's University; Damon Corgiat, Westminster University; Benjamin A. Guenther, University of Maine; William

L. Hathaway, Regent University; Meagan Lentz, Rivier University; Srinivasan Rajan Mahadevan, University of Tennessee, Knoxville; George Seror III, University of Houston, Downtown; Lael Schooler, Syracuse University; and Myeong-Ho Sohn, George Washington University.

I would also like to thank the people who read the first eight editions of my book, because much of their earlier influence remains: Chris Allan, Erik Altman, Nancy Alvarado, Jim Anderson, Walter Beagley, James Beale, Irv Biederman, Liz Bjork, Stephen Blessing, Lyle Bourne, John Bransford, Bruce Britton, Tracy Brown, Gregory Burton, Robert Calfee, Kyle Cave, Pat Carpenter, Bill Chase, Nick Chater, Micki Chi, Chung-Yiu Peter Chiu, Bill Clancy, Chuck Clifton, Lynne Cooper, Gus Craik, Bob Crowder, Ann Devlin, Mike Dodd, Thomas Donnelly, David Elmes, K. Anders Ericsson, Jonathan Evans, Martha Farah, Ronald Finke, Ira Fischler, Susan Fiske, Ellen Gagné, Michael Gazzaniga, Rochel Gelman, Barbara Greene, Alyse Hachey, Dorothea Halpert, Lynn Hasher, Evan Heit, Arturo Hernandez, Louna Hernandez-Jarvis, Robert Hines, Geoff Hinton, Kathy Hirsh-Pasek, Robert Hoffman, Martha Hubertz, Lumei Hui, Buz Hunt, Earl Hunt, Laree Huntsman, Lynn Hyah, Daniel Jacobson, Andrew Johnson, Philip Johnson-Laird, Marcel Just, Stephen Keele, Walter Kintsch, Dave Klahr, Steve Kosslyn, Al Lesgold, Clayton Lewis, Beth Loftus, Marsha Lovett, Maryellen MacDonald, Brian MacWhinney, Dominic Massaro, Jay McClelland, Michael McGuire, Karen J. Mitchell, John D. Murray, Al Newell, E. Slater Newman, Don Norman, Mike Oaksford, Gary Olson, Allan Paivio, Thomas Palmeri, Jacqueline Parke, Nancy Pennington, Jane Perlmutter, Peter Polson, Jim Pomerantz, Mike Posner, David Neil Rapp, Roger Ratcliff, Lynne Reder, Steve Reed, Russ Revlin, Phillip Rice, Lance Rips, Roddy Roediger, Daniel Schacter, Jay Schumacher, Christian Schunn, Miriam Schustack, Terry Sejnowski, Bob Siegler, Murray Singer, Scott Slotnick, Ed Smith, Kathy Spoehr, Bob Sternberg, Niels Taatgen, Roman Taraban, Charles Tatum, Joseph Thompson, Dave Tieman, Tom Trabasso, Peter Vishton, Henry Wall, Charles A. Weaver, Patricia de Winstanley, Larry Wood, Maria Zaragoza, and Xiaowei Zhao.

The Science of Cognition

Our species is called *Homo sapiens,* or "human, the wise," reflecting the general belief that our superior thought processes are what distinguish us from other animals. Today we all know that the brain is the organ of the human mind, but the connection between the brain and the mind was not always known. For instance, in a colossal misassociation, the Greek philosopher Aristotle localized the mind in the heart. He thought the function of the brain was to cool the blood. **Cognitive psychology** is the science of how the mind is organized to produce intelligent thought and how the mind is realized in the brain.

This chapter introduces fundamental concepts that set the stage for the rest of the book by addressing the following questions:

- Why do people study cognitive psychology?
- Where and when did cognitive psychology originate?
- How is the mind realized in the body?

    How do the cells in the brain process information?

    What parts of the brain are responsible for different functions?

    What are the methods for studying the brain?

Motivations for Studying Cognitive Psychology

Intellectual Curiosity

As with any scientific inquiry, the thirst for knowledge provides much of the impetus to study cognitive psychology. In this respect, the cognitive psychologist is like the tinkerer who wants to know how a clock works. The human mind is particularly fascinating: It displays a remarkable intelligence and ability to adapt. Yet we are often unaware of the extraordinary aspects of human cognition. Just as when watching a live broadcast of a distant news event we rarely consider the sophisticated technologies that make the broadcast possible, we also rarely think about the sophisticated mental processes that enable us to understand that news event. Cognitive psychologists strive to understand the mechanisms that make such intellectual sophistication possible.

The inner workings of the human mind are far more intricate than the most complicated systems of modern technology. For over half a century, researchers in the field of **artificial intelligence (AI)** have been attempting to develop programs that will enable computers to display intelligent behavior. There have been some notable successes, such as IBM's Watson (Ferrucci et al., 2010), which defeated human contestants on *Jeopardy* in 2011, and DeepMind's AlphaGo program (Silver et al., 2017), which beat the world champion Go player in 2017. Still, these are specialized programs, and no artificial intelligence system has yet come forward that matches humans in generalized **intelligence,** with human flexibility in recalling facts, solving problems, reasoning, learning, and using language.

There does not appear to be anything magical about human intelligence that would make it impossible to model in a computer. Scientific discovery, for instance, is often thought of as the ultimate accomplishment of human intelligence: Scientists supposedly make great leaps of intuition to explain extremely puzzling sets of data. Formulating a novel scientific theory is supposed to require both great creativity and special deductive powers. But is this actually the case? Herbert Simon, who won the 1978 Nobel Prize for his theoretical work in economics, spent the last 40 years of his life studying cognitive psychology. Among other things, he focused on the intellectual accomplishments involved in "doing" science. He and his colleagues (Langley, Simon, Bradshaw, & Zytkow, 1987) built computer programs to simulate the problem-solving activities involved in such scientific feats as Kepler's discovery of the laws of planetary motion and Ohm's development of his law for electric circuits. Simon also examined the processes involved in his own now-famous scientific discoveries (Simon, 1989). In all cases, he found that the methods of scientific discovery could be explained in terms of the basic cognitive processes that we study in cognitive psychology. He wrote that many of these activities are just well-understood problem-solving processes (see Chapters 8 and 9). He says:

> Moreover, the insight that is supposed to be required for such work as discovery turns out to be synonymous with the familiar process of recognition; and other terms commonly used in the discussion of creative work—such terms as "judgment," "creativity," or even "genius"—appear to be wholly dispensable or to be definable, as insight is, in terms of mundane and well-understood concepts. (Simon, 1989, p. 376)

In other words, a detailed look reveals that even what are often described as the brilliant results of human genius are produced by basic cognitive processes operating together in complex ways to produce those results.[1] Most of this book will be devoted to describing what we know about these basic processes.

> *Great feats of intelligence, such as scientific discovery, are the result of basic cognitive processes.*

[1] Weisberg (1986) comes to a similar conclusion.

Implications for Other Fields

Students and researchers interested in other areas of psychology or social science have another reason for following developments in cognitive psychology. The basic mechanisms governing human thought are important in understanding the types of behavior studied by other social sciences. For example, an appreciation of how humans think is important to understanding why certain thought malfunctions occur (clinical psychology), how people behave with other individuals or in groups (social psychology), how persuasion works (political science), how economic decisions are made (economics), why certain ways of organizing groups are more effective and stable than others (sociology), and why natural languages have certain features (linguistics). Cognitive psychology is thus the foundation on which other social sciences stand, in the same way that physics is the foundation for the other physical sciences.

Nonetheless, much social science has developed without grounding in cognitive psychology, for two related reasons. First, the field of cognitive psychology is relatively new, having really only begun in the 1950s. Second, researchers in other areas of social science have managed to find other ways to explain the phenomena in which they are interested. An interesting case in point is economics. Neoclassical economics, which dominated the last century, tried to predict the behavior of markets while completely ignoring the cognitive processes of individuals. It simply assumed that individuals behaved in ways to maximize their wealth. However, the recently developed field of behavioral economics acknowledges that the behavior of markets is affected by the flawed decision-making processes of individuals — for example, people are willing to pay more for something when they use a credit card than when they use cash (Simester & Drazen, 2001). In recognition of the importance of the psychology of decision making to economics, the cognitive psychologist Daniel Kahneman was awarded the Nobel Prize for economics in 2002.

> *Cognitive psychology is the foundation for many other areas of social science.*

Practical Applications

Practical applications of the field constitute another key incentive for the study of cognitive psychology (Groome & Eysenck, 2016). If we really understood how people acquire knowledge and intellectual skills and how they perform feats of intelligence, then we would be able to improve their intellectual training and performance accordingly.

While future applications of cognitive psychology hold great promise (Klatzky, 2009), there are a number of current successful applications. For instance, there has been a long history of research on the reliability of eyewitness testimony (e.g., Wells, Memon, & Penrod, 2006) that has led to guidelines for law enforcement personnel (U.S. Department of Justice, 1999). There have also been a number of applications of basic information processing to the design evaluations of various computer-based devices, such as modern flight management systems on aircraft (John, Patton, Gray, & Morrison, 2012). And there have been a number of applications to education, including reading instruction (Rayner, Foorman, Perfetti, Pesetsky, & Seidenberg, 2002; Seidenberg, 2013) and computer-based systems for teaching mathematics (Koedinger & Corbett, 2006). Cognitive psychology is also making important contributions to our understanding of brain disorders that reflect abnormal functioning, such as schizophrenia (Cohen & Servan-Schreiber, 1992) or autism (Dinstein et al., 2012; Just, Keller, & Kana, 2013).

At many points in this book, Implications boxes will reinforce the connections between research in cognitive psychology and our daily lives (see, for example, **Implications 1.1**).

> *The results from the study of cognitive psychology have practical applications in other fields and in our daily lives.*

Implications 1.1

What Does Cognitive Psychology Tell Us about How to Study Effectively?

Cognitive psychology has identified methods that enable humans to read and remember a textbook like this one. This research will be described in Chapters 6 and 13. The key idea is that it is crucial to identify the main points of each section of a text and to understand how these main points are organized. I have tried to help you do this by ending each section with a short summary sentence identifying its main point. I recommend that you use the following study technique to help you remember the material. This approach is a variant of the PQ4R (Preview, Question, Read, Reflect, Recite, Review) method discussed in Chapter 6.

1. Preview the chapter. Read the section headings and summary statements to get a general sense of where the chapter is going and how much material will be devoted to each topic. Try to understand each summary statement, and ask yourself whether this is something you already know or believe.

Then, for each section of the book, go through the following steps:

2. Make up a study question by looking at the section heading and thinking of a related question that you will try to answer while you read the text. For instance, for the section "Intellectual Curiosity," you might ask yourself, "What is there to be curious about in cognitive psychology?" This will give you an active goal to pursue while you read the section.

3. Read the section to understand it and answer your question. Try to relate what you are reading to situations in your own life. In the section "Intellectual Curiosity," for example, you might try to think of scientific discoveries you have read about that seemed to require creativity.

4. At the end of each section, read the summary sentence and ask yourself whether that is the main point you got out of the section and why it is the main point. Sometimes you may need to go back and reread some parts of the section.

Hanquan Chen/Getty Images

At the end of the chapter, engage in the following review process:

5. Go through the text, mentally reviewing the main points. Try to answer the questions you devised in step 2, plus any other questions that occur to you. Often, when preparing for an exam, it is a good idea to ask yourself what kind of exam questions you would make up for the chapter.

As we will learn in later chapters, such a study strategy improves one's memory of the text.

The History of Cognitive Psychology

Cognitive psychology today is a vigorous science producing many interesting discoveries. However, this productive phase was a long time coming, and it is important to understand the history of the field that led to its current form.

Early History

In Western civilization, interest in human cognition can be traced to the ancient Greeks. Plato and Aristotle, in their discussions of the nature and origin of knowledge, speculated about memory and thought. These early philosophical discussions eventually developed into a centuries-long debate between two positions: **empiricism,** which held that all knowledge comes from experience, and **nativism,** which held that children come into the world with a great deal of innate knowledge. The debate intensified in the 17th, 18th, and 19th centuries, with such British philosophers as Berkeley, Locke, Hume, and Mill arguing for the empiricist view and such continental philosophers as Descartes and Kant propounding the nativist view. Although these arguments were philosophical at their core, they frequently slipped into psychological speculations about human cognition. (For further discussion of the empiricist–nativist debate, see Chapter 14.)

During this long period of philosophical debate, sciences such as astronomy, physics, chemistry, and biology developed markedly. Curiously, however, it was not until the end of the 19th century that the scientific method was applied to the understanding of human cognition. Certainly, there were no technical or conceptual barriers to the scientific study of cognitive psychology earlier. In fact, many cognitive psychology experiments could have been performed and understood in the time of the ancient Greeks. But cognitive psychology, like many other sciences, suffered because of our egocentric, mystical, and confused attitudes about ourselves and our own nature, which made it seem inconceivable that the workings of the human mind could be subjected to scientific analysis. As a consequence, cognitive psychology as a science is less than 150 years old, and much of the first 100 years was spent freeing ourselves of the misconceptions that can arise when people engage in such an introverted enterprise as a scientific study of human cognition. It is a case of the mind studying itself.

> *Only in the last 150 years has it been realized that human cognition could be the subject of scientific study rather than philosophical speculation.*

Psychology in Germany: Focus on Introspective Observation

The date usually cited as the beginning of psychology as a science is 1879, when Wilhelm Wundt established the first psychology laboratory in Leipzig, Germany. Wundt's psychology was cognitive psychology (in contrast to other major divisions, such as comparative, clinical, or social psychology), although he had far-ranging views on many subjects. Wundt, his students, and many other early psychologists used a method of inquiry called **introspection,** in which highly trained observers reported the contents of their own consciousness under carefully controlled conditions. The basic assumption was that the workings of the mind should be open to self-observation. Drawing on the empiricism of the British philosophers, Wundt and others believed that very intense self-inspection would be able to identify the primitive experiences out of which thought arose. Thus, to develop a theory of cognition, a psychologist had only to explain the contents of introspective reports.

Let us consider a sample introspective experiment. Mayer and Orth (1901) had their participants perform a free-association task. The experimenters spoke a word to the participants and then measured the amount of time the participants took to generate responses to the word. Participants then reported all their conscious experiences from the moment of stimulus presentation until the moment of their response. To get a feeling for this method, try to come up with an association for each of the following words:

coat   book
dot   bowl

After each association, think about the contents of your consciousness during the period between reading the word and making your association.

In this experiment, many participants reported rather indescribable conscious experiences, not always seeming to involve sensations, images, or other concrete perceptions. This result started a debate over the issue of whether conscious experience could really be devoid of concrete content. As we will see in Chapters 4 and 5, modern cognitive psychology has made real progress on this issue, but not by using introspection.

> *At the turn of the 20th century, German psychologists used a method of inquiry called introspection to study the workings of the mind.*

Psychology in America: Focus on Behavior

Wundt's introspective psychology was not well accepted in America. Early American psychologists engaged in what they called "introspection," but it was not the intense analysis of the contents of the mind practiced by the Germans. Rather, it was largely an armchair avocation in which self-inspection was casual and reflective rather than intense and analytic. William James's *Principles of Psychology* (1890) reflects the best of this tradition, and many of the proposals in this work are still relevant today. The mood of American psychology was determined by the philosophical doctrines of pragmatism and functionalism. Many psychologists of the time were involved in education, and there was a demand for an "action oriented" psychology that was capable of practical application. The intellectual climate in America was not receptive to the psychology from

Germany that focused on such questions as whether or not the contents of consciousness were sensory.

One of the important figures of early American scientific psychology was Edward Thorndike, who developed a theory of learning that was directly applicable to classrooms. Thorndike was interested in such basic problems as the effects of reward and punishment on the rate of learning. To him, conscious experience was just excess baggage that could be largely ignored. Many of his experiments were done on animals, research that involved fewer ethical constraints than research on humans. Thorndike was probably just as happy that such participants could not introspect.

While introspection was being ignored at the turn of the century in America, it was getting into trouble on the continent. Various laboratories were reporting different types of introspections — each type matching the theory of the particular laboratory from which it emanated. It was becoming clear that introspection did not give one a clear window into the workings of the mind. Much that was important in cognitive functioning was not open to conscious experience. These two factors — the "irrelevance" of the introspective method and its apparent contradictions — laid the groundwork for the great behaviorist revolution in American psychology that occurred around 1920. John Watson and other behaviorists led a fierce attack not only on introspectionism but also on any attempt to develop a theory of mental operations. **Behaviorism** held that psychology was to be entirely concerned with external behavior and was not to try to analyze the workings of the mind that underlay this behavior:

> Behaviorism claims that consciousness is neither a definite nor a usable concept. The Behaviorist, who has been trained always as an experimentalist, holds further that belief in the existence of consciousness goes back to the ancient days of superstition and magic. (Watson, 1930, p. 2)

> The Behaviorist began his own formulation of the problem of psychology by sweeping aside all medieval conceptions. He dropped from his scientific vocabulary all subjective terms such as sensation, perception, image, desire, purpose, and even thinking and emotion as they were subjectively defined. (Watson, 1930, pp. 5–6)

The behaviorist program and the issues it spawned pushed research on cognition into the background of American psychology. The rat supplanted the human as the principal laboratory subject, and psychology turned to finding out what could be learned by studying animal learning and motivation. Quite a bit was discovered, but little was of direct relevance to cognitive psychology. Perhaps the most important lasting contribution of behaviorism is a set of sophisticated and rigorous techniques and principles for experimental study in all fields of psychology, including cognitive psychology.

Behaviorism was not as dominant in Europe. Psychologists such as Frederick Bartlett in England, Alexander Luria in the Soviet Union, and Jean Piaget in Switzerland were pursuing ideas that are still important in modern cognitive psychology. Cognitive psychology was an active research topic in Germany, but much of it was lost in the Nazi turmoil. A number of German psychologists immigrated to America and brought **Gestalt psychology** with them. Gestalt psychology claimed that the activity of the brain and the mind was more than the sum of its parts. This conflicted with the introspectionist program in Germany that tried to analyze conscious thought into its parts. In America, Gestalt psychologists found themselves in conflict with behaviorism for being concerned with mental structure at all. In America, Gestalt psychologists received the most attention for their claims about animal learning, and they were the standard targets for the behaviorist critiques, although some Gestalt psychologists became quite prominent in the field. For example, the Gestalt psychologist Wolfgang Kohler was elected to the presidency of the American Psychological Association. Although not a Gestalt psychologist, Edward Tolman was an American psychologist who did his research on animal learning and anticipated many ideas of modern cognitive psychology. Tolman's ideas were also frequently the target for criticism by the dominant behaviorist psychologists, although his work was harder to dismiss because he spoke the language of behaviorism.

In retrospect, it is hard to understand how American behaviorists could have taken such an anti-mental stand and clung to it for so long. The unreliability of introspection did not mean that a theory of internal mental structure and process could not be developed, only that other methods were required (consider the analogy with physics, for example, where a theory of atomic structure was developed, although that structure could only be inferred, not directly observed). A theory of internal structure makes understanding human beings much easier, and the successes of modern cognitive psychology show that understanding mental structures and processes is critical to understanding human cognition.

In both the introspectionist and behaviorist programs, we see the human mind struggling with the effort to understand itself. The introspectionists held a naïve belief in the power of self-observation. The behaviorists were so afraid of falling prey to subjective fallacies that they refused to let themselves think about mental processes. Current cognitive psychologists seem to be much more at ease with their subject matter. They have a relatively detached attitude toward human cognition and approach it much as they would any other complex system.

> *Behaviorism, which dominated American psychology in the first half of the 20th century, rejected the analysis of the workings of the mind to explain behavior.*

The Cognitive Revolution: AI, Information Theory, and Linguistics

Cognitive psychology as we know it today took form in the two decades between 1950 and 1970, in the **cognitive revolution** that overthrew behaviorism. Three main influences account for its modern development. The first was research on human performance, which was given a great boost during World War II when governments badly needed practical information about how to train soldiers to use sophisticated equipment and how to deal with problems such as the break-down of attention under stress. Behaviorism offered no help with such practical issues. Although the work during the war had a very practical bent, the issues it raised stayed with psychologists when they went back to their academic laboratories after the war. The work of the British psychologist Donald Broadbent at the Applied Psychology Research Unit in Cambridge was probably the most influential in integrating ideas from human performance research with new ideas that were developing in an area called *information theory*. Information theory is an abstract way of analyzing the processing of information. Broadbent and other psychologists, such as George Miller, Fred Attneave, and Wendell Garner, initially developed these ideas with respect to perception and attention, but such analyses soon pervaded all of cognitive psychology.

The second influence, which was closely related to the development of the information-processing approach, was a series of developments in computer science, particularly AI, which tries to get computers to behave intelligently. Allen Newell and Herbert Simon, both at Carnegie Mellon University, spent most of their lives educating cognitive psychologists about the implications of AI (and educating workers in AI about the implications of cognitive psychology). Although the direct influence of AI-based theories on cognitive psychology has always been minimal, its indirect influence has been enormous. A host of concepts have been taken from computer science and used in psychological theories. Probably more important, observing how we can analyze the intelligent behavior of a machine has largely liberated us from our inhibitions and misconceptions about analyzing our own intelligence.

The third influence on cognitive psychology was **linguistics,** the study of language (including the history, structure, acquisition, and use of language). In the 1950s Noam Chomsky, a linguist at the Massachusetts Institute of Technology, began to develop a new mode of analyzing the structure of language. His work showed that language was much more complex than had previously been believed and that many of the prevailing behaviorist formulations were incapable of explaining these complexities. Chomsky's linguistic analyses proved critical in enabling cognitive psychologists to fight off the prevailing behaviorist conceptions. George Miller, at Harvard University in the 1950s and early 1960s, was instrumental in bringing these linguistic analyses to the attention of psychologists and in identifying new ways of studying the psychology of language.

Cognitive psychology has grown rapidly since the 1950s. A milestone was the publication of Ulric Neisser's *Cognitive Psychology* in 1967, which gave a new legitimacy to the field. The book consisted of 6 chapters on perception and attention and 4 chapters on language, memory, and thought. Neisser's chapter division contrasts sharply with this book's, which has only 2 chapters on perception and attention and 10 on language, memory, and thought. My chapter division reflects a growing emphasis on higher mental processes. Following Neisser's work, another important event was the launch of the journal *Cognitive Psychology* in 1970. This journal has done much to define the field.

In the 1970s, a related new field called **cognitive science** emerged; it attempts to integrate research efforts from psychology, philosophy, linguistics, neuroscience, and AI. This field can be dated from the appearance of the journal *Cognitive Science* in 1976, which is the main publication of the Cognitive Science Society. The fields of cognitive psychology and cognitive science overlap. Speaking generally, cognitive science makes greater use of such methods as logical analysis and the computer simulation of cognitive processes, whereas cognitive psychology relies heavily on experimental techniques for studying behavior that grew out of the behaviorist era. This book draws on all methods but makes most use of cognitive psychology's experimental methodology.

> *During the 1950s–1970s, cognitive psychology broke away from behaviorism in response to developments in information theory, AI, and linguistics.*

Information-Processing Analyses

The factors described in the previous sections of this chapter have converged in the **information-processing approach** to studying human cognition, and this has become the dominant approach in cognitive psychology. The information-processing approach attempts to analyze cognition as a set of steps for processing an abstract entity called "information." Probably the best way to explain this approach is to describe a classic example of it. (See **Implications 1.2** for a general discussion of the credibility of research results in psychology and other fields.)

In a very influential paper published in 1966, Saul Sternberg described an experimental task and proposed a theoretical account of what people were doing in that task. In what has come to be called the **Sternberg paradigm,** participants were shown a memory set consisting of a small number of digits, such as "3 9 7." Then they were shown a probe digit and asked whether it was in the memory set, and they had to answer as quickly as possible. For example, 9 would be a positive probe for the "3 9 7" set; 6 would be a negative probe. Sternberg varied the number of digits in the memory set from 1 to 6 and measured how quickly participants could make this judgment. **Figure 1.1** shows his results as a function of the size of the memory set. Data are plotted separately

Figure 1.1 The Sternberg Paradigm: Recognition Time as a Function of Memory Set Size. The time needed to recognize a probe digit as a target (i.e., in the memory set) or as a foil (i.e., not in the memory set) increases with the number of items in the memory set. The straight line represents the linear function that fits the data best.

(Data from Sternberg, 1969.)

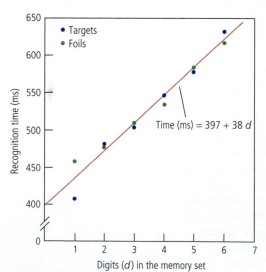

$$\text{Time (ms)} = 397 + 38\,d$$

Implications 1.2

The Replicability Crisis

This book will largely report results and conclusions based on experiments that look for effects that are different across conditions. For instance, Figure 1.1 shows increased response times in conditions where subjects have a larger set of items to remember. However, this is a result averaged from multiple trials and many subjects. Comparison of a particular pair of trials might show the reverse of the average trend — that is, a trial with a smaller set size might have a longer response time. There are many reasons for trial-to-trial variability, such as drift of attention and noise in the perceptual system. Psychology has developed statistical standards for determining if apparent effects in average data from an experiment are likely to be found reliably if the experiment were repeated. It is common to estimate what is called a **p-value,** the probability that the result would be obtained by chance. A typical threshold for believing an effect is that it have a p-value of less than .05. This would mean that there is a 95% chance that the effect is real.

However, psychology and other fields (including economics and medicine) are suffering what has been called a **replicability crisis,** meaning that experimental results reported with p-values below .05 are not replicated when the experiments are repeated. One study examined 42 cognitive psychology experiments and found that only half (21) replicated (Open Science, 2015). There are many reasons why the results of a study might not be replicated. It is often impossible to reproduce the exact conditions of the original experiment and the same population of participants. There is also a bias in which papers get published. Experiments that fail to find effects are often considered not important enough to be published. Also, journals like to publish papers with surprising, and therefore newsworthy, results, and this often pushes the journals to accept papers that they might otherwise reject. This point is supported by a study that found that researchers could predict which papers in the prestigious journals *Science* and *Nature*

reported results that would not replicate (Camerer et al., 2018). The non-replicating results in those papers violated the researchers' sense of what was likely to be found, but often the results were newsworthy because they had great social potential — for instance, that reading literary fiction makes one more sensitive to other people's perspective.

Fortunately, much of what is reported in this textbook — like the effect of set size in Figure 1.1 — has been replicated many times and seems firmly established. However, even if replicable, such well-established effects can be nuanced. For instance, while there is little question that response time increases with set size, there has been much controversy about whether it is a linear effect as Sternberg claimed and whether it is a result of the comparison process Sternberg described. In many places in this text we will describe alternative perspectives on established effects. We will also note the cases where there is some question about whether important effects can be replicated.

for positive probes, or targets, and for negative probes, or foils. Participants could make these judgments quite quickly; latencies varied from about 400 to 600 milliseconds (ms) — a millisecond is a thousandth of a second. Sternberg found a nearly linear relationship between judgment time and the size of the memory set. As shown in Figure 1.1, each one-digit increase in the size of the memory set resulted in an increase of about 38 ms in recognition time.

Sternberg's account of how participants made these judgments was very influential; it exemplified what an abstract information-processing theory is like. As illustrated in **Figure 1.2**, Sternberg assumed that when participants saw a probe stimulus such as a 9, they went through a series of information-processing stages. First the stimulus was encoded (i.e., perceived). Then the stimulus was compared to each digit in the memory set. To account for the slope of the line in Figure 1.1, Sternberg assumed that it took 38 ms to

Figure 1.2 The Sternberg Paradigm: Information-Processing Stages. Sternberg's analysis of the sequence of information-processing stages in his task.

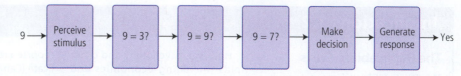

complete each one of these comparisons. Then the participant had to decide on a response and finally generate it. Sternberg showed that different variables would influence each of these information-processing stages. Thus, if he degraded the stimulus quality by making the probe harder to read, participants took longer to make their judgments. This did not affect the slope of the Figure 1.1 line, however, because it involved only the stage of stimulus perception in Figure 1.2. Similarly, if he biased participants to say yes or no, the decision-making stage, but not other stages, was affected.

It is worth noting the ways in which Sternberg's theory exemplifies a classic abstract information-processing account:

1. Information processing is discussed without any reference to the brain.
2. The processing of the information has a highly symbolic character. For example, his theory describes the human system as comparing the symbol 9 against the symbol 3, without considering how these symbols might be represented in the brain.
3. The processing of information can be compared to the way computers process information. In fact, Sternberg used the computer metaphor to explain why the comparison did not stop with the "9 = 9?" comparison in Figure 1.2. He noted that this sort of exhaustive comparison process was used by computers of that time.
4. The measurement of time to make a judgment is a critical variable, because the information processing is conceived to be taking place in discrete stages. Flowcharts such as the one in Figure 1.2 have been a very popular means of expressing the steps of information processing.

Each of these four features reflects a kind of narrowness in the classic information-processing approach to human cognition. Cognitive psychologists have gradually broadened their approach as they have begun to deal with more complex phenomena and as they have begun to pay more attention to the nature of information processing in the brain. For instance, this textbook has evolved over its editions to reflect this shift.

> *Information-processing analysis breaks a cognitive task down into a set of abstract information-processing steps.*

Cognitive Neuroscience

Over the centuries there has been a lot of debate about the possible relationship between the mind and the body. Many philosophers, such as René Descartes, have advocated a position called **dualism,** which posits that the mind and the body are separate kinds of entities. Although very few scientific psychologists believe in dualism, until recently many believed that brain activity was too obscure to provide a basis for understanding human cognition. Most of the research in cognitive psychology had relied on behavioral methods, and most of the theorizing was of the abstract information-processing sort. However, with the steady development of knowledge about the brain and methods for studying brain activity, barriers to understanding the mind by studying the brain are slowly being eliminated, and brain processes are now being considered in almost all analyses of human cognition. The field of **cognitive neuroscience** is devoted to the study of how cognition is realized in the brain (i.e., the neural basis of cognition), with exciting new findings even in the study of the most complex thought processes. The remainder of this chapter will be devoted to describing some of the neuroscience knowledge and methods that now inform the study of human cognition, enabling us to see with growing precision how cognition unfolds in the brain (for example, at the end of this chapter I will describe a study of the neural processes that are involved as one solves a mathematical equation).

Cognitive neuroscience is developing methods that enable us to understand more and more about the neural basis of cognition.

Information Processing: The Communicative Neurons

The brain is just one part of the nervous system, which also includes the various sensory systems that gather information from other parts of the body and the motor systems that control movement. In some cases, considerable information processing takes place via neurons outside the brain. From an information-processing point of view, neurons are the most important components of the nervous system.[2] A **neuron** is a cell that receives and transmits signals through electrochemical activity. The human brain contains approximately 100 billion neurons, each of which may have roughly the processing capability of a computer. A considerable fraction of these 100 billion neurons are active simultaneously and do much of their information processing through interactions with one another. Imagine the information-processing power in 100 billion interacting computers! However, there are many tasks, such as finding square roots, at which a simple calculator can outperform all 100 billion neurons. Comprehending the strengths and weaknesses of the human nervous system is a major goal in understanding the nature of human cognition.

---

[2] Neurons are by no means the majority of cells in the nervous system. There are many other cell types, such as glial cells, whose main function is thought to be supportive of the neurons.

The Neuron

Neurons come in a wide variety of shapes and sizes, depending on their exact location and function. (**Figure 1.3** illustrates some of this variety.) There is, however, a generally accepted notion of what the prototypical neuron is like, and individual neurons match up with this prototype to greater or lesser degrees. This prototype is illustrated in **Figure 1.4**. The main body of the neuron is called the *soma* (or *cell body*). Typically, the soma is 5 to 100 micrometers (μm) in diameter. Attached to the soma are short branches called **dendrites,** and extending from the soma is a long tube called the **axon**. Axons can vary in length from a few millimeters to a meter.

Axons provide the fixed paths by which neurons communicate with one another. The axon of one neuron extends toward the dendrites of other neurons. At its end, the axon branches into a large number of arborizations. Each arborization ends in terminal boutons, each of which almost makes contact with a dendrite of another neuron. The gap separating the terminal bouton and the dendrite is typically in the range of 10 to 50 nanometers (nm). This near contact between axon and dendrite is called a **synapse**. Typically, neurons communicate by releasing chemicals, called **neurotransmitters,** from the terminal bouton on one side of the synapse; these chemicals act on the membrane of the receptor dendrite to change its polarization, or electric potential. The inside of the membrane covering the entire neuron tends to be 70 millivolts (mV) more negative than the outside, due to the greater concentration of negative chemical ions inside and positive ions outside. The existence of a greater concentration of positive sodium ions on the outside

Figure 1.3 Some of the Variety of Neurons.
(a) pyramidal cell; (b) cerebellar Purkinje cell; (c) motor neuron; (d) sensory neuron.

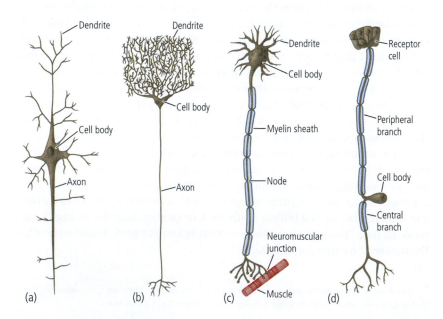

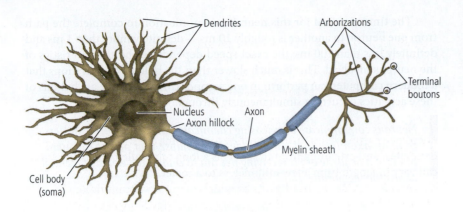

Figure 1.4 A Schematic Representation of a Typical Neuron.

of the membrane is particularly important to the functioning of the neuron. Depending on the nature of the neurotransmitter, the potential difference can decrease or increase. Synapses that release neurotransmitters that decrease the potential difference are called **excitatory synapses,** and those that increase the difference are called **inhibitory synapses**.

On average, the dendrites of a typical neuron form about 1,000 synapses with other neurons, and the terminal boutons of a typical neuron form synapses with about 1,000 other neurons. The change in electric potential due to any one synapse is rather small, but the individual excitatory and inhibitory effects will accumulate. If there is enough net excitatory input, the potential difference in the soma of the receiving neuron can drop sharply, and if the reduction in potential is large enough, a depolarization will occur at the axon hillock, where the axon joins the soma (see Figure 1.4). This depolarization is caused by a rush of positive sodium ions into the inside of the neuron. The inside of the neuron momentarily (for a millisecond) becomes more positive than the outside. This sudden change, called an **action potential** (or spike), will propagate down the axon. That is, the potential difference will suddenly and momentarily change down the axon. The rate at which this change travels can vary from 0.5 to 130 m/s, depending on the characteristics of the axon — such as the degree to which the axon is covered by a myelin sheath (the more myelination, the faster the transmission). When the nerve impulse (i.e., the action potential) reaches the end of the axon, it causes neurotransmitters to be released from the terminal boutons, thus continuing the cycle.

To review: Changes in electric potential accumulate on a cell body, reach a threshold, and cause an action potential to propagate down an axon. This pulse in turn causes neurotransmitters to be sent from the axon's terminal boutons to the dendrites of other neurons, causing changes in those neurons' membrane potential. This sequence is the core of neural information processing, yet intelligence arises from this simple system of interactions. The challenge for cognitive neuroscience is to understand how.

The time required for this neural communication to complete the path from one neuron to another is roughly 10 ms — definitely more than 1 ms and definitely less than 100 ms; the exact speed depends on the characteristics of the neurons involved. This is much slower than the billions of operations that a modern computer can perform in one second. However, there are billions of these activities occurring simultaneously throughout the brain.

> *Neurons communicate by releasing chemicals, called neurotransmitters, from an axon terminal on one side of a synapse that act on the membrane of a dendrite of the receiving neuron to change the electric potential across the membrane.*

Neural Representation of Information

Two quantities are particularly important to the representation of information in the brain. First, as we just saw, the membrane potential can be more or less negative. Second, the number of action potentials, or nerve impulses, an axon transmits per second, called its **rate of firing,** can vary from very few to upward of 100. The greater the rate of firing, the greater the effect the axon will have on the cells with which it synapses. We can contrast information representation in the brain with information representation in a computer, where individual memory cells, or bits, can have just one of two values — off (0) or on (1). A typical computer cell does not have the continuous variation of a typical neural cell.

We can think of a neuron as having an activation level that corresponds roughly to the firing rate on the axon or to the degree of depolarization on the membrane of the receiving neuron. Neurons interact by driving up the activation level of other neurons (excitation) or by driving down their activation level (inhibition). All neural information processing takes place in terms of these excitatory and inhibitory effects; they are what underlies human cognition.

How do neurons represent information? Evidence suggests that individual neurons respond to specific features of a stimulus. For instance, some neurons are most active when there is a line in the visual field at a particular angle (as described in Chapter 2), while other neurons respond to more complex sets of features. For instance, there are neurons in the monkey brain that appear to be most responsive to faces (Bruce, Desimone, & Gross, 1981; Desimone, Albright, Gross, & Bruce, 1984; Perrett, Rolls, & Caan, 1982). It is not possible, however, that single neurons encode all the concepts and shades of meaning we possess. Moreover, the firing of a single neuron cannot represent the complexity of structure in a face.

If a single neuron cannot represent the complexity of our cognition, how are complex concepts and experiences represented? How can the activity of neurons represent our concept of baseball; how can it result in our solution of an algebra problem; how can it result in our feeling of frustration? Similar questions can be asked of computer programs, which have been shown to be capable of answering questions about baseball, solving algebra problems, and displaying frustration. Where in the millions of off-and-on bits in a computer program does the concept of baseball lie? How does a change in a bit result in the solution of an algebra problem or in a feeling of frustration? However, these questions fail to see the forest for the trees. The concept of a sport, a problem solution, or an emotion occurs in large patterns of bit changes. Similarly, human cognition is achieved through large patterns of neural activity. For instance, in an early study using brain imaging (see the section "Neural Imaging Techniques" later in this chapter), Mazoyer et al. (1993) compared the brain activation of participants when they heard different kinds of speech. They found activity in more and more regions of the brain as participants went from hearing meaningless speech (i.e., speech in an unknown language) to hearing lists of words to hearing meaningful stories. This result indicates that our understanding of a meaningful story involves activity in many regions of the brain.

It is informative to think about how a computer stores information. Consider a simple case: the spelling of words. Most computers have codes by which individual patterns of binary values (1s and 0s) represent letters. **Table 1.1** illustrates the use of one coding scheme, called ASCII; the table shows a pattern of 0s and 1s that codes the words *COGNITIVE PSYCHOLOGY*.

TABLE 1.1 ASCII Coding* of the Words *COGNITIVE PSYCHOLOGY*

C	O	G	N	I	T	I	V	E
1	1	0	0	1	1	1	0	1
1	1	1	1	1	1	1	1	1
0	0	0	0	0	0	0	0	0
0	0	0	0	0	1	0	1	0
0	1	0	1	1	0	1	0	0
0	1	1	1	0	1	0	1	1
1	1	1	1	0	0	0	1	0
1	1	1	0	1	0	1	0	1

P	S	Y	C	H	O	L	O	G	Y
0	0	0	1	0	1	1	1	0	0
1	1	1	1	1	1	1	1	1	1
0	0	0	0	0	0	0	0	0	0
1	1	1	0	0	0	0	0	0	1
0	0	1	0	1	1	1	1	0	1
0	0	0	0	0	1	1	1	1	0
0	1	0	1	0	1	0	1	1	0
0	1	1	1	0	1	0	1	1	1

*7-bit with even parity. The pattern of 0s and 1s below each letter is the code for that letter.

Similarly, the brain can represent information in terms of patterns of neural activity rather than simply as cells firing. The code in Table 1.1 includes redundant bits that allow the computer to correct errors should certain bits be lost (note that each column has an even number of 1s, which reflects the added bits for redundancy). As in a computer, it seems that the brain codes information redundantly, so that even if certain cells are damaged, the brain can still determine what the pattern is encoding. It is generally thought that the brain uses schemes for encoding information and achieving redundancy that are very different from the ones a computer uses. It also seems that the brain uses a much more redundant code than a computer does because the behavior of individual neurons is not particularly reliable.

So far, we have talked only about patterns of neural activation. Such patterns, however, are transitory. The brain does not maintain the same pattern for minutes, let alone days. This means that neural activation patterns cannot encode our permanent knowledge about the world. It is thought that the memories that encode this knowledge are created by changes in the synaptic connections among neurons. By changing the synaptic connections, the brain can enable itself to reproduce specific patterns. Although there is not a great deal of growth of new neurons or new synapses in the adult, the effectiveness of synapses can change in response to experience. There is evidence that synaptic connections do change during learning, with both increased release of neurotransmitters (Kandel & Schwartz, 1984) and increased sensitivity of dendritic receptors (Lynch & Baudry, 1984). We will discuss some of this research in Chapter 6.

Information is represented by patterns of activity across many regions of the brain and by changes in the synaptic connections among neurons that allow these patterns to be reproduced.

Organization of the Brain

The central nervous system consists of the brain and the spinal cord. The major function of the spinal cord is to carry motor messages from the brain to the muscles, and sensory messages from the body to the brain. **Figure 1.5** shows a cross section of the brain with some of the more prominent neural structures labeled. The lower parts of the brain are evolutionarily more primitive. The higher portions are well developed only in the higher species.

Correspondingly, it appears that the lower portions of the brain are responsible for more basic functions. The medulla controls breathing, swallowing, digestion, and heartbeat. The hypothalamus regulates the expression of basic drives. The cerebellum plays an important role in motor coordination and voluntary movement. The thalamus serves as a relay station for motor and sensory information from lower areas to the neocortex. Although the cerebellum and thalamus serve these basic functions, they also have evolved to play an important role in higher human cognition, as we will discuss later.

The **neocortex** (the main part of the **cerebral cortex**[3]) is the most recently evolved portion of the brain. Although it is quite small and primitive in many mammals, it accounts for a large fraction of the human brain (see **Figure 1.6**). The human neocortex can be thought of as a rather thin neural sheet with a surface area of about 2,500 cm^2. To fit into the skull, it has to be highly convoluted, and the large amount of folding and wrinkling of the cortex is one of the striking physical differences between the human brain and the brains of lower mammals. A bulge of the cortex is called a **gyrus,** and a crease passing between gyri is called a **sulcus** (plural *sulci*).

The neocortex is divided into left and right hemispheres. One of the interesting curiosities of anatomy is that the right part of the body tends to be connected to the left hemisphere and the left part of the body to the right hemisphere. Thus, the left hemisphere controls motor function and sensation in the right hand. The right ear is most strongly connected to the left hemisphere. The neural receptors in either eye that receive input from the left part of the visual world are connected to the right hemisphere (as Chapter 2 will explain with respect to Figures 2.4 and 2.5).

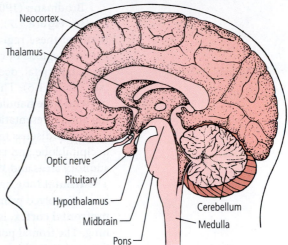

Figure 1.5 The Human Brain: Cross Section. A cross-sectional view of the brain showing some of its major components.

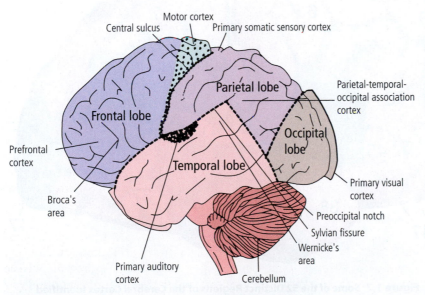

Figure 1.6 The Human Brain: Side View. A side view of the cerebral cortex showing the four lobes — frontal, temporal, parietal, and occipital — of each hemisphere (blue-shaded areas) and other major components of the cerebral cortex.

[3] The term "cerebral cortex" is widely used to refer just to the neocortex, and I have largely adopted that usage in this book, as well as using just "cortex" as a short way of referring to the cerebral cortex or neocortex. In places where the distinction is important, I have used the more specific "neocortex."

Brodmann (1909/1960) identified 52 distinct regions of the human cortex (see **Figure 1.7**), based on differences in the cell types in various regions. Many of these regions proved to have functional differences as well. The cortical regions of each hemisphere are typically organized into four lobes: frontal, parietal, occipital, and temporal, which are separated by major sulci (see Figure 1.6). The **occipital lobe** contains the primary visual areas. The **parietal lobe** handles some perceptual functions, including spatial processing and representation of the body. It is also involved in control of attention, as we will discuss in Chapter 3. The **temporal lobe** receives input from the occipital lobe and is involved in object recognition. It also has the primary auditory areas and Wernicke's area, which is involved in language processing. The **frontal lobe** has two major functions: The back portion of the frontal lobe is involved primarily with motor functions. The front portion, called the **prefrontal cortex,** is thought to control higher-level processes, such as planning. The frontal portion of the brain is disproportionately larger in primates than in most other mammals, and among primates, humans are distinguished

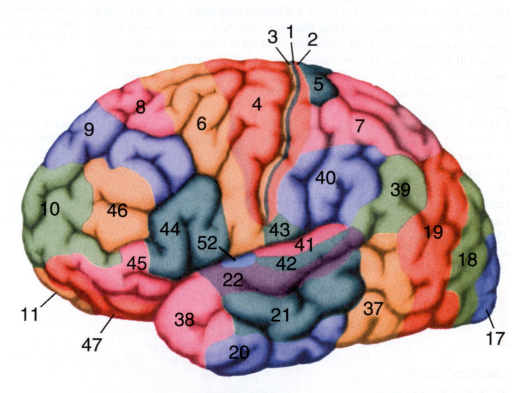

Figure 1.7 Some of the 52 Distinct Regions of the Cerebral Cortex Identified by Brodmann, Based on Cell Structure and Arrangement. Most of the numbered regions missing from this figure (areas 12–16, 23–36, and 48–51) are wrapped inside the brain and so are not visible in this exterior view.

by having disproportionately larger anterior portions of the prefrontal cortex (area 10 in Figure 1.7) (Semendeferi, Armstrong, Schleicher, Zilles, & Van Hoesen, 2001).

The neocortex is not the only region that plays a significant role in higher-level cognition. Many important circuits go from the cortex to subcortical structures and back again. A particularly significant group of subcortical structures is the limbic system, which is at the border between the cortex and lower structures. Among the structures making up the limbic system are the **amygdala** and the **hippocampus** (both of which are located inside the temporal lobe in each hemisphere). As we will see in later discussions, the amygdala is involved in emotional responses. The hippocampus appears to be critical to human memory; damage to the hippocampus and to other nearby structures produces severe amnesia, as we will see in Chapter 7. **Figure 1.8** illustrates the amygdala and hippocampus, along with the thalamus, an important subcortical structure that is not part of the limbic system.

Another important collection of subcortical structures is the **basal ganglia**. The major structures and critical connections of the basal ganglia are illustrated in **Figure 1.9**. The basal ganglia are involved both in basic motor control and in the control of complex cognition. These structures receive signals from almost all areas of the cortex and send signals to the frontal cortex. Disorders such as Parkinson's disease and Huntington's disease result from damage to the basal ganglia. Although people suffering from these diseases have dramatic motor control deficits characterized by tremors and rigidity, they also have difficulties in cognitive tasks. The cerebellum — in addition to its major role in motor control, as noted above — also seems to play a role in higher-order cognition. Many cognitive deficits have been observed in patients with damage to the cerebellum.

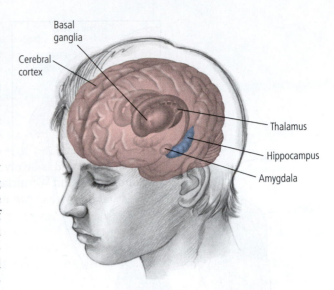

Figure 1.8 The Human Brain: Some Subcortical Structures. Structures under the cortex include tho make up the limbic system (the hippocampus, amygdala, and other structures), the thalamus, and the basal ganglia.

> The brain is organized into a number of distinct areas, which serve different types of functions, with the neocortex playing the major role in higher cognitive functions.

Localization of Function

The left and right hemispheres of the cerebral cortex appear to be somewhat specialized for different types of processing. In general, the left hemisphere seems to be associated with linguistic and analytic processing, whereas the right hemisphere is associated with perceptual and spatial processing. The left

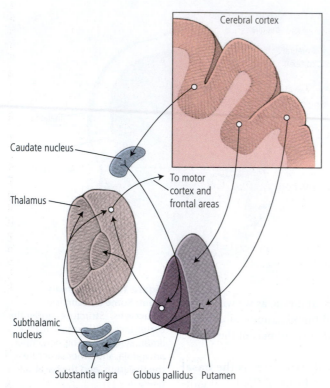

Cerebral cortex

Caudate nucleus

To motor
cortex and
frontal areas

Thalamus

Subthalamic
nucleus

Substantia nigra   Globus pallidus   Putamen

Figure 1.9 Basal Ganglia.
The major structures of the basal ganglia (blue-shaded areas) include the caudate nucleus, the subthalamic nucleus, the substantia nigra, the globus pallidus, and the putamen. The critical connections (inputs and outputs) of the basal ganglia are illustrated with arrows. *(Information from Gazzaniga, Ivry, & Mangun, 2002.)*

and right hemispheres are connected by a broad band of fibers called the **corpus callosum**. The corpus callosum has been surgically severed in some patients to prevent epileptic seizures. Such patients are referred to as **split-brain patients**. The operation is typically successful, and patients seem to function fairly well. Much of the evidence for the differences between the hemispheres comes from research with these patients. In one experiment, the word *key* was flashed on the left side of a screen the patient was viewing. Because it was on the left side of the screen, it would be received by the right, nonlinguistic hemisphere. When asked what was presented on the screen, the patient was not able to say because the left hemisphere (where linguistic processing mainly occurs) did not know. However, the patient's left hand (but not the right) was able to pick out a key from a set of objects hidden from view.

The linguistic advantage for the left hemisphere has been shown in a variety of studies with split-brain patients. For instance, commands might be presented to these patients in the right ear (and hence to the left hemisphere) or in the left ear (and hence to the right hemisphere). The right hemisphere can comprehend only the simplest linguistic commands, whereas the left hemisphere displays full comprehension. However, when tasked with arranging blocks to match a pictorial design without instruction, the left hand (and right hemisphere) does better. The right hemisphere can better follow pictorial information, whereas the left can better follow verbal information (Gazzaniga, 1967).

Research with other patients who have had damage to specific brain regions indicates that there are areas in the left hemisphere, called **Broca's area** and **Wernicke's area** (see Figure 1.6), that seem critical for speech, because damage to them results in **aphasia**, the severe impairment of speech. These may not be the only neural areas involved in speech, but they certainly are important. Different language deficits appear depending on whether the damage is to Broca's area or Wernicke's area. People with Broca's aphasia (i.e., damage to Broca's area) speak in short, ungrammatical sentences. For instance, when one patient was asked whether he drives home on weekends, he replied:

> Why, yes . . . Thursday, er, er, er, no, er, Friday . . . Bar-ba-ra . . . wife . . . and, oh, car . . . drive . . . purnpike . . . you know . . . rest and . . . teevee. (Gardner, 1975, p. 61)

In contrast, patients with Wernicke's aphasia speak in fairly grammatical sentences that are almost devoid of meaning. Such patients have difficulty with their vocabulary and generate "empty" speech. The following is the answer given by one such patient to the question "What brings you to the hospital?"

> Boy, I'm sweating, I'm awful nervous, you know, once in a while I get caught up, I can't mention the tarripoi, a month ago, quite a little, I've done a lot well. I impose a lot, while, on the other hand, you know what I mean, I have to run around, look it over, trebbin and all that sort of stuff. (Gardner, 1975, p. 68)

> *Different specific areas of the brain support different cognitive functions.*

Topographic Organization

In many areas of the cortex, information processing is structured spatially in what is called a **topographic organization**. For instance, in the visual area at the back of the cortex, adjacent areas represent information from adjacent areas of the visual field (see the discussion around Figure 2.5). A similar principle of organization governs the representation of the body in the motor cortex and the somatosensory cortex along the central sulcus. Adjacent parts of the body are represented in adjacent parts of the neural tissue. **Figure 1.10** illustrates the representation of the body along the somatosensory cortex. Note that the relative size of body parts is distorted, showing that certain areas of the body receive considerably more neural representation than other areas. It turns out that the overrepresented areas correspond to those that are more sensitive. Thus, for instance, we can make more subtle discriminations among tactile stimuli on the hands and face than we can on the back or thigh. Similarly, in the visual cortex, there is an overrepresentation of the center of our visual field, where we have the greatest visual acuity (also shown in Figure 2.5).

It is thought that topographic maps facilitate the interactions of neurons processing similar regions (Crick & Asanuma, 1986). Although there are fiber tracks that connect widely separated regions of the brain, the majority of the connections are among nearby neurons. This emphasis on local connections serves to minimize both the communication time between neurons and the amount of neural tissue that must be devoted to connecting them. The extreme of localization is seen in cortical minicolumns (Buxhoeveden & Casanova, 2002) — tiny vertical columns of about 100 neurons that have a very restricted mission. For instance, cortical minicolumns in the primary

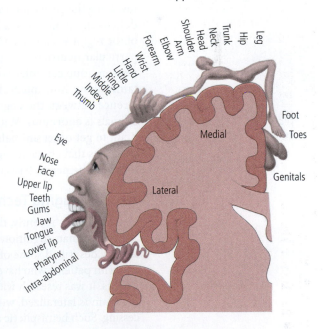

Figure 1.10 Topographic Organization of the Somatosensory Cortex. A cross section of the somatosensory cortex, showing how the human body is mapped in the neural tissue.

visual cortex are specialized to process information about one orientation of a line or an edge, from one location in the visual field, in one eye.

Neurons in a minicolumn do not represent a precise location with pinpoint accuracy but rather a range of nearby locations. This relates to another aspect of neural information processing called *coarse coding,* which refers to the fact that single neurons seem to respond to a range of events. For instance, when the neural activity from a single neuron in the somatosensory cortex is recorded, we can see that the neuron does not respond only when a single point of the body is stimulated, but rather when any point on a large patch of the body is stimulated. How, then, can we know exactly what point has been touched? That information is recorded quite accurately, but not in the response of any particular cell. Instead, different cells will respond to different overlapping regions of the body, and any point will evoke a different set of cells. Thus, the location of a point is reflected by the pattern of activation, which reinforces the idea that neural information tends to be represented in patterns of activation.

> *Adjacent cells in the cortex tend to process sensory stimuli from adjacent areas of the body, with the precise location of stimuli indicated by patterns of activation among cells.*

Methods in Cognitive Neuroscience

How does one go about understanding the neural basis of cognition? Much of the past research in neuroscience has been done on animals, sometimes involving the surgical removal of various parts of the cortex. By observing the deficits these operations have produced, it is possible to infer the functions of the regions removed. Other research has recorded the electrical activity in particular neurons or regions of neurons. By observing what activates these neurons, one can infer what they do. However, there is considerable uncertainty about how much these animal results generalize to humans. The difference between the cognitive potential of humans and that of most other animals is enormous. With the possible exception of other primates, it is difficult to get other animals to engage in even the simplest kinds of cognitive processes that characterize humans. This has been the great barrier to understanding the neural basis of higher-level human cognition.

Neural Imaging Techniques

Until relatively recently, the principal basis for understanding the role of the brain in human cognition has been the study of patient populations. We have already described some of this research, such as that with split-brain patients and with patients who have suffered damages to brain areas that cause language deficits. It was research with patient populations such as these that showed that the brain is lateralized, with the left hemisphere specialized for language processing. Such hemispheric specialization does not occur in other species.

In recent decades, there have been major advances in noninvasive methods of imaging the functioning of the brains of normal participants engaged in various cognitive activities. These advances in neural imaging are among the most exciting developments in cognitive neuroscience and will be referenced throughout this text. Although not as precise as recording from single neurons, which can be done only rarely with humans (and then as part of surgical procedures), these methods have achieved dramatic improvements in precision.

Electroencephalography (EEG) records the electric potentials that are present on the scalp. When large populations of neurons are active, this activity will result in distinctive patterns of electric potential on the scalp. In the typical methodology, a participant wears a cap of many electrodes. The electrodes detect rhythmic changes in electrical activity and record them on electroencephalograms. **Figure 1.11** illustrates some recordings typical of various cognitive states. When EEG is used to study cognition, the participant is asked to respond to some stimulus, and researchers are interested in discovering how processing this stimulus impacts general activity on the recordings. To eliminate the effects not resulting from the stimulus, many trials are averaged, and what remains is the activity produced by the stimulus. For instance, Kutas and Hillyard (1980) found that there was a large dip in the activity about 400 ms after participants heard an unexpected word in a sentence (this is discussed further in Chapter 13). Such averaged EEG responses aligned to a particular stimulus are called **event-related potentials (ERPs)**. ERPs have very good temporal resolution, but it is difficult to infer the location in the brain of the neural activity that is producing the scalp activity.

There has been a great deal of research on the use of EEG for brain–computer interfaces for applications such as helping paralyzed patients control external devices (Lotte et al., 2018). Its noninvasive nature makes it a more attractive option than approaches that involve implanting electrodes in the brain. While laboratory EEG systems can be expensive and cumbersome, there are now relatively inexpensive portable systems that approach the sensitivity of laboratory systems. A typical test application involves having a patient move a computer cursor to the left or right by imagining left or right hand movements, which can be readily distinguished in the EEG signal. One application involved flying a toy helicopter (Doud, Lucas, Pisansky, & He, 2011 — see video at Powell, 2013). The hope is that these EEG methods could be extended to enable control of devices such as wheelchairs, to input text on a computer, and to initiate calls on a telephone.

Figure 1.11 **EEG Profiles During Various States of Consciousness.** *(Alila Medical Media/ Shutterstock.)*

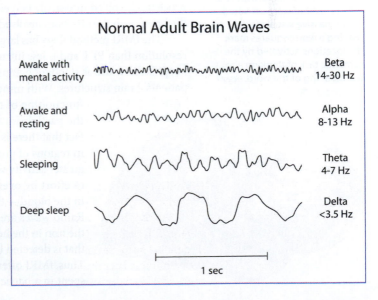

Normal Adult Brain Waves

Awake with mental activity — Beta 14-30 Hz

Awake and resting — Alpha 8-13 Hz

Sleeping — Theta 4-7 Hz

Deep sleep — Delta <3.5 Hz

1 sec

A recent variation of EEG that offers better spatial resolution is **magnetoencephalography (MEG),** which records magnetic fields produced by the brain's electrical activity. Because of the nature of the magnetic fields it measures, MEG is best at detecting activity in the sulci (creases) of the cortex and is less sensitive to activity in the gyri (bumps) or activity deep in the brain. However, like many imaging methods, MEG requires expensive equipment, making it appropriate for scientific research but not for practical applications.

Two other methods, **positron emission tomography (PET)** and **functional magnetic resonance imaging (fMRI),** provide relatively good information about the location of neural activity but rather poor information about the time course of that activity. Neither PET nor fMRI measures neural activity directly. Rather, they measure metabolic rate or blood flow in various areas of the brain, relying on the fact that more active areas of the brain require greater metabolic expenditures and have greater blood flow. PET and fMRI scans can be conceived as measuring the amount of work a brain region does.

In PET, a radioactive tracer is injected into the bloodstream (the radiation exposure in a typical PET study is equivalent to two chest X rays and is not considered dangerous). Participants are placed in a PET scanner that can detect the variation in concentration of the radioactive element. Current methods allow a spatial resolution of 5 to 10 mm. For instance, Posner, Peterson, Fox, and Raichle (1988) used PET to localize the various components of the reading process by looking at what areas of the brain are involved in reading a word. **Figure 1.12** illustrates their results. The triangles on the cortex represent areas that were active when participants were just passively looking at concrete nouns. The squares represent areas that became active when participants were asked to engage in the semantic activity of thinking of uses for these nouns. The triangles are located in the occipital lobe; the squares, in the frontal lobe. Thus, the data indicate that the processes involved in visually perceiving a word take place in a different part of the brain from the processes involved in thinking about the meaning of a word.

The fMRI methodology has largely replaced PET. It offers even better spatial resolution than PET and is less intrusive. fMRI uses the same MRI scanner that hospitals now use as standard equipment to image various structures, including patients' brain structures. With minor modification, it can be used to image the functioning of the brain. fMRI does not require injecting the participant with a radioactive tracer but relies on the fact that there is more oxygenated hemoglobin in the blood in regions of greater neural activity. (One might think that greater activity would use up oxygen, but the body responds to effort by overcompensating and increasing the oxygen in the blood — this is called the **hemodynamic response.**) Radio waves are passed through the brain, and these cause the iron in the hemoglobin to produce a local magnetic field that is detected by magnetic sensors surrounding the head. Thus, fMRI offers a measure of the amount of energy being spent in a particular brain region: The signal is stronger in

Figure 1.12 Using PET to Determine the Location of Neural Activity. Triangles mark locations in the lateral aspect of the cortex that were activated by the passive visual task of reading a word; squares mark the locations activated by the semantic task of thinking about the meaning of the word. *(Research from Posner et al., 1988.)*

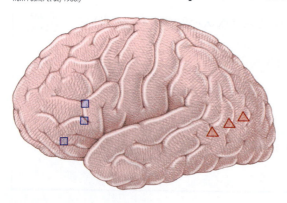

areas where there is greater activity. Among its advantages over PET are that it allows measurement over longer periods because there is no radioactive substance injected and that it offers finer temporal and spatial resolution. In the next section I will describe an fMRI study in detail to illustrate the basic methodology and what it can accomplish.

Neither PET nor fMRI is what one would call a practical, everyday measurement method. The more common method, fMRI, uses multimillion-dollar scanners that require the participant to lie motionless in a noisy and claustrophobic space. A related and more practical option is near-infrared sensing (Strangman, Boas, & Sutton, 2002). This methodology relies on the fact that light penetrates tissue (put a flashlight to the palm of your hand to demonstrate this) and is reflected back. In near-infrared sensing, light is shined on the skull, and the instrument senses the spectrum of light that is reflected back. It turns out that near-infrared light tends not to be absorbed by oxygenated tissue, and so by measuring the amount of light in the near-infrared region (which is not visible to human eyes), one can detect the oxygenation of the blood in a particular area of the brain. This methodology is cheaper and less confining than PET or fMRI and does not require movement restriction. Even now it is used with young children who cannot be convinced to remain still and with Parkinson's patients who cannot control their movements. A major limitation of this technique is that it can only detect activity 2 or 3 cm into the brain because that is as far as the light can effectively penetrate.

These various imaging techniques have revolutionized our understanding of the brain activity underlying human cognition, but they have a limitation that goes beyond temporal and spatial resolution: They provide only a limited basis for causal inference. Activity in a region of the brain during a task does not necessarily mean that the region is critical to the execution of the task. Until recently, researchers had to study patients with strokes, brain injuries, and brain diseases to get some understanding of how critical a region is. However, methods are now available that allow researchers to briefly incapacitate a region. Principal among these methods is **transcranial magnetic stimulation (TMS)**, in which a coil is placed over a particular part of the head and a magnetic pulse or pulses are delivered to the underlying region of the brain to disrupt the processing there (see **Figure 1.13**). If properly administered, TMS is safe and has no lasting effect. It can be very useful in determining the role of different brain regions. For instance, imaging techniques reveal activity in both prefrontal and parietal regions during study of an item that a participant is trying to remember. Nonetheless, the fact that TMS to the prefrontal region (Rossi et al., 2001) and not the parietal region (Rossi et al., 2006) disrupts memory formation implies a more critical role for the prefrontal region in memory formation.

Techniques such as EEG, MEG, PET, fMRI, near-infrared sensing, and TMS allow researchers to study the neural basis of human cognition with a precision starting to approach that available in animal studies.

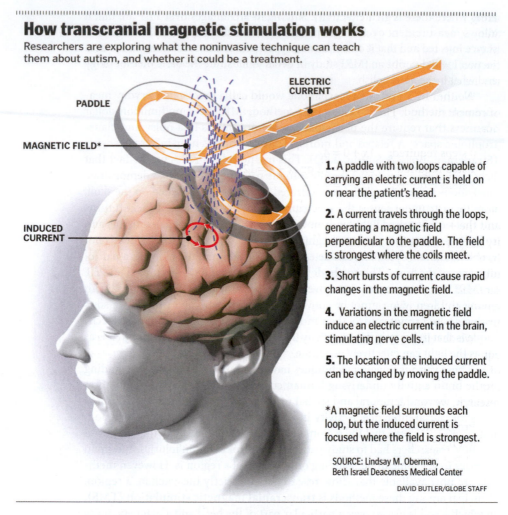

How transcranial magnetic stimulation works

Researchers are exploring what the noninvasive technique can teach them about autism, and whether it could be a treatment.

ELECTRIC CURRENT

PADDLE

MAGNETIC FIELD*

INDUCED CURRENT

1. A paddle with two loops capable of carrying an electric current is held on or near the patient's head.

2. A current travels through the loops, generating a magnetic field perpendicular to the paddle. The field is strongest where the coils meet.

3. Short bursts of current cause rapid changes in the magnetic field.

4. Variations in the magnetic field induce an electric current in the brain, stimulating nerve cells.

5. The location of the induced current can be changed by moving the paddle.

*A magnetic field surrounds each loop, but the induced current is focused where the field is strongest.

SOURCE: Lindsay M. Oberman, Beth Israel Deaconess Medical Center

DAVID BUTLER/GLOBE STAFF

Figure 1.13 Transcranial Magnetic Stimulation. TMS is delivered by a coil on the surface of the head, which generates brief put powerful magnetic pulses that induce a temporary current that disrupts neural processing in a small area on the surface of the brain with high temporal and fair spatial precision. This can provide evidence for how critical activity in a given area is for particular brain functions. *(Boston Globe/Getty Images.)*

Using fMRI to Study Equation Solving

Most brain-imaging studies have looked at relatively simple cognitive tasks, as is still true of most research in cognitive neuroscience. A potential danger of such research is that we will come to believe that the human mind is capable only of the simple tasks that are studied. However, it is possible to use brain imaging to study more complex processes. For example, I will describe a study using fMRI — for which I was one of the researchers (Qin, Anderson, Silk, Stenger, & Carter, 2004) — that looked at equation solving by children aged 11 to 14 when they were just learning to solve equations. This research illustrates the profitable marriage of information-processing analysis and cognitive neuroscience techniques.

We studied eighth-grade students as they solved equations at three levels of complexity in terms of the number of steps required to transform the equation to find the solution:

0 steps required: $1x + 0 = 4$
1 step required: $3x + 0 = 12$ or $1x + 8 = 12$
2 steps required: $7x + 1 = 29$

Note that the 0-steps equation is rather unusual, with the 1 in front of the x and the $+ 0$ after the x. This format reflects the fact that the visual complexity of different conditions must be controlled to avoid obtaining differences in the visual cortex and elsewhere just because a more complex visual stimulus has to be processed. Students kept their heads motionless while being scanned. They wore a response glove and could press a finger to indicate the answer to the problem (thumb = 1, index finger = 2, middle finger = 3, ring finger = 4, and little finger = 5).

We developed an information-processing model for the solution of such equations that involved imagined transformations of the equations, retrieval of arithmetic and algebraic facts, and programming of the motor response. **Figure 1.14** shows the sequencing of these activities. In line with existing research, we would expect that:

1. Programming of the hand would be reflected in activation in the left motor and somatosensory cortex. (See Figure 1.10; participants responded with their right hands, and so the left cortex would be involved.)
2. The imagined transformations of each equation would activate a region of the left parietal cortex involved in mental imagery (see Chapter 4).
3. The retrieval of arithmetic and algebraic information would activate a region of the left prefrontal cortex (see Chapters 6 and 7).

Figure 1.15 shows the locations of these three regions of interest. Each region is a cube with sides of approximately 15 mm. fMRI is capable of much greater spatial resolution, but the application within this study did not require this level of accuracy.

The times required to solve the three types of equation were 2.0 s for 0 steps, 3.6 s for 1 step, and 4.8 s for 2 steps. However, after students pressed the appropriate finger to indicate the answer, a long rest period followed to allow brain activity to return to baseline for the next trial. Data were obtained in terms of the percentage increase over this baseline of the **blood oxygen level dependent response (BOLD response)**. In this particular experiment, a brain scan was taken every

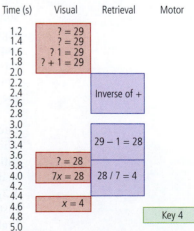

Figure 1.14 The Steps of an Information-Processing Model for Solving the Equation $7x + 1 = 29$. The model includes imagined transformations of the equation (visual processing), retrieval of arithmetic and algebraic facts, and programming of the motor response.

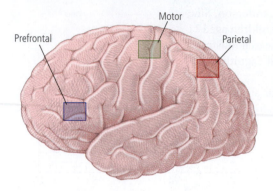

Figure 1.15 **Regions of Interest for the fMRI Scan in the Equation-Solving Experiment.** The imagined transformations would activate a region of the left parietal cortex; the retrieval of arithmetic and algebraic information would activate a region of the left prefrontal cortex; and the programming of the hand's movement would activate the left motor and somatosensory cortex.

1.2 s to obtain a reading of the BOLD response. **Figure 1.16a** shows the BOLD response in the motor region for the three conditions. The percentage increase is plotted from the time the equation was presented. Even though students solved the problem and keyed the answer to the 0-steps equation in an average of 2 s, the BOLD function did not begin to rise above baseline until the third scan after the equation was solved, and it did not reach peak until after approximately 6.6 s. This result reflects the fact that the hemodynamic response to a neural activity is delayed because it takes time for the oxygenated blood to arrive at the corresponding location in the brain. Basically, the hemodynamic response reaches a peak about 4 to 5 s after the event. In the motor region (see Figure 1.16a), the BOLD response for a 0-steps equation reached a peak at approximately 6.6 s, for a 1-step equation at approximately 7.8 s, and for a 2-step equation at approximately 9.0 s. Thus, the point of maximum activity reflects events that were happening about 4 to 5 s previously.

The BOLD function allows one to read the brain and see *when* the activity took place (at the peak of the function) and the *amount* of activity that took place (the height of the function at the peak). Note that the functions for motor activity in Figure 1.16a are of approximately equal height in the three conditions because it takes the same amount of effort to program the finger press, independent of the number of transformations needed to solve the equations.

Figure 1.16b shows the BOLD responses in the parietal region. Like the responses in the motor region, they peaked at different times, reflecting the differences in time to solve the equations. They peaked a little earlier, however, because the BOLD responses reflected the transformations being made to the mental image of the equation, which occurred before the response was emitted. Also, the BOLD functions reached very different heights, reflecting the different number of transformations that needed to be performed to solve the equation. Figure 1.16c shows the BOLD responses in the prefrontal region, which were quite similar to those in the parietal region, but with the important difference that there was no rise in the function in the 0-steps condition because it was not necessary to retrieve any information in that condition. Students could just read the answer from the mental representation of the original equation.

This experiment showed that researchers can separately track different information-processing components involved in performing a complex task. The fMRI methodology is especially appropriate for the study of complex cognition. Its temporal resolution is not very good, and so it is difficult to study in detail very brief tasks such as the Sternberg paradigm (see Figures 1.1 and 1.2). On the other hand, when a task takes many seconds, it is possible to distinguish the timing of processes, as we see in Figure 1.16. Because of its high spatial resolution, fMRI is able to separate out different components

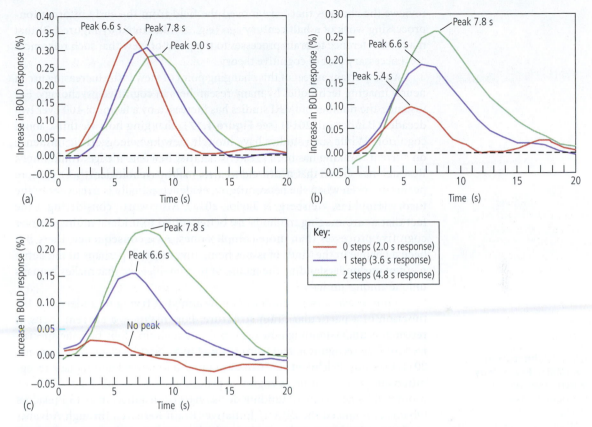

Figure 1.16 Responses of the Three Regions of Interest Shown in Figure 1.14 for Different Equation Complexities. The baseline BOLD response is indicated by the solid line at 0. (a) motor region; (b) parietal region; (c) prefrontal region.

of the overall processing. For brief cognition, EEG is often a more appropriate brain-imaging technique because it can achieve much finer temporal resolution.

> *fMRI allows researchers to track activity in the brain corresponding to different information-processing components of a complex task.*

A Cognitive Neuroscience Revolution?

The developments that we have reviewed in cognitive neuroscience have coalesced into a new attitude: that the understanding of human cognition must involve reference to brain processes. McClelland and Ralph (2015) note that cognitive neuroscience has begun to make dramatic inroads into the field of cognitive psychology, where many leading investigators have redirected their research to exploit ideas and methods from neuroscience. Kriegeskorte (2015) reviews the changes that have moved the field from the early information-processing work of a half century ago (e.g., as illustrated by Figure 1.2) that made no reference to brain processes to the point of view that such references are a necessary part of cognitive theory.

An important aspect of this changing point of view is the increasing use of neural imaging techniques by many researchers in cognitive psychology. For instance, the number of fMRI studies has increased by a factor of 100 over two decades (Bandettini, 2014) (see **Figure 1.17**), changing how we think about cognition. While such studies have brought new knowledge, their influence on current thinking has been greater than that new knowledge would imply. Research has shown that neuroscience data make psychological theories more persuasive even when the neuroimaging evidence actually is irrelevant to the theory (Hopkins, Weisberg, & Taylor, 2016). Also, worth considering is the fact that neuroimaging methods are better suited to understanding simpler cognitive processes than more complex ones. As a consequence, there has been a change in the kinds of issues being investigated, perhaps to the detriment of our understanding the nature of that intelligence that makes humans unique among animals.

More research in psychology is now aimed at trying to understand the function of a particular brain structure. For instance, a current focus of research is understanding how regions of the temporal lobe become specialized for face recognition and word reading (e.g., Nestor, Plaut, & Behrmann, 2011; Ozernov-Palchik et al., 2018), as opposed to understanding face recognition and word reading as cognitive processes. In part, this focus has been promoted by government funding decisions. For instance, in 2013 President Obama announced the BRAIN Initiative (Brain Research through Advancing Innovative Neurotechnologies), which would provide support for both increased neural recording and new technologies for neural recording.

On the theoretical side, there has been a continuing debate about the value of theories that make no reference to the brain (e.g., Griffiths, Chater, Kemp, Perfors, & Tenenbaum, 2010; McClelland et al., 2010). It is argued that explanations of cognitive function should be in terms of computations like those the brain performs. Such explanations are often described as **connectionist models**. A majority of computational models in the premier theoretical journal in psychology, *Psychological Review*, are connectionist models. A connectionist theory focuses on the connections between neuron-like elements. These connections have properties like those associated with synapses. For instance, **Figure 1.18** (Westermann & Mareschal, 2014) shows a network of such elements used in a model of how children

Figure 1.17 Increasing Use of fMRI in Psychology Research. The number of papers published each year involving studies using fMRI rose dramatically in the two decades 1995–2014. *(Data from Bandettini, 2014.)*

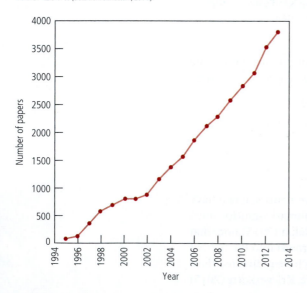

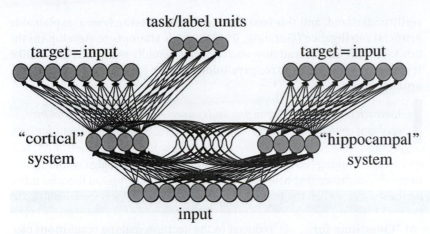

Figure 1.18 A Connectionist Model of How Perceptual Input Results in Categorical Labels. The nodes (circles) represent neuron-like elements, and the arrows represent connections with properties like synapses. The "perceptual" input at the bottom (start) of the process connects to elements in a hippocampus-like system, for targeted "memory" of the input, and to elements in a cortex-like system, for targeted "interpretation" of the input, which is then labeled as belonging to the task category.

(Republished with permission of The Royal Society of London. Westermann, G., & Mareschal, D. (2014). From perceptual to language-mediated categorization. Philosophical Transactions of the Royal Society of London B: Biological Sciences, 369(1634); permission conveyed through the Copyright Clearance Center, Inc.)

learn to label objects such as cats. The circles represent neural elements and the arrows represent connections among them. The input elements take on different patterns of activation thought to be like patterns of neural activation. Activation in elements can excite and inhibit activity in other elements that they are connected to, like activity in one neuron can change the activity in other neurons it synapses on. The behavior of these elements is simulated on computers, and the simulated behavior is remarkably humanlike. While these elements do not behave in detail like real neurons, they have general properties that are similar to the general properties of real neurons. In particular, they can change the strengths of connections among neural elements and thereby "learn" in ways that are thought to be similar to the process of neural learning.

There has been a huge surge of interest from artificial intelligence in what is called **deep learning** (LeCun, Bengio, & Hinton, 2015; Marcus, 2018). This involves learning connections in networks that have many more layers of connecting neuron-like elements than does the network shown in Figure 1.18. Deep learning systems have been shown to be capable of greater accuracy than humans in recognizing objects (see the discussion of object recognition in Chapter 2). The AlphaGo system mentioned earlier in this chapter was a deep learning system. These systems are often so complex with their many layers that it seems impossible to understand what they are actually doing, but nonetheless one cannot argue with their success. This raises the possibility that human cognition may be similarly too complex to really understand, and this issue has led to a new research area, explainable artificial intelligence (Gunning, 2017), which attempts to develop methods to help us understand how such systems actually work. It is sort of like trying to develop a cognitive psychology theory for artificial intelligence artifacts.

> *Research involving brain imaging and connectionist models of neural processing is changing the current understanding of the nature of cognition.*

Questions for Thought

Each chapter ends with a set of "Questions for Thought," designed to emphasize the core issues in the field. For this chapter, consider the following questions:

1. Research in cognitive psychology has been described as "the mind studying itself." Is this really an accurate characterization of what cognitive psychologists do in studies like those illustrated in Figure 1.1 and in Figures 1.14–1.16? Does the fact that cognitive psychologists study their own thought processes create any special opportunities or challenges? Is there any difference between the scientific study of a mental system such as memory and the scientific study of a bodily system such as digestion?

2. Notable figures such as Elon Musk, Bill Gates, and Stephen Hawking have warned of the danger that systems displaying artificial intelligence will eventually become superintelligent and replace the human race. Does this seem more likely if we assume that deep learning approaches will continue to produce ever more successful systems with underlying processing that cannot be understood by humans?

3. The scientific program of reductionism tries to reduce one level of phenomena into a lower level. For instance, this chapter has discussed how complex economic behavior can be reduced to the decision making (cognition) of individuals and how this can be reduced to the actions of individual neurons in the brain. But reductionism does not stop there. The activity of neurons can be reduced to chemistry, and chemistry can be reduced to physics. When does it help and when does it not help to try to understand one level in terms of a lower level? Why is it silly to go all the way in a reductionist program and attempt something like explaining economic behavior in terms of particle physics?

4. Humans are frequently viewed as qualitatively superior to other animals in terms of their intellectual function. What are some ways in which humans seem to display such qualitative superiority? How would these features of human cognition create problems in generalizing research from other animals to humans?

5. New techniques for imaging brain activity have had a major impact on research in cognitive psychology, but each technique has its limitations. What are the limitations of the various techniques? What would be the properties of an ideal brain-imaging technique? How do studies that actually go into the brain (almost exclusively done with nonhumans) inform the use of brain imaging?

6. What are the ethical limitations on the kinds of research that can be performed with humans and nonhumans?

Key Terms

This chapter has introduced quite a few key terms, most of which will reappear in later chapters:

action potential
amygdala
aphasia
artificial intelligence (AI)
axon
basal ganglia
behaviorism
blood oxygen level
  dependent response
  (BOLD response)
Broca's area
cerebral cortex
cognitive neuroscience
cognitive psychology
cognitive revolution
cognitive science

connectionist models
corpus callosum
deep learning
dendrites
dualism
electroencephalography
  (EEG)
empiricism
event-related potentials
  (ERPs)
excitatory synapses
frontal lobe
functional magnetic
  resonance imaging
  (fMRI)
Gestalt psychology

gyrus
hemodynamic response
hippocampus
information-processing
  approach
inhibitory synapses
intelligence
introspection
linguistics
magnetoencephalogra-
  phy (MEG)
nativism
neocortex
neuron
neurotransmitters
occipital lobe

parietal lobe
positron emission
  tomography (PET)
prefrontal cortex
p-value
rate of firing
replicability crisis
split-brain patients
Sternberg paradigm
sulcus
synapse
temporal lobe
topographic organization
transcranial magnetic
  stimulation (TMS)
Wernicke's area

Perception

Our bodies are bristling with sensory receptors — neurons that detect sights, sounds, smells, and physical contact. Billions of neurons process sensory information and deliver what they find to the higher centers in the brain. This chapter will focus on visual perception and, to a lesser extent, on audition as it is involved in the perception of speech — the two most important perceptual systems for the human species. The chapter will address the following questions:

- How does the brain extract information from the visual signal?
- How is visual information organized into objects?
- How are the sounds of speech (phonemes) recognized?
- How are visual and speech patterns recognized?
- How does context affect pattern recognition?

Visual Perception in the Brain

Humans have a big neural investment in processing visual information. This is illustrated in **Figure 2.1**, which shows some of the cortical structures devoted to processing information from vision and hearing. This investment in vision is part of our "inheritance" as primates, which have evolved to devote as much as 50% of their brains to visual processing (Barton, 1998). The enormous investment underlies the human ability to see the world.

This is vividly demonstrated by individuals with damage to certain brain regions who are not blind but are impaired at recognizing things visually, a condition called **visual agnosia.** One case of visual agnosia involved a soldier who suffered brain damage resulting from accidental carbon monoxide poisoning. He could recognize objects by their feel, smell, or sound, but he was unable to distinguish a picture of a circle from that of a square or to recognize faces or letters (Benson & Greenberg, 1969). On the other hand, he was able to discern light intensities and colors and to tell in what

Figure 2.1 Some of the Cortical Structures Involved in Vision and Audition. The visual cortex, the "where" visual pathway, and the "what" visual pathway are important in processing information from vision; the auditory cortex is important in processing information from hearing.

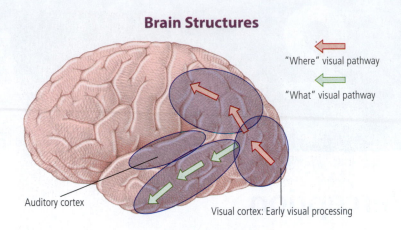

Brain Structures

"Where" visual pathway

"What" visual pathway

Auditory cortex

Visual cortex: Early visual processing

direction an object was moving. Thus, his sensory system was still able to register visual information, but the damage to his brain resulted in a loss of the ability to transform visual information into perceptual experience. This case shows that perception is much more than simply the registering of sensory information.

Generally, visual agnosia is classified as either **apperceptive agnosia** or **associative agnosia** (for a review, read Farah, 1990). Patients with apperceptive agnosia, like the soldier just described, are unable to recognize simple shapes such as circles or triangles, or to draw shapes they are shown. Patients with associative agnosia, in contrast, are able to recognize simple shapes and can successfully copy drawings, even of complex objects. However, they are unable to recognize complex objects, even after copying drawings of them. **Figure 2.2** shows the original drawing of an anchor and a copy of it made by a patient with associative agnosia (Ratcliff & Newcombe, 1982). Despite being able to produce a relatively accurate drawing, the patient could not recognize this object as an anchor (he called it an umbrella). Patients with apperceptive agnosia are generally believed to have problems with early processing of information in the visual system. In contrast, patients with associative agnosia are thought to have intact early processing but to have difficulties with pattern recognition, which occurs later. This chapter will first discuss the early processing of information in the visual stream and then the later processing of this information.

Figure 2.3 offers an opportunity for a person with normal perception to appreciate the distinction between early and late visual processing. If you have not seen this image before, it will strike you as just a bunch of ink blobs. You will be able to judge the size of the various blobs and reproduce them, just as Ratcliff and Newcombe's patient could, but you will not see

Figure 2.2 Effects of Associative Agnosia. A patient with associative agnosia was able to copy the original drawing of the anchor at left (his drawing is at right), but he was unable to recognize the object as an anchor. *(Republished with permission of Taylor & Francis, from* Human cognitive neuropsychology, *Ellis & Young, 1988; permission conveyed through Copyright Clearance Center, Inc.)*

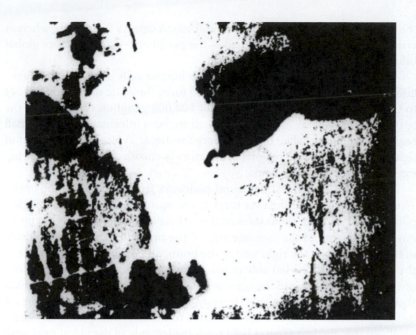

Figure 2.3 Early vs. Late Visual Processing. A scene in which we initially perceive just black and white areas; only after looking at it for some time is it possible to make out the face of a cow. *(From American Journal of Psychology. Copyright 1951 by the Board of Trustees of the University of Illinois. Used with permission of the University of Illinois Press. Research from Dallenbach, 1951.)*

any patterns. If you keep looking at the image, however, you may be able to make out a cow's face (nose slightly to the left of center at the bottom). Now your pattern perception has succeeded, and you have interpreted what you have seen.

> *Visual perception can be divided into an early phase, in which shapes and objects are extracted from the visual scene, and a later phase, in which the shapes and objects are recognized.*

Early Visual Information Processing

Early visual information processing begins in the eye. Light coming through the eye falls on the **retina,** the innermost layer of cells within the eye. Photoreceptor cells in the retina contain light-sensitive molecules that undergo structural changes when exposed to light, initiating a photochemical process that converts light into neural signals. There are two distinct types of photoreceptors in the eye: **cones** and **rods.** Cones are involved in color vision and produce high resolution (i.e., greater visual acuity). Less light energy is required to trigger a response in the rods, but they produce poorer resolution and no information about color. As a consequence, they are principally responsible for the less acute, black-and-white vision we experience at night. Cones are especially concentrated in a small area of the retina called the **fovea.** When we focus on an object, we move our eyes so that the image of the object falls on the fovea, which enables us to take full advantage of the high resolution of the cones in perceiving the object. Foveal vision detects fine details, whereas vision in the rest of the visual field — the periphery — detects more global information, including movement.

The photoreceptor cells synapse onto bipolar cells and these onto ganglion cells, whose axons leave the eye and form the optic nerve, which goes to the brain. Altogether there are about 800,000 ganglion cell axons in the optic nerve of each eye. Each ganglion cell encodes information from a small region of the retina called the cell's **receptive field.** Typically, the amount of light stimulation in that region of the retina is encoded by the neural firing rate on the ganglion cell's axon.

Figure 2.4 illustrates the neural pathways from the eyes to the brain. The optic nerves from the eyes meet at the optic chiasma, where the ganglion cell axons from the insides of the retinas (the sides nearest the nose) cross over and go to the opposite side of the brain (axons from the inside of the left eye go to the right side of the brain, and axons from the inside of the right eye go to the left side of the brain). The axons from the outsides of the retinas continue to the same side of the brain as the eye from which they emanate. This means that the right halves of both eyes are connected to the right hemisphere and the left halves to the left hemisphere. As Figure 2.4 illustrates, the lens focuses light from the left side of the visual field onto the right half of each eye and light from the right half of the visual field onto the left half of each eye. Thus, information about the left side of the visual field goes to the right brain, and information about the right side of the visual field goes to the left brain. This is one instance of the general fact, discussed in Chapter 1, that the left hemisphere processes information about the right part of the world and the right hemisphere processes information about the left part.

Once inside the brain, the fibers from the ganglion cells synapse onto cells in various subcortical structures. These subcortical structures (such as the lateral geniculate nucleus and superior colliculus in Figure 2.4) are connected to the primary visual cortex (area 17 in Figure 1.7). The **primary visual cortex** is the first cortical area to receive visual input, but there are many other visual areas. **Figure 2.5** illustrates the topographic representation of the visual field in the primary visual cortex (as discussed in Chapter 1). The fovea receives a disproportionate representation while the peripheral areas receive less representation (Figure 1.9 illustrates a similar disproportionate neural representation in the somatosensory cortex). Figure 2.5 shows that the left visual field is represented in the right cortex and the right in the left cortex. It also illustrates

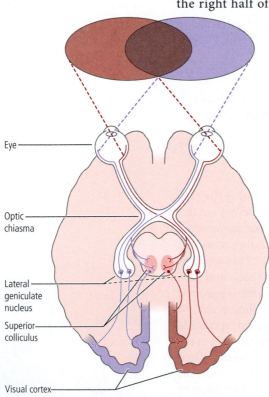

Figure 2.4 Neural Pathways from the Eye to the Brain. The optic nerves from the left and right eyes meet at the optic chiasma. Information about the left side of the visual field goes to the right brain, and information about the right side of the visual field goes to the left brain. Optic nerve fibers synapse onto cells in subcortical structures, such as the lateral geniculate nucleus and superior colliculus. Both structures are connected to the visual cortex.

Eye

Optic chiasma

Lateral geniculate nucleus

Superior colliculus

Visual cortex

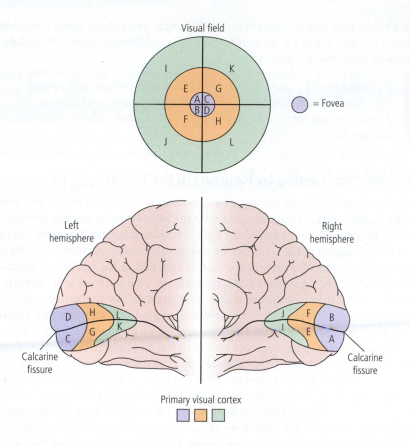

Visual field

= Fovea

Left hemisphere

Right hemisphere

Calcarine fissure

Calcarine fissure

Primary visual cortex

Figure 2.5 The Orderly Mapping of the Visual Field onto the Primary Visual Cortex. The upper parts of the visual field are mapped below the calcarine fissure and the lower parts are mapped above the fissure. Note the disproportionate representation given to the fovea, which is the region of greatest visual acuity. *(Information from Kandel, Schwartz, & Jessell, 1991.)*

another "reversal" of the mapping—the upper part of the visual field is represented in the lower part of the visual cortex and the lower part is represented in the upper region.

From the primary visual cortex, information tends to follow two pathways, a "what" pathway and a "where" pathway (look back at Figure 2.1). The **"what" visual pathway** goes to regions of the temporal cortex that are specialized for identifying objects. The **"where" visual pathway** goes to parietal regions of the brain that are specialized for representing spatial information and for coordinating vision with action. Research has shown that monkeys with lesions in the "what" pathway have difficulty learning to identify objects, whereas monkeys with lesions in the "where" pathway have difficulty learning to identify specific locations (Pohl, 1973; Ungerleider & Brody, 1977). Other researchers (e.g., Milner & Goodale, 1995) have made the point that the "where" pathway is specialized for action. They cite research showing that patients with agnosia because of damage to the temporal lobe, but with intact parietal lobes, can often take actions appropriate

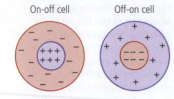

On-off cell   Off-on cell

Figure 2.6 Receptive Fields of On-off and Off-on Cells. Ganglion cells in the retina and cells in the lateral geniculate nucleus increase (+) or decrease (−) their firing rate in response to light falling on the center vs. the surround of their receptive field, depending on whether they are on-off cells or off-on cells.

to objects they cannot recognize. For instance, one patient could correctly reach out and grasp a door handle that she could not recognize (Goodale, Milner, Jakobson, & Carey, 1991).

> *A photochemical process converts light energy into neural activity carrying visual information, which progresses by various neural tracts to the primary visual cortex and thence along "what" and "where" pathways through the brain.*

Information Coding by Neurons in the Visual System

Kuffler's (1953) research showed how information is encoded by the ganglion cells in the retina. These cells generally fire at some spontaneous rate even when the eyes are not receiving any light. For some ganglion cells, if light falls on a small region of the retina at the center of the cell's receptive field, their spontaneous rates of firing will increase. If light falls in the region just around this sensitive center, however, the spontaneous rate of firing will decrease. Light farther from the center elicits no change in the spontaneous firing rate — neither an increase nor a decrease. Ganglion cells that respond in this way are known as on-off cells. There are also off-on ganglion cells: Light at the center decreases the spontaneous rate of firing, and light in the surrounding areas increases that rate. Cells in the lateral geniculate nucleus respond in the same way. **Figure 2.6** illustrates the receptive fields of such cells (i.e., the locations on the retina that increase or decrease the firing rate of the cell).

Hubel and Wiesel (1962), in their study of the primary visual cortex in the cat, found differently configured receptive fields than those of ganglion cells and cells in the lateral geniculate nucleus. **Figure 2.7** illustrates four patterns that have been observed in cortical cells. These receptive fields all have an elongated shape, in contrast to the circular receptive fields of the on-off and off-on cells. The types shown in Figures 2.7a and 2.7b are **edge detectors.** They respond positively to light on one side of a line and negatively to light on the other side. They respond most if an edge of light falls exactly along the boundary. The types shown in Figures 2.7c and 2.7d are **bar detectors.** They respond positively to light in the center and negatively to light in the periphery, or vice versa. Thus, a bar detector with a positive center will respond most if a bar of light just covers its center.

Both edge and bar detectors are specific with respect to position, orientation, and width. That is, they respond only to stimulation in a small area of the visual field, to bars and edges in a small range of orientations, and to bars and edges of certain widths. Different detectors are tuned to different locations, widths, and orientations. Any bar or edge anywhere in the visual field, at any orientation, and of any width will elicit a maximum response from some subset of detectors.

Hubel and Wiesel (1977) found that the visual cortex is divided into 2×2 mm regions, which they called *hypercolumns* (see **Figure 2.8**). Each hypercolumn represents a particular region of the visual field. As noted in Chapter 1, the organization of the visual cortex is topographic, and so adjacent areas

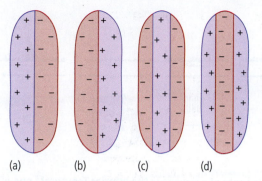

(a) (b) (c) (d)

Figure 2.7 Response Patterns of Cells in the Visual Cortex. (a) and (b) illustrate the receptive fields of edge detectors, cells that respond positively to light on one side of a line and negatively to light on the other side. (c) and (d) illustrate the receptive fields of bar detectors, cells that respond positively to light in the center and negatively to light at the periphery, or vice versa.

of the visual field are represented in adjacent hypercolumns. Figure 2.8 shows that each hypercolumn itself has a two-dimensional (2-D) organization. Along one dimension, cells in alternating rows receive input from the right or left eye. Along the other dimension, the rows vary in the orientation to which the cells in the row are most sensitive, with cells in adjacent rows representing similar orientations. This organization should impress upon us how much information is encoded about the visual scene. Hundreds of regions of space are represented separately for each eye, and within these regions many different orientations are represented. In addition, different cells code for different sizes and widths of line (an aspect of visual coding not illustrated in Figure 2.8). Thus, an enormous amount of information has been extracted from the visual signal even before it leaves the first cortical areas.

In addition to this rich representation of line orientation, size, and width, the visual system extracts other information from the visual signal. For instance, we also perceive the colors of objects and whether they are moving. Livingstone and Hubel (1988) proposed that the visual system processes these various dimensions (form, color, and movement) separately. Many different visual pathways and many different areas of the cortex are devoted to visual processing (32 visual areas in the count by Van Essen & DeYoe, 1995). Different pathways have cells that are differentially sensitive to color, movement, and orientation. Thus, the visual system analyzes a stimulus into many independent features in specific locations. Such a spatial representation of visual features is called a **feature map** (Wolfe, 1994), with separate maps for color, orientation, and movement. Thus, if a vertical red bar is moving at a particular location, separate feature maps represent its color as red, its orientation as vertical, and its movement as occurring in that location.

As one progresses down the ventral stream (the "what" visual pathway in Figure 2.1) one finds neurons that have more complex response functions (Roe et al., 2012). Even in the primary visual cortex there is a distinction between simple cells like those in Figure 2.7 that respond to patterns in specific visual locations and complex cells that respond to similarly simple patterns but in many locations. By the time the ventral stream gets to the inferior

Figure 2.8 Representation of a Hypercolumn in the Visual Cortex. The hypercolumn is organized in one dimension according to whether input is coming from the right eye (R) or left eye (L). In the other dimension, it is organized according to the orientation of lines to which the receptive cells are most sensitive. Adjacent layers of cells represent similar orientations. (Information from Horton, 1984.)

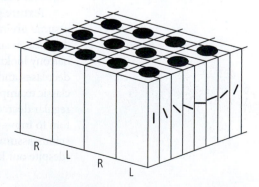

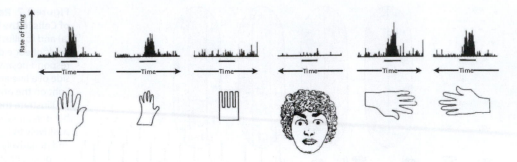

Figure 2.9 Responses of a Neuron in the Inferior Temporal Lobe of a Macaque Monkey. The graphs show the rate of firing of the cell over the time when each stimulus image was in view (horizontal bar under each graph) *(Desimone, R., Albright, T. D., Gross, C. G., & Bruce, C. (1984). Stimulus selective properties of inferior temporal neurons in the macaque. Journal of Neuroscience, 4, 2051–2062.)*

temporal cortex, we find cells that respond to complex patterns like hands and faces (Gross, 2008). For example, **Figure 2.9** shows the responses of a neuron found in the inferior temporal lobe of a macaque monkey (Desimone, Albright, Gross, & Bruce, 1984). This cell responds to stimuli to the degree that they look like hands and seems somewhat insensitive to the orientation of the hand.

> *The encoding of information by neurons in the visual system progresses from simple features to more and more complex features.*

Depth and Surface Perception

Even after the visual system has identified edges and bars in the environment, a great deal of information processing must still be performed to enable visual perception of the world. Crucially, it is necessary to determine where those edges and bars are located in space, in terms of their relative distance, or depth. The fundamental problem is that the information laid out on the retina is inherently 2-D, whereas we need to construct a three-dimensional (3-D) representation of the world. The visual system uses a number of cues to infer distance, including texture gradient, stereopsis, and motion parallax (other important cues involve features such as size, position, and lighting).

Texture gradients cue our perception of distance when elements that we assume are more or less equal in size and evenly spaced appear to regularly decrease in size and pack more closely together — for instance, if you stand on a balcony looking out over a large crowd of people, the apparent size of the people decreases and the apparent density of the crowd increases with distance. In the classic examples shown in **Figure 2.10** (Gibson, 1950), the texture change — the regular decrease in the size of and distance between the ovals and lines from bottom to top — creates the perception of increasing distance, based on our unconscious assumption that the ovals or lines are about equal in size and spacing (despite our knowledge that these elements are all equally distant on a flat page).

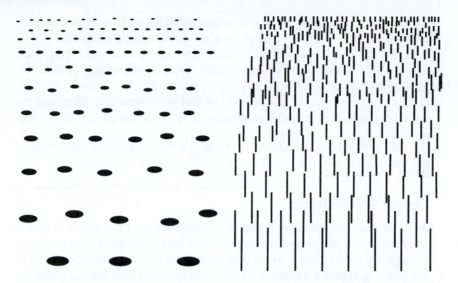

Figure 2.10 Texture Gradients. We unconsciously assume that the elements in these two examples are more or less equal in size and evenly spaced; the regular bottom-to-top decrease in actual size and increase in density make the elements appear to be increasingly further away. *(From Gibson, J. J. (1950). The perception of the visual world. Houghton Mifflin. Used with permission of Cengage.)*

Stereopsis is the ability to perceive 3-D depth based on the fact that each eye receives a slightly different view of the world. The 3-D glasses used to view some movies and some exhibits in theme parks achieve this by filtering the light coming from a single 2-D source (say, a movie screen). Two slightly different images are projected onto the screen and the 3-D glasses allow each eye to see only one image, which would be what that eye would receive if the scene was 3-D rather than a flat 2-D movie screen. The perception of a 3-D structure resulting from stereopsis can be quite compelling.

Motion parallax provides information about 3-D structure when the observer and/or the objects in a scene are in motion: The images of distant objects will move across the observer's retina more slowly than the images of closer objects. For an interesting demonstration, look at a nearby tree with one eye closed and without moving your head. Denied stereoscopic information, you will have the sense of a very flat image in which it is hard to see the relative depths of the leaves and branches. But if you move your head, the 3-D structure of the tree will suddenly become clear, because the images of nearby leaves and branches will move across the images of more distant ones, providing clear information about depth.

Although it is easy to demonstrate the importance to depth perception of such cues as texture gradient, stereopsis, and motion parallax, it has been a challenge to understand how the brain actually processes such information. A number of researchers in the area of computational vision have worked on the problem. For instance, David Marr (1982) made the influential proposal that these various sources of information work together to create what he calls a **2½-D sketch** that identifies where various visual features are located in space relative to the viewer. While a lot of information processing is required to produce this 2½-D sketch, a lot more is required to convert that sketch into actual perception of the world. In particular, such a sketch represents only parts of surfaces and does not yet identify how these parts go together to form images of objects in the environment (the problem we had with Figure 2.3). Marr used the term **3-D model** to refer to such a later representation of objects in a visual scene.

> Cues such as texture gradient, stereopsis, and motion parallax combine to create a representation of the locations of surfaces in 3-D space.

Object Segmentation

A major problem in constructing a representation of the world is object segmentation. Knowing where the lines and bars are located in space is not enough; we need to know which ones go together to form objects. Consider the scene in **Figure 2.11**: Many lines go this way and that, but somehow we put them together to come up with the perception of a set of objects.

We group elements into units according to a set of principles called the **gestalt principles of organization,** after the Gestalt psychologists who first proposed them (e.g., Wertheimer, 1912/1932). These groupings help determine object boundaries. **Figure 2.12** illustrates some of the basic gestalt principles:

- Figure 2.12a illustrates the principle of proximity: Elements close together tend to be grouped together. Thus, we perceive four pairs of lines rather than eight separate lines. Guided by this grouping, one might perceive the figure as consisting of parts of four objects (vertical bars that stretch beyond the figure).

Figure 2.11 Object Perception. This illustration provides an example of how we aggregate the perception of many broken lines into the perception of solid objects. *(From Winston, P. H. (1970). Learning structural descriptions from examples (Tech. Rep. No. 231). Copyright © 1970 Massachusetts Institute of Technology. Reprinted by permission.)*

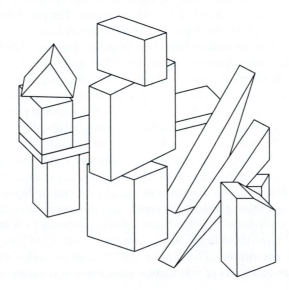

- Figure 2.12b illustrates the principle of similarity: Elements that look alike tend to be grouped together. In this case, we tend to see this array as rows of o's alternating with rows of x's.
- Figure 2.12c illustrates the principle of good continuation. We perceive two lines, one from *A* to *B* and the other from *C* to *D*, although there is no reason why this sketch could not represent another pair of lines, one from *A* to *D* and the other from *C* to *B*. However, the lines from *A* to *B* and from *C* to *D* display better continuation than the lines from *A* to *D* and from *C* to *B*, which have a sharp turn.
- Figure 2.12d illustrates the principles of closure and good form. The objects we see are two circles, one partly occluded by the other. Of course, the occluded part of the object on the left could simply be missing or could have any of an infinite number of possible shapes. However, the principle of closure means that we perceive the large arc as part of a complete shape, not just as a curved line that breaks off at the border of the occluding object; and the principle of good form means that we perceive the occluded part as part of a circle, not as a wiggly, jagged, or broken border.

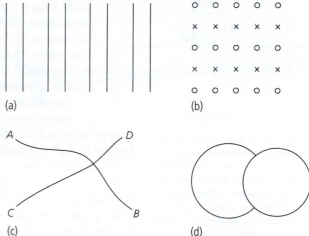

Figure 2.12 Gestalt Principles of Organization. (a) the principle of proximity, (b) the principle of similarity, (c) the principle of good continuation, (d) the principle of closure.

These principles will organize completely novel stimuli into units. Palmer (1977) studied the shapes such as the ones shown in **Figure 2.13**. He first showed participants a stimulus such as Figure 2.13a and then asked them to decide whether the fragments depicted in Figures 2.13b through 2.13e were part of the original stimulus. The gestalt principles of organization predict that the stimulus in Figure 2.13a will tend to organize itself into a triangle (principle of closure) and a bent letter *n* (principle of good continuation). Palmer found that the most rapidly recognized fragments were those predicted by the gestalt principles. So the stimuli in Figures 2.13b and 2.13c were recognized more rapidly than those in Figures 2.13d and 2.13e. Thus, we see that recognition depends critically on the initial segmentation of the figure. Recognition

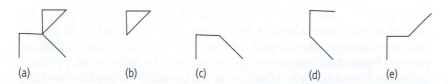

Figure 2.13 Examples of Stimuli Used by Palmer (1977) for Studying Segmentation of Novel Figures. (a) is the original stimulus that participants saw; (b) through (e) are the subparts of the stimulus presented for recognition. The stimuli shown in (b) and (c) were recognized more rapidly than those shown in (d) and (e).

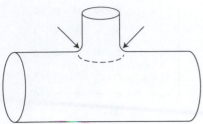

Figure 2.14 Segmentation of an Object into Subobjects. The lines at the concavities indicated by the arrows do not fully exhibit good continuation, leading us to perceive this object as two subobjects joined together along the dashed line. *(Neil Stillings, Mark H. Feinstein, Jay L. Garfield, Edwina L. Rissland, David A. Rosenbaum, and Steven E. Weisler,* Cognitive Science, *Figure 12.17, p. 495, © 1987 Massachusetts Institute of Technology, by permission of The MIT Press.)*

can be impaired when this gestalt-based segmentation contradicts the actual pattern structure. FoRiNsTaNcEtHiSsEnTeNcEiShArDtOrEaD. The reasons for this difficulty are (a) that the gestalt principle of similarity makes it hard to perceive adjacent letters of different case as going together and (b) that removing the spaces between words has eliminated the proximity cues.

The gestalt principles of organization can be extended to describe how more complex 3-D structures are perceived. **Figure 2.14** illustrates a proposal by Hoffman and Richards (1985) for how gestaltlike principles can be used to segment an outline representation of an object into subobjects. They observed that where one segment joins another, there is typically a concavity in the line outline (e.g., the concavities indicated by the arrows in Figure 2.14). Basically, people exploit the gestalt principle of good continuation: The lines at the points of concavity are not good continuations of one another, and so viewers do not group these parts together.

Gestalt principles of organization help explain how the brain segments visual scenes into objects.

Visual Pattern Recognition

We have now discussed visual information processing to the point where we organize the visual world into objects. There still is a major step before we see the world, however: We also must identify what these objects are. This task is called *pattern recognition*. Much of the research on this topic has focused on the question of how we recognize the identity of letters, a special kind of object. For instance, how do we recognize a presentation of the letter *A* as an instance of the pattern *A*? We will first discuss pattern recognition with respect to letter identification and then move on to a more general discussion of how we recognize the full variety of objects that occupy our world.

Template-Matching Models

Perhaps the most obvious way to recognize a pattern is by means of **template matching.** The template-matching theory of perception proposes that a retinal image of an object is faithfully transmitted to the brain, and the brain attempts to compare the image directly to various stored patterns, called *templates*. For example, in recognizing a letter of the alphabet, the basic idea is that the perceptual system compares the image of the letter to the templates it has for different patterns. **Figure 2.15** illustrates template matching for different letter patterns and shows various examples of successful and unsuccessful template matching. In each case, an attempt is made to achieve a correspondence between the retinal cells stimulated and the retinal cells specified for a template pattern for a letter.

Figure 2.15a shows a case in which a correspondence is achieved and an *A* is recognized. Figure 2.15b shows a case in which no correspondence

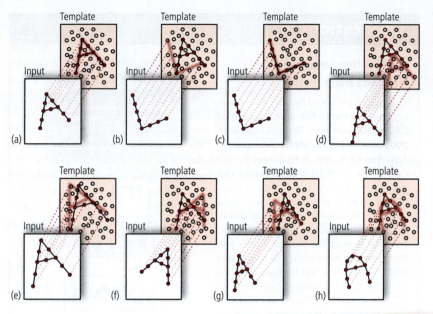

Figure 2.15 Attempts to Match Templates to the Letters *A* and *L*. The little circles on the "Input" patterns represent the cells actually stimulated on the retina by a presentation of the letter *A* or *L*, and the little circles on the "Template" patterns are the retinal cells specified by a template pattern for a letter. (a) and (c) are successful template-matching attempts; (b) and (d)–(h) are failed attempts.

is reached between the input of an *L* and the template pattern for an *A*. But *L* is matched in Figure 2.15c by the *L* template. However, things can very easily go wrong even when trying to match a letter with a template for that letter. Figure 2.15d shows a mismatch that occurs when the image falls on the wrong part of the retina, and Figure 2.15e shows the problem when the image is the wrong size. Figure 2.15f shows what happens when the image is in a wrong orientation, and Figures 2.15g and 2.15h show the difficulty when the images are nonstandard *A*'s.

Despite these difficulties with template matching, it is one of the methods used in machine vision (see Ullman, 1996), where procedures have been developed for rotating, stretching, and otherwise modifying images to match. Template matching is also used in fMRI brain imaging (see Chapter 1). Each human brain is anatomically different, much as each human body is different. When researchers claim regions like those in Figure 1.15 display activation patterns like those in Figure 1.16, they typically are claiming that the same region in the brains of each of their participants displayed that pattern. To determine that it is the same region, they map the individual brains to a reference brain by a sophisticated computer-based 3-D template-matching procedure. Although template matching has enjoyed some success, there seem to be limitations to the abilities of computers to use template matching to recognize patterns, as suggested in **Implications 2.1.**

> *Template matching is a way to identify objects by aligning the retinal image of a stimulus to a stored template of a pattern.*

Implications 2.1

CAPTCHAs: Separating Humans from Bots

The special nature of human visual perception motivated the development of CAPTCHAs (Von Ahn, Blum, & Langford, 2002). CAPTCHA stands for "Completely Automated Public Turing test to tell Computers and Humans Apart." The motivation for CAPTCHAs comes from real-world problems such as those faced by YAHOO!, which offers free email accounts. The problem is that automatic bots will sign up for such accounts and then use them to send spam. To test that the user is a real human, the system can present images like those in **Figure 2.16**. Use of such CAPTCHAs is quite common on the Internet. Although template-based approaches may fail to recognize such figures, more sophisticated feature-based character recognition algorithms have had a fair degree of success (e.g., Mori & Malik, 2003). This has led to more and more difficult CAPTCHAs being used, which unfortunately humans also have great difficulty in decoding (Bursztein, Bethard, Fabry, Mitchell, & Jurafsky, 2010). You can visit the CAPTCHA Web site and contribute to the research at http://www.captcha.net/.

Figure 2.16 CAPTCHAs. These are examples of CAPTCHAs that humans can read but template-based computer programs have great difficulty with. *(Staff KRT/Newscom.)*

Test yourself

To stay ahead of hackers, programmers are making it more difficult for computers to read CAPTCHAs, tests to differentiate between computers and humans. Try your hand at these examples:

A. Blogger.com

tnytq

B. Paypal.com

PA4XE

C. Yahoo.com

yLF8zr

D. Apple.com

hNx4

E. AOL.com

TP PPi

F. Hotmail.com

K686AXSE

Answers:

A. tnytq   **D.** ghNx4
B. PA4XE   **E.** TP PPi
C. yLF8zr   **F.** K686AXSE

© 2014 MCT
Source: Blogger.com, Paypal, Yahoo!, Apple, AOL, Hotmail
Graphic: The Dallas Morning News

Feature Analysis

Partly because of the difficulties posed by template matching, psychologists have proposed that pattern recognition occurs through **feature analysis.** In this model, stimuli are thought of as combinations of elemental features. **Table 2.1** from Gibson (1969) shows her proposal for the representation of the letters of the alphabet in terms of features. For instance, the capital letter *A* can be seen as consisting of a horizontal, two diagonals in opposite orientations, line intersections, symmetry, and a feature she called vertical discontinuity. Some of these

TABLE 2.1 Gibson's Proposal for the Features Underlying the Recognition of Letters

Features	A	B	C	D	E	F	G	H	I	J	K	L	M	N	O	P	Q	R	S	T	U	V	W	X	Y	Z
Straight																										
Horizontal	+				+	+	+	+				+								+						+
Vertical		+		+	+	+		+	+		+	+	+	+		+		+		+					+	
Diagonal /	+							+			+											+	+	+	+	+
Diagonal \	+							+			+		+	+								+	+	+	+	
Curve																										
Closed		+		+											+	+	+	+								
Open V									+												+					
Open H			+			+			+										+							
Intersection	+	+			+	+		+								+	+	+		+				+		
Redundancy																										
Cyclic change		+			+								+						+				+			
Symmetry	+	+	+	+	+			+	+				+		+					+	+	+	+	+	+	
Discontinuity																										
Vertical	+					+		+	+		+		+	+		+		+		+					+	
Horizontal					+	+						+								+						+

+ indicates features for a particular letter.

features, like the straight lines, can be thought of as outputs of the edge and bar detectors in the visual cortex (see Figure 2.7).

You might wonder how feature analysis represents an advance beyond the template model. After all, what are the features but miniature templates? The feature-analysis model does have a number of advantages over the template model, however. First, because the features are simpler, it is easier to see how the system might try to correct for the kinds of difficulties faced by the template-matching model in recognizing full patterns, as in Figure 2.15. Indeed, to the extent that features are just line strokes, the bar and edge detectors we discussed earlier can extract such features. Second, feature analysis makes it possible to specify those relationships among the features that are most important to the pattern. For example, in the case of the letter *A*, the critical point is that there are three lines that intersect, two diagonals (in different directions), and one horizontal. Many other details are unimportant. Thus, all the following patterns are *A*'s:

ʌ ʌ ʌ ʌ

Finally, the use of features rather than larger patterns reduces the number of templates needed. In the feature-analysis model, we would not need a template for each possible pattern but only for each feature. Because the same features tend to occur in many patterns, the number of distinct entities to be represented would be reduced considerably.

There is a fair amount of behavioral evidence for the existence of features as components in pattern recognition. For instance, when letters share features — for example, *C* and *G* share a feature called "open H," according to the feature set in Table 2.1 — evidence suggests that people are particularly prone to confuse them (Kinney, Marsetta, & Showman, 1966). When such letters are presented for very brief intervals, people often misclassify one stimulus as the other. So, for instance, participants in the Kinney et al. experiment made 29 errors when presented with the letter *G*. Of these errors, there were 21 misclassifications as *C*, 6 misclassifications as *O*, 1 misclassification as *B*, and 1 misclassification as *9*. No other errors occurred. It is clear that participants were choosing items with similar feature sets as their responses. Such a response pattern is what we would expect if participants were using features as the basis for recognition. If participants could extract only some of the features in the brief presentation, they would not be able to decide among stimuli that shared these features.

Another kind of experiment that yields evidence in favor of a feature-analysis model involves stabilized images. The eye has a very slight tremor, called *psychological nystagmus*, which occurs at the rate of 30 to 70 cycles per second. Also, the eye's direction of gaze drifts slowly over an object. Consequently, the retinal image of the object on which a person tries to focus is not perfectly constant; its position changes slightly over time. This retinal movement is critical for perception. When techniques are used to keep an image in the exact same position on the retina regardless of eye movement, parts of the object start to disappear from our perception. If the exact same retinal and nervous pathways are used uninterruptedly, they become fatigued and stop responding.

The most interesting aspect of this phenomenon is the way the stabilized object disappears. It does not simply fade away or vanish all at once. Instead, different portions drop out over time. **Figure 2.17** illustrates the fate of one of the stimuli used in an experiment by Pritchard (1961). The leftmost item is the image that was presented; the four others are various fragments that were reported after the original image started to disappear. Two points are important. First, whole features such as a vertical bar seemed to be lost. This finding suggests that features are the important units in perception. Second, the stimuli that remained tended to constitute complete letter or number

Figure 2.17 Disintegration of an Image That Is Stabilized on the Eye. At far left is the original image displayed. The partial outlines to the right show various patterns reported as the stabilized image began to disappear. *(Information from Pritchard, 1961.)*

patterns, indicating that the remaining features are combined into recognizable patterns. Thus, even though our perceptual system may extract features, what we actually perceive are patterns composed from these features. The feature-extraction and feature-combination processes that underlie pattern recognition are not available to conscious awareness; all that we are aware of are the resulting patterns.

> *Feature analysis involves recognizing first the separate features that make up a pattern and then their combination.*

Object Recognition by Deep Convolutional Networks

One of the major challenges in artificial intelligence has been object recognition. **Figure 2.18** shows the kinds of pictures in a large database of thousands of images that have been used to test computer vision programs. Try to label the objects in these pictures before reading the caption. It can be difficult even if you are given some training on the possible labels. Part of the reason is the specificity of the answers required — for instance, it is not enough to label 2.18f as "dog," but you must recognize the breed, keeshond. Until the last decade, computer vision programs performed worse than humans on such tests. Recently, however, taking an approach that has striking similarities to the way the human visual system works, computer vision programs have been able to match and now outperform humans in this sort of object recognition task.

Figure 2.18 Test Pictures Like Those Used in ImageNet Large-Scale Visual Recognition, a Benchmark for Machine Category Classification. (a) Flamingo, (b) Partridge, (c) Persian cat, (d) Lynx, (e) Dalmatian, (f) Keeshond. *(Research from Russakovsky et al., 2015. (a) Evannovostro/ Shutterstock, (b) NCaan/Shutterstock, (c) ArxOnt/Getty Images, (d) Martin Mecnarowski/Shutterstock, (e) Adrian Sherratt/Alamy, (f) Anagramm/Getty Images.)*

(a)　　　(b)　　　(c)

(d)　　　(e)　　　(f)

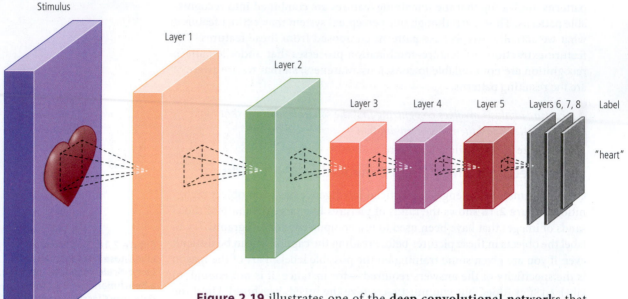

Stimulus

Layer 1

Layer 2

Layer 3   Layer 4   Layer 5   Layers 6, 7, 8   Label

"heart"

Figure 2.19 An Eight-Layer Deep Convolutional Network. The stimulus is a pixel representation that can be thought of as similar to activity in the retina. The connections from the stimulus to Layer 1 and from each layer to the next illustrate how the neural elements in a receptive field of one layer converge to an element in the next layer. Layers 6–8 are fully connected and determine the label. *(Research from Cichy, Khosla, Pantazis, Torralba, & Oliva, 2016.)*

Figure 2.19 illustrates one of the **deep convolutional networks** that was used in this type of research (Krizhevsky, Sutskever, & Hinton, 2012). Its image processing starts from the stimulus — a pixel representation of the image — followed by five layers of pattern recognizers. The initial pixel representation can be thought of as similar to the activity in the retina. Elements in small regions of pixels converge on elements in Layer 1, which detect patterns in these small regions. Layer 1 elements converge on Layer 2 elements that detect patterns of these patterns in small regions of Layer 1, and so on until Layer 5, after which there are three fully connected layers, leading to a response label. These are called convolutional networks because the same pattern in a higher layer is matched against each region of the next lower layer. After Krizhevsky et al. produced this system in 2012, subsequent years have seen the development of even deeper networks with as many as 150 or more layers (He, Zhang, Ren, & Sun, 2016) that perform still better than the eight-layer network in Figure 2.19. However, the interest in psychology has been on shallower deep convolutional networks like the one in Figure 2.19 because they appear to have properties like those of the human visual system.

These networks learn to recognize objects by being trained on millions of images and their associated labels. As learning progresses, a structure emerges wherein early layers respond to simple features and later layers respond to more complex patterns, as shown in **Figure 2.20**. In Layer 1, there are elements that behave much like the bar and edge detectors in the primary visual cortex, By the time we get to Layer 5, we find elements that respond to complex patterns like faces, similar to cells in the inferior temporal lobe. Not only do these networks have a similar structure to that of the human visual system, but it has been shown that objects that produce similar fMRI patterns of activity in the human inferior temporal lobe are represented similarly in Layer 5 of the deep network in Figure 2.19 (Güçlü & van Gerven, 2015). Similarly, in an fMRI study of the monkey visual system, earlier occipital regions of the visual system responded similarly to earlier layers of the network, while later cells in the inferior temporal lobe responded similarly to later layers (Yamins et al., 2014).

Despite such similarities, there are many ways in which these networks are not like the human visual system. The elements are not in detail like real neurons, and the method by which these networks learn (called *back propagation*) is not considered a realistic model of human learning. However, the results obtained with deep convolutional networks do support the conjecture that human object recognition works by starting with the detection of simple features in the input and gradually combining them to form more complex features.

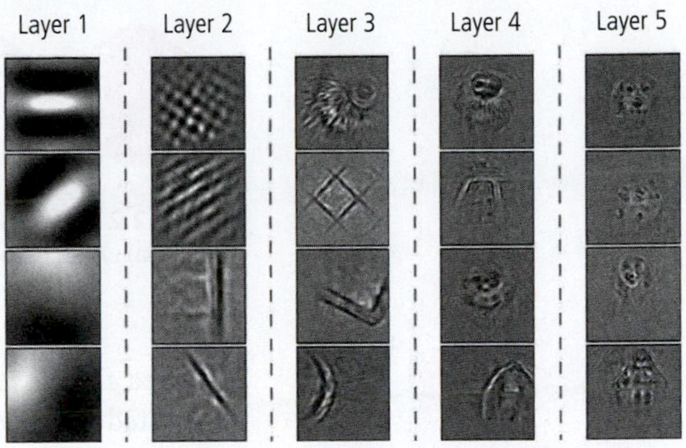

> *Excellent object recognition has been achieved by computer vision systems that use deep convolutional networks, layers of neural elements like those found in the "what" pathway of the brain.*

Figure 2.20 Reconstructions of the Internal Representations in the Layers of a Deep Convolutional Network. These reconstructions show the images that produced the greatest response for different neural elements in the layers. *(Güçlü, U., & van Gerven, M. A. (2015). Deep neural networks reveal a gradient in the complexity of neural representations across the ventral stream. Journal of Neuroscience, 35(27), 10005–10014.)*

Face Recognition

Faces make up one of the most important categories of visual stimuli, and some evidence suggests that we have special mechanisms for recognizing faces. Special cells that respond preferentially to the faces of other monkeys have been found in the temporal lobes of monkeys (Baylis, Rolls, & Leonard, 1985; Rolls, 1992—but see also the hand recognition cell in Figure 2.9). Damage to the temporal lobe in humans can result in a deficit called **prosopagnosia,** in which people have selective difficulties in recognizing faces. Brain-imaging studies using fMRI have found a particular region of the temporal lobe, called the **fusiform gyrus,** that responds when faces are present in the visual field (e.g., Ishai, Ungerleider, Martin, Maisog, & Haxby, 1997; Kanwisher, McDermott, & Chun, 1997; McCarthy, Puce, Gore, & Allison, 1997). The response is much stronger in the right fusiform gyrus.

Other evidence that the processing of faces is special comes from research that examined the recognition of faces turned upside down. In one of the original studies, Yin (1969) found that people are much better at recognizing faces presented in their upright orientation than they are at recognizing other categories of objects, such as houses, presented in their upright orientation. When a face is presented upside down, however, there is a dramatic decrease in its recognition; and this is not true of other objects. Thus, it appears that we are specially attuned to recognizing faces. Studies have also found somewhat

Figure 2.21 Greebles. "Greeble experts" show activity in the fusiform gyrus (the so-called face area) when recognizing these objects. *(Image courtesy of Michael J. Tarr.)*

reduced fMRI response in the fusiform gyrus when upside-down faces are presented (Haxby et al., 1999; Kanwisher, Tong, & Nakayama, 1998). In addition, we are much better at recognizing parts of a face (a nose, say) when it is presented in context, whereas recognizing parts of a house (for example, a window) is not as context dependent (Tanaka & Farah, 1993). All this evidence leads some researchers to think that we are specifically predisposed to identify whole faces, and it is sometimes argued that this special capability was acquired through evolution.

Other research questions whether the fusiform gyrus is specialized for just face recognition and presents evidence that it is involved in making fine-grained distinctions generally. For instance, Gauthier, Skudlarski, Gore, and Anderson (2000) found that bird experts or car experts showed high activation in the fusiform gyrus when they made judgments about birds or cars. In another study, people given a lot of practice at recognizing a set of unfamiliar objects called *greebles* (see **Figure 2.21**) showed activation in the fusiform gyrus. Studies like these support the idea that, because of our great familiarity with faces, we are good at making such fine-grained judgments in recognizing them, but similar effects can be found with other stimuli with which we have had a lot of experience. (See **Implications 2.2** for a discussion of face recognition by deep convolutional networks.)

> *The right fusiform gyrus, located in the temporal lobe, becomes active when people recognize faces.*

Speech Recognition

Up to this point, we have considered only visual pattern recognition. An interesting test of the generality of our conclusions is whether they extend to speech recognition. Although we will not discuss the details of early speech processing, it is worth noting that similar issues arise, especially the issue of segmentation. Speech is not broken into discrete units the way printed text is. Although we seem to perceive well-defined gaps between words in speech, these gaps are often an illusion. If we examine the actual physical speech signal, we often find undiminished sound energy at word boundaries. Indeed, gaps in sound energy are as likely to occur within a word as

Implications 2.2

New Developments in Face-Recognition Software

Recent years have seen rapid improvements in face-recognition software. The classic approach to face recognition is to identify key features like eyes and nose and to recognize faces on the basis of features around these landmarks. A number of recent systems, including Facebook's Deep-Face (Taigman, Yang, Ranzato, & Wolf, 2014) and Google's FaceNet (Schroff, Kalenichenko, & Philbin, 2015), take a different approach using deep convolutional networks like those that have enjoyed recent success in object recognition (e.g., the deep convolutional network depicted in Figure 2.19). These systems achieve better than human accuracy in recognizing faces. The tests can be quite demanding. **Figure 2.22** shows pairs of faces that these systems were asked to recognize as belonging to the same individual. Google's FaceNet achieved 99% accuracy in making such identifications. Such systems are used for many purposes beyond identifying faces in social media. For example, they are used by Apple's Face ID to identify authorized users, by police to identify individuals in a crowd, and by some countries (e.g., Australia) to verify that visitors match their passport photos. Most Americans have their photos on record (e.g., for driver's licenses), and the FBI can use its face-recognition system to match persons of interest to these photos.

Not surprisingly, such advances in face recognition have raised privacy concerns. With the ubiquity of video cameras (an estimated 60 million surveillance cameras in the United States) and the frequency with which faces appear in social media, there is fear that the way is open for government agencies or large technology companies to track our every move. As an example, in the Chinese city of Xiangyang surveillance cameras identify jaywalkers; then, to shame the jaywalkers, their photos, names, and government IDs are displayed on a big outdoor screen (Mozur, 2018). Use of face recognition for criminal identification is also controversial because it can be prone to errors, particularly in the case of minorities like African Americans and Latinos. There have been lawsuits filed against private organizations such as Facebook and government organizations such as the U.S. Department of Justice concerning their use of large databases of faces in conjunction with their face-recognition software.

Figure 2.22 Pairs of Faces Used to Test Face-Recognition Systems. These are examples of the 1% of face pairs that Google's FaceNet was *not* able to recognize as belonging to the same person. *(Republished with permission of IEEE, from Facenet: A unified embedding for face recognition and clustering. In Proceedings of the IEEE Conference on Computer Vision and Pattern Recognition; Schroff, F., Kalenichenko, D., & Philbin, J. (2015); permission conveyed through Copyright Clearance Center.)*

between words. This property of speech becomes particularly compelling when we listen to someone speaking an unfamiliar language. The speech appears to be a continuous stream of sounds with no obvious word boundaries. It is our familiarity with our own language that leads to the illusion of word boundaries.

Within a single word, even greater segmentation problems exist. These intraword problems involve the identification of **phonemes.** Phonemes are the basic units for speech recognition.[1] A phoneme is defined as the minimal unit of speech that can result in a difference in the spoken message. To illustrate, consider the word *bat.* This word is composed of three phonemes: /b/, /a/, and /t/. Replacing /b/ with the phoneme /p/, we get *pat;* replacing /a/ with /i/ we get *bit;* replacing /t/ with /n/, we get *ban.* Obviously, a one-to-one correspondence does not always exist between letters and phonemes. For example, the word *one* consists of the phonemes /w/, /ə/, and /n/; *school* consists of the phonemes /s/, /k/, /ú/, and /l/; and *knight* consists of /n/, /ī /, and /t/. It is the lack of perfect letter-to-phoneme correspondence that makes English spelling so difficult.

A segmentation problem arises when the phonemes composing a spoken word need to be identified. The difficulty is that speech is continuous, and phonemes are not discrete in the way letters are on a printed page. Segmentation at this level is like recognizing a handwritten (not printed) message, where one letter runs into another. Also, as in the case of writing, different speakers vary in the way they produce the same phonemes. The variation among speakers is dramatically clear, for instance, when a person first tries to understand a speaker with a strong and unfamiliar regional accent (e.g., when a Texan listens for the first time to a speaker from Australia — or vice versa). Examination of the speech signal, however, will reveal that even among speakers with the same accent, considerable variation exists. For instance, the voices of women and children normally have a much higher pitch than those of men, some people speak much more rapidly or much more slowly than average, and so on.

A further difficulty in speech perception involves a phenomenon known as coarticulation (Liberman, 1970). As the vocal tract is producing one sound — say, the /b/ in *bag* — it is moving toward the configuration it needs for the /a/. As it is saying the /a/, it is moving to produce the /g/. In effect, the various phonemes overlap. This means additional difficulties in segmenting phonemes, and it also means that the actual sound produced for one phoneme will be determined by the context of the surrounding phonemes.

Speech perception poses information-processing demands that are in many ways greater than those involved in other kinds of auditory perception. Researchers have identified a number of patients who have lost just the ability to recognize speech as a result of injury to the left temporal lobe (see Goldstein, 1974, for a review) but whose ability to detect and recognize other sounds and to speak is intact. Thus, their deficit is specific to speech perception. Occasionally, such patients have some success if the speech they are

---

[1] Massaro (1996) presents an often-proposed alternative — that the basic perceptual units are consonant-vowel and vowel-consonant combinations.

trying to perceive is very slow (see, e.g., Okada, Hanada, Hattori, & Shoyama, 1963), which suggests that part of the problem might lie in segmenting the speech stream.

> *Speech recognition involves segmenting words and the phonemes within words from the continuous speech stream.*

Feature Analysis of Speech

Feature-analysis and feature-combination processes seem to underlie speech perception, much as they do visual object recognition. As with individual letters, individual phonemes can be analyzed into a number of features. These features refer to aspects of how the phoneme is generated by the vocal apparatus. Among the features of phonemes are the consonantal feature, voicing, and the place of articulation (Chomsky & Halle, 1968). The **consonantal feature** is the consonant-like quality of a phoneme (in contrast to a vowel-like quality). **Voicing** is a feature of phonemes produced by vibration of the vocal cords. For example, the phoneme /z/ in the word *zip* has voicing, whereas the phoneme /s/ in the word *sip* does not. You can detect this difference between /z/ and /s/ by placing your fingers on your larynx as you generate the buzzing sound *zzzz* versus the hissing sound *ssss*. You will feel the vibration of your larynx for *zzzz* but not for *ssss*.

Place of articulation refers to the location at which the vocal tract is closed or constricted in the production of a consonant phoneme. (It is closed or constricted at some point in the utterance of most consonants.) For instance, /p/, /m/, and /w/ are considered to have a bilabial place of articulation because the lips are closed (or constricted, in the case of /w/) while they are being generated. The phonemes /f/ and /v/ are considered labiodental because the bottom lip is pressed against the front teeth. Two different phonemes are represented by /th/ — one in *thy* (with voicing) and the other in *thigh* (without voicing). Both are dental because the tongue presses against the teeth. The phonemes /t/, /d/, /s/, /z/, /n/, /l/, and /r/ are all alveolar because the tongue presses against the alveolar ridge of the gums just behind the upper front teeth. The phonemes /sh/, /ch/, /j/, and /y/ are all palatal because the tongue presses against the roof of the mouth just behind the alveolar ridge. The phonemes /k/ and /g/ are velar because the tongue presses against the soft palate, or velum, in the rear roof of the mouth.

Consider the phonemes /p/, /b/, /t/, and /d/. All share the feature of being consonants. The four can be distinguished, however, by voicing and place of articulation. **Table 2.2** classifies these four phonemes according to these two features.

Considerable evidence exists for the role of such features in speech perception. For instance, Miller and Nicely (1955) had participants try to recognize phonemes such

TABLE 2.2 The Classification of /b/, /p/, /d/, and /t/ According to Voicing and Place of Articulation

Place of Articulation	Voicing	
	Voiced	Unvoiced
Bilabial	/b/	/p/
Alveolar	/d/	/t/

as /b/, /d/, /p/, and /t/ by distinguishing between the sounds *ba*, *da*, *pa*, and *ta* presented in noise.[2] Participants exhibited confusion, thinking they had heard one sound in the noise when in reality another sound had been presented. The experimenters were interested in which sounds participants would confuse with which other sounds. Participants most often confused consonants that were distinguished by just a single feature. To illustrate, when presented with /p/, participants more often thought that they had heard /t/ than that they had heard /d/. The phoneme /t/ differs from /p/ only in place of articulation, whereas /d/ differs both in place of articulation and in voicing. Similarly, participants presented with /b/ more often thought they heard /p/ (differing only in voicing) than /t/ (differing in both features).

This experiment is an earlier demonstration of the kind of logic we saw in the Kinney et al. (1966) study on letter recognition. When the participant could identify only a subset of the features underlying a pattern (in this case, the pattern is a phoneme), the participant's responses reflected confusion among the patterns (i.e., phonemes) sharing the same subset of features.

> *Phonemes are recognized in terms of features involved in their production, such as place of articulation and voicing.*

Categorical Perception

The features of phonemes result from the ways in which they are articulated. What properties of the acoustic stimulus encode these articulatory features? This issue has been particularly well researched in the case of voicing. In the pronunciation of syllables beginning with such consonants as /b/ and /p/ (e.g., the syllables *pa* and *ba*), two things happen: The closed lips open, releasing air, and the vocal cords begin to vibrate (voicing). In the case of syllables beginning with the voiced consonant /b/, the release of air and the vibration of the vocal cords are nearly simultaneous, and the vocal cord vibration continues into the articulation of the following vowel /a/. In the case of the unvoiced consonant /p/, the release occurs 60 ms before the vibration begins for the vowel. What we are detecting when we perceive a voiced versus an unvoiced consonant is the presence or absence of a 60-ms interval between release and voicing. This period of time is referred to as the *voice-onset time*. The difference between /p/ and /b/ is illustrated in **Figure 2.23**. Similar differences exist in other voiced–unvoiced pairs, such as /d/ and /t/. Again, the factor controlling the perception of a phoneme is the delay between the release of air and the vibration of the vocal cords.

Lisker and Abramson (1970) performed experiments with artificial (computer-generated) syllables in which the delay between the release of air and the onset of voicing was varied from –150 ms (voicing occurred 150 ms before release) to +150 ms (voicing occurred 150 ms after release). The

---

[2] It is not possible to present /b/, /d/, /p/, or /t/ alone without something that will sound like a vowel.

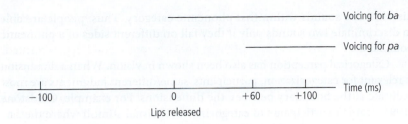

Figure 2.23 Voice-Onset Time for *ba* versus *pa*. The difference between syllables beginning with the voiced consonant /b/ and the unvoiced consonant /p/ is the delay in the case of /p/ between the release of the lips and the onset of voicing. *(Data from Clark & Clark, 1977.)*

participant's task was to identify which syllables began with /b/ and which with /p/. **Figure 2.24** plots the percentage of /b/ identifications and /p/ identifications against voice-onset time. Throughout most of the continuum, participants agreed 100% on what they heard, but there was a sharp switch from /b/ to /p/ at about 25 ms. At a 10-ms voice-onset time, participants were in nearly unanimous agreement that the sound was a /b/; at 60 ms, they were in nearly unanimous agreement that the sound was a /p/. Because of this sharp boundary between identifications of the voiced and unvoiced phonemes, perception of this feature is referred to as *categorical*. **Categorical perception** is the perception of stimuli as belonging in distinct categories and the failure to perceive the gradations among stimuli within a category.

Other evidence for categorical perception of speech comes from discrimination studies (see Studdert-Kennedy, 1976, for a review). People are very poor at discriminating between pairs of syllables beginning with /b/ or pairs beginning with /p/ that differ in voice-onset time but are on the same side of the phonemic boundary. However, they are good at discriminating between pairs that have the same difference in voice-onset time when one item of the pair is on the /b/ side of the boundary and the other item is on the /p/ side. It seems that people can identify the phonemic category of a sound but cannot

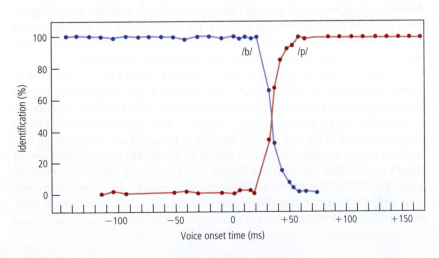

Figure 2.24 Percentage Identification of /b/ versus /p/ as a Function of Voice-Onset Time. A sharp shift from /b/ to /p/ in these identification functions occurred at a voice-onset time of about +25 ms. *(Data from Lisker & Abramson, 1970.)*

discriminate sounds within that phonemic category. Thus, people are able to discriminate two sounds only if they fall on different sides of a phonemic boundary.

Categorical perception has also been shown in vision. When a dimension is relevant for categorization, participants' same/different judgments are most accurate at the boundary between the dimensions. For example, Goldstone (1994) trained participants to categorize novel visual stimuli where the categories were determined by either the size or the brightness of the stimuli. Participants showed increased ability to make perceptual discriminations on whichever dimension was relevant to categorization.

There are at least two views of exactly what is meant by categorical perception, which differ in the strength of their claims about the nature of perception. The weaker view is that we experience stimuli as coming from distinct categories. There seems to be little dispute that the perception of phonemes is categorical in this sense. A stronger viewpoint is that we cannot discriminate among stimuli within a category. Massaro (1992) has taken issue with this viewpoint, arguing that there is some residual ability to discriminate within categories. Even if there is discriminability within categories, people are typically better able to make discriminations that cross category boundaries (Goldstone & Hendrickson, 2010). Thus, there is increased discriminability between categories (acquired distinctiveness) and decreased discriminability within categories (acquired equivalence).

There is also considerable debate about what the mechanism is behind categorical perception in speech. Some researchers (e.g., Liberman & Mattingly, 1985) have argued that categorical perception of speech reflects special speech perception mechanisms that enable people to perceive how the sounds were generated. Consider, for instance, the categorical distinction between how voiced and unvoiced consonants are produced — either the vocal cords vibrate during the consonant or they do not. This has been used to argue that we perceive voicing by unconsciously determining how the consonants are spoken. This theory, referred to as *analysis by synthesis,* asserts that we determine how we would generate the speech sounds and that we recognize them in terms of the generation process. Thus, the reason for the categorical discrimination between voiced and unvoiced is that they are generated in distinct ways (i.e., with or without vocal cord vibrations, respectively).

However, there is evidence that categorical perception is not tied to human processing of language but rather reflects a general property of how certain sounds are perceived. For instance, Pisoni (1977) created nonlinguistic tones that had a distinguishing acoustic feature similar to the feature of voice-onset time in voicing — a low-frequency tone that was either simultaneous with a high-frequency tone or lagged it by 60 ms. His participants showed abrupt boundaries like those in Figure 2.24 for speech signals. In another study, Kuhl (1987) trained chinchillas to discriminate between *da* (beginning with voiced /d/) and *ta* (beginning with voiceless /t/). Even though these animals do not have a human vocal tract, they showed the sharp perceptual boundary between these stimuli that humans do. Thus, it seems that categorical perception depends on neither the signal being speech (Pisoni, 1977) nor the perceiver having a human vocal or auditory system (Kuhl, 1987). Diehl, Lotto, and Holt (2004) have argued that the phonemes we use are chosen because they match up with boundaries already present in our auditory system. So it is more a case of our perceptual system determining our speech behavior rather than vice versa.

> *Speech sounds differing on continuous dimensions but falling on different sides of some perceptual boundary are perceived as coming from distinct categories.*

Context and Pattern Recognition

So far, we have considered pattern recognition as if the only information available to a pattern-recognition system were the information in the physical stimulus to be recognized. This is not the case, however. Objects occur in context, and we can use context to help us recognize objects. Consider the example in **Figure 2.25**. We perceive the words *THE* and *CAT*, even though the symbols for *H* and *A* are identical. The general context provided by the two words makes us see the letters as different. When context or general knowledge of the world guides perception, we refer to the processing as **top-down processing,** because high-level general knowledge contributes to the interpretation of the low-level perceptual units. A general issue in perception is how such top-down processing is combined with the **bottom-up processing** of information from the stimulus itself, without regard to the general context.

One important line of research in top-down effects comes from a series of experiments on letter identification, starting with those of Reicher (1969) and Wheeler (1970). Participants were presented very briefly with either a letter (such as *D*) or a word (such as *WORD*). Immediately afterward, they were given a pair of alternatives and instructed to report which alternative they had seen. (The initial presentation was sufficiently brief that participants made a good many errors in this identification task.) If they had been shown the letter *D*, they might be presented with *D* and *K* as alternatives. If they had been shown *WORD*, they might be given *WORD* and *WORK* as alternatives. Note that both choices differed only in the letter *D* or *K*. Participants were about 10% more accurate in identifying the word than in identifying the letter alone. Thus, they discriminated between *D* and *K* better in the context of a word than as letters alone — even though, in a sense, they had to process four times as many letters in the word context. This phenomenon is known as the **word superiority effect.**

Figure 2.26 illustrates an explanation given by Rumelhart and Siple (1974) and Thompson and Massaro (1973) for why people are more accurate when identifying the letter in the word context. The

Figure 2.25 A Demonstration of Context. The same stimulus is perceived as an *H* or an *A*, depending on the context. *(Republished with permission of Association for Computing Machinery, from Proceedings of the March 1–3, 1955, Western Joint Computer Conference, Selfridge, 1955; permission conveyed through Copyright Clearance Center, Inc.)*

TAE CAT

(a)

(b)

Figure 2.26 Incomplete Perception of Words. The parts of the words that are not obscured provide a hypothetical set of features that might be extracted on a trial in an experiment on word perception: In (a), only the last letter is unidentifiable; in (b), both the second and third letters are unidentifiable.

figure illustrates the products of incomplete perception: In both (a) and (b), certain parts of the word have not been detected. In (a) just the last letter is unidentifiable (it could be *K* or *R*). A participant shown just the partially obscured last letter in (a) would not be able to say whether that letter was a *K* or an *R*. That is, the stimulus information alone would not be enough to identify the letter; but neither would the context alone be enough — the first three letters in (a) are clearly *WOR,* but there are a number of four-letter words that begin *WOR*: *WORD, WORE, WORK, WORM, WORN, WORT.* However, if the participant combines the information from the stimulus with the information from the context, it becomes clear that the whole word must be *WORK* (since *WORR* is not a word), which implies *K* was the last letter. It is not that participants see the *K* better in the context of *WOR* but that they are better able to infer that *K* is the fourth letter. The participants are not conscious of inferences like this, however; so they are said to make unconscious inferences in the act of perception. Note that this analysis is not restricted to the case where the context letters are unambiguous, as in (a). In (b), multiple letters are unidentifiable (the second letter could be *O* or *U* and the third letter could be *B, P,* or *R*). Still, there is enough information in these letter fragments so that *WORK* is the only possible word.

This example illustrates the redundancy present in many complex stimuli such as words. These stimuli consist of many more features than are required to distinguish one stimulus from another. Thus, perception can proceed successfully when only some of the features are recognized, with context filling in the remaining features. In language, this redundancy exists on many levels besides the feature level. For instance, redundancy occurs at the letter level. We do not need to perceive every letter in a string of words to be able to read it. To xllxstxatx, I cxn rxplxce xvexy txirx lextex of x sextexce xitx an x, anx yox stxll xan xanxge xo rxad xt — ix wixh sxme xifxicxltx.

> *Word context can be used to supplement feature information in the recognition of letters.*

Massaro's FLMP Model for Combination of Context and Feature Information

We have reviewed the effects of context on pattern recognition in a variety of perceptual situations, but the question of how to understand these effects still remains. Massaro has argued that the perceptual information provided

Figure 2.27 Recognizing *c* versus *e*. Contextual clues used by Massaro (1979) to study how participants combine stimulus information from a letter with context information from the surrounding letters. *(From D. W. Massaro, Letter information and orthographic context in word perception, Journal of Experimental Psychology: Human Perception and Performance, 5, 595–609. Copyright © 1979 American Psychological Association. Reprinted by permission.)*

by the stimulus and the information provided by the context are independent sources of information about the identity of the stimulus, which are combined to provide the best inference about what the stimulus might be. **Figure 2.27** shows examples of the material Massaro used in a test of recognition of the letter *c* versus the letter *e*.

Figure 2.28 Probability of an *e* Response as a Function of the Stimulus Value of the Test Letter and of the Orthographic Context. The lines reflect the predictions of Massaro's FLMP model, and the symbols (● + × ●) show the results of experiments (clearly supporting the predictions). *(Data from Massaro, 1979.)*

The four quadrants in Figure 2.27 represent four variations in the amount of contextual evidence: *(top left)* only an *e* can make a word; *(bottom left)* only a *c* can make a word; *(top right)* either *e* or *c* can make a word; *(bottom right)* neither *e* nor *c* can make a word. As one reads down any column within a quadrant, the image of the ambiguous letter provides more evidence for *e* and less for *c*. Participants were briefly exposed to the individual four-letter stimuli and asked to identify the ambiguous letter. **Figure 2.28** shows the probability of an *e* identification as a function of the stimulus value (i.e., how *e*-like the ambiguous letter is) and the context information (i.e., whether the four-letter stimulus makes a word with *e* only, with *c* only, with both, or with neither). The lines reflect the predictions of Massaro's model for how people combine stimulus and context information to make such identifications, a model Massaro called **FLMP (fuzzy logical model of perception)**; the symbols reflect the actual results of experiments. In all four contexts, as the image of the letter itself provided more evidence for an *e*, the probability of the participants' identifying an *e* went up. Similarly, the probability of identifying an *e* increased as the context provided more evidence for *e*.

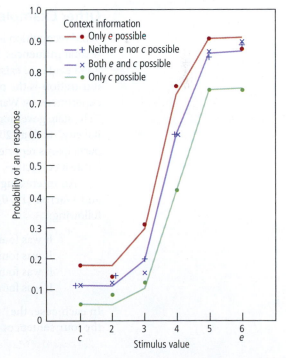

Massaro argued that these data reflect an independent combination of evidence from the context and evidence from the letter stimulus. He assumed that the letter stimulus represents some evidence L_c for the letter c and that the context also provides some evidence C_c for the letter c. He assumed that these evidences can be scaled on a range of 0 to 1 and can be thought of basically as probabilities, which he called "fuzzy truth values." Because probabilities sum to 1, the evidence for e from the letter stimulus is $L_e = 1 - L_c$, and the evidence from the context is $C_e = 1 - C_c$. Given these probabilities, then, the overall probability for a c is

$$p(c) = \frac{L_c \times C_c}{(L_c \times C_c) + (L_e \times C_e)}$$

and, therefore, the overall probability for an e is $p(e) = 1 - p(c)$. In general, as illustrated by Figure 2.28, Massaro's FLMP theory has done a very good job of accounting for the combination of context and stimulus information in pattern recognition.

> *Massaro's FLMP model of perception proposes that contextual information combines independently with stimulus information to determine what pattern is perceived.*

Other Examples of Context and Recognition

Word recognition is one case for which there have been detailed analyses of contextual influences, but contextual effects are ubiquitous. For instance, equally good evidence exists for the role of context in the perception of speech. A nice illustration is the **phoneme-restoration effect,** originally demonstrated in an experiment by Warren (1970). He asked participants to listen to the sentence "The state governors met with their respective legislatures convening in the capital city," with a 120-ms tone replacing the middle s in *legislatures.* Only 1 in 20 participants reported hearing the pure tone, and that participant was not able to locate it correctly.

An interesting extension of this first study was an experiment by Warren and Warren (1970). They presented participants with sentences such as the following:

It was found that the *eel was on the axle.
It was found that the *eel was on the shoe.
It was found that the *eel was on the orange.
It was found that the *eel was on the table.

In each case, the * denotes a phoneme replaced by a nonspeech sound. For the four sentences above, participants reported hearing *wheel, heel, peel,* and *meal,* depending on context. The important feature to note about each of these sentences is that they are identical through the critical word and beyond, up to the last word. The identification of the critical word is determined by what occurs after it — that is, by the last word. Thus, the identification of words often is not instantaneous but can depend on the perception of subsequent words.

An interesting context effect in speech perception is known as the *McGurk effect,* named after Harry McGurk (McGurk and MacDonald, 1976 — there are numerous YouTube demonstrations). The effect involves watching the lips of someone making a sound like *ga* while hearing the sound *ba.* Depending on various factors such as the quality of the acoustic input, listeners report hearing *da* (a fusion or compromise perception — this type of compromise is the McGurk effect), the combination *bga,* the actual sound *ba,* or *ga,* corresponding to the visual input (Jiang & Bernstein, 2011). Even when listeners are aware that the sound is *ba,* they will often hear something else. They are merging the acoustic stimulus with the context provided by the lips.

Context also appears to be important for the perception of complex visual scenes. Biederman, Glass, and Stacy (1973) looked at the perception of objects in novel scenes. **Figure 2.29** illustrates the two kinds of scenes presented to their participants. Figure 2.29a shows a normal, coherent scene; in Figure 2.29b, the same scene is jumbled. Participants viewed one of the scenes briefly on a screen, and immediately thereafter an arrow pointed to a position on a now-blank screen where an object had been moments before.

(a)

(b)

Figure 2.29 Context and Visual Recognition. These scenes were used by Biederman, Glass, and Stacy (1973) in their study of the role of context in the recognition of complex visual scenes: (a) a coherent scene; (b) a jumbled scene. Objects in the jumbled scene are harder to recognize. *(From Biederman, Glass, & Stacy, 1973. Reprinted by permission of the publisher. © 1973 by the American Psychological Association.)*

Figure 2.30 Change Blindness. *(left to right)* An unknowing participant (pointing) is giving directions to an experimenter when worker accomplices carrying a door pass between the experimenter and the participant, allowing one of the accomplices to switch places with the experimenter. Only 7 of the 15 participants noticed the change.

Participants were asked to identify the object that had been in that position in the scene. For example, the arrow might have pointed to the location of the fire hydrant. Participants were considerably more accurate in their identifications when they had viewed the coherent picture than when they had viewed the jumbled picture. Thus, as with the processing of written text or speech, people are able to use context in a visual scene to help in their identification of an object.

One of the most dramatic examples of the influence of context on perception involves a phenomenon called **change blindness.** As Chapter 3 will discuss in detail, people are unable to keep track of all the information in a typical complex scene. If elements of the scene change at the same time as some retinal disturbance occurs (such as an eye movement or a scene-cut in a motion picture), people often fail to detect the change. The original studies on change blindness (McConkie & Currie, 1996) introduced large changes in pictures that participants were viewing while they were making an eye movement. For instance, the color of a car in the picture might change and the change might not be noticed. **Figure 2.30** illustrates a dramatic instance of change blindness (Simons & Levin, 1998) where it seems context is also promoting the insensitivity to change. The experimenter stopped pedestrians on Cornell University's campus and asked for directions. While the unwitting participant was giving the directions, worker accomplices carrying a door passed between the experimenter and the participant, and one of the accomplices switched places with the experimenter. Only 7 of the 15 participants noticed the change. In the scene shown in Figure 2.30, the participants thought of themselves as giving instructions to a student, and as long as the switched accomplice fit that interpretation, they did not process him as different. In a laboratory study of the ability to detect changes in people's faces, Beck, Rees, Frith, and Lavie (2001) found greater activation in the fusiform gyrus (see the earlier discussion of face recognition) when face changes were detected than when they were not.

> *Contextual information biases perceptual processing in a wide variety of situations.*

Conclusions

This chapter discusses how neurons process sensory information and deliver it to higher centers in the brain, and how the information is then processed and combined with contextual information to perceive and recognize objects. **Figure 2.31** depicts the overall flow of information processing in the case of vision perception. Perception begins with light energy from the external environment. Receptors, such as those in the retina, transform this energy into neural information. Early sensory processing makes initial sense of the information by extracting features to yield what Marr (1982) called a **primal sketch.** These features are combined with depth information to get a representation of the location of surfaces in space; this is Marr's 2½-D sketch. The gestalt principles of organization are applied to segment the elements in the 2½-D sketch into objects; this is Marr's 3-D model. Finally, information about the features of these objects and general context information are combined to recognize the objects. The output of this last level is a representation of the objects and their locations in the environment, and this is what we are consciously aware of in perception. This information is then input to higher-level cognitive processes. Figure 2.31 illustrates an important point: A great deal of information processing must take place before we are consciously aware of the objects we are perceiving.

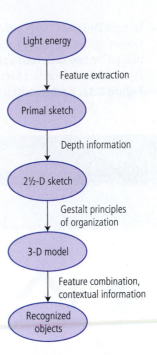

Figure 2.31 How Information Flows from the Environment and Is Processed into Our Perceptual Representation of Recognized Objects. The ovals represent different levels of information in Marr's (1982) model, and the lines are labeled with the perceptual processes that transform one level of information into the next.

Questions for Thought

1. **Figure 2.32a** illustrates an optical illusion called *Mach bands*, after the Austrian physicist and philosopher Ernst Mach, who discovered the illusion. Each band is a uniform shade of gray, and yet the bands appear lighter on the left, next to a darker band, and darker on the right, next to a lighter band. Can you explain why, using on-off cells, edge detectors, and bar detectors in your explanation (see Figures 2.6 and 2.7)?

2. Use the gestalt principles of organization to explain why we tend to perceive two triangles in Figure 2.32b.

3. Figure 2.28 shows that participants presented with the stimulus "cdit" exhibit an increased tendency to say that they have seen "edit," which makes a word. Some people describe this as a case of context distorting perception. Do you agree that this is a case of distortion? Explain your answer.

4. In Luis Buñuel's 1977 movie *That Obscure Object of Desire*, the principal female role is played by two different actresses, Carole Bouquet and Angela Morina (left and right in Figure 2.32c), who switch from scene to scene. Most viewers who are not warned ahead of time are not aware that the switch is happening. Is this an example of the movie context impairing or facilitating perceptual recognition? Explain your answer.

(a)

(b)

(c)

Figure 2.32 Figures for Question for Thought. (a) Mach bands; (b) demonstration of gestalt principles of organization; (c) Carole Bouquet (left) and Angela Morina (right). *(Allan Tannenbaum/Getty Images.)*

Key Terms

2½-D sketch	deep convolutional	gestalt principles of	retina
3-D model	networks	organization	rods
apperceptive agnosia	edge detectors	phoneme-restoration	template matching
associative agnosia	feature analysis	effect	top-down processing
bar detectors	feature map	phonemes	visual agnosia
bottom-up processing	FLMP (fuzzy logical	place of articulation	voicing
categorical perception	model of perception)	primal sketch	"what" visual pathway
change blindness	fovea	primary visual cortex	"where" visual pathway
cones	fusiform gyrus	prosopagnosia	word superiority effect
consonantal feature		receptive field	

Attention and Performance

Chapter 2 described how the human visual system and other perceptual systems simultaneously process information from all over their sensory fields. However, we have limits on how much we can do in parallel. In many situations, we can attend to only one spoken message or one visual object at a time. This chapter explores how higher-level cognition determines what to attend to and how attention affects performance on various types of tasks. We will consider the following questions:

- What are bottlenecks in human information processing?
- In a busy world filled with sounds, how do we select what to listen to?
- How do we find meaningful information within a complex visual scene?
- What role does attention play in putting visual patterns together as recognizable objects?
- How do we coordinate parallel activities like driving a car and holding a conversation?

Serial Bottlenecks

Psychologists have proposed that there are **serial bottlenecks** in human information processing, points at which it is no longer possible to continue processing everything in parallel. For example, it is generally accepted that there are limits to parallelism in the motor systems. Although most of us can perform separate actions simultaneously when the actions involve different motor systems (such as walking and chewing gum), we have difficulty in getting one motor system to do two things at once. For example, even though we have two hands, we have only one system for moving our hands, so it is hard to get our two hands to move in different ways at the same time. Think of the familiar problem of trying to pat your head while rubbing your stomach. It is hard to prevent one of the movements from dominating—if you are like me, you tend

Figure 3.1 *The Garden of Earthly Delights* **(right panel).** The right panel of this triptych by the Dutch artist Hieronymus Bosch (c. 1450–1610) is a depiction of Hell. *(Historic Images/Alamy.)*

to wind up rubbing or patting both parts of the body.[1] The many human motor systems — one for moving feet, one for moving hands, one for moving eyes, and so on — can and do work independently and simultaneously, but it is difficult to get any one of these systems to do two things at the same time.

One question that has occupied psychologists is how early do the bottlenecks occur: before we perceive the stimulus, after we perceive the stimulus but before we think about it, or only just before motor action is required? Common sense suggests that some things cannot be done at the same time. For instance, it is basically impossible to add two digits and multiply them simultaneously. Still, there remains the question of just where the bottlenecks in information processing lie. Various theories about where they happen are referred to as **early-selection theories** or **late-selection theories,** depending on where they propose that bottlenecks take place. Wherever there is a bottleneck, our cognitive processes must select which pieces of information to attend to and which to ignore. The study of **attention** is concerned with where these bottlenecks occur and how information is selected at these bottlenecks.

A major distinction in the study of attention is between control by goal-directed factors (**goal-directed attention,** sometimes called *endogenous control*) and control by stimulus-driven factors (**stimulus-driven attention,** sometimes called *exogenous control*). To illustrate the distinction, Corbetta and Shulman (2002) ask us to imagine ourselves at Madrid's El Prado Museum, looking at the right panel of Hieronymus Bosch's painting *The Garden of Earthly Delights* (see **Figure 3.1**). Initially, our eyes will probably be drawn to large, salient objects like the white object in the center of the picture. This would be an instance of stimulus-driven attention — it is not that we wanted to attend to the white object; it just grabbed our attention. However, our guide may start to comment on a "small animal playing a musical instrument." Now we have a goal and will direct our attention over the picture to find the object being described. Continuing their story, Corbetta and Shulman ask us to imagine that we hear an alarm system starting to ring in the next room. Now, a stimulus-driven factor has intervened, and our attention will be drawn away from the picture and switch to the adjacent room. Corbetta

---

[1] Drummers (including my son) are particularly good at doing this — I definitely am not a drummer. This suggests that the real problem might be motor timing.

and Shulman argue that somewhat different brain systems control goal-directed attention versus stimulus-driven attention. For instance, neural imaging evidence suggests that the goal-directed attentional system is more left lateralized, whereas the stimulus-driven system is more right lateralized.

The brain regions involved in attention—that is, the regions that select information to process—can be distinguished (to an approximation) from those that process the information selected. Among the regions highlighted in **Figure 3.2** is the parietal cortex, which influences information processing in regions such as the visual cortex and auditory cortex. Figure 3.2 also highlights prefrontal regions that influence processing in the motor area and more posterior regions. These prefrontal regions include the dorsolateral prefrontal cortex and, well below the surface, the anterior cingulate cortex. As this chapter proceeds, it will elaborate on the research concerning the various brain regions in Figure 3.2.

> *Attentional systems select information to process at serial bottlenecks where it is no longer possible to do things in parallel.*

Brain Structures

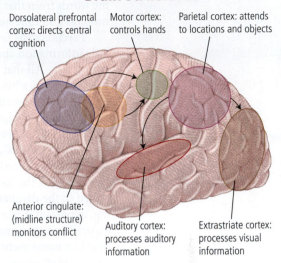

Dorsolateral prefrontal cortex: directs central cognition

Motor cortex: controls hands

Parietal cortex: attends to locations and objects

Anterior cingulate: (midline structure) monitors conflict

Auditory cortex: processes auditory information

Extrastriate cortex: processes visual information

Figure 3.2 Some of the Brain Areas Involved in Attention and Some of the Perceptual and Motor Regions They Control. The parietal regions are particularly important in directing perceptual resources. The prefrontal regions (dorsolateral prefrontal cortex, anterior cingulate) are particularly important in executive control.

Auditory Attention

Some of the early research on attention was concerned with auditory attention, and much of this research centered on the **dichotic listening task.** In a typical dichotic listening experiment, illustrated in **Figure 3.3**, participants wear a set of headphones. They hear two messages at the same time, one in

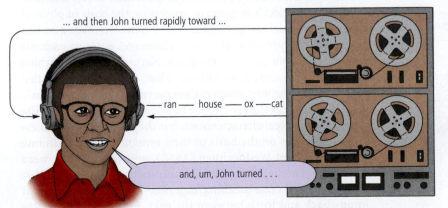

... and then John turned rapidly toward ...

ran — house — ox — cat

and, um, John turned . . .

Figure 3.3 A Typical Dichotic Listening Task. Different messages are presented to the left and right ears, and the participant attempts to "shadow" the message entering one ear.

each ear, and are asked to "shadow" one of the two messages (i.e., repeat back the words from that message only). Most participants are able to attend to one message and tune out the other.

Psychologists (e.g., Cherry, 1953; Moray, 1959) have discovered that very little information about the unattended message is processed in a dichotic listening task. All that participants can report about the unattended message is whether it was a human voice or a noise; whether the human voice was male or female; and whether the sex of the speaker changed during the test. They cannot tell what language was spoken or remember any of the words, even if the same word was repeated over and over again. An analogy is often made between performing this task and being at a party, where a guest tunes in to one message (a conversation) and filters out others. This is an example of goal-directed processing — the listener selects the message to be processed. However, to return to the distinction between goal-directed and stimulus-driven processing, important stimulus information can disrupt our goals. We have probably all experienced the situation in which we are listening intently to one person and hear our name mentioned by someone else. It is very hard in this situation to keep your attention on what the original speaker is saying.

The Filter Theory

Broadbent (1958) proposed an early-selection theory called the **filter theory** to account for these results. His basic assumption was that sensory information comes through the system until some bottleneck is reached. At that point, a person chooses which message to process on the basis of some physical characteristic. The person is said to filter out the other information. In a dichotic listening task, the theory proposed that the message to each ear was registered but that at some later point the participant selected one message to listen to on the basis of the specified ear, thus filtering out the message in the other ear. At a crowded party, we pick which speaker to follow on the basis of other physical characteristics, such as the pitch or loudness of the speaker's voice.

A crucial feature of Broadbent's original filter model is its proposal that we select a message to process on the basis of physical characteristics such as ear or pitch. This hypothesis made a certain amount of neurophysiological sense. Messages entering each ear arrive at the brain on different nerves. Nerves also vary in which frequencies they carry from each ear. Thus, we might imagine that the brain, in some way, selects certain nerves to "pay attention to."

People can certainly choose to attend to a message on the basis of its physical characteristics, but they can also select messages to process on the basis of their semantic content. In one study, Gray and Wedderburn (1960), who at the time were undergraduate students at Oxford University, demonstrated that participants can use meaningfulness to follow a message that jumps back and forth between the ears. **Figure 3.4** illustrates

Figure 3.4 The Shadowing Task in the Gray and Wedderburn (1960) Experiment: Shadow the Meaningful Message. The participant follows the meaningful message as it moves from ear to ear.

the participants' task in their experiment. In one ear they might be hearing the words *dogs six fleas,* while at the same time hearing the words *eight scratch two* in the other ear. Instructed to shadow the meaningful message, participants would report *dogs scratch fleas.* Thus, participants can shadow a message on the basis of meaning rather than on the basis of what each ear physically hears.

Treisman (1960) looked at a situation in which participants were instructed to shadow a particular ear (see **Figure 3.5**). The message in the ear to be shadowed was meaningful up to a certain point; then it turned into a random sequence of words. Simultaneously, the meaningful message switched to the other ear — the one to which the participant had not been attending. Some participants switched ears, against instructions, and continued to follow the meaningful message. Others continued to follow the shadowed ear. Thus, it seems that sometimes people use a physical characteristic (e.g., a particular ear) to select which message to follow and that sometimes they use semantic content.

> *Broadbent's filter model proposes that we use physical features, such as ear or pitch, to select one message to process, but it has been shown that people can also use the meaning of the message as the basis for selection.*

Figure 3.5 The Shadowing Task in the Treisman (1960) Experiment: Shadow the Input in the Specified Ear. The meaningful message moves to the other ear, and the participant sometimes continues to shadow it against instructions.

The Attenuation Theory and a Late-Selection Theory

To account for these kinds of results, Treisman (1964) proposed an early-selection theory that is a modification of the Broadbent model and has come to be known as the **attenuation theory.** This model hypothesized that certain messages would be attenuated (weakened) but not filtered out entirely on the basis of their physical properties. Thus, in a dichotic listening task, participants would minimize processing of the signal from the unattended ear but not eliminate it. Semantic selection criteria could apply to all messages, whether they were attenuated or not. If the message were attenuated, it would be harder to apply these selection criteria, but it would still be possible. Treisman (personal communication, 1978) emphasized that in her experiment illustrated in Figure 3.5, most participants actually continued to shadow the prescribed ear. Apparently, participants found it easier to follow the message that was not being attenuated than to apply semantic criteria to switch attention to the attenuated message.

An alternative explanation had been offered by J. A. Deutsch and D. Deutsch (1963) in their late-selection theory, which proposed that all the information is processed completely without attenuation. Their hypothesis was that the capacity limitation is in the response system, not the perceptual system. That is, their claim was that people can perceive multiple messages but that they can say only one message at a time. Thus, people need some basis for selecting which message to shadow. If they use meaning as the criterion (either according to or in contradiction to instructions), they will switch ears to follow the message. If they use the ear of origin in deciding what to attend to, they will shadow the chosen ear.

The difference between this late-selection theory and the early-selection attenuation theory is illustrated in **Figure 3.6**. Both models assume that there is some filter, or bottleneck, in processing. Treisman's attenuation theory (Figure 3.6a) assumes that a perceptual filter selects which message to attend to (message #1) and that the unselected message (message #2) is therefore attenuated (dashed arrows); thus, only message #1 is fully analyzed for verbal content. In contrast, Deutsch and Deutsch's late-selection theory (Figure 3.6b) assumes that a response filter operates after both messages have been fully analyzed.

Figure 3.6 also illustrates how Treisman and Geffen (1967) tested the difference between these two theories using a dichotic listening task in which participants had to shadow one message (in the figure, this is message #1) while also processing both messages for a target word. If they heard the target word, they were to signal by tapping. According to the Deutsch and Deutsch late-selection

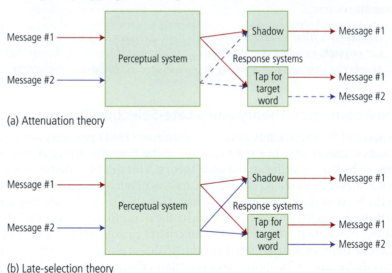

(a) Attenuation theory

(b) Late-selection theory

Figure 3.6 Information Processing from Message to Response in a Dichotic Listening Experiment: Attenuation Theory versus Late-Selection Theory. In this illustration of Treisman and Geffen's (1967) experiment, the task is to shadow message #1 while also trying to detect and respond with a tap to a target word, which could occur in either message. (a) In Treisman's (1964) attenuation theory, the perceptual system filters message #2, which is therefore attenuated when sent to the response systems for shadowing and tapping (dashed arrows, versus solid arrows for unattenuated message #1). (b) In Deutsch and Deutsch's (1963) late-selection theory, the perceptual system processes both messages equally. The response system for shadowing filters out message #2, but the response system for detecting the target word and then tapping should also process both messages equally. (Information from Treisman & Geffen, 1967.)

theory, messages from both ears would be analyzed for verbal content, so participants should have been able to detect the target word equally well in either ear. In contrast, the attenuation theory predicted much less detection of the target word in the message in the unshadowed ear because the unshadowed message would be attenuated. The results of the experiment strongly supported the attenuation theory: participants detected 87% of the target words in the shadowed ear and only 8% in the unshadowed ear. Other evidence consistent with the attenuation theory was reported by Treisman and Riley (1969) and by Johnston and Heinz (1978).

Neural evidence for a version of the attenuation theory supports the idea that there is not only attenuation of the signal from the unattended ear, but also enhancement of the signal coming from the attended ear. The primary auditory cortex (part of the auditory cortex, shown in Figure 3.2) shows an enhanced response to auditory signals coming from the ear the listener is attending to and a decreased response to signals coming from the other ear. Through ERP recording, Woldorff et al. (1993) showed that these responses occur between 20 and 50 ms after stimulus onset. The enhanced responses occur much sooner in auditory processing than the point at which the meaning of the message can be identified. Other studies also provide evidence for enhancement of the message in the primary auditory cortex on the basis of features other than location. For instance, Zatorre, Mondor, and Evans (1999) found in a PET study that when people attend to a message on the basis of pitch, the primary auditory cortex shows enhancement (registered as increased activation). This study also found increased activation in the parietal areas that direct attention.

Although auditory attention can enhance processing in the primary auditory cortex, there is no reliable evidence of effects of attention on earlier stages of auditory processing, such as in the auditory nerve or the brain stem (Picton & Hillyard, 1974). The various results we have reviewed suggest that the primary auditory cortex is the earliest area to be influenced by attention to auditory stimuli. It should be stressed that the effects at the primary auditory cortex are a matter of attenuation and enhancement. Messages are not completely filtered out, and so it is still possible to select them at later points of processing.

> *Attention can enhance or reduce the magnitude of response to an auditory signal in the primary auditory cortex.*

Visual Attention

The bottleneck in visual information processing is even more apparent than the one in auditory information processing. As we saw in Chapter 2, the retina varies in acuity, with the greatest acuity in a very small area, the fovea (see Figure 2.4). Although the human eye registers a large part of the visual field, the fovea registers only a small fraction of that field. Thus, in choosing where to focus our vision, we also choose to devote our most powerful visual processing resources to a particular part of the visual field, and we limit the

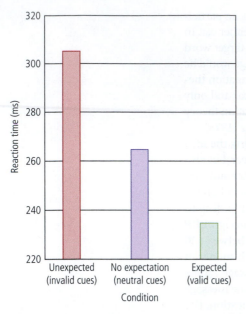

Figure 3.7 Reaction Time to Stimuli in Expected, Unexpected, or Neutral Locations. The stimuli appeared 7° to the left or right of the fixation point. Participants reacted faster to stimuli in expected locations and slower to stimuli in unexpected locations.

(Data from Posner et al., 1978.)

resources allocated to processing other parts of the field. Usually, we are attending to that part of the visual field on which we are focusing. For instance, as we read, we move our eyes so that we are fixating the words we are attending to.

The focus of visual attention is not always identical with the part of the visual field being processed by the fovea, however. People can be instructed to fixate on one part of the visual field (making the focused image of that part fall on the fovea) while attending to another, nonfoveal region of the visual field.[2] In one experiment, Posner, Nissen, and Ogden (1978) had participants fixate on a constant point and then presented them with a stimulus 7° to the left or the right of the fixation point. In each trial, before the stimulus appeared, participants would see a cue near the fixation point, providing information about where to expect the stimulus. In a third of the trials, the cue would point to the left of the fixation point; in a third, the cue would point to the right; and in the other third, the cue would be neutral, not indicating either direction. The cues indicating left or right were correct 80% of the time (valid cues), but 20% of the time the stimulus appeared on the unexpected side (invalid cues). After neutral cues, the stimulus appeared equally often left and right. The researchers monitored the participants' eye movements and included only those trials in which the eyes had stayed on the fixation point. **Figure 3.7** shows the time required to react to the stimulus if it appeared after a valid cue, in the expected location; if it appeared after a neutral cue; and if it appeared after an invalid cue, in the unexpected location. Participants were faster when the stimulus appeared in the expected location and slower when it appeared in the unexpected location. Thus, they were able to shift their attention from where their eyes were fixated.

Posner, Snyder, and Davidson (1980) found that people can attend to regions of the visual field as far as 24 degrees from the fovea. Although visual attention can be moved without accompanying eye movements, people usually do move their eyes, so that the fovea processes the portion of the visual field to which they are attending. Posner (1988) pointed out that successful control of eye movements actually *requires* us to attend to places outside the fovea. That is, we must attend to and identify an interesting nonfoveal region so that we can guide our eyes to fixate on that region to achieve the greatest acuity in processing it. Thus, a shift of attention often precedes the corresponding eye movement.

To process a complex visual scene, we must move our attention around in the visual field to track the visual information. This process is like shadowing a conversation. Neisser and Becklen (1975) performed the visual analogue of the auditory shadowing task. As illustrated in **Figure 3.8**, they had participants observe two videotapes superimposed over each other, one showing two pairs of hands playing a hand-slapping game (Figure 3.8a), the other showing some

---

[2] This is what quarterbacks are supposed to do when deciding where to pass the football, so that they don't "give away" the position of the intended receiver.

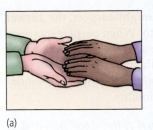  

(a)   (b)   (c)

Figure 3.8 **Illustrations of Frames from Videotapes Used by Neisser and Becklen (1975) in Their Visual Analog of the Auditory Shadowing Task.** (a) The "hand-game" video; (b) the basketball video; and (c) the two videos superimposed. *(Information from Neisser & Becklen, 1975.)*

people passing around a basketball (Figure 3.8b). Figure 3.8c illustrates how the superimposed videotapes would have appeared to the participants. They were instructed to pay attention to one of the two films and to watch for odd events, such as the two players in the hand-slapping game pausing and shaking hands. Participants were able to monitor one film successfully and reported filtering out the other. When asked to monitor both films for odd events, the participants experienced great difficulty and missed many of the critical events.

As Neisser and Becklen (1975) noted, this situation involved an interesting combination of the use of physical cues and the use of content cues. Participants moved their eyes and focused their attention in such a way that the critical aspects of the monitored event fell on their fovea and the center of their attentive spotlight. The only way they could know where to move their eyes to focus on a critical event was by making reference to the content of the event. Thus, the content of the event facilitated their processing of the film, which in turn facilitated extracting the content.

Figure 3.9 shows an example of the overlapping stimuli used in an experiment by O'Craven, Downing, and Kanwisher (1999) to study the neural consequences of attending to one object or the other. Participants in their experiment saw a series of pictures that consisted of faces superimposed on houses. They were instructed to look for either repetition of the same face in the series or repetition of the same house. Recall from Chapter 2 that there is a region of the temporal cortex in the fusiform gyrus (a region known as the *fusiform face area*), which becomes more active when people are observing faces. There is another area within the temporal cortex, known as the *parahippocampal place area*, that becomes more active when people are observing places. What is special about these pictures is that they consisted of both faces and places. Which region would become active — the fusiform face area or

Figure 3.9 **A Picture Used in a Study of Visual Attention by O'Craven et al. (1999).** When the face is attended, there is activation in the fusiform face area, and when the house is attended, there is activation in the parahippocampal place area. *(Paul Downing & Nancy Kanwisher.)*

the parahippocampal place area? As the reader might suspect, the answer depended on what the participant was attending to. When participants were looking for repetition of faces, the fusiform face area became more active; when they were looking for repetition of places, the parahippocampal place area became more active. Attention determined which region of the temporal cortex was engaged in the processing of the stimulus.

> *People can focus their attention on nonfoveal parts of the visual field and can change their focus of attention to process what they are interested in.*

The Neural Basis of Visual Attention

It appears that the neural mechanisms underlying visual attention are very similar to those underlying auditory attention. Just as auditory attention directed to one ear enhances the cortical signal from that ear, visual attention directed to a spatial location appears to enhance the cortical signal from that location. If a person attends to a particular spatial location, a distinct neural response (detected using ERP records) in the visual cortex occurs within 70 to 90 ms after the onset of a stimulus. On the other hand, when a person is attending to a particular object (attending to a chair rather than a table, say) rather than to a particular location in space, we do not see a response for more than 200 ms. Thus, it appears to take more effort to direct visual attention on the basis of content than on the basis of physical features, just as is the case with auditory attention.

Mangun, Hillyard, and Luck (1993) had participants fixate on the center of a computer screen, then judge the lengths of bars presented in positions different from the fixation location (upper left, lower left, upper right, and lower right). **Figure 3.10** shows the distribution of scalp activity detected by ERP when a participant was attending to each of these four different regions of the visual array (while fixating on the center of the screen). Consistent with the topographic organization of the visual cortex, there was greatest activity over the side of the scalp opposite the side of the visual field where the object appeared. Recall from Chapters 1 and 2 (see Figure 2.5) that the visual cortex (at the back of the brain) is topographically organized, with each visual field (left or right) represented in the opposite hemisphere. Thus, it appears that there is enhanced neural processing in the portion of the visual cortex corresponding to the location of visual attention.

A study by Roelfsema, Lamme, and Spekreijse (1998) illustrates the impact of visual attention on information processing in the primary visual cortex of the macaque monkey. In this experiment, the researchers trained monkeys to perform the rather complex task illustrated in **Figure 3.11**. While a monkey performed this task, Roelfsema et al. recorded from cells in the monkey's primary visual cortex (where cells with receptive fields like those in Figure 2.7 are found). The square in Figure 3.11 represents the receptive field of one of these cells, a cell that shows increased response when a line falls on that part of the visual field. A trial would begin with the monkey

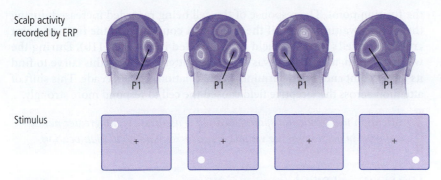

Scalp activity recorded by ERP

Stimulus

Figure 3.10 Results from an Experiment by Mangun, Hillyard, and Luck (1993) on the Neural Basis of Visual Attention. Distribution of scalp activity was recorded by ERP when a participant was attending to a stimulus in each of the four different regions of the visual array indicated by the white circles in the displays at bottom while fixating on the center of the screen. The greatest activity (the areas labeled "P1") was recorded over the side of the scalp opposite the side of the visual field where the object appeared, confirming that there is enhanced neural processing in portions of the visual cortex corresponding to the location of visual attention. *(David E. Meyer and Sylvan Kornblum, eds., Attention and Performance XIV, Figure 10.5, © 1993 Massachusetts Institute of Technology, by permission of The MIT Press.)*

keeping its gaze on a fixation point in the visual field (the display shown in Figure 3.11a). Then, a stimulus would appear — two curves that ended in blue dots (the curves and target points shown in Figure 3.11b), with only one of these curves connected to the fixation point. The monkey had to keep looking at the fixation point for 600 ms and then perform the saccade shown in Figure 3.11c — an eye movement to the target point that was connected to

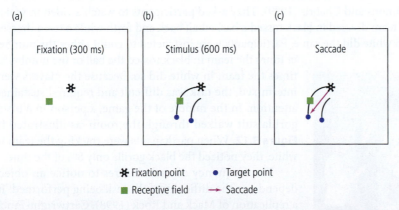

✳ Fixation point ● Target point
■ Receptive field → Saccade

Figure 3.11 The Experimental Procedure in Roelfsema et al. (1998), Studying How Attention Affects the Response of Cells in the Visual Cortex of Macaque Monkeys. (a) The monkey fixates on the star. (b) Two curves and target points are presented, one of which links the start point to a target point (in the trial illustrated here, the curve crosses the receptive field of a cell being recorded). (c) The monkey saccades to the target point connected to the fixation point, which means that the monkey's attention crosses the receptive field of the cell being recorded.

the fixation point. The response of the cell being recorded increased during the 600-ms waiting period if the curve that connected to the fixation point crossed the cell's receptive field (as illustrated in Figure 3.11b). During the waiting period, the monkey was shifting its attention along this curve to find its target point and thus determine the destination of the saccade. This shift of attention across the receptive field caused the cell to respond more strongly.

> *Attention to a particular spatial location is associated with greater neural response in portions of the visual cortex corresponding to that location.*

Inattentional Blindness

We think we are generally aware of everything in our environment, but research indicates that this is largely an illusion — we are only aware of what we are attending to. The term **inattentional blindness** (Mack & Rock, 1998) refers to the phenomenon that we are often unaware of what is in our direct field of view if we are not paying attention to it. In their classic demonstration of this phenomenon, Mack and Rock had participants perform a perceptual task in which they judged whether the horizontal or vertical bar of a cross was longer. After a number of trials, there would be a surprise trial in which an additional stimulus such as a rectangle would appear on the screen along with the cross. When asked after the trial, many subjects failed to report seeing the additional stimulus. This experiment only included a single surprise trial with each participant, but in their original research Mack and Rock tested 5000 participants. Interestingly, they found that participants were more likely to notice the surprise stimulus if it was their name rather than a rectangle or another name.

A striking demonstration of inattentional blindness was reported by Simons and Chabris (1999). They asked participants to watch a video in which a team dressed in black tossed a basketball back and forth while a team dressed in white did the same. Participants were instructed to count either the number of times the team in black tossed the ball or the number of times the team in white did so. Because the players were intermixed, the task was difficult and required sustained attention. In the middle of the game, a person in a black gorilla suit walked through the room, as illustrated in **Figure 3.12**. When participants were tracking the team in white, they noticed the black gorilla only 8% of the time.

The frequency of such failures to notice an object depends on the difficulty of the task being performed. In a replication of Mack and Rock (1998), Cartwright-Finch and Lavie (2007) found that 80% of their participants failed to detect a surprise square when performing the difficult line-length discrimination task. However, in another condition participants had only to identify which of the bars was green (the other was blue). In this

Figure 3.12 Illustration of a Single Frame from the Video Used by Simons and Chabris (1999) to Demonstrate Inattentional Blindness. When participants were intent on tracking the ball passed among the players dressed in white T-shirts, they tended not to notice the person in the black gorilla suit walking across the room. *(Information from Simons & Chabris, 1999.)*

simple color-discrimination task, only 45% of the participants failed to notice the square.

A similar effect of task difficulty has been reported in audition. Raveh and Lavie (2015) presented a surprise tone while participants were searching for a target letter in a display where distracter letters were the same size as the target letter (a high-difficulty task) or where distracter letters were smaller than the target letter (a low-difficulty task). In the high-difficulty condition, participants failed to detect the tone in 55% of the trials, versus a failure rate of only 18% in the low-difficulty condition. The researchers called this phenomenon *inattentional deafness*. Remember also the shadowing experiments illustrated in Figure 3.3, where performing the demanding shadowing task made it difficult for participants to identify what was in the unattended ear.

Exactly what is happening when subjects fail to detect the surprise stimulus is a matter of continuing debate. Wolfe (1999) argued that what was happening was really a matter of inattentional amnesia—that the object was really noticed but then immediately forgotten; and indeed, it can be shown that there are effects of object presentation even when the presentation is not noticed. For instance, Butler and Klein (2009) found that unnoticed words are more easily seen in a later brief presentation than words that were not originally presented. Thus, at some level a seemingly unnoticed word must have registered, facilitating its later recognition. If so, it is argued, the word must have been forgotten in the brief period after its presentation and before a follow-up question about whether there had been anything unusual about the trial. This inattentional amnesia explanation is not universally accepted, with other researchers (e.g., Ward & Scholl, 2015) arguing that it is implausible to assume we immediately forget something we have just become aware of. Whatever the explanation of inattentional blindness, the phenomenon is real and can have important consequences. For instance, after the fatal crash of a small aircraft in New Zealand in 2016, when it struck high voltage power lines, the investigative report stated, "It is considered likely that the pilot's attention was engaged on [another] aircraft and it was possible he experienced inattentional blindness and failed to perceive the visual stimuli" (*Gisborne Herald*, 2018).

> We often fail to see objects in plain view, particularly when our attention is engaged in another task.

Visual Search

We often find ourselves looking for an object like a friend or a book. In some such cases, as when the friend is in a crowd or the book is on a shelf with other books, it seems that we search through the possible objects in our visual field one by one, looking for the one that has the desired properties. Much of the research on visual attention has focused on how people perform such searches. Rather than study how people find faces in a crowd or books on a shelf, however, researchers have tended to use simpler materials. **Figure 3.13**,

```
TWLN
XJBU
UDXI
HSFP
XSCQ
SDJU
PODC
ZVBP
PEVZ
SLRA
JCEN
ZLRD
XBOD
PHMU
ZHFK
PNJW
CQXT
GHNR
IXYD
QSVB
GUCH
OWBN
BVQN
FOAS
ITZN
```

Figure 3.13 Find the *K*. Lines 7–31 of the letter array used in Neisser's (1964) visual search experiment. *(Data from Neisser, 1964.)*

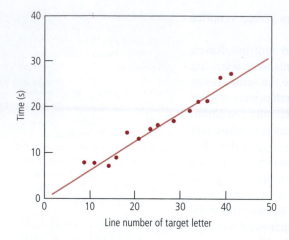

Figure 3.14 Results from Neisser's (1964) Visual Search Experiment. The graph shows the time required to find a target letter in the full array partially shown in Figure 3.13 as a function of the line number in which the letter first appears. *(Data from Neisser, 1964.)*

for instance, shows a portion of the display that Neisser (1964) used in one of the early studies. Try to find the first *K* in the set of letters displayed.

Presumably, you tried to find the *K* by going through the letters row by row, looking for the target. **Figure 3.14** graphs the average time it took participants in Neisser's experiment to find the letter as a function of which row it appeared in. The slope of the best-fitting function in the graph is about 0.6, which implies that participants took about 0.6 s to scan each line. When people engage in such searches, they appear to be allocating their attention intensely to the search process. For instance, brain-imaging experiments have found strong activation in the parietal cortex during such searches (see Kanwisher & Wojciulik, 2000, for a review).

Although a search can be intense and difficult, it is not always that way. Sometimes we can find what we are looking for without much effort. For instance, one circle in **Figure 3.15a** pops out of the display because it is uniquely red. Similarly, if we know that our friend has a red umbrella, it would be easy to find her in a crowd like the one in Figure 3.15b. These searches depend on stimulus-driven attention: If there is some distinctive feature in an array, we can find it without an object-by-object search.

Treisman studied the ability of distinctive features to guide search (the basis of the popout in Figure 3.15). For instance, Treisman and Gelade (1980) instructed participants to try to detect a **T** in a 30-letter array where the distracters were **I**'s and **Y**'s (**Figure 3.16a**). They reasoned that participants could do this relatively quickly and easily by looking for the crossbar feature of the

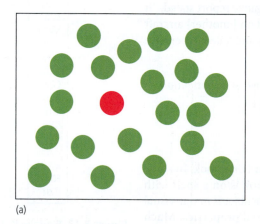

(a)

(b)

Figure 3.15 Visual Popout. (a) One circle in the display grabs our attention. (b) It can be easy to find someone in this crowd if we know she is holding a red umbrella. *(Song_about_summer/Shutterstock.)*

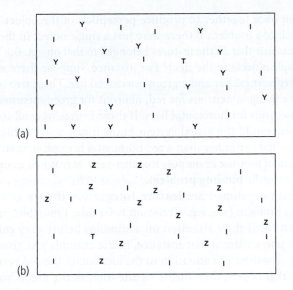

(a)

(b)

Figure 3.16 Stimuli Used by Treisman and Gelade (1980) in Their Study of How Distinctive Features Are Used to Guide Visual Search. Participants were quicker to find the target letter **T** in (a) than in (b). In (a), the target letter has a single feature (the horizontal bar) that distinguishes it from the distracter letters (**I**'s and **Y**'s). In (b), the same target letter has no single feature that distinguishes it from both the distracters (**I**'s and **Z**'s), so the search required participants to find a conjunction of features (a horizontal bar combined with a vertical bar). *(Data from Treisman & Gelade, 1980.)*

T that distinguishes it from all **I**'s and **Y**'s. Participants took an average of about 400 ms to perform this task. Treisman and Gelade also asked participants to detect a **T** in an array where the distracters were **I**'s and **Z**'s (Figure 3.16b). In this task, they could not use just the vertical bar or just the horizontal bar of the **T** (the **I** also has a vertical bar, and the **Z** also has a horizontal bar); they had to look for the conjunction of these features and perform the feature combination required in pattern recognition. It took participants more than 800 ms, on average, to find the target letter in this case. Thus, a task requiring them to recognize the conjunction of features took about twice as long as one in which perception of a single feature was sufficient. Moreover, as shown in **Figure 3.17**, when Treisman and Gelade varied the number of letters in the array, they found that the number of letters affected participants' reaction times much more in the task that required recognition of the conjunction of features.

> *It is necessary to search through a visual array for a target object only when a unique visual feature does not distinguish that object.*

The Binding Problem

As discussed in Chapter 2, there are different types of neurons in the visual system that respond to different features, such as colors, lines at various orientations, and objects in motion. A single object in our visual field will involve a number of features; for instance, a red vertical line combines the vertical feature and the red feature. The fact that different features of the same object are represented by different neurons gives rise to a logical question: How are these

Figure 3.17 Results from the Treisman and Gelade (1980) Experiment. The graph plots the average reaction times required to detect a target letter as a function of the size of the array (the number of letters in the array). The array size has more of an effect on reaction time when the target letter differs from the distracters by a combination of features than when it differs by a single feature. *(Data from Treisman & Gelade, 1980.)*

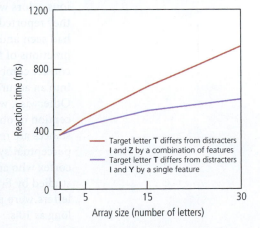

Reaction time (ms)

Array size (number of letters)

— Target letter **T** differs from distracters
I and **Z** by a combination of features
— Target letter **T** differs from distracters
I and **Y** by a single feature

features put back together to produce perception of the object? This would not be much of a problem if there were just a single object in the visual field. We could assume that all the features belonged to that object. But what if there were multiple objects in the field? For instance, suppose there were just two objects: a red vertical bar and a green horizontal bar. These two objects might result in the firing of neurons for red, neurons for green, neurons for vertical bars, and neurons for horizontal bars. If these firings were all that occurred, though, how would the visual system know it saw a red vertical bar and a green horizontal bar rather than a red horizontal bar and a green vertical bar? The question of how the brain puts together various features in the visual field is referred to as the **binding problem.**

Treisman developed her **feature-integration theory** as an answer to the binding problem (see, e.g., Treisman & Gelade, 1980). She proposed that people must focus their attention on a stimulus before they can synthesize its features into a pattern. For instance, in the example just given, the visual system can first direct its attention to the location of the red vertical bar and synthesize that object, then direct its attention to the green horizontal bar and synthesize that object. According to Treisman, people must search through an array when they need to synthesize features to recognize an object (for instance, when trying to identify a **K**, which consists of a vertical line and two diagonal lines). In contrast, when an object in an array has a single unique feature, such as a red jacket or a line at a particular orientation, we can attend to it without searching the array.

The binding problem is not just a hypothetical dilemma — it is something that humans actually experience. One source of evidence comes from studies of **illusory conjunctions,** in which people report combinations of features that did not occur. For instance, Treisman and Schmidt (1982) looked at what happens to feature combinations when the stimuli are out of the focus of attention. Participants were asked to report the identity of two black digits flashed in one part of the visual field, so this was where their attention was focused. In an unattended part of the visual field, letters in various colors were presented, such as a pink *T,* a yellow *S,* and a blue *N.* After they reported the numbers, participants were asked to report any letters they had seen and the colors of these letters. They reported seeing illusory conjunctions of features (e.g., a pink *S*) almost as often as they reported seeing correct combinations. Thus, it appears that we are able to combine features into an accurate perception only when our attention is focused on an object. Otherwise, we perceive the features but may well combine them into a perception of objects that are not really there. Although rather special circumstances are required to produce illusory conjunctions in people with normal perceptual systems, there are certain patients with damage to the parietal cortex who are particularly prone to such illusions. For instance, one patient studied by Friedman-Hill, Robertson, and Treisman (1995) confused which letters were presented in which colors even when shown the letters for as long as 10 s.

A number of studies have been conducted on the neural mechanisms involved in binding together the features of a single object. Luck, Chelazzi, Hillyard, and Desimone (1997) trained macaque monkeys to fixate on a certain part of the visual field and recorded neurons in a region of the visual cortex called *V4*. The neurons in this region have large receptive fields (several degrees of visual angle). Therefore, the images of multiple objects in a display may fall within the receptive field of a single neuron. They found neurons that were specific to particular types of objects, such as a cell that responded to a blue vertical bar. What happens when both a blue vertical bar and a green horizontal bar are presented within the receptive field of this cell? If the monkey attended to the blue vertical bar, the rate of firing of the cell was the same as when there was only a blue vertical bar. In contrast, if the monkey attended to the green horizontal bar, the rate of firing of this same cell was greatly depressed. Thus, the same stimulus (blue vertical bar plus green horizontal bar) can evoke different responses depending on which object is attended to. It is speculated that this phenomenon occurs because attention suppresses responses to all features in the receptive field except those at the attended location. Similar results have been obtained in fMRI experiments with humans. Kastner, DeWeerd, Desimone, and Ungerleider (1998) measured the fMRI signal in visual areas that responded to stimuli presented in one region of the visual field. They found that when attention was directed away from that region, the fMRI response to stimuli in that region decreased; but when attention was focused on that region, the fMRI response was maintained. These experiments indicate enhanced neural processing of attended objects and locations.

> *For feature information to be synthesized into a pattern, the information must be in the focus of attention.*

Neglect of the Visual Field

We have discussed the evidence that visual attention to a spatial location results in enhanced activation in the corresponding portion of the primary visual cortex. The neural structures that control the direction of attention, however, appear to be located elsewhere, particularly in the parietal cortex (Behrmann, Geng, & Shomstein, 2004). Damage to the parietal lobe (see Figure 3.2) has been shown to result in deficits in visual attention. For instance, Posner, Walker, Friederich, and Rafal (1984) showed that some patients with parietal lobe injuries have difficulty in disengaging attention from one side of the visual field.

Damage to the right parietal region produces distinctive patterns of deficit, as can be seen in a study of one such patient by Posner, Cohen, and Rafal (1982). Like the participants in the Posner, Nissen, and Ogden (1978) experiment discussed earlier (see Figure 3.7), the patient was cued to expect a stimulus to the left or right of the fixation point in a display (i.e., in the left or right visual field).

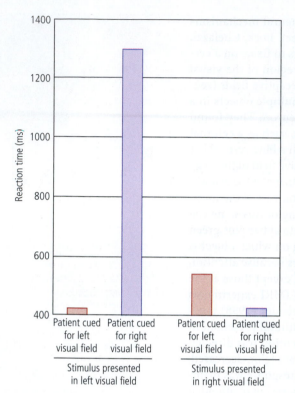

Figure 3.18 The Attention Deficit Shown by a Patient with Right Parietal Lobe Damage When Switching Attention to the Left Visual Field. When cued to attend to the right visual field, it takes this patient a long time (about 1300 ms) to switch attention to the left visual field and detect a stimulus there. In contrast, the corresponding switch of attention to the right visual field takes less than 600 ms.
(Data from Posner, Cohen, & Rafal, 1982.)

As in the earlier experiment, 80% of the time the stimulus appeared in the expected field, but 20% of the time it appeared in the unexpected field. **Figure 3.18** shows the time required to detect the stimulus as a function of which visual field it was presented in and which field had been cued. When the stimulus was presented in the right field, the patient showed only a little disadvantage if inappropriately cued. If the stimulus appeared in the left field, however, the patient showed a large deficit if inappropriately cued. Because the right parietal lobe processes the left visual field, damage to the right lobe impairs its ability to draw attention back to the left visual field once attention is focused on the right visual field. This sort of one-sided attentional deficit can be temporarily created in normal individuals by applying transcranial magnetic stimulation (TMS) to the parietal cortex (Pascual-Leone et al., 1994—see Chapter 1 for discussion of TMS).

A more extreme version of this attentional disorder is called *unilateral visual neglect*. In this condition, patients with damage to the right hemisphere completely ignore the left side of the visual field, and patients with damage to the left hemisphere ignore the right side of the visual field. **Figure 3.19** shows the performance of a patient with damage to the right hemisphere who had been instructed to put slashes through all the circles (Albert, 1973). As can be seen, the right hemisphere damage caused her to ignore the circles in the left part of her visual field. Such patients will often behave peculiarly. For instance, one patient failed to shave half of his face (Sacks, 1985). These effects can also show up in nonvisual tasks. For instance, a study of patients with neglect of the left visual field showed a systematic bias in making judgments about the midpoint in sequences of numbers and letters: when asked to judge what number is midway between *1* and *5*, they showed a bias to respond *4*; and when asked to judge what letter is midway between *P* and *T*, they showed a tendency to respond *S* (Zorzi, Priftis, Meneghello, Marenzi, & Umiltà, 2006). In both cases, this can be interpreted as a tendency to ignore the items to the left of the actual midpoint in the sequence.

It seems that the right parietal lobe is involved in allocating spatial attention in many modalities, not just the visual (Zatorre et al., 1999). For instance, when one attends to the location of auditory or visual stimuli, there is increased activation in the right parietal region. It also appears that the right parietal lobe is more responsible for the spatial allocation of attention than is the left parietal lobe and that this is why right parietal damage tends to produce such dramatic effects. Left parietal damage tends to produce a subtler pattern of deficits. Robertson and Rafal (2000) argue that the right parietal region is responsible for attention to such global features as spatial location, whereas the left parietal region is responsible for directing attention to local aspects of objects. **Figure 3.20** is a striking illustration of the different types of deficits associated with left and right parietal damage. Patients with right parietal damage were able to reproduce the specific components of the pictures but had little success in reproducing their spatial configuration. In contrast, patients with left parietal damage (Figure 3.20) were able to reproduce the overall configuration but not the detail. Similarly, brain-imaging studies have found more activation of the right parietal region when a person is responding to global patterns and more activation of the left parietal region when a person is attending to local patterns (Fink et al., 1996; Martinez et al., 1997).

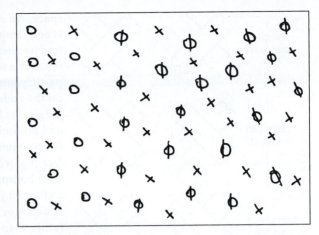

> *Parietal regions are responsible for the allocation of attention, with the right hemisphere more concerned with global features and the left hemisphere with local features.*

Object-Based Attention

So far we have talked about **space-based attention,** where people allocate their attention to a region of space. There is also evidence for **object-based attention,** where people focus their attention on particular objects rather than regions of

Figure 3.19 Performance of a Patient with Damage to the Right Hemisphere. The patient had been asked to put slashes through all the circles. Because of the damage to the right hemisphere, she ignored the circles in the left part of her visual field. *(Research from Ellis & Young, 1988.)*

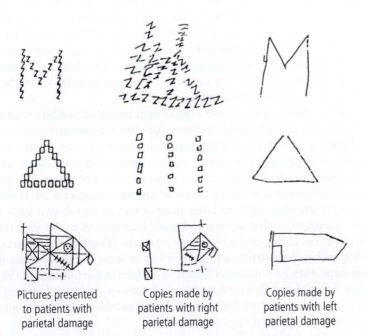

Pictures presented to patients with parietal damage

Copies made by patients with right parietal damage

Copies made by patients with left parietal damage

Figure 3.20 Comparison of Deficits Associated with Damage to the Right and Left Parietal Lobes. Patients with right-hemisphere damage could reproduce the specific components of a picture but not their spatial configuration. Patients with left-hemisphere damage could reproduce the overall configuration but not the detail. *(Research from Robertson & Lamb, 1991.)*

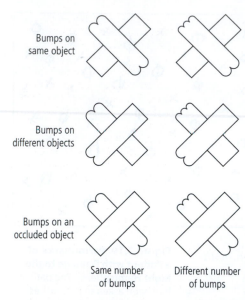

Bumps on same object

Bumps on different objects

Bumps on an occluded object

Same number of bumps

Different number of bumps

Figure 3.21 Object-Based Attention. These stimuli were used in an experiment by Behrmann, Zemel, and Mozer (1998) to demonstrate that it is sometimes easier to attend to an object than to a location. Participants were quicker to judge whether the numbers of bumps were the same or different when the bumps were on the same object (top and bottom rows), even if the object was partially occluded (bottom row). *(Behrmann, M., Zemel, R. S., & Mozer, M. C. (1998). Object-based attention and occlusion: Evidence from normal participants and computational model. Journal of Experimental Psychology: Human Perception and Performance, 24, 1011–1036. Copyright © 1988 American Psychological Association. Reprinted by permission.)*

space. An experiment by Behrmann, Zemel, and Mozer (1998) is an example of research demonstrating that people sometimes find it easier to attend to an object than to a location. **Figure 3.21** illustrates some of the stimuli used in the experiment, in which participants were asked to judge whether the numbers of bumps on the ends of objects were the same. Participants made these judgments faster when the bumps were on the same object (top and bottom rows in Figure 3.21) than when they were on different objects (middle row). This result occurred despite the fact that when the bumps were on different objects, the ends with bumps were located closer together, which should have facilitated judgment if attention were space based. Behrmann et al. argue that participants attended to one object at a time rather than one location at a time. Therefore, judgments were faster when the bumps were on the same object because participants did not need to shift their attention between objects. Using a variant of the paradigm in Figure 3.21, Chen and Cave (2008) presented the stimulus either for 1 s or for just 0.12 s. The advantage of the within-object effect disappeared when the stimulus was present for only the brief period. This indicates that it takes time for object-based attention to develop.

Other evidence for object-centered attention involves a phenomenon called **inhibition of return.** Research indicates that if we have looked at a particular region of space, we find it a little harder to return our attention to that region. If we move our eyes to location A and then to location B, we are slower to return our eyes to location A than to some new location C. This is also true when we move our attention without moving our eyes (Posner, Rafal, Chaote, & Vaughn, 1985). This phenomenon confers an advantage in some situations: If we are searching for something and have already looked at a location, we would prefer our visual system to find other locations to look at rather than return to an already searched location.

Tipper, Driver, and Weaver (1991) demonstrated inhibition of return in studies that also provided evidence for object-based attention. In their experiments, participants viewed three squares in a frame, similar to what is shown in Frame 1 at the bottom of each part of **Figure 3.22**. In the condition illustrated in Figure 3.22a, the squares did not move. The participants' attention was first drawn to one of the outer squares when it flickered (Frame 2), and then, 200 ms later, their attention was drawn back to the center square when that square flickered (Frame 3). A probe stimulus was then presented in one of the two outer positions (Frame 4 alternatives), and participants were instructed to press a key as soon as they saw the probe. On average, they took 420 ms to react to a probe at the location of the outer square that had not flickered, versus 460 ms to a probe at the location of the outer square that had flickered. This 40-ms advantage is an example of

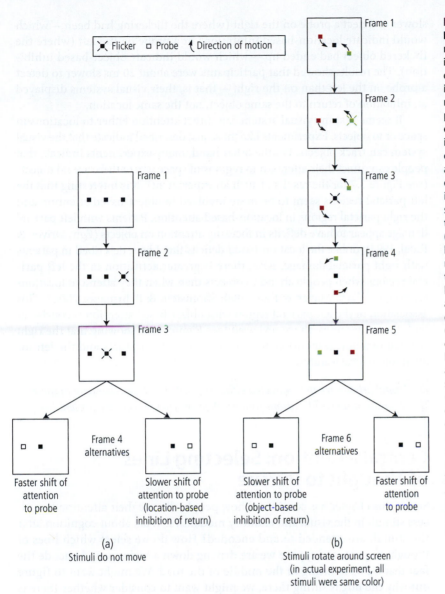

Figure 3.22 Inhibition of Return. (a) With stimuli that do not move, participants' attention is first drawn to one of the outer stimuli by a flicker (here, in Frame 2, the stimulus on the right). Next, another flicker draws participants' attention back to the center (Frame 3). Then, a probe is presented to either the left or the right of center (Frame 4 alternatives). Participants in this condition show location-based inhibition of return—they are slower to shift their attention to the previously attended location. (b) With stimuli (color coded here to help you follow the movement) that rotate around the screen, when the stimuli are horizontally aligned, participants' attention is first drawn to one of the outer stimuli by a flicker (Frame 2—here also, the stimulus on the right), and then drawn back to the center (Frame 3). After a full rotation, with the outer stimuli having switched locations (Frame 5), a probe is presented either to the left or right of center (Frame 6 alternatives). But in this condition, participants show object-based inhibition of return—they are slower to shift their attention to the previously attended object, even though it is in a previously unattended location. *(Information from Tipper, Driver, & Weaver, 1991.)*

location-based inhibition of return. People are slower to shift their attention to a previously attended location than to a new location.

Figure 3.22b illustrates the other condition of their experiment, in which the objects rotated around the screen. At the end of a full rotation (Frame 5), the object that had flickered on one side was now on the other side — the two outer objects had traded positions. In trials like the one illustrated in Figure 3.22b, the question of interest was whether participants would be slower to detect a probe on the right (where the flickering had been — which would indicate location-based inhibition) or a probe on the left (where the flickered object had ended up — which would indicate object-based inhibition). The results showed that participants were about 20 ms slower to detect a probe on the left than on the right — that is, their visual systems displayed an inhibition of return to the same object, not the same location.

It seems that the visual system can direct attention either to locations in space or to objects. Experiments like those just described indicate that the visual system can track objects. On the other hand, many experiments indicate that people can direct their attention to regions of space where there are no objects (see Figure 3.7 for the results of such an experiment). It is interesting that the left parietal regions seem to be more involved in object-based attention and the right parietal regions in location-based attention. Patients with left parietal damage appear to have deficits in focusing attention on objects (Egly, Driver, & Rafal, 1994), unlike the location-based deficits that I have described in patients with right parietal damage. Also, there is greater activation in the left parietal regions when people attend to objects than when they attend to locations (Arrington, Carr, Mayer, & Rao, 2000; Shomstein & Behrmann, 2006). This association of the left parietal region with object-based attention is consistent with the earlier research we reviewed (see Figure 3.20) showing that the right parietal region is responsible for attention to global features and the left for attention to local features.

> *Visual attention can be directed either toward objects independent of their location or toward locations independent of what objects are present.*

Central Attention: Selecting Lines of Thought to Pursue

So far, this chapter has considered how people allocate their attention to process stimuli in the visual and auditory modalities. What about cognition after the stimuli are attended to and encoded? How do we select which lines of thought to pursue? Suppose we are driving down a highway and encode the fact that a dog is sitting in the middle of the road. We might want to figure out why the dog is sitting there, we might want to consider whether there is something we should do to help the dog, and we certainly want to decide how best to steer the car to avoid an accident. Can we do all these things at once? If not, how do we select the most important problem of deciding how to steer and save the rest for later? It appears that people allocate central attention to competing lines of thought in much the same way they allocate perceptual attention to competing objects.

In many (but not all) circumstances, people are able to pursue only one line of thought at a time. This section will describe two laboratory experiments: one in which it appears that people have no ability to overlap two tasks and another in which they appear to have almost total ability to do so. Then we will address how people can develop the ability to overlap tasks and how they select among tasks when they cannot or do not want to overlap them.

The first experiment, which Mike Byrne and I did (Byrne & Anderson, 2001), illustrates the claim made at the beginning of the chapter about the impossibility of multiplying and adding numbers at the same time. Participants in this experiment saw a string of three digits, such as "3 4 7." Then they were asked to do one or both of two tasks:

- Task 1: Judge whether the first two digits add up to the third and press a key with the right index finger if they do or another key with the left index finger if they do not. In this case, they do, because $3 + 4 = 7$.

- Task 2: Report verbally the product of the first and third numbers. In this case, the answer is 21, because $3 \times 7 = 21$.

Figure 3.23 compares the time required to do each task in the single-task condition versus the time required for each task in the dual-task condition. Participants took almost twice as long to do either task when they had to perform the other as well. In the dual task, they sometimes gave the answer for the multiplication task first (59% of the time) and sometimes the addition task first (41%). The bars in Figure 3.23 for the dual task reflect the time to respond with an answer, regardless of whether the answer came first or second. The horizontal dashed line near the top of Figure 3.23 represents the time participants took to give both answers. This time (1.99 s) is greater than the sum of the time for the addition verification task by itself (0.88 s) and the time for the multiplication task by itself (1.05 s). The extra time probably reflects the cost of shifting between tasks (for reviews of task switching, see Kiesel et al., 2010; Monsell, 2003). In any case, it appears that the participants were not able to overlap the addition and multiplication computations at all.

The second experiment, reported by Schumacher et al. (2001), illustrates what is referred to as **perfect time-sharing.** The tasks were much simpler than the tasks in the Byrne and Anderson (2001) experiment. Participants simultaneously saw a single letter on a screen and heard a tone and, as in the Byrne and Anderson experiment, had to perform one or both of two tasks:

- Task 1: Press a left, middle, or right key according to whether the letter occurred on the left part of the screen, in the middle, or on the right.

- Task 2: Say "one," "two," or "three" according to whether the tone was low, middle, or high in frequency.

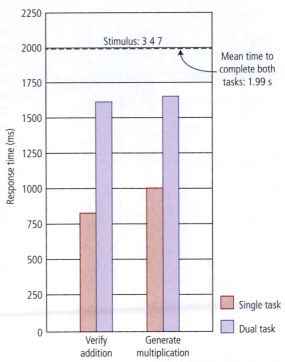

Figure 3.23 Results of an Experiment by Byrne and Anderson (2001) to See Whether People Can Overlap Two Tasks. The bars show the response times required to solve two problems—one of addition and one of multiplication—when done individually (single task) and when done together (dual task). The results indicate that the participants were not able to overlap the addition and multiplication computations. *(Data from Byrne & Anderson, 2001.)*

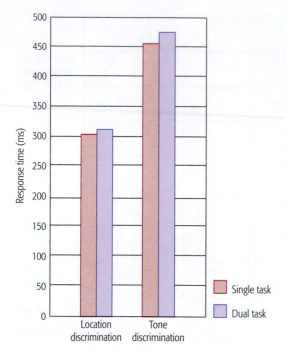

Figure 3.24 Results of an Experiment by Schumacher et al. (2001) Illustrating Near Perfect Time-Sharing. The bars show the response times required to perform two simple tasks—a location discrimination task and a tone discrimination task—when done individually (single task) and when done together (dual task). The times were nearly unaffected by the requirement to do both tasks, indicating that the participants were able to almost completely overlap the two tasks—that is, participants achieved almost perfect time-sharing. *(Data from Schumacher et al., 2001.)*

Figure 3.24 compares the times required to do each task in the single-task condition and the dual-task condition. As can be seen, these times are nearly unaffected by the requirement to do the two tasks. There are many differences between this task and the Byrne and Anderson task, but the most apparent is the complexity of the tasks. Participants were able to do the individual tasks in the second experiment in a few hundred milliseconds, whereas the individual tasks in the first experiment took around a second. Significantly more thought was required in the first experiment, and it is hard for people to engage in two streams of thought simultaneously. Also, participants in the second experiment achieved perfect time-sharing only after five sessions of practice, whereas participants in the first experiment had only one session of practice.

Figure 3.25 presents an analysis of what occurred in the Schumacher et al. (2001) experiment. It shows what was happening at various points in time in five streams of processing: (1) perceiving the visual location of a letter, (2) generating manual actions, (3) central cognition, (4) perceiving auditory stimuli, and (5) generating speech. Task 1 involved visually encoding the location of the letter, using central cognition to select which key to press, and then performing the actual finger movement. Task 2 involved detecting and encoding the tone, using central cognition to select which word to say ("one," "two," or "three") and then saying it. The lengths of the boxes in Figure 3.25 represent estimates of the duration of each component based on human performance studies. Each of these streams can go on in parallel with the others. For instance, during the time the tone is being detected and encoded, the location of the letter is being encoded (which happens much faster), a key is being selected by central cognition, and the motor system is starting to program the action. Although all these streams can go on in parallel, within each stream only one thing can happen at a time. This could create a bottleneck in the central cognition stream, because central cognition must direct all activities (e.g., in this case, it must serve both task 1 and task 2). In this experiment, however, the length of time devoted to central cognition was so brief that the two tasks did not contend for the resource. The five days of practice in this experiment played a critical role in reducing the amount of time devoted to central cognition.

Although the discussion here has focused on bottlenecks in central cognition, there can be bottlenecks in any of the processing streams. Earlier, we reviewed evidence that people cannot attend to two locations at once; they must shift their attention across locations in the visual array serially. Similarly, they can process only one speech stream at a time, move their hands in one way at a time, or say one thing at a time. Even though all these

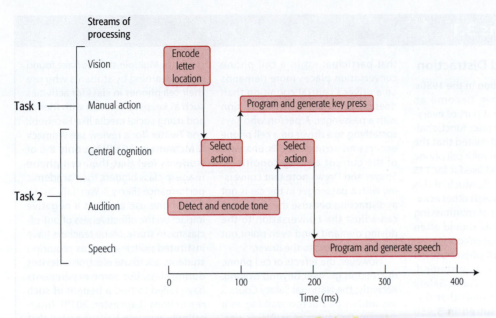

Figure 3.25 Timing of Events in Five Streams of Processing During Execution of the Dual Task in the Schumacher et al. (2001) Experiment. Participants were required to identify the location of a letter on a screen and press a corresponding key, while also identifying the frequency of a tone and saying a corresponding word. These tasks involved multiple simultaneous streams of processing, including vision, manual action, central cognition, audition, and speech.

peripheral processes can have bottlenecks, it is generally thought that bottlenecks in central cognition can have the most significant effects, and they are the reason we seldom find ourselves thinking about two things at once. The bottleneck in central cognition is referred to as the **central bottleneck.** (**Implications 3.1** looks at the consequences of attentional bottlenecks for cell phone use.)

> *People can process multiple perceptual modalities at once and execute actions in multiple motor systems at once, but they cannot process multiple things in a single system, including central cognition.*

Automaticity: Expertise through Practice

The near perfect time-sharing in Figure 3.25 only emerged after five days of practice. The general effect of practice is to reduce the central cognitive component of information processing. When one has practiced the central cognitive component of a task so much that the task requires little or no thought, we say that doing the task is automatic. **Automaticity** is a matter of degree.

Implications 3.1

Cell Phones and Distraction

Since their introduction in the 1980s, mobile phones have become an increasingly prevalent part of everyday life, with ever greater functionality. In 2016 it was estimated that the average user touched their cell phone 2,617 times a day and used it for 145 minutes (dscout, 2016). Much of this use is in conjunction with other activities, requiring types of multitasking that research suggests should often be difficult to carry out effectively.

The impact of cell phone use on driving has been heavily studied. The National Highway Traffic Safety Administration estimates that distracted driving resulted in 3,450 deaths in the United States in 2016. Strayer and Drews (2007) review the evidence that people are more likely to miss traffic lights and other critical information while talking on a cell phone. Strayer and Drews suggest that participating in a cell phone conversation places more demands on a driver's central cognition than does participating in a conversation with a passenger. A person who says something to a driver on a cell phone expects an answer and is unaware of the current driving conditions. Strayer and Drews note that conversing with a passenger in the car is not as distracting because the passenger can adjust the conversation to the driving demands and even point out potential dangers to the driver.

However, the effects of cell phone distraction go well beyond driving. Recently, the National Safety Council has added distracted walking as a category for causes of accidents, noting the increase in fatalities among pedestrians as they walk along looking at their cell phones. Teachers are increasingly concerned about the impact of cell phone use among students. Multiple studies have found poorer learning by students who use their cell phones in class for activities such as keeping in touch with friends and using social media like Facebook and Twitter (for a review see Womack & McNamara, 2017). Yet only 8% of students feel that their cell phone usage in class hinders their academic performance (Berry & Westfall, 2015). Cell phone use also has a negative impact on the effectiveness of out-of-classroom study. Many teachers have instituted policies such as requiring students not to use electronic devices during class, but some experiments have failed to find a benefit of such restrictions (Lancaster, 2018). Interestingly, research has suggested that merely having a cell phone within reach can lead to cognitive impairment, even if it is not used (Ward, Duke, Gneezy, & Bos, 2017), because one is still thinking about it.

A nice example is driving. For experienced drivers in unchallenging conditions, driving has become so automatic that they can carry on a conversation while driving with little difficulty. Experienced drivers are much more successful than novices at doing secondary tasks such as changing the radio station (Wikman, Nieminen, & Summala, 1998). Experienced drivers also often have the experience of traveling long stretches of highway with no memory of what they did.

There have been a number of dramatic demonstrations in the psychological literature of how practice can enable parallel processing. For instance, Underwood (1974) reports a study on the psychologist Neville Moray, who had spent many years studying shadowing. During that time, Moray practiced shadowing a great deal, and unlike most participants in experiments, he was very good at reporting what was contained in the unattended channel. Through a great deal of practice, the process of shadowing had become partially automatic for Moray, and he had capacity left over to attend to the unshadowed channel.

Spelke, Hirst, and Neisser (1976) provided an interesting demonstration of how a highly practiced skill ceases to interfere with other ongoing behaviors. (This was a follow-up of a demonstration pioneered by the writer Gertrude Stein when she was an undergraduate working with William James at Harvard University.) Their participants had to perform two tasks simultaneously: read a text silently for comprehension while copying words dictated by the experimenter. At first, this was extremely difficult. Participants had to read much more slowly than normal in order to copy the words accurately. After six weeks of practice, however, the participants were reading at normal speed. They had become so skilled at copying automatically that their comprehension scores were the same as for normal reading. For these participants, reading while copying had become no more difficult than reading while walking. It is of interest that participants reported no awareness of what it was they were copying. Much as with driving, the participants lost their awareness of the automated activity.[3]

Another example of automaticity is transcription typing. A typist is simultaneously reading the text and executing the finger strokes for typing. In this case, we have three systems operating in parallel: perception of the text to be typed, central translation of the perceived letters into keystrokes, and the actual typing of the letters. It is the central processes that get automated. Skilled transcription typists often report little awareness of what they are typing, because this task has become so automated. Skilled typists also find it impossible to stop typing instantaneously. If suddenly told to stop, they will hit a few more letters before quitting (Salthouse, 1985, 1986).

> *As tasks become practiced, they become more automatic and require less and less central cognition to execute.*

The Stroop Effect

Automatic processes not only require little or no central cognition to execute but also appear to be difficult to prevent. A good example is word recognition for practiced readers. It is virtually impossible to look at a common word and not read it. This strong tendency for words to be recognized automatically has been studied in a phenomenon known as the **Stroop effect,** after the psychologist who first demonstrated it, J. Ridley Stroop (1935). The task requires participants to say the ink color in which words are printed. **Figure 3.26** provides an illustration of such a task. Try saying the colors of the words in each column as fast as you can. Which column was easiest to read? Which was hardest?

The three columns illustrate three of the conditions in which the Stroop effect is studied. The first column illustrates a neutral, or control, condition in which the words are not color words. The second column illustrates the congruent condition in which the words are color words that match the color of the ink they are printed in. The third column illustrates the conflict condition in which the words are color words that do not match their ink colors. A typical modern experiment, rather than having participants respond to a whole column of words, will present a single word at a time in random order of neutral, congruent, and conflict conditions, while measuring the time taken to name the

House	Green	Red
Cat	Red	Yellow
Ball	Blue	Green
Table	Yellow	Red
Rock	Red	Blue
Tree	Green	Yellow
Book	Yellow	Blue
Rope	Red	Yellow
Fish	Blue	Green
Water	Green	Red
Spoon	Blue	Red
Gun	Yellow	Red
Foot	Blue	Green
Dog	Green	Blue
Baby	Blue	Yellow

Figure 3.26 Stimuli for the Stroop Task. Try naming the colors of the words in each column as fast as you can.

---

[3] When given further training with the intention of having participants remember what they were transcribing, participants were also able to recall this information.

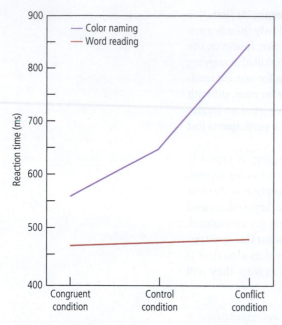

Figure 3.27 Performance Data for the Standard Stroop Task. The curves show the average reaction time of the participants as a function of the condition tested: congruent (the word was the name of the ink color); control (the word was not related to color at all); and conflict (the word was the name of a color different from the ink color). *(Data from Dunbar & MacLeod, 1984.)*

color of each word or, conversely, to read the word aloud. **Figure 3.27** shows the results from such an experiment on the Stroop effect by Dunbar and MacLeod (1984). In the color naming task, participants were somewhat faster in the congruent condition — when the word was the name of the ink color — than in the control condition of a neutral word. In the conflict condition, when the word was the name of a different color, they named the ink color much more slowly. For instance, they had great difficulty in saying "green" when the ink color of the word "red" was green. Figure 3.27 also shows the results when the task is switched and participants are asked to read the word and not name the color. The results in the two tasks are asymmetrical; that is, individual participants experienced very little difficulty in reading a color word that was different from its ink color. Additionally, in all three conditions, participants could read a word much faster than they could name its ink color. Reading is such an automatic process that not only is it unaffected by the color, but participants are unable to inhibit reading the word, and that reading can interfere with the color naming.

MacLeod and Dunbar (1988) looked at the effect of practice on performance in a variant of the Stroop task. They used an experiment in which the participants learned to associate color names with random shapes. **Figure 3.28a** illustrates shape-color associations they might learn. The

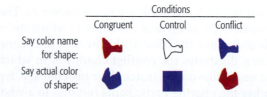

Figure 3.28 Illustrative Materials and Tasks in the MacLeod & Dunbar (1988) Experiment. Participants learned arbitrary color names for shapes and then were tested on shape naming and color naming under three conditions (congruent, control, and conflict). *(Information from MacLeod & Dunbar, 1988.)*

experimenters then presented the participants with test shapes and asked them to say either the color name associated with the shape or the actual color of the shape. As in the original Stroop experiment, there were three conditions (see Figure 3.28b):

1. **Congruent:** The shape was the same color as its name.
2. **Control:** Outlined white versions of the learned shapes were presented when participants were to say the color name for the shape; colored squares were presented when they were to say the actual color of the shape. (The square shape was not associated with any color.)
3. **Conflict:** The shape was a different color from its name.

As shown in **Figure 3.29a**, before participants were given practice at shape naming, color naming was much more automatic than shape naming and was relatively unaffected by congruence with the shape, whereas shape naming was affected both by congruence with the color and especially by conflict with the color. In contrast, as shown in Figure 3.29b, after 20 days of practice at naming the shapes, participants became much faster at shape naming under all three conditions, and, in the conflict condition, shape naming now interfered with color naming rather than vice versa. Thus, the consequence of the training was to make shape naming more automatic than color naming, so

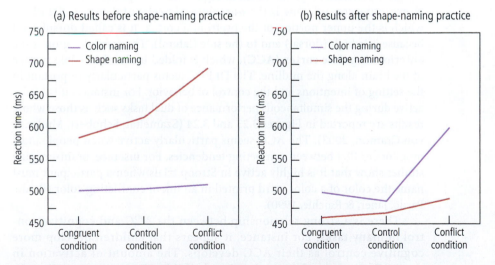

Figure 3.29 Results from the MacLeod and Dunbar (1988) Experiment to Evaluate the Effect of Practice on the Performance of a Stroop Task. (a) Before practice, color naming is more automatic than shape naming and, as shown in the conflict condition, interferes with shape naming. (b) After 20 days of practice, shape naming is more automatic, like word reading, and it interferes with color naming. *(Data from MacLeod and Dunbar, 1988.)*

that it affected color naming, just as all of our practice reading words created the original Stroop effect.

> *Reading a word is such an automatic process that it is difficult to inhibit, and it will interfere with processing other information about the word.*

Prefrontal Sites of Executive Control

We have seen that the parietal cortex is important in the allocation of attention in the perceptual domain. There is evidence that prefrontal regions are particularly important in the direction of central cognition, often known as **executive control.** The prefrontal cortex is that portion of the frontal cortex anterior to the premotor region (the premotor region is area 6 in Figure 1.7). Just as damage to parietal regions results in deficits in the deployment of perceptual attention, damage to prefrontal regions results in deficits of executive control. Patients with such damage often seem totally driven by the stimulus and fail to control their behavior according to their intentions. A patient who sees a comb on the table may be unable to inhibit the action of picking it up and beginning to comb her hair; another who sees a pair of glasses cannot help putting them on, even if he already has a pair on his face. Patients with damage to prefrontal regions show marked deficits in the Stroop task and often cannot refrain from saying the word rather than naming the color (Janer & Pardo, 1991).

Two prefrontal regions shown in Figure 3.2 seem particularly important in executive control. One is the **dorsolateral prefrontal cortex (DLPFC),** which is the upper portion of the prefrontal cortex. It is called dorsolateral because it is high (dorsal) and to the side (lateral). The second region is the **anterior cingulate cortex (ACC),** which is folded under the visible surface of the brain along the midline. The DLPFC seems particularly important in the setting of intentions and the control of behavior. For instance, it is highly active during the simultaneous performance of dual tasks such as those whose results are reported in Figures 3.23 and 3.24 (Szameitat, Schubert, Muller, & von Cramon, 2002). The ACC seems particularly active when people must monitor conflict between competing tendencies. For instance, brain-imaging studies show that it is highly active in Stroop trials when a participant must name the color of a color word printed in an ink of conflicting color (Pardo, Pardo, Janer, & Raichle, 1990).

There is a strong relationship between the ACC and cognitive control in many tasks. For instance, it appears that children develop more cognitive control as their ACC develops. The amount of activation in the ACC appears to be correlated with children's performance in tasks requiring cognitive control (Casey et al., 1997a). Developmentally, there also appears to be a positive correlation between performance and sheer volume of the ACC (Casey et al., 1997b). Weissman, Roberts, Visscher, and Woldorff (2006) studied trial-to-trial variation in activity of the ACC when participants were performing a simple judgment task. When there was a decrease in ACC activation, participants showed an increase in time to make the judgment. Weissman et al.'s interpretation was that lapses in attention are produced by decreases in ACC activation.

A nice paradigm for demonstrating the development of cognitive control in children is the "Simon says" task. In one study, Jones, Rothbart, and Posner (2003) had children receive instructions from two dolls — a bear and an elephant — such as, "Elephant says, 'Touch your nose.'" The children were told to follow the instructions from one doll (the act doll) and ignore the instructions from the other (the inhibit doll). All children successfully followed the act doll but many had difficulty ignoring the inhibit doll. From the age of 36 to 48 months, children progressed from 22% success to 91% success in ignoring the inhibit doll. Some children used physical strategies to control their behavior such as sitting on their hands or distorting their actions — pointing to their ear rather than their nose.

Another way to appreciate the importance of prefrontal regions in cognitive control is to compare the performance of humans with that of other primates. As reviewed in Chapter 1, a major dimension of the evolution from lower primates to humans has been the increase in the size of prefrontal regions. Primates can be trained to do many tasks that humans do, and so they permit careful comparison. One such task involving a variant of the Stroop task presents participants with a display of numerals (e.g., five 3s) and pits naming the number of objects against indicating the identity of the numerals. **Figure 3.30** provides an example of this task in the same form as the original Stroop task (Figure 3.26): trying to count the number of numerals in each line versus trying to name the numeral in each line. The stronger interference in this case is from the numeral naming to the counting (Windes, 1968). This paradigm has been used to compare Stroop-like interference in humans versus rhesus monkeys who had been trained to associate the numerals with their relative quantities — for example, they

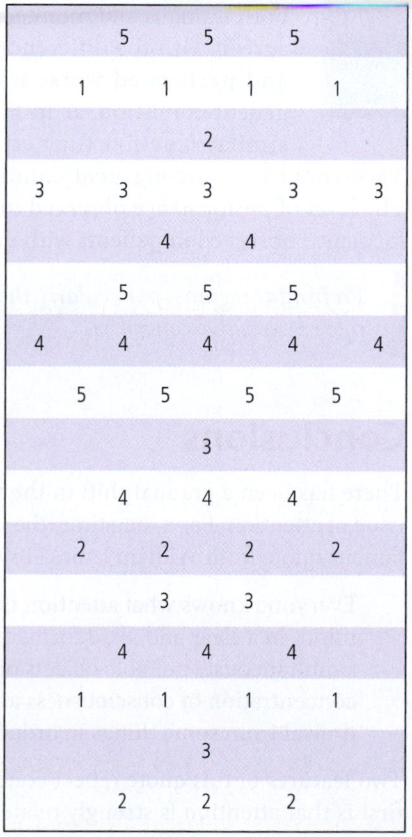

Figure 3.30 A Numerical Stroop Task Comparable to the Color Stroop Task (see Figure 3.26). The task is to name the numeral in each line or to say the number of numerals in each line.

TABLE 3.1 Accuracy (%) and Mean Response Time (ms) in a Numerical Stroop Task as a Function of Species and Condition

	Rhesus Monkeys (N = 6)	Human Participants (N = 28)
Congruent numerals	92% 676 ms	99% 584 ms
Baseline (letters)	86% 735 ms	99% 613 ms
Incongruent numerals	73% 829 ms	97% 661 ms

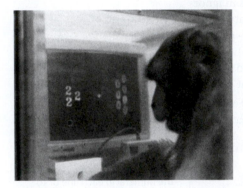

Figure 3.31 A Monkey Engaged in the Numerical Stroop Task. The monkey reaches through its cage to manipulate the joystick so as to bring the cursor into contact with one of the arrays. *(Republished with permission of Sage Publications from Washburn, D. A. (1994). Stroop-like effects for monkeys and humans: Processing speed or strength of association. Psychological Science, 5(6). Permission conveyed through Copyright Clearance Center, Inc.)*

had learned that "5" represented a larger quantity than "2" (Washburn, 1994). Both monkeys and humans were shown two arrays and were required to indicate which had more numerals independent of the identity of the numerals (**Figure 3.31** shows a monkey engaged in this task). **Table 3.1** shows the performance of the monkeys and humans. Compared to a baseline where they had to judge which array of letters had more objects, both humans and monkeys performed better when the numerals agreed with the difference in cardinality (congruent condition) and performed worse when the numerals disagreed (incongruent condition, as in Figure 3.30). Both populations showed similar reaction time effects, but whereas the humans made 3% errors in the incongruent condition, the monkeys made 27% errors. The level of performance observed in the monkeys was like the level of performance observed in patients with damage to their frontal lobes.

> *Prefrontal regions, particularly the DLPFC and the ACC, play a major role in executive control.*

Conclusions

There has been a gradual shift in the way cognitive psychology perceives the issue of attention. For a long time, the implicit assumption was captured by this famous quote from William James (1890, pp. 403–404) over a century ago:

> Everyone knows what attention is. It is the taking possession by the mind, in a clear and vivid form, of one out of what seem several simultaneously possible objects or trains of thought. Focalization, concentration of consciousness are of its essence. It implies withdrawal from some things in order to deal effectively with others.

Two features of this quote reflect conceptions once held about attention. The first is that attention is strongly related to consciousness — we cannot attend to something unless we are conscious of it. The second is that attention, like consciousness, is a unitary system. More and more, cognitive psychology is beginning to recognize that attention also operates at an unconscious level. For instance, people often are not conscious of where they have moved their eyes. Along with this recognition has come the realization that attention is multifaceted (e.g., Chun, Golumb, & Turk-Browne, 2011). We have seen that it makes sense to separate auditory attention from visual attention and to distinguish between attention in perceptual processing, attention in executive control, and attention in response generation. The brain consists of a number of parallel processing systems for the various perceptual systems, for motor systems, and for central cognition. Each of these parallel systems seems to suffer bottlenecks — points at which it must focus its processing on a single thing. Attention is best conceived as the processes by which each of these systems is allocated to potentially competing information-processing demands. The amount of interference that occurs among tasks making demands on the same system is a function of the overlap in timing among those demands.

Questions for Thought

1. The chapter discussed how processing one spoken message makes it difficult to process a second spoken message. Do you think that participating in a conversation on a cell phone while driving makes it harder to process other sounds, such as a car horn honking? Explain your answer.

2. Which should produce greater parietal activation: searching Figure 3.16a for a **T** or searching Figure 3.16b for a **T**? Why?

3. Describe circumstances where it would be advantageous to focus one's attention on an object rather than a region of space, and describe circumstances where the opposite would be true.

4. We have discussed how automatic behaviors can interfere with other behaviors and how some aspects of driving can become automatic. Consider the situation in which a passenger in a car is a skilled driver whose driving automaticity is evoked while being a passenger. Can you think of examples where a passenger's driving automaticity would seem to affect the passenger's behavior in a car? Might this help explain why having a conversation with a passenger in a car is not as distracting as having a conversation over a cell phone?

Key Terms

anterior cingulate cortex (ACC)
attention
attenuation theory
automaticity
binding problem
central bottleneck

dichotic listening task
dorsolateral prefrontal cortex (DLPFC)
early-selection theories
executive control
feature-integration theory

filter theory
goal-directed attention
illusory conjunction
inattentional blindness
inhibition of return
late-selection theories
object-based attention

perfect time-sharing
serial bottleneck
space-based attention
stimulus-driven attention
Stroop effect

Mental Imagery

Try answering these two questions:

- How many windows are in your house?
- How many nouns are in the American Pledge of Allegiance?

Most people who answer these questions have the same experience. For the first question they imagine themselves walking around their house and counting windows. For the second question, if Americans do not actually say the Pledge of Alliance out loud, they imagine themselves saying the Pledge of Allegiance. In both cases they are creating mental images of what they would have perceived.

Visual imagery is particularly important. As a result of our primate heritage, a large portion of our brain processes visual information, and we use these brain structures almost constantly. Even in the absence of a visual signal from the outside world, we are often creating mental images in our heads. Some of humankind's most creative acts involve visual imagery. For instance, Einstein claimed he developed the theory of relativity by imagining himself traveling beside a beam of light.

A major debate in cognitive psychology has been the degree to which the processes behind visual imagery are the same as the perceptual and attentional processes that we considered in the previous two chapters. Some researchers (e.g., Pylyshyn, 1973, in an article sarcastically titled "What the Mind's Eye Tells the Mind's Brain") have argued that our perceptual experience when doing something like picturing the windows in our house is an **epiphenomenon;** that is, it is a mental experience that does not have any functional role in information processing. The philosopher Daniel Dennett (1969) also argued that mental images are epiphenomenal:

> Consider the Tiger and his Stripes. I can dream, imagine or see a striped tiger, but must the tiger I experience have a particular number of stripes? If seeing or imagining is having a mental image, then the image of the tiger *must* — obeying the rules of images in

general — reveal a definite number of stripes showing, and one should be able to pin this down with such questions as "more than ten?", "less than twenty?". (p. 136)

Dennett's argument is that if seeing a tiger is actually having a mental image, we should be able to count its stripes just like we could if we saw a picture of a tiger and counted its actual stripes. If we cannot count the stripes in a mental image of a tiger, we are not having a real perceptual experience. This argument is not considered decisive, but it does illustrate the discomfort some people have with the claim that mental images are actually perceptual in character.

This chapter will review some of the experimental evidence showing the ways that mental imagery does play a role in information processing. We will define **mental imagery** broadly as the processing of perceptual-like information in the absence of an external source for the perceptual information. We will consider the following questions:

- How do we process the information in a mental image?
- How is imaginal processing related to perceptual processing?
- What brain areas are involved in mental imagery?
- How do we develop mental images of our environment and use these to navigate through the environment?

Verbal Imagery Versus Visual Imagery

Cognitive neuroscience has provided increasing evidence that several different brain regions are involved in mental imagery. This evidence has come both from studies of patients suffering damage to various brain regions and from studies of the brain activation of normal individuals as they engage in various imagery tasks. In one of the early studies of brain activation patterns during mental imagery, Roland and Friberg (1985) identified many of the brain regions that have been investigated in subsequent research. The investigators measured changes in blood flow in the brain as participants either mentally rehearsed a nine-word circular jingle or mentally rehearsed finding their way around streets in their neighborhoods. **Figure 4.1** illustrates the principal areas they identified. When participants engaged in the verbal jingle task, there was activation in the prefrontal cortex near Broca's area and in the parietal-temporal region of the posterior cortex near Wernicke's area (see Figure 1.6). As discussed in Chapter 1, patients with damage to these regions show deficits in language processing. When participants engaged in the visual task, there was activation in the parietal cortex, occipital cortex, and temporal cortex. All these areas are involved in visual perception and attention, as we saw in Chapters 2 and 3. Thus, when people process verbal imagery or visual imagery, some of the same brain areas are active as when they process actual

Brain Structures

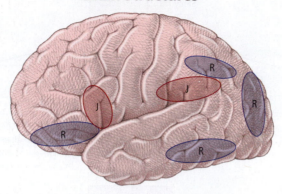

Figure 4.1 Regions Activated During Mental Imagery. Roland and Friberg's (1985) study of brain activation patterns during mental imagery revealed regions of the left cortex that showed increased blood flow when participants imagined a jingle (J) (verbal imagery) or a route (R) (visual imagery).

speech or visual information. (**Implications 4.1** reviews research on how patterns of brain activation can be used to reveal the content of the information being processed.)

An experiment by Santa (1977) demonstrated the functional consequence of representing information in a visual image versus representing it in a verbal image. The two conditions of Santa's experiment are shown in **Figure 4.2**. In the geometric condition (Figure 4.2a), participants studied an array of three geometric shapes, arranged with one shape centered below the other

Implications 4.1

Using Brain Activation to Read People's Minds

Scientists are learning how to decode the brain activity of people to determine what they are thinking. For instance, Nishimoto et al. (2011) reconstructed movie clips from the brain activity of participants watching the clips (view the original and reconstructed clips at https://www.youtube.com/watch?v=nsjDnYxJ0bo). While blurry, the reconstructed clips capture some of the content from the originals. Researchers have since gone beyond this and asked whether they can identify participants' thoughts. For instance, is it possible to identify the visual images a person is experiencing? There has been some success at this, and, interestingly, the brain areas involved seem to be the same areas as those involved in actual viewing of the objects corresponding to the visual images (Cichy, Heinzle, & Haynes, 2012; Stokes, Thompson, Cusack, & Duncan, 2009). Other research has reported success in identifying the concepts participants are thinking about (Mitchell et al., 2008) and what participants are thinking while solving an equation (Anderson, Betts, Ferris, & Fincham, 2010). Could these methods be used in interrogations to determine what people are really thinking and whether they are lying? This question has been the subject of debate, but the consensus is that the methodology is a long way from being reliable, and it has not been allowed in court (read the August 26, 2012, *Washington Post* article "Debate on Brain Scans as Lie Detectors Highlighted in Maryland Murder Trial," by Michael Laris). Not surprisingly, such research has received a lot of press — for instance, see the *60 Minutes* report "Reading Your Mind" and the *PBS NewsHour* report "It's Not Mind-Reading, but Scientists Exploring How Brains Perceive the World," both of which you can find on YouTube.

Figure 4.2 Santa's (1977) Experiment Demonstrating That Visual and Verbal Information Are Represented Differently in Mental Images. Participants studied an initial array of objects or words (the study array) and then had to decide whether a test array contained the same elements. Geometric shapes were used in (a) and words for the shapes in (b).

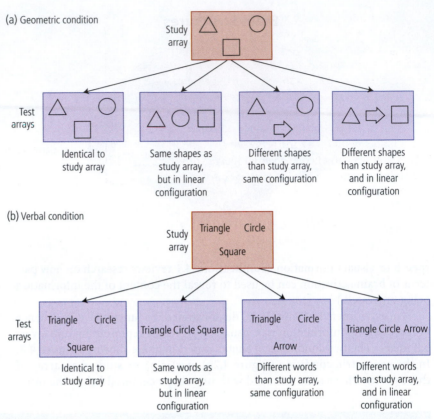

two. As can be seen without much effort, this array has a facelike property (eyes and a mouth). After participants studied the array, it was removed, and they had to hold the information in their minds. Then they were presented with one of the test arrays shown in the figure. The participants' task was to indicate whether the test array contained the same elements as the study array, even if not in the same spatial configuration. Thus, participants should have responded positively to the two leftmost test arrays in Figure 4.2a and negatively to the two rightmost. The interesting results concern the difference between the two positive test arrays. The first was identical to the study array. In the second array, the shapes were displayed in a line (linear configuration). Santa predicted that participants would make a positive identification more quickly in the first case, where the configuration was identical to the study array — because, he hypothesized, the mental image for the study array would preserve spatial information. **Figure 4.3** shows the results for both conditions in Santa's experiment when the test array had the same elements as the study array but could differ in configuration (the verbal condition is discussed below). The results for the geometric condition confirm Santa's predictions: participants were faster in their judgments when the test array had the same configuration as the study array.

e 4.4 **Illustrative**
li in the Shepard and
er (1971) Study on
al Rotation. (a) The
ts have an 80° angular
·ity in the picture
(two dimensions).
e objects have an 80°
ar disparity in depth
dimensions. (c) The
ts are not identical and
annot be rotated into
uence. *(Research from Shepard &*
971.)

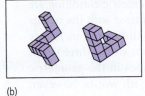
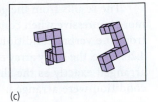

(a)   (b)   (c)

Their first experiment was reported in the journal *Science* (Shepard & Metzler, 1971). Participants were presented with pairs of 2-D representations of 3-D objects, like those in **Figure 4.4**. Their task was to determine whether the objects were identical except for orientation. (the objects in panels [a] and [b] are identical, those in panel [c] are not). Participants reported that to determine whether the two shapes matched, they mentally rotated one of the objects in each pair to see if it could be made congruent with the other object.

The graphs in **Figure 4.5** show the times required for participants to decide that matching pairs were identical, plotted as a function of the angular disparity between the objects in the pair (the angular disparity is the amount one object would have to be rotated to match the other object in orientation). Reaction time is plotted for two different kinds of rotation: Figure 4.5a shows the results for 2-D rotation (rotation in the picture plane — i.e., by rotating the page), and Figure 4.5b shows the results for 3-D rotation (rotation in depth — i.e., by rotating the object into the page). Note that the two functions are very similar and that the relationship in both functions is linear — for every increment in angular disparity, there is an equal increment in reaction time. Processing an object in depth (in three dimensions) does not appear to have taken longer than processing an object in the picture plane. Hence, participants must have been operating on 3-D mental images of the objects in both the picture-plane and depth conditions.

re 4.5 Results of
Shepard and Metzler
1) Study on Mental
ation. The mean time
·ired to determine that
objects have the same
shape is plotted as a
·tion of the angular
·arity in their portrayed
·ntations. (a) Plot for
s differing by a rotation
·e picture plane (two
·ensions). (b) Plot for
s differing by a rotation
·epth (three dimensions).
from Metzler & Shepard, 1974.)

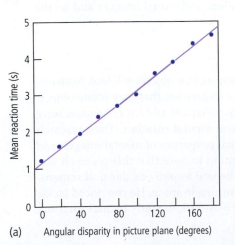

(a)   Angular disparity in picture plane (degrees)

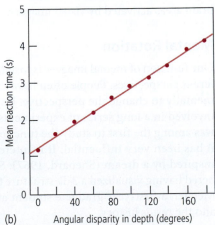

(b)   Angular disparity in depth (degrees)

The results from the geometric condition are more impressive when contrasted with the results from the verbal condition, illustrated in Figure 4.2b. Here, the study array consisted of three words arranged exactly as the shapes in the geometric condition were arranged. With words, however, the study array did not suggest a face or have any other pictorial properties. Santa speculated that participants would read the array left to right and top to bottom and encode a verbal image with the verbal information but not the spatial information. So, given the study array, participants would encode it as "Triangle Circle Square." After they studied the initial array, one of the test arrays was presented and participants had to indicate whether the words were identical to those in the study array. All the test arrays involved words, but otherwise they presented the same possibilities as the test arrays in the geometric condition. The two positive stimuli exemplify the same linear configuration. Note that the order of words in the linear-configuration array was the same as in the study array. Santa predicted that, unlike the geometric condition, because participants had encoded the words into a linearly ordered verbal image, they would be faster when the test array was linear. As Figure 4.3 illustrates, his predictions were again confirmed.

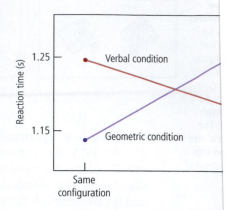

> Different parts of the brain are involved in verbal and visual imagery, and they represent and process information differently.

Visual Imagery

Most of the research on mental imagery has involved visual imagery, and this will be the principal focus of this chapter. In the following sections, we will review research on various mental operations with visual imagery and on the brain areas activated by visual imagery.

Mental Rotation

One function of mental imagery is to anticipate how objects will look from different perspectives. People often have the impression that they rotate objects mentally to change the perspective. Roger Shepard and his colleagues were involved in a long series of experiments on **mental rotation.** Their research was among the first to study the functional properties of mental images, and it has been very influential. It is interesting to note that this research was inspired by a dream (Shepard, 1967): Shepard awoke one day and remembered having visualized a 3-D structure turning in space. He convinced Jackie Metzler, a first-year graduate student at Stanford, to study mental rotation, and the rest is history.

Figu Stim Metz Men obje dispa plane (b) T angu (thre obje thus con *Metzler,*

Figure 4.3 F **(1977) Exper** data confirme hypotheses: (condition, par make a positiv more quickly configuration when it was li the visual ima array would p information. (2 condition, par make a positiv more quickly v configuration when it was id participants wo words from the linearly, in acc normal reading

Fig the (19 Ro req twe 3-D fun dis ori pa in dir pa in (Da

These data seem to indicate that participants rotated the mental image of the object in a 3-D space within their heads. The greater the angle of disparity between the two objects, the longer participants took to complete the mental rotation. Though the participants were obviously not actually rotating a real object in their heads, the mental process appears to be analogous to physical rotation.

A great deal of subsequent research has examined the mental rotation of all sorts of different objects, typically finding that the time required to complete a rotation varies with the angular disparity. There have also been a number of brain-imaging studies that looked at what regions are active during mental rotation. Consistently, the parietal region (roughly the horizontally oriented region labeled R at the upper back of the brain in Figure 4.1) has been activated across a range of tasks. This finding corresponds with the results we reviewed in Chapter 3 showing that the parietal region is important in spatial attention. Some tasks involve activation of other areas. For instance, Kosslyn, DiGirolamo, Thompson, and Alpert (1998) found that imagining the rotation of one's hand produced activation in the motor cortex.

Neural recordings of monkeys have provided some evidence about neural representation during mental rotation involving hand movement. Georgopoulos, Lurito, Petrides, Schwartz, and Massey (1989) had monkeys perform a task in which they moved a handle counterclockwise to a specific position in response to a given stimulus. Georgopoulos et al. found cells that fired for movements to particular positions. So, for instance, there were cells that fired most strongly when the monkeys were moving the handle to the 9 o'clock position and other cells that responded most strongly when the monkeys were moving it to the 12 o'clock position. In the base condition, monkeys just moved the handle to the position of the stimulus. In the rotation condition, the monkeys had to move the handle to a position rotated some number of degrees from the stimulus. For instance, a stimulus at the 12 o'clock position required that they move the handle to 9 o'clock, and a stimulus at the 6 o'clock position required that they move the handle to 3 o'clock. In the rotation condition, Georgopoulos et al. found that various cells fired at different times during the task. At the beginning of a trial, when the stimulus was presented, the cells that fired most were associated with a move in the direction of the stimulus. By the end of the trial, when the monkeys actually moved the handle, maximum activity occurred in cells associated with the movement. Between the beginning and the end of a trial, cells representing intermediate directions were most active. These results suggest that mental rotation involves gradual shifts of firing from cells that encode the initial stimulus (the handle at its initial angle) to cells that encode the response (the handle at its final angle).

Mental rotation of a visual image to make a comparison involves rotation of the image through the intermediate positions until it reaches the desired orientation.

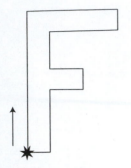

Figure 4.6 Block Diagram Used in Brooks (1968) Study of Visual Image Scanning. The asterisk and arrow show the starting point and the direction for scanning the image. *(Data from Brooks, 1968.)*

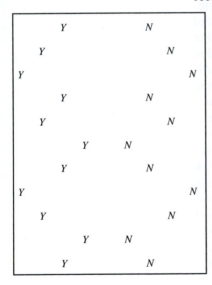

Figure 4.7 Sheet Used for Pointing to Responses in Brooks (1968) Study of Visual Image Scanning. If an *N* response came first, participants had to point to the topmost *N*; if the next response was a *Y*, participants had to point to the second *Y* from the top; and so on. The letters are staggered to force careful visual monitoring of pointing. *(Research from Brooks, 1968.)*

Image Scanning

Something else we often do with mental images is to scan them for critical information. For instance, when people are asked how many windows there are in their house (the task described at the beginning of this chapter), many report mentally going through the house visually and scanning each room for windows. Researchers have studied whether people are actually scanning perceptual representations in such tasks, as opposed to just retrieving abstract information. For instance, are we really "seeing" each window in the room or are we just remembering how many windows are in the room?

Brooks (1968) performed an important series of experiments on the scanning of visual images. He had participants scan imagined diagrams such as the one shown in **Figure 4.6**. For example, the participant was to scan around an imagined block F from a prescribed starting point and in a prescribed direction, categorizing each corner of the block as a point on the top or bottom (assigned a *yes* response) or as a point in between (assigned a *no* response). In the example (beginning with the starting corner), the correct sequence of responses is yes, yes, yes, no, no, no, no, no, no, yes. For a nonvisual contrast task, Brooks also gave participants sentences such as "A bird in the hand is not in the bush." Participants had to scan the sentence while holding it in memory, deciding whether each word was a noun or not. A second experimental variable was how participants made their responses. Participants responded in one of three ways: (1) said *yes* or *no*; (2) tapped with the left hand for *yes* and with the right hand for *no*; or (3) pointed to specific *Y*'s or *N*'s on a sheet of paper such as the one shown in **Figure 4.7**.

Table 4.1 gives the results of Brooks's experiment in terms of the mean time spent in classifying the sentences or diagrams in each of the three response modes. The important result for our purposes is that participants took much longer to respond to diagrams in the pointing mode than in the other two modes, but this was not the case when responding to sentences. Apparently, scanning a physical visual object conflicted with scanning a mental image (recall the discussion in Chapter 3 of bottlenecks when trying to process multiple tasks in a single processing stream). This result strongly reinforces the conclusion that when people are scanning a mental image, they are scanning a representation that is analogous to a physical picture.

One might think that Brooks's result was due to the conflict between engaging in a visual pointing task and scanning a visual image. Subsequent research makes it clear, however, that the interference is not a result of the visual character of the pointing task per se. Rather, the problem is spatial and not specifically visual; it arises from the conflicting directions in which participants had to scan the physical visual array and the mental image. Evidence for this interpretation comes from another experiment in which Brooks found similar interference when participants had their eyes closed and indicated *yes* or *no* by scanning an array of raised *Y*'s and *N*'s with their fingers. In this case, the actual stimuli were tactile, not visual. Thus, the conflict is indeed spatial, not specifically visual.

TABLE 4.1 Results of Brooks's (1968) Experiment Showing Conflict Between Scanning a Visual Image and Scanning a Physical Picture

Stimulus Material	Mean Response Time (s) by Output Mode		
	Vocal	*Tapping*	*Pointing*
Diagrams	11.3	14.1	28.2
Sentences	13.8	7.8	9.8

Data from Brooks, 1968.

Baddeley and Lieberman (reported in Baddeley, 1976) performed an experiment that further supports the view that the nature of the interference in the Brooks task is spatial rather than visual. Participants were required to perform two tasks simultaneously. All participants performed the Brooks letter-image task illustrated in Figure 4.6. However, participants in one group simultaneously monitored a series of stimuli of two possible brightness levels and had to press a key whenever a brighter stimulus appeared. This task involved the processing of visual but not spatial information. Participants in the other group were blindfolded and seated in front of a swinging pendulum. The pendulum emitted a tone and contained a photocell, and participants had to try to keep the beam of a flashlight on the swinging pendulum. Whenever they were on target, the photocell caused the tone to change frequency, thus providing auditory feedback. This test involved the processing of spatial but not visual information. The spatial auditory tracking task produced far greater impairment in the image-scanning task than did the brightness judgment task. This result also indicates that the nature of the impairment in the Brooks task was spatial, not visual.

> *People suffer interference in scanning a mental image if they simultaneously have to process a conflicting perceptual structure.*

Mental Comparison of Magnitudes

A fair amount of research has focused on the way people judge the details of objects in their mental images. One line of research has asked participants to discriminate between objects based on some dimension such as size. This research has shown that when participants try to discriminate between two objects based on their relative size, the time it takes them to do so decreases continuously as the difference in size between the two objects increases.

Moyer (1973) was interested in the speed with which participants could judge the relative size of two animals from memory — for example, the speed with which participants could answer questions such as "Which is larger,

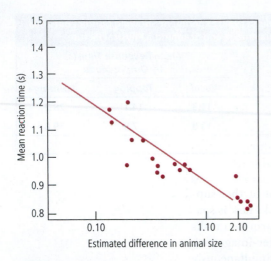

Figure 4.8 **Results from Moyer's (1973) Experiment on Size Comparisons.** Participants were asked to compare their estimated sizes of two animals. The mean time required to judge which of two animals is larger is plotted as a function of the estimated difference in size of the two animals. The time decreases as the difference in estimated size increases, but the logarithmic scale used for estimated size indicates that increasing size estimates have a decreasing effect. *(Data from Moyer, 1973.)*

moose or roach?" and "Which is larger, wolf or lion?" Many people report that in making these kinds of judgments, particularly for items that are similar in size, they generate mental images of the two objects and compare the sizes of the objects in their images.

Moyer also asked participants to estimate the absolute size of these animals. **Figure 4.8** plots the time required to compare the imagined sizes of two animals as a function of the difference between the two animals' estimated absolute size. The individual points in Figure 4.8 represent comparisons between pairs of items. In general, the judgment times decreased as the difference in estimated size increased (e.g., the lower points in the graph, at the right, might represent the reaction times for deciding about ant vs. elk or flea vs. bear; and the higher points, at the left, might represent hog vs. cow or louse vs. roach). The graph shows that judgment time decreases linearly with increases in the difference between the estimated sizes of the two animals, but note that the differences have been plotted logarithmically. This makes the distance between small estimated differences large relative to the same distances between large differences, which means that increasing the difference in estimated size has a diminishing effect on reaction time.

Significantly, very similar results are obtained when people visually compare the size of actual physical objects. For instance, Johnson (1939) asked participants to judge which of two simultaneously presented lines was longer. **Figure 4.9** plots participant judgment time as a function of the difference in line length, again on a logarithmic scale (as in the Moyer experiment), and again a linear relation is obtained. It is reasonable to expect that the more similar the lengths being compared, the longer will be the time for perceptual judgments, because the difficulty of the task increases as the difference in lengths decreases. The fact that similar functions are obtained when mental images are compared (Figure 4.8) and when physical objects are compared (Figure 4.9) indicates that making mental comparisons involves the same processes as those involved in perceptual comparisons.

> *People experience greater difficulty in judging the relative size of two objects or of two mental images as similarity in size increases.*

Are Visual Images Like Visual Perception?

Can people recognize patterns in mental images in the same way that they recognize patterns in things they actually see? In an experiment designed to investigate this question, Finke, Pinker, and Farah (1989) asked participants to create mental images and then engage in a series of transformations of those images. Here are two examples of the problems that they read to their participants:

- Imagine a capital letter N. Connect a diagonal line from the top right corner to the bottom left corner. Now rotate the figure 90° to the right. What do you see?
- Imagine a capital letter D. Rotate the figure 90° to the left. Now place a capital letter J at the bottom. What do you see?

Participants closed their eyes and tried to imagine these transformations as they were read to them. The participants were able to recognize their composite images just as if they had been presented with them on a screen. In the first example, they saw an hourglass; in the second, an umbrella. The ability to perform such tasks illustrates an important function of imagery: It enables us to construct new objects in our minds and inspect them. It is just this sort of visual synthesis that structural engineers or architects must perform as they design new bridges or buildings.

Chambers and Reisberg (1985) reported a study that seemed to indicate differences between a mental image and visual perception of the real object. Their research involved the processing of reversible figures, such as the duck-rabbit shown in **Figure 4.10**. Participants were briefly shown the figure and asked to form an image of it. They had only enough time to form one interpretation of the picture before it was removed. When they were then asked to find a second interpretation, they were not able to do so. But when they were asked to draw the image on paper to see whether they could reinterpret it, they were successful. This result suggests that mental images differ from pictures in that one can interpret visual images, even images of ambiguous figures, only in one way.

Subsequently, Peterson, Kihlstrom, Rose, and Gilsky (1992) were able to get participants to reverse mental images by giving them more explicit instructions. For instance, participants might be told how to reverse another figure or be given the instruction to consider the back of the head of the animal in their mental image as the front of the head of another animal. This result indicates that although it may be more difficult to reverse an image than a picture, both can be reversed. In general, it seems harder to process an image than the actual stimulus. Given a choice, people will almost always choose to process an actual picture rather than imagine it. For instance, players of Tetris prefer to rotate shapes on the screen to find an appropriate orientation rather than rotate them mentally (Kirsh & Maglio, 1994).

It is possible to make many of the same kinds of detailed judgments about mental images that we make about things we actually see, though it is more difficult.

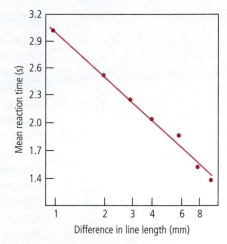

Figure 4.9 Results from Johnson's (1939) Experiment on Size Comparisons. Participants judged which of two lines was longer. The mean time required to judge which line was longer is plotted as a function of the difference in line length. As in the graph of results of the Moyer (1973) experiment shown in Figure 4.8, difference in size (here, actual line length, vs. estimated animal size in the Moyer experiment) is shown on a logarithmic scale. The results of the two experiments are very similar, demonstrating that making mental comparisons (in Moyer, 1973) involves difficulties of discrimination similar to those involved in making perceptual comparisons (in this experiment).

Figure 4.10 Duck–Rabbit. This ambiguous figure was used in Chambers and Reisberg's (1985) study of the processing of reversible figures. *(American Psychological Association.)*

Visual Imagery and Brain Areas

Brain-imaging studies indicate that the same regions are involved in visual perception as in visual imagery. As already noted, the parietal regions that are involved in attending to locations and objects (see Chapter 3) are also involved in mental rotation. O'Craven and Kanwisher (2000) performed an experiment that further illustrates how closely the brain areas activated by imagery correspond to the brain areas activated by perception. As discussed in Chapters 2 and 3, the **fusiform face area (FFA)** in the temporal cortex responds preferentially to faces, and another region of the temporal cortex, the **parahippocampal place area (PPA),** responds preferentially to pictures of locations (i.e., indoor or outdoor scenes). O'Craven and Kanwisher asked participants either to view faces and scenes or to imagine faces and scenes. The same areas were active when the participants were viewing as when they were imagining. As shown in **Figure 4.11**, every time the participants viewed or imagined a face, there was increased activation in the FFA, and this activation went away when they viewed or imagined a scene. Conversely, when they viewed

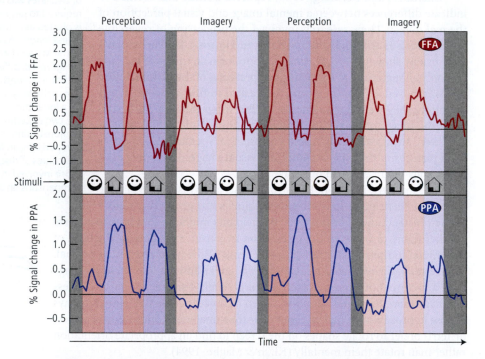

Figure 4.11 Results from the O'Craven and Kanwisher (2000) Study of Brain Activation During Mental Imagery. Participants alternately perceived (or imagined) faces and places, and brain activation was correspondingly seen in the fusiform face area (FFA, upper panel) or the parahippocampal place area (PPA, lower panel). These results show that visual images are processed in the same way as actual perceptions and by many of the same neural structures. *(O'Craven and Kanwisher, Mental imagery of faces and places activates corresponding stimulus-specific brain regions [2000]. The Journal of Cognitive Neuroscience.)*

or imagined scenes, there was increased activation in the PPA that went away when they viewed or imagined faces. The responses during imagery were very similar to the responses during perception, although a little weaker. The fact that the response was weaker during imagery is consistent with the behavioral evidence we have reviewed suggesting that it is more difficult to process an image than a real perception.

There are many studies like these that show that cortical regions involved in high-level visual processing are activated during the processing of visual imagery. However, the evidence is less clear about activation in the primary visual cortex (areas 17 and 18 in Figure 1.7; see also Figure 2.5), where visual information first reaches the brain. The O'Craven and Kanwisher (2000) study did find activation in the primary visual cortex during imagery. Such results are important because they suggest that visual imagery includes relatively low-level perceptual processes. However, other studies have not always found activation in the primary visual cortex. For instance, the Roland and Friberg (1985) study illustrated in Figure 4.1 did not find activation in this region (see also Roland, Eriksson, Stone-Elander, & Widen, 1987). Kosslyn and Thompson (2003) reviewed 59 brain-imaging studies that looked for activation in early visual areas during imagery. About half of these studies find activation in early visual areas and half do not. Kosslyn and Thompson's analysis suggests that the studies that find activation in these early visual areas tend to emphasize high-resolution details of the images and tend to focus on shape judgments. For example, Kosslyn et al. (1993) found activation in area 17 in a study where participants were asked to imagine block letters. In one of their experiments, participants were asked to imagine large versus small letters. In the small-letter condition, activity in the visual cortex occurred in a more posterior region, closer to where the center of the visual field is represented. This makes sense because a small image would be more concentrated at the center of the visual field.

Imaging studies like these show that perceptual regions of the brain are active when participants engage in mental imagery, but they do not establish whether these regions are actually critical to imagery. To return to the epiphenomenon critique at the beginning of the chapter, it could be that the activation plays no role in the participants' experience of the imagery. A number of experiments have used transcranial magnetic stimulation (TMS) (see Figure 1.13) to investigate the causal role of these regions in the performance of the underlying task. For instance, Kosslyn et al. (1999) presented participants with four-quadrant arrays like those in **Figure 4.12** and asked them to form a mental image of the array. Then, with their eyes closed, participants had to use their image to answer questions like "Which has longer stripes: Quadrant 1 or Quadrant 2?" and "Which has more stripes: Quadrant 1 or Quadrant 4?" Application of TMS to disrupt processing in area 17 in the primary visual cortex significantly increased the time participants took to answer these questions. The fact

Figure 4.12 Illustration of Stimuli Used in Kosslyn et al. (1999). The numbers 1, 2, 3, and 4 were used to label the four quadrants, each of which contained a set of stripes. After memorizing the display, the participants closed their eyes, visualized the entire display, heard the names of two quadrants, and then heard the name of a comparison term (for example, "length"); the participants then decided whether the stripes in the first-named quadrant had more of the named property than those in the second. (*Research from Kosslyn et al., 1999.*)

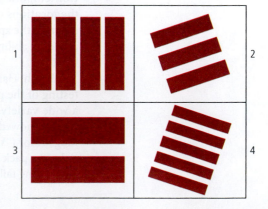

that temporarily disrupting these visual regions results in slower performance in the visual imagery task suggests that they do play a causal role in mental imagery.

> Brain regions involved in visual perception are also involved in visual imagery tasks, and disruption of these regions results in disruption of the imagery tasks.

Imagery Involves Both Spatial and Visual Components

There is an important distinction to be made between the spatial and visual attributes of imagery. We can encode the position of objects in space by seeing where they are, by feeling where they are, or by hearing where they are. Such encodings use a common spatial representation that integrates information that comes in from any sensory modality. (One type of evidence for this common spatial representation is provided by the interference that participants experienced in scanning a mental image like Figure 4.6 while also performing a tactile or auditory task.) In contrast, certain aspects of visual experience, such as color, are unique to the visual modality and seem separate from spatial information. Imagery involves both spatial and visual components. In the discussion of the visual system in Chapter 2, we reviewed the evidence that there is a "where" pathway for processing spatial information and a "what" pathway for processing object-recognition information (see Figure 2.1). Corresponding to this distinction, there is evidence (Mazard, Fuller, Orcutt, Bridle, & Scanlan, 2004) that parietal regions support the spatial component of visual imagery, whereas temporal regions support the visual aspects. We have already noted that mental rotation, a spatial task, tends to produce activation in the parietal cortex. Similarly, temporal structures are activated when people imagine visual properties of objects (Thompson & Kosslyn, 2000).

Studies of patients with brain damage also support this association of spatial imagery with parietal areas and visual imagery with temporal areas. Levine, Warach, and Farah (1985) compared two patients, one who suffered bilateral parietal-occipital damage and the other who suffered bilateral inferior temporal damage. The patient with parietal damage could not describe the locations of familiar objects or landmarks from memory, but he could describe the appearance of objects. The patient with temporal damage had an impaired ability to describe the appearance of objects but could describe their locations.

Farah, Hammond, Levine, and Calvanio (1988) carried out more detailed testing of the patient with temporal damage, comparing his performance on a wide variety of imagery tasks to that of normal participants. They found that he showed deficits in only a subset of these tasks: ones in which he had to judge color ("What is the color of a football?"), sizes ("Which is bigger, a popsicle or a pack of cigarettes?"), the lengths of animals' tails ("Does a kangaroo have a long tail?"), and whether two U.S. states had similar shapes. In contrast, he did not show any deficit in performing tasks that seemed to involve a substantial amount of spatial processing: mental rotation, image scanning, letter scanning (as in Figure 4.7), or judgments of where one U.S. state was relative to another state. Thus, this patient's temporal damage seemed to affect only those imagery tasks that required access to visual detail, not those that required spatial judgments.

The blind are an interesting population to study with regard to this question of spatial versus visual imagery. Blind individuals are capable of forming spatial imagery, using information gained through nonvisual modalities such as haptic perception (touch) and auditory perception (for a review, see Renzi, Cattaneo, Vecchi, & Cornoldi, 2013). Blind individuals can then use such a mental representation of their environment to navigate through it. Congenitally blind participants who routinely navigate their environment unassisted (not all do) were shown to be as good as sighted participants in judging where things are from a verbal description of the layout of the environment (Schmidt, Tinti, Fantino, Mammarella, & Cornoldi, 2013). Like sighted individuals, blind participants can explore two objects haptically and judge whether they are rotations of one another, and, like sighted individuals, their response times are affected by the degree of rotation (Carpenter & Eisenberg, 1978) (see Figure 4.5).

> *Neuropsychological evidence suggests that imagery of spatial information is supported by parietal structures, and that imagery of objects and their visual properties is supported by temporal structures.*

Individual Difference in Visual Imagery

Individuals vary in how vivid their experience of visual imagery is, as measured by the Vividness of Visual Imagery Questionnaire (VVIQ) (Marks, 1973). The questionnaire asks the participant to perform activities such as forming an image of a friend and focusing on things like the exact contour of face, head, shoulders, and body. Participants are asked to rate the vividness of the image, and ratings vary from saying that the experience is just like really seeing the person to saying that the image is moderately clear to saying that there is no image at all. One might think people who report very vivid images are generally good at tasks that rely on visual imagery, but the actual results of tests on such tasks are more nuanced than this.

For example, in the paper-folding test (Ekstrom, French, Harman, & Dermen, 1976), participants are asked to imagine a sheet of paper folded in certain ways and then punched with a hole, as illustrated in the left part of **Figure 4.13**. The participant is then asked to imagine what the pattern of holes would be if the paper were unfolded, as illustrated by the choices presented in the right part of Figure 4.13. On average, participants who score high on vividness of visual imagery actually do worse at this task than those who report less vivid imagery (Kozhevnikov, Kosslyn, & Shephard, 2005). Other studies

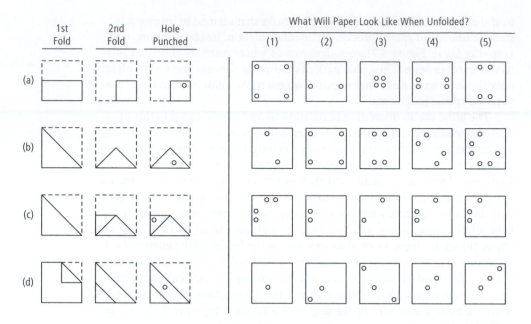

Figure 4.13 Example Problems on a Paper-Folding Test. Participants must imagine that the paper is folded as indicated and a hole punched as indicated, and then visualize what the pattern of holes will be when the paper is unfolded. (a) Paper is folded in half horizontally and then folded in half vertically. (b) Paper is folded in half diagonally from upper left to lower right and then from lower left to upper right. (c) Paper is folded in half diagonally from upper left to lower right and then folded horizontally. (d) Upper right quarter of paper is folded diagonally from upper left to lower right, and then the paper is folded across the long diagonal. *(Research from Ekstrom et al., 1976.)*
Answers: a4, b4, c1, d5.

Figure 4.14 (Test) A Degraded Pictures Task. Can you find the object hidden in the picture? (Turn a page to see the answer.)

have failed to find a relationship between VVIQ and measures of spatial ability in tasks such as mental rotation (see Figure 4.4) (Dean & Morris, 2003). The consistent and surprising result is that there does not seem to be a positive relationship between performance on such tests of spatial ability and vividness of visual imagery.

However, there are tests on which vivid imagers do better, such as the task illustrated in **Figure 4.14 (Test)**. Participants are asked to find the object hidden in the degraded image (turn a page to see the answer). In this case, participants who reported vivid imagery showed a marginally significant advantage over those who did not. A similar advantage for participants with vivid imagery was found in tests that asked participants to identify pictures of real objects presented at different levels of blurriness, from very blurry to sharp and detailed (Vannucci, Mazzoni, Chiorri, & Cioli, 2008). In fMRI studies of the relationship between VVIQ scores and brain activation when engaging in a mental image, participants with less vivid imagery tend to activate a wider range of brain areas than people with more vivid imagery (Fulford et al., 2018). This suggests that vivid imagers find it easier to create the images and have to engage these regions less.

Blazhenkova and Kozhevnikov (2009) argue that there are two distinct kinds of imagery ability, one spatial and one object oriented. This would be in line with the neural evidence we have reviewed showing that spatial and visual imagery are associated with the "where" and "what" visual pathways, respectively. But a curious result is that these two types of imagery ability are at least somewhat negatively related — that is, people who score high on one tend to score low on the other. In a related result, Kozhevnikov, Blazhenkova, & Becker (2010) found that students specializing in the visual arts tend to score high on object visualization and low on spatial visualization, whereas the reverse is true for students specializing in science. As we will discuss more thoroughly in Chapter 14, most measures of cognitive ability tend to be somewhat positively related — people who score high on one measure tend to score high on others. (**Implications 4.2** reviews research on correlations between spatial skills and success in STEM fields.)

> *The ability to experience vivid and detailed visual images is not related to the ability to make judgments that involve spatial imagery.*

Implications 4.2

Spatial Skills and STEM Education

There is a relationship between spatial ability (measured by tests like the paper folding problems illustrated in Figure 4.13) and success in learning science, technology, engineering, and mathematics (STEM disciplines). In studies following students over many years, performance on spatial ability tests predicts both course grades and whether students will go on to work in STEM fields (Wai, Lubinski, & Benbow, 2009). Approximately half of all people who earn PhDs in STEM fields perform in the top 5% of individuals on tests of spatial ability. There are very few PhDs in STEM fields who perform below average on such tests. The correlation between high spatial ability and success in STEM fields holds even in studies that control for mathematical and verbal ability. However, in a study of 40,000 high-school students, Wai et al. (2009) found that males and students of higher socioeconomic status tend to score higher in spatial abilities. Such results are worrisome because they suggest that differences in spatial ability might be limiting diversity in STEM fields.

In a review of the literature, Uttal et al. (2013) found that spatial training programs — for example, training on drawing engineering designs — can have a large impact on measures of spatial skills. Uttal et al. suggest that systematic training might increase success and broaden participation in STEM fields. However, they note the possibility that training-related improvements in spatial skills would not be accompanied by improvements in STEM performance. Nevertheless, a recent study (Sorby, Veurink, & Streiner, 2018) did find that training in spatial skills did correlate with improved grades of first-year engineering students with weak spatial skills (the improvement averaged about half a grade point on a 4.0 GPA scale).

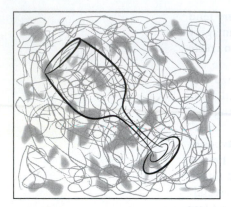

Figure 4.14 (Answer)

Cognitive Maps

Another important function of visual imagery is to help us understand and remember the spatial structure of our environment. Our imaginal representations of the world are often referred to as **cognitive maps.** The connection between imagery and action is particularly apparent in cognitive maps. We often find ourselves imagining our environment as we plan how we will get from one location to another and as we actually move between locations.

An important distinction can be made between cognitive maps that are route maps and those that are survey maps (Hart & Moore, 1973). A **route map** is a path that indicates specific places but contains no spatial information. It can even be a verbal description of a path ("Straight until the light, then turn left; two blocks later at the intersection . . ."). Thus, with a pure route map, if your route from location 1 to location 2 were blocked, you would have no general idea of where location 2 was, and so you would be unable to construct a detour. Also, if you knew (in the sense of a route map) two routes from a location, you would have no idea whether these routes formed a 90° angle or a 120° angle with respect to each other. A **survey map,** in contrast, contains this type of information — it is basically a spatial image of the environment. When you ask for directions from online mapping services, they will typically provide both a route map and a survey map to support both types of mental representations of space.

Thorndyke and Hayes-Roth (1982) investigated workers' knowledge of the large, mazelike Rand Corporation Building in Santa Monica, California (see **Figure 4.15**). People who work in the Rand Building quickly

Figure 4.15 Floor Plan for the First Floor of the Rand Corporation Building in Santa Monica, California. Workers at Rand quickly acquired route maps for getting from one place to another (e.g., from the administrative conference room to the common room) but took years to acquire the knowledge represented by survey maps (e.g., the knowledge that the supply room is due west of the cashier). *(Information from Thorndyke & Hayes-Roth, 1982.)*

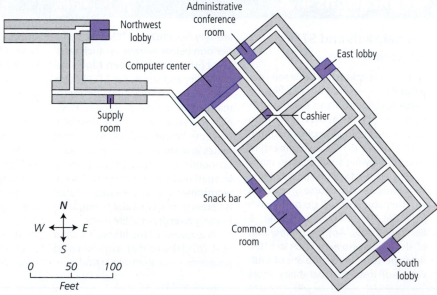

acquire the ability to find their way from one specific place in the building to another — for example, from the supply room to the cashier. This type of knowledge represents a route map. Typically, though, workers had to have years of experience in the building before acquiring survey-map knowledge, such as the direction of the snack bar from the administrative conference room (due south).

Hartley, Maguire, Spiers, and Burgess (2003) used fMRI to look at differences in brain activity when people used route maps versus survey maps. They had participants navigate virtual reality towns under one of two conditions: *route-following* (involving a route map) or *way-finding* (involving a survey map). In the route-following condition, participants learned to follow a fixed path through the town, whereas in the way-finding condition, participants first freely explored the town and then had to find their way between locations. The results of the experiment are illustrated in **Figure 4.16**. In the way-finding task, participants showed greater activation in a number of regions that have also been found to show greater activation in other studies of visual imagery, including the parietal cortex. There was also greater activation in the hippocampus (see Figure 1.8), a region that has been implicated in navigation in many species. In contrast, in the route-following task participants showed greater activation in more anterior regions and motor regions. It would seem that the survey map is more like a visual image and the route map is more like an action plan. This is a distinction that is supported in other fMRI studies of route maps versus survey maps (e.g., Shelton & Gabrieli, 2002).

Landmarks serve as an important part of survey maps and enable flexible action. Using a virtual environment navigation system, Foo, Warren, Duchon, and Tarr (2005) performed an experiment that used the presence

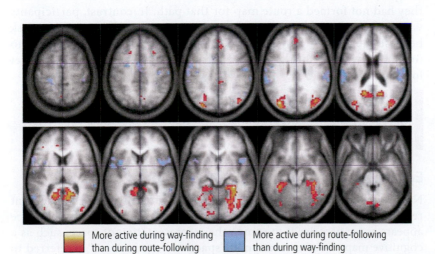

More active during way-finding than during route-following

More active during route-following than during way-finding

Figure 4.16 Brain Activation: Survey Maps (Way-Finding) Versus Route Maps (Route-Mapping). These results from Hartley et al. (2003) illustrate areas that were more active in the survey map task than in the route map task versus areas that were more active in the route map task than in the survey map task.

(Republished with permission of Elsevier Global Rights, from The well-worn route and the path less traveled, Hartley et al., 37, 5, 2003. Permission conveyed through Copyright Clearance Center, Inc., Elsevier Global Rights.)

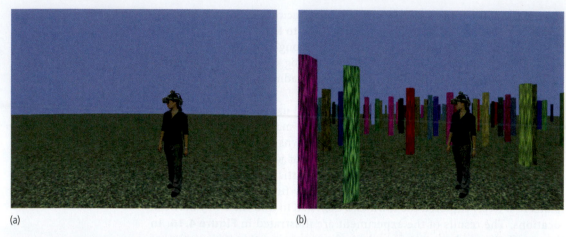

(a)   (b)

Figure 4.17   Displays Used in the Virtual Reality Study of Foo et al. (2005).   (a)The desert world consisted of a textured ground plane only. (b) The forest world included many colored posts scattered randomly throughout, serving as potential landmarks. *(Foo, P., Warren, W. H., Duchon, A., & Tarr, M. J. (2005). Do humans integrate routes into a cognitive map? Map- versus landmark-based navigation of novel shortcuts.* Journal of Experimental Psychology: Learning, Memory, and Cognition, *31(2), 195-215, Mar 2005, American Psychological Association, reprinted with permission.)*

or absence of landmarks ("desert" or "forest" condition) to promote creation of different types of mental maps. In both conditions, participants practiced navigating from a home position to two target locations. In the "desert" condition, there were no landmarks (see **Figure 4.17a**); in the "forest" condition, there were "trees" (the posts in Figure 4.17b). After these practicing sessions, participants were asked to navigate from one of the target locations to the other, having never done so before. Participants who had practiced in the "desert" condition were very poor at this task because they had not formed a route map for that path. In contrast, participants who had practiced in the "forest" condition were much better at the task because the colored posts served as landmarks enabling participants to form a survey map of the entire environment including the two target locations.

> *Our knowledge of our environment can be represented in either survey maps that emphasize spatial information or route maps that emphasize action information.*

Egocentric and Allocentric Representations of Space

Navigation becomes difficult when we must tie together multiple different representations of space. In particular, we often need to relate the way space appears as we perceive it to some other representation of space, such as a cognitive map. A representation of "space as we perceive it" is referred to

Figure 4.18 An Egocentric Representation. A view from the Tidal Basin in Washington, D.C., during cherry blossom time. *(OGphoto/Getty Images.)*

as an **egocentric representation. Figure 4.18** illustrates an egocentric representation that one might have when looking through the cherry blossoms at the Tidal Basin in Washington, D.C. Even young children have little difficulty understanding how to navigate in space as they *see* it — if they see an object they want, they go for it. Problems arise when one wants to relate what one sees to such representations of the space as cognitive maps, be they route maps or survey maps. Similar problems arise when one wants to deal with physical maps, such as the map in **Figure 4.19**. This kind of map is referred to as an **allocentric representation** because it is not specific to a particular

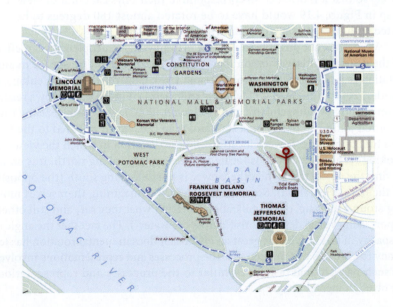

Figure 4.19 An Allocentric Representation: Washington's National Mall and Memorial Parks. The stick figure shows the position of an observer experiencing the egocentric representation shown in Figure 4.18. *(National Park Service.)*

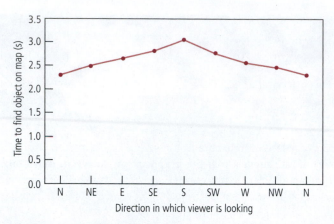

Figure 4.20 Results from Gunzelmann and Anderson (2002) Study of the Coordination of Different Representations of Space. The time required for participants to find an object on a map is plotted as a function of the angle of disparity between a standard map (looking north) and the observer's viewpoint (i.e., the difference in orientation between the allocentric representation of the map and the observer's egocentric representation). *(Data from Gunzelmann & Anderson, 2002.)*

viewpoint, though, as is true of most maps, north is oriented to the top of the image. Using the map in Figure 4.19, assuming the perspective of the stick figure (looking south), try to identify the building in Figure 4.18. When people try to make such judgments, the degree to which the map is rotated from their actual viewpoint has a large effect. Indeed, people will often rotate a map so that it is oriented to correspond to their physical point of view. The map in Figure 4.19 would have to be rotated almost 180 degrees to be oriented with the representation shown in Figure 4.18.

When it is not possible to rotate a map physically, people show an effect of the degree of misorientation that is much like the effect we see for mental rotation (e.g., Boer, 1991; Easton & Sholl, 1995; Gugerty, deBoom, Jenkins, & Morley, 2000; Hintzman, O'Dell, & Arndt, 1981). **Figure 4.20** shows results from a study by Gunzelmann and Anderson (2002), who looked at the time required to find an object on a standard map (i.e., north oriented to the top) as a function of the viewer's location and the direction in which the viewer is looking. When the viewer is located to the south, looking north, it is easier to find the object than when the viewer is north looking south (the opposite of the map orientation). Some people describe imagining themselves moving around the map, others talk about rotating what they see, and still others report using verbal descriptions ("across the water"). The fact that the angle of disparity in this task has as great an effect as it does in mental rotation has led many researchers to conclude that the processes and representations involved in such navigational tasks are similar to the processes and representations involved in mental imagery.

Physical maps seem to differ from cognitive maps in one important way: Physical maps show the effects of orientation, and cognitive maps do not. For example, imagine yourself standing against various walls of your bedroom, and point to the location of the front door of your home or apartment. Most people can do this equally well no matter which position they take. In contrast, when given a map like the one in Figure 4.19, people find it much easier to point to various objects on the map if they are oriented in the same way the map is.

Recordings from single cells in the hippocampal region (inside the temporal lobe) of rats suggest that the hippocampus plays an important role in maintaining an allocentric representation of the world. There are cells in the hippocampus that fire maximally when the animal is in a particular location in its environment, such as the southwest corner of its cage (O'Keefe & Dostrovsky, 1971). Similar cells have been found in recordings from human patients during a procedure to map out the brain before surgery to control epilepsy (Ekstrom et al., 2003). Brain-imaging studies have shown high hippocampal activation when humans are navigating their environment (Maguire et al., 1998). Another study (Maguire et al., 2000) showed that the hippocampal volume of London taxi drivers was greater than that of people who did not drive taxis. The longer they had been taxi drivers, the greater the volume of their hippocampus. It took about three years of intensive training to gain enough knowledge of London streets to be a successful taxi driver, and this training had an impact on the structure of the brain.* The amount of activation in hippocampal structures has also been shown to correlate with age-related differences in navigation skills (Pine et al., 2002) and may relate to gender differences in navigational ability (Gron, Wunderlich, Spitzer, Tomczak, & Riepe, 2000).

Whereas the hippocampus appears to be important in supporting allocentric representations, the parietal cortex seems particularly important in supporting egocentric representations (Burgess, 2006). In one fMRI study comparing egocentric and allocentric spatial processing (Zaehle et al., 2007), participants were asked to make judgments that emphasized either an allocentric or an egocentric perspective. In the allocentric conditions, participants would read a description like "The blue triangle is to the left of the green square. The green square is above the yellow triangle. The yellow triangle is to the right of the red circle." Then they would be asked a question like "Is the blue triangle above the red circle?" In the egocentric condition, they would read a description like "The blue circle is in front of you. The yellow circle is to your right. The yellow square is to the right of the yellow circle." They would then be asked a question like "Is the yellow square to your right?" There was greater hippocampal activation when participants were answering questions in the allocentric condition than in the egocentric

---

*In 2018, Uber regained its license to operate in London. Traditional cabbies had lobbied against this decision, arguing that they have better knowledge of the streets of London than what GPS systems provide Uber drivers (German, 2018).

condition. Although there was considerable parietal activation in both conditions, it was greater in the egocentric condition.

> *Our representation of space includes both allocentric representations of where objects are in the world and egocentric representations of where they are relative to ourselves.*

Map Distortions

Our mental maps often have a hierarchical structure in which smaller regions are organized within larger regions. For instance, the structure of my bedroom is organized within the structure of my house, which is organized within the structure of my neighborhood, which is organized within the structure of Pittsburgh. Consider your mental map of the United States. It is probably divided into regions, and these regions into states, and cities are presumably pinpointed within the states. It turns out that certain systematic distortions arise because of the hierarchical structure of these mental maps. Stevens and Coupe (1978) documented a set of common misconceptions about North American geography. Consider the following questions taken from their research:

- Which is farther east: San Diego or Reno?
- Which is farther north: Seattle or Montreal?
- Which is farther west: the Atlantic or the Pacific entrance to the Panama Canal?

The first choice is the correct answer in each case, but most people hold the opposite opinion. Reno seems to be farther east because most of Nevada is east of most of California, but due to the westward curve in California's coastline, Reno is actually west of San Diego. Montreal seems to be north of Seattle because most of Canada is north of most of the United States, but the border dips south in the east. And the Atlantic is east of the Pacific — but consult a map if you need to be convinced about the location of the entrances to the Panama Canal. The geography of North America is quite complex, and people resort to abstract facts about the relative locations of large areas (e.g., California and Nevada) to make judgments about smaller locations (e.g., San Diego and Reno).

Stevens and Coupe were able to demonstrate such confusions with experimenter-created maps. Different groups of participants learned the maps shown in **Figure 4.21**. The important feature of the incongruent maps is that the relative locations of the Alpha and Beta counties are inconsistent with the locations of the X and Y cities. After learning the maps, participants were asked a series of questions about the locations of cities, including "Is X east or west of Y?" for the horizontal-condition maps and "Is X north or south of Y?" for the vertical-condition maps. Participants made errors on 18% of the questions for the congruent maps, 15% for the homogeneous maps, but 45% for the incongruent maps. Participants were using information about the locations of the

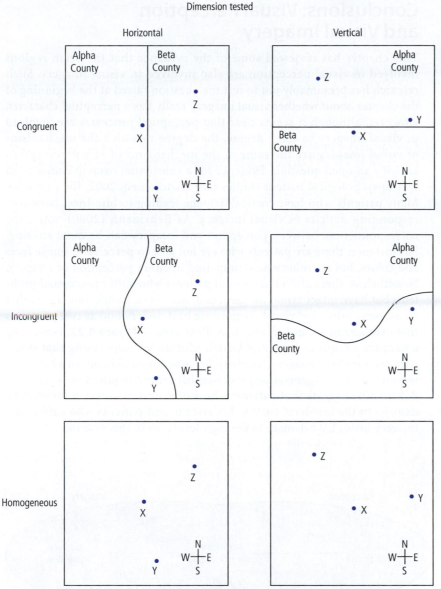

Figure 4.21 Maps Studied by Participants in the Experiments of Stevens and Coupe (1978). The results demonstrated the effects of higher-order information (location of county lines) on participants' recall of city locations. *(Data from Stevens & Coupe, 1978.)*

counties to help them remember the city locations. This reliance on higher order information led them to make errors, just as similar reasoning can lead to errors in answering questions about North American geography.

> *When people have to work out the relative positions of two locations, they will often reason in terms of the relative positions of larger areas that contain the two locations.*

Conclusions: Visual Perception and Visual Imagery

This chapter has reviewed some of the evidence that the brain regions involved in visual perception are also involved in visual imagery. Such research has presumably put to rest the question raised at the beginning of the chapter about whether visual imagery really has a perceptual character. However, although it seems clear that perceptual processes are involved in visual imagery to some degree, the degree to which the mechanisms of visual imagery are the same as the mechanisms of visual perception remains an open question. Evidence for a substantial overlap comes from neuropsychological patient studies (see Bartolomeo, 2002, for a review). Many patients who have cortical damage leading to blindness have corresponding deficits in visual imagery. As Behrmann (2000) notes, the correspondences between perception and imagery can be quite striking. For instance, there are patients who are not able to perceive or image faces and colors, but are otherwise unimpaired in either perception or imagery. Nonetheless, there also exist cases of patients who suffer perceptual problems but have intact visual imagery, and vice versa. Behrmann argues that visual perception and visual imagery are best understood as two processes that overlap but are not identical, as illustrated in **Figure 4.22**. Perceiving a kangaroo requires low-level visual information processing that is not required for visual imagery. Similarly, forming a mental image of a kangaroo requires high-level generation processes that are not required by perception. Behrmann suggests that patients who suffer only perceptual losses have damage to the low-level part of this system, and patients who suffer only imagery losses have damage to the high-level part of this system.

Figure 4.22 Visual Perception and Visual Imagery: Overlap in Processing. Visual perception and visual imagery both involve some intermediate-level processing. But visual perception involves some low-level processing not involved in visual imagery, and visual imagery involves some high-level processing not involved in visual perception. *(John Crux/ Shutterstock.)*

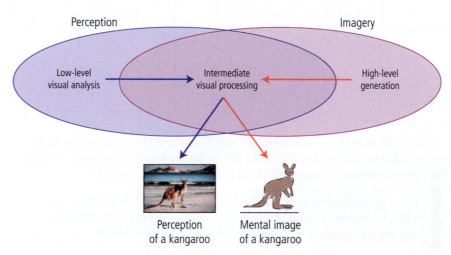

Questions for Thought

1. It has been hypothesized that our perceptual system regularly uses mental rotation to recognize objects in nonstandard orientations. In Chapter 2 we contrasted template and feature models for object recognition. Would mental rotation be more important to a template model or a feature model? Explain your answer.

2. Consider the following problem:

   Imagine a wire-frame cube resting on a tabletop with the front face directly in front of you and perpendicular to your line of sight. Imagine the long diagonal that goes from the bottom, front, left-hand corner to the top, back, right-hand corner. Now imagine that the cube is reoriented so that this diagonal is vertical and the cube is resting on one corner. Place one fingertip about a foot above the tabletop and let this mark the position of the top corner on the diagonal. The corner on which the cube is resting is on the tabletop, vertically below your fingertip. With your other hand, point to the spatial locations of the other corners of the cube.

   Hinton (1979) reports that only one out of over 20 researchers was able to perform this task successfully. In light of the successes we have reviewed for mental imagery, why is this task so hard? To aid you in answering this question, here is an illustration of the cube standing on its corner (the dashed red line is the diagonal):

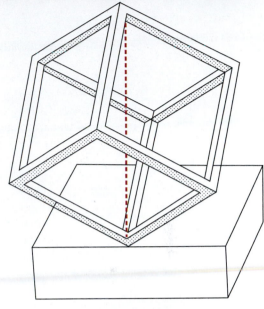

3. The chapter reviewed the evidence that many different regions of the brain are activated in mental imagery tasks — parietal and motor areas in mental rotation, temporal regions in judgments of object attributes, and hippocampal regions in reasoning about navigation. Why would mental imagery involve so many regions?

4. Consider map distortions such as the tendency to believe San Diego is west of Reno. Are these distortions in an egocentric representation, an allocentric representation, or something else?

Key Terms

allocentric representation

cognitive maps

egocentric representation

epiphenomenon

fusiform face area (FFA)

mental imagery

mental rotation

parahippocampal place area (PPA)

route maps

survey maps

Representation of Knowledge

In Chapter 2 we discussed how information comes in through perception, and in Chapter 4 we discussed how we can mentally manipulate perceptual information. This might naturally lead to the assumption that the knowledge we have about the world consists of just our perceptual experiences, something like a movie recording our life. However, what we encode from our experience proves to be more complex than that.

Recall a wedding you attended a while ago. Presumably, you can remember who married whom, where the wedding was, many of the people who attended, and some of the things that happened. You would probably be hard pressed, however, to say exactly what all the participants wore, the exact words that were spoken, or the way the bride walked down the aisle, although you probably registered many of these details at the time. It is not surprising that our memories lose information over time, but what is interesting is that our loss of information is selective: We tend to forget the less significant and remember the more significant aspects of what happened.

It might seem that it would be ideal if we had the capacity to remember all the details of our experiences. Parker, Cahill, and McGaugh (2006) describe a case of an individual with highly detailed memories.[1] Although she can remember many details from years ago in her life, she had difficulty in school and seems to perform poorly on tasks of abstract reasoning such as processing analogies. A more recent study of 11 such individuals (LePort et al., 2012) finds that although they can remember an enormous amount of detail from their personal lives, they are no better than average on many standard laboratory memory tasks. They probably would not do better than others in remembering the information from a text like this. It seems like their ability to remember insignificant details does not confer any special ability to remember critical information.

---

[1] She has written her own biography, *The Woman Who Can't Forget* (Price, 2008).

In many situations, we need to rise above the details of our experience and get to their true meaning and significance. Understanding how we do this is the focus of this chapter, where we will address the following questions:

- How do we represent the significant aspects of our experience?
- Do we represent knowledge in ways that are not tied to specific perceptual modalities?
- How do we represent categorical knowledge, and how does this affect the way we perceive the world?

Knowledge and Regions of the Brain

Figure 5.1 shows some of the brain regions involved in the representation of knowledge. Some prefrontal regions are associated with extracting meaningful information from verbal and visual material, with the left prefrontal region more involved in processing verbal material and the right prefrontal region more involved in processing visual material (Gabrieli, 2001). There is also strong evidence that categorical (conceptual) information is represented in posterior regions, particularly the temporal cortex (Visser, Jefferies, & Ralph, 2010). In addition, there is fairly consistent evidence for greater activation throughout the left hemisphere when categorical information is presented verbally (e.g., Binder, Desai, Graves, & Conant, 2009).

At points in this chapter, we will review neuroscience data on the localization of semantic information in the brain, but our focus will be on the striking results from behavioral studies that examine what people remember or forget after an event.

> *Prefrontal regions of the brain are associated with meaningful processing of verbal and visual information, and posterior regions, such as the temporal cortex, are associated with representing categorical information.*

Figure 5.1 Cortical Regions Involved in the Processing of Meaning and the Representation of Concepts.

Brain Structures

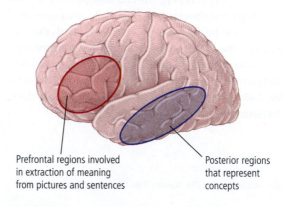

Prefrontal regions involved in extraction of meaning from pictures and sentences

Posterior regions that represent concepts

Memory for Meaningful Interpretations of Events

In this section, we will see that meaningfulness is an important determinant of what people remember, for both verbal and visual information. Then we will discuss some of the implications of that fact when it comes to remembering arbitrary associations (e.g., names and faces) or random groups of items (e.g., shopping lists).

Memory for Verbal Information

A dissertation study by Eric Wanner (1968) illustrates circumstances in which people do and do not remember the exact wording of verbal information. Wanner asked participants to come into the laboratory and listen to tape-recorded instructions. For one group of participants, the warned group, the tape began this way:

> The materials for this test, including the instructions, have been recorded on tape. Listen very carefully to the instructions because you will be tested on your ability to recall particular sentences which occur in the instructions.

The participants in the second group received no such warning and so had no idea that they would be responsible for remembering the instructions verbatim. After this point, the instructions were the same for both groups. At a later point in the instructions, one of four possible critical sentences was presented:

1. When you score your results, do nothing to correct your answers but mark carefully those answers which are wrong.
2. When you score your results, do nothing to correct your answers but carefully mark those answers which are wrong.
3. When you score your results, do nothing to your correct answers but mark carefully those answers which are wrong.
4. When you score your results, do nothing to your correct answers but carefully mark those answers which are wrong.

Note that some sentences differ in style but not in meaning (sentences 1 and 2, and 3 and 4), whereas other sentences differ in meaning but not in style (sentences 1 and 3, and 2 and 4), and that the sentences in each of these four pairs differ only in the ordering of two words. Immediately after one of these sentences was presented, all participants (warned or not) heard the following conclusion to the instructions:

> To begin the test, please turn to page 2 of the answer booklet and judge which of the sentences printed there occurred in the instructions you just heard.

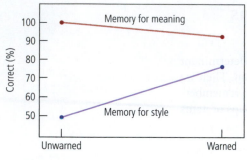

Figure 5.2 Memory for Meaning Versus Style of Verbal Material. The ability of participants to remember a wording difference that affected meaning versus one that affected only style is plotted as a function of whether or not the participants were warned that they would be tested on their ability to remember the exact wording of sentences.

(Data from Wanner, 1968.)

On page 2, they found two sentences: the critical sentence they had just heard and a sentence that differed just in style or just in meaning. For example, if they had heard sentence 1, they might have to choose between sentences 1 and 2 (different in style but not in meaning) or between sentences 1 and 3 (different in meaning but not in style). Thus, by looking at participants' ability to discriminate between different pairs of sentences, Wanner was able to measure their ability to remember the meaning versus the style of the sentence and to determine how this ability was affected by whether or not they were warned.

The relevant data are presented in **Figure 5.2**. The percentage of correct identifications of sentences heard is displayed as a function of whether participants had been warned. The percentages are plotted separately for participants who were asked to discriminate a meaningful difference in wording and for those who were asked to discriminate a stylistic difference. If participants were just guessing, they would have scored 50% correct by chance; thus, we would not expect any values below 50%.

The implications of Wanner's experiment are clear. First, memory is better for the meaning of the sentence in the instructions than for the style of the sentence. The superiority of memory for meaning indicates that people normally extract the meaning from a linguistic message and do not necessarily remember its exact wording. Moreover, memory for meaning was unaffected by whether participants were warned or not. (The slight advantage for unwarned participants does not approach statistical significance.) Thus, participants retained the meaning of a message as a normal part of their comprehension process. They did not have to be cued (warned) to remember the meaning of the sentence.

The second implication of these results is that people are capable of remembering exact wording if that is their goal — the warning did have a significant effect on memory for style. The unwarned participants remembered the style of the sentence in the instructions at about the level of chance, whereas the warned participants remembered it almost 80% of the time. Thus, although we do not normally retain much information about exact wording, we can do so when we are cued to pay attention to such information.

> *After processing a linguistic message, people usually remember just its meaning and not its exact wording.*

Memory for Visual Information

Our memory for what we see seems often much better than our memory for what we hear. Shepard (1967) performed one of the early experiments comparing memory for pictures with memory for verbal material. In the picture-memory task, participants first studied a set of magazine pictures one at a time, then were presented with pairs of pictures consisting of one picture they had studied and one they had not, and then had to indicate which picture had been studied. In the sentence-memory task, participants studied sentences one at a time and were similarly tested on their ability to recognize those sentences. Participants made errors on the verbal task 11.8% of the time but only 1.5% of the time on the visual task. In other words, memory for verbal information was quite good, but memory for visual information was virtually perfect. Many subsequent experiments have demonstrated our high capacity for remembering pictures. For example, Brady, Konkle, Alvarez, and Oliva (2008) had participants first study a set of 2,500 pictures and then identify individual pictures from the set when paired with a similar alternative (**Figure 5.3** shows some of these pairs). Participants were able to achieve almost 87.5% accuracy in making such discriminations.

However, people do not always show such good memory for pictures — it depends on the circumstances. Nickerson and Adams (1979) performed a classic study showing lack of memory for visual detail. They asked 36 American students to indicate which of the pictures in **Figure 5.4** was the actual U.S. penny. Despite having seen this object literally thousands of times, 21 of the participants were not able to identify the actual penny with certainty. What accounts for the difference in results between studies showing good memory for visual detail and a study like this one, showing poor memory for visual detail? It seems that the answer is that the details of the penny are not something people attend to. In experiments showing good visual memory, the participants are told to attend to the details. The role of attention was confirmed in a study by Marmie and Healy (2004) following up on the Nickerson and Adams study. Participants examined a novel coin for a minute and then, a week later, were asked to remember the details. In this study, participants achieved much higher accuracy than in the penny study.

How do people actually deploy their attention when studying a complex visual scene? Typically, people attend to, and remember, what they consider to be the meaningful or important aspects of the scene. This is illustrated in an experiment by Mandler and Johnson (1976) in which participants studied pictures of scenes, like the scene in

Figure 5.3 Memory for Visual Information. Participants in Brady et al. (2008) studied one of the pictures in each of 2,500 pairs like these. The numbers next to the pairs show how many participants were able to remember which picture they had studied (e.g., when the pair of cylinder pictures at top left was presented, 13 of 14 participants were able to remember which one they had studied). *(Brady, T. F., Konkle, T., Alvarez, G. A., & Oliva, A. (2008). Visual long-term memory has a massive storage capacity for object details. Proceedings of the National Academy of Sciences, 105(38), 14325–14329. Figure 1. © 2008 National Academy of Sciences, U.S.A.)*

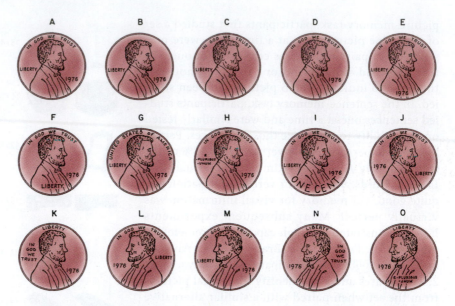

Figure 5.4 Which Is the Real Penny? In an experiment by Nickerson and Adams (1979), participants viewed 15 drawings of pennies like these and had to decide which was the actual U.S. penny. *(Research from Nickerson & Adams, 1979.)*

Figure 5.5a. After studying eight such pictures for 10 s each, participants were presented with a series of pictures consisting of the exact pictures they had studied (target pictures) and distracter pictures, which included token distracters and type distracters for each target. A token distracter differed from its target only in a relatively unimportant visual detail (e.g., Figure 5.5b is a token distracter because the pattern on the teacher's pants is an unimportant detail). In contrast, a type distracter differed from the target in a relatively important visual detail (e.g., Figure 5.5c is a type distracter because the difference between an artwork and the world map in the target is an important detail that indicates the subject being taught). Participants recognized the original pictures 77% percent of the time; they rejected the token distracters only 60% of the time, but rejected the type distracters 94% of the time.

The conclusion in this study is very similar to that in the Wanner (1968) experiment reviewed earlier. Wanner found that participants were much more sensitive to significant (i.e., meaningful) changes in a sentence than to changes in style; Mandler and Johnson (1976) found that participants were more sensitive to significant changes in a picture than to changes in minor details. This is not because people are incapable of remembering such details, but rather because people do not attend to details that do not seem important. Had participants viewing a picture like Figure 5.5a been told that the picture

(a)

(b)   (c)

Figure 5.5 Memory for Significant Versus Insignificant Details in Pictures.
Mandler and Johnson (1976) used pictures like these to demonstrate that people
distinguish between the meaning of a picture and the physical picture itself. (a) A target
picture studied by participants. (b) A token distracter—a picture that differs from the
target in an insignificant detail. (c) A type distracter—a picture that differs from the
target in a significant way. Participants were much less likely to incorrectly identify type
distracters as pictures they had studied than they were to identify token distracters.

illustrated the style of the teacher's clothing, the result would probably have
been quite different.

> *When people see a picture, they attend to and remember best those
> aspects that they consider meaningful.*

Importance of a Meaningful Interpretation to Memory

So far we have considered memory for verbal and pictorial materials that have a
clear interpretation. However, what if the material does not seem to have a meaningful interpretation, such as a hard-to-follow written description? Consider the
following passage that was used in a study by Bransford and Johnson (1972):

> The procedure is actually quite simple. First you arrange items into
> different groups. Of course, one pile may be sufficient depending
> on how much there is to do. If you have to go somewhere else due
> to lack of facilities that is the next step, otherwise you are pretty well

Figure 5.6 Memory for Snowflakes. Four snowflakes like those used by Goldstein and Chance (1970) in their memory experiment. *(Herbert/Getty Images.)*

set. It is important not to overdo things. That is, it is better to do too few things at once than too many. In the short run this may not seem important but complications can easily arise. A mistake can be expensive as well. At first the whole procedure will seem complicated. Soon, however, it will become just another facet of life. It is difficult to foresee any end to the necessity for this task in the immediate future, but then one never can tell. After the procedure is completed one arranges the materials into different groups again. Then they can be put into their appropriate places. Eventually they will be used once more and the whole cycle will then have to be repeated. However, that is part of life. (p. 722)

Figure 5.7 Memory for Abstract Pictures. Two of the pictures that participants had a hard time remembering in an experiment by Oates and Reder (2010). *(Dr. Lynne Reder.)*

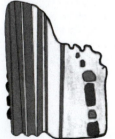

Presumably, you find this description hard to make sense of; one group of participants did, too, and showed poor recall of the passage. However, another group of participants were told before reading this passage that it was about washing clothes. With that one piece of information, which made the passage much more interpretable, they were able to recall twice as much as the uninformed group.

Similar effects are found in memory for pictorial material. One study (Goldstein & Chance, 1970) compared memory for faces versus memory for snowflakes. Individual snowflakes are highly distinct from one another, more so than faces (see **Figure 5.6**). However, participants do not know what sense to make of snowflakes, whereas they often assign interpretations to faces, based on subtle differences. In a test 48 hours after viewing pictures of faces and snowflakes, participants were able to recognize 74% of the faces and only 30% of the snowflakes. In another study, provocatively titled "Sometimes a Picture Is Not Worth a Single Word," Oates and Reder (2010) compared recognition memory for words with recognition memory for abstract pictures like those in **Figure 5.7**. They found that participants' memory for these pictures was quite poor — only half as good as their memory for words.

Bower, Karlin, and Dueck (1975) reported an amusing demonstration of the fact that people's good memory for pictures is tied to their ability

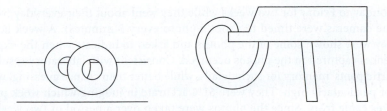

Figure 5.8 Recalling "Droodles." (left) Two donuts rolling down the street together. (right) A piano playing itself.

to make sense of those pictures. **Figure 5.8** shows two drawings like the ones they used, called "droodles." Participants studied the drawings, with or without an explanation of their meaning, and then were given a memory test in which they had to redraw the pictures. Participants who had been given an explanation when studying the pictures showed better recall (70% correctly reconstructed) than those who were not given an explanation (51% correctly reconstructed). Thus, memory for the drawings depended critically on participants' ability to give them a meaningful interpretation.

> *Memory is better for material if we are able to meaningfully interpret that material.*

Memory for the Detail of Everyday Experiences In the laboratory studies we have just reviewed, researchers create controlled experiences for participants and investigate what participants can remember from these experiences. The assumption is that the properties discovered in the laboratory will be the properties that govern our memory for what we experience in everyday life. Recently, the development of wearable cameras has allowed researchers to test that assumption.

In a study using still photos (see **Figure 5.9**), Yim, Garrett, Baker, and Dennis (2018) had participants wear a camera during waking hours from

Figure 5.9 Memory for Real Experience, 1. In an experiment by Yim et al. (2018), participants wore an Android phone (left) set to take a photo every 5 minutes. After two weeks, participants were asked to identify when specific photos (like the one at right) were taken. *(Dr. Hyungwook Yim.)*

Monday to Friday for two weeks while they went about their everyday lives (the cameras were timed to shoot a photo every 5 minutes). A week later they were shown some of the photos and asked to indicate when the experiences captured in the photos occurred. Consistent with laboratory results, participants' memory for such details, while better than chance guessing, was not particularly high. They were 61% accurate in judging which week pictures came from. Since the photos were taken over a period of two weeks, chance guessing would yield 50% accuracy. They were 34% accurate in judging which day of the week (chance 20%) and 22% accurate in judging the hour (chance 8.3%). They were much more accurate at judging the time of events that they considered important, consistent with the idea that the significance of an event is a main determinant of whether the event is represented in detail in memory.

In a rather different study, Misra, Marconi, and Kreiman (2018) had multiple participants walk the same 2.1 mile route in Cambridge, Massachusetts, while wearing a video camera and an eye tracker. The next day, each participant was presented with a series of 1 s video clips, each of which was from the participant's own walk or from another participant's walk (see **Figure 5.10**), and they had to identify the clips that were from their own experience. Participants were only about 60% accurate (chance is 50%). Their accuracy (such as it was) depended on remembering significant things they encountered during their walk, such as someone talking.

In a similar walking experiment, Jeunehomme and D'Argembeau (2018) asked camera-wearing participants to perform a series of tasks that involved walking around the campus of the University of Liege. Right after the walk, they were shown a pair of pictures taken by their camera that spanned a period

Frames from 1 s video clips
during walk by participant 1

Frames from 1 s video clips
during walk by participant 2

Figure 5.10   Memory for Real Experience, 2. Participants in Misra et al. (2018) wore video cameras and eye trackers while walking the same path. They were then shown 1-second video clips and asked to identify the clips that represented their own experience. *(Harvard University.)*

of time and asked what they remembered happening during that period. The number of things that participants remembered per period varied — when they were just walking, they remembered only about two things per minute of the period, but when they were achieving a goal (like posting a letter), they remembered about eight things per minute. Participants also generally thought that the time that passed during the period spanned by the pictures was less than it actually was. The fewer things they could remember from the period, the shorter they thought it was. The authors suggest that we judge how long a period is by jumping from thing to thing that we can remember — the more jumps, the longer the estimated length of time. Overall, our memory for what we experience tends to have large gaps, particularly for unimportant experiences.

> *We remember relatively little detail from our daily life, and what we remember tends to be that which we consider important.*

Implications of Good Memory for Meaning We have seen that people have relatively good memory for meaningful interpretations of information. So when faced with material to remember, it will help if they can give it some meaningful interpretation. Unfortunately, many people are unaware of this fact, and their memory performance suffers as a consequence. I can still remember the traumatic experience I had in my first paired-associates experiment, in a sophomore class in experimental psychology. For reasons I have long since forgotten, we had designed a class experiment that involved learning 16 pairs of meaningless syllables, such as DAX-GIB. Our task was to recall the second half of each pair when prompted with the first half, and I was determined to outperform the other members of my class. My personal theory of memory at that time, which I applied to this task, was that if you try hard and focus intensely, you can remember anything well. For the impending experimental situation, this meant that during the learning period I should say (as loud as was seemly) the paired associates over and over again, as fast as I could. I believed that this method would burn the paired associates into my mind forever. To my chagrin, I wound up with the worst score in the class.

My theory of "loud and fast" was directly opposed to the true means of improving memory. I was trying to memorize a meaningless verbal pair. But the material discussed in this chapter so far suggests that we have the best memory for meaningful information. I should have been trying to convert each pair of syllables into something more meaningful. For instance, DAX is like *dad* and GIB is the first part of *gibberish*. So I might have created an image of my father speaking some gibberish to me. This would have been a simple **mnemonic technique** ("mnemonic" means "memory assisting") and would have worked quite well as a means of associating the two elements.

Implications 5.1

Mnemonic Techniques for Remembering Vocabulary Items

One domain where we have to learn arbitrary associations is foreign language vocabulary. For instance, consider trying to learn that the Italian word *formaggio* (pronounced "for-MAH-jo") means *cheese*. There is a memorization technique, called the *keyword method*, for learning vocabulary items, which some students are taught and others discover on their own. The first step is to think of some word or phrase in one's native language that sounds like the foreign word. For example, we might associate *formaggio* with *for much dough*. The second step is to create a meaningful connection between the sound-alike term and the meaning. For example, we might imagine expensive cheese being sold for much money or *for much dough*. As another example, consider the Italian word *carciofi* (pronounced "car-CHOH-fee"), which means *artichokes*. We might associate *carciofi*

with "car trophy" and then imagine a winning car at an auto show with a trophy shaped like an artichoke. The intermediate sound-alike term (e.g., *for much dough* or *car trophy*) is called the *keyword*, although in both of these examples they are really key phrases. There has been extensive research on this technique (for a review, see Kroll & De Groot,

(Ted Tamburo/Getty Images.)

2005), showing that, as with many things, one needs to take a nuanced approach in evaluating its effectiveness. There is no doubt that it results in more rapid vocabulary learning in many situations, but there are potential costs. One might imagine that having to go through the intermediate keyword slows down the speed of translation when listening to or producing speech, and the keyword method has been shown to result in slower retrieval compared to retrieval of items that are directly associated without an intermediate. Moreover, going through an intermediate has been shown to result in poorer long-term retention. Finally, evidence suggests that although the method may help in passing an immediate vocabulary test in a class and hurt in a delayed test that we have not studied for, its ultimate impact on achieving real language mastery is minimal. (For discussion of the issues involved in foreign language mastery, see Chapter 12.)

(See **Implications 5.1** for a more detailed discussion of this type of mnemonic technique.)

We do not often need to learn pairs of nonsense syllables outside the classroom or the laboratory. In many situations, however, we do have to associate various combinations that do not have much inherent meaning. We have to remember shopping lists, names for faces, telephone numbers, rote facts in a college class, vocabulary items in a foreign language, and so on. In all cases, we can improve memory if we associate the items to be remembered with a meaningful interpretation.

> *It is easier to commit arbitrary associations to memory if they are converted into something more meaningful.*

Propositional Representations

We have shown that in many situations people do not remember exact physical details of what they have seen or heard but rather the meaningful aspects of what they have encountered. In an attempt to become more precise about what is meant by "meaning," cognitive psychologists developed what is called a **propositional representation.** The concept of a **proposition,** borrowed from logic and linguistics, is central to such analyses. A proposition is the smallest unit of knowledge that can stand as a separate assertion — that is, the smallest unit that one can meaningfully judge as true or false. Thus, a propositional representation is a representation of the meaning of something as a set of propositions. Propositional analysis applies most clearly to linguistic information, and I will develop the topic here in terms of such information.

Consider the following sentence:

Lincoln, who was president of the United States during a bitter war, freed the slaves.

The information conveyed in this sentence can be communicated by the following simpler sentences.

A. Lincoln was president of the United States during a war.
B. The war was bitter.
C. Lincoln freed the slaves.

If any of these simple sentences were false, the complex sentence also would be false. These sentences correspond closely to the propositions that underlie the meaning of the complex sentence. Each simple sentence expresses a primitive unit of meaning. Like these simple sentences, each separate element of our propositional representations must correspond to a unit of meaning.

However, the theory of propositional representation does not claim that a person remembers simple sentences like these when encoding the meaning of a complex sentence. Rather, the claim is that the material is encoded in a more abstract way. For instance, the propositional representation proposed by Kintsch (1974) represents the meaning of each sentence as a list containing a **relation** followed by an ordered list of **arguments.** The relations organize the arguments and typically correspond to the verbs (in this case, *free*), adjectives (*bitter*), and other relational terms (*president of*). The arguments refer to particular times, places, people, or things, typically corresponding to the nouns (*Lincoln, United States, war, slaves*). The relations assert connections among the entities these nouns refer to. Kintsch represents each proposition by a list consisting of a relation plus arguments, enclosed in parentheses. As an example, the propositions corresponding to sentences A through C would be represented by the following structures:

A. (president of: Lincoln, United States, war)
B. (bitter: war)
C. (free: Lincoln, slaves)

Note that each relation takes a different number of arguments: *president of* takes three, *free* takes two, and *bitter* takes one. Whether a person heard the original complex sentence or heard

> The slaves were freed by Lincoln, the president of the United States during a bitter war.

the meaning of the message would be represented by propositions A through C.

Bransford and Franks (1971) provided an interesting demonstration of the psychological reality of propositional units. In this experiment, participants studied 12 sentences, including the following:

> The ants ate the sweet jelly, which was on the table.
> The rock rolled down the mountain and crushed the tiny hut.
> The ants in the kitchen ate the jelly.
> The rock rolled down the mountain and crushed the hut beside the woods.
> The ants in the kitchen ate the jelly, which was on the table.
> The tiny hut was beside the woods.
> The jelly was sweet.

The propositional units in each of these sentences come from one of two sets of four propositions.[2] One set can be represented as

1. (eat: ants, jelly, past)
2. (sweet: jelly)
3. (on: jelly, table, past)
4. (in: ants, kitchen, past)

The other set of four propositions can be represented as

1. (roll down: rock, mountain, past)
2. (crush: rock, hut, past)
3. (beside: hut, woods, past)
4. (tiny: hut)

---

[2] In these propositional representations, the term *past* appears as a time argument, filling a role like the role of the argument *war* in the propositional representation of the Lincoln sentence.

Bransford and Franks looked at participants' recognition memory for the following three kinds of sentences:

1. Old: The ants in the kitchen ate the jelly.
2. New: The ants ate the sweet jelly.
3. Noncase: The ants ate the jelly beside the woods.

"Old" sentences were the sentences actually studied. "New" sentences were not studied but consisted of a combination of propositions that occurred in the studied sentences — for example, sentence 2 consists of these propositions from the first list above: (eat: ants, jelly, past) and (sweet: jelly). "Noncase" sentences consisted of words that were studied (ants, ate, jelly, beside, woods), but did not consist entirely of propositions that were studied — for example, one of the propositions composing sentence 3 is (beside: jelly, woods), and this is a new proposition. Bransford and Franks found that participants had almost no ability to discriminate between "old" and "new" sentences and were equally likely to say that they had actually heard either. In contrast, participants were quite confident that they had not heard the "noncase" sentences.

The experiment shows that people remember propositions but are quite insensitive to the actual way propositions are combined into sentences. Indeed, the participants in this experiment were *most* likely to say that they had heard a sentence consisting of all four propositions, such as

The ants in the kitchen ate the sweet jelly, which was on the table.

even though they had not in fact studied this sentence.

> *According to propositional analyses, people remember a complex sentence as a set of abstract meaning units (propositions) that represent the simple assertions in the sentence.*

Amodal Versus Perceptual Symbol Systems

The propositional representations that we have just considered are examples of what Barsalou (1999) called an **amodal symbol system.** By this he meant that the elements within the system are inherently nonperceptual. The original stimulus might be a picture or a sentence, but the representation is abstracted away from the verbal or visual modality. Given this abstraction, one would predict that participants in experiments would be unable to remember the exact words they heard or the exact picture they saw.

As an alternative to such representations, Barsalou proposed the hypothesis that information is represented by what he called the **perceptual symbol system.** This hypothesis claims that information is always represented in terms that are specific to a particular perceptual modality (vision, audition, etc.). The perceptual symbol system hypothesis is an extension of Paivio's (1971, 1986) earlier **dual-code theory,** which claimed that we represent information in combined verbal and visual codes. Paivio suggested that when we hear a sentence, we also develop a visual image of what it describes. If we later remember the visual image and not the sentence, we will remember what the sentence was about, but not its exact words. Analogously, when we see a picture, we might describe to ourselves the significant features of that picture. If we later remember our description and not the picture, we will not remember details we did not think important to describe (such as the clothes the teacher was wearing in Figure 5.5).

According to the dual-code theory, memory for wording versus memory for meaning depends on the relative attention that people give to the verbal versus the visual representation. A number of experiments indicate that when participants pay attention to wording, they show better memory for wording. For instance, Holmes, Waters, and Rajaram (1998), in a replication of the Bransford and Franks (1971) study that we just reviewed, asked participants to count the number of letters in the last word of each sentence that they studied. This increased their attention to the wording of the sentence and resulted in an increased ability to discriminate sentences they had studied from sentences with similar meanings that they had not — although participants still showed considerable confusion among similar-meaning sentences.

But how can an abstract concept (e.g., honesty) be represented in a purely perceptual cognitive system? One can be very creative in combining perceptual representations. Consider a pair of sentences from an old, unpublished study of mine.[3] Participants studied one of the following two sentences:

1. The lieutenant wrote his signature on the check.
2. The lieutenant forged a signature on the check.

Later, we asked participants to recognize which sentence they had studied. They could make such discriminations more successfully than they could distinguish between pairs such as

1. The lieutenant enraged his superior in the barracks.
2. The lieutenant infuriated a superior in the barracks.

In the first pair of sentences, there is a big difference in meaning; in the second pair, little difference. However, the difference in wording between the sentences in the two pairs is equivalent. When I did the study, I thought it showed that people could remember meaning distinctions that did not have perceptual differences, since there is no difference between watching someone sign a check or forge a check. The distinction between signing one's own signature and forging someone else's is not in what the person does but

---

[3] It was not published because at the time (1970s) it was considered too obvious a result given studies like those described earlier in this chapter.

in his or her intentions and the relationship between those intentions and implicit social contracts. Barsalou (personal communication, March 12, 2003) suggested that we represent the distinction between the two sentences by internally reenacting what seems like a plausible history behind each sentence. So even if the actual act of writing and forging might be the same, the history of what a person said, thought, felt, and did in getting to that point would be different. Thus, the perceptual features involved in forging (but not in signing) might include the sensations of tension that one has when one is in a difficult situation.

Barsalou, Simmons, Barbey, and Wilson (2003) cited evidence that when people understand a sentence, they often actually come up with a perceptual representation of that sentence. For instance, in one study by Stanfield and Zwaan (2001), participants read a sentence about a nail being pounded into either the wall or the floor. Then they viewed a picture of a nail oriented either horizontally or vertically and were asked whether the object in the picture was mentioned in the sentence that they just read. If they had read a sentence about a nail being pounded into the wall, they recognized a horizontally oriented nail more quickly. When they had read a sentence about a nail being pounded into the floor, they recognized a vertically oriented nail more quickly. In other words, they responded faster when the orientation implied by the sentence matched the orientation of the picture. Thus, their representation of the sentence seemed to contain this perceptual detail. As further evidence of the perceptual representation of meaning, Barsalou et al. (2003) cited neuroscience studies showing that concepts are represented in brain areas similar to those that process perceptions.

> *An alternative to amodal representations of meaning is the view that meaning is represented as a combination of encodings in different perceptual modalities.*

Embodied Cognition

Barsalou's hypothesis of the perceptual symbol system reflects a growing emphasis in psychology on understanding how the environment and our bodies contribute to shaping our cognition. As Thelen (2000) describes the viewpoint:

> To say that cognition is *embodied* means that it arises from bodily interactions with the world and is continually meshed with them. From this point of view, therefore, cognition depends on the kinds of experiences that come from having a body with particular perceptual and motor capabilities that are inseparably linked and that together form the matrix within which reasoning, memory, emotion, language and all other aspects of mental life are embedded. (p. 5)

The **embodied cognition** perspective emphasizes the contribution of motor action and how it connects us to the environment. For instance, Glenberg (2007) argues that our understanding of language often depends on an inner acting out of what the language describes. He points to an fMRI study by Hauk, Johnsrude, and Pulvermuller (2004), who recorded brain activation while people listened to verbs that involved face, arm, or leg actions (e.g., *lick*, *pick*, or *kick*). The researchers looked for activity along the motor cortex in separate regions associated with the face, arm, and leg. **Figure 5.11** shows that each type of verb produced greater activation in the part of the motor cortex associated with the corresponding action.

A theory of how meaning is represented in the human mind must explain how different perceptual and motor modalities connect with one another. For instance, part of understanding a word such as *kick* is our ability to relate it to a picture of a person kicking a ball, enabling us to describe that picture. As another example, part of our understanding of someone performing an action is our ability to relate it to our own motor system, enabling us to mimic the action. Interestingly, **mirror neurons** have been found in the motor cortex of monkeys; these are active when the monkeys perform an action like ripping a paper or when the monkeys see the experimenter rip a paper or hear the experimenter rip the paper without seeing the action (Rizzolatti & Craighero, 2004). Although one cannot typically do single-cell recordings with humans, brain-imaging studies have found increased activity in the motor region when people observe actions, particularly with the intention to mimic the action (Iacoboni et al., 1999).

In the last decade, serious questions have been raised about the significance of the evidence for embodied cognition (e.g. Goldinger, Papesh, Barnhart, Hansen, & Hout, 2016; Mahon, 2015). Most of the evidence cited in favor of embodied cognition is not evidence against abstract representations of knowledge — the two perspectives are not mutually exclusive. That is, many of the experimental results supporting embodied cognition would be predicted by a theory that assumed there were both abstract and embodied representations.

Figure 5.11 Brain Activation in Different Motor Regions as Participants Listened to Different Types of Verbs. Face, arm, and leg verbs describe actions associated with the face, arm, and leg, such as *lick, pick,* and *kick,* respectively. Activation was greatest in the region of the motor cortex devoted to the body part associated with the verb. Thus, *lick* produced greatest activation in the motor region for the face, *pick* in the region for the arm, and *kick* in the region for the leg. *(Data from Hauk, Johnsrude, & Pulvermuller, 2004.)*

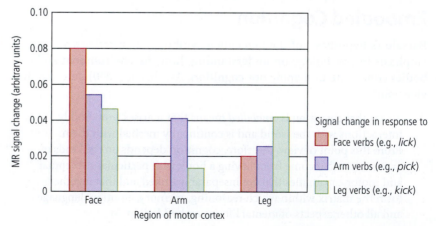

One would expect activation to spread between brain regions generating an abstract representation of a concept like *kicking* and perceptual and motor regions associated with the action of kicking. This spreading of activation would be necessary for someone to recognize an action as an instance of kicking or to perform a kicking action if asked to. What happens to the conceptual representations of individuals who have suffered neural damage to their perceptual or motor systems? In a review of the literature, Binder and Desai (2011) conclude that "conceptual deficits in patients with sensory-motor impairments, when present, tend to be subtle rather than catastrophic." They argue that information is represented in both concrete (perceptual, motor) and abstract (amodal) ways.

Figure 5.12 illustrates two conceptions of how mappings might take place between different representations. One possibility is illustrated in the **multimodal hypothesis,** which holds that we have various representations, each tied to a different perceptual or motor system, and that we have systems for directly converting one representation to another. For instance, the arrow going from the visual to the motor representation would be a system for converting a visual representation into a motor representation. The parallel arrow going from the motor to the visual representation would be a system for converting the representations in the opposite direction. The alternative **amodal hypothesis** is that there is an intermediate abstract "meaning" system, perhaps involving propositional representations like those we described earlier. According to this hypothesis, we have systems for converting any type of perceptual or motor representation into an abstract representation of its meaning (arrows going from the representations to the meaning in Figure 5.12), and we have systems for converting abstract representation into any type of perceptual or motor representation (arrows going from the meaning to the representations).

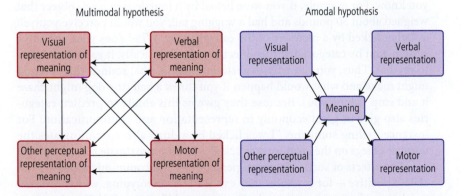

Figure 5.12 Two Hypotheses About How Information Is Related Between Different Perceptual and Motor Modalities. The multimodal hypothesis holds that there is a mechanism for translating in either direction between the meaning represented in one modality and the meaning represented in any other modality. The amodal hypothesis holds that there is a mechanism for translating from the representation in any modality to a central meaning representation and a mechanism for translating from that central meaning representation to a representation in any other modality.

So to convert a visual representation of a picture into a motor representation of an action, one first converts the visual representation into an abstract representation of its meaning and then converts that representation into a motor representation. These two approaches offer alternative explanations for the research we reviewed earlier that indicated people remember the meaning of what they experience, but not the details. The amodal hypothesis holds that this information is retained in a central system for representing meanings. The multimodal hypothesis holds that the information is retained in one or another perceptual or motor modality, either the modality in which the information was first represented or a modality to which the person has converted the information.

> *The multimodal hypothesis proposes that meaning is represented in the perceptual and motor systems that we use to interact with the world; in contrast, the amodal hypothesis proposes that meaning is represented in an abstract system.*

Conceptual Knowledge

When we look at the picture in Figure 5.5a, we do not see it as just a collection of specific objects. Rather, we see it as a picture of a teacher instructing a student on geography. That is, we see the world in terms of categories (i.e., concepts), such as *teacher, student, instruction,* and *geography.* As we saw, people tend to remember categorical information and not specific details. For instance, the participants in the Mandler and Johnson (1976) experiment forgot what the teacher wore but remembered the subject she taught.

You cannot help but experience the world in terms of the categories you know. For example, if you were licked by a four-legged furry object that weighed about 50 pounds and had a wagging tail, you would perceive yourself as being licked by a member of the category *dog.* What does your cognitive system gain by categorizing the object as a dog? Basically, it gains the ability to predict. Thus, you can have expectations about what sounds this creature might make and what would happen if you threw a ball (the dog might chase it and stop licking you). Because they give us this ability to predict, categories also give us great economy in representation and communication. For instance, telling someone, "I was licked by a dog," also communicates the number of legs on the creature that licked you, its approximate size, and so on.

The effects of such categorical perceptions and communications are not always positive — for instance, they can lead to stereotyping, which can lead to false conclusions. In one study, Dunning and Sherman (1997) had participants study sentences such as

Elizabeth was not very surprised upon receiving her math SAT score.

or

Bob was not very surprised upon receiving his math SAT score.

Participants who had heard the first sentence showed a tendency to falsely believe they had heard "Elizabeth was not very surprised upon receiving her low math SAT score," whereas if they had heard the second sentence, they showed a tendency to falsely believe they had heard "Bob was not very surprised upon receiving his high math SAT score." Categorizing Elizabeth as female, the participants brought the stereotype of females as poor at math to their memory of the first sentence. Categorizing Bob as male, they brought the opposite stereotype to their memory of the second sentence. This was even true among participants (both male and female) who were rated as not being sexist in their attitudes. They could not help but be influenced by their implicit stereotypes.

Research on categorization has focused both on how we form these categories in the first place and on how we use them to interpret experiences. It has also been concerned with notations for representing conceptual knowledge. In this section, we will consider a number of proposed notations, starting with two early theories, one based on semantic networks and the other based on schemas. Then we will discuss abstraction theories and exemplar theories, designed to overcome inadequacies in the early theories. We will end with a consideration of natural categories and how they are represented in the brain.

The categorical organization of our knowledge strongly influences the way we encode and remember our experiences.

Semantic Networks

Quillian (1966) proposed that people store information about various categories—such as canaries, robins, fish, and so on—in **semantic networks** structured like the network shown in **Figure 5.13**. In this illustration, we

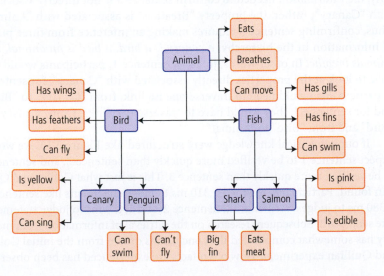

Figure 5.13 A Semantic Network. Quillian (1966) proposed that people store information about categories in a hierarchical network structure that represents both categorical facts, such as that a canary is a bird and a bird is an animal, and the properties associated with each category. Properties associated with higher-level categories are also associated with lower-level categories, by inference—for example, the information that fish have gills and that sharks are fish allows the inference that sharks have gills. *(Research from Collins & Quillian, 1969.)*

represent a hierarchy of categorical facts, such as that a canary is a bird and a bird is an animal, by linking the nodes for two categories (blue boxes) with an **isa link** (blue arrow). Properties (orange boxes) are linked to the highest-level category that they are true of. Properties that are true of higher-level categories are also true of lower-level categories. Thus, one can infer from this representation that canaries can breathe because animals breathe. A diagram like Figure 5.13 can also represent information about exceptions — for instance, birds generally can fly, but penguins have the property "Can't fly."

Collins and Quillian (1969) did an experiment to test the psychological reality of such networks by having participants respond to assertions about concepts, such as

1. Canaries can sing.
2. Canaries have feathers.
3. Canaries breathe.

Participants were shown true assertions like these along with false assertions such as "apples have feathers," and they had to indicate which were true and which were false. The false assertions were included mainly to keep participants "honest"; Collins and Quillian were really interested in how quickly participants could indicate the truth of assertions like sentences 1 through 3, above.

Consider how participants would answer such questions if their knowledge of a category such as "Canary" were represented in a network like Figure 5.13. The information needed to confirm sentence 1 is directly associated with "Canary." The information for sentence 2, however, is not directly associated with "Canary"; instead, the property "Has feathers" is associated with "Bird." Thus, confirming sentence 2 requires making an inference from two pieces of information in the hierarchy: *a canary is a bird* and *birds have feathers*. Similarly, the information needed to confirm sentence 3 is not directly associated with "Canary"; rather, the property "Breathes" is associated with "Animal." Thus, confirming sentence 3 requires making an inference from three pieces of information in the hierarchy: *a canary is a bird, a bird is an animal*, and *animals breathe*. In other words, to verify sentence 1, participants would just have to look at the properties directly associated with "Canary"; for sentence 2, participants would need to traverse one isa link, from "Canary" to "Bird"; and for sentence 3, they would have to traverse two links, from "Canary" to "Bird" and from "Bird" to "Animal."

If our categorical knowledge were structured like Figure 5.13, we would expect sentence 1 to be verified more quickly than sentence 2, and sentence 2 to be verified more quickly than sentence 3. This is just what Collins and Quillian found. Participants required 1,310 ms to judge statements like sentence 1; 1,380 ms to judge statements like sentence 2; and 1,470 ms to judge statements like sentence 3. Subsequent research on the retrieval of information from memory has somewhat complicated the conclusions drawn from the initial Collins and Quillian experiment. How often facts are experienced has been observed to have strong effects on retrieval time (e.g., Conrad, 1972). Some facts that are experienced quite often, such as *apples are eaten,* are verified as fast as or faster than facts such as *apples have dark seeds,* even though the property "Is eaten" is associated with a higher-level category such as "Food," whereas the property "Has dark seeds" is associated more directly with the category "Apple." It seems that if a fact about a concept is encountered frequently, it will be associated with that concept, even if it could also be inferred from a more general concept. The following statements about the organization of facts in semantic memory and their retrieval times seem to be valid conclusions from the research:

1. If a fact about a concept is encountered frequently, it will be associated with that concept even if it could be inferred from a higher-order concept.
2. The more frequently a fact about a concept is encountered, the more strongly that fact will be associated with the concept. The more strongly facts are associated with concepts, the more rapidly they are verified.
3. Inferring facts that are not directly associated with a concept takes a relatively long time.

> *When a property is not associated directly with a concept, people can retrieve it from a higher-order concept.*

Schemas

Consider the many things we know about houses, such as

- Houses are a type of building.
- Houses have rooms.
- Houses can be built of wood, brick, or stone.
- Houses serve as human dwellings.
- Houses tend to have rectilinear and triangular shapes.
- Houses are usually larger than 100 square feet and smaller than 10,000 square feet.

The importance of a category is that it is associated with predictable information about specific instances of that category. So when someone mentions a house, for example, we have a rough idea of the size of the object being referred to.

Semantic networks, which just associate properties with concepts, cannot represent our general knowledge about properties — for instance, our knowledge about the typical size or shape of a house. Early in the history of cognitive science, researchers (e.g., Rumelhart & Ortony, 1976) proposed a way of representing both categorical knowledge and knowledge about properties, thus a way that seemed more useful than the semantic network representation. **Schemas** represent categorical knowledge according to a **slot** structure, in which slots are attributes that members of a category possess, and each slot is filled with one or more values, or specific instances, of that attribute. So we have the following partial schema representation of a house:

House
- *Isa:* building
- *Parts:* rooms
- *Materials:* wood, brick, stone
- *Function:* human dwelling
- *Shape:* rectilinear, triangular
- *Size:* 100–10,000 square feet

In this representation, the slots labeled *Parts, Materials, Function, Shape,* and *Size* are the attributes, and the terms *rooms, wood, brick, stone, human dwelling, rectilinear, triangular,* and *100–10,000 square feet* are the values. Each pair of a slot and a value specifies a typical feature. Values like these are called **default values** because they are the typical features of the attributes but do not exclude other possibilities. For instance, the fact that houses are usually built of materials such as wood, brick, and stone does not mean that something built of cardboard or plastic could not be a house. Similarly, the fact that our schema for "Bird" specifies that birds can fly does not prevent us from categorizing penguins as birds. We simply overwrite this default value in our schema for a penguin.

A special slot in each schema is its *isa slot,* which points to the superset. Basically, a concept inherits the features of its superset in the isa slot (unless contradicted, as in the case of penguins, birds, and the feature of being able to fly). Thus, with the schema for "Building," the superset of "House," we would store such features as that it has a roof and walls and that it is found on the ground. This information is not represented in the schema for "House" because it can be inferred from "Building." Both in schema representations and in semantic network representations like Figure 5.13, isa links create a structure called a *generalization hierarchy* (i.e., the features of higher-level categories, or supersets, generalize down to the lower-level categories in the hierarchy).

Schemas have another type of structure, called a *part hierarchy*: The values paired with the *Parts* attribute have their own schema representations. Thus, the parts of houses, such as walls and rooms, would have schemas representing information about their own parts (e.g., walls have windows, and rooms have ceilings). Thus, the part hierarchy would enable us to infer that houses have windows and ceilings.

Schemas are abstractions that can be used to make inferences about instances of the concepts they represent. If we know something is a house, we can use the default values in the schema to infer that it is probably made of wood, brick, or stone and that it probably has walls, windows, and ceilings. And as we have seen above, the inferential processes for schemas must also be able to deal with exceptions: We can understand that a building without windows may still be a house. Finally, it is necessary to understand the constraints between the slots of a schema. If we hear of a house that is underground, for example, we can infer that it does not have windows.

> Schemas represent concepts in terms of supersets, parts, and other slot–value pairs.

Psychological Reality of Schemas Brewer and Treyens (1981) provided an interesting demonstration of how inferences from schemas can influence memory. Thirty participants were brought individually to the room shown in **Figure 5.14**. Each was told that this was the experimenter's office and was asked to wait there while the experimenter went to the laboratory to see whether the previous participant had finished. After 35 s, the experimenter returned and took the waiting participant to a nearby seminar room. Here, the participant was instructed:

> We would like you to draw everything you can remember about the room on the provided floor plan. . . . Represent each object in the location you remember it, and try to draw each object's size to scale. Label each object which you draw with its name. (p. 215)

What would you be able to recall?

Figure 5.14 The "Office Room" Used in Brewer and Treyens (1981) to Demonstrate the Effects of Schemas on Memory. As predicted, participants' recall of the contents of the room was strongly influenced by inferences from their schema of what an office contains. *(William F. Brewer.)*

Brewer and Treyens predicted that their participants' recall would be strongly influenced by their schema of what an office contains. Participants would recall very well items that are default values of that schema, they would recall much less well items that are not default values of the schema, and they would falsely recall items that are default values of the schema but were not in this office. Brewer and Treyens found just this pattern of results. For instance, 29 of the 30 participants recalled that the office had a chair, a desk, and walls. Only 8 participants, however, recalled that it had a bulletin board or a skull. On the other hand, 9 participants recalled that it had books, which it did not. Thus, we see that a person's memory for the properties of a location is strongly influenced by that person's default assumptions about what is typically found in the location. A schema is a way of encoding those default assumptions.

> *People will infer that an object has the default values for its category, unless they explicitly notice otherwise.*

Degree of Category Membership One of the important features of schemas is that they allow variation in the objects associated with a schema. There are constraints on what typically occupies the various slots of a schema, but few absolute prohibitions. Thus, if schemas encode our knowledge about various object categories, we ought to see a shading from less typical to more typical members of the category as the features of the members better satisfy the default values and the schema constraints. There is now considerable evidence that natural categories such as *birds* have the kind of structure that would be expected of a schema.

Rosch did early research documenting such variations in category membership. In one experiment (Rosch, 1973), she instructed participants to rate the typicality of various members of a category on a 1 to 7 scale, where 1 meant very typical and 7 meant very atypical. Participants consistently rated some members as more typical than others. In the bird category, *robin* got an average rating of 1.1, and *chicken* a rating of 3.8. In reference to sports, *football* was thought to be very typical (1.2), whereas *weight lifting* was not (4.7). *Murder* was rated a very typical crime (1.0), whereas *vagrancy* was not (5.3). *Carrot* was a very typical vegetable (1.1); *parsley* was not (3.8).

Rosch (1975) also asked participants to identify the category of pictured objects. People are faster to judge a picture as an instance of a category when it presents a typical member of the category. For instance, apples are seen as fruits more rapidly than are watermelons, and robins are seen as birds more rapidly than are chickens. Thus, typical members of a category appear to have an advantage in perceptual recognition as well.

Rosch (1977) demonstrated another way in which some members of a category are more typical. She had participants compose sentences for category names. For *bird,* participants generated sentences such as

I heard a bird twittering outside my window.
Three birds sat on the branch of a tree.
A bird flew down and began eating.

Rosch replaced the category name "bird" in these sentences with a typical member (robin), a less typical member (eagle), or a peripheral member (chicken) and asked participants to rate the sensibleness of the resulting sentences. Sentences involving typical members got high ratings, sentences with less typical members got lower ratings, and sentences with peripheral members got the lowest ratings. This result indicates that when participants wrote the sentences, they were thinking of typical members of the category.

Failing to have a default or typical value does not disqualify an object from being a member of a category, but people's judgments about nontypical objects tend to vary a great deal. McCloskey and Glucksberg (1978) looked at people's judgments about what were or were not members of various categories. They found that although participants did agree on some items, they disagreed on many. For instance, whereas all 30 participants agreed that *cancer* was a disease and *happiness* was not, 16 thought *stroke* was a disease and 14 did not. Again, all 30 participants agreed that *apple* was a fruit and *chicken* was not, but 16 thought *pumpkin* was a fruit and 14 disagreed. Once again, all participants agreed that a *fly* was an insect and a *dog* was not, but 13 participants thought a *leech* was and 17 disagreed. Thus, it appears that people do not always agree on what is a member of a category. McCloskey and Glucksberg tested the same participants a month later and found that many had changed their minds about the disputed items. For instance, 11 out of 30 reversed themselves on *stroke*, 8 reversed themselves on *pumpkin*, and 3 reversed themselves on *leech*. Thus, disagreement about category boundaries does not occur just *among* participants — people are very uncertain *within* themselves exactly where the boundaries of a category should be drawn.

Figure 5.15 shows a set of materials used by Labov (1973) in studying which items participants would call *cups* and which they would call *bowls*. How would you classify each item? The interesting point is that these concepts do not appear to have clear-cut boundaries. In one experiment, Labov used items 1 through 4 shown in Figure 5.15 plus a fifth item that continued the ever-increasing ratio of width to depth. For item 1, that ratio is 1, whereas for item 4 it is 1.9, and for the fifth item, 2.5. **Figure 5.16** shows the percentage of participants who called each of the five objects a cup and the percentage who called each a bowl, under two different conditions. In one condition (neutral context, indicated by solid lines), participants were simply presented with pictures of the objects. As can be seen, the percentage of *cup* responses gradually decreased with increasing width, but there is no clear-cut point where participants stopped using *cup*. At the extreme 2.5 width ratio, about 25% percent of the participants still gave the *cup* response, whereas another 25% gave *bowl*. (The remaining 50% gave other responses.) In the other condition (food context, indicated by dashed lines), participants were asked to imagine the object filled with mashed potatoes

Figure 5.15 Illustrations Used in Labov's (1973) Experiment on the Boundaries of the Cup Category. Participants were asked to categorize each object as a cup or a bowl. *(Figure: Numbered cups/glasses © 1973 by Georgetown University Press. Labov, W. (1973). The boundaries of words and their meanings. In C.-J. N. Bailey & R.W. Shuy (Eds.), New ways of analyzing variations in English (p. 354). Washington, DC: Georgetown University Press. Reprinted with permission. www.press.georgetown.edu.)*

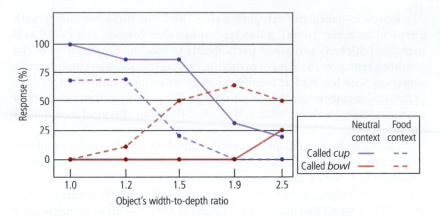

Figure 5.16 Results from Labov's (1973) Experiment on the Boundaries of the Cup Category. The percentage of participants who used the term *cup* versus the term *bowl* to describe the objects shown as items 1–4 in Figure 5.15 (plus a fifth, even wider, object) is plotted as a function of the objects' width-to-depth ratio. In the neutral-context condition, participants just saw the illustrations in Figure 5.15; in the food-context condition, participants were told to imagine the objects as filled with mashed potatoes and placed on a table. *(Data from Labov, 1973.)*

and placed on a table. In this context, fewer *cup* responses and more *bowl* responses were given (especially for item 3, the midpoint of the sequence, with a 1.5 width-to-depth ratio), but the data show the same gradual shift from *cup* to *bowl*. Thus, it appears that people's classification behavior varies continuously not only with the properties of an object but also with the context in which the object is imagined or presented. These influences of perceptual features and context on categorization judgments are very much like the similar influences of these features on perceptual pattern recognition (see Chapter 2).

> *Different objects are judged to be members of a category to different degrees, with the more typical members of a category having an advantage in processing.*

Event Concepts Just as objects have a conceptual structure that can be expressed in terms of category membership, so also do various kinds of events, such as going to a movie or going to a restaurant. Schemas have been proposed as ways of representing such categories, allowing us to encode our knowledge about events according to their typical parts. For instance, going to a movie typically involves going to the theater, buying a ticket, buying refreshments, seeing the movie, and leaving the theater. Schank and Abelson (1977) proposed versions of event schemas that they called **scripts,** based on their observation that many events typically involve certain specific sequences of

TABLE 5.1 The Script for Going to a Restaurant	
Scene I: Entering	**Scene 3: Eating**
Customer enters restaurant	Cook gives food to waitress
Customer looks for table	Waitress brings food to customer
Customer decides where to sit	Customer eats food
Customer goes to table	
Customer sits down	**Scene 4: Exiting**
	Waitress writes bill
Scene 2: Ordering	Waitress goes over to customer
Customer picks up menu	Waitress gives bill to customer
Customer looks at menu	Customer gives tip to waitress
Customer decides on food	Customer goes to cashier
Customer signals waitress	Customer gives money to cashier
Waitress comes to table	Customer leaves restaurant
Customer orders food	
Waitress goes to cook	
Waitress gives food order to cook	
Cook prepares food	
(Information from Schank & Abelson, 1977.)	

actions. **Table 5.1**, for example, represents the components of a script for dining at a restaurant like a diner, based on Schank and Abelson's hunch as to what the most typical aspects of such an occasion might be.

Bower, Black, and Turner (1979) reported a series of experiments in which the psychological reality of the script notion was tested. They asked participants to name what they considered the 20 most important actions typically involved in an event, such as going to a restaurant. With 32 participants, they failed to get complete agreement on what these actions were. No particular action was listed as part of the event by all participants, although considerable consensus was reported. **Table 5.2** lists the actions named. The items in green type were given by at least 25% of the participants; the items in blue type were given by at least 48%; and the items in red type were given by at least 73%. Using 73% as a criterion, we find that the stereotypical sequence was *sit down, look at menu, order meal, eat food, pay bill,* and *leave.*

Bower et al. (1979) went on to show that such event scripts have a number of effects on memory for stories. They had participants study stories that included some but not all of the typical events from a script. Participants were then asked to recall the stories (in one experiment) or to recognize whether various statements came from the story (in another experiment). When recalling these stories, participants tended to report statements that were parts of the script but that had not been presented as parts of the stories. Similarly, in the recognition test, participants thought they had studied script items that had not actually been in the stories. However, participants showed a greater

TABLE 5.2 Agreement About the Actions Typically Involved in Going to a Restaurant	
Open door	Eat salad or soup
Enter	Meal arrives
Give reservation name	**Eat food**
Wait to be seated	Finish meal
Go to table	Order dessert
Sit down	Eat dessert
Order drinks	Ask for bill
Put napkin on lap	Bill arrives
Look at menu	**Pay bill**
Discuss menu	Leave tip
Order meal	Get coats
Talk	**Leave**
Drink water	

Color code:
Items listed by at least 73% of the participants.
Items listed by at least 48% of the participants.
Items listed by at least 25% of the participants.

(Data from Bower, Black, & Turner, 1979.)

tendency to recall actual items from the stories or to recognize actual items than to misrecognize foils that were not in the stories, despite the distortion in the direction of the general schema.

In another experiment, these same investigators read to participants stories composed of 12 stereotypical actions in an event; 8 of the actions occurred in their standard temporal position, but 4 were rearranged — for example, in the restaurant story, the bill might be paid at the beginning and the menu read at the end. In recalling these stories, participants showed a strong tendency to put the actions back into their normal order. In fact, about half of the statements were put back. This experiment serves as another demonstration of the powerful effect of general schemas on memory for stories.

These experiments indicate that new events are encoded with respect to general schemas and that subsequent recall is influenced by the schemas. One might be tempted to say that participants were misrecalling the stories, but it is not clear that *misrecalling* is the right characterization. Normally, if a certain standard event, such as paying a check at a restaurant, is omitted in a story, we are supposed to assume it occurred. Similarly, if the storyteller says the check was paid before the meal was ordered, we have some reason to doubt the storyteller. Event schemas, or scripts, exist because they encode the predominant sequence of actions making up a particular kind of event. Thus, they can serve as a valuable basis for filling in missing information and for correcting errors in information.

Scripts are event schemas that people use to reason about stereotypical events.

Prototype Theories Versus Exemplar Theories

We have described semantic networks and schemas as two ways of representing conceptual knowledge. Although each has merits, the field of cognitive psychology has concluded that both fail to fully capture conceptual structure. We have already noted that semantic networks do not capture the graded character of categorical knowledge such that different objects or events are seen as better or worse members of a category. Schemas can do this, but it has never been clear in detail how to relate them to our actual mental processing. Much ongoing research in cognitive psychology is aimed at discriminating between two different proposals about the general ways in which we capture conceptual knowledge: prototype theories and exemplar theories.

Prototype theories hold that we store a single prototype of what a member of a category is like and classify specific objects or events in terms of their similarity to that prototype (e.g., Reed, 1972). These prototypes are averages of individual members of the category. Some prototype models further assume that the prototype includes information about the allowable variation of instances from the prototype (e.g., Anderson, 1991; Hayes-Roth & Hayes-Roth, 1977).

Exemplar theories, such as those of Medin and Schaffer (1978) and Nosofsky (1986), could not be more different. These models assume that we store no central concept like a prototype but only specific instances, so when it comes time to judge, for example, how typical a specific bird is in the general category of birds, we compare the specific bird to other specific birds in our experience and make some sort of judgment of difference from the average.

Given that prototype and exemplar theories differ so greatly in what they propose the mind does, it is surprising that they generate such similar predictions over a wide range of experiments. For instance, both types predict better processing of the most typical members of a category. Prototype theories predict this because typical instances are more similar to the abstract representation of the concept. Exemplar theories predict this because typical instances will be more similar, on average, to other instances of a category.

There are subtle differences between the predictions of the two types of theories, however. Exemplar theories predict that specific instances in our experience should have effects that would not be predicted by a prototype theory. Thus, although we may think that dogs in general bark, we may have experienced a peculiar-looking dog that did not, and we would then tend to expect that another similar-looking dog would also not bark. Such effects of specific instances have been found in some experiments (e.g., Medin & Schaffer, 1978; Nosofsky, 1991), but, in contrast, other research has shown that people infer tendencies that are not in the specific instances (Elio & Anderson, 1981). For example, if we have encountered many dogs that chase balls and many dogs that bark at the postman, we might consider a dog that both chases balls and barks at the postman to be prototypical. However, we may never have observed any specific dog that both chases balls and barks at the postman.

While much of the early research aimed at trying to determine if categories are represented by exemplars or prototypes, it may be more reasonable to assume that both sorts of representations are available to us.

Smith (2014) argues that some categories might be better represented by exemplars and others by prototypes. It is also becoming clear that there are other aspects to our understanding of concepts, as we will discuss in the next section.

> *Categories can be represented either by abstracting their central tendencies or by storing many specific instances.*

Rule-Based and Theory-Based Structures of Categories

People often have explicit rules for what is a category member, as opposed to using prototype or exemplar theories to make such judgments. For instance, our rule for deciding whether a number is a prime number is to determine whether the number can be divided evenly by 1 and itself only (any such number is prime). It appears that different brain regions are engaged when judging instances of concepts that are represented by rules rather than by similarity to other instances (exemplars). Patalano, Smith, Jonides, and Koeppe (2001) had participants learn to classify a set of 10 animals like those shown in **Figure 5.17** by indicating whether each animal was from Saturn or Venus. Participants in one group were encouraged to use the following rule: "An animal lives on VENUS if it has at least 3 out of the following 5 features: hoofed feet, curly tail, long legs, red, and antenna ears. Otherwise, it lives on SATURN." Participants in a second group were encouraged simply to memorize the category of each of the 10 animals. Patalano et al. found very different patterns of brain activation as participants classified the stimuli. Regions in the prefrontal cortex tended to be activated in the participants who used the rule, whereas regions in the occipital visual areas and the cerebellum were activated in the participants who memorized instances (exemplars). Smith and Grossman (2008) review

Figure 5.17 Artificial Animals Like Those Used in the PET Studies of Patalano et al. (2001). Participants had to classify each animal as living on Venus or Saturn, either by memorizing where each animal lives or by applying a rule ("An animal lives on VENUS if it has at least 3 out of the following 5 features: hoofed feet, curly tail, long legs, red, and antenna ears. Otherwise, it lives on SATURN"; by this rule, only the animal on the far right lives on Saturn).

evidence that using exemplars also activates brain regions supporting memory, such as the hippocampus (see Figure 1.7).

Our understanding of a category can depend on our more general knowledge about the nature of the world, which may indicate that certain features are critical to being a member of the category and other features are not. For instance, when black swans were first observed by Europeans in Australia they were still recognized as swans even though Europeans had believed that all swans were white. This indicates that the feature "white" was not an essential part of their concept "Swan." Researchers have studied the development of such theory-based understanding. Keil (1992) told children a story about an animal that looked like a raccoon but actually had the organs of a skunk and had skunk parents and children. With increasing age they come more and more to believe that this animal is really a skunk. Other researchers have shown that encouraging participants to explain category structure changes what they learn about the category. For instance, Williams and Lombrozo (2013) had subjects learn to classify two types of robots into indoor and outdoor robots. The features they chose for categorization depended on whether they were encouraged to explain why these robots were outdoor or indoor robots. Those encouraged to explain tended to focus on relevant features such as the nature of the robot feet.

People have theories about the features that are critical to the different categories of living things and different categories of artifacts. Much of the research documenting these theories has been done with primary-school children who are still learning the categories. For instance, if primary-school children are told that a human has a spleen, they will conclude that dogs have a spleen too (Carey, 1985). Similarly, if they are told that a red apple has pectin inside, they will assume that green apples also have pectin (Gelman, 1988). Apparently, children assume that if something is an inherent part of a member of a biological category, it is an inherent part of all members of the category. In contrast, if children are told that a particular artifact has a feature (e.g., that a cup is made of ceramic), they do not conclude that all such artifacts have that feature (i.e., they do not conclude that all cups are made of ceramic). The pattern is just the opposite with respect to actions. For instance, if told that a cup is used for "imbibing" (a term they do not know), they conclude that all cups are used for imbibing. In contrast, if told that they can "repast" with a particular red apple, they do not necessarily conclude that they can repast with a green apple. Thus, artifacts seem distinguished by the fact that there are actions considered appropriate to a whole category of artifacts. In summary, children come to believe that all things in a biological category have the same parts (like pectin in apples) and that all things in an artifact category have the same function (like imbibing for cups).

> *Categories can be organized by rules, and these rules can be influenced by our general knowledge about the world and by our theories about living things versus artifacts.*

Natural Categories and Their Brain Representations

Cognitive neuroscience data suggest that biological and artifact categories are represented differently in the brain. Much of this evidence comes from patients with semantic dementia, who suffer deficits in their categorical knowledge because of brain damage. Patients with damage to different regions show different deficits. Patients who have damage to the temporal lobes show deficits in their knowledge about biological categories such as animals, fruits, and vegetables (Saffran & Schwartz, 1994; Warrington & Shallice, 1984). These patients are unable to recognize such objects as ducks, and one patient who was asked what a duck is was only able to say "an animal." However, knowledge about artifacts such as tools and furniture is relatively unaffected in these patients. In contrast, patients with frontoparietal lesions show deficits in their knowledge about artifact categories but are unaffected in their knowledge of biological categories. **Table 5.3** compares descriptions of biological categories and artifact categories by two patients with temporal lobe damage. (These types of patients are more common than patients with frontoparietal damage resulting in deficits in their knowledge of artifacts.)

It has been suggested (e.g., Farah & McClelland, 1991; Warrington & Shallice, 1984) that these deficits occur because biological categories are more associated with perceptual features such as shape, whereas artifact categories are more associated with the actions that we perform with them. Farah and McClelland developed a computer model of these deficits in which the model first learns associations among words, pictures, visual semantic features, and functional semantic features. Then, by selectively

TABLE 5.3	Definitions Given by Two Patients with Impaired Knowledge of Living Things	
Patient	**Definitions of Living Things**	**Definitions of Artifacts**
1	*Parrot:* Don't know *Daffodil:* Plant *Snail:* An insect animal *Eel:* Not well *Ostrich:* Unusual	*Tent:* Temporary outhouse, living home *Briefcase:* Small case used by students to carry papers *Compass:* Tool for telling direction you are going *Torch:* Handheld light *Dustbin:* Bin for putting rubbish in
2	*Duck:* An animal *Wasp:* Bird that flies *Crocus:* Rubbish material *Holly:* What you drink *Spider:* A person looking for things, he was a spider for his nation or country	*Wheelbarrow:* Object used by people to take material about *Towel:* Material used to dry people *Pram:* Used to carry people, with wheels and a thing to sit on *Submarine:* Ship that goes underneath the sea

(Data from Farah & McClelland, 1991.)

damaging the visual features in their computer model, the researchers were able to produce a deficit in knowledge of living things; and by selectively damaging the functional features, they were able to produce a deficit in knowledge of artifacts. This suggests that loss of categorical information in human patients is related to loss of the feature information that defines the categories.

Brain-imaging data also seem consistent with this conclusion (see Martin, 2001, for a review). In particular, it has been shown that when people process pictures of artifacts or words denoting artifacts, activation tends to occur in the same regions of the brain shown to produce category-specific deficits when damaged. Processing of both animals and tools activates regions of the temporal cortex, but the tool regions tend to be located above (superior to) the animal regions. There is also activation of occipital regions (visual cortex) when processing animals. In general, the evidence seems to point to a greater visual involvement in the representation of animals and a greater motor involvement in the representation of artifacts. However, there is some debate in the literature over whether the real distinction in mental processing is between natural categories and artifacts or between visual-based and motor-based categories (Caramazza, 2000).

While research studying semantic dementia has focused on specific brain regions, there is evidence that knowledge of these categories is distributed throughout the brain. Huth, de Heer, Griffiths, Theunissen, and Gallant (2016) had participants listen to two hours of stories from the Moth Radio Hour and examined their brain activity in response to different words (for a video illustrating their results visit https://www.youtube.com/watch?v=k61nJkx5aDQ&feature=youtu.be). They found that many areas of the brain responded to individual words, but they also found that different regions of the brain responded most to different semantic categories of words, and they identified 12 categories: **Figure 5.18** shows a color-coded representation of the brain indicating which regions seemed to be most responsive to which categories. The authors note that the 12 categories showed a strong tendency to organize along two dimensions according to whether the word belonged to the domain of humans and social interaction or to the domain of perceptual and quantitative information. Using these activity patterns, Huth et al. were able to predict with some accuracy what word the participant was hearing at any point in time.

Figure 5.18 shows a remarkable patterning of activity over the whole brain, but a word of caution is important in interpreting these results. The fact that a particular region of the brain shows greater activation in response to a certain category of words does not necessarily mean that the region is critical in processing the meaning of words in that category. As we noted above, semantic dementia is only associated with damage to certain areas

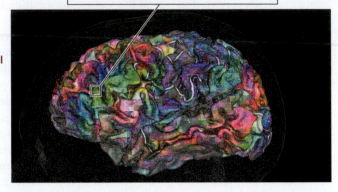

"Visual" words that produced greatest activity in one voxel in frontal region

beads brown cloth coat colored fur leather lighter metallic plastic powder purple skin sleeve thick thicker thin thinner wool

Semantic Categories

abstract	professional
communal	social
emotional	tactile
locational	temporal
mental	violent
numeric	visual

Figure 5.18 Brain Activation in Response to Semantic Categories. Huth et al. (2016) found that different regions of the brain respond most strongly to different semantic categories of words. *(left)* The 12 semantic categories identified in the experiment, which fell into two dimensions: human/social and perceptual/quantitative. *(right)* Warm colors (red/orange end of the spectrum) indicate greater activation in response to words along the human/social dimension; cool colors (blue/green end of the spectrum) indicate greater activation in response to words along the perceptual/quantitative dimension. A voxel (a 2.4 mm long, 2.4 mm wide, and 4.1 mm high region) in the frontal lobe was most strongly activated by words in the *visual* category. *(Dr. Alexander Huth.)*

of the brain, predominantly with temporal lobe damage. So, for instance, a person with damage, say, in the region of the frontal lobe where the voxel highlighted in Figure 5.18 is located, would not be predicted to have a deficit in processing the meaning of a biological word such as "skin."

> *Different categories produce distinct patterns of activity across the brain. Damage to specific regions, particularly the temporal lobe, will result in loss of information about the categories.*

Conclusions

Estimates of the storage capacity (e.g., Moll & Miikkulainen, 1997; Treves & Rolls, 1994) of the brain differ substantially, but they are all many orders of magnitude less than what would be required to store a faithful video recording of our whole life. This chapter has reviewed studies of what we retain and what we forget — for instance, for Figure 5.5, what subject was being taught, but not what the teacher was wearing; or for Figure 5.14, that the room was an office, but not what was in the office. The chapter also reviewed three perspectives on the basis for this selective memory.

1. The multimodal hypothesis (Figure 5.12 left), which proposes that we select important aspects of our experience to remember and often convert meanings from one modality to another. For instance, we may describe a room (visual) as an "office" (verbal).

2. The amodal hypothesis (Figure 5.12 right), which proposes that we convert our experience into some abstract representation that just encodes what is important. For instance, the chapter discussed how propositions captured the connections among the concepts in our understanding of a sentence.

3. Theories proposing that we remember our experiences in terms of the categories that they seem to exemplify. We discussed a varied set of such category representations: semantic networks, schemas, scripts, exemplar, prototype, and rule based.

These hypotheses are not mutually exclusive, and cognitive scientists are actively engaged in trying to understand when a particular kind of knowledge representation is used to encode experience.

Questions for Thought

1. Jill Price, the person with superior autobiographical memory described at the beginning of the chapter, can remember what happened on almost any day of her life (see her interview with Diane Sawyer: https://www.youtube.com/watch?v=aAbQvmf0YOQ). For instance, if you ask her, she can tell you the date of the last show of any former TV series she watched. In contrast, she reported great difficulty in remembering the dates of events discussed in her history class. Why do you think this is?

2. Take some sentences at random from this book and try to develop propositional representations for them.

3. Consider the debate between amodal theories and multimodal theories and the debate between exemplar and prototype theories. In what ways are these debates similar and in what ways are they different?

4. We noted that there are brain regions that become active in normal individuals when they think about particular concepts. However, patients with damage to these areas are often not impaired in thinking about these concepts. Why might that be?

Key Terms

amodal hypothesis	exemplar theories	perceptual symbol	relation
amodal symbol system	isa link	system	schema
arguments	mirror neurons	proposition	scripts
default values	mnemonic technique	propositional	semantic networks
dual-code theory	multimodal	representation	slot
embodied cognition	hypothesis	prototype theories	

Human Memory: Encoding and Storage

Previous chapters have discussed how we perceive what is in our present and encode it for storage. Now we turn to discussing memory, which is the means by which we can perceive our past. People who lose the ability to create new memories become effectively blind to their past. The movie *Memento* (released in the year 2000) provides a striking characterization of what this would be like. The protagonist of the film, Leonard, can remember his past up to the point of a terrible crime during which he suffered traumatic injuries that left him with amnesia. He can keep track of what is in the immediate present, but as soon as his attention is drawn to something else, he forgets what has just happened. So, for instance, he is constantly meeting people he has met before, who have often manipulated him, but he does not remember them, nor can he protect himself from being manipulated further. Although Leonard incorrectly labels his condition as having no short-term memory, this movie is an accurate portrayal of *anterograde amnesia* — the inability to form new long-term memories. It focuses on the amazing ways Leonard tries to connect the past with the immediate present.

This chapter and the next can be thought of as being about what worked and did not work for Leonard. This chapter will answer the following questions:

- How do we maintain our short-term memory of what just happened? This allows us to manipulate that information in working memory and is what still worked for Leonard.

- How does information we are currently maintaining in working memory prime knowledge in our long-term memory?

- How do we create long-term memories of our experiences? This is what did not work anymore for Leonard.

- What factors influence our success in creating new long-term memories?

Memory and the Brain

Throughout the brain, the connections among neurons are capable of changing in response to experience. This neural plasticity provides the basis for memory. Regions in all areas of the brain play a role in memory, but two regions illustrated in **Figure 6.1** have played the most prominent role in research on human memory. First, there is a region within the temporal cortex that includes the hippocampus, whose role in memory was discussed in Chapter 1 and is further discussed later in this chapter. The hippocampus and surrounding structures play an important role in the storage of new memories. This is where Leonard had his difficulties. Second, research has found that prefrontal brain regions are strongly associated with both the encoding of new memories and the retrieval of old memories. These regions include those involved in the meaningful encoding of pictures and sentences (see Figure 5.1) and those involved in the retrieval of arithmetic and algebraic facts (see Figure 1.15).

These prefrontal regions exhibit laterality effects similar to those noted at the beginning of Chapter 5 (Gabrieli, 2001). Specifically, study of verbal material tends to engage the left hemisphere more than the right hemisphere, whereas study of pictorial material tends to engage the right hemisphere more.

> *Human memory depends heavily on prefrontal structures of the brain for the creation and retrieval of memories and on temporal structures for the permanent storage of these memories.*

Figure 6.1 Brain Structures Involved in the Creation, Storage, and Retrieval of Memories. Prefrontal regions are responsible for the creation and retrieval of memories. The hippocampus and surrounding structures in the temporal cortex are responsible for the permanent storage of memories.

Brain Structures

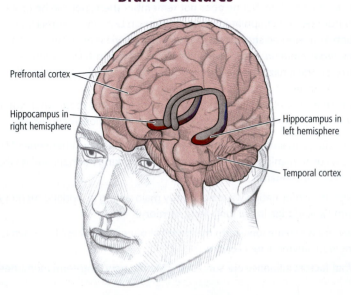

Prefrontal cortex

Hippocampus in right hemisphere

Hippocampus in left hemisphere

Temporal cortex

Sensory Memory

Before reaching the structures in Figure 6.1, information must be processed by perceptual systems, and these systems display a brief memory. There has been extensive research into the nature of these brief sensory memories.

Visual Sensory Memory

Many studies of visual sensory memory have used a procedure in which participants are presented with a visual array of items, such as the letters shown in **Figure 6.2**, for a brief period of time (e.g., 50 ms). When asked to recall the items, participants are typically able to correctly report three, four, five, or at most six items. One might think that only this much material can be held in visual memory — yet participants report that they were aware of more items but the items faded before they could attend to them and report them.

An important methodological variation on this task was introduced by Sperling (1960). He presented arrays consisting of three rows of four letters, like the array in Figure 6.2. Immediately after this stimulus was turned off, participants were cued to attend to their memory of just one row of the display and to report only the letters in that row (the cues were in the form of different tones: high for top row, medium for middle, and low for bottom). Sperling's method was called the **partial-report procedure,** in contrast to the **whole-report procedure** used previously. Participants in Sperling's experiments were able to recall all or most of the items from a row of four. Because participants did not know beforehand which row would be cued, Sperling argued that they must have had most or all of the items stored in some sort of short-term visual memory. Given the cue right after the visual display was turned off, they could attend to that row in their short-term visual memory and report the letters in that row. In contrast, in experiments using the whole-report procedure, participants could not report more items because items had faded from this visual memory before participants could attend to them.

In the partial-report experiments just described, the tone cue was presented immediately after the display was turned off. Sperling also varied the length of the delay between the removal of the display and the tone. The results he obtained, in terms of the number of letters recalled in the cued row, are presented in **Figure 6.3**. As the delay increased to 1 s, the participants' performance declined to what would be expected based on the results from experiments using the whole-report procedure, where participants typically reported 4 or 5 items from an array of 12 items. That is, participants in partial-report experiments were reporting about a third of the items from the cued row, just as participants in whole-report experiments reported about a third of the 12 items in the entire display. Thus, it appears that the memory of the whole display decays very rapidly and is essentially gone by the end of 1 s. All that is left

Figure 6.2 The Kind of Display Used in a Visual-Report Experiment. The display is presented briefly to participants, who are then asked to report the letters it contains.

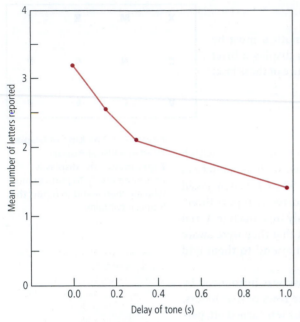

Figure 6.3 **Results from Sperling's (1960) Experiment Demonstrating the Existence of a Brief Visual Sensory Store.** Participants were shown arrays consisting of three rows of four letters (as in Figure 6.2). After the display was turned off, they were cued by a tone, either immediately or after a delay, to report the letters in a particular one of the three rows. The results show that the number of items reported decreased as the delay in the tone increased. *(Data from Sperling, 1960.)*

is what the participant has had time to attend to and convert to a more permanent form.

Sperling's experiments indicate the existence of a **visual sensory store** (sometimes called *iconic memory*) — a memory system that can briefly store visual information. While information is being held in this store, we can attend to it and report it, but information that is not attended to and processed further is quickly lost. The decay time of this sensory store appears to be particularly dependent on the amount of continuing visual input, as Sperling (1967) demonstrated in an experiment in which he varied the postexposure field (the participants' visual field after the display was turned off). He found that when the postexposure field was bright (high visual input), the information in the sensory store was completely gone after only 1 s, but when the field was dark (low visual input), some information remained for a full 5 s. Thus, a bright postexposure field tends to "wash out" memory for the display. And not surprisingly, a postexposure field consisting of another display of characters also destroys the memory for the first display.

Auditory Sensory Memory

Speech comes in over time, which means that auditory information must be held long enough to determine the meaning of what is being said. The existence of an **auditory sensory store** (sometimes called *echoic memory*) has been demonstrated behaviorally by experiments showing that people can report an auditory stimulus with considerable accuracy if probed for it soon after onset (e.g., Darwin, Turvey, & Crowder, 1972; Glucksberg & Cowan, 1970; Moray, Bates, & Barnett, 1965), similar to Sperling's experiments demonstrating visual sensory memory.

One of the more interesting measures of auditory sensory memory involves an ERP measure called *mismatch negativity*. When a sound is presented that is different from recently heard sounds in pitch or loudness (or is a different phoneme), there is an increase in the negativity of the ERP recording 150 to 200 ms after the discrepant sound (for a review, see Näätänen, 1992). In one study, Sams, Hari, Rif, and Knuutila (1993) presented one tone followed by another at various intervals. If the delay between the two tones was less than 10 s, a mismatch negativity was produced whenever the second tone was different from the first. This indicates that an auditory sensory memory can last up to 10 s, consistent with other behavioral measures. It appears that the source of this neural response in the brain is at or near the primary auditory cortex. Similarly, it appears that the neural responses involved in visual sensory memory occur in or near the primary visual cortex. Thus, these basic perceptual regions of the cortex hold a brief representation of sensory information for further processing.

> **Visual and auditory sensory memories are held briefly in corresponding basic perceptual regions of the cortex.**

Short-Term Memory and Working Memory

We have just seen that brief memories of perceptual information are held in sensory stores, and later in this chapter we will discuss how information can be held for long periods in long-term memory. Now, in this section, we will review various proposals for an intermediate memory system that allows us to hold information in mind while we engage in activities such as considering the dinner options offered by a waiter or solving a simple math problem like 32 + 8. We will discuss how such an intermediate memory system might work and how it might relate to the perceptual and long-term memory systems.

A Theory of Short-Term Memory

A very important event in the history of cognitive psychology was the development of a theory of **short-term memory** in the 1960s. The theory clearly illustrated the power of the new cognitive methodology to account for a great deal of data in a way that had not been possible with previous behaviorist theories. Broadbent (1958) had anticipated the theory, and Waugh and Norman (1965) gave an influential formulation of it. However, it was Atkinson and Shiffrin (1968) who gave the theory its most systematic development. It has had an enormous influence on psychology, and although few researchers still accept the original formulation, similar ideas play a crucial role in some of the more recent theories that we will be discussing.

The basic theory begins with the ideas discussed in the preceding sections — information coming in from the environment tends to be held in transient sensory stores from which it is lost unless attended to. As illustrated in **Figure 6.4**, the theory proposed that attended information went into an intermediate, limited-capacity short-term memory system; that information rehearsed in short-term memory could go into long-term memory for relatively permanent storage; and that unrehearsed information would be lost. At one time, the capacity of short-term memory was identified with the **memory span,** the number of elements one can immediately repeat back in the correct order after hearing a list. To test your memory span, have a friend make up lists of digits of various lengths and read them to you. See how many digits you can immediately repeat back in the right order. You will probably find that you are able to correctly repeat back no more than around seven or eight digits (in the 1960s, this was considered convenient because American phone

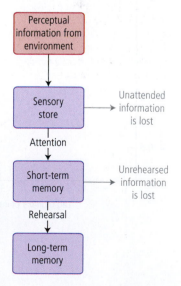

Figure 6.4 A Model of Memory with an Intermediate Short-Term Memory. Information coming in from the environment is briefly held in a sensory store. Attended information goes into an intermediate short-term memory with a limited capacity to hold information (unattended information in the sensory store is lost). Information in short-term memory must be rehearsed before it can move into a relatively permanent long-term memory.

numbers consisted of seven digits). Experimental results on similar tasks led many researchers to conclude that the capacity of short-term memory was about seven elements, although some theorists (e.g., Broadbent, 1975) proposed that its capacity was smaller.

In a typical memory experiment, it was assumed that participants rehearsed the contents of short-term memory. For instance, in a study of memory span, participants might rehearse the digits by saying them over and over again to themselves. It was also assumed that every time an item was rehearsed, there was an increase in the probability that the information would be transferred to a relatively permanent long-term memory. An item that left short-term memory before transfer to long-term memory would be lost forever. One could not keep information in short-term memory indefinitely because new information would always be coming in and pushing out old information from the limited-capacity short-term memory.

An experiment by Shepard and Teghtsoonian (1961) is a good illustration of these ideas. Participants listened to a long sequence of 200 three-digit numbers and were asked to indicate when a number was repeated. The investigators were interested in how participants' ability to recognize a repeated number changed as more numbers intervened between the first appearance of the number and its repetition. The number of intervening items is referred to as the *lag*. The prediction was that recognition for numbers with short lag (i.e., with just a few intervening numbers) would be good, because the most recent numbers would tend to still be present in short-term memory, and that recognition would get progressively worse as the lag increased, because older numbers would be pushed out of short-term memory. The level of recall for numbers with long lag would reflect the amount of information that got into long-term memory. As shown in **Figure 6.5**, the results confirmed these predictions: Recognition of "old" numbers drops off rapidly as the lag increases to 10, but then the drop-off slows and appears to be leveling off between about 50% and 60%.[1] The rapid drop-off can be interpreted as reflecting the decreasing likelihood that the numbers are being held in short-term memory.

A critical element in this theory was the idea that the amount of rehearsal determines whether information is transferred to long-term memory. In one test of this idea, Rundus (1971) asked participants to rehearse out loud, and the results showed that the more that participants rehearsed

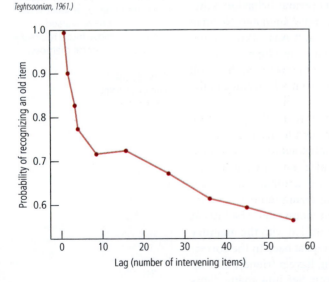

Figure 6.5 Recognition of Previously Seen Items in a Long List. Participants in an experiment by Shepard and Teghtsoonian (1961) listened to a sequence of 200 three-digit numbers, trying to recognize when a number was repeated (i.e., "old"). The probability of an "old" response to a repeated item is plotted as a function of the number of intervening items (the lag). The decline in recognition with increasing lag demonstrates that information cannot be kept in short-term memory indefinitely because new information pushes out old information. *(Data from Shepard & Teghtsoonian, 1961.)*

[1] The level of recall was not really between 50% and 60% (the hit rate) because participants also incorrectly indicated that more than 20% of the new items were repeats (the false alarm rate). Thus, the actual level of recall was really around 30% to 40% (the difference between the hit rate and the false alarm rate).

an item, the more likely they were to remember it. Data of this sort were perhaps the most critical to the theory of short-term memory because they reflected the fundamental property of short-term memory: It is a necessary stop on the way to long-term memory. Information has to "do time" being rehearsed in short-term memory to get into long-term memory, and results like this indicated that the more time done, the more likely information is to be remembered.

However, there is evidence that simply saying a word over and over again does not improve recall, if the person is saying the word without attending to it. For instance, Glenberg, Smith, and Green (1977) had participants study a four-digit number for 2 s, then repeat a word out loud for 2, 6, or 18 s, and then recall the four-digit number. Participants thought that their task was to recall the number and that they were just rehearsing the word to fill the time. Then, when they were given a final surprise test for the words, participants recalled, on average, 11%, 7%, and 13% of the words they had rehearsed for 2, 6, and 18 s, respectively. Not only was their recall poor, but it also showed little relationship to the amount of rehearsal. In another experiment, Souza and Oberauer (2018) instructed participants either to say out loud the items to be remembered (i.e., to rehearse the items) or to say a nonsense term ("babibu") unrelated to the items. There was no difference between the two groups in terms of their ability to recall lists of six items.

In an influential article, Craik and Lockhart (1972) argued that what was critical was not how long information is rehearsed, but rather the depth to which it is processed. This theory, called **depth of processing,** held that rehearsal improves memory only if the material is rehearsed in a deep way that involves assigning meaning to the material (see the Chapter 5 section "Memory for Meaningful Interpretations of Events" for exploration of this idea). Kapur et al. (1994) did a PET study of the difference between brain correlates of the deep and shallow processing of words. In the shallow processing task, participants had to indicate whether each word contained a particular letter; in the deep processing task, they had to indicate whether each word described a living thing. Even though the presentation time was the same for each word in the two tasks (each word was displayed on a screen for 0.5 s), participants later remembered 75% of the deeply processed words and only 57% of the shallowly processed words. Kapur et al. found that there was greater activation during deep processing in the left prefrontal region indicated in Figure 6.1, and a number of subsequent studies have also shown that this region of the brain is more active during deep processing (for a review, see Wagner, Bunge, & Badre, 2004).

> *Atkinson and Shiffrin's theory of short-term memory postulated that information rehearsed in a limited-capacity short-term memory is transferred to long-term memory, but later studies indicate that depth of processing, not rehearsal, determines what goes into long-term memory.*

Baddeley's Theory of Working Memory

Baddeley (1986) proposed a theory of the rehearsal processes that did not tie them to storage in long-term memory. He hypothesized that there are two systems, a **visuospatial sketchpad** and a **phonological loop,** which he called "slave systems" for maintaining information, and he speculated that there might be more such systems. These systems compose part of what he called **working memory** (replacing the prior concept of short-term memory). Baddeley's working memory is a system for holding the information needed to perform a task. For instance, try multiplying 35 by 23 in your head. You may find yourself developing a visual image of part of a written multiplication problem (this visual image would be information held in the visuospatial sketchpad), and you may find yourself rehearsing partial products like 105 (this would be information held in the phonological loop). **Figure 6.6** illustrates Baddeley's overall conception of how these two slave systems interact with a **central executive,** which controls how the slave systems are used. That is, the central executive can put information into and retrieve information from either slave system and can translate information from one system to the other. Baddeley also proposed that the central executive has its own temporary store of information, which would be needed to make decisions about how to control the slave systems.

The phonological loop has received much more extensive investigation than the visuospatial sketchpad. Baddeley proposed that the phonological loop consists of two components, including an articulatory rehearsal process and a phonological store. The **articulatory process** functions as an "inner voice" that rehearses verbal information, as when we're told a phone number and we then mentally or vocally rehearse it while trying to dial it. Many brain-imaging studies (see Smith & Jonides, 1995, for a review) have found activation in Broca's area when participants are trying to remember an ordered list of items like the digits making up a phone number or an unordered list like a shopping list, and this activation occurs even if the participants are not actually talking out loud to themselves (Broca's area — see Figure 1.6 — is in the frontal region labeled "J" in Figure 4.1). Patients with damage to this region show deficits in tests of short-term memory (Vallar, Di Betta, & Silveri, 1997).

The **phonological store** is, in effect, an "inner ear" that hears the inner voice and stores the information in a phonological form. It has been proposed that the phonological store is associated with the parietal-temporal region of the brain (the more posterior region labeled "J" in Figure 4.1). A number of brain-imaging studies have found activation of this region during the processing of verbal information (Henson, Burgess, & Frith, 2000; Jonides et al., 1998).

Figure 6.6 Baddeley's Theory of Working Memory. The visuospatial sketchpad and phonological loop are "slave systems" controlled by the central executive.

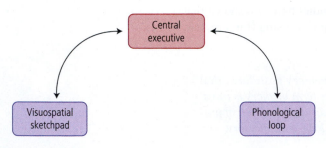

Like patients with damage to Broca's area, patients with lesions in this region (which includes Wernicke's area — see Figure 1.6) suffer deficits of short-term memory (Vallar et al., 1997).

One of the most compelling pieces of evidence for the existence of the articulatory loop is the word length effect (Baddeley, Thomson, & Buchanan, 1975). Read the five words below and then try to repeat them without looking back at the page:

wit, sum, harm, bay, top

Most people can do this. Baddeley et al. found that participants were able to repeat back an average of 4.5 out of 5 such one-syllable words. Now read and try to repeat the following five words without looking back:

university, opportunity, hippopotamus, constitutional, auditorium

Participants were able to recall an average of only 2.6 out of 5 such five-syllable words. The crucial factor appears to be how long it takes to say the words. Baddeley et al. looked at recall for words that varied from one to five syllables. They also measured how many words of the various lengths participants could say in a second. **Figure 6.7** shows the results. Note that the slopes of the two

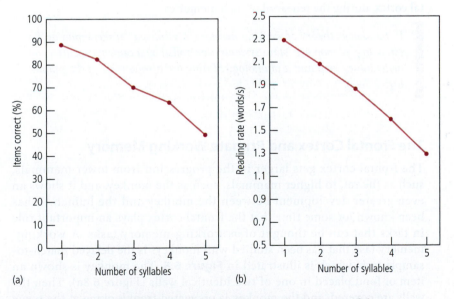

(a)

(b)

Figure 6.7 Results of Baddeley et al. (1975) Showing the Existence of the Articulatory Loop. In each trial, participants were shown a sequence of 5 words with the same number of syllables, at a rate of 2 seconds per word. They were then given 12 seconds to rehearse the sequence vocally before attempting to repeat it back. (a) The percentage of words correctly recalled as a function of the number of syllables. (b) The participants' average reading rate (the number of words that could be read aloud per second) as a function of the number of syllables. *(Data from Baddeley et al., 1975.)*

curves almost exactly match — that is, as the number of syllables increases, the decline in the percent of words correctly recalled almost exactly matches the decline in reading rate.

Trying to maintain information in working memory is much like the efforts of entertainers who spin plates on sticks. The performer will get one plate spinning on one stick, then another on another stick, then another, and so on. Then he runs back to the first plate to respin it before it slows down and falls off, then respins the second, and so on. He can keep only so many plates spinning at the same time. Baddeley proposed that it is the same situation with respect to working memory. If we try to keep too many items in working memory, by the time we get back to rehearse the first one, it will have decayed to the point that it takes too long to retrieve and re-rehearse. Baddeley proposed that we can keep about 1.5 to 2.0 seconds' worth of material rehearsed in the articulatory loop.

There is considerable evidence that this articulatory loop truly involves speech. For instance, Conrad (1964) showed that participants suffered more confusion when they tried to remember sequences of letters in which a high proportion of the letters rhymed (such as *BCTHVZ*) than when they tried to remember non-rhyming sequences (such as *HBKLMW*). Also, as we just discussed, there is evidence for activation in Broca's area, part of the left prefrontal cortex, during the rehearsal of such memories.

> *In Baddeley's theory of working memory, a visuospatial sketchpad and a phonological loop are "slave systems" controlled by a central executive; an articulatory loop and a phonological store are components of the phonological loop.*

The Frontal Cortex and Primate Working Memory

The frontal cortex gets larger in the progression from lower mammals, such as the rat, to higher mammals, such as the monkey, and it shows an even greater development between the monkey and the human. It has been known for some time that the frontal cortex plays an important role in tasks that can be thought of as working-memory tasks. A working-memory task that has been studied with monkeys is the delayed match-to-sample task, which is illustrated in **Figure 6.8**. The monkey is shown an item of food placed in one of two identical wells (Figure 6.8a). Then the wells are covered, and the monkey is prevented from looking at the scene for a delay period — typically 10 s (Figure 6.8b). Finally, the monkey is given the opportunity to retrieve the food, but it must remember in which well it was hidden (Figure 6.8c). Monkeys with lesions in the frontal cortex cannot perform this task (Jacobsen, 1935, 1936). A human infant cannot perform similar tasks until its frontal cortex has matured somewhat, usually at about 1 year of age (Diamond, 1991).

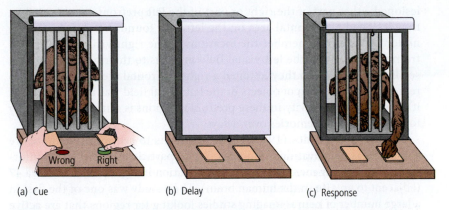

(a) Cue   (b) Delay   (c) Response

Figure 6.8 **The Delayed Match-to-Sample Task.** (a) Food is placed in the well on the right and covered. (b) A curtain is drawn for the delay period. (c) The curtain is raised, and the monkey can lift the cover from one of the wells. *(Information from Goldman-Rakic, 1987.)*

When a monkey must remember where a food item has been placed, a region called Brodmann area 46 (see **Figure 6.9**; also see Figure 1.7), on the side of the frontal cortex, is involved (Goldman-Rakic, 1988). Lesions in this area produce deficits in this task. It has been shown that neurons in this region fire only during the delay period of the task, as if they are keeping information active during that interval. They are inactive before and after the delay. Moreover, different neurons in that region seem tuned to remembering objects in different portions of the visual field (Funahashi, Bruce, & Goldman-Rakic, 1991).

Goldman-Rakic (1992) examined monkey performance on other tasks that require maintaining other types of information over a delay interval. In one task, monkeys had to remember different objects. For example, the animal would have to remember to select a red circle and not a green square. It appears that a different area of the prefrontal cortex is involved in this type of task. Different neurons in this area will fire depending on whether a red circle or a green square is being remembered. Goldman-Rakic speculated that the prefrontal cortex is parceled into many small regions, each of which is responsible for remembering a different kind of information.

Like many neuroscience studies, these experiments are correlational — they show a relationship between neural activity and memory function, but they do not show that the neural activity is essential for the memory function. In an effort to show a causal role, Funahashi, Bruce, and Goldman-Rakic (1993) trained monkeys to remember the location of objects in their visual field and then selectively

Figure 6.9 **Brodmann Areas in the Frontal Lobe of a Human (Top) and of a Monkey (Bottom).** Brodmann area 46 is the region shown in orange. *(Information from Goldman-Rakic, 1987.)*

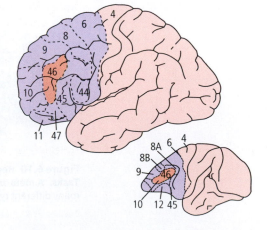

lesioned either part of the right or part of the left prefrontal cortex. When they lesioned a prefrontal area on the left they found that monkeys were no longer able to remember the locations in the right visual field (recall from Chapter 2 that the left visual field projects to the right hemisphere; see Figure 2.5). When they lesioned a right prefrontal area, their ability to remember the location of objects in the left visual field was impaired. Thus, it does seem that activity in these prefrontal regions is critical to the ability to maintain these memories over delays.

Smith and Jonides (1995) used PET scans to see whether there are similar areas of activation in humans. When participants held visual information in working memory, there was activation in right prefrontal area 47 (adjacent to area 46 in the human brain). Their study was one of the first in a large number of neural imaging studies looking for regions that are active when people maintain information in a working-memory task. This research has revealed a stable core of prefrontal and parietal regions that are active across many different types of tasks. In a meta-analysis of 189 fMRI studies, Rottschy et al. (2012) identified the regions shown in **Figure 6.10** and pointed out that activity in these areas occurs across a range of tasks, not just working-memory tasks. One possibility is that activity in these areas corresponds to the functioning of Baddeley's central executive (see Figure 6.6). Postle (2006, 2015) has argued that this activity may reflect the operation of brain systems that play a role in controlling the representation of information in more specialized regions of the brain. For instance, in a visual memory task the information may be maintained in visual areas — the analogue of Baddeley's visuospatial sketchpad — and prefrontal regions like those found by Smith and Jonides may control the activation of this information in other brain regions.

> *Different areas of the frontal and parietal cortex appear to be responsible for maintaining different types of information in working memory.*

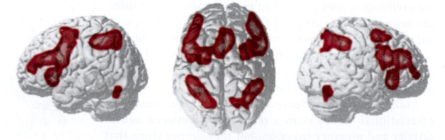

Figure 6.10 Regions of the Brain That Consistently Activate Across a Range of Tasks. A meta-analysis of 189 fMRI studies revealed that these regions are active across many different types of tasks, including working-memory tasks *(Data from Rottschy et al., 2012.)*

Activation and Long-Term Memory

So far, we have discussed how information from the environment comes into working memory and is maintained by rehearsal. There is another source of information besides the environment, however: long-term memory. For instance, rather than reading a new phone number and holding it in working memory, we can retrieve a familiar number from long-term memory and hold it in working memory. Part of our working memory is formed by information we can quickly access from long-term memory — something that Ericsson and Kintsch (1995) called *long-term working memory*. Similarly, Cowan (2005) argues that working memory includes the activated subset of long-term memory. The ability to bolster our working memory with information from long-term memory helps explain why the memory span for meaningful sentences is about twice the span for unrelated words (Potter & Lombardi, 1990). Many of the phrases in a sentence (like the phrase "memory span" in the previous sentence) already have long-term representations.

Information in long-term memory can vary from moment to moment in terms of how easy it is to retrieve it into working memory. Different theories use different terminology to describe the same basic idea. The language I use in this chapter is similar to that used in my ACT (Adaptive Control of Thought) theory (Anderson, 2009).

Activation Calculations

In the ACT theory, the level of **activation** determines both the probability that some given piece of information will be retrieved from long-term memory and the speed with which that retrieval will be accomplished. The free-association technique is sometimes used to get at levels of activation in memory. In free association, a person is presented with information (e.g., one or more words) and is asked to free-associate by responding with whatever first comes to mind. The responses can be taken as reflecting the things that the presented information activates most strongly among all the currently active information in long-term memory. For example, what do you think of when you read the three words below?

> Bible
> animals
> flood

If you are like the students in my classes, you will think of the story of Noah. The curious fact is that when I ask students to associate to just the word *Bible,* they typically come up with words like *Moses* and *Jesus* — almost never *Noah.* When I ask them to associate to just *animals,* they come up with words like *farm* and *zoo,* but almost never *Noah;* and when I ask them to associate to just

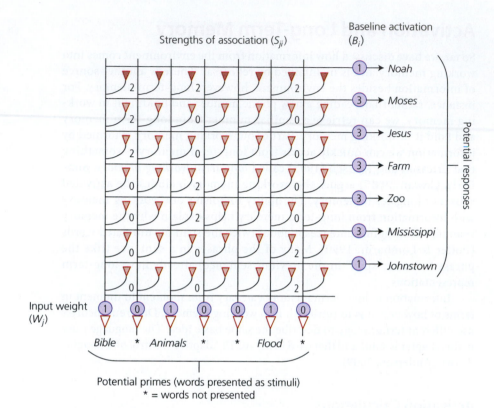

Figure 6.11 A Representation of Activation in a Network. In the ACT theory, activation coming from stimulus words (potential primes) — such as *Bible, animals,* and *flood* — spreads activation to associated concepts (potential responses) — such as *Noah, Moses,* and *farm.*

flood, they come up with words like *Mississippi* and *Johnstown* (the latter being perhaps a Pittsburgh-specific association), but almost never *Noah.* So why do they come up with *Noah* when given all three terms together? **Figure 6.11** represents this phenomenon in terms of activation computations and shows three kinds of things:

- Potential responses: terms that are currently active in long-term memory and so could potentially come to mind, such as *Noah, Moses, Jesus, farm, zoo, Mississippi,* and *Johnstown.*
- Potential primes: terms that might be used to elicit responses from long-term memory, such as *Bible, animals,* and *flood.*
- The strength of the association between each potential prime and each potential response: the triangular connections with curved tails.

In the ACT theory, the following equation represents how the activation A_i of any potential response, such as a word or an idea, reflects the strength of associations in a network like the one in Figure 6.11:

$$A_i = B_i + \sum_j W_j S_{ji}$$

In this equation

- A_i is the activation of any potential response i.
- B_i is the baseline activation of the potential response i before priming. Figure 6.11 illustrates the idea that some concepts, such as *Jesus* and *Mississippi*, are more common than others, such as *Noah*, and so would have greater baseline activation. Just to be concrete, in Figure 6.11 the baseline activation for *Jesus* and *Mississippi* is assumed to be 3 and for *Noah* is assumed to be 1.
- W_j is the weight given to each potential prime j. For instance, in Figure 6.11 we assume that the weight for any presented word is 1 and that the weight for any word not presented is 0. The Σ indicates that we are summing over all of the potential primes j.
- S_{ji} is the strength of the association between any potential prime j and any potential response i. To keep things simple, in Figure 6.11 we assume that the strength of association is 2 in the case of related pairs such as *Bible–Jesus* and *flood–Mississippi* and 0 in the case of unrelated pairs such as *Bible–Mississippi* and *flood–Jesus*.

With this equation, these concepts, and these numbers, we can explain why the students in my class associate *Noah* when prompted with all three words but almost never do so when presented with any word individually. Consider what happens when I present just the word *Bible*. In this case, the activation of *Noah* is

$$A_{\text{Noah}} = 1 + (1 \times 2) = 3$$

where the first 1 is *Noah's* baseline activation (B_{Noah}), the second 1 is *Bible's* weight (W_{Bible}), and the 2 is the strength of association between *Bible* and *Noah* ($S_{\text{Bible–Noah}}$). In contrast, the activation for *Jesus* is higher because it has a higher baseline activation, reflecting its greater frequency:

$$A_{\text{Jesus}} = 3 + (1 \times 2) = 5$$

The reason *Jesus* and not *Noah* comes to mind in response to *Bible* is that *Jesus* has higher activation. Now let's consider what happens when

I present all three words — *Bible, animals,* and *flood.* The activation of *Noah* will be

$$A_{\text{Noah}} = 1 + (1 \times 2) + (1 \times 2) + (1 \times 2) = 7$$

where there are three (1×2) expressions because all three of the words have an association with *Noah*. In contrast, the activation equation for *Jesus* remains

$$A_{\text{Jesus}} = 3 + (1 \times 2) = 5$$

because only *Bible* has an association with *Jesus.* Thus, the extra associations to *Noah* have raised the activation of *Noah* above that of *Jesus,* despite the fact that *Noah* has a lower baseline activation.

There are two critical factors in this activation equation: the baseline activation of each potential response, which sets a starting activation for the idea, and the activation received through associations with potential primes, which adjusts the baseline activation to reflect the current context. The next section will explore this associative activation, and the section after that will discuss the baseline activation.

> *The probability and speed of accessing a concept in memory are determined by the concept's level of activation, which in turn is determined by its baseline activation and the activation it receives from associated concepts.*

Spreading Activation

Spreading activation is the term often used to refer to the process by which currently attended items can make associated memories more available. Many studies have examined how memories are primed by what we attend to. One of the earliest was a study by Meyer and Schvaneveldt (1971) in which participants were asked to judge whether or not both items in a pair were words. **Table 6.1** shows examples of the materials used in their experiments, along with participants' judgment times (in positive pairs, both items were words; in negative pairs, either or both were not words). The pairs were presented with one item above the other (as in the table), and if either item was not a word, participants were to respond *no*. The judgment times for the negative pairs suggest that participants first judged the top item and then the bottom item. When the top item was not a word, participants were faster to reject the pair than when only the bottom item was not a word. (When the top item was not a word, participants did not have to judge the bottom item and so could respond sooner.) The major interest in this study was in the positive pairs, which could consist of unrelated words, such as *nurse* and *butter,* or of words with an associative relation, such as *bread* and *butter.* Participants were 85 ms faster on the

TABLE 6.1 Examples of Pairs Used to Demonstrate Associative Priming				
Positive Pairs		**Negative Pairs**		
Unrelated	*Related*	*Nonword First*	*Nonword Second*	*Both Nonwords*
Nurse	Bread	Plame	Wine	Plame
Butter	Butter	Wine	Plame	Reab
940 ms*	855 ms	904 ms	1,087 ms	884 ms

*Judgment time (time to indicate whether both items in the pair are words).

(Data from Meyer & Schvaneveldt, 1971.)

related pairs. This result can be explained by a spreading-activation analysis. When the participant read the first word in the related pair, activation would spread from it to associated words, including the second word, making that word easier to judge. The implication of this result is that the spreading of activation through associations can increase the rate at which words are read. Thus, we can read material that has a strong associative coherence more rapidly than we can read incoherent material where the words seem unrelated.

Kaplan (1989), in his dissertation research, reported an effect of associative priming at a very different timescale of information processing. The "participants" in the study were members of his dissertation committee. I was one of these participants, and it was a rather memorable and somewhat embarrassing experience. He gave us riddles to solve, and each of us was able to solve about half of them. One of the riddles that I was able to solve was

What goes up a chimney down but can't come down a chimney up?

The answer is *umbrella*. Another faculty member was not able to solve this one, and he has his own embarrassing story to tell about it — much like the one I have to tell about the following riddle that I could not get:

On this hill there was a green house. And inside the green house there was a white house. And inside the white house, there was a red house. And inside the red house there were a lot of little blacks and whites sitting there. What place is this?

More or less randomly, different faculty members were able to solve various riddles.

Then Kaplan gave us each a microphone and tape recorder and told us that we would be beeped at various times over the next week. When it beeped we were supposed to record what we had thought about our unsolved riddles and whether we had solved any of them. He said that he was interested in the steps by which we came to solve these problems. That was essentially a lie to cover the true purpose of the experiment, but it did keep us thinking about the riddles over the week.

What Kaplan had done was to split the riddles each of us could not solve randomly into two groups. For half of these unsolved problems, he seeded our environment with clues to the solution. He was quite creative in how he did this: In the case of the riddle above that I could not solve, he drew a picture of a watermelon as a graffito in the men's restroom. Sure enough, shortly after seeing this graffito I thought again about this riddle and came up with the answer — *watermelon!* I congratulated myself on my great insight, and when I was next beeped, I proudly recorded how I had solved the problem — quite unaware of the role the bathroom graffito had played in my solution.

Of course, that might just be one problem and one foolish participant. Averaged over all the problems and all the participants (which included a Nobel laureate), however, we were twice as likely to solve those riddles that had been primed in the environment than those that had not been. Basically, activation from the primes in the environment spread activation to the solutions and made them more available when trying to solve the riddles. We were all unaware of the manipulation that was taking place. This example illustrates the importance of priming to issues of insight (a topic we will consider at length in Chapter 8) and also shows that one is not aware of the associative priming that is taking place, even when one is trained to spot such things, as I am.

> *Activation spreads from presented items through a network to memories related to that prime item.*

Practice and Memory Strength

Spreading activation explains how the context can make some memories more available than others. However, some memories are always more available, because they are recalled frequently in a wide range of contexts. So, for instance, you can recall the names of close friends almost immediately, anywhere and anytime. The quantity that determines this inherent availability of a memory is sometimes referred to as its **strength** (a different term for the same concept as baseline activation in the discussion above of the ACT theory). In contrast to the activation level of a memory, which can have rapid fluctuations depending on whether associated items are being attended, the strength of a memory changes more gradually. Each time we recall a memory, it increases a little in strength. The strength of a memory determines in part how active it can become and hence how accessible it will be, and as we will see next, the strength of a memory can be gradually increased by repeated practice.

The Power Law of Learning

The effects of practice on memory retrieval are extremely regular and very large. In one study (Pirolli & Anderson, 1985), participants practiced recalling a set of sentences for 25 days and were tested to see how the speed with

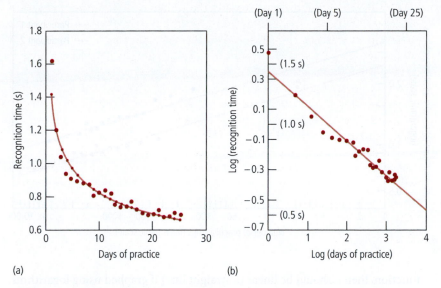

Figure 6.12 Results of Pirolli and Anderson (1985) on the Effects of Practice on Recognition Time. (a) The time required to recognize sentences is plotted as a function of the number of days of practice. Each of the 25 data points represents the average recognition time for each of the 25 days of practice, and the curve is the best fit to the data points. (b) When recognition time and days of practice are represented by their logarithms, the best-fitting curve is a straight line, revealing that this is a power function. (Times and days are indicated in parentheses.) *(Data from Pirolli & Anderson, 1985.)*

which they could recognize the sentences varied with the number of days of practice. The data points in **Figure 6.12a** plot how participants' time to recognize a sentence decreased with practice. As can be seen, participants sped up from about 1.6 s to about 0.7 s, cutting their retrieval time by more than 50%. The figure also shows that the rate of improvement decreases with more practice — that is, increasing practice has diminishing returns. The data are nicely fit by a power function of the form

$$T = 1.40\, P^{-0.24}$$

where T is the recognition time and P is the number of days of practice. This is called a **power function** because the amount of practice P is being raised to a power. This power relationship between performance (measured in terms of response time or any of several other variables) and amount of practice is a ubiquitous phenomenon in learning. One way to see that data correspond to a power function is to use logarithms, as shown in Figure 6.12b, where the logarithm of recognition time is plotted against the logarithm of days of practice. If a function graphed using nonlogarithmic variables is indeed a power

Figure 6.13 Data from Blackburn's (1936) Study on the Effects of Practicing Addition Problems for 10,000 Trials. Participant 1 was consistently faster than Participant 2 at adding two numbers, but the rate of improvement with practice was about the same for the two participants. The fact that both sets of data are best fit by a straight line when plotted on logarithmic scales indicates that both are power functions. *(Data from Blackburn, 1936, and Crossman, 1959.)*

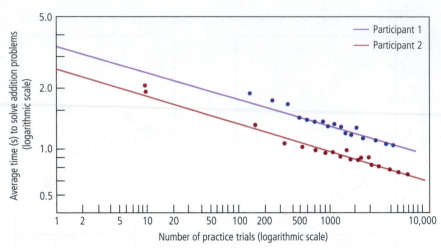

function, then it should be linear (a straight line) if graphed using logarithms. As can be seen in Figure 6.12b, the relationship is quite close to this linear function:

$$\ln T = 0.34 - 0.24 \ln P$$

Newell and Rosenbloom (1981) refer to the way that memory performance improves as a function of practice as the **power law of learning. Figure 6.13** shows some data from Blackburn (1936), who looked at the effects of practicing addition problems for 10,000 trials by two participants. The data are plotted on logarithmic scales, and there is a linear relationship. On this graph and on some others in this book, the original numbers (i.e., like those given in parentheses in Figure 6.12b) are plotted on a logarithmic scale but are expressed in normal form (not as logarithms). Blackburn's data show that the power law of learning extends to amounts of practice far beyond that shown in Figure 6.12. Figures 6.12 and 6.13 reflect the gradual increase in memory strength with practice. As memories become stronger, they reach higher levels of activation and so can be retrieved more rapidly.

As a memory is practiced, it is strengthened according to a power function.

Neural Correlates of the Power Law

What really underlies the power law of learning? Some evidence suggests that the law may be related to neural changes that occur during learning. One such neural change that has attracted much attention is called **long-term potentiation (LTP),** which occurs in the hippocampus and in cortical areas.

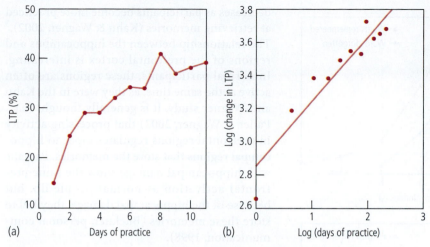

(a) Days of practice
(b) Log (days of practice)

Figure 6.14 Results from Barnes's (1979) Study of Long-Term Potentiation (LTP). When a neural pathway is stimulated, cells along that pathway show increased sensitivity to further stimulation. The growth in LTP is plotted as a function of number of days of practice (a) on normal scales and (b) on logarithmic scales. *(Data from Barnes, 1979.)*

When a neural pathway is stimulated with a high-frequency electric current, cells along that pathway show increased sensitivity to further stimulation. Barnes (1979) looked at LTP in rats by stimulating the hippocampus each day for 11 successive days and measuring the percentage increase in excitatory postsynaptic potential (EPSP) over its initial value.[2] The results shown in **Figure 6.14a** indicate a diminishing increase in LTP as the amount of practice increases. The plot of the same data points on logarithmic scales in Figure 6.14b shows that the relationship is approximately a power function (the best-fitting curve is linear). Thus, it does seem that neural activation changes with practice in the same way that behavioral measures do.

Note that the activation measure shown in Figure 6.14a increases more and more slowly, whereas recognition time (see Figure 6.12a) decreases more and more slowly. In other words, a performance measure such as recognition time is an inverse reflection of the growth of strength that is happening internally. As the strength of the memory increases, the performance measures improve (which means shorter recognition times and fewer errors). You remember something faster after you've thought about it more often.

The hippocampal region observed in rats in Barnes (1979) is the equivalent of the region that was damaged in the fictional character Leonard in the movie *Memento,* discussed at the beginning of the chapter. Damage to this region often results in amnesia.

Studies of the effects of practice on participants without brain damage have found that activation in the hippocampus and the prefrontal regions

---

[2] As discussed in Chapter 1, the difference in electric potential between the outside and inside of the cell decreases as the dendrite and cell body of a neuron become more excited. EPSP is described as increasing when this difference decreases.

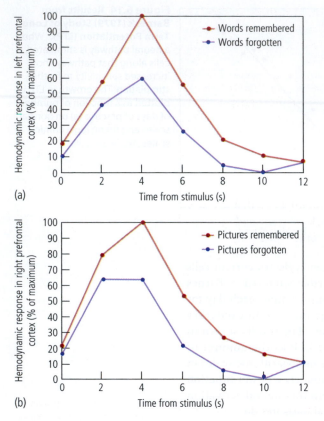

(a)

(b)

Figure 6.15 The Role of the Prefrontal Cortex in Forming New Memories. Results from two studies show that brain activation (hemodynamic response) is greater when participants study items that are later remembered versus items that are later forgotten. (a) Activation in the left prefrontal cortex while participants studied words. *(Data from Wagner et al., 1998.)* (b) Activation in the right prefrontal cortex while participants studied pictures. *(Data from Brewer et al., 1998.)*

decreases as participants become more practiced at retrieving memories (Kahn & Wagner, 2002).[3] The relationship between the hippocampus and regions of the prefrontal cortex is interesting. In normal participants, these regions are often active at the same time, as they were in the Kahn and Wagner study. It is generally thought (e.g., Paller & Wagner, 2002) that processing activity in prefrontal regions regulates input to hippocampal regions that store the memories. Patients with hippocampal damage show the same prefrontal activation as normal people do, but because of the hippocampal damage, they fail to store these memories (Buckner, personal communication, 1998).

Two studies illustrating the role of the prefrontal cortex in forming new memories in normal participants (i.e., without hippocampal damage) appeared back-to-back in the same issue of *Science* magazine. One study (Wagner et al., 1998) investigated memory for words; the other (Brewer, Zhao, Desmond, Glover, & Gabrieli, 1998) investigated memory for pictures. In both cases, participants remembered some of the items and forgot others. Using fMRI measures of the hemodynamic response, the researchers contrasted the brain activation at the time of study for those words and pictures that were subsequently remembered and those that were subsequently forgotten. Wagner et al. found that activity in left prefrontal regions was predictive of memory for words (see **Figure 6.15a**), whereas Brewer et al. found that activity in right prefrontal regions was predictive of memory for pictures (see Figure 6.15b). In both parts of Figure 6.15, the rise in the hemodynamic response is plotted as a function of the time from stimulus presentation. As discussed in Chapter 1, the hemodynamic response lags, reaching a maximum at about 4–5 s after the actual neural activity. The correspondence between the results from the two laboratories is striking. In both cases, remembered items corresponded with greater activation in the prefrontal regions, supporting the conclusion that prefrontal activation is indeed

[3] Note that neural activation decreases with practice because it takes less effort to retrieve the memory. This can be a bit confusing—practice increases the baseline activation of a memory, which results in lower brain activation when the memory is retrieved. You can avoid confusion by keeping in mind that memory activation and brain activation refer to different concepts: memory activation reflects the availability of the memory, whereas brain activation reflects the effort (the hemodynamic expenditure) required to retrieve the memory.

critical for storing a memory successfully. Also, note that these studies are a good example of the lateralization of prefrontal processing, with verbal material involving the left hemisphere to a greater extent and visual material involving the right hemisphere to a greater extent.

> *Activation in prefrontal regions appears to drive long-term potentiation in the hippocampus. This activation results in the creation and strengthening of memories.*

Factors Influencing Memory

A reasonable inference from the preceding discussion might be that the only thing determining memory performance is how much we study and practice. In this section, we will review a number of factors other than practice that have been thought to be critical to how well we remember things. Some prove to be important and others not.

Spacing Effects

The spacing of items to be studied and recalled can have large effects. Pavlik and Anderson (2005) showed participants a set of English–Japanese vocabulary items, giving participants either 1, 2, or 4 opportunities to restudy these items. A restudy opportunity consisted, first, of a test of whether they could recall the English translation of a Japanese word; then, if they could not recall a translation, they got another opportunity to study it. Not surprisingly, the more opportunities participants had to study an item, the better they did.

Figure 6.16 Spacing Effects. Repeated study closely spaced is more effective for immediate recall (a) but not for delayed recall (b). *(Data from Pavlik & Anderson, 2005.)*

Participants went through a long sequence of 480 presentations in which the initial study of items and restudy opportunities for items were intermixed. This enabled a second important manipulation, which was how far apart the restudy opportunities were. Participants were retested on a particular item after either 2, 14, or 98 intervening presentations of other items. **Figure 6.16a** shows how well they did on their last test on the first day. As can be seen, the fewer the number of intervening items between study opportunities, the better was participants' performance. Best performance was 98.8% correct for items with 4 restudy opportunities with 2 intervening items.

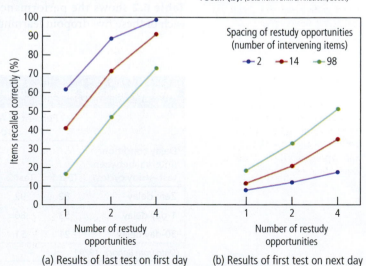

(a) Results of last test on first day

(b) Results of first test on next day

However, the results were completely reversed when the participants came back the next day and were tested for what they remembered (Figure 6.16b). For instance, items restudied just once with 98 intervening items (leftmost data point on green curve) were recalled as well as items restudied 4 times with just 2 intervening items (rightmost data point on blue curve). This illustrates the typical effect of spacing when studying something to be remembered: Massing study opportunities produces better immediate recall but worse delayed recall.

Bahrick (1979) did a study of spacing effects where the interval between restudy opportunities was as long as 30 days. All participants began with a study session that consisted of being shown 50 English–Spanish word pairs, with each pair displayed for 5 s as the experimenter pronounced the Spanish word. Participants were then immediately tested on the 50 pairs by being shown the English words in random order to see if they were able to give the Spanish equivalent. Any words not correctly recalled were then immediately tested again, and so on until all words had been correctly recalled. This procedure of retesting the items answered incorrectly until all answers are correct is called a *dropout learning procedure.*

Participants were divided into three groups to be tested five times each under three different conditions: zero delay, 1-day delay, and 30-day delay.

- In the zero-delay condition, this same dropout learning procedure was repeated 5 more times.
- In the 1-day delay condition, the dropout learning procedure was repeated at 1-day intervals — thus, the 5 cycles occurred over the course of 5 days.
- In the 30-day delay condition, there was a 30-day delay between dropout learning procedures — thus, the 5 cycles occurred over the course of 150 days.

Table 6.2 shows the performance of the participants at the beginning of each of these five dropout learning cycles. As can be seen, their performance

TABLE 6.2 Recall of Spanish Words Under Three Different Delay Conditions

Delay condition (interval between test–study cycles)	Percent of Words Correctly Recalled at the Beginning of Each Dropout Learning Cycle					Final test (30 days after Test 5)
	Test 1	Test 2	Test 3	Test 4	Test 5	
Zero delay	82	92	96	96	98	68
1-day delay	53	86	94	96	98	86
30-day delay	21	51	72	79	82	95

(Data from Bahrick, 1979.)

improved as would be expected, but as in Figure 6.16a, their performance was better with shorter delays.

All three groups had a final test 30 days after their last test–study cycle. Table 6.2 also shows that the groups who studied at shorter intervals and had done better on earlier tests now had the worst performance, as in Figure 6.16b. Thus, once again we see that spacing study sessions close together helps immediate recall but hinders longer retention.

Bahrick's study makes particularly apparent the tragedy of cramming for an exam. If one wants to score well on an exam it makes sense to mass one's study as close to the exam as possible. However, if one is interested in long-term retention of the material, it is better to study the material at long delays. Results like this have led to a number of programs that try to deliberately manipulate the spacing of students' study sessions. For instance, Kapler, Weston, and Wiseheart (2015) had undergraduates complete an online review of meteorological concepts either 1 day or 7 days after a lecture. The students who reviewed the material after 7 days did better on a test 35 days after the review. In another application of spacing principles, Lindsey, Shroyer, Pashler, and Mozer (2014) were able to improve middle-school students' learning of Spanish.

Elaborative Processing

There is evidence that memory is helped by **elaborative processing** — thinking of information that relates to and expands on the information that needs to be remembered. For instance, my graduate advisor and I did an experiment that demonstrated the importance of elaboration (Anderson & Bower, 1972). We had participants try to remember simple sentences such as *The doctor hated the lawyer*. In one condition, participants just studied the sentence; in the other, they were asked to generate an elaboration of their choosing — such as *because of the malpractice suit*. Later, participants were presented with the subject and verb of the original sentence (e.g., *The doctor hated*) and were asked to recall the object (e.g., *the lawyer*). Participants who just studied the original sentences were able to recall 57% of the objects, but those who generated the elaborations recalled 72%. This advantage resulted from the redundancy created by the elaboration. If the participants could not originally recall *lawyer* but could recall the elaboration *because of the malpractice suit*, they might then be able to recall *lawyer*.

A series of experiments by Stein and Bransford (1979) showed why self-generated elaborations are often better than experimenter-provided elaborations. In one of these experiments, participants were asked to remember 10 sentences like *The fat man read the sign* and were later asked to recall the adjective (*fat* in this case). There were four conditions of study.

- In the base condition, participants studied just the sentence.
- In the self-generated elaboration condition, participants were asked to continue the sentence with an elaboration of their own.

- In the imprecise elaboration condition, participants were given a continuation that was poorly related to the meaning of the sentence, such as *that was two feet tall*.

- In the precise elaboration condition, participants were given a continuation that gave context to the sentence, such as *warning about the ice*.

After studying the material, participants in all conditions were presented with such sentence frames as *The _____ man read the sign*, and they had to recall the missing adjective. Participants recalled 4.2 of the 10 adjectives in the base condition and 5.8 of the 10 when they generated their own elaborations. Obviously, the self-generated elaborations had helped. Participants could recall only 2.2 of the 10 adjectives in the imprecise elaboration condition, replicating the typical inferiority found for experimenter-provided elaborations relative to self-generated ones. However, participants' recall was best in the precise elaboration condition (7.8 of the 10 adjectives). So, by careful choice of words, experimenter elaborations can be made better than self-generated ones. (For further research on this topic, see Pressley, McDaniel, Turnure, Wood, & Ahmad, 1987.)

It appears that the critical factor is not whether the participant or the experimenter generates the elaborations but how effectively the elaborations prompt the material to be recalled. Participant-generated elaborations are effective because they reflect the idiosyncratic constraints of each particular participant's knowledge. As Stein and Bransford demonstrated, however, it is possible for the experimenter to construct elaborations that facilitate even better recall.

Otten, Henson, and Rugg (2001) noted that the prefrontal and hippocampal regions involved in memory for material that is processed meaningfully and elaborately seem to be the same regions that are involved in memory for material that is processed shallowly. High activity in these regions is predictive of subsequent recall for all kinds of material (see Figure 6.15). Meaningful, elaborative processing tends to evoke higher levels of activation during recall than shallow processing (Wagner et al., 1998). Thus, it appears that meaningful, elaborate processing is effective because it is better at driving the brain processes that result in successful recall. (**Implications 6.1** describes a method of elaborative processing—the method of loci.)

Memory for material improves when it is processed with more meaningful elaborations.

Techniques for Studying Textual Material

Frase (1975) found evidence of the benefit of elaborative processing with text material. He compared how participants in two groups remembered text when preparing for a test: One group was given what are called "advance

Implications 6.1

How Does the Method of Loci Help Us Organize Recall?

Mental imagery is an effective method for developing meaningful elaborations. A classic mnemonic technique, the **method of loci,** depends heavily on visual imagery and the use of spatial knowledge to organize recall. This technique, used extensively in ancient times when speeches were given without written notes or teleprompters, is still used today. Cicero (in *De Oratore*) credits the method to a Greek poet, Simonides, who had recited a lyric poem at a banquet. After his recitation, he was called from the banquet hall by the gods Castor and Pollux, whom he had praised in his poem. While he was absent, the roof fell in, killing all the people at the banquet. The corpses were so mangled that relatives could not identify them. Simonides was able to identify each corpse, however, according to where each person had been sitting in the banquet hall. This feat of total recall convinced Simonides of the usefulness of an orderly arrangement of locations into which a person could place objects to be remembered. This story may be rather fanciful, but whatever its origin, the method of loci is well documented as a useful technique for remembering a list of items, such as the points a person wants to make in a speech (e.g., Christen & Bjork, 1976; Ross & Lawrence, 1968). (The painting at right — *Cicero Denounces Catiline,* a fresco by Cesare Maccari — depicts Cicero making a lengthy speech before the Roman Senate.)

To use the method of loci, one imagines a specific path through a familiar area with some fixed locations along the path. For instance, if we were familiar with a path from a bookstore to a library, we might use it. To remember a series of objects, we simply walk along the path mentally, associating the objects with the fixed locations. As an example, consider a grocery list of six items — milk, hot dogs, dog food, tomatoes, bananas, and bread. To associate the milk with the bookstore, we might imagine books lying in a puddle of milk in front of the bookstore. To associate hot dogs with a coffee shop (the next location on the path from the bookstore), we might imagine someone stirring their coffee with a hot dog. The pizza shop is next, and to associate it with dog food, we might imagine a dog-food pizza (well, some people even like anchovies). Then we come to an intersection; to associate it with tomatoes, we can imagine an overturned vegetable truck with tomatoes splattered everywhere. Next we

come to a bicycle shop and create an image of a bicyclist eating a banana. Finally, we reach the library and associate it with bread by imagining a huge loaf of bread serving as a canopy under which we must pass to enter. To re-create the list, we need only take an imaginary walk down this path, reviving the association for each location. This technique works well even with very much longer lists; all we need is more locations. There is considerable evidence (e.g., Christen & Bjork, 1976) that the same loci can be used over and over again in the learning of different lists.

Two important principles underlie this method's effectiveness. First, the technique imposes organization on an otherwise unorganized list. We are guaranteed that if we follow the mental path at the time of recall, we will pass all the locations for which we created associations. The second principle is that imagining connections between the locations and the items forces us to process the material meaningfully, elaboratively, and with visual imagery.

(Ataspix/Alamy.)

organizers" (Ausubel, 1968), questions to think about before reading the text, and were asked to find answers to these questions as they read the text. Trying to answer the questions should have forced them to process the text more carefully and to think about its implications. The other group (a control group) simply read the text. The advance-organizer group answered 64% of the test questions correctly, whereas the control group answered only 57% correctly. The questions in the test were either relevant or irrelevant to the advance organizers. For instance, a test question about an event that precipitated America's entry into World War II would be considered relevant if the advance questions directed participants to learn why America entered the war. The same test question would be considered irrelevant if the advance questions only directed participants to learn about the economic consequences of World War II. The advance-organizer group correctly answered 76% percent of the relevant questions and 52% of the irrelevant ones. Thus, they did only slightly worse than the control group on topics for which they had been given only irrelevant advance questions but did much better on topics for which they had been given relevant advance questions.

Many college study-skills departments, as well as private firms, offer courses designed to improve students' memory for text material. These courses teach study techniques mainly for texts such as those used in the social sciences, not for the denser texts used in the physical sciences and mathematics or for literary materials such as novels. The study techniques from different courses are rather similar, and their success has been fairly well documented. One example of such a study technique is the PQ4R method (Thomas & Robinson, 1972). (Implications 1.1 describes a slight variation on this technique as a method for studying this book.)

The PQ4R method derives its name from the six phases it advocates for studying a chapter in a textbook:

1. *Preview.* Survey the chapter to determine the general topics being discussed. Identify the sections to be read as units. Apply steps 2 through 5 to each such section.

2. *Questions.* Make up one or more questions about each section. Often, simply transforming a section heading results in a relevant question (e.g., the heading of this section could be transformed to "What are some techniques for studying textual material?").

3. *Read.* Read each section carefully, trying to answer the questions you have made up about it.

4. *Reflect.* Reflect on the text as you are reading it. Try to understand it, to think of examples, and to relate the material to your prior knowledge.

5. *Recite.* After finishing a section, try to recall the information in it. If you cannot recall enough, reread the portions you had trouble remembering. Try again to answer the questions you made up for the section.

6. *Review.* After you have finished the chapter, go through it mentally, recalling its main points. Again try to answer the questions you made up.

The central features of the PQ4R technique are the generation and answering of questions. There is reason to think that the most important aspect of these features is that they encourage deeper and more elaborative processing of the text material. This point is supported by the results of the Frase (1975) experiment discussed at the beginning of this section: Reading a text with a set of advance questions in mind is beneficial in answering test items related to the questions.

An important aspect of such techniques is testing one's memory rather than simply studying the material. As Marsh and Butler (2013) review, memory researchers for over a century have documented that testing one's memory results in substantial improvement in retention, but only recently has the educational importance of this research been emphasized. In one demonstration, Roediger and Karpicke (2006) had participants study prose pages from the reading comprehension section of a test-preparation book for the Test of English as a Foreign Language. After studying a passage from the book for 7 minutes, participants were either given a 7-minute opportunity to study the passage and answer the questions or given an equal 7 minutes to just recall the passage. Then a retention test was given after various delays. **Figure 6.17** shows that there was little difference in retention when the test was given after a delay of just 5 minutes but that, as the delay increased, there was an increasing advantage for the group that spent the second 7 minutes testing their memory for the passage. If you are like many other students, you will study for a test by rereading the material (Karpicke, Butler, & Roediger, 2009). However, results like these suggest that you should consider inserting a self-test into your study regimen.

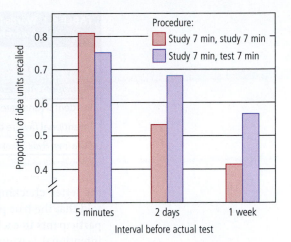

Figure 6.17 Self-testing Improves Recall of Textual Material. These results from Roediger and Karpicke (2006) show that self-testing improves long-term recall of idea units. *(Data from Roediger & Karpicke, 2006.)*

> *Study techniques that involve generating and answering questions lead to better memory for text material.*

Incidental Versus Intentional Learning

So far, we have talked about factors that affect memory. Now we will turn to a factor that does not affect memory, despite people's intuitions to the contrary: It does not seem to matter whether people intend to learn material; what is important is how they process it. This fact is illustrated in an experiment by Hyde and Jenkins (1973) in which participants were asked to perform what was called an *orienting task* while studying a list of 24 words. For one group of participants, the orienting task was to check whether each word had an *e* or a *g* in it. For the other group, the task was to rate the pleasantness of each word on a five-point scale. It is reasonable to assume that the pleasantness rating involved more meaningful and deeper processing than

TABLE 6.3 Words Recalled as a Function of Orienting Task and Participant Awareness That True Learning Purpose Was to Recall Words

Participant Awareness	Words Recalled (%)	
	Orienting Task: Rate Pleasantness	Orienting Task: Check Letters
Incidental (unaware of learning purpose)	68	39
Intentional (aware of learning purpose)	69	43

(Data from Hyde & Jenkins, 1973.)

the letter-checking task. Another variable was whether participants were told that the true purpose of the experiment was to learn the words. Half the participants in each group were told the true purpose of the experiment (the intentional-learning condition). The other half of participants in each group thought the true purpose of the experiment was to rate the words or check for letters (the incidental-learning condition). Thus, there were four conditions: pleasantness–intentional, pleasantness–incidental, letter checking–intentional, and letter checking–incidental.

After completing their task, the participants in each condition were asked to recall as many words as they could. **Table 6.3** presents the results from this experiment in terms of percentage of the 24 words recalled. Two results are noteworthy. First, participants' knowledge of the true purpose of studying the words had relatively little effect on performance. Second, a large depth-of-processing effect was demonstrated; that is, participants showed much better recall in the pleasantness-rating condition versus the letter-checking condition. In rating a word for pleasantness, participants had to think about its meaning — that is, process the word elaboratively.

The Hyde and Jenkins (1973) experiment illustrates an important finding that has been proved over and over again in the research on intentional versus incidental learning: Whether a person intends to learn or not really does not matter (see Postman, 1964, for a review of the old literature). What matters is how the person processes the material during its presentation. If one engages in identical mental activities when processing the material, one gets identical memory performance, regardless of whether one is intending to learn the material or not. People do typically show better memory when they intend to learn because they are likely to engage in activities more conducive to good memory, such as rehearsal and elaborative processing. The small advantage for participants in the intentional-learning conditions of the Hyde and Jenkins experiment may reflect some small variation in processing. Experiments in which great care is taken to control processing find that intention to learn (or, equivalently, the amount of motivation to learn) has no effect (see Nelson, 1976).

There is an interesting everyday example of the relationship (or lack of relationship) between intention to learn and type of processing. Many students claim they find it easier to remember material from a novel, which they are not trying to remember, than from a textbook, which they are trying to remember. The reason is that students typically find it much easier to elaborate on a novel, because novels invite such elaborations (e.g., Why did the suspect deny knowing the victim?).

> *Type of processing, and not whether one intends to learn, determines the amount of material remembered.*

Flashbulb Memories

Although it does not appear that intention to learn affects memory, a different question is whether people display better memory for events that are important to them? One class of research involves **flashbulb memory** — memory for events so important that they seem to burn themselves permanently into our minds. Brown and Kulik (1977) coined the term *flashbulb memory* in a discussion of memory reports about the assassination of President John F. Kennedy in 1963, a traumatic event of major importance to Americans at that time. They found that most people still had vivid memories of the event 13 years later, and they proposed that people have a special biological mechanism guaranteeing memory of particularly important events. This interpretation of their result is problematic, however, because Brown and Kulik were not able to assess the accuracy of the reported memories.

Since the Brown and Kulik proposal, a number of studies have been done to determine what participants remembered about a traumatic event immediately after it occurred and what they remembered later. For instance, McCloskey, Wible, and Cohen (1988) did a study involving the 1986 space shuttle *Challenger* explosion. At that time, many people felt that this was a particularly traumatic event they had watched with horror on television. McCloskey et al. interviewed participants 1 week after the event and then again 9 months later. Nine months after the accident, one participant reported:

> When I first heard about the explosion I was sitting in my freshman dorm room with my roommate and we were watching TV. It came on a news flash and we were both totally shocked. I was really upset and I went upstairs to talk to a friend of mine and then I called my parents. (Neisser & Harsch, 1992, p. 9)

McCloskey et al. found that although participants reported vivid memories 9 months after the event, their memories were often inaccurate. For instance, the participant just quoted had actually learned about the *Challenger* explosion in class a day after it happened and had then watched it on television.

Palmer, Schreiber, and Fox (1991) came to a somewhat different conclusion in a study of memories of the 1989 San Francisco earthquake. They compared participants who had experienced the earthquake firsthand with those who had only watched it on TV. Those who had experienced it in person showed much superior long-term memory of the event. Conway et al. (1994) argued that McCloskey et al. (1988) failed to find a memory advantage in the *Challenger* study because their participants did not have true flashbulb memories. They contended that flashbulb memories are produced only if an event is consequential to the individual remembering it. That explains why only people who actually experienced the San Francisco earthquake, and not those who saw it on TV, had flashbulb memories of the event. Conway et al. studied memory for Margaret Thatcher's resignation as prime minister of the United Kingdom in 1990. They compared participants from the United Kingdom, the United States, and Denmark, all of whom had followed news reports of the resignation. It turned out that 11 months later, 60% of the participants from the United Kingdom showed perfect memory for the events surrounding the resignation, whereas only 20% of those who did not live in the United Kingdom showed perfect memory. Conway et al. argued that this was because the Thatcher resignation was really consequential only for the U.K. participants.

On September 11, 2001, Americans suffered a particularly traumatic event, the terrorist attacks that have come to be known simply as "9/11." Hirst et al. (2015) report a very extensive study of memory for the events of 9/11, involving over 3,000 individuals from seven American cities. They conducted four surveys: 1 week after the attack, 11 months later, 35 months later, and 10 years later. **Table 6.4** shows that there was some loss of memory for the principal events over the 10-year period but that people were still 80% correct 10 years later. Table 6.4 also shows that memory for the relatively minor fact

	Facts Recalled Correctly (%)			
Fact	Survey date: Sept. 17–21, 2001	Survey date: Aug. 5–26, 2002	Survey date: Aug. 9–20, 2004	Survey date: Aug. 1–15, 2011
Number of planes	95	89	86	88
Airline names	88	75	54	55
Crash sites	95	94	90	90
Order of events	89	89	83	89
Location of President Bush	90	60	85	83
Saw Michael Moore's film	90	59	90	87
Did not see film	90	62	80	83
Overall	91	80	81	81

TABLE 6.4 Accuracy of Memories for Facts about 9/11

(Data from Hirst et al., 2015.)

of where President Bush was during the attack dropped substantially from the first to the second survey but then jumped up on the third survey. As the table suggests, a possible explanation for this memory pattern is whether the participants had seen Michael Moore's film *Fahrenheit 911*, which had been released during the interval between Survey 2 and Survey 3. The film features the fact that Bush was reading a storybook to children in a Florida elementary school at the time. Those participants who saw the movie showed an especially strong boost on the third survey in their ability to remember the location of President Bush. Hirst et al. (2009) tracked the reporting of 9/11 events in the media and found that this factor had a strong influence on people's memory for the events. They also found a relationship between how much people remembered and how often they talked about specific events.

The term "flashbulb memories" is sometimes reserved just for memories of the personal details surrounding where and how one learned about an important event. Hirst et al. (2015) obtained participants' reports about this information right after 9/11 and then again in later surveys, by asking the following six questions:

1. How did you first learn about it (what was the source of the information)?
2. Where were you?
3. What were you doing?
4. How did you feel when you first became aware of the attack?
5. Who was the first person with whom you communicated about the attack?
6. What were you doing immediately before you became aware of the attack?

On later surveys, participants answered only about 60% of these questions with the same answers they gave immediately after the event. Interestingly, they became increasingly consistent in the different answers they gave. So for instance, in response to the question of where they were (question 2), one participant gave the following answers in the four surveys:

Survey 1: Kitchen, making breakfast
Survey 2: In dorm room, folding laundry
Survey 3: Ironing in dorm room
Survey 4; In dorm room, ironing

It seems that this participant had come to believe the wrong answer first given in the second survey. The inaccurate reports for such personal details contrast with the highly accurate reports of information like the order of the events, information that is repeatedly given accurately by the media and other sources. Basically, flashbulb memories behave like other memories — they reflect what is practiced, either to ourselves or by external sources.

> *People report having better memories for particularly important events, but these memories seem no different than other memories.*

Conclusions

This chapter has focused on the processes involved in getting information into memory. We saw that a great deal of information gets registered in sensory memory, but relatively little can be maintained in short-term or working memory and even less survives for long periods of time. However, an analysis of what actually gets stored in long-term memory really needs to consider how that information is retained and retrieved — which is the topic of the next chapter. Many of the issues considered in this chapter are complicated by retrieval issues. This is certainly true for the effects of elaborative processing that we have just discussed. There are important interactions between how a memory is processed at study and how it is processed at test. Even in this chapter, we were not able to discuss the effects of such factors as practice without discussing the activation-based retrieval processes that are facilitated by these factors. Chapter 7 will also have more to say about the activation of memories.

Questions for Thought

1. Many people write notes on their bodies to remember things like phone numbers. In the movie *Memento*, Leonard tattoos information that he wants to remember on his body. Describe instances where storing information on the body works like sensory memory, where it is like working memory, and where it is like long-term memory.

2. The discussion of Kaplan (1989) mentions a colleague of mine who was stuck solving the riddle, "What goes up a chimney down but can't come down a chimney up?" How would you have seeded the environment to subconsciously prime a solution to the riddle? To see what Kaplan did, read Anderson (2007, pp. 93–94).

3. Figures 6.12 and 6.13 show how participants' memories improve when they practice facts many times. Can you describe situations in your schooling where this sort of practice improved your memory for facts?

4. Think of the most traumatic events you have experienced. How have you rehearsed and elaborated upon memories about these events? What influence might such rehearsal and elaboration have on these memories? Could rehearsal and elaboration cause you to remember things that did not happen?

Key Terms

activation	flashbulb memories	phonological loop	strength
articulatory process	long-term potentiation (LTP)	phonological store	visual sensory store
auditory sensory store		power function	visuospatial sketchpad
central executive	memory span	power law of learning	whole-report procedure
depth of processing	method of loci	short-term memory	working memory
elaborative processing	partial-report procedure	spreading activation	

Human Memory: Retention and Retrieval

Popular fiction sometimes includes a protagonist who is unable to recall some critical information — either because of a head injury or because of repression due to a traumatic experience, or just because the passage of time has seemed to erase the memory. The critical event in the story occurs when the protagonist is able to recover the memory — perhaps because of hypnosis, clinical treatment, returning to an old context, or (particularly improbable) sustaining another head injury. Although our everyday struggles with our memory are seldom so dramatic, we all have had experiences with memories that are just on the edge of availability. For instance, try remembering the name of someone who sat beside you in class in grade school or the name of a grade school teacher. Often, we can picture the person but struggle to retrieve the person's name — a struggle at which we may or may not succeed. This chapter will answer the following questions:

- How does memory for information fade with the passage of time?
- How do other memories interfere with the retrieval of a desired memory?
- How can other memories support the retrieval of a desired memory?
- How does a person's internal and external context influence the retrieval of a memory?
- How can our past experiences influence our behavior without our being able to recall these experiences?
- What role do temporal (and particularly hippocampal) regions of the brain play in memory?

Are Memories Really Forgotten?

Figure 7.1 identifies the prefrontal and temporal structures that have proved important in studies of memory (see Figure 6.1 for a different view of these regions). An early study on the role of the temporal cortex in memory seemed to provide evidence that forgotten memories are still there even though we cannot retrieve them. As part of a neurosurgical procedure, Penfield (1959) electrically stimulated portions of patients' brains and asked them to report what they experienced (patients were conscious during the surgery, but the stimulation was painless). In this way, Penfield determined the functions of various portions of the brain. Stimulation of the temporal lobes led to reports of memories that patients were unable to report in normal recall, such as events from childhood. This seemed to provide evidence that much of what seems forgotten is still stored in memory. Unfortunately, it is hard to know whether the patients' memory reports were accurate — that is, whether the reported events actually occurred. Therefore, although suggestive, the Penfield experiments are generally discounted by memory researchers.

A better experiment, conducted by Nelson (1971), also indicated that forgotten memories still exist. He had participants learn a list of 20 paired associates, each consisting of a number for which the participant had to recall a noun (e.g., *43-dog*). The subjects studied the list and were tested on it until they could recall all the items without error. Participants returned for a retest 2 weeks later and were able to recall 75% of the associated nouns when cued with the numbers. However, the research question concerned the 25% that they could no longer recall — were these items really forgotten? Participants were given new learning trials on the 20 paired associates. The paired associates they had missed were either kept the same or changed. For example, participants who had learned *43-dog* but failed to recall the response *dog* to *43* might now be trained on either *43-dog* (unchanged) or *43-house* (changed).

Figure 7.1 Brain Structures Involved in the Creation and Storage of Memories. Prefrontal regions are responsible for the creation of memories. The hippocampus and surrounding structures in the temporal cortex are responsible for the permanent storage of these memories.

Brain Structures

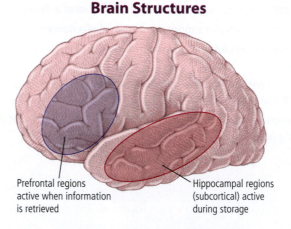

Prefrontal regions active when information is retrieved

Hippocampal regions (subcortical) active during storage

Participants were tested after studying the new list once. If the participants had lost all memory for the forgotten pairs, there should have been no difference between recall of changed and unchanged pairs. However, participants correctly recalled 78% of the unchanged items formerly missed, but only 43% of the changed items. This large advantage for unchanged items indicates that participants had retained some memory of the original paired associates, even though they had been unable to recall them initially.

Johnson, McDuff, Rugg, and Norman (2009) report a brain-imaging study that also shows that there are records of experiences in our brain that we can no longer remember. Participants saw a list of words and, for each word, were asked either to imagine how an artist would draw the object denoted by the word or to imagine uses for the object. The researchers trained a pattern classifier (a program for analyzing patterns of brain activity, as discussed in Implications 4.1) to distinguish between words assigned to the artist task and words assigned to the uses task, based on differences in brain activity during the two tasks. Later, the classifier was applied to participants' brain activation patterns while they were shown the words again and asked to recall the type of task they had assigned to each word. The classifier was able to recognize from these patterns what task the word had been assigned to with better than chance accuracy. It was successful at recognition both for words that participants could recall studying and for words they could not remember, although the accuracy was somewhat lower for the words they could not remember. This indicates that even though we may have no conscious memory of something, aspects of how we experienced it may be retained in our brains.

These experiments do not prove that everything is remembered. They show only that appropriately sensitive tests can find evidence for remnants of some memories that appear to have been forgotten. In this chapter, we will discuss first how memories become less available with time, then some of the factors that determine our success in retrieving these memories.

> *Even when people appear to have forgotten memories, there is evidence that they still have some of these memories stored.*

The Retention Function

The processes by which memories become less available are extremely regular, and psychologists have studied their mathematical form. Wickelgren did early, systematic research on memory retention functions, and his data are still used today. In one recognition experiment (Wickelgren, 1975), he presented participants with a sequence of words to study and then examined the probability of their recognizing the words after delays ranging from 1 min to 14 days. **Figure 7.2** shows performance as a function of delay. The performance measure Wickelgren used is called d' (pronounced d-prime), which is derived from the probability of recognition. Wickelgren interpreted d' as a measure of memory strength.

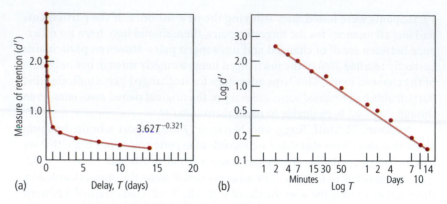

(a) Delay, *T* (days) (b)

Figure 7.2 Results from Wickelgren's (1975) Experiment on Memory Retention.
(a) Success at word recognition, as measured by *d′*, as a function of delay *T*. (b) The data
in (a) replotted on logarithmic scales. *(Data from Wickelgren, 1975.)*

Figure 7.2 shows that this measure of memory systematically deteriorates with delay. However, the memory loss is *negatively accelerated* — that is,
the rate of change gets smaller and smaller as the delay increases. Figure 7.2b
replots the data as the logarithm *d′* versus the logarithm of delay. Marvelously,
the function becomes linear:

$$\log d' = A - b \log T$$

where *A* is the value of the function at 1 min [$\log(1) = 0$] and *b* is the slope of
the function in Figure 7.2b ($= 0.321$ in this case).

This equation can be transformed to

$$d' = cT^{-b}$$

where $c = 10^A$ ($= 3.62$ in this case). Such a functional relationship is called a
power function because the independent variable (the delay *T* in this case)
is raised to a power ($-b$ in this case) to produce the performance measure
(*d′* in this case). In a review of research on forgetting, Wixted and Ebbesen
(1991) concluded that retention functions are generally power functions. This
relationship is called the **power law of forgetting.** Recall from Chapter 6 that
there is also a power law of learning: Both power functions are negatively
accelerated, but with an important difference: Whereas the practice functions
associated with the power law of learning show diminishing improvement
with practice (see Figure 6.12), the retention functions associated with the
power law of forgetting show diminishing loss with delay (see Figure 7.2).

A very extensive investigation of the negative acceleration in retention functions was produced by Bahrick (1984), who looked at participants' retention of
English–Spanish vocabulary items anywhere from immediately to 50 years after

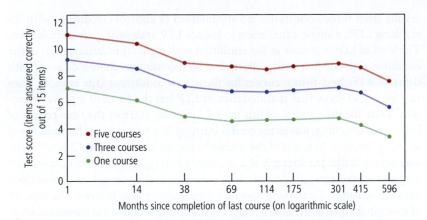

Figure 7.3 Results from Bahrick's (1984) Experiment Measuring Retention of English–Spanish Vocabulary Items over Various Time Periods. The number of items correctly recalled out of a total of 15 items is plotted as a function of the logarithm of the time since course completion. *(Data from Bahrick, 1984.)*

they had completed courses in high school and college. **Figure 7.3** plots the number of items correctly recalled out of a total of 15 items as a function of the logarithm of the time since course completion. Separate functions are plotted for students who had one, three, or five courses. The data show a slow decay of memory combined with a substantial practice effect (the greater the number of courses, the better the recall, regardless of time since completion). In Bahrick's data, the retention functions are nearly flat between 3 and 25 years (as would be predicted by a power function), with some further drop-off from 25 to 50 years (which is more rapid than would be predicted by a power function). Bahrick (personal communication, circa 1993) suspects that this final drop-off is probably related to memory deterioration associated with old age.

There is some evidence that the explanation for these retention functions may be found in the associated neural processes. In Chapter 6, we saw that long-term potentiation (LTP, an increase in neural responsiveness that occurs as a reaction to prior electrical stimulation) mirrors the power law of learning (see Figure 6.14). Raymond and Redman (2006) found a decrease in LTP in the rat hippocampus with delay after electrical stimulation. **Figure 7.4** shows their

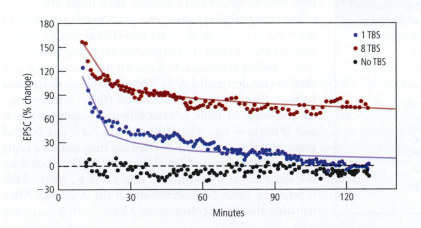

Figure 7.4 Neural Forgetting Mirrors Behavioral Forgetting. At 10 minutes in this experiment, Raymond and Redman (2006) stimulated rats' hippocampus with 1 or 8 theta-burst stimulations (TBS). The decrease in ESPC (excitatory postsynaptic current—a measure of LTP) with delay (the two lines represent the best-fitting power functions) mirrors the decline in memory with delay (e.g., the power function in Figure 7.2a). The "No TBS" results represent a control condition that received no stimulation.

results from three conditions: no stimulation (a control condition, with no resulting LTP), a single stimulation to induce LTP, and eight such stimulations. The level of LTP is greater in the condition with eight stimulations than in the condition with one (a learning effect), but both conditions show a drop-off with delay, and the best-fitting curves for those two conditions (the smooth lines in Figure 7.4) show that maintenance of LTP has the form of a power function. Thus, the time course of this neural forgetting mirrors the time course of behavioral forgetting, just as the neural learning function mirrors the behavioral learning function. In terms of the strength concept introduced in Chapter 6, the assumption is that the strength of a memory decays with time. The data on LTP suggest that this strength decay involves changes in the strength of connections between synapses. Thus, there may be a direct relationship between the concept of strength defined at the behavioral level and strength defined at the neural level.

The idea that memories simply decay in strength with time is one of the common explanations of forgetting; it is called the **decay theory** of forgetting. In the next section, we will review one of the major competitors of this theory.

> The strength of a memory decays as a power function of the period of time over which it is retained.

How Interference Affects Memory

The discussion to this point might lead one to infer that the only factor affecting loss of memories is the passage of time. However, it turns out that retention is strongly impacted by another factor, interfering material — this is the **interference theory** of forgetting. Much of the original research on interference investigated how learning a list of paired associates would affect memory for a previously learned list. **Table 7.1** illustrates paired-associates lists made up by associating nouns as stimuli to two-digit numbers as responses. While various experiments will involve many sorts of pairings besides nouns and numbers, such items are typical of the rather arbitrary associates participants are asked to learn. As in the table, there are two critical groups, experimental and control. The experimental group learns two lists of paired associates, first the list designated A–B and then the list designated A–D. These lists are so designated because they share common stimuli (the A terms — e.g., *cat* and *house* in Table 7.1) but different responses (the B and D terms — e.g., *43* and *82* in Table 7.1). The control group also first studies the A–B list but then studies a completely different second list, designated C–D, which does not share any stimuli with the first list (e.g., none of the C terms in Table 7.1 matches any of the A terms). After learning their respective second lists, both groups are

TABLE 7.1 Sample Paired-Associates Lists in a Typical Interference Experiment	
Experimental Group	*Control Group*
Learn A–B	*Learn A–B*
cat-43	cat-43
house-61	house-61
apple-29	apple-29
etc.	etc.
Learn A–D	*Learn C–D*
cat-82	bone-82
house-37	cup-37
apple-45	chair-45
etc.	etc.

retested for memory of their first list (the same A–B list in both cases). Often, this retention test is administered after a considerable delay, such as 24 hours or a week. In general, the experimental group, which learns the A–D list, does not do as well as the control group, which learns the C–D list: The experimental group shows both a slower rate of learning of the second list and poorer retention of the original A–B list (see Keppel, 1968, for a review). Such experiments provide evidence that learning the A–D list interferes with retention of the A–B list, causing it to be forgotten more rapidly.

More generally, research has shown that it is difficult to maintain multiple associations to the same items. It is harder both to learn new associations to old items and to retain the old ones if new associations are learned. These results might seem to have rather a dismal implication for our ability to remember information: that it would become increasingly difficult to learn new information about a concept — for example, every time we learned a new fact about a friend, we would be in danger of forgetting an old fact about that person. Fortunately, there are important additional factors that counteract such interference. Before discussing these factors, however, we need to examine in more detail the basis for interference effects. It turns out that a rather different experimental paradigm has been helpful in identifying the cause of those effects.

> *Learning additional associations to an item can cause old ones to be forgotten.*

The Fan Effect: Networks of Associations

The interference effects discussed above can be understood in terms of how much activation spreads to stimulate a memory structure (refer back to the activation equation in Chapter 6). The basic idea is that when participants are presented with a stimulus such as *cat,* activation will spread from this source stimulus to all of its associated memory structures. However, the total amount of activation that can spread from a source is limited; thus, the greater the number of associated memory structures, the less the amount of activation that will spread to any one structure.

In one of my dissertation studies illustrating these ideas (Anderson, 1974), I asked participants to memorize 26 sentences of the form a-person-is-in-a-location, like the four example sentences listed below. As you can see from these examples, some persons were paired with only one location (1–1 and 1–2) and some locations with only one person (1–1 and 2–1), whereas other persons were paired with two locations (2–1 and 2–2) and other locations with two persons (1–2 and 2–2):

1. The doctor is in the bank. (1–1)
2. The fireman is in the park. (1–2)
3. The lawyer is in the church. (2–1)
4. The lawyer is in the park. (2–2)

TABLE 7.2 Recognition of Studied Sentences When Presented with Re-paired Sentences	
Sentence Type	*Recognition Time (s)*
1–1 (person appears in 1 studied sentence, location appears in 1 studied sentence)	1.11
1–2 (person appears in 1 studied sentence, location appears in 2 studied sentences)	1.17
2–1 (person appears in 2 studied sentences, location appears in 1 studied sentence)	1.17
2–2 (person appears in 2 studied sentences, location appears in 2 studied sentences)	1.22
(Data from Anderson, 1974.)	

Participants were drilled on 26 sentences like these until they knew the material well. Then participants were presented with a set of test sentences that consisted of studied sentences mixed in with new sentences created by re-pairing people and locations from the study set, and participants had to recognize the sentences from the study set.

The recognition times displayed in **Table 7.2** show that recognition time increases as a function of the sum of the two numbers used to classify the example sentences above — that is, sentences that could be labeled 1–1 are fastest to be recognized (sum of associations = 2), sentences that could be labeled 1–2 or 2–1 are next fastest (sum of associations = 3), and sentences that could be labeled 2–2 are slowest (sum of associations = 4). The increase in recognition time from fastest to slowest is not much more than a hundred milliseconds $(1.22 \, s \, – \, 1.11 \, s \, = \, 0.11 \, s \, = \, 110$ milliseconds$)$, but such effects can add up in situations like taking a test under time pressure: Taking a little more time to answer each question could mean not finishing the test.

These interference effects — that is, the increases in recognition time — can be explained in terms of activation spreading through network structures, like the network structure in **Figure 7.5**, which represents the four example sentences above. According to the spreading-activation theory, recognizing a sentence (i.e., retrieving the memory of that sentence) would involve the following discrete steps:

1. Presentation of a sentence activates the representations of the concepts in the sentence. In Figure 7.5, the concepts are *doctor, lawyer, fireman, bank, church,* and *park,* which are each associated with either one or two of the four sentences.

2. Activation spreads from these source concepts to memory structures representing the associated sentences. In Figure 7.5, the ovals represent these memory structures, and the arrows represent the activation pathways from the concepts. However, as noted above, the total amount of activation that can spread from a source is limited. This means,

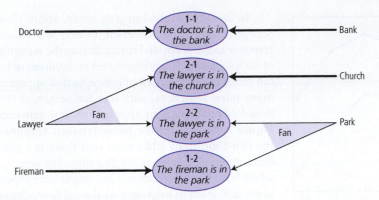

Figure 7.5 How Spreading Activation Works. The ovals are the memory structures of the sentences to be remembered (from Anderson, 1974). Each memory structure is labeled with the number of associations of the person and location in the sentence — e.g., in the 2–1 sentence, the person (*lawyer*) has 2 associations and the place (*church*) has 1 association. The sources of activation are the concepts *doctor, lawyer, fireman, bank, church,* and *park;* the arrows represent the activation pathways; and the thickness of each arrow represents the amount of activation along that pathway.

for example, that each of the two pathways from *lawyer* carries less activation than the single pathway from *doctor.* In Figure 7.5, the thickness of each arrow represents the amount of activation it carries.

3. As activation spreading down the pathways converges on the memory structures, the memory structures are activated to various levels. These activations sum to produce an overall level of activation of the memory structure. Because of the limitation on the total activation from any one source, a memory structure's activation level is inversely related to the sum of associations of the source concepts.

4. A sentence is recognized in an amount of time that is inversely related to the activation level of its memory structure — that is, the greater the activation level, the less time required to retrieve the memory and recognize the sentence. Or, to put it in terms of associations, the greater the number of associations of the source concepts, the more time required to recognize the sentence.

So, given a structure like that shown in Figure 7.5, participants should be slower to recognize the sentence involving *lawyer* and *park* than the one involving *doctor* and *bank* (as is the case in Table 7.2) because more paths emanate from the first set of concepts. That is, in the *lawyer* and *park* case, two paths point from each of the concepts to the two sentences in which each was studied, whereas only one path leads from each of the *doctor* and *bank* concepts. The increase in reaction time related to an increase in the number of memory structures associated with a concept is called the **fan effect.** It is so named because the increase in reaction time is related to an increase in the fan of activations emanating from the network representation of the concept (see the fans in Figure 7.5).

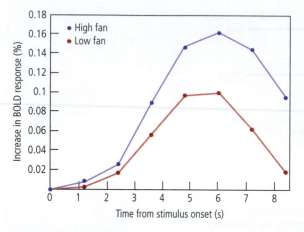

Figure 7.6 Hemodynamic Response in the Prefrontal Cortex During Retrieval of Low-Fan vs. High-Fan Sentences. The increase in BOLD response is plotted against the time from stimulus onset. The greater response for high-fan sentences reflects the greater amount of mental work required to retrieve them from memory.

(Data from Sohn et al., 2003.)

In an fMRI brain-imaging study, Sohn, Goode, Stenger, Carter, and Anderson (2003) looked at the response in the prefrontal cortex during the recognition of such sentences. They contrasted recognition of high-fan sentences (composed of concepts that appeared in many other sentences) with low-fan sentences (composed of concepts that appeared in few sentences). **Figure 7.6** compares the hemodynamic response in the two conditions and shows that there is a greater hemodynamic response for the high-fan sentences, which have lower activation. One might have expected lower activation to map onto weakened hemodynamic response. However, the prefrontal structures must work harder to retrieve memories with lower activation. As we will see throughout the later chapters of this text, in which we look at higher mental processes like problem solving, more difficult conditions are associated with higher metabolic expenditures, reflecting the greater mental work required under more difficult conditions.

> *The more facts associated with a concept, the slower the retrieval of any one of the facts.*

The Interfering Effect of Preexisting Memories

Do such interference effects occur with material learned outside of the laboratory? As one way to address this question, Lewis and Anderson (1976) investigated whether the fan effect could be obtained with material the participant knew before the experiment. We had participants learn fantasy "facts" about public figures, in the form of statements such as *Napoleon Bonaparte was from India*. Participants studied from zero to four such fantasy facts about each public figure. After learning these "facts," they proceeded to a recognition test phase, in which they saw three types of sentences: (1) statements they had studied in the experiment; (2) true statements about the public figures (e.g., *Napoleon Bonaparte was an emperor*); and (3) statements about the public figures that were false in the real world and had not been studied. Participants had to respond to the first two types of statements as true and to the last type as false.

Figure 7.7 presents participants' times in making these judgments as a function of the number (or fan) of the fantasy facts studied about the person. Note that the recognition time increased with the fan for all types of statements. Also note that participants responded much faster to actual true statements than to the fantasy facts they had studied. The advantage of true statements can be explained by the observation that these facts would be much more strongly encoded in memory than the fantasy facts studied. The most important result to note in Figure 7.7 is that the more fantasy facts participants learned about an individual such as Napoleon Bonaparte, the longer they took to recognize a fact that they already knew about the individual (e.g., *Napoleon Bonaparte was an emperor*). This shows that we can produce interference with preexperimental material. (For further research on this topic, see Peterson & Potts, 1982.)

> *Material learned in the laboratory can interfere with material learned outside of the laboratory.*

Both Decay and Interference?

We have discussed two mechanisms that can produce forgetting: decay of memory strength and interference from other memories. There has been some speculation among researchers that what appears to be decay may really reflect interference. That is, the reason memories appear to decay over a retention interval is that they are interfered with by additional memories that the participants have stored. Objections have been raised to decay theories because they do not identify the psychological factors that produce the forgetting but rather just assert that forgetting occurs spontaneously with time. It is possible, however, that there is no explanation of decay at the purely psychological level. The explanation may be physiological, as we saw with respect to the LTP data (see Figure 7.4). Thus, it seems that the best conclusion, given the available data, is that both interference and decay contribute to forgetting (Sadeh, Ozubko, Winocur, & Moscovitch, 2016).

> *Forgetting results both from decay in memory strength and from interference from other memories.*

An Inhibitory Explanation of Forgetting?

A more recent controversy in psychology concerns the issue of whether interference effects are due to an inhibition process that actively suppresses the competing memories rather than being a passive side effect of storing and strengthening memories. The inhibition account has been championed by Michael Anderson (e.g., Anderson, 2003). Evidence for this account comes from a variety of paradigms that show that trying to retrieve certain items causes others to be forgotten. For instance, participants might learn a list of category–exemplar pairs where there are multiple instances of the same category. After the initial study, participants are given practice on only some of the pairs studied; then they are given a recall test in which they see the category names and have to recall all the instances they studied. For example, pairs such as the four below might be studied (among others), followed by practice on *Red–Blood* but not on the other three pairs, followed by a recall

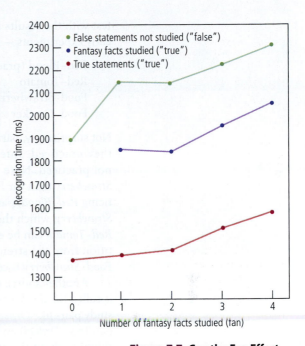

Figure 7.7 Can the Fan Effect Be Obtained Using Already Known Material? In Lewis and Anderson (1976), participants studied 0–4 fantasy "facts" about public figures and then saw a mix of those statements, true statements about the public figures, and false statements about them that they had not studied. The task was to respond "true" to the first two types of statements and "false" to the last type. Participants' recognition times are plotted as a function of the number (or fan) of the fantasy facts studied. The time participants took to make all three judgments increased as they learned more fantasy facts. *(Data from Lewis and Anderson, 1976.)*

test with the results shown in parentheses (these results are from one of the early experiments — Anderson & Spellman, 1995):

Red–Blood (practiced)   (74% correct recall)
Red–Tomato   (22% correct recall)
Food–Strawberry   (22% correct recall)
Food–Cracker   (36% correct recall)

Not surprisingly, participants showed the highest recall for *Red–Blood,* which they practiced. Interest focuses on recall of the other pairs, which were not practiced. Note that recall was lower for both *Red–Tomato* and *Food–Strawberry* than for *Food–Cracker.* Michael Anderson argues that while practicing *Red–Blood,* participants were inhibiting all other red things, including *Strawberry,* which they did not even study as a red thing. The lower recall for *Red–Tomato* can be explained by other types of interference, such as competition from the strengthened *Red–Blood* association, but the lower recall of *Food-Strawberry* is considered evidence for the inhibition account.

Another source of evidence for the inhibition account comes from what is called the *think/no-think paradigm* (Anderson & Green, 2001). Participants study pairs like *Ordeal–Roach.* Then they are presented with the first item in a pair (e.g., *Ordeal*) and asked either to think about the response or to suppress thinking about the other item in the pair (e.g., *Roach*). Participants are then tested with a probe like *Insect–R,* where their task is to produce a word from the pairs studied that is associated to the first term (*Insect*) and that begins with the given first letter (*Roach* in this example). Participants are less likely to recall the target word (*Roach*) if they have been suppressing it.

Unfortunately for the purposes of presenting firm conclusions, there have been a number of recent critiques of this research (e.g., Raaijmakers & Jakab, 2013; Verde, 2012). Other researchers sometimes can replicate these results but oftentimes cannot. Much effort has been put into trying to elucidate the cause of this mixed empirical picture. One idea that has emerged is that the occurrence of these "inhibition" effects may be the result of unobserved strategies used by participants. For instance, in the think/no-think paradigm, participants may think of some other insect to prevent themselves from thinking of *Roach.* In the first experiment we discussed, when subjects are given the stimulus *Food,* they might be tempted to respond with items associated with the category *Red,* because some of the food items were red. Thus, what appears to be the result of inhibition of a response item like *Roach* or *Strawberry* may actually be the result of competition from other, implicit stimuli generated by the participant's strategy. Such strategies could vary with many factors, and this strategy variation could explain the inconsistent results. There is some evidence for the existence of such covert strategies (e.g., Camp, Pecher, & Schmidt, 2005), although the evidence has been disputed (see Huddleston & Anderson, 2012).

In some ways retrieval-induced suppression is not a new idea. It hearkens back to Freud, who argued that we suppress unpleasant memories.

Freud's hypothesis was thought to apply only to highly emotional memories, and even there it is controversial (see the later section of this chapter on the false memory controversy). Freud's original account of the mechanisms that produced suppressed memories is not generally accepted. One of the criticisms of current inhibition ideas is that proponents have not described mechanisms that might produce such inhibition. This is similar to the criticisms of decay theory for not describing mechanisms that might produce the decay. (Regardless of the exact mechanisms behind forgetting, there is evidence that forgetting itself may be adaptive from an evolutionary standpoint — see **Implications 7.1** for discussion of this idea.)

It has been argued that forgetting may also be produced by active inhibition (suppression) of memories, but the evidence is inconclusive.

Implications 7.1

Is Forgetting Adaptive?

We tend to view the fact we forget things as an annoying feature of our brains. However, Schooler and Anderson (2017) argue that forgetting is actually quite adaptive. That argument begins with the observation that it is impossible for any physical system to store everything. Libraries throughout history have had only so much space for books (or, before books, for scrolls), meaning that hard decisions had to be made about what to keep and what to discard (Agee & Naper, 2007). Likewise, there is only so much storage available in the human brain. Even in the current digital age, with the immense storage capacity available, there are limits. For instance, in response to the search query "cognitive psychology," Google reports that it has millions of related results. However, if you explore those results, you will find that only a few hundred pages are available. The strength of search engines is that they make the best results available — users do not go beyond the first page of results for 94% of all searches (Buddenbrock, 2016).

Likewise, human memory makes some information much more available than other information. While we might struggle to remember the name of our third grade teacher, we do not have that problem with the name of our significant other, parent, or best friend.

Schooler and Anderson observed that human memory tends to forget what is less useful and tends to make most available what is most useful. For instance, consider the power law of forgetting (see Figure 7.2), describing how the probability of remembering some piece of information decreases with the delay since the information was last recalled. Across a wide range of environments, the longer it has been since we have encountered something, the less likely we are to encounter it again and hence it is less costly to lose memory access to it. The striking observation is that the probability of encountering some person or thing declines as a power function, just like human forgetting. Interestingly, **Figure 7.8** shows that this observation is true of both humans and chimpanzees. Figure 7.8a

(data from Pachur, Schooler, & Stevens, 2014) shows how the probability of meeting someone declines as a function of how long it has been since the last face-to-face meeting. Figure 7.8b (data from Stevens, Marewski, Schooler, & Gilby, 2016) shows that a similar relationship holds for chimpanzee meetings in the wild. In both the human and chimpanzee cases, the rate of decline closely fits a power function like the function for the human law of forgetting. This match between species suggests that the human forgetting function may have been shaped through a long history of evolutionary adaptations, consistent with what we see with respect to long-term potentiation (Figure 7.4).

As another example of the adaptiveness of human memory, Anderson and Schooler review evidence that memories typically need to be accessed in particular contexts. For instance, in the gym the thing I am most likely to need to remember is the combination of the lock on my locker. Fortunately memories do tend to be more available in the context in which they are experienced

Implications 7.1 (*Continued*)

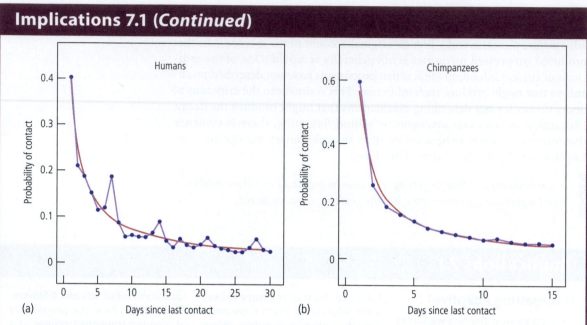

Figure 7.8 Probability of Contact as a Function of Time Since Last Contact. (a) For people going about their daily lives, the probability of a face-to-face encounter with a specific other person declines at a rate that is proportional to the time since the last encounter. *(Data from Pachur et al., 2014, and Stevens et al., 2016.)* (b) The same is true for chimpanzees in the wild encountering a specific other chimpanzee. *(Data from Stevens et al., 2016.)* For both species, the rate of decline in this probability is a power function, like the power function that describes the power law of forgetting. (The smooth curves are the best-fitting power functions.)

(see Figure 7.12). Some cues tend to be associated with particular facts. For instance, my lock is nearly uniquely associated with its combination whereas other cues (like my clothes) are associated with many things. Correspondingly, human memory gives more reliable and more rapid access to memories when cued with items that are uniquely associated with the memory (see Tables 7.1 and 7.2). This kind of context-dependent access is similar to having a web page show up high in the results for a search query when items in the query are found only on that web page.

Relatedness Protects Against Interference

There is a major qualification about the situations in which interference effects are seen: Interference occurs only when one is learning multiple pieces of information that have no intrinsic relationship to one another. In contrast, interference does not occur when the pieces of information are meaningfully related. An experiment by Bradshaw and Anderson (1982) illustrates the contrasting effects of related versus unrelated information. These researchers looked at participants' ability to learn some little-known information about famous people, under three conditions: single, unrelated, and related:

- In the single condition, they had participants study just one fact:

  Newton became emotionally unstable and insecure as a child.

- In the unrelated condition, they had participants learn a target fact about the individual:

  Locke was unhappy as a student at Westminster.

plus two unrelated facts:

  Locke felt fruits were unwholesome for children. Locke had a long history of back trouble.

TABLE 7.3 Recall of Related and Unrelated Information

Condition	Recall of Target Facts (% of participants)	
	Immediately	After 1 Week
Single	92	62
Unrelated	80	45
Related	94	73

(Data from Bradshaw & Anderson, 1982.)

- In the related condition, participants learned a target fact:

  Mozart made a long journey from Munich to Paris.

plus two additional facts that were causally related to the target fact:

  Mozart wanted to leave Munich to avoid a romantic entanglement. Mozart was intrigued by musical developments coming out of Paris.

Participants were then tested for their ability to recall the target facts immediately after studying them and after a week's delay. In each test, they were presented with names such as Newton, Mozart, and Locke and asked to recall what they had studied. **Table 7.3** shows the results in terms of the percentage of participants who recalled the target facts. Comparing the unrelated condition with the single condition, we see the standard interference effect: Recall was worse when there were more facts to be learned about an item. However, the result is quite different when we compare the related condition to the single condition. Here, particularly after a week's delay, recall was better when there were more facts to be learned, presumably because the additional facts were causally related to the target facts.

To understand why the effects of interference are eliminated or even reversed when there is relatedness among the materials to be learned requires that we move on to discussing the retrieval process and, in particular, the role of inferential processes in retrieval.

> *Learning related material does not interfere with retrieval of a target memory and may even facilitate retrieval.*

Retrieval and Inference

Often, when people cannot remember a particular fact, they are able to retrieve related facts and so infer the target fact on the basis of the related facts. For example, in the case of the Mozart facts just discussed, if the participants who could not recall the target fact (that Mozart made a long journey from Munich to Paris) were able to retrieve the other two facts, they might have then been able to infer the target fact. There is considerable evidence that people make such inferences at the time of recall. They seem unaware that they are making inferences but rather think that they are directly recalling what they studied.

Bransford, Barclay, and Franks (1972) reported an experiment that demonstrates how inference can lead to incorrect recall. They had participants study one of the following sentences:

1. Three turtles rested beside a floating log, and a fish swam beneath them.
2. Three turtles rested on a floating log, and a fish swam beneath them.

Participants who had studied sentence 1 were later asked whether they had studied this sentence:

3. Three turtles rested beside a floating log, and a fish swam beneath it.

Not many participants thought they had studied this sentence. Participants who had studied sentence 2 were tested with:

4. Three turtles rested on a floating log, and a fish swam beneath it.

The participants in this group judged that they had studied sentence 4 much more often than participants in the other group judged that they had studied sentence 3. Sentence 4 is implied by sentence 2, whereas sentence 3 is not implied by sentence 1. Thus, participants thought that they had actually studied what was implied by the studied material.

A study by Sulin and Dooling (1974) illustrates how inference can bias participants' memory for a text. They asked participants to read the following passage:

Gerald Martin's Seizure of Power
Gerald Martin strove to undermine the existing government to satisfy his political ambitions. Many of the people of his country supported his efforts. Current political problems made it relatively easy for Martin to take over. Certain groups remained loyal to the old government and caused Martin problems. He confronted these groups directly and so silenced them. He became a ruthless, uncontrollable dictator. The ultimate effect of his rule was the downfall of his country.

A second group of participants read the same passage, except that the name *Adolf Hitler* was substituted for *Gerald Martin*. A week after reading the passage, participants were given a recognition test in which they were presented with a sentence and asked to judge whether it had occurred in the passage they read originally. One of the critical test sentences was *He hated the Jews particularly and so persecuted them*. Only 5% of participants who read the Gerald Martin passage accepted this sentence, but a full 50% of the participants who read the Adolf Hitler version thought they had read the sentence. The second group of participants had elaborated the story with facts they knew about Adolf Hitler. Thus, it seemed reasonable to them at test that this sentence had appeared in the studied material, but in this case their inference was wrong.

We might wonder whether an inference such as *He hated the Jews particularly and so persecuted them* was made while the participant was studying the passage or only at the time of the test. This is a subtle issue, and participants certainly do not have reliable intuitions about it. However, a couple of techniques seem to yield evidence that some inferences are being made at test. One method is to determine whether the inferences increase in frequency with delay. With delay, participants' memory for the studied passage should deteriorate, and if they are making inferences at test, they will have to do more reconstruction via inference, which in turn will lead to more inferential errors. Both Dooling and Christiaansen (1977) and Spiro (1977) found evidence for increased inferential intrusions with increased delay of testing. Dooling and Christiaansen used another technique with the Gerald Martin passage to show that inferences were being made at test. They had the participants study the passage and then told them a week later, just before test, that Gerald Martin really was Adolf Hitler. In this situation, participants also made many inferential errors, accepting such sentences as *He hated the Jews particularly and so persecuted them.* Because they did not know that Gerald Martin was Adolf Hitler until test, they must have made the inferences at test. Thus, it seems that participants do make such reconstructive inferences at time of test.

> *In trying to remember material, people will use what they can remember to infer what else they might have studied.*

Plausible Retrieval

In the foregoing analysis, we spoke of participants as making errors when they recalled or recognized facts that were not explicitly presented. In real life, however, such acts of recall often would be regarded not as errors but as intelligent inferences. Reder (1982) has argued that much of recall in real life involves plausible inference rather than exact recall. For instance, in deciding that Darth Vader was evil in *Star Wars,* a person does not search memory for the specific proposition that Darth Vader was evil, although it may have been directly asserted in the movie. The person infers that Darth Vader was evil from memories about the *Stars Wars* movies.

Reder demonstrated that people will display very different behavior, depending on whether they are asked to engage in exact retrieval or plausible retrieval. She had participants study passages such as the following:

> The heir to a large hamburger chain was in trouble. He had married
> a lovely young woman who had seemed to love him. Now he
> worried that she had been after his money after all. He sensed that
> she was not attracted to him. Perhaps he consumed too much beer
> and French fries. No, he couldn't give up the fries. Not only were
> they delicious, he got them for free.

Then she had participants judge sentences such as

1. The heir married a lovely young woman who had seemed to love him.
2. The heir got his French fries from his family's hamburger chain.
3. The heir was very careful to eat only healthy food.

The first sentence was studied; the second was not studied, but is plausible; and the third neither was studied nor is plausible. Participants in the exact condition were asked to make exact recognition judgments, in which case the correct responses would have been to accept the first sentence and reject the second two. Participants in the plausible condition were asked to judge whether the sentence was plausible given the story, in which case the correct responses would have been to accept the first two and reject the last. Reder tested participants immediately after studying the story, 20 min later, or 2 days later.

Reder was interested in the response time for participants in the two conditions, exact versus plausible. **Figure 7.9** shows the results from her experiment, plotted as the average response times as a function of delay. As might be expected, participants' response times increased with delay in the exact condition. However, the response times actually decreased in the plausible condition. They started out slower in the plausible condition than in the exact condition, but this trend was reversed after 2 days. Reder argued that participants respond more slowly in the exact condition after a lengthy delay because the memories of exact wording are getting weaker. A plausibility judgment, however, does not depend on any particular memory and so is not similarly vulnerable to forgetting. Participants respond faster in the plausible condition with delay because they no longer try to retrieve facts, which often have been forgotten, but instead immediately begin making inferences on which to base plausibility judgments.

In another experiment, Reder and Ross (1983) compared exact versus plausible judgments after participants had studied sentences such as

Alan bought a ticket for the 10:00 a.m. train.
Alan heard the conductor call, "All aboard."
Alan read a newspaper on the train.
Alan arrived at Grand Central Station.

They manipulated the number of sentences that participants had to study about a particular person such as Alan. Then they looked at the times participants took to recognize sentences such as

1. Alan heard the conductor call, "All aboard."
2. Alan watched the approaching train from the platform.
3. Alan sorted his clothes into colors and whites.

In the exact condition, participants had to judge whether the sentence had been studied. So, given the foregoing material, participants would accept sentence 1 and reject sentences 2 and 3. In

Figure 7.9 Exact Retrieval vs. Plausible Retrieval. In Reder (1982), participants in the exact condition had to recognize whether presented information exactly matched the information studied, whereas participants in the plausible condition had to judge whether presented information was plausible based on the information studied. Exact judgments were made faster than plausible judgments immediately after study, but slower after a delay of 2 days. *(Data from Reder, 1982.)*

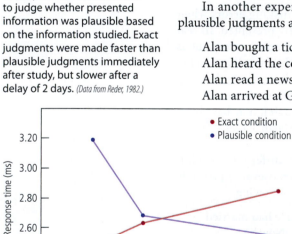

the plausible condition, participants had to judge whether it was plausible that Alan was involved in the activity, given what they had studied. Thus, participants would accept sentences 1 and 2 and reject sentence 3.

In the exact condition, Reder and Ross found that participants' response times increased when they had studied more facts about Alan. This is basically a replication of the fan effect discussed earlier in this chapter. In the plausible condition, however, participants' response times decreased when they had learned more facts about Alan. The more facts they knew about Alan, the more ways there were to judge a particular fact to be plausible. Thus, plausibility judgments did not have to depend on retrieval of a particular fact.

> *People will often judge what plausibly might be true rather than try to retrieve exact facts.*

The Interaction of Elaboration and Inferential Reconstruction

In Chapter 6, we discussed how people tend to display better memories if they elaborate the material being studied. We also discussed how semantic elaborations are particularly beneficial. Such semantic elaborations should facilitate the process of inference by providing more material from which to infer. Thus, we expect elaborative processing to lead to both an increased recall of what was studied and an increase in the number of inferences recalled. An experiment by Owens, Bower, and Black (1979) confirms this prediction. Participants (college students divided into two conditions, a theme condition and a neutral condition) studied a story that followed the principal character, a college student, through a day in her life: making a cup of coffee in the morning, visiting a doctor, attending a lecture, shopping for groceries, and attending a party. The following is a passage from the story:

> Nancy went to see the doctor. She arrived at the office and checked in with the receptionist. She went to see the nurse, who went through the usual procedures. Then Nancy stepped on the scale and the nurse recorded her weight. The doctor entered the room and examined the results. He smiled at Nancy and said, "Well, it seems my expectations have been confirmed." When the examination was finished, Nancy left the office.

The only difference between the two groups of participants was that those in the theme condition had read the following additional information at the beginning:

> Nancy woke up feeling sick again and she wondered if she really were pregnant. How would she tell the professor she had been seeing? And the money was another problem.

Participants in the theme condition characterized Nancy as an unmarried student who is afraid she is pregnant as a result of an affair with a college professor. Participants in the neutral condition, who had not read this opening passage,

TABLE 7.4 The Interactive Effects of Elaboration and Inference		
	Number of Propositions Recalled	
	Theme Condition	Neutral Condition
Studied propositions	29.2	20.3
Inferred propositions	15.2	3.7
(Data from Owens, Bower, & Black, 1979.)		

had no reason to suspect that there was anything special about Nancy. We would expect participants in the theme condition to make many more theme-related elaborations of the story than participants in the neutral condition.

Participants were asked to recall the story 24 hours after studying it. Those in the theme condition introduced a great many more inferences that had not actually been studied. For instance, many participants reported that the doctor told Nancy she was pregnant. Intrusions of this variety are expected if participants reconstruct a story on the basis of their elaborations. **Table 7.4** reports some of the results from the study. As can be seen, many more inferences were added in recall for the theme condition than for the neutral condition. A second important observation, however, is that participants in the theme condition also recalled more of the propositions they had actually studied. This indicates that the additional elaborations these participants made enabled them to recall more of the story.

We might question whether participants really benefited from their elaborations, because they also mistakenly recalled many things that did not occur in the story. However, it is wrong to characterize these inferences as errors. Given the theme information, participants were perfectly right to make inferences. In a nonexperimental setting, such as recalling information for an exam, we would expect these participants to recall such inferences as easily as they recalled material they had actually read.

> *When participants elaborate on material while studying it, they tend to recall more of what they studied and also tend to recall inferences that they did not study but made themselves.*

Eyewitness Testimony and the False-Memory Controversy

The ability to elaborate on and make inferences from information, both while it is being studied and when our recall is being tested, is essential to using our memory successfully in everyday life. Inferences made while studying material allow us to extrapolate from what we actually heard and saw to what is probably true. When we hear that someone found out she was pregnant during a visit to a doctor, it is a reasonable inference that the doctor told her. So such inferences usually lead to a much more coherent and accurate understanding of the world. There are circumstances, however, in which we need to be able to separate what we actually saw and heard from our inferences. The difficulty of doing so can lead to false memories that may have negative consequences; the Gargoil example in **Implications 7.2** represents only the tip of the iceberg.

Implications 7.2

How Have Advertisers Used Knowledge of Cognitive Psychology?

Advertisers often capitalize on our tendency to embellish what we hear with plausible inferences. Consider the following description of a portion of an old Listerine commercial:

"Wouldn't it be great," asks the mother, "if you could make him cold proof? Well, you can't. Nothing can do that." [Boy sneezes.] "But there is something that you can do that may help. Have him gargle with Listerine Antiseptic. Listerine can't promise to keep him cold free, but it may help him fight off colds. During the cold-catching season, have

him gargle twice a day with full-strength Listerine. Watch his diet, see he gets plenty of sleep, and there's a good chance he'll have fewer colds, milder colds this year."

A verbatim text of this commercial, with the product name changed to "Gargoil," was used in an experiment conducted by Harris (1977). After hearing this commercial, all 15 of his

participants recalled that "gargling with Gargoil Antiseptic helps prevent colds," although this assertion was clearly not made in the commercial. The Federal Trade Commission explicitly forbids advertisers from making false claims, but does the Listerine ad make a false claim? In a landmark case, the courts ruled against Warner-Lambert, makers of Listerine, for implying false claims in this commercial. As a corrective action the court ordered Warner-Lambert to include in future advertisements the disclaimer "contrary to prior advertising, Listerine will not help prevent colds or sore throats or lessen their severity." They were required to continue this disclaimer until they had expended an amount of money equivalent to their prior 10 years of advertisements.

One situation in which it is critical to separate inference from actual experience is in eyewitness testimony. It has been shown that eyewitnesses are often inaccurate in their testimony, even though jurors accord it high weight. One reason for the low accuracy is that people confuse what they actually observed about an incident with what they learned from other sources. Loftus (Loftus & Zanni, 1975; Loftus, Miller, & Burns, 1978) showed that subsequent information can change a person's memory of an observed event. In one study, for instance, Loftus asked participants who had witnessed a traffic accident about the car's speed when it passed a Yield sign. Although there was no Yield sign, many participants subsequently remembered having seen one, confusing the implication of the question they were asked with what they had actually seen.

The Loftus study provided an early example of errors in memory reports arising from confusion about the source of information, about whether information came from what was observed or from some other source. Identifying the source of one's memory is crucial for avoiding errors in eyewitness testimony (Davis & Loftus, 2017). Such errors, called *source monitoring errors* (Johnson et al., 1993), can affect eyewitness testimony in many ways. For instance, Brown, Deffenbacher, and Sturgill (1977) found that seeing a person's face when reviewing a series of mugshots can make participants in an experiment more likely to identify that person in a lineup as the person they saw committing a crime. Such misidentifications happen in reality as well as in experiments. For instance, a man named Walter Snyder was wrongly convicted of rape in 1985 and later exonerated on the basis of DNA evidence. The victim had seen his face in a mugshot and did not identify him at that time as the perpetrator, but upon actually seeing him months later she identified him as her rapist (Scheck, Neufeld, & Dwyer, 2000). Source monitoring errors can also arise when keeping straight what one actually observed versus what was reported in the media or by other witnesses, or even versus what was just imagined. For instance, over 40% of participants in a U.K. study (Ost, Vrij, Costall, & Bull, 2002) claimed to have seen a video of the car crash in which Diana, Princess of Wales, died, even though there is no such video.

Another kind of memory confusion — the so-called **false-memory syndrome** — has produced a great deal of controversy in cases where individuals claim to have recovered previously suppressed memories of childhood sexual abuse (Schacter, 2001). Many of these memories are recovered in the process of therapy, and some memory researchers have questioned whether these recovered memories reflect what really happened and have hypothesized that such memories might have been implanted as a result of therapists' suggestions. For instance, one therapist said to patients, "You know, in my experience, a lot of people who are struggling with many of the same problems you are, have often had some kind of really painful things happen to them as kids — maybe they were beaten or molested. And I wonder if anything like that ever happened to you?" (Forward & Buck, 1988, p. 161). Given the evidence we have reviewed about how people will put information together to make inferences that they then "remember," one could wonder whether patients hearing such suggestions from their therapist might remember what did not happen.

A number of researchers have shown that it is indeed possible to create false memories by use of suggestive interview techniques. For instance, Loftus and Pickerall (1995) had adult participants read four stories from their childhood written by an older relative — three were true, but one was a false story about being lost in a mall at age 5. After reading the story, about 25% of participants claimed to remember the event of being lost in a mall. In another study, Wade, Garry, Read, and Lindsay (2002) inserted an actual photo from the participants' childhood into a picture of a hot-air balloon ride that never happened (see **Figure 7.10**). Fifty percent of their participants then reported false memories about the experience. There is a lot of room for error in the process by which we distinguish between memory and imagination, and it is easy to become confused about the source of information. Of course, it would not be ethical to intentionally try to implant false memories about something as traumatic as childhood sexual abuse, and there are questions about whether it is even possible to create false memories about such awful events (e.g., Pope, 1996).

Figure 7.10 Remembering What Did Not Happen. The actual childhood photo on the left was embedded into the picture on the right to help create a false childhood memory of a balloon ride. *(Reprinted with permission from Kimberly Wade.)*

The intense debate about how much credibility should be given to recovered memories of childhood abuse might tempt one to conclude either that all reports of recovered memories of abuse should be believed or that all should be discounted, but the truth does not appear to be so simple. In some cases, recovered memories of abuse seem to be strongly supported by documentation (Sivers, Schooler, & Freyd, 2002), whereas in other cases people who claimed to have recovered such memories have subsequently retracted their claims and said they were misled in their memories (Schacter, 2001).

A similarly nuanced conclusion seems appropriate with regard to eyewitness testimony. While there are certainly cases where wrongful convictions were based on inaccurate eyewitness testimony, Wixted, Mickes, and Fisher (2018) argue that eyewitness testimony is often quite accurate. They argue that, just as major precautions need to be taken not to contaminate DNA evidence, similar efforts should be taken not to contaminate the memories of eyewitnesses. Eyewitnesses who have not had contaminating experiences, such as seeing photos in mugshots before seeing suspects in person, are typically very confident and very accurate in their identifications (Wixted & Wells, 2017). **Table 7.5** lists recommendations from Wixted and Wells for best practices in conducting a lineup, and some jurisdictions have begun to adopt such practices.

> *Serious errors of memory can occur when people fail to separate what they actually experienced from what they inferred, imagined, or were told. In cases with serious personal or legal consequences, care must be taken to avoid such contamination of memory.*

TABLE 7.5 Best Practices in Conducting a Lineup
1. Include only one actual suspect per lineup.
2. Make sure that the suspect does not stand out in the lineup.
3. Caution the eyewitness that the offender might not be in the lineup.
4. Use double-blind testing (i.e., neither the eyewitness nor those conducting the lineup should know who the suspect is in the lineup).
5. If the eyewitness makes an identification at the lineup, collect a confidence statement at that time (i.e., a statement by the eyewitness of how confident he or she is in the identification).
(Data from Wixted & Wells, 2017.)

False Memories and the Brain

Using less exotic paradigms than the one illustrated in Figure 7.10, researchers have developed the ability to explore the neural basis of false memories. In experiments based on the **Deese-Roediger-McDermott paradigm** — originally developed by Deese (1959) and elaborated by Roediger and McDermott (1995) — participants study lists of words and then have their brain activity monitored as they are tested on their recall of which words they studied. One such list of words might contain *thread, pin, eye, sewing, sharp, point, prick, thimble, haystack, thorn, hurt, injection, syringe, cloth, knitting*; a second list might contain *bed, rest, awake, tired, dream, wake, snooze, blanket, doze, slumber, snore, nap, peace, yawn, drowsy*. In the later test, participants are shown a series of words and must decide whether they have studied each word. There are three types of words:

True (e.g., *sewing, awake*) — words that were in the lists studied
False (e.g., *needle, sleep*) — words that are strongly associated with words in the lists studied but were not in those lists
New (e.g., *door, candy*) — words that were not in the lists studied and are unrelated to any of the words in those lists

Typically, participants say they have studied most of the true words and reject most of the new words, but they have difficulty rejecting the false words. For example, Cabeza, Rao, Wagner, Mayer, and Schacter (2001) found that 88% of the true words and only 12% of the new words were accepted, but 80% of the false words were also accepted — almost as high a percentage as the true words.

Cabeza et al. examined the activation patterns that these different types of words produced in the cortex. **Figure 7.11** illustrates such activation profiles in hippocampal and parahippocampal structures. In the hippocampus proper, true words and false words produced almost identical fMRI responses, which were stronger than the responses produced by the new words. Thus, these hemodynamic responses appear to match up pretty well with the behavioral data, where participants cannot discriminate between true words and

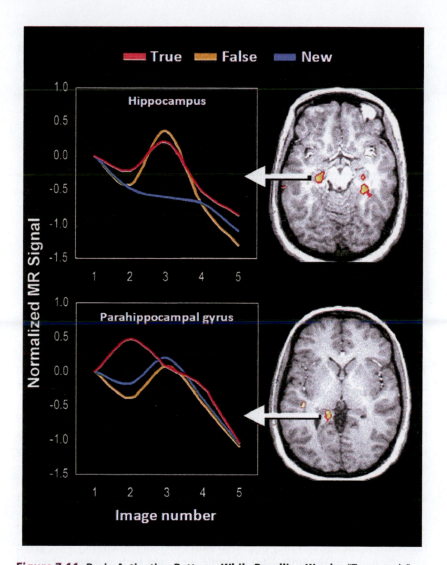

Figure 7.11 Brain Activation Patterns While Recalling Words. "True words" were in lists of words that participants studied; "false" words were not in the lists studied but were strongly associated with words in the lists; "new" words were not in the lists studied and were unrelated to any words in those lists. In the hippocampus (top), hemodynamic responses align with behavioral data: participants are almost equally likely to accept true words and false words as being in the lists studied, but reject new words. In contrast, in the parahippocampal gyrus (bottom), hemodynamic responses for both false words and new words were weaker than for true words, perhaps reflecting the parahippocampal area's closer connection to sensory areas. *(Cabeza et al., Can medial temporal lobe regions distinguish true from false? Proceedings of the National Academy of Sciences Apr 2001, 98(8) 4805–4810; Copyright (2001) National Academy of Sciences, U.S.A.)*

false words. However, in the parahippocampal gyrus, an area just adjacent to the hippocampus, both false and new words produced weaker responses than the true words. The parahippocampus is more closely connected to sensory regions of the brain than is the hippocampus, and Cabeza et al. suggested that the parahippocampus retains the original sensory experience of seeing the word, whereas the hippocampus maintains a more abstract representation, which would explain why true words produce a larger hemodynamic response in the parahippocampus. Schacter (e.g., Dodson & Schacter, 2002a, 2000b) has suggested that people can be trained to pay more attention to these distinctive sensory features and so improve their resistance to false memories. For instance, distinctiveness training could be used to help elderly patients who find it hard to remember whether they have seen something or just imagined it (Henkel, Johnson, & DeLeonardis, 1998).

> *Activation in the hippocampus is about the same for false memories and true memories, reflecting our difficulties in discriminating between what was experienced, what was inferred, and what was imagined.*

Associative Structure and Retrieval

The spreading-activation theory described in Chapter 6 implies that we can improve our ability to retrieve particular memories by prompting ourselves with closely associated memories. You may find yourself practicing this technique when you try to remember the name of an old classmate. You may prompt your memory with names of other classmates or memories of things you did with that classmate. Often, the name does seem to come to mind as a result of such efforts. An experiment by Tulving and Pearlstone (1966) provides one demonstration of this technique. They had participants learn lists of 48 words that included words from particular categories — for example, a list might include the words *dog, cat, horse,* and *cow,* which belong to the category of domesticated mammals. Participants were asked to try to recall all the words in the list, and they displayed better memory when they were given category names as prompts — for example, a prompt such as *mammal* would cue their memory for the words denoting members of that category.

The Effects of Encoding Context

Among the cues that can become associated with a memory are those from the context in which the memory was formed. This section will review some of the ways that such contextual cues influence memory.

Smith, Glenberg, and Bjork (1978) performed an experiment that showed the importance of physical context. In their experiment, participants learned two lists of paired associates on different days and in different physical settings. On day 1, participants learned the paired associates in a windowless room in a building near the University of Michigan campus. The experimenter was neatly groomed, dressed in a coat and a tie, and the paired associates were shown on slides. On day 2, participants learned the paired associates in a tiny room with windows on the main campus. The experimenter was dressed sloppily in a flannel shirt and jeans (it was the same experimenter, but some participants did not recognize him), and the paired associates were presented via a tape recorder. A day later, participants were tested for their recall of half the paired associates in one setting and half in the other setting. They could recall 59% of the list learned in the same setting as the one in which they were tested, but only 46% of the list learned in the other setting. Thus, it seems that recall is better if the context during test is the same as the context during study.

Perhaps the most dramatic manipulation of context was performed by Godden and Baddeley (1975). They had divers learn a list of 40 unrelated words either on the shore or 20 feet under the sea. The divers were then asked to recall the list either in the same environment or in the other environment. **Figure 7.12** displays the results of this study. Participants clearly showed superior memory when they were asked to recall the list in the same environment in which they studied it. So, it seems that contextual elements do get associated with memories and that memory is better when participants are provided with these contextual elements when being tested. This result actually has serious implications for diver instruction, because most of the instructions are given on dry land but must be recalled underwater.

The degree to which such contextual effects are obtained has proved to be quite variable from experiment to experiment (Roediger & Guynn, 1996). Fernandez and Glenberg (1985) reported a number of failures to find any context dependence; and Saufley, Otaka, and Bavaresco (1985) reported a failure to find such effects in a classroom situation. Eich (1985) argued that the magnitude of such contextual effects depends on the degree to which the participant integrates the context with the memories. In his experiment, he read lists of nouns to two groups of participants. In one condition, participants were instructed to imagine the referents of the nouns alone (e.g., imagine a *kite*); in the other, they were asked to imagine the referents integrated with the experimental context (e.g., imagine a *kite* on the table in the corner of the room). Participants were then tested for their recall of the nouns in one of two contexts, either in the same room where they had heard the nouns or in a different room. Eich found that participants had much better memory for the nouns that they had imagined as integrated with the experimental context, but only when participants were tested in that same context.

Bower, Monteiro, and Gilligan (1978) showed that emotional context can have the same effect as physical context. They instructed participants to learn two lists.

Figure 7.12 Context Effects on Recall of Words. Divers learned lists of words either on shore or underwater and were then tested for recall either on shore or underwater. Participants' recall was better when the environment at test matched the environment at study. *(Data from Godden & Baddeley, 1975.)*

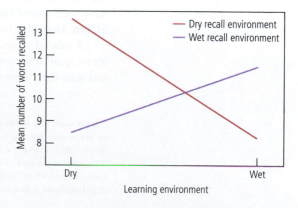

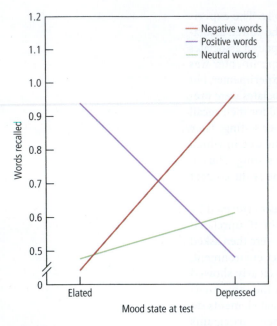

Figure 7.13 Mood Congruence. At study, participants in a neutral mood learned a list of positive, negative, and neutral words. Then, at test, participants were induced into either an elated or a depressed mood. Participants recalled more of the words that matched their mood at test. *(Data from Teasdale & Russell, 1983.)*

For one list, they hypnotically induced a positive state by having participants review a pleasant episode in their lives; for the other, they hypnotically induced a negative state by having participants review a traumatic event. A later recall test was given under either a positive or a negative emotional state (again hypnotically induced). Better memory was obtained when the emotional state at test matched the emotional state at study.[1]

Not all research shows such mood-dependent effects. For instance, Bower and Mayer (1985) failed to replicate the Bower et al. (1978) result. Eich and Metcalfe (1989) found that mood-dependent effects tend to be obtained only when participants integrate what they are studying with mood information. Thus, like the effects of physical context, mood-dependent effects occur only in special study situations.

While an effect of match between study mood and test mood is only sometimes found, there is a more robust effect called **mood congruence:** Memories are easier to recall when the emotional content of the memory matches the mood at recall. In other words, memories of events that made one happy are easier to recall when one is in a happy mood, and memories of events that made one sad are easier to recall when one is in a sad mood. Thus, mood congruence is an effect of the content of the memories rather than the emotional state of the participant during study. For instance, Teasdale and Russell (1983) had participants learn a list of positive, negative, and neutral words in a neutral mood. Then, at test, they induced either an elated or a depressed mood. Their results, illustrated in **Figure 7.13**, show that participants recalled more of the words that matched their mood at test. When a particular mood is created at test, elements of that mood will prime memories that share these elements. Thus, mood elements can prime both memories whose content matches the mood, as in the Teasdale and Russell experiment, and memories that have such mood elements integrated as part of the study procedure (as in Eich & Metcalfe, 1989).

A related phenomenon is **state-dependent learning.** People find it easier to recall information if they can return to the same emotional and physical state they were in when they learned the information. For instance, it is

---

[1] As an aside, it is worth commenting that, despite popular reports, the best evidence is that hypnosis per se does nothing to improve memory (see Hilgard, 1968; Lynn, Lock, Myers, & Payne, 1997; Smith, 1982), although it can help memory to the extent that it can be used to re-create the contextual factors at the time of test. However, much of a learning context can also be re-created by nonhypnotic means, such as through free association about the circumstances of the event to be remembered (e.g., Geiselman, Fisher, Mackinnon, & Holland, 1985).

TABLE 7.6 State-Dependent Learning: The Effects of Drugged State at Study and at Test

At Study	Words Correctly Recalled at Test (%)		
	Ordinary Cigarette	Marijuana Cigarette	Average
Ordinary cigarette	25	20	23
Marijuana cigarette	12	23	18
(Data from Eich et al., 1975.)			

often casually claimed that when heavy drinkers are sober, they are unable to remember where they hid their alcohol when drunk, and when drunk, they are unable to remember where they hid their money when sober. In fact, some experimental evidence does exist for this state dependency of memory with respect to alcohol, but the more important factor seems to be that alcohol has a general debilitating effect on the acquisition of information (Parker, Birnbaum, & Noble, 1976). Marijuana has been shown to have similar state-dependent effects. In one experiment (Eich, Weingartner, Stillman, & Gillin, 1975), participants studied a list of words after smoking either a marijuana cigarette or an ordinary cigarette. Participants were tested 4 hours later — again after smoking either a marijuana cigarette or a regular cigarette. **Table 7.6** shows the results from this study. Two effects were seen, both of which are typical of research on the effects of psychoactive drugs on memory. First, there is a state-dependent effect reflected by better recall when the state at test matched the state at study. Second, there is an overall higher level of recall when the material was studied in a nonintoxicated state.

> *People show better memory if their external context and their internal states are the same at the time of study and the time of test.*

The Encoding-Specificity Principle

Memory for studied material can also depend heavily on the context of the other material in which it is embedded at study and at test. A series of experiments (e.g., Tulving & Thomson, 1973; Watkins & Tulving, 1975) illustrate how memory for a word can depend on how well the test context matches the original study context. There were three phases to a typical experiment in this series:

1. *Study.* Participants learned pairs of words, such as *train–black*, and were told that they were responsible for remembering only the second word, referred to as the "to-be-remembered word" (in this example, *black*).

2. *Generate and recognize.* Participants were presented with words not studied and asked to generate four free associates to each word. The presented words were chosen to have a high probability of eliciting to-be-remembered words. For instance, participants might be presented with *white* and might generate the free associates *snow, black, wool,* and *pure* (*white* has a high probability of eliciting *black*). For each presented word, participants were asked to indicate which of the four associates they generated was a to-be-remembered word. In cases where a to-be-remembered word was generated, participants correctly chose it only 54% of the time. Because participants were always forced to indicate a choice, some of these correct choices must have been lucky guesses. Thus, true recognition was lower than 54%.

3. *Cued recall.* Participants were presented with the original context words (the first word in each pair studied — e.g., *train*) and asked to recall the to-be-remembered words (in this case, *black*). Participants recalled 61% of the to-be-remembered words — better than their 54% recognition rate without any correction for guessing. Moreover, Watkins and Tulving found that 42% of the words recalled in this phase had not been recognized earlier when the participants gave them as free associates.[2]

Recognition is usually superior to recall. Thus, in the experiment just described, we would expect participants' recognition rate in phase 2 to be better than their recall rate in phase 3; in particular, we would expect that participants who could not recognize a word would be unable to recall it (just as we expect to do better on a multiple-choice test than on a recall-the-answer test). Experiments such as this provided dramatic reversals of such standard expectations. The results can be understood in terms of the similarity of the test context to the study context. The test context in the generate-and-recognize phase was quite different from the context in which the words had originally been studied. The test context in the cued-recall phase, by contrast, matched the study context. This shows that, if contextual factors are sufficiently weighted in favor of recall, recall can be superior to recognition. Tulving interprets these results as illustrating what he calls the **encoding-specificity principle:** The probability of recalling an item at test depends on the similarity of the context during encoding at test to the context during encoding at study.

> *People show better word memory if the words are tested in the context of the same words with which they were studied.*

[2] A great deal of research has been done on this phenomenon (for a review, see Nilsson & Gardiner, 1993.)

The Hippocampal Formation and Amnesia

In Chapter 6, we discussed the fictional character Leonard from the movie *Memento*, who suffered amnesia resulting from hippocampal damage. A large amount of evidence points to the great importance of the hippocampal formation, a structure embedded within the temporal cortex, for the establishment of permanent memories. In animal studies (typically rats or primates; for a review, see Eichenbaum, Dudchenko, Wood, Shapiro, & Tanila, 1999; Squire, 1992), lesions in the hippocampal formation produce severe impairments to the learning of new associations, particularly those that require remembering combinations or configurations of elements. Damage to the hippocampal area also produces severe **amnesia** (memory loss) in humans. One of the most studied amnesic patients is known in the literature as H.M.[3] In 1953, when he was 27 years old, large parts of his temporal lobes were surgically removed to cure epilepsy. His epilepsy after the surgery was much less severe, but he suffered one of the most profound amnesias ever recorded and was studied for decades. He had normal memories of his life up to the age of 16 but forgot most of the subsequent 11 years preceding the surgery. Moreover, he was almost totally unable to remember new information and events. He appeared in many ways as a normal person with a clear self-identity, but his identity was largely as the person he was when he was 16, when his memories stopped (although he realized he was older, and he had learned some general facts about the world). His surgical operation involved complete removal of the hippocampus and surrounding structures, and this is considered the reason for his profound memory deficits (Squire, 1992).

Only rarely is there a reason for surgically removing the hippocampal formation from humans. However, humans can suffer severe damage to this structure and the surrounding parts of the temporal lobe. One common cause is a severe blow to the head, but other frequent causes include brain infections (such as encephalitis) and chronic alcoholism, which can result in a condition called **Korsakoff syndrome.** Such damage (including the damage associated with Korsakoff syndrome) can result in two types of amnesia: **retrograde amnesia** (loss of memory for events that occurred before an injury) and **anterograde amnesia** (an inability to store new things in memory).

In the case of a blow to the head, the amnesia often is not permanent but displays a particular pattern of recovery. **Figure 7.14** displays the pattern of recovery for a patient who was in a coma for 7 weeks following a head injury that did not require surgery. Tested 5 months after the injury, the patient showed total anterograde amnesia — he could not remember anything that had happened since the injury. He also displayed total retrograde amnesia

---

[3] Henry Gustav Molaison died in 2008 at the age of 82. There is an interesting discussion of him in the article "The Man Who Forgot Everything," by Steven Shapin (*New Yorker*, October 14, 2013).

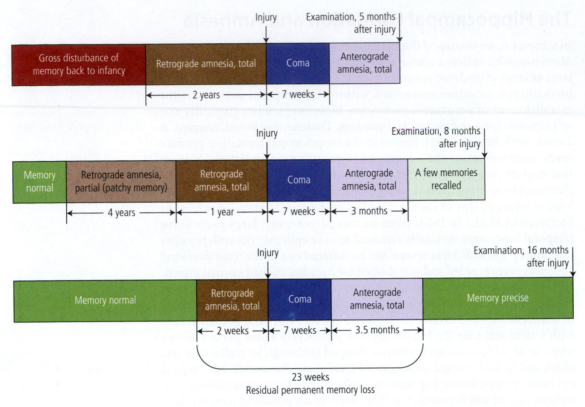

Figure 7.14 Recovery from Amnesia Caused by a Head Injury. This patient's time course of anterograde and retrograde amnesia over a period of 16 months following a head injury is typical. The severity of amnesia symptoms can vary among patients, but memories for events close in time to the injury (both before and after) are generally never recovered. *(Data from Barbizet, 1970.)*

for the 2 years preceding the injury and substantial disturbance of memory beyond that. When tested 8 months after the injury, the patient showed some ability to remember new experiences (but still had total anterograde amnesia for the 3 months following the injury), and the period of total retrograde amnesia had shrunk to 1 year. When tested 16 months after injury, the patient had full ability to remember new events and had only what proved to be a permanent 2-week period of total retrograde amnesia and a permanent 3.5-month period of total anterograde amnesia preceding and following the time of the injury (and of course total amnesia for the time in coma). It is characteristic that retrograde amnesia is for events close in time to the injury and that events just before the injury are never recovered. In general, anterograde and retrograde amnesia show this pattern of occurring and recovering together, although the severity of the retrograde and the anterograde symptoms can differ in different patients.

A number of striking features characterize cases of amnesia. The first is that anterograde amnesia can occur along with some preservation of long-term memories. This was particularly the case for H.M., who remembered many things from his youth but was unable to learn new things. The existence of such cases indicates that the neural structures involved in forming new memories are distinct from those involved in maintaining old ones. It is thought that the hippocampal formation is particularly important in creating new memories and that old memories are maintained in the cerebral cortex. It is also thought that events just prior to an injury are particularly susceptible to retrograde amnesia because they still require the hippocampus for support. A second striking feature of these amnesia cases is that the memory deficit is not complete: the patient can still acquire certain kinds of memories (this feature will be discussed in the next section, on implicit and explicit memory). A third striking feature of amnesia is that patients might remember things for short periods but then forget them. Thus, H.M. would be introduced to someone and told the person's name, would use that name for a short time, and would then forget it after a half minute. Thus, the problem in anterograde amnesia is retaining memories for more than 5 or 10 seconds.

> *Patients with damage to the hippocampal formation show both retrograde amnesia and anterograde amnesia.*

Implicit Versus Explicit Memory

Another famous case of amnesia involves the British musicologist Clive Wearing, who suffered herpesviral encephalitis that attacked his brain, particularly the hippocampus. His case is documented by his wife (Wearing, 2011) in *Forever Today: A Memoir of Love and Amnesia* and in the ITV documentary "The Man with a 7 Second Memory" (you can probably find videos by searching the Internet for "Clive Wearing"). He has nearly no memory for his past at all, and yet he remains a proficient pianist. Thus, while he cannot recall facts, he has perfect knowledge of all that is needed to play a piano. This illustrates the distinction between **explicit memory,** what we can consciously recall, and **implicit memory,** what our actions imply we remember in the absence of conscious memory.

While Clive Wearing is an extreme example, we all have implicit memories for things that we cannot consciously recall. However, because there is no conscious involvement, we are not aware of the extent of such memories. One example that some people can relate to is memory for the location of the keys of a computer keyboard. Many proficient typists cannot recall the arrangement of the keys except by imagining themselves typing (Snyder, Ashitaka, Shimada, Ulrich, & Logan, 2014). Clearly, their fingers know where the keys are, but they have no conscious access to this knowledge. Such implicit memory demonstrations highlight the significance of retrieval conditions in

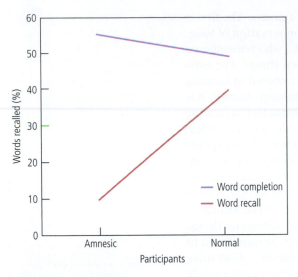

Figure 7.15 Word Recall and Word Completion in Amnesic versus Normal Participants. Both groups of participants studied lists of words and were then tested on their recall of the studied words. Then they were given the task of completing words when presented with the first three letters of studied words. Amnesic participants did much worse than normal participants on the word-recall task, but amnesic and normal participants were about equally likely to produce studied words in the word-completion task. *(Data from Graf, Squire, & Mandler, 1984.)*

assessing memory. If we asked typists to tell us where the keys are, we would conclude they had no knowledge of the keyboard. If we tested their typing, we would conclude that they had perfect knowledge. This section discusses such contrasts, or **dissociations,** between explicit and implicit memory. In the keyboard example above, explicit memory shows no knowledge, while implicit memory shows total knowledge.

A considerable amount of research has been done on implicit memory in amnesic patients. For instance, Graf, Squire, and Mandler (1984) compared amnesic versus normal participants with respect to their memories for a list of words. After studying the list, participants were asked to recall the words. As shown in **Figure 7.15**, amnesic participants did much worse than normal participants. Then participants were given a word-completion task. They were shown the first three letters of a word they had studied (e.g., *banana*) and were asked to complete it to make an English word (e.g., they might be asked to complete *ban-*). There is less than a 10% probability that participants will generate a word such as *banana* just given the prompt *ban-* without having studied the word, but the results show that participants in both groups came up with the studied word more than 50% of the time. There was no significant difference between the amnesic and normal participants in the word-completion task. Clearly, then, the amnesic participants did have memory for the word list, although they could not gain conscious access to that memory in a free-recall task. Rather, they displayed implicit memory in the word-completion task. The patient H.M. was also capable of implicit learning. For example, he was able to improve on various perceptual-motor tasks from one day to the next, although each day he had no memory of the task from the previous day (Milner, 1962).

> *Amnesic patients often cannot consciously recall a particular event but will show in implicit ways that they have some memory for the event.*

Implicit Versus Explicit Memory in Normal Participants

A great deal of research (for reviews, see Richardson-Klavehn & Bjork, 1988; Schacter, 1987) has also looked at dissociations between implicit and explicit memory in normal individuals. It is often impossible with normal participants to obtain the dramatic dissociations we see in amnesic individuals, who can show no explicit memory but have normal implicit memory (as in the Graf et al., 1984, experiment discussed above). It has been possible, however, to demonstrate that certain variables have different effects on tests of explicit memory than on tests of implicit memory. For instance, Jacoby (1983) had participants respond to words under three different conditions: In the no-context condition, participants studied each word alone (e.g., *woman*); in the context condition, participants studied each word in the presence of an antonym (e.g., *man–woman*); and in the generate condition, participants would see a word and have to generate an antonym (e.g., see *man* and have to say *woman*). Participants were then tested in two ways, designed to tap either explicit memory or implicit memory. In the explicit memory test, participants were presented with a list of words, some studied or generated and some not, and asked to recognize the studied or generated words. In the implicit memory test, participants were presented with a studied or generated word for a very brief period (40 ms) and asked to identify the word. **Figure 7.16** shows the results.

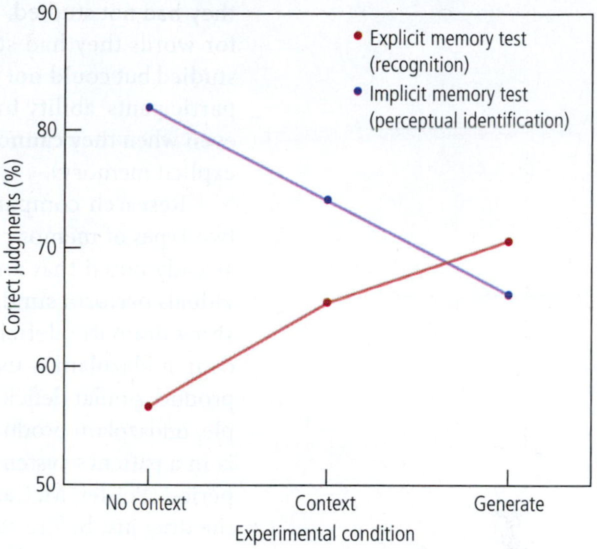

Performance on the explicit memory test was best in the generate condition, which involved more semantic and generative processing — consistent with the research we have reviewed on elaborative processing. In contrast, performance on the implicit perceptual identification was worst in the generate condition and best in the no-context condition. All three conditions showed better perceptual identification than would have been expected if the participants had not studied the word at all (there is 60% correct perceptual identification for non-studied words). This enhancement of perceptual identification is referred to as **priming,** and Jacoby argues that participants show greatest priming in the no-context condition because that is the condition in which they had to rely most on perceptual encoding to recognize or identify the word.[4] In the generate condition, participants did not even have the word to read. Similar contrasts have been shown in memory for pictures: Elaborative processing of a picture will improve explicit memory for the picture but not affect implicit perceptual identification (e.g., Schacter, Cooper, Delaney, Peterson, & Tharan, 1991).

In another experiment, Jacoby and Witherspoon (1982) tested whether participants would display more priming for words they could recognize than for words they could not. Participants first studied a set of words. Then, in one phase of the experiment (involving explicit memory), participants had to recognize the words they had studied. In another phase (involving implicit memory), participants had simply to say what word they had seen after a very brief presentation. Participants showed better ability to identify the briefly presented words that they had studied than words

Figure 7.16 Explicit Memory versus Implicit Memory in Normal Participants. In the explicit memory test, participants were presented with a list of words and had to recognize which words had been studied (in either the context or no-context condition) or generated (in the generate condition). In the implicit memory test, participants had to identify studied or generated words on the basis of a very brief presentation (too brief for conscious recognition). These results indicate that explicit memory improves as the amount of elaborative processing increases (from no context to context to generate) but that implicit memory is best in the no-context condition, where perceptual processing is most prominent. *(Data from Jacoby, 1983.)*

---

[4] Not all research has found better implicit memory in the no-context condition. However, all research finds an interaction between study condition and type of memory test. (For further discussion, see Masson & MacLeod, 1992.)

they had not studied. However, their identification success was no different for words they had studied and could recognize than for words they had studied but could not recognize. Thus, exposure to a word improves normal participants' ability to perceive that word (i.e., improves implicit memory), even when they cannot recall having studied the word (i.e., in the absence of explicit memory).

Research comparing implicit and explicit memory suggests that the two types of memory are supported rather differently in the brain. We have already noted that amnesics with hippocampal damage and normal individuals perform similarly in studies of priming, whereas such amnesics can show dramatic deficits in explicit memory. Research has shown that the drug midazolam — used for sedation in patients undergoing surgery — can produce similar deficits in normal patients (Victoria & Reder, 2010). For example, midazolam produces severe anterograde amnesia for the period of time it is in a patient's system, although the patient functions normally during that period (Polster, McCarthy, O'Sullivan, Gray, & Park, 1993). Participants given the drug just before studying a list of words showed greatly impaired explicit memory for the studied words but intact priming for these words (Hirshman, Passannante, & Arndt, 2001). Midazolam has its effect on neurotransmitters that are found throughout the brain but that are particularly abundant in the hippocampus and prefrontal cortex. Thus, the explicit memory deficits it produces are consistent with the association of the hippocampus and the prefrontal cortex with explicit memory. The drug's lack of implicit memory effects suggests that implicit memories are supported elsewhere in the brain.

Neuroimaging studies suggest that implicit memories are supported in the cortex. As we have discussed, there is increased hippocampal activity when memories are explicitly retrieved (Schacter & Badgaiyan, 2001). During priming, in contrast, there is often decreased activity in various cortical regions. For instance, in one fMRI study (Koutstaal et al., 2001), priming produced decreased activation in visual areas responsible for the recognition of pictures. (As discussed earlier in relation to fMRI studies, decreased activation reflects the fact that the brain regions responsible for the processing have to work less and so produce a weaker fMRI response).

A general interpretation of these results would seem to be that new explicit memories are formed in the hippocampus and prefrontal cortex; but with experience, this information is transferred elsewhere in the cortex. That is why hippocampal damage does not eliminate old memories formed before the damage. The permanent knowledge deposited in the cortex includes such information as word spelling and what things look like. These cortical memories are strengthened when they are primed and become more available in a later retest.

New explicit memories are built in hippocampal regions, but old knowledge can be implicitly primed in cortical structures.

Procedural Memory

Implicit memory is defined as memory without conscious awareness. By this definition, rather different things can be considered implicit memories. Sometimes, implicit memories involve perceptual information relevant to recognizing words. These types of memories result in the priming effects we saw in experiments such as the one illustrated in Figure 7.16. In other cases, implicit memories involve knowledge about how to perform tasks. An important type of implicit memory involves **procedural knowledge,** the knowledge of how to perform a task such as riding a bike. Most of us have learned to ride a bike but, if asked, would have little ability to say explicitly what it is we have learned. Memory for such procedural knowledge is spared in amnesic individuals.

An experiment by Berry and Broadbent (1984) involved a procedural learning task with a more cognitive character than riding a bike. They asked participants to try to control the monthly output of a hypothetical sugar factory by manipulating the size of the workforce (all simulated by a computer program). Participants would see the factory's sugar output for the current month (in thousands of tons — e.g., 6,000 tons) and current workforce (in hundreds of workers — e.g., 500 workers) and then have to choose the next month's workforce (e.g., 700). They would then see the next month's sugar output with that new workforce (e.g., 8,000 tons) and have to pick the workforce for the following month (e.g., keep it at 700 or reduce to 600). The goal was to keep sugar production within the range of 8,000–10,000 tons. **Table 7.7** shows a series of participant interactions with the hypothetical sugar factory.

The relationship of sugar output to workforce is rule governed, but the series of interactions in Table 7.7 does not make the rule particularly obvious. The computer program used the following formula to relate the next month's sugar output in thousands of tons (S) to the size of the next month's workforce in hundreds of workers (W), given the current month's sugar output in thousands of tons (S_1):

$$S = 2W - S_1$$

In addition, a fluctuation of 1,000 tons of sugar was randomly added to or subtracted from S, and S and W were constrained to stay within the bounds of 1 to 12. Oxford undergraduates given 60 trials at trying to control the factory output got quite proficient at it. However, they were unable to state what the rule was and claimed they made their responses on the basis of "some sort of intuition" or because it "felt right." Thus, participants were able to acquire implicit knowledge of how to operate such a factory without acquiring the corresponding explicit knowledge. Amnesic participants have also been shown to be capable of acquiring this type of implicit knowledge (Phelps, 1989).

TABLE 7.7 Procedural Memory: A Series of Choices for Workforce Size in a Hypothetical Sugar Factory When Trying to Produce a Desired Output

Workforce Size (number of workers)	Output (tons of sugar)
700	8,000
900	10,000
800	7,000
1,000	12,000
900	6,000
1,000	12,000
1,000	8,000

Sequence learning (Curran, 1995) has also been used to study the nature of procedural memory, including its realization in the brain. There are a number of sequence-learning models, but in the basic procedure, a participant observes a sequence of lights flash and must press corresponding buttons. For instance, there may be four lights with a button under each, and the task is to press the buttons in the same order as the lights flash. The typical manipulation is to introduce a repeating sequence of lights and contrast how much faster participants can press the keys in this sequence than when the sequence is random. For instance, in the original Nissen and Bullemer (1987) study, the repeating sequence might be 4-2-3-1-3-2-4-3-2-1. After a sufficient number of repeats, people are faster with such a repeating sequence than when the lights come up in a random order. There has been much interest in the question of whether participants are aware that there is a repeating sequence. In some experiments, they are aware of the repetition; but in many others, they are not. They tend not to notice the repeating sequence when the experimental pace is fast or when they are performing some secondary task. However, participants are faster at the repeated sequence whether they are aware of it or not.

It does not appear that the hippocampus is critical to developing proficiency with the repeated sequence, because amnesics show an advantage for the repeated sequence, as do normal patients with pharmacologically induced amnesia. Rather, a set of subcortical structures, referred to as the *basal ganglia* (see Figure 1.8), does appear to be critical for sequence learning. It has long been known that the basal ganglia are critical to motor control, because damage to these structures produces the deficits associated with Huntington's and Parkinson's diseases, which are characterized by uncontrolled movements. However, there are rich connections between the basal ganglia and the prefrontal cortex, and it is now known that the basal ganglia are also important in cognitive functions. They have been shown to be active during the learning of a number of skills, including sequence learning (Middleton & Strick, 1994). Nonhuman primates are capable of mastering sequence tasks and have been used to study the neural basis of sequence learning. Such primate studies have shown that the basal ganglia are critical to early learning of a sequence. For instance, Miyachi, Hikosaka, Miyashita, Karadi, and Rand (1997) were able to impair early sequential learning in monkeys by injecting their basal ganglia with a chemical that temporally inactivated it. Other neural structures appear to be involved in sequence learning as well. For instance, similar chemical inactivation of structures in the cerebellum impairs later learning of a sequence. All in all, the evidence is pretty compelling that procedural learning involves structures different from those involved in explicit learning.

Procedural learning is another type of implicit learning and is supported by the basal ganglia.

Conclusions: The Many Varieties of Memory in the Brain

Figure 7.17 shows the different types and subtypes of memory proposed by Squire (1987). The major distinction in his classification is between explicit memory and implicit memory, which he calls *declarative memory* and *nondeclarative memory*. It appears that the hippocampus is particularly important for the establishment of declarative memories. Within the declarative memory system, there is a distinction between episodic and semantic memory. Episodic memories include information about where and when they were acquired. For example, a memory of a particular newscast can be considered an episodic memory. This chapter and Chapter 6 have discussed these kinds of memories. Semantic memories, discussed in Chapter 5, reflect general knowledge of the world, such as what a dog is or what a restaurant is.

Figure 7.17 makes it clear that there are many kinds of nondeclarative, or implicit, memories. We have just completed a discussion of procedural memories and the critical role of the basal ganglia and cerebellum in their formation. We also talked about priming and the fact that priming seems to entail changes to cortical regions directly responsible for processing the information involved. There are other kinds of learning that we have not discussed but that are particularly important in studies of animal learning. These include conditioning and the two types of memory labeled *nonassociative* in Figure 7.17, habituation and sensitization, all of which have been demonstrated in species ranging from sea slugs to humans. Evidence suggests that conditioning in mammals involves many different brain structures (Anderson, 2000), as do many other types of learning, with different brain structures supporting different kinds of learning.

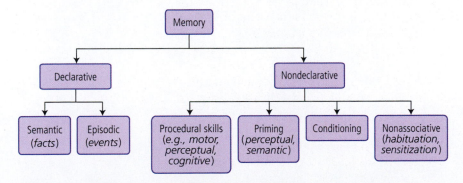

Figure 7.17 The Varieties of Memory Proposed by Squire. This classification system suggests that there are two memory systems (declarative and nondeclarative, corresponding to explicit memory and implicit memory), presumably supported by different brain structures. (*Research from Squire, 1987.*)

Questions for Thought

1. One of the exceptions to the decay of memories with time is the "reminiscence bump" (Berntsen & Rubin, 2002) — people show better memory for events that occurred in their late teens and early 20s than for earlier or later events. What might be the explanation of this effect?

2. The story is told about David Starr Jordan, an ichthyologist (someone who studies fish), who was the first president of Stanford University. He tried to remember the names of all the students but found that whenever he learned the name of a student, he forgot the name of a fish. Does this seem a plausible example of interference in memory?

3. Do the false memories created in the Deese-Roediger-McDermott paradigm reflect the same sort of underlying processes as false memories of childhood events?

4. It is sometimes recommended that students study for an exam in the same room that they will be tested in. According to Eich (1985), discussed earlier in this chapter, how would one have to study to make this an effective procedure? Would this be a reasonable way to study for an exam?

5. Squire's classification in Figure 7.17 would seem to imply that explicit and implicit memories involve different memory systems (declarative and nondeclarative) and, presumably, different brain structures. However, Reder, Park, and Keiffaber (2009) argue that the same memory system and the same brain structures are sometimes involved in both types of memories (ones of which we are consciously aware and others of which we are not). How could one determine whether implicit memory and explicit memory correspond to different memory systems?

Key Terms

amnesia
anterograde amnesia
decay theory
Deese-Roediger-
    McDermott paradigm

dissociations
encoding-specificity
    principle
explicit memory
false-memory syndrome

fan effect
implicit memory
interference theory
Korsakoff syndrome
mood congruence

power law of forgetting
priming
procedural knowledge
retrograde amnesia
state-dependent learning

Problem Solving

Human ability to solve novel problems greatly surpasses that of any other species. This ability stems from the advanced evolution of our prefrontal cortex. As noted in Chapter 1, the prefrontal cortex plays a crucial role in a number of higher level cognitive functions, such as language, imagery, and memory. It is generally thought that in addition to these specific functions, the prefrontal cortex also plays a major role in the overall organization of behavior. The regions of the prefrontal cortex that we have discussed so far tend to be ventral (toward the bottom) and posterior (toward the back), and many of these regions are left lateralized. In contrast, dorsal (toward the top), anterior (toward the front), and bilateral prefrontal structures tend to be more involved in the organization of behavior.

Goel and Grafman (2000) describe a patient, P.F., who suffered damage to his right anterior prefrontal cortex as the result of a stroke. Like many patients with damage to the prefrontal cortex, P.F. appears normal and even intelligent, scoring in the superior range on an intelligence test. Nonetheless, despite these surface appearances of normality, P.F. shows profound intellectual deficits. He had been a successful architect before his stroke but was forced to retire because he had lost his ability to design; he was then only able to find work as a draftsman. As part of their study, Goel and Grafman gave P.F. a problem that involved redesigning their laboratory space. Although he was able to speak coherently about the problem, he was unable to make any real progress on the solution (a comparably trained architect without brain damage achieved a good solution in a couple of hours). It seems that the stroke affected only P.F.'s most highly developed intellectual abilities.

This chapter and Chapter 9 will look at what we know about the nature and the neural basis of human problem solving. In this chapter, we will answer the following questions:

- What does it mean to characterize human problem solving as a search of a problem space?
- How do humans learn methods, called *operators*, for searching a problem space?

- How do humans select among different operators for searching a problem space?
- How can past experience affect the availability of different operators and the success of problem-solving efforts?

The Nature of Problem Solving

We begin our investigation of problem solving by looking at some differences in brain structure between humans and other mammals, focusing on chimpanzees and using an example of problem solving by a chimpanzee to define the essential features of problem solving. We then show how the problem-solving process can be characterized as searching a problem space — a space consisting of the possible states of the problem — in order to transform the problem from its start state through some intermediate states to its goal state (the solution), using operators to effect the transformations from one state to another.

A Comparative Perspective on Problem Solving

Humans have larger brains than most species of animals, but the more dramatic difference is the relative size of the prefrontal cortex, as **Figure 8.1** illustrates. The larger prefrontal cortex in humans supports the advanced problem

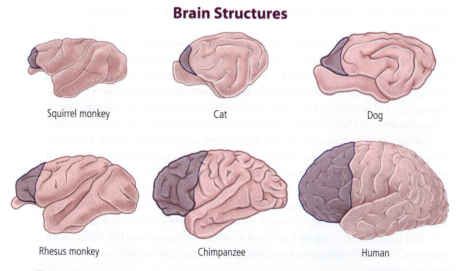

Brain Structures

Squirrel monkey   Cat   Dog

Rhesus monkey   Chimpanzee   Human

Figure 8.1 The Prefrontal Cortex in Six Mammals. The shaded areas show the portion of each brain occupied by the prefrontal cortex. (The brains are not drawn to scale—in particular, the human brain is much larger than it appears here relative to the other brains—but the relative size of the prefrontal cortex in each brain is accurately represented. *(Research from Fuster, 1989.)*

solving of which only humans are capable. None-theless, one can find instances of interesting problem solving in other species, particularly in the higher apes, such as chimpanzees. The study of problem solving in other species offers perspective on our own abilities. The German Gestalt psychologist Wolfgang Köhler, who came to America in the 1930s, performed some of the classic studies on chimpanzee problem solving (Köhler, 1927). During World War I, he found himself trapped on Tenerife in the Canary Islands. On the island, he found a colony of captive chimpanzees, which he studied, taking particular interest in the problem-solving behavior of the animals. His best participant was a chimpanzee named Sultan. One problem posed to Sultan was to get some bananas that were outside his cage. Sultan had no difficulty when he was given a stick that could reach the bananas; he simply used the stick to pull the bananas into the cage. The problem became harder when Sultan was provided with two poles, neither of which could reach the food. After unsuccessfully trying to use the poles to get to the food, the frustrated ape sulked in his cage. Suddenly, he went over to the poles and put one inside the other, creating a pole long enough to reach the bananas (see **Figure 8.2**).

Figure 8.2 Köhler's Ape, Sultan. The chimpanzee solved the two-stick problem by joining two short sticks to form a pole long enough to reach the food outside his cage. *(Republished with permission of Taylor & Francis UK, from* The mentality of apes, *Wolfgang Köhler, © 1925; permission conveyed through Copyright Clearance Center, Inc.)*

What are the essential features that qualify this episode as an instance of problem solving? There seem to be three:

1. *Goal directedness.* The behavior is organized toward achieving a goal — in this case, getting the food.
2. *Subgoal decomposition.* If Sultan could have obtained the food simply by reaching for it, the behavior would have been problem solving, but only in the most trivial sense. Critically, Sultan decomposed the original goal into **subgoals,** such as getting the poles and putting them together.
3. *Operator application.* Decomposing the overall goal into subgoals is useful because the ape knows operators that can help him achieve these subgoals. The term **operator** refers to an action that will transform the problem state into another problem state (in this case, putting the poles together is an operator that transforms the problem state from a state in which there is no usable tool for reaching the bananas to a state in which there is such a tool). The solution of the overall problem is a sequence involving these known operators.

Problem solving is goal-directed behavior that often involves setting sub-goals to enable the application of operators.

The Problem-Solving Process: Problem Space and Search

Often, problem solving is described in terms of searching a **problem space** (also called a *state space*), which consists of the various states of the problem along with the operators for transforming one problem state into another. A **state** is a representation of the problem in some degree of solution. The initial situation of the problem is referred to as the *start state*; the situations on the way to the goal, as *intermediate states*; and the situation in which the problem is solved, as the **goal state.** In the start state and in each intermediate state, there are many ways in which the problem solver can change the state (i.e., there are many operators available). For instance, in the start state of Sultan's problem, he could reach for a stick, stand on his head, sulk, or try other approaches. Suppose he reaches for a stick. Now he has entered a new state, an intermediate state that he can transform into yet another state—for example, he could let go of the stick (thereby returning to the earlier state), reach for the food with the stick, throw the stick at the food, or reach for the other stick. Suppose he reaches for the other stick. Again, he has created a new state. From this state, Sultan can choose to try, say, walking on the sticks, putting them together, or eating them. Suppose he chooses to put the sticks together. In this new state, he can choose to reach for the food, throw the sticks away, or separate them. If he reaches for the food and pulls it into his cage, he will have achieved the goal state.

The various states that the problem solver can produce define a problem space. Problem-solving operators can be thought of as ways to change one state in the problem space into another. We can think of the problem space as a maze of states and of the operators as paths for moving among them. The challenge is to find some possible sequence of operators in the problem space that leads from the start state to the goal state. Given such a characterization, solving a problem can be described as engaging in a **search;** that is, the problem solver must find an appropriate path through a maze of states. This conception of problem solving as a search through a state space was developed by Allen Newell and Herbert Simon whose work culminated in the publication of the classic book *Human Problem Solving* (1972). This approach became the major approach to problem solving, in both cognitive psychology and artificial intelligence.

A good example of a problem space characterized as a set of states and operators is provided by the eight puzzle, which consists of eight numbered, movable tiles occupying all but one of the nine cells in a 3 × 3 frame. Any tile adjacent to the empty cell can be moved into the empty cell (thereby "moving" the empty cell as well). The goal is to achieve a particular configuration of tiles, starting from a different configuration. For instance, a problem might be to transform the configuration on the left to the one on the right:

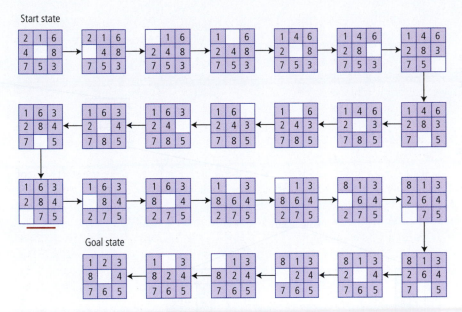

Figure 8.3 A Solution to an Eight Puzzle. The author's less-than-optimal sequence of 26 moves for solving the eight puzzle shown in the text above.

The possible states of this problem are represented as configurations of tiles in the eight puzzle. So, the configuration on the left is the start state and the configuration on the right is the goal state. The operators that change the states are movements of tiles into empty spaces. **Figure 8.3** reproduces a solution I found to this problem involving 26 moves, each move being an operator that changed the state of the problem (the move marked by the red bar is discussed later in this chapter). Can you find a shorter sequence of moves? (The shortest sequence possible, with just 18 moves, is shown in Figure A8.1 in the appendix at the end of the chapter.)

Often, discussions of problem solving involve the use of a **search tree**. **Figure 8.4** gives a partial search tree for the following, simpler eight puzzle:

Figure 8.4 is like an upside-down tree with a single trunk (the start state) and branches leading out from it. The tree shows all three states reachable from the start state, and if it were complete, it would then show all the states reachable from those three states, and so on. Any path through such a tree represents a possible sequence of moves that a problem solver might make. By generating a complete tree, we can also find the shortest sequence of operators between the start state and the goal state. Figure 8.4 illustrates some of the problem space. In discussions of such examples, often only a path through

Figure 8.4 Part of a Search Tree for an Eight Puzzle. The heavy dark lines show the shortest path (i.e., the shortest sequence of operators, five moves deep) from the start state to the goal state of the eight puzzle shown in the text above. If complete, this search tree would include a very large number of other possible paths.

(Data from Nilsson, 1971.)

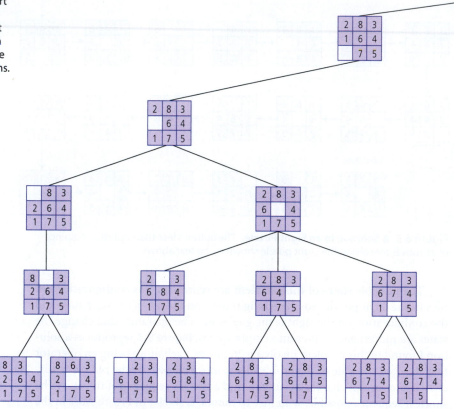

the problem space that leads to the solution is presented (as in Figure 8.3). Figure 8.4 gives a better idea of the size of the problem space of possible moves for this kind of problem.

> *Problem-solving operators generate a space of possible states through which the problem solver must search to find a path to the goal.*

Problem-Solving Operators

The search space approach discussed above describes the possible steps that a problem solver might take. But there are still two important questions to answer before we can explain the behavior of a particular problem solver. First, what determines the operators that are available to the problem solver?

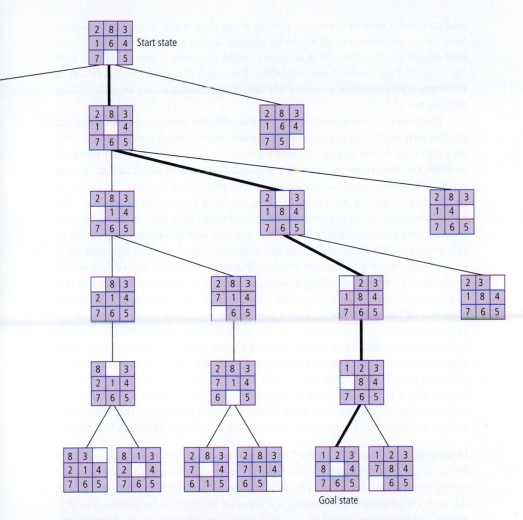

Goal state

Second, how does the problem solver select a particular operator when several are available? An answer to the first question determines the problem space in which the problem solver is working. An answer to the second question determines which path the problem solver takes.

Acquisition of Operators

There are at least three ways to acquire new problem-solving operators: by discovery, by being told about them, and by example (i.e., by observing someone else use them).

Discovery We might find that a new service station has opened nearby and so learn by discovery a new operator for repairing our car. Children might discover that their parents are particularly susceptible to temper tantrums and so learn a new operator for getting what they want. We might discover how a new microwave oven works by playing with it and so learn a new operator for preparing food. Or a scientist might discover a new drug that kills bacteria and so invent a new operator for combating infections. (Each of these examples involves a variety of reasoning processes that we will explore in Chapter 10.)

Discovery of new operators can involve complex reasoning in humans, but it is the only method that most other creatures have to learn new operators, and they certainly do not engage in complex reasoning. In a famous study reported in 1898, the American psychologist Edward Thorndike placed cats in "puzzle boxes." The boxes could be opened by various nonobvious means. For instance, in one box, if the cat hit a loop of wire, the door would fall open. The cats, which were hungry, were rewarded with food when they got out. Initially, a cat would move about randomly, clawing at the box and behaving ineffectively in other ways until it happened to hit the unlatching device. After repeated trials in the same puzzle box, the cats eventually arrived at a point where they would immediately hit the unlatching device and get out. A controversy exists to this day over whether the cats ever really "understood" the new operator they had acquired or just gradually formed a mindless association between getting out of the box and hitting the unlatching device. It has been argued that it need not be an either–or situation. Daw, Niv, and Dayan (2005) review evidence that there are two bases for learning such operators from experience — one involves the basal ganglia (see Figure 1.8), where simple associations are gradually reinforced, whereas the other involves the prefrontal cortex, where a mental model is built of how these operators work. It is reasonable to suppose that the second system becomes more important in mammals with larger prefrontal cortices.

Learning by Being Told or by Example We can acquire new operators by being told about them or by observing someone else use them. These are examples of social learning. The first method is uniquely human because it depends on language. The second is a capacity thought to be common in primates: "Monkey see, monkey do." However, the capacity of nonhuman primates for learning by imitation has often been overestimated.

It might seem that the most efficient way to learn new problem-solving operators would be simply to be told about them, but seeing an example of how a problem can be solved is often at least as effective as being told what to do. **Table 8.1** shows two forms of instruction about an algebraic concept, called a *pyramid expression* (Anderson & Fincham, 2014), which is unfamiliar to most undergraduates. In tests of which form is more effective, students either study the explanation, which describes a pyramid expression in words, or study the example, which shows a sample pyramid expression with labels to clarify some terminology. Then students are asked to evaluate pyramid expressions, like this one:

TABLE 8.1 What Is a Pyramid Expression?

Explanation

N$M is a pyramid expression for designating repeated addition where each term in the sum is one less than the previous.
N, the base, is the first term in the sum.
M, the height, is the number of terms you add to the base.

Example

$$\overset{\text{base}}{\underset{\text{height}}{7\$3}} = 7 + 6 + 5 + 4 = 22$$

Which form of instruction do you think would be more useful? Lee, Fincham, and Anderson (2015) found that participants did equally well with the two forms in learning mathematical concepts like the one illustrated in Table 8.1. The researchers performed a brain imaging study to see which regions were most active when participants were studying verbal instructions and when studying an example. They also looked at which brain regions were most active when solving problems after either form of instruction. Studying a verbal explanation tended to produce activity in visual regions of the occipital lobe (at the bottom of the brain image in **Figure 8.5a**), reflecting the reading process, whereas studying an example tended to produce activity in parietal and frontal areas (as shown in Figure 8.5b), where activity is often seen when participants are engaged in mathematical operations. Interestingly, brain activity when participants were solving problems was virtually identical following the two modes of study (see Figures 8.5c and 8.5d). This suggests that the two forms of instruction, when successful, lead to similar states of understanding, which is reflected in the similar brain activity during problem solving.

Many studies have been performed comparing the effectiveness of worked examples and verbal instructions in learning mathematical problem-solving skills (for a review, see Lee & Anderson, 2013). Of course, real mathematics instruction typically involves a mix of these two types of instruction. A large number of studies have also investigated how much verbal instruction adds to worked examples. Typically, providing instruction in addition to

Figure 8.5 Learning by Being Told and Learning by Example. Brain activity when studying a verbal explanation of a mathematical concept (a) occurs mainly in visual areas of the occipital lobe, whereas activity when studying an example of a mathematical concept (b) is concentrated in parietal and frontal areas. However, brain activity when solving a mathematical problem after verbal instruction (c) is virtually identical to activity when solving a problem after studying an example (d). *(John R. Anderson.)*

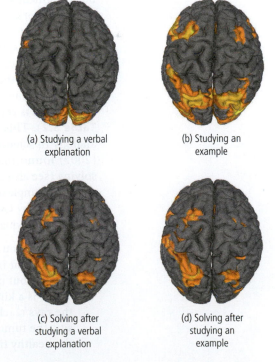

(a) Studying a verbal explanation

(b) Studying an example

(c) Solving after studying a verbal explanation

(d) Solving after studying an example

examples helps learning; but sometimes it actually hurts, and sometimes there is no effect. Verbal instruction is particularly helpful with examples that are obscure or suggest incorrect conclusions. For instance, if children are shown an example such as

$$3 \times 2 + 5 = 6 + 5 = 11$$

and are then asked to solve a problem like this

$$4 + 6 \times 2 = ?$$

many children will give 20 as the answer, mistakenly adding 4 and 6 to get 10 and then multiplying that by 2. Instruction can teach them to perform multiplication first $(6 \times 2 = 12)$ and then perform addition $(4 + 12 = 16)$, even though in this case addition is the first operation in the expression.

> *Problem-solving operators can be acquired by discovery, by direct instruction, or by example.*

Analogy and Imitation

In problem solving, **analogy** is the process by which a problem solver extracts the operators used to solve an example and maps them onto a solution for another problem. Sometimes, the process of analogy can be straightforward. For instance, a student may take the structure of an example worked out in a section of a mathematics text and easily map it into the solution for a problem in the exercises at the end of the section. At other times, the mapping can be more complex. For example, in 1911 the British physicist Ernest Rutherford demonstrated the validity of an analogy using the solar system as a model for the structure of the atom, in which electrons revolve around the nucleus of the atom in the same way as the planets revolve around the sun (Gentner, 1983; Koestler, 1964 — see **Table 8.2**). This is a particularly famous example of the frequent use of analogy in science and engineering. In one study, Christensen and Schunn (2007) found that engineers made 102 analogies in 9 hours of problem solving (see also Dunbar & Blanchette, 2001).

An example of the power of analogy in problem solving is provided in an experiment by Gick and Holyoak (1980). They presented their participants with the following problem (adapted from Duncker, 1945):

> Suppose you are a doctor faced with a patient who has a malignant tumor in his stomach. It is impossible to operate on the patient, but unless the tumor is destroyed, the patient will die. There is a kind of ray that can be used to destroy the tumor. If the rays reach the tumor all at once at a sufficiently high intensity, the tumor will be destroyed. Unfortunately, at this intensity the healthy tissue that the rays pass through on the way to the

TABLE 8.2 Analogy: Mapping the Structure of the Solar System onto a Model of the Atom	
Solar System	**Atom**
The sun attracts the planets.	The nucleus attracts the electrons.
The sun is more massive than the planets.	The nucleus is more massive than the electrons.
The planets revolve around the sun.	The electrons revolve around the nucleus.
The planets revolve around the sun because of the attraction and the mass difference.	The electrons revolve around the nucleus because of the attraction and the mass difference.
The planet Earth has life on it.	No mapping.

(Information from Gentner, 1983.)

tumor will also be destroyed. At lower intensities the rays are harmless to healthy tissue, but they will not affect the tumor either. What type of procedure might be used to destroy the tumor with the rays, and at the same time avoid destroying the healthy tissue? (pp. 307–308)

This is a very difficult problem, and few people are able to solve it. However, Gick and Holyoak presented their participants with the following story:

A small country was ruled from a strong fortress by a dictator. The fortress was situated in the middle of the country, surrounded by farms and villages. Many roads led to the fortress through the countryside. A rebel general vowed to capture the fortress. The general knew that an attack by his entire army would capture the fortress. He gathered his army at the head of one of the roads, ready to launch a full-scale direct attack. However, the general then learned that the dictator had planted mines on each of the roads. The mines were set so that small bodies of men could pass over them safely, since the dictator needed to move his troops and workers to and from the fortress. However, any large force would detonate the mines. Not only would this blow up the road, but it would also destroy many neighboring villages. It therefore seemed impossible to capture the fortress. However, the general devised a simple plan. He divided his army into small groups and dispatched each group to the head of a different road. When all was ready he gave the signal and each group marched down a different road. Each group continued down its road to the fortress so that the entire army arrived together at the fortress at the same time. In this way, the general captured the fortress and overthrew the dictator. (p. 351)

(a)

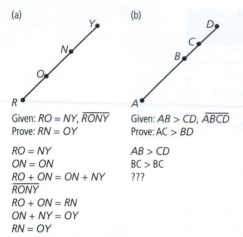

Given: $RO = NY$, $\overline{RONY}$
Prove: $RN = OY$

$RO = NY$
$ON = ON$
$RO + ON = ON + NY$
$\overline{RONY}$
$RO + ON = RN$
$ON + NY = OY$
$RN = OY$

(b)

Given: $AB > CD$, $\overline{ABCD}$
Prove: $AC > BD$

$AB > CD$
$BC > BC$
???

Figure 8.6 Using Analogy Incorrectly. (a) A proof given in a geometry text. (b) One student's misguided attempt to use analogy to apply the solution in (a) to a superficially similar problem.

Told to use this story as the model for solving the tumor problem, most participants were able to develop an analogous solution.

Figure 8.6 shows an interesting example of an unsuccessful attempt to use analogy to solve a geometry problem. Figure 8.6a gives the steps of a solution that a student's textbook used as an example, and Figure 8.6b shows the student's attempt to use that example to guide his solution to a homework problem. In Figure 8.6a, two segments of a straight line are given as equal in length, and the goal is to prove that two larger segments have equal length. In Figure 8.6b, the student is given two line segments as unequal in length, and his task is to prove the same inequality for two larger segments.

The student noted the obvious similarity between the two problems and proceeded to develop the apparent analogy. He thought he could simply substitute points on one line for points on another, and inequality for equality. That is, he tried to substitute A for R, B for O, C for N, D for Y, and $>$ for $=$. With these substitutions, he got the first line correct: Analogous to $RO = NY$, he wrote $AB > CD$. Then he had to write something analogous to $ON = ON$, so he wrote $BC > BC$! This example illustrates the danger in using analogy to create operators for problem solving without asking whether the analogy makes sense.

Another difficulty with analogy is finding appropriate examples from which to analogize operators. Often, participants do not notice when an analogy is possible. Gick and Holyoak (1980) did an experiment in which they first read participants the story about the general and the dictator and then gave them Duncker's (1945) ray problem (both shown above). Very few participants spontaneously noticed the relevance of the story to solving the problem. To achieve success, participants had to be explicitly told to use the general and dictator story as an analogy for solving the ray problem.

When participants do spontaneously use previous examples to solve a problem, they are often guided by superficial similarities in their choice of examples. For instance, Ross (1984, 1987) taught participants several methods for solving probability problems. These methods were taught by reference to specific examples, such as finding the probability that a pair of tossed dice will sum to 7. Participants were then tested with new problems that were superficially similar to prior examples. The similarity was superficial because both the example and the problem involved the same content (e.g., dice) but not necessarily the same principle of probability. Participants tried to solve the new problem by using the operators illustrated in the superficially similar prior example. When the principle illustrated in the example was the same as the principle required to solve the problem, participants were able to solve the problem, but when the principles were not the same, they were unable to solve the problem. Reed (1987) found similar results with algebra story problems.

In solving homework problems, students often use proximity in the textbook as a cue to determine which examples to use in making analogies.

For instance, a student working on physics problems at the end of a chapter expects that the methods used to solve example problems within the chapter will be the same methods needed to solve the problems at the end of the chapter (Chi, Bassok, Lewis, Reimann, & Glaser, 1989).

> *Problem solving by analogy involves identifying a past problem solution that is relevant to a current problem and then mapping the elements from that solution to produce an operator for the current problem.*

Analogy and Imitation from an Evolutionary and Brain Perspective

It has been argued that analogical reasoning is a hallmark of human cognition (Halford, 1992). The capacity to solve problems analogically is almost uniquely human. There is some evidence for this ability in chimpanzees (Oden, Thompson, & Premack, 2001), but lower primates such as monkeys seem totally incapable of such tasks. For instance, Premack (1976) reported that Sarah, a chimpanzee used in studies of language (see Chapter 12), was able to solve analogies such as the following:

> Key is to a padlock as what is to a tin can?
> The answer: can opener.

In more careful study of Sarah's abilities, however, Oden et al. (2001) found that although Sarah could solve such problems more often than chance, she was much more prone to error than human participants.

Brain-imaging studies have looked at the cortical regions that are activated in analogical reasoning. **Figure 8.7a** shows stimuli similar to those used in a study by Whitaker, Vendetti, Wendelken, and Bunge (2018) where participants were presented with visual stimuli that pose an analogy problem. The example in Figure 8.7a presents the analogy

> *dress* is to *closet* as *milk carton* is to *what*?

Participants had to identify the correct choice (in this case, the refrigerator) from a set of four choices. The 138 participants ranged in age from 6 to 19. Older participants chose correctly more often, but the researchers' real interest was in the brain activity predictive of choosing correctly. Figure 8.7b shows that activity in a left anterior prefrontal region was predictive of success. This is a region that shows considerable development over this age range. In another study, Wendelken, O'Hare, Whitaker, Ferrer, and Bunge (2011) found that, in children, activity in this region does not vary appropriately with the difficulty of the task, whereas it does vary appropriately in adults.

In problems like the one in Figure 8.7, completing the analogy is the end goal. From the perspective of this chapter, however, the real importance of analogy is that it can be used to acquire new problem-solving

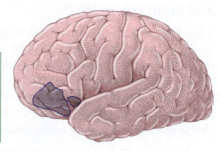

(a) Analogy problem

(b) Brain activity predictive of choosing correctly

Figure 8.7 Analogy and Brain Activity. (a) An analogy problem used by Whitaker et al. (2018). Participants had to choose the refrigerator to complete the analogy correctly: *dress* is to *closet* as *milk carton* is to *refrigerator* (i.e., a dress is stored in a closet, and a milk carton is stored in a refrigerator). (b) An increase in activity in a left anterior prefrontal region predicted successful completion of the analogy in trials across all participants, aged 6–19, after correcting for the effects of age. *(Research from Whitaker et al., 2018; dress: Leonid Nyshko/Alamy; wardrobe: Ingram Publishing/Alamy; milk: Gts/Shutterstock; cow: Eric Isselee/Shutterstock; clock: Kateryna Moiseyenko/Shutterstock; racket: pukach/Shutterstock; fridge: CoolPhotoGirl/Shutterstock.)*

operators for solving similar problems, as in the case of worked examples in mathematical instruction. Humans have a special ability to imitate others in solving problems. When we ask someone how to use an unfamiliar device, the person is likely to show us how, not tell us how. In comparison, despite the proverb "Monkey see, monkey do," monkeys and even the higher apes are quite poor at imitation (Tomasello & Call, 1997). Thus, it seems that one of the things that makes humans such effective problem solvers is that we have special abilities to acquire new problem-solving operators by using analogical processes to incorporate the operators we see others use.

> *Analogical problem solving appears to be a capability nearly unique to humans and to depend on the advanced development of the prefrontal cortex.*

Operator Selection

As noted earlier, in any particular state, multiple problem-solving operators can be applicable, and a critical task is to select the one to apply. In principle, a problem solver may select operators in many ways, and the field of artificial intelligence has succeeded in enumerating various powerful techniques. However, it seems that most methods are not particularly natural as human problem-solving approaches. Here we will review three criteria that humans use to select operators: backup avoidance, difference reduction, and means–ends analysis.

Backup avoidance biases the problem solver against any operator that undoes the effect of one or more previous operators. For instance, in the eight puzzle, people show great reluctance to take back a step even if this might be necessary to solve the problem. However, backup avoidance by itself, while eliminating certain operators, provides no basis for choosing among the remaining operators.

Difference reduction refers to the human tendency to select the operator that most reduces the difference between the current state and the goal. This is a very general principle that also describes the behavior of many other types of creatures. For instance, Köhler (1927) described how a chicken will move directly toward desired food and will not go around a fence that is blocking it. The poor creature is effectively paralyzed, being unable to move forward and unwilling to back up and go around because this would increase its distance from the food. Difference reduction and backup avoidance seem to be a chicken's only principles for selection of operators. This leaves it without a solution to the problem.

In contrast, the chimpanzee Sultan (see Figure 8.2) did not just claw at his cage trying to get the bananas. He created a new tool that enabled him to obtain the food. In effect, he pursued a new subgoal — the creation of a new means for achieving the main goal. **Means–ends analysis** is the term used to describe the creation of new subgoals (ends) to enable operators (means) to apply. By using means–ends analysis, humans and other higher primates can be more resourceful in achieving goals than they could be if they used only difference reduction and backup avoidance. In the next sections, we will discuss the roles of both difference reduction and means–ends analysis in operator selection.

> *Humans use backup avoidance, difference reduction, and means–ends analysis to guide their selection of operators.*

Difference Reduction

A common method of problem solving, particularly in unfamiliar domains, is to try to reduce the difference between the current state and the goal state. For instance, consider my solution to the eight puzzle in Figure 8.3. There were four options (operators) for the first move: to move tile 1, 4, 5, or 8 into the empty cell. I chose to move tile 4. Why? Because it seemed to get me closer to my end goal — I was moving the tile 4 closer to its final destination. (Moving tile 8 would have had the same effect.) Human problem solvers are often strongly governed by difference reduction or, conversely, by similarity increase. That is, they choose operators that transform the current state into a new state that reduces the difference from the goal state (or, equivalently, increases the similarity to the goal state). Difference reduction is sometimes called *hill climbing*. If we imagine the goal as the top of the highest point in some area of land, one approach to reaching it is always to take steps that go up, thereby reducing the difference (in height, in this case) between the goal state and the current state. Hill climbing has a potential flaw, however: We might reach the top of a hill lower than the highest point that is the goal. Thus, difference reduction is not guaranteed to work. It is myopic in that it considers only whether the next step is an improvement and does not ask whether the larger plan will work. (Means–ends analysis, which we will discuss later, is an attempt to take a more global perspective on problem solving.)

When applying difference reduction, problem solvers can improve operator selection by using more sophisticated measures of similarity. In the eight puzzle shown in Figure 8.3, my first move was intended simply to get a tile closer to its final destination. After working with many such tile problems, we may begin to notice the importance of sequence — that is, whether noncentral tiles are followed by their appropriate successors. For instance, after the 14th move in Figure 8.3 (the move marked with a red bar), tiles 3 and 4 are in sequence because they are followed by their successors, 4 and 5, respectively, but tile 5 is not in sequence because it is followed by 7 rather than 6. Trying first to move tiles into sequence proves to be more important than trying to move them to their final destinations right away. Thus, using sequence as a measure of increasing similarity leads to more effective problem solving based on difference reduction (see Nilsson, 1971, for further discussion).

The difference-reduction technique relies on evaluation of the similarity between the current state and the goal state, but in some problem-solving situations, a correct solution involves going against the grain of similarity. A good example is provided by a type of problem known as a river-crossing problem. Consider this problem involving hobbits and orcs:

> On one side of a river are three hobbits and three orcs. They have a boat on their side that is capable of carrying two creatures at a time across the river. Their goal is for all six of them to cross to the other side of the river. At no point on either side of the river can orcs outnumber hobbits (or the orcs would eat the outnumbered hobbits). How, then, can all six creatures get across the river without the hobbits ever being outnumbered?

Stop reading and try to solve this problem. **Figure 8.8** shows a correct sequence of moves, starting from the initial state (1), in which the hobbits (H) and

Figure 8.8 The Hobbits and Orcs Problem. In the initial state (1), three hobbits (H) and three orcs (O) and a boat are on side 1 of the river. The goal is for all six creatures to cross to side 2. At no point can orcs outnumber hobbits on either side of the river. The boat can carry two creatures at a time. The sequence of boat trips moving from state 1 to state 12 is a solution to the problem.

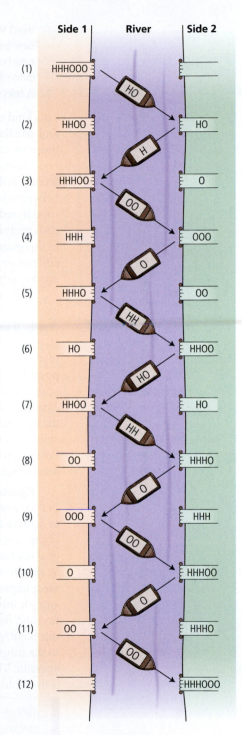

orcs (O) and the boat all start on one side of the river. Then a hobbit and an orc cross to side 2 (state 2). In state 3, one hobbit has taken the boat back, and so on until the problem is solved in state 12. Each state in the figure represents a different configuration of hobbits and orcs. In a study by Jeffries, Polson, Razran, and Atwood (1977), participants had a particular problem with the transition from state 6 to state 7—about a third of all participants chose to send two hobbits back to side 1—thereby recreating state 5—rather than sending a hobbit and an orc to side 1, to create state 7 (see also Greeno, 1974). One reason for this difficulty is that transporting a hobbit and an orc to side 1 involves moving two creatures back to the wrong side of the river, which appears to be a move away from the desired solution. Even though going back to state 5 simply undoes their previous move, participants would rather do that than move to a state that appears to be further from the goal.

It is worth noting that people do not get stuck in suboptimal states only while solving puzzles. Hill climbing can also produce suboptimal results when we are making serious life choices. A classic example is someone trapped in a suboptimal job because he or she is unwilling to get the education needed for a better job. The person is unwilling to endure the temporary deviation from the goal (of earning as much as possible) to get the skills needed to earn a higher salary.

> *People experience difficulty in solving a problem at points where the correct solution involves increasing the difference between the current state and the goal state.*

Means–Ends Analysis

Means–ends analysis is a more sophisticated method of operator selection than difference reduction. This method was extensively studied by Newell and Simon, who used it in a computer simulation program called the **General Problem Solver (GPS)** that modeled human problem solving. They describe means–ends analysis as typified by the following kind of commonsense argument:

> I want to take my son to nursery school. What's the difference between what I have and what I want? One of distance. What changes distance? My automobile. My automobile

won't work. What is needed to make it work? A new battery. What has new batteries? An auto repair shop. I want the repair shop to put in a new battery; but the shop doesn't know I need one. What is the difficulty? One of communication. What allows communication? A telephone . . . and so on. (Newell & Simon, 1972, p. 416)

This kind of analysis — classifying things in terms of the functions they serve and oscillating among ends, functions required, and means that perform those functions — forms the basic system of GPS.

Means–ends analysis can be viewed as a more sophisticated version of difference reduction. Like difference reduction, it tries to eliminate differences between the current state and the goal state. For instance, in this example, it tried to reduce the distance between the son and the nursery school. Means–ends analysis identifies the biggest difference first and tries to eliminate it. Thus, in this example, the focus is first on the difference in the general location of son and nursery school. The difference between where the car will be parked at the nursery school and the location of the classroom has not yet been considered.

Means–ends analysis offers a major advance over difference reduction because it will not abandon an operator just because it cannot be applied immediately. If the car did not work, for example, difference reduction would have one start transporting one's son to the nursery school on foot. The essential feature of means–ends analysis is that it focuses on enabling a blocked operator by temporarily turning the means into an end. That is, the problem solver deliberately ignores the final goal and focuses on the subgoal of enabling the means. In the example we have been discussing, the problem solver set a subgoal of repairing the automobile, which was the means of achieving the original goal of getting the child to nursery school. New operators can be selected to achieve this subgoal. For instance, installing a new battery was chosen. If this operator is blocked, yet another subgoal could be set (i.e., in this case, calling the repair shop).

Figure 8.9 shows two flowcharts representing the procedures used by GPS in means–ends analysis. A general feature of this approach is that GPS attempts to achieve a larger goal via intermediate subgoals. As shown in Flowchart 1 in Figure 8.9, GPS first analyzes the current state into a set of differences from the goal state and sets the elimination of each difference as a separate subgoal. Then, as shown in Flowchart 2, GPS tries to find an operator that will eliminate the most important remaining difference. If an operator is found but GPS cannot apply it immediately because a difference exists between the operator's condition and the state of the environment, GPS tries to eliminate *that* difference. At this point, enabling the means has become the end, and GPS applies Flowchart 2 to the subgoal of eliminating a difference that is blocking the application of an operator. The term *operator subgoal* is used to refer to a subgoal whose purpose is to eliminate a difference that is blocking application of an operator.

Means–ends analysis involves creating subgoals to eliminate differences blocking the application of desired operators.

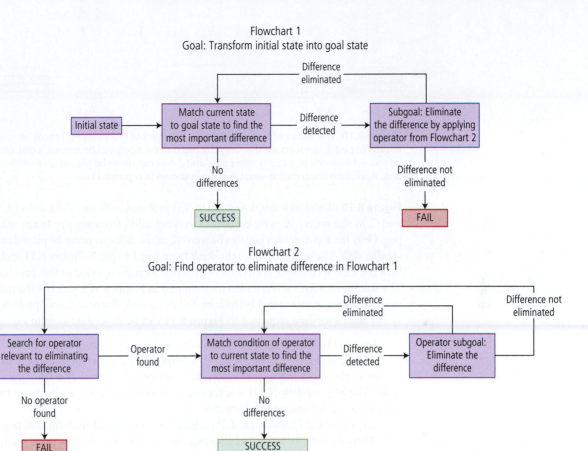

Figure 8.9 Means–Ends Analysis by Newell and Simon's General Problem Solving (GPS) Program. In Flowchart 1, GPS analyzes the current state into a set of differences from the goal state and sets a subgoal of eliminating the most important difference. In Flowchart 2, GPS tries to find an operator to eliminate that most important difference. If an operator is found but its application is blocked because of a difference between the operator's current condition and the condition of the environment, GPS sets an operator subgoal of eliminating that difference.

The Tower of Hanoi Problem

Means–ends analysis has proved to be a generally applicable and extremely powerful method of problem solving. Ernst and Newell (1969) discussed its application to the modeling of monkey and bananas problems (such as Sultan's predicament described at the beginning of the chapter), algebra problems, calculus problems, and logic problems. Here, however, we will illustrate means–ends analysis by applying it to the Tower of Hanoi problem, in which a stack of disks in size order on one of three pegs must be moved to another peg according to certain rules.

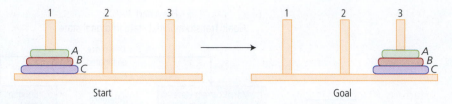

Figure 8.10 The Tower of Hanoi Problem. The stack of disks on peg 1 must be moved to peg 3. The rules are that only the top disk on a peg can be moved, a disk can be moved from any peg to any other peg, and a disk can never be placed on a smaller disk. A solution using means–ends analysis is shown in Figure 8.11.

Figure 8.10 illustrates a simple version of this problem, with just three disks (A, B, and C, in size order). A move consists of moving a disk from any peg to any other peg. Only the top disk on a peg can be moved, and a disk can never be placed on a smaller disk. The goal is to move the stack from peg 1 to peg 3. **Figure 8.11** shows how the GPS techniques illustrated in Figure 8.9 can be applied to this problem. The solution involves seven moves (highlighted in Figure 8.11), which is the minimum number of moves needed to solve the three-disk Tower of Hanoi problem.

The line-by-line sequence in Figure 8.11 can be described as follows:

Line 1: The final goal is to move disks A, B, and C from peg 1 to peg 3.

Lines 2 and 3: Per Flowchart 1 in Figure 8.9, GPS identifies what it perceives as the most important difference between the goal and the current state: The biggest disk (C) is not on peg 3. A subgoal is set to eliminate this difference, which takes us to Flowchart 2.

Lines 4–6: Per Flowchart 2, GPS selects the operator of moving C to peg 3. GPS then detects differences blocking this operator — A and B are on top of C. An operator subgoal is created to eliminate the most important of those differences — remove B from C — which takes us back to the start of Flowchart 2.

Lines 7–9: The operator chosen the second time in Flowchart 2 is to move B to peg 2. However, this operator cannot immediately be applied because GPS detects the difference that A is on top of B. Therefore, another operator subgoal — remove A from B — is set up, again taking us back to the start of Flowchart 2.

Lines 10–12: GPS finds that the operator relevant to achieving this subgoal is to move A to peg 3. No differences are detected between the conditions for this operator and the current state, and GPS applies the operator.

Lines 13–15: The subgoal of moving A to peg 3 is achieved. Now GPS returns to the earlier subgoal of moving B to peg 2. There are no differences between the condition of the operator (move B to peg 2) and the current state, and B is moved to peg 2.

Line 16–18: The subgoal of removing B from C is achieved, but GPS now detects the difference that A is on peg 3 and sets up the operator subgoal of removing A from peg 3 to eliminate this difference.

Line 19–21: To accomplish this subgoal, GPS finds the operator of moving A to peg 2. GPS detects no difference between the current state and this operator's condition and so applies that operator.

Lines 22–24: The subgoal of removing *A* from peg 3 is achieved, and GPS can finally apply the original operator of moving *C* to peg 3.

Lines 25–27: Having moved *C* to peg 3, GPS sets the new subgoal of eliminating the biggest remaining difference — *B* is not on peg 3.

Lines 28–45: GPS achieves this subgoal (line 37) by first moving *A* to peg 1 (lines 28–33) and then *B* to peg 3 (lines 34–37). The remaining difference is that *A* is not on peg 3, and this difference is eliminated in lines 38–43. In lines 44 and 45, GPS verifies that no differences now exist between the current state and the goal state and that the original goal has therefore been achieved.

Note that subgoals are created in service of other subgoals. For instance, to achieve the subgoal of moving the largest disk, GPS creates a subgoal of moving the second-largest disk, which is on top of it. It then creates a further subgoal of moving the smallest disk, which is on top of the second-largest disk (this logical dependency of one subgoal on another is indicated in Figure 8.11 by indenting the processing of each such subgoal). It appears that creating such goals and subgoals can be quite costly timewise. Both Anderson, Kushmerick, and Lebiere (1993) and Ruiz (1987) found that the time required to make a move in the Tower of Hanoi problem is a function of the number of subgoals that must be created. For instance, before the first move in Figure 8.11 (*A* to peg 3, on line 12), three subgoals have to be created, whereas no subgoals have to be created before the next move (*B* to peg 2, on line 15). Correspondingly, Anderson et al. (1993) found that it took participants 8.95 s on average to make the first move but just 2.46 s to make the second move.

In solving the Tower of Hanoi problem, could participants avoid the cost of setting subgoals by using the simpler difference-reduction method instead of the means–ends approach illustrated in Figure 8.11? The answer is no — a simple difference-reduction method would not be effective, because solving the Tower of Hanoi problem demands that one look beyond what is currently possible and have a more global plan of attack. That is, the only first move that difference reduction could make in Figure 8.10 would be to move the top disk (*A*) to the target peg (3), but then difference reduction would provide no further guidance because no second move would reduce the difference

1. Goal: Move *A*, *B*, and *C* to peg 3
2. : Difference is that *C* is not on 3
3. : Subgoal: Make *C* on 3
4. : Operator is to move *C* to 3
5. : Difference is that *A* and *B* are on *C*
6. : Subgoal: Remove *B* from *C*
7. : Operator is to move *B* to 2
8. : Difference is that *A* is on *B*
9. : Subgoal: Remove *A* from *B*
10. : Operator is to move *A* to 3
11. : No difference with operator's condition
12. : Apply operator (move *A* to 3)
13. : Subgoal achieved
14. : No difference with operator's condition
15. : Apply operator (move *B* to 2)
16. : Subgoal achieved
17. : Difference is that *A* is on 3
18. : Subgoal: Remove *A* from 3
19. : Operator is to move *A* to 2
20. : No difference with operator's condition
21. : Apply operator (move *A* to 2)
22. : Subgoal achieved
23. : No difference with operator's condition
24. : Apply operator (move *C* to 3)
25. : Subgoal achieved
26. : Difference is that *B* is not on 3
27. : Subgoal: Make *B* on 3
28. : Operator is to move *B* to 3
29. : Difference is that *A* is on *B*
30. : Subgoal: Remove *A* from *B*
31. : Operator is to move *A* to 1
32. : No difference with operator's condition
33. : Apply operator (move *A* to 1)
34. : Subgoal achieved
35. : No difference with operator's condition
36. : Apply operator (move *B* to 3)
37. : Subgoal achieved
38. : Difference is that *A* is not on 3
39. : Subgoal: Make *A* on 3
40. : Operator is to move *A* to 3
41. : No difference with operator's condition
42. : Apply operator (move *A* to 3)
43. : Subgoal achieved
44. : No difference
45. Goal achieved

Figure 8.11 Applying GPS to the Tower of Hanoi. The GPS program illustrated in Figure 8.9 goes through a sequence of 45 steps (including the seven actual moves highlighted) in solving the three-disk Tower of Hanoi problem shown in Figure 8.10.

between the current state and the goal state. Participants would have to make a random move. In a study of the way people actually approach the Tower of Hanoi problem, Kotovsky, Hayes, and Simon (1985) found that there was an initial problem-solving period during which participants did adopt this fruitless difference-reduction strategy but that they then switched to a means–ends strategy, after which the solution to the problem came quickly.

> *The Tower of Hanoi problem is solved by adopting a means–ends strategy in which subgoals are created.*

Goal Structures and the Prefrontal Cortex

It is significant that complex goal structures, particularly those involving operator subgoals, have been observed with any frequency only in humans and higher primates — for example, in Sultan's solution to the two-stick problem (see Figure 8.2). Novel tool building, a clear instance of operator subgoaling, is almost unique to the higher apes (Beck, 1980). The process of handling complex goal structures with subgoals is performed by the prefrontal cortex — which, as Figure 8.1 illustrates, is much larger in the higher primates than in most other mammals, and is larger in humans than in apes. Chapter 6 discussed the role of the prefrontal cortex in holding information in working memory. One of the major prerequisites to developing complex goal structures is the ability to maintain these goal structures in working memory.

Goel and Grafman (1995) looked at how patients with severe prefrontal damage performed in solving the Tower of Hanoi problem. Many were veterans of the Vietnam War who had lost large amounts of brain tissue as a result of penetrating missile wounds (bullets, shrapnel, etc.). Although they had normal IQs, they showed much worse performance than normal participants on the Tower of Hanoi task. There were certain moves that these patients had particular difficulty in finding. As we noted in discussing how means–ends analysis applies to the Tower of Hanoi problem, it is necessary to make moves that deviate from the prescriptions of hill climbing (difference reduction). One might have a disk at the correct position but have to move it away to enable another disk to be moved to that position. It was exactly at these points where the patients had to move "backward" that they had their problems. Only by maintaining a set of goals and subgoals in working memory can one see that a backward move is necessary for a solution.

More generally, it has been noted that patients with prefrontal damage have difficulty inhibiting a predominant response (e.g., Roberts, Hager, & Heron, 1994). For instance, in the Stroop task (see Chapter 3), these patients have trouble not saying the word itself when they are supposed to say the color of the word. The predominant response — saying the word they are reading — overrides the goal of saying the color and not the word, forcing that goal out of working memory.

There is increased activation in the prefrontal cortex during many tasks that involve organizing novel and complex behavior (Gazzaniga, Ivry, & Mangun, 1998).

Fincham, Carter, van Veen, Stenger, and Anderson (2002) did an fMRI study of students while they were solving Tower of Hanoi problems and looked at brain activation as a function of the number of goals that the students had to set. These students were solving much more complicated problems, involving more disks than the simple three-disk problem shown in Figure 8.10. For instance, the problem of moving a five-disk tower requires maintaining as many as five goals and subgoals to reach a solution. **Figure 8.12** shows the fMRI BOLD response of a region in the prefrontal cortex during a sequence of eight problem-solving steps in which the number of goals being held in working memory varied from one to four. There seems to be a striking match between the goal load and the magnitude of the fMRI response.

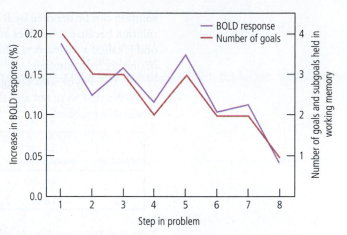

Figure 8.12 Brain Activation and Number of Goals While Solving a Tower of Hanoi Problem. Across a sequence of eight steps in solving the problem, the magnitude of the fMRI BOLD response in a region in the right, anterior, dorsolateral prefrontal cortex varied in synchrony with the number of goals being held in working memory. *(Data from Fincham et al., 2002.)*

> *The prefrontal cortex plays a critical role in maintaining goal structures.*

Giving Up on Problem Solving

We have been discussing how people search a problem space for a solution. What if the problem has no solution? Payne and Duggan (2011) studied participants trying to solve classic water jug problems in which participants imagine they have three jugs (A, B, and C) of different capacities and an unlimited water supply. The task is to measure out a specified quantity of water. Two example problems are shown in this table:

| | Capacity (cups) | | | Desired |
Problem	Jug A	Jug B	Jug C	Quantity
1	5 cups	40 cups	18 cups	28 cups
2	21 cups	127 cups	3 cups	100 cups

Participants are told to imagine that they have a sink so that they can fill jugs from the tap and pour water into the sink or from one jug into another. The jugs start out empty. The rules are that when filling a jug from the tap, participants must fill the jug to capacity, and that when pouring the water from a jug, participants must empty the jug completely. The goal in problem 1 is to get 28 cups using three jugs with capacities of 5 cups, 40 cups, and 18 cups. To solve this problem, participants would fill jug *A* and pour it into *B*, fill *A* again and pour it into *B*, and fill *C* and pour it into *B*. This solution can be denoted by $2A + C$. The solution for problem 2, with a desired quantity of 100 cups, is to fill jug *B*; fill *A* from *B*, leaving 106 cups in *B*; fill *C* from *B*, leaving 103 cups in *B*; empty *C*; and fill *C* again from *B*, leaving the goal of 100 cups in *B*. This solution can be denoted by $B - A - 2C$. The first solution is called an *addition solution* because it involves adding the contents of the jugs together; the second is called a *subtraction solution* because it involves subtracting the contents of one jug from another.

In the Payne and Duggan experiment, participants were also given problems that were not solvable. Different participants saw one of these two unsolvable problems:

Problem	Size of Problem Space	Capacity (cups)			Desired Quantity
		Jug A	Jug B	Jug C	
1	Smaller	18 cups	36 cups	9 cups	14 cups
2	Larger	15 cups	36 cups	9 cups	14 cups

Note that the capacities of all the jugs in problem 1 are divisible by 9, while the capacities of all the jugs in problem 2 are only divisible by 3. As a consequence, one can only reach states that are multiples of 9 in problem 1 and only reach states that are multiples of 3 in problem 2. Because there are many more states that are multiples of 3 than multiples of 9, problem 2 has a much larger problem space. **Table 8.3** indicates that two conditions influenced the amount of time participants spent on average before giving up trying to solve the problem. First, participants spent longer before giving up on problems with a larger problem space, which seems reasonable because they have more options to explore. Second, participants who were told that 75% of the problems were solvable spent longer before giving up than participants who were told that only 25% of the problems were solvable.

Giving up sooner makes sense when one thinks problems are unlikely to be solvable, but there is evidence that in many real-world situations people are too pessimistic about their ability to solve problems. It has been shown that, in many situations, people underestimate how much they could achieve if they just kept trying (e.g., Lucas & Nordgren, 2015). Such premature goal abandonment can be particularly problematic for individuals who believe that success is a matter of innate talent rather than effort (Dweck, 2008). One study found that lower SES (socioeconomic status) children were more likely than higher SES children to give up when stuck on a math problem. Similarly, women are more likely to give up than men when faced with failure in a mathematics contest (Buser & Yuan, 2016). Perhaps this reflects a phenomenon known as *stereotype threat,* reflected in overly pessimistic estimates of one's ability to solve a problem when one fears behaving according to a negative stereotype of one's social group (defined, for example, by gender, ethnicity, religion, or other such factors). For instance, when a test is perceived as related to gender differences in math ability, women perform worse than men, but no difference is found when the same test is not so perceived (Spencer, Steele, & Quinn, 1999).

TABLE 8.3 Time Spent Before Abandoning Problem Solving

Proportion of Problems Thought to Be Solvable	Size of Problem Space	
	Smaller	Larger
0.75	3.30 min.	4.55 min
0.25	2.85 min.	3.55 min

(Data from Payne & Duggan, 2011.)

> *Judgments about when to give up on solving a problem are based on properties of the problem, the person's history of past success at solving such problems, and perceptions of one's ability to solve such problems.*

Problem Representation

We have analyzed solving problems as a process consisting of identifying problem states and finding operators for changing states. The tasks we have discussed as being involved in this process are acquiring operators, selecting the appropriate ones, and deciding when to give up on solving a problem. However, there are also important effects of how one represents both the problem itself and the functions of the objects in the environment.

The Importance of the Correct Representation

A famous example illustrating the importance of problem representation is the mutilated-checkerboard problem (Kaplan & Simon, 1990). Suppose we have a checkerboard from which two diagonally opposite corner squares have been cut out, leaving 62 squares, as illustrated in **Figure 8.13**. Now suppose that we have 31 dominoes, each of which can exactly cover two squares of the board. Can you find some way of arranging these 31 dominoes on the board so that they cover all 62 squares? If it can be done, explain how. If it cannot be done, prove that it cannot. Perhaps you would like to ponder this problem before reading on. Relatively few people are able to solve it without some hints, and very few see the answer quickly.

The answer is that the dominoes cannot cover the checkerboard. The trick to seeing this is to include in your representation of the problem the fact that each domino must cover one black and one white square, not just any two squares. There is just no way to place a domino on two squares of the checkerboard without having it cover one black and one white square. So with 31 dominoes, we can cover 31 black squares and 31 white squares. But the mutilation has removed two white squares. Thus, there are 30 white squares and 32 black squares. It follows that the mutilated checkerboard cannot be covered by 31 dominoes.

Contrast this problem with the following "marriage" problem that occurs with many variations in its statement:

> In a village in Eastern Europe lived an old marriage broker. He was worried. Tomorrow was St. Valentine's Day, the village's traditional betrothal day, and his

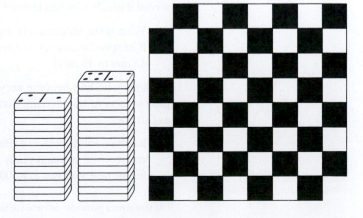

Figure 8.13 The Importance of Representation: The Mutilated Checkerboard Problem. Each of the 31 dominoes stacked on the left can cover two of the 62 squares in the mutilated checkerboard on the right. Can all the squares be covered by the dominoes? *(Information from Kaplan and Simon, 1990.)*

job was to arrange weddings for all the village's eligible young people. There were 32 eligible young women and 32 eligible young men in the village. This morning he learned that two of the young women had run away to the big city to found a company to build phone apps. Was he going to be able to get all the young folk paired off?

People almost immediately see that this problem cannot be solved[1] since there are no longer enough women to pair up with the men.

Both problems require the same insight of matching pairs (black with white squares in the case of the checkerboard, and men with women in the case of marriage), so why is the mutilated-checkerboard problem so hard and the marriage problem so easy? The answer is that we tend not to represent the checkerboard in terms of matching black and white squares, whereas we do tend to represent marriages in terms of matching brides and grooms. For either the checkerboard problem or the marriage problem, using such a matching representation allows the critical operator to apply (i.e., checking for parity).

Another problem that depends on correct representation is the 27-apples problem. Imagine 27 apples packed together in a crate 3 apples high, 3 apples wide, and 3 apples deep. A worm is in the center apple. Its life's ambition is to eat its way through all the apples in the crate, but it does not want to waste time by visiting any apple twice. The worm can move from apple to apple only by going from the side of one to the side of another, moving only horizontally (into the apple directly to the left, right, back, or front of its current apple) or vertically (into the apple directly above or below its current apple), not diagonally. Can you find a path by which the worm, starting from the center apple, can reach all the apples without going through any apple twice? If not, can you prove it is impossible? (*Hint:* The solution is based on a partial 3-D analogy to the solution for the mutilated-checkerboard problem; it is given in the appendix at the end of the chapter.)

Inappropriate problem representations often cause students to fail to solve problems even when they have the appropriate knowledge, which often frustrates teachers. Bassok (1990) and Bassok and Holyoak (1989) studied high-school students who had learned to solve physics problems such as the following:

> What is the acceleration (increase in speed each second) of a train, if its speed increases uniformly over a period of 12 seconds from 15 m/s to 45 m/s?

Students who had become very effective at solving such problems had very little success in transferring that knowledge to solving algebra problems such as this one:

> Juanita went to work as a teller in a bank at a salary of $19,400 per year and received constant yearly increases. After 12 years of work, her salary for the next year was $26,600. What was her yearly salary increase?

---

[1] At least given a particular definition of marriage.

The students failed to see that their experience with the physics problems was relevant to solving such algebra problems, which actually have the same structure. This happened because students did not appreciate that the knowledge associated with continuous quantities such as speed (m/s) was relevant to problems posed in terms of discrete quantities such as salaries (dollars/year).

> *Successful problem solving depends on representing problems in such a way that appropriate operators can be seen to apply.*

Functional Fixedness

Sometimes solutions to problems depend on the solver's ability to represent the objects in his or her environment in novel ways. This fact has been demonstrated in a series of studies by different experimenters. A typical experiment in the series is the two-string problem of Maier (1931), illustrated in **Figure 8.14**. The two strings hanging from the ceiling are to be tied together, but they are so far apart that the participant

Figure 8.14 Functional Fixedness I: The Two-String Problem. How could you tie the two strings together? Only 39% of the participants in Maier (1931) were able to see the solution within 10 minutes. A large majority of the participants did not perceive the pliers as a weight that could be used to transform a string into a pendulum.

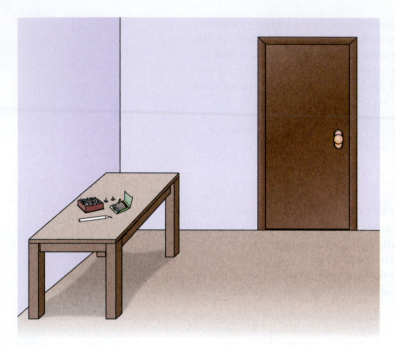

Figure 8.15 Functional Fixedness II: The Candle Problem. Can you figure out how to use the objects on the table to support the candle on the wall? *(Research from Duncker, 1945.)*

cannot grasp both at once. Among the objects in the room are a chair and a pair of pliers. Participants try various solutions involving the chair (e.g., standing on the chair or trying to use the chair to drag the free string closer), but these do not work. The only solution that works is to tie the pliers to one string and set that string swinging like a pendulum; then get the other string, bring it to the center of the room, and wait for the string with the pliers to swing close enough to catch. Only 39% of Maier's participants were able to see this solution within 10 minutes. The difficulty is that the participants did not perceive the pliers as a weight that could be used as a pendulum. This phenomenon is called **functional fixedness,** so named because people are fixed on representing an object according to its conventional function and fail to represent it as having a novel function.

An experiment by Duncker (1945) provides another demonstration of functional fixedness. Participants were asked to support a candle on a wall, ostensibly for an experiment on vision. As illustrated in **Figure 8.15**, a box of tacks, a book of matches, and the candle are on a table in the room. The solution is to empty the box of tacks, tack the box to the wall, and then use the box as a platform for the candle. This task is difficult because participants see the box as a container, not as a platform. If the box is filled with tacks at the start (as illustrated), participants have greater difficulty with the task than if the box starts out empty with some tacks lying next to it, because the full box reinforces participants' perception of the box as a container.

These demonstrations of functional fixedness are consistent with the idea that representation has an effect on operator selection. For instance, to solve Duncker's candle problem, participants needed to represent the tack box in such a way that it could be used by the problem-solving operators that were looking for a support for the candle. When the box was conceived of as a container and not as a support, it was not available to the support-seeking operators. There has been recent work on methods of getting participants to see the full range of potential functions for specific objects. For instance, McCaffrey (2012) trained participants to decompose objects into their primitive parts and features. If participants did this with the items in Figure 8.15, they would describe the parts of the tack box — their material and their shape. Such training improved solution rates on functional-fixedness problems from 49% to 83%. (**Implications 8.1** discusses human versus computerized approaches to solving a certain type of problem.)

> *Functional fixedness refers to people's tendency to see objects as serving conventional problem-solving functions and thus failing to see possible novel functions.*

Implications 8.1

When Humans Are Better at Solving Problems Than Computers

Much research has been done in both computer science and cognitive psychology on what is called the *traveling salesman problem*: A salesman wants to visit a set of cities and must find the shortest route that would let him visit each city just once and finish by getting back to the original city. While this is the popular way of stating the problem, it appears more abstractly as a computational problem in many areas, including DNA sequencing. In its traveling salesman form, the problem is typically presented to human participants as a set of dots like **Figure 8.16a**; participants try to draw a line connecting all the dots to make the shortest complete path. (Try solving this; then turn the page to see the optimal solution in **Figure 8.16b**. A gamified version of the problem — the traveling snakesman problem [Kickmeier-Rust & Holzinger, 2018] — is on the web at https://iml.hci-kdd.org/TravellingSnakesmanWS.)

Figure 8.17a shows how the amount of time that people take to solve this type of problem increases linearly with the number of points they have to connect. The figure shows the average total time to find a solution with various numbers of points and, for each number of points, breaks that total into the amount of time spent thinking about moves and the amount spent drawing the path line. This linear trend is interesting because it is not what computers show when solving for the optimal path — the time to solve the problem increases much more dramatically as the number of points increases (the best-known computer algorithms more than double their computation time with each additional point). However, unlike the computer algorithms, humans do not always find the optimal path. Figure 8.17b shows average path length of participants' solutions for various numbers of points versus the estimated optimal (shortest) path. Humans come close, but they tend to find the optimal path only when there are very few points to connect.

Like humans, a number of computer algorithms produce approximate solutions, but while faster than algorithms that produce optimal solutions, they still show a greater-than-linear increase in solution time as the number of points increases. This raises the question of why humans find a computationally hard problem relatively easy. It should also be noted that such problems are easy for other creatures who have to travel routes, such as rats (Bellizzi, Goldsteinholm, & Blaser, 2015) and honeybees (Lihoreau et al., 2012). The foraging paths used by these creatures closely approximate the optimal paths. Young children

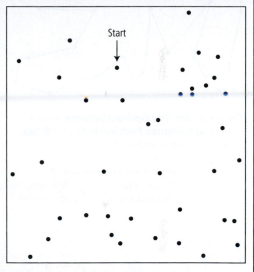

Figure 8.16a The Traveling Salesman Problem. Find the shortest path that goes through each dot once and returns to the start point.

Implications 8.1 (*Continued*)

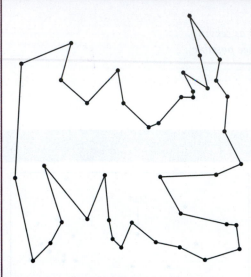

Figure 8.16b The Optimal Solution to the Traveling Salesman Problem in Figure 8.16a.
(Research from Dry, Lee, Vickers, & Hughes, 2006.)

(e.g., 7-year-olds) also do well in solving traveling salesman problems (van Rooij, Schactman, Kadlec, & Stege, 2006). One important factor in this better-than-computers performance is that we and other creatures can take advantage of the heavy investment that our brains have made in visual and spatial processing (as discussed in Chapters 2 and 4). For instance, people can perceive the boundary surrounding the points (called the *convex hull* in computer science), which helps in solving the problem (MacGregor and Chu,

2011). Many explanations of the human approach to these problems make reference to visual factors such as the Gestalt principles of good continuation and good form (Frisby & Stone, 2010). Some computer simulations of human solutions make heavy use of visual information (e.g., Pizlo et al., 2006), but a great deal of computation is required to perform visual analysis. Typical computer applications for traveling-salesman-type problems (e.g., in telecommunication or genetics) would not have a reason for investing effort to achieve human-level visual processing. However, in the course of evolution, the brains of humans have made that investment for other purposes, and we can deploy this capacity when confronted with a traveling salesman problem.

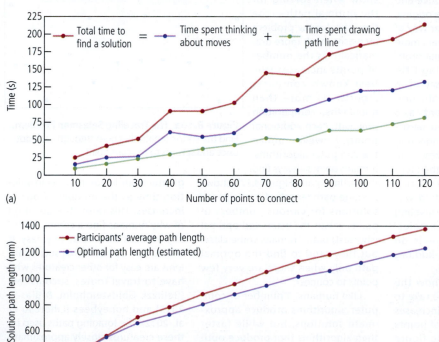

Figure 8.17 Human vs. Computer Performance on the Traveling Salesman Problem. (a) The average total time that participants take to solve a traveling salesman problem increases approximately linearly as the number of points increases. The components of that total time (thinking about moves and drawing the path line) also increase approximately linearly. (b) The average length of the paths drawn by participants versus the length of the optimal paths found by computer algorithms.
(Data from Dry et al., 2006.)

Set Effects

People's experiences can bias them to prefer certain operators when solving a problem. Such biasing is referred to as a **set effect**. A good illustration involves the water jug problems studied by Luchins (1942) and Luchins and Luchins (1959) (see the discussion of water jug problems in the section "Giving Up on Problem Solving" earlier in this chapter). In one experiment, Luchins (1942) first gave participants a series of problems that all could be solved by adding quantities of water together. This created a set effect that resulted in these participants being able to solve new addition problems faster, but subtraction problems (where water has to be poured out of a jug) slower, than participants who had had no practice. That is, the participants who had practiced addition problems were biased toward looking for solutions involving addition, which made them slower to find solutions involving subtraction.

TABLE 8.4 Water Jug Problems Used to Illustrate the Einstellung Effect

Problem	Capacity (cups)			Desired Quantity
	Jug A	Jug B	Jug C	
1	21	127	3	100
2	14	163	25	99
3	18	43	10	5
4	9	42	6	21
5	20	59	4	31
6	23	49	3	20
7	15	39	3	18
8	28	76	3	25
9	18	48	4	22
10	14	36	8	6

(Research from Luchins, 1942.)

The set effect that Luchins (1942) is most famous for demonstrating is the **Einstellung effect** (or *mechanization of thought*), which is illustrated by the series of problems shown in **Table 8.4**. Participants in one group were given all 10 problems in the order shown in the table and were required to find a solution for each problem. Participants in a control group were given just problems 6–10. Take time out from reading this text and try to solve each of the 10 problems.

The following chart shows which problems can be solved by which of three methods: $B - 2C - A$, $A + C$, or $A - C$ (for problems that can be solved by two of these methods, an asterisk identifies the simpler solution).

Problem	Can Be Solved By		
	$B - 2C - A$	$A + C$	$A - C$
1	✓		
2	✓		
3	✓		
4	✓		
5	✓		
6	✓		✓*
7	✓	✓*	
8	✓		✓
9	✓	✓*	
10	✓		✓*

This chart shows that problems 1–5 can be solved only by the $B - 2C - A$ method, whereas problems 6–10 can be solved by simpler methods. The $B - 2C - A$ method can also solve the last 5 problems except for problem 8. The following chart compares the performance of participants who worked on all 10 problems with that of the control participants, who worked on problems 6–10 only.

Performance	Participants Who Worked on Problems 1–10	Participants Who Worked Only on Problems 6–10
Used $B - 2C - A$ on problems 6 and 7	83%	< 1%
Failed to solve problem 8	64%	5%
Used $B - 2C - A$ on problems 9 and 10	79%	< 1%

These results indicate that working on the first five problems, which can be solved only by $B - 2C - A$, created a powerful bias for a particular solution that hurt the solution of problems 6–10. However, even though these effects are quite dramatic, they sometimes are relatively easy to reverse with the exercise of cognitive control. Luchins found that simply warning participants by saying "Don't be blind" after problem 5 allowed more than 50% of them to overcome the set for the $B - 2C - A$ solution.

Another kind of set effect in problem solving has to do with the influence of general semantic factors. This effect is well illustrated in the experiment of Safren (1962) on anagram solutions. Safren presented participants with lists such as the following, in which each set of letters was to be unscrambled and made into a word:

kmli graus teews recma foefce ikrdn

This is an example of an organized list, in which the individual words are all associated with drinking coffee. Safren found that the median solution time for each anagram in an organized list was 7.4 s, versus 12.2 s for each anagram in an unorganized list. Presumably, the facilitation evident with an organized list occurred because the earlier items in the list associatively primed, and so made more available, the later words. This anagram experiment contrasts with the water jug experiment in that no particular procedure was being strengthened. Rather, what was being strengthened was part of the participant's factual (declarative) knowledge about spellings of associatively related words.

In general, set effects occur when some knowledge structures become more available than others. These structures can be either procedures, as in the water jug problems, or declarative information, as in the anagram problems. If the available knowledge is what participants need to solve the problem, their problem solving will be facilitated. If the available knowledge is not what is needed, problem solving will be inhibited. It is good to realize that sometimes set effects can be dissipated easily (as with Luchins's "Don't be blind" instruction). If you find yourself stuck on a problem and you keep generating similar unsuccessful approaches, it is often useful to force yourself to back off, change set, and try a different kind of solution.

Set effects result when the knowledge relevant to a particular type of problem solution is strengthened.

Incubation Effects

People often report that after trying to solve a problem and getting nowhere, they can put it aside for hours, days, or weeks and then, upon returning to it, can see the solution quickly. The notable French mathematician Henri Poincaré (1929) reported many examples of this pattern, including the following:

> Then I turned my attention to the study of some arithmetical questions apparently without much success and without a suspicion of any connection with my preceding researches. Disgusted with my failure, I went to spend a few days at the seaside, and thought of something else. One morning, walking on the bluff, the idea came to me, with just the same characteristics of brevity, suddenness, and immediate certainty, that the arithmetic transformations of indeterminate ternary quadratic forms were identical with those of non-Euclidean geometry. (p. 388)

Such a phenomenon, called an **incubation effect,** was nicely demonstrated in an experiment by Silveira (1971) in which participants were asked to solve the cheap-necklace problem, illustrated in **Figure 8.18**. Participants were given the following instructions:

> You are given four separate pieces of chain that are each three links in length. It costs 2¢ to open a link and 3¢ to close a link. All links are closed at the beginning of the problem. Your goal is to join all 12 links of chain into a single circle at a cost of no more than 15¢.

Try to solve this problem yourself. (A solution is provided in the appendix at the end of this chapter.) Silveira tested three groups, each given a total time of half an hour to work on the problem. A control group worked on the problem for half an hour straight; 55% of these participants solved the problem. For one experimental group, the time spent on the problem was interrupted by a half-hour break in which the participants did other activities; 64% of these participants solved the problem. A second experimental group had a 4-hour break, and 85% of these participants solved the problem. Silveira required her participants to speak aloud as they tried to solve the problem. She found that they did not come back to the problem after a break with solutions completely worked out. Rather, they began by trying to solve the problem much as before. This result is evidence

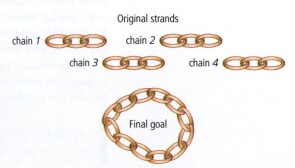

Figure 8.18 The Cheap-Necklace Problem. If it costs 2¢ to open a link and 3¢ to close a link, how can you connect the four pieces of chain into a single circle at a cost of no more than 15¢? Silveira (1971) used this problem to investigate the incubation effect.

Original strands

chain 1 chain 2

chain 3 chain 4

Final goal

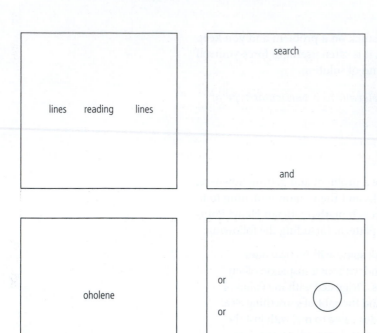

Figure 8.19 Find the Familiar Phrase. These puzzles were used by Smith and Blakenship to test the hypothesis that incubation effects occur because people "forget" inappropriate ways of solving problems. Participants had to figure out what familiar phrase was represented by each image. (Answers: top left: "reading between the lines"; top right: "search high and low"; lower left: "a hole in one"; lower right: "double or nothing.")

against a common misconception that people are subconsciously solving a problem during the period that they are away from it.

The best explanation for incubation effects relates them to set effects. During initial attempts to solve a problem, people set themselves to think about the problem in certain ways and bring to bear certain knowledge structures. If this initial set is appropriate, they will solve the problem. If the initial set is not appropriate, however, they will be stuck throughout the session with inappropriate procedures. Going away from the problem allows activation of the inappropriate knowledge structures to dissipate, and people are able to take a fresh approach.

The basic argument is that incubation effects occur because people "forget" inappropriate ways of solving problems. Smith and Blakenship (1989, 1991) performed a fairly direct test of this hypothesis. They had participants solve problems like those shown in **Figure 8.19**, where the goal is to think of the familiar phrase represented by each image (try this without looking at the answers in the figure caption). They provided half of their participants, the fixation group, with inappropriate ways to think about the problems, thus deliberately inducing incorrect sets. For instance, for the problem at the lower left in Figure 8.19, they told participants to think about chemicals. Not surprisingly, the fixation participants solved fewer of the problems than the control participants (who were not given any such "hints"). The interesting issue, however, was how much incubation effect these two groups of participants showed. Half of both the fixation and control participants worked on the problems for a continuous period of time, whereas the other half had an incubation period inserted in the middle of their problem-solving efforts. The fixation participants showed a greater benefit from the incubation period than did the control participants. When the researchers asked the fixation participants what the misleading hint had been, they found that the hint had been forgotten by more of the participants who had had an incubation period than by those who had not had an incubation period. Apparently, the incubation effect for the fixation participants occurred because they had forgotten the inappropriate hint about how to solve the problem.

Incubation effects occur when people forget the inappropriate strategies they were using to solve a problem.

Insight

A common misconception about learning and problem solving is that there are magical moments of insight when everything falls into place and we suddenly see a solution. This is called the "aha" experience, and many of us can report uttering that very exclamation after a long struggle with a problem that we suddenly solve. The incubation effect just discussed has been used to argue that the subconscious is deriving this insight during the incubation period. As we saw, however, what really happens is that participants simply let go of poor ways of solving problems.

Metcalfe and Wiebe (1987) came up with an interesting way to define an **insight problem** as one in which people are not aware that they are close to a solution. They proposed that problems like the cheap-necklace problem (see Figure 8.18) are insight problems, whereas problems requiring multistep solutions, like the Tower of Hanoi problem (see Figure 8.10), are noninsight problems. To test this, they gave participants problems of both types and asked them to judge every 15 s how close they felt they were to the solution. Typically, with noninsight problems, 15 s before they actually solved a problem, participants were fairly confident they were close to a solution. In contrast, with insight problems, participants had little idea they were close to a solution, even 15 s before they actually solved the problem.

Kaplan and Simon (1990) studied participants while they solved the mutilated-checkerboard problem (see Figure 8.13), which is another insight problem. They found that some participants noticed key features of the solution to the problem — such as that a domino covers one square of each color — early on. Sometimes, though, these participants did not judge those features to be critical and went off and tried other methods of solution; only later did they come back to the key feature. So, it is not that solutions to insight problems cannot come in pieces, but rather that participants do not recognize which pieces are key until they see the final solution. It reminds me of the time I tried to find my way through a maze, cut off from all cues as to where the exit was. I searched for a very long time, was quite frustrated, and was wondering if I was ever going to get out — and then I made a turn and there was the exit. I believe I even exclaimed, "Aha!" It was not that I solved the maze in a single turn; it was that I did not appreciate which turns were on the way to the solution until I made that final turn.

Sometimes, insight problems require only a single step (or turn) to solve, and it is just a matter of finding that step. What is so difficult about these problems is just finding that one step, which can be a bit like trying to find a needle in a haystack. As an example of such a problem, consider the following:

> What is greater than God
> More evil than the Devil
> The poor have it
> The rich want it
> And if you eat it, you'll die.

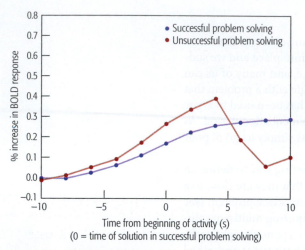

Figure 8.20 Brain Activity While Trying to Solve Remote Association Problems. Activity in a prefrontal region that is sensitive to memory retrieval increases with increasing time on task, but when solution attempts are successful, activity drops off shortly after the solution (at time 0). *(Data from Anderson et al, 2009.)*

Reportedly, schoolchildren find this problem easier than college undergraduates. If so, it is because they consider fewer possibilities as an answer. (If you are frustrated and cannot solve this problem, you can find the answer by searching the Web — many people have posted this problem on their Web pages.)

As a final example of insight problems, consider the remote association problems introduced by Mednick (1962). In one version of these problems (Mednick, 1962), participants are asked to find some word that can be combined with three words to make a compound word. So, for instance, given *fox, man,* and *peep,* the solution is *hole* (*foxhole, manhole, peephole*). Here are some examples of these word problems to try (the solutions are given in the appendix):

> print/berry/bird
> dress/dial/flower
> pine/crab/sauce

Jung-Beeman et al. (2004) conducted studies of brain activity while people tried to solve these problems, whose solution is often accompanied by a sudden feeling of insight (as is characteristic of insight problems in general). **Figure 8.20** shows results from our laboratory involving activity in a left prefrontal region that has been associated with retrieval from declarative memory (see Figures 1.16c and 7.6). Activity increases as the search for a solution progresses, reflecting increasing effort as the search goes on. However, when the search is successful, there is an abrupt drop in activity after the insight (time-lagged from the moment of insight at time 0, as we would expect with the BOLD response). It should be emphasized that other regions of the brain, such as the motor region, show a rise in activity at this point, associated with the generation of the response. Thus, the drop in activity in the prefrontal cortex, reflecting the end to the search for the solution, is strikingly different from the rise in activity in other brain regions. Typically, participants had been retrieving different possible answers, one after another, until finally getting the right answer, and the feeling of insight at that point corresponds to the moment when retrieval finally succeeds and activity drops in the retrieval area.

> *Insight problems are ones in which solvers cannot recognize when they are getting close to the solution.*

Conclusions

This chapter has been built around the Newell and Simon model of problem solving as a search through a state space defined by operators. We have looked at problem-solving success as determined by the operators available and the methods used to guide the search for operators. This analysis is particularly appropriate for first-time problems, whether a chimpanzee's quandary (see Figure 8.2) or a human's predicament when shown a Tower of Hanoi problem for the first time (see Figure 8.10). The next chapter will focus on the other factors that come into play after repeated practice at problem solving.

Questions for Thought

1. We discussed the issue of giving up on trying to solve a problem. A special case that students face concerns time-pressured tests that contain more problems than one might be able to solve in the given time (like a math SAT). In such situations one cannot spend too much time on any one problem. When you take such a test, how do you decide when to give up on a problem and move on to the next problem? This question is a topic in many test preparation courses.

2. In the modern world, humans frequently want to learn how to use devices such as a microwave oven or software such as a spreadsheet package. When do you try to learn such things by discovery, by following an example, and by following instructions? How often are your learning experiences a mixture of these modes of learning?

3. A common goal for students is getting a good grade in a course. There are many different things that you can do to try to improve your grade. How do you select among them? When do your efforts to obtain good grades constitute hill climbing (difference reduction) and when do they constitute means–ends analysis?

4. **Figure 8.21** illustrates the nine-dots problem (Maier, 1931). The problem is to connect all nine dots by drawing four straight lines, never lifting your pen from the page. Summarizing a variety of studies, Kershaw and Ohlsson (2001) report that given only a few minutes, only 5% of undergraduates can solve this problem. Try it, and if you get frustrated, you can find an answer by Googling "nine-dots problem." After you have tried to solve the problem, use some of the key terms listed below to describe the difficulties posed by this problem and what people need to do to solve it successfully.

Figure 8.21 The Nine-Dots Problem.

Key Terms

analogy
backup avoidance
difference reductions
Einstellung effect
functional fixedness

General Problem Solver (GPS)
goal state
incubation effect
insight problem

means–ends analysis
operator
problem space
search
search tree

set effect
state
subgoals

Appendix: Solutions

Solution to the eight puzzle (page 248). **Figure A8.1** shows the shortest sequence of moves for solving the problem solved less efficiently in Figure 8.3.

Figure A8.1 The Minimum-Path Solution for the Eight-Tile Problem. A less efficient solution is shown in Figure 8.3.

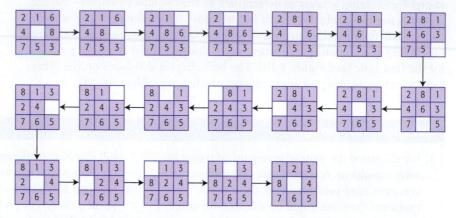

Solution to the problem of the 27 apples (page 270). The worm cannot succeed. To see that this is the case, imagine that the apples alternate in color, green and red, in a 3-D checkerboard pattern. If the apples were cubical, they would look like this:

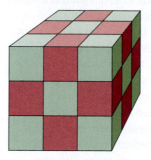

If the center apple from which the worm starts is red (like the hidden center cube in the illustration above), there are 13 red apples and 14 green apples in all. Each time the worm moves, it goes from an apple of one color to an apple of the other color. Because the worm starts from a red apple, it cannot reach more green apples than red apples—that is, once it reaches the 13th and last red apple, there will still be two green apples it has not reached. Thus, it cannot visit all 14 green apples if it also visits each of the 13 red apples just once.

Solution to the cheap-necklace problem (page 277). To solve the problem shown in Figure 8.18, open all three links in one chain (at a cost of 6¢) and then use the three open links to connect the remaining three chains (at a cost of 9¢).

Solutions to the three remote association problems (page 280). *Blue* (*blueprint, blueberry,* and *bluebird*), *sun* (*sundress, sundial,* and *sunflower*), and *apple* (*pineapple, crabapple,* and *applesauce*).

Expertise

It has been speculated that the expansion of the human brain from *Homo erectus* to modern *Homo sapiens* was driven by the need to quickly learn how to exploit the novel features of the new environments that our ancient ancestors were moving into (Skoyles, 1999). This ability to become expert at new things allowed humans to spread throughout the world and permitted the development of the technology that has created modern civilization. Humans are the only species that display this kind of behavioral plasticity — becoming experts at agriculture in Inca society, navigating the oceans by stars and other means in Polynesian society, and designing apps for modern smartphones in our society. William G. Chase, late of Carnegie Mellon University, was one of our local experts on human expertise. He emphasized two well-known sayings that summarize much of the nature of expertise and its development:

- No pain, no gain.
- When the going gets tough, the tough get going.

"No pain, no gain" refers to the fact that no one develops expertise without a great deal of hard work. John R. Hayes (1985), another former Carnegie Mellon faculty member, studied geniuses in a wide range of fields, including music, science, and chess. He found that no one reached genius levels of performance without at least 10 years of practice.

"When the going gets tough, the tough get going" refers to the fact that the difference between relative novices and relative experts increases as we look at more difficult problems. For instance, there are many chess duffers who could play a decent, if losing, game against a master if given unlimited time to choose moves. However, duffers would lose embarrassingly against masters if forced to play lightning chess, where each player is permitted only 5 seconds per move.

In Chapter 8, we reviewed some of the general principles governing problem solving, particularly in novel domains. These principles provide a framework for analyzing the development of expertise in problem solving. Expertise has been a major area of research in cognitive science and has been particularly exciting because of the important contributions it can make to the teaching of technical or formal skills in mathematics, science, and engineering.

This chapter will address the following questions about the nature of human expertise:

- What are the phases in the development of expertise?
- How does the organization of a skill change as one becomes expert?
- What are the contributions of practice versus talent to the development of skill?
- How much can skill in one domain transfer to a new domain?
- What are the implications of our knowledge about expertise for teaching new skills?

Skill Acquisition and Brain Activity

As people become more proficient at a task, they seem to use less of their brains to perform that task. **Figure 9.1** shows fMRI data from Qin et al. (2003), who were looking at areas of the brain activated over the course of five days, as college students learned to perform transformations on equations in an artificial algebra system. As the students achieved greater efficiency, regions of activity dropped out or shrank. The activity in these regions corresponds to metabolic expenditure, so as they developed expertise, the students were spending less mental energy doing these tasks.

A general goal of research on expertise is to characterize both the qualitative and the quantitative changes that take place with expertise. Figure 9.1, for example, depicts a quantitative change — more practice resulted in more efficient mental execution. We will look at a number of quantitative measures, particularly latency, that indicate this increased efficiency. However, there are also qualitative changes in how a skill is performed with practice.

Figure 9.1 does not reveal such changes — it just seems to indicate that fewer areas and smaller areas, rather than different areas, take part. However, this chapter will describe the results of other brain-imaging and behavioral studies that indicate that the way in which we perform a task and the associated brain activity can indeed change qualitatively as we become expert at it.

> *Through extensive practice, we can develop high levels of expertise in novel domains, a capacity that has supported the evolution of human civilization.*

Figure 9.1 Brain Activity during Skill Acquisition. Activity was much more extensive on day 1 than on day 5, as students practiced a complex mathematical skill. Note that these images depict "transparent" brains: the activation shown is not just on the surface of the brain but also below the surface. *(Research from Qin et al., 2003.)*

Brain Structures

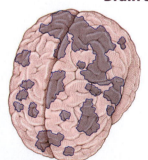

Day 1 of Practice

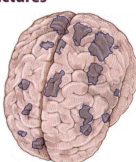

Day 5 of Practice

General Characteristics of Skill Acquisition

As we will see in this section, skill acquisition occurs across three phases, as skills are practiced to the point where they become virtually automatic. We will also see that the progression from novice to expert, in terms of the time taken to complete skill-related tasks, is reflected in a power law analogous to the power laws discussed in earlier chapters.

Three Phases of Skill Acquisition

The development of a skill typically can be characterized as passing through three phases (Anderson, 1983; Fitts & Posner, 1967). In the first phase, termed the **cognitive phase** by Fitts and Posner, participants develop a declarative encoding of the skill; that is, they commit to memory a set of facts relevant to the skill. Essentially, these facts define the tasks involved in performing the skill. Learners typically rehearse these facts as they first practice performing the skill. For instance, when I was first learning to shift gears in a standard transmission car, I memorized the location of the gears (e.g., "reverse is up, left" for an old 3-speed transmission) and the correct sequence of engaging the clutch and moving the stick shift. I rehearsed this information as I practiced performing the skill.

The information that I had learned about the location and function of the gears amounted to a set of problem-solving operators for driving the car. For instance, if I wanted to get the car into reverse, there was the operator of moving the gear to the upper left. Despite the fact that my knowledge about what to do next was clear, my driving performance was hardly skilled. My use of the knowledge was very slow because that knowledge was still in a declarative form. I had to retrieve specific facts and interpret them to solve my driving problems. I did not have the knowledge in a procedural form. (Procedural knowledge is discussed in Chapter 7.)

In the second phase of skill acquisition, the **associative phase,** two main things happen. First, errors in the initial understanding are gradually detected and eliminated. So, I slowly learned to coordinate the release of the clutch in first gear with the application of gas so as not to kill the engine. Second, the connections among the various elements required for successful performance are strengthened. Thus, I no longer had to try to remember how to get to second gear from first; I just did it. Basically, the outcome of the associative phase is a successful procedure for performing the skill. However, it is not always the case that the procedural representation of the knowledge replaces the declarative representation. Sometimes, the two forms of knowledge can coexist side by side, as when we can speak a foreign language fluently and still remember many rules of grammar. However, it is procedural knowledge, not declarative knowledge, that governs skilled performance.

The third phase in the standard analysis of skill acquisition is the **autonomous phase,** in which the procedure becomes more and more automatic and rapid. The concept of automaticity was introduced in Chapter 3, where we discussed how central cognition drops out of the performance of a task as we become more skilled at it. Complex skills such as driving a car or playing chess gradually evolve in the direction of becoming more automatic and requiring fewer processing resources. For instance, driving a car can become so automatic that a driver can engage in a conversation while driving and have no memory of the trip.

> *The three phases of skill acquisition are the cognitive phase, the associative phase, and the autonomous phase.*

Power Law of Learning

Chapter 6 documented the way in which the retrieval of simple associations improved as a function of practice according to a power law. It turns out that the performance of complex skills, requiring the coordination of many such associations, also improves according to a power law. **Figure 9.2** illustrates a classic example of such skill acquisition: the development of cigar-making ability by workers in a factory. The figure uses logarithmic coordinates to plot the time to make a cigar against the number of years of practice, and the nearly straight line until about the second year implies that the relationship up to that point is a power function (as discussed in Chapters 6 and 7). Why does the improvement appear to stop after the fifth year? It turns out that workers were approaching the limits of the cigar-making machinery (the line labeled

Figure 9.2 Learning to Make a Cigar. The time required to produce a cigar decreases as a function of the amount of experience. The relationship is a power function until the worker's speed approaches the limit imposed by the cigar-making machinery, after about two years of experience. *(Data from Crossman, 1959.)*

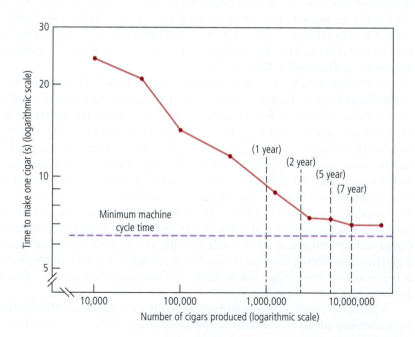

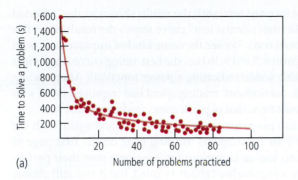
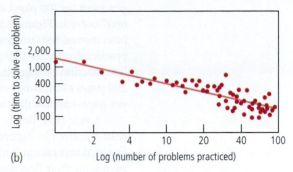

(a) Number of problems practiced

(b) Log (number of problems practiced)

Figure 9.3 Learning to Prove Theorems. (a) The time required to generate a proof in a geometry-like proof system declined as a function of the number of proofs already done. (b) Plotting the function in (a) on logarithmic scales yields a linear best-fitting curve, showing that it is a power function. *(Data from Neves & Anderson, 1981.)*

"Minimum machine cycle time" in Figure 9.2) and therefore could improve no more. As is usually the case in skill acquisition, there is a limit on how much improvement can be achieved, determined by the equipment, the person's age and physical condition, and so on. However, there is no limit on how much the cognitive component of a skill can speed up — it will go to zero, given enough practice.

In domains of complex problem solving, such as giving justifications for geometry-like proofs, performance also improves with practice according to a power function, as shown in **Figure 9.3** (Neves & Anderson, 1981). Such functions illustrate that the benefit of further practice rapidly diminishes but that, no matter how much practice we have had, further practice will help a little.

Kolers (1979) used normal and spatially transformed reading materials like those illustrated in **Figure 9.4** to investigate the acquisition of reading skills. Text N is normal; in text R, each line has been reversed (turned upside down and backward); in text I, each line has been inverted (turned upside down); and text M is a mirror image of normal text. In one experiment, Kolers looked at the effect of massive practice on reading inverted (I) text. Initially, before any practice, participants took more than 16 min to read a page of inverted text, compared with 1.5 min per page for normal text. After this initial test, participants

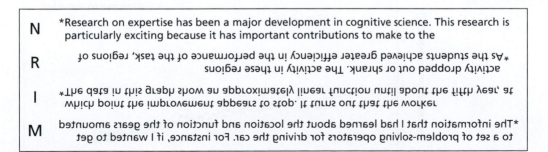

Figure 9.4 Spatially Transformed Texts. Kolers (1979) used materials like these in his studies of the acquisition of reading skills. The asterisks indicate the starting point for reading.

practiced on 200 pages of inverted text, with the results shown by the "inverted text" curve in **Figure 9.5a** (the "normal text" curve shows the results for a few interspersed tests on normal text). We see the same kind of improvement with practice that we see in Figures 9.2 and 9.3b (i.e., the best-fitting curve is a straight line function on logarithmic scales, indicating a power function). After reading 200 pages of inverted text, participants' reading speed had improved to 1.6 min per page—almost the same rate as that of participants reading normal text.

A year later, Kolers had his participants read inverted text again, with the results shown in Figure 9.5b. Participants' reading time on the first page of inverted text (about 3 min) was an enormous improvement over their performance on their first page a year earlier (about 16 min), but it was still almost twice as long as their reading time per page after 200 pages of training a year earlier (about 1.6 min). They had clearly forgotten something. Nevertheless,

Figure 9.5 Reading Speed on Inverted Text. (a) The time participants took to read a page of inverted text improved from about 16 min initially (before any practice) to about 1.6 min after 200 pages of practice (pages of normal text were occasionally interspersed). (b) A year later, participants' initial performance was about 3 min per page, and they reached their original level of performance after just 50 pages of practice (again with normal text occasionally interspersed). In both panels, the best-fitting straight line on logarithmic scales shows that the relationship between performance and practice is a power function. *(Data from Kolers, 1976.)*

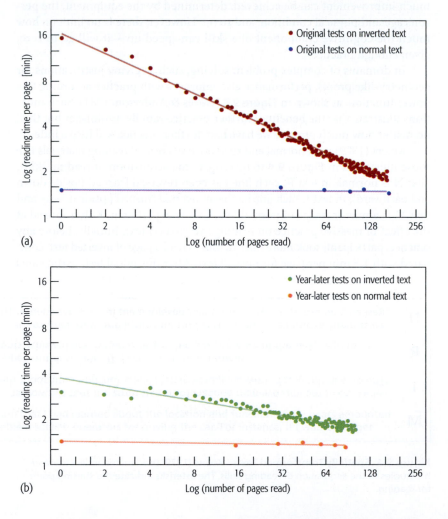

participants' performance again improved with practice in a power-function relationship, as shown by the best-fitting straight line in Figure 9.5b. The same level of performance that participants had initially reached after 200 pages of training was now reached after 50 pages. This example illustrates the fact that skills generally show very high levels of retention. In many cases, complex skills can be maintained for years with no retention loss. Someone coming back to a skill — skiing, for example — after many years of absence often requires just a short warm-up period before the skill is reestablished (Schmidt, 1988).

In an fMRI study, Poldrack and Gabrieli (2001) investigated the brain correlates of the changes taking place as participants learn to read transformed texts like those in Figure 9.4. They found increased activity in the basal ganglia and decreased activation in the hippocampus as learning progressed. Recall from Chapters 6 and 7 that the basal ganglia are associated with procedural knowledge, whereas the hippocampus is associated with declarative knowledge. Similar changes in the activation of brain areas were found by Poldrack et al. (1999) as participants developed skill in classifying stimuli. Participants appeared to move from the cognitive phase to the associative phases — that is, to direct recognition of the stimuli. Thus, the results of this brain-imaging research reveal changes consistent with the switch discussed in the preceding section, between the cognitive and the associative phases. In other words, qualitative changes appear to be contributing to the quantitative changes captured by the power function. We will consider these qualitative changes in more detail in the next section.

> *Performance of a cognitive skill improves as a power function of practice and shows modest declines only over long retention intervals.*

The Nature of Expertise

So far in this chapter we have considered some of the phenomena associated with skill acquisition. An understanding of the mechanisms behind these phenomena has come from examining the nature of expertise in various fields, such as mathematics, chess, computer programming, and physics. This research compares people at different levels of development of their expertise. Sometimes this research is truly longitudinal, following specific groups of students from their introduction to a field to their development of some expertise. More typically, such research samples people at different levels of expertise. For instance, research on medical expertise might look at students just beginning medical school, residents, and doctors with many years of medical practice. This research has begun to identify some of the ways in which problem solving becomes more effective with experience. The following subsections describe some of these dimensions of the development of expertise.

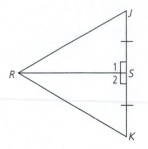

Given: ∠1 and ∠2 are right angles
$\overline{JS} \cong \overline{KS}$
Prove: ΔRSJ ≅ ΔRSK

Figure 9.6 Proving That Two Triangles Are Congruent: I. The first geometry-proof problem encountered by a student after studying the side-side-side and side-angle-side postulates.

Figure 9.7 Proving That Two Triangles Are Congruent: II. The sixth geometry-proof problem encountered by a student after studying the side-side-side and side-angle-side postulates.

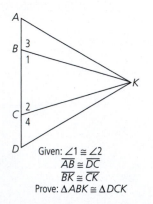

Given: ∠1 ≅ ∠2
$\overline{AB} \cong \overline{DC}$
$\overline{BK} \cong \overline{CK}$
Prove: ΔABK ≅ ΔDCK

Proceduralization

The degree to which participants rely on declarative versus procedural knowledge changes dramatically as expertise develops, as is illustrated in my own work on the development of expertise in geometry (Anderson, 1982). One student had just learned the side-side-side (SSS) and side-angle-side (SAS) postulates for proving triangles congruent. The side-side-side postulate states that, if three sides of one triangle are congruent to the corresponding sides of another triangle, the triangles are congruent. The side-angle-side postulate states that, if two sides and the included angle of one triangle are congruent to the corresponding parts of another triangle, the triangles are congruent. **Figure 9.6** shows the first problem that the student had to solve. As part of the study, the student was required to think aloud, and the following passage indicates that he began by trying to decide which postulate to use:

> If you looked at the side-angle-side postulate [long pause] well *RK* and *RJ* could almost be [long pause] what the missing [long pause] the missing side. I think somehow the side-angle-side postulate works its way into here [long pause]. Let's see what it says: "Two sides and the included angle." What would I have to have to have two sides *JS* and *KS* are one of them. Then you could go back to *RS* = *RS*. So that would bring up the side-angle-side postulate [long pause]. But where would Angle 1 and Angle 2 are right angles fit in [long pause] wait I see how they work [long pause]. *JS* is congruent to *KS* [long pause] and with Angle 1 and Angle 2 are right angles that's a little problem [long pause]. OK, what does it say — check it one more time: "If two sides and the included angle of one triangle are congruent to the corresponding parts." So I have got to find the two sides and the included angle. With the included angle you get Angle 1 and Angle 2. I suppose [long pause] they are both right angles, which means they are congruent to each other. My first side is *JS* is to *KS*. And the next one is *RS* to *RS*. So these are the two sides. Yes, I think it is the side-angle-side postulate. (Anderson, 1982, pp. 381–382)

After a series of four more problems (two solved by SAS and two by SSS), the student applied the SAS postulate in solving the problem illustrated in **Figure 9.7**, as indicated in the following passage:

> Right off the top of my head I am going to take a guess at what I am supposed to do: Angle *DCK* [angle 4] is congruent to Angle *ABK* [angle 3]. There is only one of two and the side-angle-side postulate is what they are getting to. (Anderson, 1982, p. 382)

A number of things seem striking about the contrast between these two passages. One is that the process of deciding about which postulate to apply has clearly sped up. Another is that there is no verbal rehearsal of the statement of the postulate in the second passage — that is, the student is no longer calling a declarative representation of the postulate into working memory. Note also that, in the first passage, working memory fails a number of times — points at which the student had to recover information that he had forgotten. A third contrast is that, in the first passage, application of the postulate is piecemeal; the student separately identifies each element of the postulate. In the second passage, the student appears to match the postulate to the problem in a single step.

The transition from the first passage to the second passage is like the transition that Fitts and Posner (1967) characterized as marking the movement from the cognitive to the associative phase of skill acquisition. The student is no longer relying on verbal recall of the postulate but has advanced to the point where he can simply recognize the application of the postulate as a pattern. Pattern recognition is an important part of the procedural embodiment of a skill. We no longer have to think about what to do next; we just recognize what is appropriate for the situation. The process of converting the deliberate use of declarative knowledge into pattern-driven application of procedural knowledge is called **proceduralization.**

In Anderson (2007), I reviewed a number of studies in our laboratory looking at the effects of practice on the performance of mathematical problem-solving tasks like the ones we have been discussing in this section. We were interested in the effects of this sort of practice on the three brain regions illustrated in Figure 1.15:

Motor region: involved in programming the actual motor movements in writing out the solution.

Parietal region: involved in representing the problem internally.

Prefrontal region: involved in retrieving information such as the task instructions.

In addition we looked at a fourth region:

Anterior cingulate cortex (ACC): involved in the control of cognition (see Figure 3.2 and the later discussion in the Chapter 3 section "Prefrontal Sites of Executive Control").

Figure 9.8 shows the mean level of activation in these regions initially and after 5 days of practice. The activation for motor movements and for cognitive control (in the ACC) does not change much after practice. There is some reduction in activation in the parietal region, suggesting that the representational demands may decrease a bit after practice. However, the dramatic

Figure 9.8 Brain Activity in Four Regions while Performing Mathematical Problem-Solving Tasks: Before and after Practice. Five days of practice do not have much effect on activity in motor regions or on activity in the ACC. The reduction in activity in the parietal region indicates that the mental effort involved in representing problems decreases with practice. The major reduction in activity in the prefrontal region indicates that much less retrieval of declarative knowledge is needed after practice.

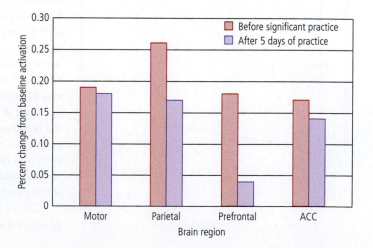

change is in activation in the prefrontal region, where a major decrease after practice indicates that task instructions are no longer being retrieved; rather, knowledge of task instructions is being directly applied.

> Proceduralization *refers to the process by which people switch from explicit use of declarative knowledge to direct application of procedural knowledge, which enables them to perform a task without thinking about it.*

Tactical Learning

As students practice problems, they come to learn the sequences of actions required to solve them or the actions required to solve their component parts. Learning to execute such sequences of actions is called **tactical learning.** A tactic is a method of accomplishing a particular goal. For instance, Greeno (1974) found that it took only about four repetitions of the hobbits and orcs problem (see the discussion surrounding Figure 8.8) before participants learned the tactic that enabled them to solve the problem perfectly. In this experiment, participants were learning the sequence of moves for getting the six creatures across the river. Once they had learned the sequence, they could simply recall it and did not have to figure it out.

Logan (1988) argued that a general mechanism of skill acquisition involves learning that enables us to recall solutions to problems that formerly had to be figured out. A nice illustration of this mechanism is from a domain called alpha-arithmetic, which entails solving problems such as $F + 3$, in which the participant is supposed to say the letter that is the corresponding number of letters forward in the alphabet — in this case, $F + 3 = I$. Logan and Klapp (1991) performed an experiment in which they gave participants problems with numbers (termed *addends*) from 2 (e.g., $C + 2$) through 5 (e.g., $G + 5$). **Figure 9.9** shows the time taken by participants to solve these problems initially and then after 12 sessions of practice on the same set of problems, repeated again and again across the sessions. Initially, participants took 1.5 seconds longer on problems with addend 5 than on problems with addend 2, because it takes longer to count five letters forward in the alphabet than it does to count two letters. However, after the repeated practice, participants became faster on all problems, reaching the point where they could solve with 5 as quickly as with 2. They had memorized the answers and so were not going through the procedure of solving each problem by counting.

There is evidence that, as people become more practiced at a task and shift from computation to

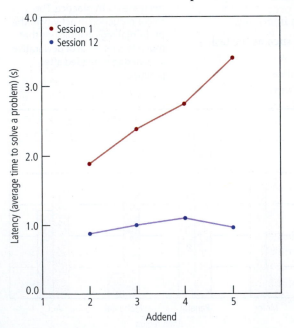

Figure 9.9 Solving Alpha-Arithmetic Problems: Before and after Practice. After 12 sessions, participants not only solved alpha-arithmetic problems in considerably less time, but also were able to solve addend 5 problems as quickly as addend 2 problems, because they had memorized the answers. *(Data from Logan & Klapp, 1991.)*

retrieval, brain activation shifts from the prefrontal cortex to more posterior areas of the cortex. For instance, Jenkins, Brooks, Nixon, Frackowiak, and Passingham (1994) looked at participants learning to make various sequences of finger presses on a keyboard, such as ring-index-middle-little-middle-index-ring-index. They compared participants initially learning these sequences with participants practiced in them. Using PET imaging, the researchers found that there was more activation in frontal areas early in learning than late in learning, whereas later in learning, there was more activation in the hippocampus, which is a structure associated with memory. Such results indicate that, early in learning a task, there is significant involvement of the ACC in organizing the behavior needed to accomplish the task, but that, late in learning, participants are just recalling the process from memory. Thus, these neurophysiological data are consistent with Logan's proposal.

> *Tactical learning is a process by which people learn specific procedures for solving specific problems.*

Strategic Learning

Many types of smaller problems repeat so often that we can solve them using tactical learning — that is, by memorizing the sequences of actions involved in solving the problems. Although large and complex problems tend not to repeat exactly, they still can be similar in overall structure, and one can learn how to organize one's solution in relation to that structure. This process — learning how to organize one's problem solving to capitalize on the general structure of a class of problems — is referred to as **strategic learning.** The contrast between tactical and strategic learning in skill acquisition is analogous to the distinction between tactics and strategy in the military. In the military, tactics refers to smaller-scale battlefield maneuvers, whereas strategy refers to higher-level organization of a military campaign. Similarly, tactical learning involves learning new pieces of skill, whereas strategic learning is concerned with putting the pieces together.

One of the clearest demonstrations of strategic learning occurs in the domain of physics problem solving. Researchers have compared novice and expert solutions to problems like the one depicted in **Figure 9.10**. A block of mass m begins at rest at the top of an inclined plane of length l and then starts sliding down the plane; the coefficient of friction is μ; and θ is the angle between the plane and the horizontal (Figure 9.10 depicts a time after the block has begun sliding down). The participant's task is to find the velocity of the block when it reaches the bottom of the plane. The novices in these studies are beginning college students, and the experts are their teachers.

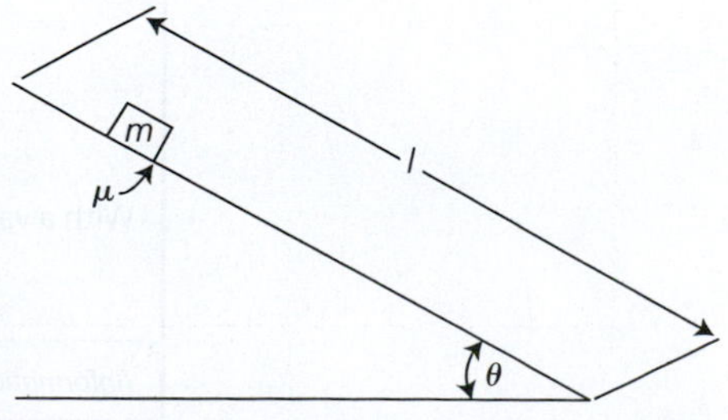

Figure 9.10 Solving a Physics Problem: Novices vs. Experts. A block is sliding down an inclined plane of length l at an angle θ with the horizontal; μ is the coefficient of friction. What will be the velocity v of the block when it reaches the bottom of the plane? Tables 9.1 and 9.2 contrast novice and expert approaches to solving this problem. *(Information from Larkin, 1981.)*

Larkin (1981) found a difference in how novices and experts approached the problem, as shown in **Table 9.1** (a typical novice's solution) and **Table 9.2** (a typical expert's solution). The novice's solution typifies the method of reasoning backward, which starts with the unknown — in this case, the velocity v. Then the novice finds an equation for calculating v. However, to calculate v by this equation, it is necessary to calculate a, the acceleration. So the novice finds an equation for calculating a; and the novice chains backward in this way until a set of equations is found for solving the problem.

The expert, in contrast, uses similar equations but in the completely opposite order. The expert starts with quantities that can be directly computed, such as gravitational force, and works toward the desired velocity. It is also apparent that the expert is speaking a bit like the physics teacher that he is, leaving the final substitutions for the student.

Unlike Larkin (1981), a study by Priest and Lindsay (1992) failed to find a difference in problem-solving direction between novices and experts. Participants in their study included British university students rather than American students, and they found that both novices and experts predominantly reasoned forward. However, their experts were much more successful in doing so than their novices were. Priest and Lindsay suggest that the experts have the

---

TABLE 9.1 Typical Novice Solution to a Physics Problem

To find the desired final speed v requires a principle with v in it — say

$$v = v_0 + 2at$$

But both a and t are unknown; so that seems hopeless. Try instead

$$v^2 - v_0^2 = 2ax$$

In that equation, v_0 is zero and x is known; so it remains to find a. Therefore, try

$$F = ma$$

In that equation, m is given and only F is unknown; therefore, use

$$F = \Sigma F's$$

which in this case means

$$F = F_g'' - f$$

where F_g'' and f can be found from

$$F_g'' = mg \sin \theta$$
$$f = \mu N$$
$$N = mg \cos \theta$$

With a variety of substitutions, a correct expression for speed can be found:

$$v = \sqrt{2(g \sin \theta - \mu g \cos \theta)}$$

(Information from Larkin, 1981.)

TABLE 9.2 Skilled Solution to a Physics Problem

The motion of the block is accounted for by the gravitational force,

$$F_g'' = mg \sin \theta$$

directed downward along the plane, and the frictional force,

$$f = \mu mg \cos \theta$$

directed upward along the plane. The block's acceleration a is then related to the (signed) sum of these forces by

$$F = ma$$

or

$$mg \sin \theta - \mu mg \cos \theta = ma$$

Knowing the acceleration a, it is then possible to find the block's final speed v from the relations

$$l = \frac{1}{2}at^2$$

and

$$v = at$$

(Information from Larkin, 1981.)

necessary experience to know which forward inferences are appropriate for a problem. It seems that novices have two choices — reason forward, but often fail (Priest & Lindsay's students) or reason backward, which is hard (Larkin's students).

Reasoning backward is hard because it requires setting goals and subgoals and keeping track of them. For instance, students must remember that they are calculating F so that a can be calculated in order for v to be calculated. Thus, reasoning backward puts a severe strain on working memory, which can lead to errors. Reasoning forward eliminates the need to keep track of subgoals. However, to reason forward successfully, one must know which of the many possible forward inferences are relevant to the solution, and this is what an expert learns with experience. That is, experts learn to associate various inferences with various patterns of features in the problems. The novices in Larkin's study seemed to prefer struggling with backward reasoning, whereas the novices in Priest and Lindsay's study tried forward reasoning without much success.

Not all domains show this advantage for forward reasoning in problem solving. In computer programming, for example (Anderson, Farrell, & Sauers, 1984; Jeffries, Turner, Polson, & Atwood, 1981; Rist, 1989), both novice and expert programmers develop programs in a top-down manner — that is, they work from the statement of the problem to subproblems to sub-subproblems, and so on, until they solve the problem. This top-down development is basically the same as reasoning backward in the context of geometry or physics. However, there are differences between expert programmers and novice programmers. Experts tend to develop problem solutions breadth first, in which they will completely work out the high-level solution, then decompose that into more detail, and so on, until they get to the final code. In contrast, novices will completely code individual parts of the problem before really working out the overall solution. Physics and geometry problems have a rich set of givens that are more predictive of solutions than is the goal, and this enables forward problem solving. In contrast, nothing in the typical statement of a programming problem would guide a working forward (or bottom-up) solution. The typical problem statement only describes the goal and often does so with information that will guide a top-down solution. Thus, we see that expertise in particular domains means adopting the problem-solving approaches that tend to be successful in those domains.

In summary, the transition from novice to expert does not entail the same changes in strategy in all domains. Different problem domains have different structures that make different strategies optimal. Physics experts learn to reason forward; programming experts learn breadth-first expansion.

> *Strategic learning refers to a process by which people learn to organize their problem solving.*

Problem Perception

As they acquire expertise, problem solvers learn to perceive problems in ways that enable more effective problem-solving procedures to apply. This dimension of learning can be nicely demonstrated in the domain of physics, an intellectually deep subject where the principles for solving a problem are typically not explicitly represented in the statement of the problem. Experts learn to see these implicit principles and represent problems in terms of them.

A study by Chi, Feltovich, and Glaser (1981) brings out this difference between novices and experts. Participants were asked to classify a large set of physics problems into similar categories. **Figure 9.11a** shows a pair of problems that novices thought were similar and the novices' explanations of the similarity. As can be seen, the novices chose surface features (inclined planes, friction, angles) as their bases for classification. (Being a physics novice myself, I have to admit that these seem very intuitive bases for ascribing similarity.) Contrast this classification with the classification by experts of the pair of problems in Figure 9.11b, where problems that seem completely different on the surface were seen as similar because they both involved conservation of energy. Thus, experts have the ability to map the surface features of a problem onto deeper principles. This ability is very useful because the deeper principles are more predictive of the method of solution. This shift in classification from reliance on simple, superficial features to reliance on more complex, deeper features has been found in a number of domains, including

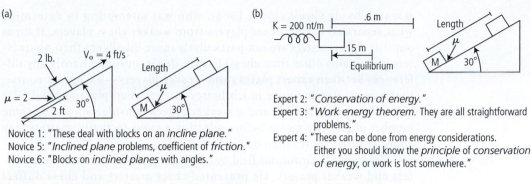

(a)

2 lb. $V_o = 4$ ft/s

$\mu = 2$ 30° 2 ft

Length μ M 30°

Novice 1: "These deal with blocks on an *incline plane*."
Novice 5: "*Inclined plane* problems, coefficient of *friction*."
Novice 6: "Blocks on *inclined planes* with angles."

(b)

$K = 200$ nt/m $.6$ m

$.15$ m

Equilibrium

Length μ M 30°

Expert 2: "*Conservation of energy.*"
Expert 3: "*Work energy theorem.* They are all straightforward problems."
Expert 4: "These can be done from energy considerations. Either you should know the *principle* of *conservation of energy*, or work is lost somewhere."

Figure 9.11 Similarity of Physics Problems: Novices vs. Experts. (a) A pair of problems that three novices categorized as similar, and the reasons they gave for that classification. (b) A pair of problems categorized as similar by three experts, and their explanations. *(Information from Chi et al., 1981.)*

mathematics (Schoenfeld & Herrmann, 1982; Silver, 1979), computer programming (Weiser & Shertz, 1983), and medical diagnosis (Lesgold et al., 1988).

A good example of this shift from superficial to deep processing of perceptual features comes from the interpretation of X rays. **Figure 9.12** is a schematic of one of the X rays diagnosed by participants in the research by Lesgold et al. The sail-like area in the right lung (shown on the left side of the figure) is a shadow caused by a collapsed lobe of the lung that created a denser image in that portion of the X ray than did other parts of the lung. Medical students interpreted this shadow as an indication of a tumor because tumors are the most common cause of shadows on X rays of the lung. Radiological experts, in contrast, were able to correctly interpret the shadow as an indication of a collapsed lobe. They saw that features such as the size of the sail-like region are counterindicative of a tumor. Radiologists — who are experts at examining X rays — do not rely on a simple association between shadows on the lungs and tumors, but are aware of the complexities involved in interpreting such shadows.

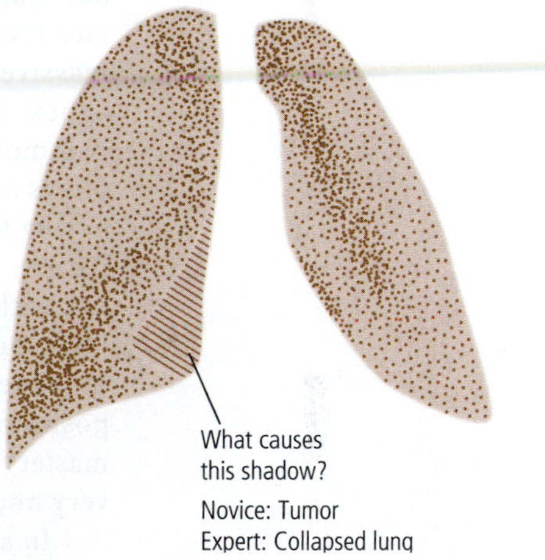

> *An important dimension of growing expertise is learning to perceive problems in ways that enable more effective problem-solving procedures to apply.*

What causes this shadow?

Novice: Tumor
Expert: Collapsed lung

Figure 9.12 X ray Interpretation: Novices vs. Experts. A shadow on a lung X ray could be caused by a tumor or by a collapsed lung lobe. Experts have the experience and knowledge needed to tell the difference. *(Information from Lesgold, et al., 1988.)*

Pattern Learning and Memory

A surprising discovery about expertise is that experts seem to display especially enhanced memory for information about problems in their domains of expertise. This enhanced memory was first discovered in research by de Groot (1965, 1966), who was attempting to determine what separated master chess players from weaker chess players. It turns out that chess masters are not particularly more intelligent than nonmasters in domains other than chess. In fact, de Groot found hardly any differences between expert players and weaker players — except, of course, that expert players chose much better moves when playing chess. For instance, a chess master and a weaker player consider about the same number of possible moves before selecting a move (actually, masters may consider fewer moves than do chess duffers).

However, de Groot did find one intriguing difference between masters and weaker players. He presented chess masters and chess duffers with chess positions (i.e., chessboards with pieces in a configuration that could occur in a game) for just 5 seconds and then removed the chess pieces. The chess masters were able to accurately reconstruct the positions of more than 20 pieces after just 5 seconds of study. In contrast, the chess duffers could reconstruct the positions of only 4 or 5 pieces — a number much more in line with the traditional capacity of working memory (see the discussion of memory capacity in Chapter 6). As a result of the massive amount of experience that they have had with chess, masters appear to have memorized patterns of 4 or 5 pieces that correspond to common board configurations. Thus, they remember not individual pieces but these patterns, and their memory task is reduced from remembering the individual positions of 20+ pieces (which is what the duffers have to do) to remembering the positions of a few familiar patterns. In line with this analysis, when masters and duffers were presented with random chessboard positions rather than ones that are actually encountered in games, they showed no difference in their ability to reconstruct the positions — both were able to position only a few pieces correctly. (The masters also complained that the chaotic board positions made them feel very uncomfortable and disturbed.)

In a systematic analysis, Chase and Simon (1973) compared novices, Class A (advanced) players, and masters with respect to their ability to reproduce actual game positions versus randomized counterparts of those positions, as illustrated in **Figure 9.13** (both of the randomized positions shown in Figure 9.13 are impossible in actual games). As shown in **Figure 9.14**, memory was poorer for all groups for the random positions, and if anything, masters were worst at reproducing these positions. However, masters showed a considerable advantage over advanced players for the actual board positions, and advanced players showed a considerable advantage over beginners. This basic phenomenon of superior expert memory for meaningful problems has been demonstrated in a large number of domains, including the game of Go (Reitman, 1976), electronic circuit diagrams (Egan & Schwartz, 1979), bridge hands (Charness, 1979; Engle & Bukstel, 1978), and computer programming (McKeithen, Reitman, Rueter, & Hirtle, 1981; Schneiderman, 1976).

Middle game

Actual position

Black

Randomized position

Black

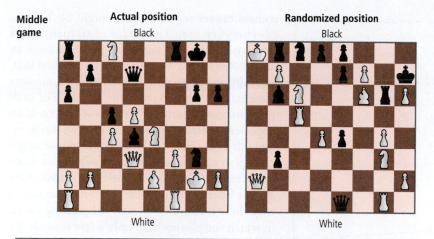

White

White

Figure 9.13 Actual Chess Positions and Their Randomized Counterparts. Typically, chess games can be divided into an opening, a middle game, and an end game, with progressively fewer pieces on the board. The rules of chess make the randomized positions shown here impossible in an actual game.

End game

Actual position

Black

Randomized position

Black

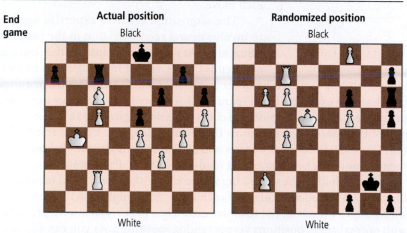

White

White

Chase and Simon (1973) also used a chessboard-reproduction task to examine the nature of the patterns, or "chunks," used by chess masters. The participants' task was simply to reproduce the positions of pieces of a target chessboard on a test chessboard. In this task, participants glanced at the target board, placed some pieces on the test board, glanced back to the target board, placed some more pieces on the test board, and so on. Chase and Simon defined a "chunk" as a group of pieces that participants moved after one glance. They found that these chunks tended to define meaningful game relations among the pieces. For instance, more than half of the masters' chunks were pawn chains (configurations of pawns that occur frequently in chess).

Simon and Gilmartin (1973) estimated that chess masters have acquired 50,000 different chess chunks, that they can quickly recognize such patterns on a chessboard, and that this ability is what underlies their superior memory performance in chess. This estimate of 50,000 patterns does not seem unreasonable when one considers the years of dedicated study that becoming

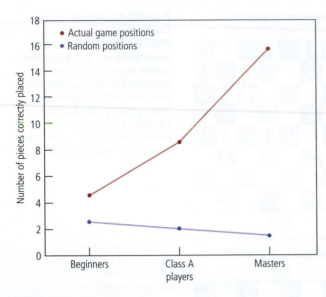

Figure 9.14 Reconstruction of Actual Chess Positions and Their Randomized Counterparts: Beginners vs. Advanced Players vs. Masters. The advanced (Class A) players and the masters are no better (and maybe a bit worse) than beginners at reconstructing the randomized counterparts of actual chess positions, but with actual positions masters were much more successful than Class A players, who were, in turn, much more successful than beginners. *(Data from Chase & Simon, 1973.)*

a chess master requires. What might be the relation between their knowledge of so many chess patterns and their superior performance in chess? Newell and Simon (1972) speculated that, in addition to learning many patterns, masters have learned what to do in the presence of such patterns. For instance, if the chunk pattern of an opponent's pieces is symptomatic of weakness on one side of the board, the player's response might be to plan an attack on the weak side. Thus, masters effectively "see" possibilities for moves; they do not have to think them out, which explains why chess masters do so well at lightning chess, in which the players have only a few seconds for each move.

The acquisition of chess expertise appears to involve neural reorganization in the fusiform visual area. As we saw in Chapter 2, the fusiform area tends to be engaged in recognition of faces but can also be engaged by other stimuli for which people have acquired high levels of expertise (see Figure 2.23). The fusiform area also appears to be engaged in the development of chess expertise. **Figure 9.15a** shows examples of the board configurations that Bilalić, Langner, Ulrich, and Grodd (2011) presented to chess experts and to novices, which included positions found in normal chess games and random positions. Participants' tasks were to indicate whether the white king was in check (the Check task) or whether the position included a knight of each color (the Knight task). Figure 9.15b shows activity levels in the fusiform area when participants were presented with normal chess positions versus random positions. As you can see, activation in the fusiform area was considerably higher for experts than for novices, in response to both types of positions. Also, for experts, the normal chess positions produced greater activation than did the random chess positions; in contrast, for novices, normal versus random positions produced no significant difference in activation.

To summarize, chess experts have stored the solutions to many problems that duffers must solve as novel problems. Duffers have to analyze different configurations, try to figure out their consequences, and act accordingly, whereas masters already have this information stored in memory. Thus, masters have advantages over duffers. First, they do not risk making errors in solving the problems for which they have stored the solutions. Second, because they have stored correct analyses of so many positions, they can focus their problem-solving efforts on more subtle and sophisticated aspects and strategies of chess.

Experts' pattern learning and better memory for board positions is part of tactical learning. The way humans become expert at chess reflects the fact

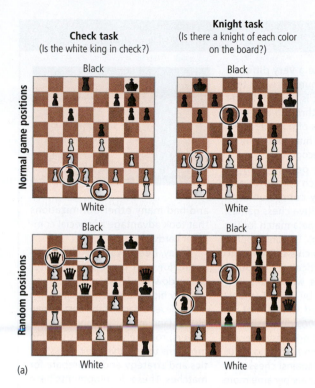

Check task
(Is the white king in check?)

Knight task
(Is there a knight of each color
on the board?)

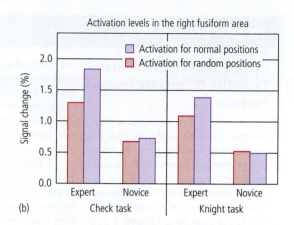

(b)

**Figure 9.15 Recognition
of Chess Positions and
Corresponding Activity in
the Right Fusiform Area:
Novices vs. Experts.** (a) In the
Check task, participants had
to indicate whether the white
king was in check (in both the
normal position and the random
position, the answer is yes, as
indicated by the arrows); in the
Knight task, participants had
to indicate whether there were
knights of both colors on the
board (again, the answer is yes
in both positions, as indicated by
the circles). (b) Activation levels
(percent signal change relative
to baseline) in the right fusiform
area in experts and novices when
executing the Check and Knight
tasks (the blue bars show activity
for normal positions; the red
bars show activity for random
positions). *(Research from Bilalić et al., 2011.)*

that we are very good at pattern recognition but relatively poor at things like mentally searching through sequences of possible moves. As described in **Implications 9.1,** human strengths and weaknesses lead to a very different way of achieving expertise at chess than we see in computer programs for playing chess.

> *Experts can recognize patterns of elements that repeat in many problems, and they know what to do in the presence of such patterns without having to think them through.*

Long-Term Memory and Expertise

One might think that the memory advantage shown by experts is just a working-memory advantage, but research has shown that their advantage extends to long-term memory. Charness (1976) compared experts' memory for chess positions immediately after they had viewed the positions or after a 30-second delay filled with an interfering task. Class A chess players showed no loss in recall over the 30-second interval, unlike weaker participants, who showed a great deal of forgetting. Thus, expert chess players, unlike duffers, have an increased capacity to store information about chess. Interestingly,

Implications 9.1

Computers Achieve Chess Expertise Differently Than Humans Do

In Chapter 8, we discussed how human problem solving can be viewed as a search of a problem space that consists of various states. The initial situation is the start state, the situations on the way to the solution are the intermediate states, and the solution is the goal state. Chapter 8 also described how people use certain methods, such as backup avoidance, difference reduction, and means–ends analysis, to move through the states. Often, when humans search a problem space, they actually manipulate the physical world, as in solving an eight puzzle (see Figures 8.3 and 8.4). However, sometimes they imagine states, as when playing chess and contemplating how an opponent might react to a move one is considering, how one might react to the opponent's move, and so on. Computers are very effective at representing such hypothetical states and searching through them for the optimal move toward the goal state (in the case of chess, a won game). Artificial intelligence algorithms have been developed that are successful at all sorts of problem-solving applications, including playing chess. This has led to the development of chess-playing programs that use a very different style of play than humans when they play chess — that is, the computer programs search through and evaluate vast numbers of possible chess positions, whereas humans rely much more on pattern recognition.

At first, many people thought that, although such computer programs could play competent and modestly competitive chess games, they would never be a match for the best human players. The philosopher Hubert Dreyfus, a chess duffer who was famously critical of computer chess in the 1960s, was beaten by a program written by an MIT undergraduate, Richard Greenblatt, in 1966 (Boden, 2006, discusses the intrigue surrounding these events). The programs of the 1960s and 1970s performed poorly against chess masters, but as computers became more powerful and could search larger spaces (i.e., represent and evaluate increasing numbers of possible positions), they became increasingly competitive with expert human players. Then, in May 1997, IBM's Deep Blue program defeated the reigning world champion, Gary Kasparov. Deep Blue was able to evaluate 200 million imagined chess positions per second. It also had stored records of 4,000 opening positions and 700,000 games between masters (Hsu, 2002)

and had many other optimizations that took advantage of special computer hardware.

Today, freely available chess programs for your personal computer can be downloaded over the Web and will play highly competitive chess at a master level. In fact, all the best human players (and many thousands of other players) routinely use chess-playing programs to improve their chess tactics and strategy and to prepare for matches. These developments have led to a profound shift in the understanding of intelligence. It once was thought that there was only one way to achieve high levels of intelligent behavior, and that was the human way. Nowadays it is increasingly accepted that intelligence can be achieved in different ways and that the human way may not always be the best. Also, curiously, as a consequence some researchers no longer view the ability to play expert chess as a reflection of the essence of human intelligence.

these expert participants showed the same poor memory for three-letter trigrams as do ordinary participants. Thus, their increased long-term memory is only for the domain of expertise.

Experts appear to be able to remember more patterns as well as larger patterns. For instance, Chase and Simon (1973; see Figures 9.13 and 9.14) tried to identify the patterns that their participants used to reconstruct the chess positions. They found that participants would tend to recall a pattern, pause, recall another pattern, pause, and so on. The researchers found that a 2-second pause identified the boundary between recall of patterns. With this objective definition of what a pattern is, they could then explore how many patterns were recalled and how large these patterns were. In comparing a master chess player with a beginner, they found large differences in both measures. First, the pattern size of the master averaged 3.8 pieces, whereas it was only 2.4 for the beginner. Second, the master also recalled an average of 7.7 patterns per board, whereas the beginner recalled an average of only 5.3. Thus, it seems that the experts' memory advantage is based not only on larger patterns but also on the ability to recall more patterns.

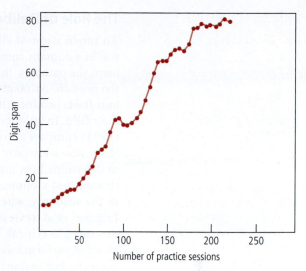

Figure 9.16 Digit Span Increase with Practice. Notice how the number of digits that this participant (SF) can recall increases gradually but steadily with the number of practice sessions. *(Data from Chase & Ericsson, 1982.)*

Additional compelling evidence that expertise requires the ability to remember more patterns as well as larger patterns comes from Chase and Ericsson (1982), who studied the development of a simple but remarkable skill. They watched a participant, called SF, increase his digit span with practice (the digit span is the number of digits that a person can repeat in sequence after one presentation). As discussed in Chapter 6, the normal digit span is about 7 or 8 items. After about 200 hours of practice, SF was able to recall a sequence of 81 random digits presented at the rate of 1 digit per second. **Figure 9.16** illustrates how his digit span grew with practice.

What was behind this apparently superhuman feat of memory? In part, SF was learning to chunk the digits into meaningful patterns. He was a long-distance runner, and part of his technique was to convert digits into running times. So, he would take 4 digits, such as 3492, and convert them into "Three minutes, 49.2 seconds — near world-record mile time." Using such a strategy, he could convert a memory span for 7 digits into a memory span for 7 patterns consisting of 3 or 4 digits each. This would get him to a digit span of more than 20, which was still far short of his eventual performance. In addition to this chunking, he developed what Chase and Ericsson called a "retrieval structure," which enabled him to recall 22 such patterns. This retrieval structure was very specific; it did not generalize to retrieving letters rather than digits. Chase and Ericsson hypothesized that part of what underlies the development of expertise in other domains, such as chess, is the development of retrieval structures, which allows superior recall for past patterns.

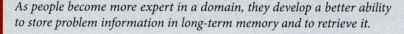

As people become more expert in a domain, they develop a better ability to store problem information in long-term memory and to retrieve it.

The Role of Deliberate Practice

An implication of all the research that we have reviewed is that expertise in a domain comes only with an investment of a great deal of time to learn the patterns, the methods, and the appropriate overall approach for the domain. As mentioned earlier, John Hayes found that geniuses in various fields produce their best work only after 10 years of apprenticeship in their field. In another research effort, Ericsson, Krampe, and Tesch-Römer (1993) compared the best violinists at a music academy in Berlin with those who were only very good. They looked at diaries and self-estimates to determine how much the two populations had practiced and estimated that the best violinists had practiced more than 7,000 hours before coming to the academy, whereas the very good had practiced only 5,000 hours. Ericsson et al. reviewed a great many fields where, like music, time spent practicing is critical. Time on task is important not only in achieving high levels of performance in a domain like music, but also in mastering school subjects. For instance, Anderson, Reder, and Simon (1998) noted that a major reason for the higher achievement in mathematics of students in Asian countries is that those students spend twice as much time practicing mathematics as students elsewhere.

Ericsson et al. (1993) make the strong claim that almost all of expertise is to be accounted for by the amount of practice. They point to the research of Bloom (1985a, 1985b), who looked at the histories of children who became great in fields such as music and tennis. Bloom found that most of these children got started by playing casually, but after a short time they typically showed some promise and were encouraged by their parents to start serious training with a teacher. However, the early natural abilities of these children were surprisingly modest and did not predict ultimate success in the domain (Ericsson et al., 1993). Rather, the critical factor seems to be parents who come to believe that their child is talented and consequently pay for the child's instruction and equipment as well as support their time-consuming practice. Ericsson et al. speculated that the resulting training is sufficient by itself to account for the development of children's success.

Ericsson et al. are careful to note, however, that not all practice leads to the development of expertise. They note that many people spend a lifetime playing chess or some sport without ever getting much better. What is critical, according to Ericsson et al., is what they call **deliberate practice,** in which learners are motivated to learn (not just perform), are given feedback on their performance, and carefully monitor how well their performance corresponds to the correct performance and where there are deviations (so they can focus on eliminating these points of discrepancy). The importance of deliberate practice in the acquisition of expertise is similar to the importance of deep and elaborative processing in improving memory, versus passive study, which yields few memory benefits (see the discussions in Chapters 6 and 7).

An important function of deliberate practice in both children and adults may be to drive the neural growth that is necessary to enable expertise. It was once thought that adults do not grow new neurons, but it now appears that they do (Gross, 2000). An interesting recent discovery is that extensive practice appears to drive neural growth in the adult brain. For instance, Elbert, Pantev, Wienbruch, Rockstroh, and Taub (1995) found that violinists, who finger strings with the left hand, show increased development of the right cortical regions that correspond to their fingers. In another study, Maguire et al. (2000), previously discussed in Chapter 4, used imaging to examine the brains of London taxi drivers. It takes at least three years for London taxi drivers to acquire all of the knowledge necessary to navigate expertly through the streets of London. The taxi drivers were found to have significantly more gray matter in the hippocampal region than did their matched controls. This finding corresponds to the increased hippocampal volume reported in small mammals and birds that engage in behavior requiring navigation (Lee, Miyasato, & Clayton, 1998). For instance, food-storing birds show seasonal increases in hippocampal volume corresponding to times of the year when they need to remember where they stored food.

> *A great deal of deliberate practice is necessary to develop expertise in any field.*

Talent versus Deliberate Practice

The extreme position is that achieving high-levels of expertise is all a matter of putting the time and effort into learning and that there is no role for talent. The American behaviorist psychologist John Watson once proclaimed:

> Give me a dozen healthy infants, well-formed, and my own
> specified world to bring them up in and I'll guarantee to take any
> one at random and train him to become any type of specialist
> I might select — doctor, lawyer, artist, merchant-chief and, yes,
> even beggar-man and thief, regardless of his talents. . . . (Watson,
> 1930, p. 104)

This idea has seen a recent revival in popular writings. Relying heavily on research on deliberate practice, Malcolm Gladwell (2008) argues that putting in 10,000 hours of such practice is sufficient to achieve extremely high levels of performance in a wide range of domains. People have acted on such advice. For instance, Dan McLaughlin, who had never played a round of golf, set about to put in 10,000 hours of deliberate practice with the goal of becoming a professional golfer (Phillips, 2017), only to be sidelined by an injury after 6,003 hours. At one point he had achieved a handicap of 2.6, which is achieved by less than 6% of golfers, but still not what is required for entry into the Professional Golfers Association qualifying tournament.

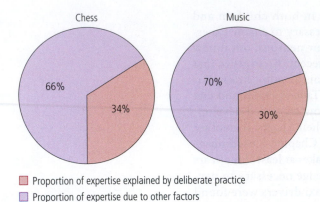

Chess   Music

66%   34%   70%   30%

■ Proportion of expertise explained by deliberate practice
■ Proportion of expertise due to other factors

Figure 9.17 Proportion of Expertise Explained by Deliberate Practice. (a) Time spent studying chess accounts for 34% of the variation in ratings of chess players (from intermediate to grandmasters). (b) Time spent practicing accounts for 30% of the variation in ratings of musicians' performance. *(Data from Hambrick et al., 2014.)*

In contrast to the extreme position, a recent surge of research argues for the importance of talent in addition to practice. In many domains, experts differ considerably in their levels of achievement, and much of these differences cannot be explained by differences in the amount of practice (Hambrick et al., 2014; Macnamara, Hambrick, & Oswald, 2014). In these studies, information about the amount of practice comes from self-reports, diary records, and observations. Level of achievement is judged by measures such as rankings and performance ratings. Both the amount of practice and the level of achievement show wide variation. **Figure 9.17** shows the amount of variation in the level of achievement in two domains, chess and music, that Hambrick et al. (2014) were able to explain by deliberate practice. The other factors involved in explaining variation in achievement could be differences in starting age, in environmental support, or in talent.

Studies comparing musical performance of monozygotic twins (identical genetically) and dizygotic twins (who have no more genetic overlap than non-twin siblings) indicate that practice does have some effect but that, overall, monozygotic twins are more similar in their musical performance than are dizygotic twins (Hambrick & Tucker-Drob, 2015; Ullén, Mosing, & Madison, 2015). That is, both genetic factors and practice seem to combine to determine level of achievement, suggesting that there is indeed some role for talent in expertise. In addition, there are some interesting interactions between genetic similarity and practice. For instance, Hambrick et al. (2014) found that the more monozygotic twins practiced, the more similar they became to one another in level of achievement. There will always be some differences in how much each member of a twin pair practices. Ullén et al. (2015) compared in each pair the twin who practiced more with the twin who practiced less. In the case of dizygotic twins, they found that the one who practiced more tended to play better but that this was not so for pairs of monozygotic twins. In part, this may reflect the fact that monozygotic twins tend not to differ much in their amount of practice. (See Chapter 14 for further discussion of the idea that an important genetic effect on achievement may be in controlling the kinds of experiences that individuals choose to have.)

> *Genetic factors as well as practice determine level of achievement.*

Transfer of Skill

Expertise can often be quite narrow. As noted earlier, participant SF (Chase & Ericsson, 1982) was unable to transfer memory span skill from digits to letters. This is almost a ridiculously extreme example of a frequent pattern in the development of cognitive skills — that these skills can be quite narrow and can fail to transfer to other activities. Chess grandmasters do not appear to be better thinkers in other domains, despite their genius in chess. An amusing example of the narrowness of expertise is provided by a study of the mathematical strategies used by Brazilian schoolchildren who also worked as street vendors (Carraher, Carraher, & Schliemann, 1985). On the job, these children used quite sophisticated strategies for calculating the total cost of orders consisting of different numbers of different objects (e.g., the total cost of 4 coconuts and 12 lemons); what's more, they could perform such calculations reliably in their heads. Carraher et al. actually went to the trouble of going to the streets and posing as customers for these children, making certain kinds of purchases and recording the percentage of correct calculations. The experimenters then asked the children to come with them to the laboratory, where they were given written mathematics tests that included the same numbers and mathematical operations that they had manipulated successfully in the streets. For example, if a child had correctly calculated the total cost of 5 lemons at 35 cruzeiros apiece on the street, the child was given the following written problem:

$$5 \times 35 = ?$$

Whereas children correctly solved 98% of the problems presented in the real-world context, they solved only 37% of the problems presented in the laboratory context using the exact same numbers and mathematical operations. Interestingly, if the problems were stated in the form of word problems in the laboratory, performance improved to 74%. This improvement runs counter to the usual finding, which is that word problems are more difficult than equivalent "number" problems (Carpenter & Moser, 1982). Apparently, the additional context provided by the word problem allowed the Brazilian children to make contact with their pragmatic strategies.

Carraher et al. (1985) found a curious failure of expertise to transfer from the real world to the laboratory, but educators typically have the opposite concern — whether what is taught in one class will transfer to other classes and the real world. Early in the 20th century, when educators were fairly optimistic that such transfer would occur, a number of educational psychologists subscribed to what has been called the "doctrine of formal discipline" (Angell, 1908; Pillsbury, 1908; Woodrow, 1927), which held that studying such esoteric subjects as Latin and geometry was of significant value because it served to discipline the mind to operate in ways that would facilitate other studies. Those who believed in formal discipline subscribed to the faculty view of mind, which extends back to Aristotle and was first formalized by Thomas Reid in the late 18th century (Boring, 1950). The faculty view held that the mind is composed of a collection of general faculties, such as observation, attention, discrimination, and reasoning, which could be exercised in much the same way as a set of muscles. The content of the

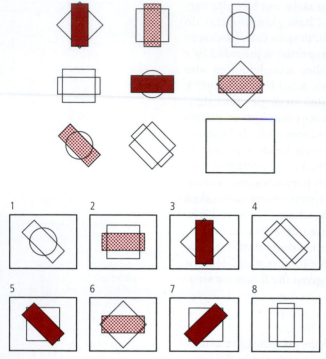

Figure 9.18 Raven's Progressive Matrices Test: Example Question. Which configuration of shapes 1–8 should be put into the blank box to correctly complete the progression?[1] A typical test contains 60 items like this.

exercise made little difference; most important was the level of exertion (hence the fondness for Latin and geometry). In such a view, transfer is broad and takes place at a general level, sometimes spanning domains that have no content in common.

A recent spate of research has investigated whether deliberate working-memory practice would provide a basis for training mental abilities in general, achieving what proponents of the doctrine of formal discipline thought geometry and Latin would do. For instance, Jaeggi, Buschkuehl, Jonides, and Perrig (2008) published a report on the effectiveness of what they called the "dual *n*-back" training program. In a typical *single n*-back task, participants see or hear a long series of stimuli and have to say whether each new stimulus is the same as the one that occurred *n* items back. For example, in a single 2-back task with letters, participants might see

T L H C **H** O C **O** R R K C **K** M

and would respond yes to the three cases in boldface. In Jaeggi et al. (2008), participants had the very demanding *dual n*-back task of simultaneously tracking a sequence of letters presented auditorily and the locations of squares presented visually. The experimenters varied *n* (the length of the gap participants had to monitor) from 1 to 4, raising it as participants got better. To see whether training on this task improved participants' general mental abilities, Jaeggi et al. had participants take the Raven's Progressive Matrices test (**Figure 9.18** shows an example question), a general test of intelligence, before training and after different amounts of training. The results, shown in **Figure 9.19**, seem to indicate that training on a difficult cognitive task that challenges working memory can indeed raise general intelligence.

Results like this led to a glowing article in the *New York Times Magazine* titled "Can You Make Yourself Smarter?" (Hurley, 2012). Numerous commercial companies sprang up marketing cognitive training programs to individuals and schools. However, more careful investigations by cognitive scientists led to questions, and just one year later the *New Yorker* published an article titled "Brain Games are Bogus" (Cook, 2013). The early studies

[1] The correct answer is 5, which can be deduced from these three observations:
    1. Each row contains a circle, a square, and a diamond.
    2. Each row contains three bars (one solid color, one patterned, and one clear).
    3. Within each row, the three bars have the same orientation (vertical, horizontal, or diagonal).

showing positive results had small sample sizes, and more adequately powered studies have often failed to find positive results (Chooi & Thompson, 2012; Redick et al., 2013). Probably the best conclusion is captured by the title of this article: "Working Memory Training Remains a Work in Progress" (Shipstead, Hicks, & Engle, 2012).

There appears to be a similar state of uncertainty about whether playing video games can improve general cognitive abilities. There is concern about violent video games although a large-scale study failed to find any positive cognitive effects or negative social effects (Ferguson, Garza, Jerabeck, Ramos, & Galindo, 2013). Some research does suggest that playing action video games may have positive effects on some perceptual and attentional abilities, such as greater visual acuity and greater ability to track objects moving rapidly and randomly in a display (Bavelier, Green, Pouget, & Schrater, 2012). This seems a plausible sort of transfer because these games often require monitoring rapidly changing visual displays. However, many of the existing studies of the effects of playing video games have been criticized because they compare video-game players with non–video-game players, and different sorts of people — that is, people with better visual and attentional skills — may choose to play action video games (Boot, Blakely, & Simons, 2011). However, there have been better controlled studies that assigned novices to learn either action video games or some other type of game, such as Tetris (e.g., Green & Bavelier, 2006). Many of these studies find positive effects of training on action video games, but a few have failed to find effects (van Ravenzwaaij, Boekel, Forstmann, Ratcliff, & Wagenmakers, 2013). Bediou et al. (2018) suggest that failure to find transfer in well-controlled studies occurred because those studies had used massed practice instead of using the spaced practice typical of video game play (see the discussion of spaced versus massed practice in Chapter 6).

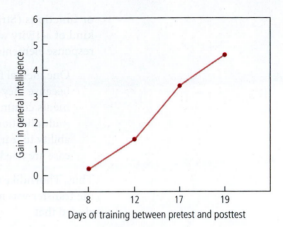

Figure 9.19 Does Training on a Difficult Cognitive Task Improve General Intelligence? The gain in general intelligence is measured by the posttest score (after training) minus the pretest score (before any training) on the Raven's Progressive Matrices test. These results suggest that working-memory training can indeed improve general intelligence (the more training, the greater the improvement), but later studies raise doubts.

(Data from Jaeggi et al., 2008.)

> *There is often failure to transfer skills to similar domains and virtually no transfer to very different domains.*

Theory of Identical Elements

A century ago, Edward Thorndike criticized the doctrine of formal discipline, which holds that the mind can be trained like a muscle, and instead proposed his **theory of identical elements.** According to Thorndike, the mind is not composed of general faculties, but rather of specific habits and associations, which provide a person with a variety of narrow responses to very specific stimuli. This corresponded with the prevalent view during Thorndike's time that the mind was just a convenient name for countless special operations or functions (Stratton, 1922). Thorndike's theory held that training in one kind of activity would transfer to another only if the activities had situation-response elements in common:

> One mental function or activity improves others in so far as and because they are in part identical with it, because it contains elements common to them. Addition improves multiplication because multiplication is largely addition; knowledge of Latin gives increased ability to learn French because many of the facts learned in the one case are needed in the other. (Thorndike, 1906, p. 243)

Thus, Thorndike was happy to accept transfer between diverse skills as long as the transfer was mediated by identical elements. Generally, however, he concluded that

> The mind is so specialized into a multitude of independent capacities that we alter human nature only in small spots, and any special school training has a much narrower influence upon the mind as a whole than has commonly been supposed. (p. 246)

Although the doctrine of formal discipline was too broad in its predictions of transfer, Thorndike formulated his theory of identical elements in what proved to be an overly narrow manner. For instance, he argued that skill in solving geometry problems in which one set of letters is used to label the points in a diagram would not transfer to solving geometry problems with a different set of letters. The research on analogy examined in Chapter 8 indicates that this is not true — that is, transfer is not tied to the identity of surface elements. In some cases, there is very large positive transfer between skills that have the same logical structure but different surface elements (see Singley & Anderson, 1989, for a review). For instance, there is large positive transfer between different word-processing systems, between different programming languages, and between using calculus to solve economics problems and using calculus to solve problems in solid geometry. Singley and Anderson argued that there are, however, definite bounds on how far skills will transfer and that becoming an expert in one domain will have little positive benefit on becoming an expert in a very different domain. There will be positive transfer only to the extent that the two domains use the same facts, rules, and patterns — that is, the same knowledge.

A positive side to this specificity in the transfer of skill is that there seldom seems to be **negative transfer,** in which learning one skill makes a person worse at learning another skill. Interference, such as that which occurs in memory for facts (see Chapter 7), is almost nonexistent in skill acquisition. Polson, Muncher, and Kieras (1987) provided a good demonstration of lack of negative transfer in the domain of text editing on a computer (using the command-based word processors that were common at the time). They asked participants to learn one text editor and then learn a second, which was designed to be maximally confusing in relation to the first. For example, the command to go down a line of text might be n and the command to delete a character might be *k* in one text editor, but in the other text editor *n* would mean to delete a character and *k* would mean to go down a line. However, participants experienced very strong positive transfer in going from one text editor to the other because the two text editors worked in the same way, even though the surface commands had been scrambled.

The Einstellung effect (discussed in Chapter 8) is a kind of negative transfer that can occur in problem solving. In such cases, people learn ways of solving problems in one domain that are not optimal for solving problems in another domain. So, for instance, someone may learn tricks in algebra to avoid having to perform difficult arithmetic computations and may then waste time and effort by using those tricks to perform unnecessary simplifications when doing computations with a calculator. This is not a case of failure to transfer; rather, it is a case of transferring knowledge to an activity where that knowledge is not useful.

> *There is transfer between skills only when these skills have the same abstract knowledge elements.*

Educational Implications

With this analysis of skill acquisition and transfer, we can ask the question: What are the implications for the training of cognitive skills? Traditional high-school algebra, for example, has been estimated to require the acquisition of many thousands of rules (Anderson, 1992). Instruction can be improved by an analysis of what these individual elements are. Approaches to instruction that begin with an analysis of the elements to be taught are called **componential analyses.** A description of the application of componential approaches to the instruction of a number of topics in reading and mathematics can be found in Anderson (2000). Generally, students show higher achievement in programs that include componential analyses.

A particularly effective part of such componential programs is **mastery learning,** in which instructors follow students' performance on each of the components underlying the cognitive skill and ensure that all components are mastered. Typical instruction, without mastery learning, leaves some students not knowing some of the material. This failure to learn some of the components can snowball in a course in which mastery of earlier material is a prerequisite for mastery of later material. There is a good deal of evidence that mastery learning leads to higher achievement (Guskey & Gates, 1986; Kulik, Kulik, & Bangert-Downs, 1986).

Probably the most extensive use of componential analysis is for **intelligent tutoring systems** (Graesser, Hu, & Sottilare, 2018), computer systems that interact with students while they are learning and solving problems, much as a human tutor would. Prominent versions of such tutoring systems are called *cognitive tutors* (Anderson, Corbett, Koedinger, & Pelletier, 1995), which

Figure 9.20 A Screen Shot from the Cognitive Tutor for Algebra. *(Carnegie Learning Cognitive Tutor Software Algebra I. Reproduced by permission of Carnegie Learning.)*

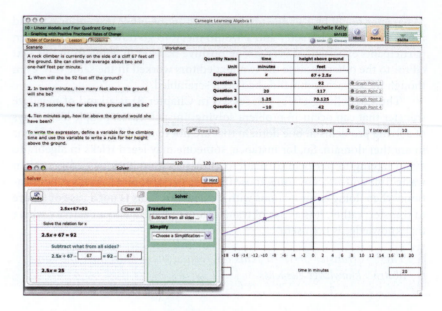

involve a computer model of how students solve problems. This model is used to interpret and respond to each student's actions and to select problems appropriate for each student's current state of learning. Cognitive tutors have particularly focused on instructing middle-school and high-school mathematics.[2] **Figure 9.20** shows a screen shot from a widely used product, a tutor for high-school algebra. A large-scale study conducted by the Rand Corporation (Pane, Griffin, McCaffrey, & Karam, 2013) indicated that this tutor can provide real, if modest, gains for high-school students.

A motivation for research on intelligent tutoring is the evidence showing that private human tutoring is very effective. Human tutors can improve student success by almost a letter grade. Studies of intelligent tutoring systems find that they are as effective as human tutors and more effective than both classroom instruction and other kinds of computer-based instruction (Kulik & Fletcher, 2016; Ma, Adesope, Nesbit, & Liu, 2014; VanLehn, 2011).

> *Instruction is improved by approaches that identify the underlying knowledge components and ensure that students master them all. Intelligent tutoring systems are computer-based systems that achieve this.*

[2] Cognitive mathematics tutors distributed by Carnegie Learning (spun off by Carnegie Mellon University in 1998) have been deployed to thousands of schools nationwide and have interacted annually with hundreds of thousands of students (Koedinger & Corbett, 2006; Ritter, 2011; Ritter, Anderson, Koedinger, & Corbett, 2007; see also www.carnegielearning.com).

Conclusions

This chapter began by noting the remarkable ability of humans to acquire the complexities of culture and technology. In fact, in today's world people routinely acquire whole new sets of skills over their lifetimes. For instance, I now use my phone for instant messaging, GPS navigation, and surfing the Web — functions that I could not have imagined when I was a young man, let alone associated with a phone. This chapter has emphasized the role of practice in acquiring such skills, and certainly it has taken me some considerable practice to master them. However, human flexibility depends on more than time on task — other creatures could never acquire such skills. Critical to human expertise are the higher-order problem-solving skills that we reviewed in Chapter 8. Also critical is our human ability to reason, make decisions, and communicate by language. These are the topics of the forthcoming chapters.

Questions for Thought

1. An interesting case study of skill acquisition was reported by Ohlsson (1992), who looked at the development of Isaac Asimov's writing skill. Asimov was one of the most prolific authors of our time, writing approximately 500 books in a career that spanned 40 years. Reportedly, he sat down at his keyboard every day at 7:30 a.m. and wrote until 10:00 p.m. **Figure 9.21** shows the average number of months he took to write a book as a function of practice. The linear best-fitting curve shows that it corresponds closely to a power function. At what phase of writing-skill acquisition do you think Asimov was at the end of his career?

2. The chapter discussed how chess experts have learned to recognize appropriate moves just by looking at the chessboard. It has been argued (Charness, 1981; Holding, 1992; Roring, 2008) that experts also learn to engage in more search and more effective search for winning moves. Relate these two kinds of learning (learning specific moves and learning how to search) to the concepts of tactical and strategic learning.

3. In a 2006 *New York Times* article, Stephen J. Dubner and Steven D. Levitt (of "Freakonomics" fame) noted that elite soccer players are much more likely to be born in the early months of

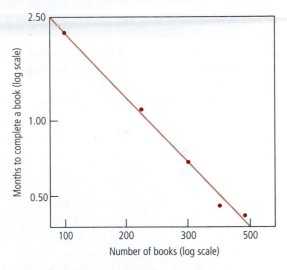

Figure 9.21 How Fast Could Isaac Asimov Write? Asimov was an incredibly disciplined writer, spending long hours daily at his desk, across a career that spanned four decades. After about 400 books worth of practice, he was able to complete a book in half a month or less. *(Data from Ohlsson, 1992.)*

the year than the late months. Anders Ericsson argues they have an advantage in youth soccer leagues, which organize teams by birth year. Because they are older and tend to be bigger than other children of the same birth year, they are more likely to get selected for elite teams and receive the benefit of deliberate practice. Can you think of any other explanations for the fact that elite soccer players tend to be born in the first months of the year?

4. One reads frequent complaints about the performance level of American students in studies of mathematics achievement, where they are greatly outperformed by children from other countries, such as Japan. Frequently proposed remedies point to changing the nature of the mathematics curriculum or improving teacher quality. Seldom mentioned is the fact that American children actually spend much less time learning mathematics than do the better-performing children in other countries

(see Anderson et al., 1998). What does this chapter imply about the importance of instruction versus amount of learning time? Can improvements in one of these areas increase American achievement levels without improvements in the other?

5. Niels Taatgen (2013) argued that the transfer we see from working-memory training such as the dual *n*-back task (see Figure 9.19) might be explained in terms of transfer of identical elements rather than training of a mental muscle. What might the identical elements be that are shared between performing the dual *n*-back task and solving a Raven's puzzle like the one in Figure 9.18?

Key Terms

associative phase
autonomous phase
cognitive phase
componential analyses

deliberate practice
intelligent tutoring
   systems
mastery learning

negative transfer
proceduralization
strategic learning
tactical learning

theory of identical
   elements

10

Reasoning

As noted in Chapter 1, superior intelligence is thought to be the feature that distinguishes humans as a species. In Chapters 8 and 9, we examined humans' enormous capacity for solving problems and acquiring new intellectual skills. In light of this particular capacity, we might expect that the research on human reasoning (the topic of this chapter) and decision making (the topic of the next chapter) would reveal how we achieve our superior intellectual performance. Historically, however, most psychological research on reasoning and decision making has started with prescriptions derived from logic and mathematics about how humans *should* behave, has then compared these prescriptions to what humans actually do, and has found humans deficient compared to these standards.

The opposite conclusion seems to come from older research in artificial intelligence (AI), where researchers tried to create artificial systems for reasoning and decision making using the same prescriptions from logic and mathematics. For instance, Shortliffe (1976) created an expert computer-based system for diagnosing infectious diseases. Similar approaches based on formal reasoning were used in developing the first generation of robots to help them reason about how to navigate through the world. Researchers were very frustrated with such systems, noting that they lacked common sense and would do the stupidest things, things that no human would do. In response to such frustrations, researchers are now creating systems based less on logical computations and, often, more on emulating how neurons in the brain compute (e.g., Russell & Norvig, 2009).

Thus, we have a paradox: Human reasoning is judged as deficient when compared against the standards of logic and mathematics, but AI systems built on these very standards are judged as deficient when compared against humans. This apparent contradiction might lead one to conclude either that logic and mathematics are wrong or that humans have some mysterious intuition-based process that guides their thinking. However, the real problem seems to be with the way the principles of logic and mathematics have been applied, not with the principles themselves. New research is showing that the situations faced by people are more complex than has often been assumed. We can better understand human behavior when we expand our analyses of human reasoning to include such complexities. In this chapter and the next, we will

315

review a number of the models used to predict how people arrive at conclusions when presented with certain evidence, research on how people deviate from these models, and then research based on newer and richer analyses of human reasoning.

This chapter will address the following questions about the way people reason:

- How do people reason about situations described in conditional language (e.g., "if-then")?

- How do people reason about situations described with quantifiers, such as *all, some,* and *none*?

- How do people reason from specific examples and pieces of evidence to general conclusions?

Reasoning and the Brain

Research on which brain areas are involved in reasoning suggests that people can bring different systems to bear on different types of reasoning problems. Consider an fMRI experiment by Goel, Buchel, Frith, and Dolan (2000) in which participants reasoned about logical **syllogisms**, arguments consisting of two premises and a conclusion. Participants were presented with congruent problems (i.e., logically correct arguments with promises and conclusions that reflect standard beliefs), such as

> All poodles are pets.
> All pets have names.
> *Therefore:* All poodles have names.

With this type of congruent problem, participants correctly judged 84% of the time that the third statement logically followed from the first two. Goel et al. contrasted this type of problem with incongruent problems (i.e., logically correct arguments with premises and conclusions that violate standard beliefs), such as

> All pets are poodles.
> All poodles are vicious.
> *Therefore:* All pets are vicious.

With this type of problem, participants correctly judged only 74% of the time that the third statement was true if the first two were. Finally, Goel et al. contrasted both of these types with logically correct arguments involving abstract concepts, such as

> All P are B.
> All B are C.
> *Therefore:* All P are C.

In this case, participants judged 77% of the time that the argument was correct.

Although logicians would call all three kinds of syllogism valid, the reader might wonder whether it makes sense to say that a participant is mistaken in rejecting an incongruent but logically valid conclusion such as "All pets are vicious." We will return to this question in the second section of this chapter,

Brain Structures

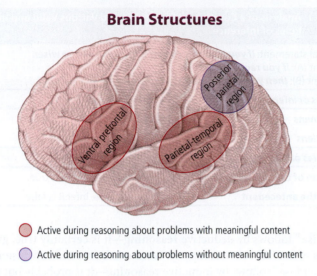

○ Active during reasoning about problems with meaningful content

○ Active during reasoning about problems without meaningful content

Figure 10.1 Brain Activation during Reasoning about Material with Meaningful Content versus Reasoning about Material without Content. Reasoning about material with meaningful content activates left ventral prefrontal and left temporal–parietal regions (regions associated with language processing), whereas reasoning about content-free material activates parietal regions (regions activated when solving algebraic equations).

but for now, of greater interest are the brain regions that Goel et al. found to be active when participants were judging these different types of syllogisms. Contrasting material with content (like the two syllogisms about pets) and material without content (like the syllogism about P, B, and C), they found the regions illustrated in **Figure 10.1**. When participants were judging content-free material, parietal regions that have been found to have roles in solving algebraic equations were active (see Figure 1.16b). In contrast, when participants were judging material with meaningful content, left ventral prefrontal and left temporal–parietal areas that are associated with language processing were active (see Figure 4.1). This indicates that people do not process all syllogisms in the same way; rather, different brain regions are active when the syllogisms are based on content than when they are content free.

> *Faced with logical problems, people can engage either brain regions associated with the processing of meaningful content or regions associated with the processing of more abstract information.*

Reasoning About Conditionals

The first body of research we will cover looks at **deductive reasoning**, which is concerned with conclusions that follow with certainty from the premises. It is distinguished from **inductive reasoning**, which is concerned with conclusions that follow probabilistically from the premises. To illustrate the distinction, suppose someone is told, "Fred is the brother of Mary" and "Mary is the mother of Lisa." Then, one might conclude both that "Fred is the uncle of Lisa" and that "Fred is older than Lisa." The first conclusion, "Fred is the

TABLE 10.1 Analysis of a Conditional Statement and Various Valid and Invalid Rules of Inference	
Conditional statement: *If you read this chapter, then you will be wiser.* Antecedent (A): *If you read this chapter* Consequent (B): *then you will be wiser*	
Valid Rules of Inference	*Valid Inferences*
Modus ponens	Given A is true, infer B is true.
Modus tollens	Given B is false, infer A is false.
Invalid Rules of Inference	*Invalid Inferences*
Affirmation of the consequent	Given B is true, infer A is true.
Denial of the antecedent	Given A is false, infer B is false.

uncle of Lisa," follows by deductive reasoning—it is certainly true, given the definitions of familial relationships. In contrast, the second conclusion, "Fred is older than Lisa," follows by inductive reasoning—it is probably but not certainly true (i.e., it is logically possible, and not all that uncommon in the real world, for an uncle to be younger than a niece).

Our first topic will concern human deductive reasoning using the conditional connective *if*. A **conditional statement** is an assertion such as *If you read this chapter, then you will be wiser*, in which the *if* part (*If you read this chapter*) is called the **antecedent**, and the *then* part (*then you will be wiser*) is called the **consequent**. **Table 10.1** lays out the structure of conditional statements and various valid and invalid rules of inference, as discussed in the next two sections.

Two Valid Rules of Inference

A particularly central rule of inference in the logic of conditional statements is known as ***modus ponens*** (which loosely translates from Latin as "method of affirming"). It allows us to infer that the consequent of a conditional statement is true if both the statement itself and the antecedent are true. Thus, given that both the conditional statement *If A, then B* and its antecedent *A* are true, we can infer that its consequent *B* is true. This rule of inference is illustrated by the following example in which the two premises are the conditional statement and its antecedent, and the conclusion is the consequent:

Modus Ponens
If Joan understands this book, then she will get a good grade.
Joan understands this book.
Therefore: Joan will get a good grade.

Although this example illustrates a valid deduction, it also illustrates the artificiality of applying logic to real-world situations. How is one to really know whether Joan understands the book? One can only assign a certain probability to her understanding. Also, even if Joan does understand the book, at best it is only likely—not certain—that she will get a good grade. However, in research investigating how people reason, participants are asked to suspend their real-world knowledge about such matters and treat these types of statements as if they were certainly true. Or, more precisely, they are asked to reason about what would follow for certain if these statements were true. Participants do not find these instructions particularly strange, but as we will see, they are not always able to make logically correct inferences.

Another valid rule of inference is known in logic as **modus tollens** (which loosely translates as "method of denying"). It allows us to infer that the antecedent of a conditional statement is false if the statement itself is true and the consequent is false. Thus, given that the conditional statement *If A, then B is true* and given that its consequent *B* is false, we can infer that its antecedent *A* is false. This rule of inference is illustrated by the following example:

Modus Tollens
If Joan understands this book, then she will get a good grade.
Joan will not get a good grade.
Therefore: Joan does not understand this book.

This conclusion might strike the reader as less than totally compelling because, again, in the real world such statements are not typically treated as certain.

> *If a conditional statement is true, **modus ponens** allows us to infer the consequent from the antecedent, and **modus tollens** allows us to infer that the antecedent is false if the consequent is false.*

Two Invalid Patterns of Inference

People sometimes accept two patterns of inference that are invalid—that is, they are fallacies because the conclusion does not logically follow from the premises. The first, called **affirmation of the consequent**, asserts that, if a conditional statement is true and if the consequent is true, then the antecedent must also be true, as illustrated by the following example:

Fallacy: Affirmation of the Consequent
If Joan understands this book, then she will get a good grade.
Joan will get a good grade.
Therefore: Joan understands this book.

The other invalid pattern, called **denial of the antecedent**, asserts that, if a conditional statement is true and if the antecedent is false, then the consequent must also be false, as illustrated by this example:

Fallacy: Denial of the Antecedent
If Joan understands this book, then she will get a good grade.
Joan does not understand this book.
Therefore: Joan will not get a good grade.

In both of these cases, the inference is invalid because there might be other ways in which Joan could get a good grade.

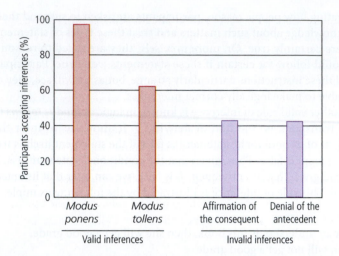

Figure 10.2 Acceptance of Valid and Invalid Inferences. Participants almost always accept valid *modus ponens* inferences, but acceptance of valid *modus tollens* inferences is only slightly greater than acceptance of the two invalid types of inferences. *(Data from Evans, 1993.)*

Evans (1993) reviewed a large number of studies that compared the frequency with which people accept the valid *modus ponens* and *modus tollens* inferences to the frequency with which they accept these two types of invalid inferences (see **Figure 10.2**). As can be seen, people rarely fail to accept a *modus ponens* inference, but the frequency with which they accept the valid *modus tollens* is only slightly greater than the frequencies with which they accept the invalid inferences.

> *People show high levels of logical reasoning with* **modus ponens** *only.*

Causal Reasoning

People often interpret statements with *if-then* clauses as reflecting a causal relationship rather than a logical relationship. Consider, for example, the contrast between the following pair of statements (Weidenfeld, Oberauer, & Hörnig, 2005):

1. If the church bells are ringing in Manchester, then the workmen in *Manchester* knock off work.
2. If the church bells are ringing in Manchester, then the workmen in *London* knock off work.

Both of these statements may be true, but readers are inclined to interpret the first as expressing a causal relationship (the workmen knock off *because* they hear the church bells), the second as expressing just a statistical regularity. A causal interpretation of the first statement affects the inferences that follow. For example, if you were told the bells did not ring in Manchester, it would be reasonable to infer that the workmen did not knock off work. However, from a logical standpoint, that inference would be invalid, because it would be based on the fallacy of denying the antecedent (the workmen might have knocked off work for some other reason, even though the church bells did not ring).

Research has shown that the way people reason about conditional statements given a causal interpretation differs from the way they reason about non-causally interpreted conditionals. Errors of inference for conditionals given a logical interpretation are not errors for a causal interpretation. For instance, Sloman and Lagnado (2005) described a situation in causal terms to one group of participants and in logical, conditional terms to another group. In the causal description, Sloman and Lagnado used the word "cause" rather than an *if-then* statement to avoid ambiguity as to whether a causal relation held:

> *Causal description:* There are three billiard balls on a table that act in the following way: Ball 1's movement causes Ball 2 to move. Ball 2's movement causes Ball 3 to move.

In contrast, Sloman and Lagnado used the word "logical" and *if-then* terminology to reinforce the conditional interpretation:

> *Conditional description:* Someone is showing off her logical abilities. She is moving balls without breaking the following rules: If Ball 1 moves, then Ball 2 moves. If Ball 2 moves, then Ball 3 moves.

They then told participants to imagine Ball 2 could not move and asked them to judge whether Ball 1 could move and whether Ball 3 could move. Both groups tended to think that Ball 3 could not move, but there was a big difference between the two groups in their judgments about Ball 1. Logically, if given the premises *If Ball 1 moves, then Ball 2 moves* and *Ball 2 does not move*, a valid inference (using *modus tollens*) is *Ball 1 does not move*. However, in the causal interpretation, preventing Ball 2 from moving has no implications for whether Ball 1 is moving. The results of the study support this contrast: 55% of the participants given the conditional statement concluded that Ball 1 could not move, whereas only 5% of the participants given the causal statement came to that conclusion.

When *if-then* statements can be seen as implying causal relationships, participants often interpret them in terms of things they know about the real world. Cummins, Lubart, Alksnis, and Rist (1991) presented participants with pairs of arguments like these:

1. If Mary jumped into the swimming pool, then she got wet.
   Mary jumped into the swimming pool.
   Therefore, she got wet.
2. If fertilizer was put on the plants, then they grew quickly.
   Fertilizer was put on the plants.
   Therefore, they grew quickly.

Even though these statements are given in *if-then* terms and are valid inferences using *modus ponens*, participants seemed to place causal interpretations on them, affecting how they reasoned about the conclusions. Participants were willing to accept the conclusion less frequently in the second case than in the first because they knew that other things are necessary for plants to grow quickly. In another test, participants were presented with pairs of arguments like these:

1. If the trigger was pulled, then the gun fired.
   The gun fired.
   Therefore, the trigger had been pulled.
2. If Mary jumped into the swimming pool, then she got wet.
   Mary got wet.
   Therefore, she had jumped into the swimming pool.

In both cases accepting the conclusion is an example of the fallacy of affirming the consequent. However, participants were more willing to accept the conclusion in the first case because they could think of few ways for a gun to fire other than by having the trigger pulled, whereas, in the second case, participants could think of many ways for Mary to get wet.

Results like these show that when participants place a causal interpretation on an *if-then* statement, they reason about the statement in terms of their knowledge about causes in the real world (e.g., water is necessary for a plant to grow, and a person can get wet by being out in the rain). Pearl (1988) introduced Bayes nets as a graphical formalism to use in work on artificial intelligence for reasoning about real-world knowledge, a formalism that has proven useful for understanding how humans reason about causal relationships. **Figure 10.3a** shows an example of a Bayes net from Holyoak and Cheng (2011), representing a situation

Figure 10.3 Bayes Nets.
(a) This network shows that both viral pneumonia and bacterial pneumonia cause headache, cough, and fever (generative causes). Antibiotics are given to cure bacterial pneumonia, and aspirin is administered to relieve headache (preventive causes). How should an artificial intelligence system (or a human being) use the causal relationships depicted in this network along with knowledge about the real world to reason about how to deal with a medical situation? *(Information from Holyoak and Cheng, 2011.)* (b) This abstract network, which can be described in both causal terms and conditional terms, was used by Sloman and Lagnado (2005) to reveal differences in how people reason, depending on which description they are given.

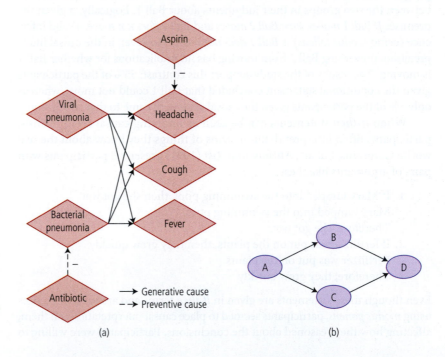

in which two types of pneumonia cause the same three symptoms. It also shows a way of curing one type of pneumonia and a way of treating one of the symptoms.

Much work with such Bayes nets uses Bayesian inference (to be discussed in Chapter 11) to deal with reasoning about the probabilities that these causal relationships hold, but researchers also study how the network structure affects causal reasoning (see Sloman & Lagnado, 2015, for a critical review). For instance, Sloman and Lagnado (2005) described the network in Figure 10.3b in either causal or conditional terms:

Causal	Conditional
A causes B.	If A then B.
A causes C.	If A then C.
B causes D.	If B then D.
C causes D.	If C then D.
D definitely occurred.	D is true.

In the causal case, participants were asked, "If B had not occurred, would D still have occurred?"; and in the conditional case, they were asked the parallel question, "If B were false, would D still be true?" Participants were more likely to think D occurred in the causal case than they were to think D is true in the conditional case. In the causal case, even if B does not occur, D could still occur through the path from A to C to D; but in the conditional case, it is less clear how to reason logically through the relationships.

> If-then *statements can be interpreted as logical conditionals or as causal statements. When people place a causal interpretation on an if-then statement, they reason differently and are more influenced by prior knowledge.*

The Wason Selection Task

Some deviations from logical reasoning can be explained by assuming that people are engaging in causal reasoning, but this assumption does not account for participant errors in a long series of experiments initiated by Peter Wason (for a review of the early research, see Evans & Over, 2004). These errors have been taken as a striking demonstration of human inability to reason about conditionals correctly. In a typical experiment in this research, four cards like the following were placed in front of participants:

E   K   4   7

Participants were told that a letter appeared on one side of each card and a number on the other, according to the following rule:

If a card has a vowel on one side, then it has an even number on the other side.

The participants' task was to turn over only those cards that had to be turned over in order to verify the correctness of the rule. This task, typically referred to as the **Wason selection task**, has been the subject of a great deal of research. (Note that only the E and the 7 need to be turned over—the E because revealing an odd number on the other side would disconfirm the rule, and the 7 because revealing a vowel on the other side would also disconfirm the rule. Turning over the K is pointless because the rule says nothing about the number opposite a consonant, and turning over the 4 is also pointless because the rule does not say that an even number could not be opposite a consonant.)

Averaging over a large number of experiments (Oaksford & Chater, 1994), about 90% of the participants have been found to select E, a logically correct choice, as noted above. However, only about 25% elected to turn over the 7 (also a logically correct choice), whereas about 60% chose to turn over the 4 (a logically incorrect choice), and about 15% elected to turn over the K (also a logically incorrect choice).

Thus, participants tend to display two types of logical errors in the task. First, turning over the 4 is an example of the fallacy of affirming the consequent. Second, and even more striking, is the failure by about 75% of the participants to apply the rule of *modus tollens*—that is, not turning over the 7 means they miss the chance of finding a vowel, which would disconfirm the rule.

In these studies, the number of participants who make the right combination of choices, turning over only the E and the 7, is often only about 10%, which has been taken as a damning indictment of human reasoning. Early in the history of research on this task, Wason gave a talk at the IBM Research Center in which he presented this same problem to an audience filled with PhDs, many in mathematics and physics. He got the same poor results from this audience, who reportedly were so embarrassed that they harassed Wason with complaints about how the problem was not accurately presented or the correct answer was not really correct. This question of what the right answer is has been explored, but before considering that research, we will see what happens when one puts content into this type of problem.

> When presented with abstract material in the Wason selection task, people have particular difficulty in recognizing the importance of exploring whether the consequent is false.

Permission Interpretation of the Conditional

A person's performance on the Wason selection task can sometimes be greatly enhanced by using meaningful content. Griggs and Cox (1982) were among the first to demonstrate this enhancement in a paradigm that is formally equivalent to the Wason task. Participants were instructed to imagine that they were police officers responsible for ensuring that the following regulation was being followed: *If a person is drinking beer, then the person must be over 19.* They were presented with four cards that represented people sitting around a table. On one side of each card was a label giving the age of the person drinking and on the other side was the beverage that the person was drinking. The sides of the cards in view were labeled "Drinking beer," "Drinking Coke," "16 years of age," and "22 years of age." The task was to select which cards had to be turned over in order to determine whether the drinking law was being violated. In this situation, 74% of the participants selected both logically correct cards (namely, "Drinking beer" and "16 years of age").[1]

It has been argued that the better performance in this task depends on the fact that the conditional statement is being interpreted as a rule about a social norm, according to the **permission schema** (i.e., interpreting a conditional statement as the antecedent specifying the situations in which the consequent is permitted). Society has many rules about how its members should conduct themselves, and the argument is that people are good at applying such social rules (Cheng & Holyoak, 1985). An alternative argument is that better performance with meaningful content in this task depends not on the permission schema but on the familiarity of the participants with the content. The participants in Griggs and Cox (1982) were Florida undergraduates, and this rule about drinking age was in force in Florida at the time. Would the participants have been able to reason as accurately about a similar but unfamiliar rule? To answer this question, Cheng and Holyoak (1985) performed an experiment in which participants saw four forms with the following labels: "Transit," "Entering," "cholera, typhoid, hepatitis," and "typhoid, hepatitis." One group of participants was asked to select the forms that would need to be turned over to evaluate the following apparently senseless rule: "If the form says 'entering' on one side, then the other side includes cholera among the list of diseases." Another group was given the same rule as well as the rationale that a person must have been vaccinated for cholera in order to satisfy immigration officials upon entering a particular country. This rationale was intended to invoke reasoning according to the permission schema by leading participants to interpret one side as indicating whether someone was entering the country or in transit, and the other side as listing the diseases for which the person had been vaccinated. The performance of the group given the rationale was much better than that of the group given just the apparently senseless rule; that is, participants in the "rationale" group were significantly more successful than the participants in the "senseless" group at selecting the forms labeled "Entering" and "typhoid, hepatitis" as the ones necessary to turn over. Because both groups of participants were equally unfamiliar with the rule, the good performance of the "rationale" group apparently depended on reasoning according to the permission schema and not on practice in applying the specific rule.

---

[1] Interestingly, patients with damage to the ventromedial prefrontal cortex do not show this advantage with meaningful content (Adolphs, Tranel, Bechara, Damasio, & Damasio, 1996). We will discuss this patient population more thoroughly in Chapter 11.

Cosmides (1989) and Gigerenzer and Hug (1992) argued that our good performance with such rules (which they call *social contract rules*) depends on our skill at detecting cheaters. Gigerenzer and Hug had participants evaluate the following rule:

> If a student is assigned to Grover High School, then that student must live in Grover City.

They saw cards that stated whether the students attended Grover High School or not on one side and whether they lived in Grover City or not on the other side. As in the original Wason experiment, they had to decide which cards to turn over in order to verify the rule. In one condition, called the "cheating" condition, participants were asked to take the perspective of a member of the Grover City School Board looking for students who were illegally attending the high school. In the "noncheating" condition, participants were asked to take the perspective of a visiting official from the German government who just wants to find out whether this rule is in effect at Grover High School. Gigerenzer and Hug were interested in the frequency with which participants would choose just the two logically correct cards to turn over: the card saying the student attended Grover High School and the card saying the student did not live in Grover City. In the cheating condition, where they took the perspective of a school board member, 80% of the participants chose just these two cards, replicating other results with permission rules. In the noncheating condition, where they took the perspective of a disinterested visitor, only 45% of the participants chose just these two.

> *When participants take the perspective of someone interested in detecting whether a social rule has been violated, they make a large proportion of logically correct choices in tasks that are formally identical to the Wason selection task.*

Probabilistic Interpretation of the Conditional

The research just reviewed demonstrates that people reason well when they adopt a permission interpretation of the conditional. What, then, accounts for participants' poor reasoning performance in the original Wason selection task, where they are not making a permission interpretation? Oaksford and Chater (1994) argued that people tend to interpret conditional statements like those in the original task as probabilistic statements about the real world, not just as logical statements without any relationship to the real world. That is, statements of the form *If A, then B* are interpreted as meaning that B will probably occur when A occurs. Even more important to the Oaksford and Chater argument is the idea that people typically tend to assume that events A and B have low probabilities of occurring in the real world—because that is what would make such a statement informative. To understand their argument, suppose you visited a city and a friend told you that the following rule held about cars in that city:

If a car has a broken headlight, it will have a broken taillight.

Events A and B (broken headlight and broken taillight) are both rare, and consequently asserting that one implies the other is informative. Suppose you go to a large parking lot in which there are hundreds of cars; some are parked with their fronts exposed and others with their rears exposed. Most do not have a broken headlight or a broken taillight, but there are one or two with a broken headlight and one or two with a broken taillight. On which cars would you check the end not exposed to test your friend's claim? Let us consider the following possibilities:

1. *A car with a broken headlight:* If you saw such a car, like participants in all of these experiments, you would be inclined to check its taillight. Almost everyone sees that this would be the sensible thing to do.

2. *A car without a broken headlight:* You would not be inclined to check this car, like most of the participants in these experiments, and again, everyone agrees that you would be right.

3. *A car with a broken taillight:* You would be sorely tempted to see whether that car did not have a broken headlight (despite the fact that it is unnecessary or "illogical" with regard to verifying your friend's claim), and Oaksford and Chater agree with you. The reason is that a car with a broken taillight is so rare that, if it did have a broken headlight, you would be inclined to believe the claim. The coincidence would be too much to shrug off.

4. *A car without a broken taillight:* You would be reluctant to check every car in the lot that met this condition (despite the fact that it is the logical thing to do), and again, Oaksford and Chater would agree with you. The reason is that the odds of finding a broken headlight on such a car are low because a broken headlight is rare, and so many cars would have to be checked. Checking those hundreds of normal cars just does not seem worthwhile.

Oaksford and Chater developed a mathematical analysis of the optimal behavior that explains why the typical errors in the original Wason task make sense. Their analysis, which predicts the frequency of choices in the Wason task, depends on the assumption that properties such as "broken headlight" and "broken taillight" are rare. For this reason, checking cars with a broken taillight, as in possibility 3, is much more likely to be informative than is checking cars without a broken taillight, as in possibility 4. Although the properties in such situations in real life might not always be as rare as in this example, Oaksford and Chater argued that they generally are rare. For instance, more things are not dogs than are dogs and more things don't bark than do, and so the same analysis would apply to a rule such as "If an animal is a dog, then it will bark" (and many other such rules). There is an apparent weakness in the Oaksford and Chater argument, however, when applied to the original Wason experiment, where the participants were reasoning about even numbers: There are not more odd numbers than even numbers. Nonetheless, Oaksford argued that people carry their beliefs that properties are rare into Wason-type situations. There is evidence that manipulations of the probabilities of these properties do change people's behavior in the expected way (Oaksford & Wakefield, 2003).

> *The "incorrect" reasoning in the Wason card selection task can be explained if we assume that participants select cards that will be informative under a probabilistic model.*

Final Thoughts on the Connective *If*

The logical connective *if* can be interpreted in many different ways, reflecting the richness of human cognition. We have considered evidence for its causal interpretation, its probabilistic interpretation, and its permission interpretation. People are also capable of adopting the logical interpretation, which is what logicians and students of logic do when working with logic. Studies of their reasoning with the connective *if* (Lewis, 1985; Scheines & Sieg, 1994) find it to be similar to mathematical reasoning, as in the domain of geometry discussed in Chapter 9. That is, people are able to take a problem-solving approach to formal reasoning with the connective *if*. In an fMRI study, Qin et al. (2003) looked at participants solving abstract logic tasks and found activation in the same parietal regions that Goel et al. (2000) found active with their content-free material (see Figure 10.1).

An amusing result is that training in logic does not necessarily result in better behavior on the original Wason selection task. In a study by Cheng, Holyoak, Nisbett, and Oliver (1986), college students who had just taken a semester course in logic did only 3% better on the Wason selection task than those who had no formal training in logic. It was not that they did not know the rules of logic; rather, they did not think to apply them in the experiment. When presented with these problems outside the logic classroom, the students chose to adopt some other interpretation of the word *if*. However, this is not necessarily a flaw in human reasoning. To repeat a point made before, many researchers in AI wish their programs were as adaptive as humans are in interpreting information.

> *People use different problem-solving operators, depending on their interpretation of the logical connective* **if**.

Reasoning about Quantifiers

Much of human knowledge is expressed with **logical quantifiers** such as *all* or *some*. Witness this famous statement often attributed to Abraham Lincoln: "You can fool all of the people some of the time, and you can fool some of the people all of the time, but you can't fool all of the people all of the time." In this section, we will review research on how people reason about such quantifiers when they appear in simple sentences. As was the case for the logical connective *if,* we will see that there are differences between the logician's interpretation of quantifiers and the interpretations that people frequently use when reasoning about sentences with quantifiers.

Categorical Syllogisms

Modern logic is greatly concerned with analyzing the meaning of quantifiers such as *all, no,* and *some* in statements like this:

> All philosophers read books.

If you believe that this statement is true, a logician would then say that you are therefore committed to the belief that there is no philosopher who does not read books. However, most of us have no trouble accepting the idea that we might find somewhere in the world an illiterate person who deserves to be identified as a philosopher. This example illustrates the fact that when we use *all* in real life, we frequently mean "most" or "with high probability." Similarly, when we use *no* as in

> No doctors are poor.

we often mean "hardly any" or "with small probability." Logicians call both the *all* and *no* statements **universal statements** because they interpret these statements as blanket claims with no exceptions. Roger Schank, a well-known AI researcher, was once observed to make the assertion

> No one uses universals.

which surely is a sign that people use these quantifiers in a richer and more complex way than is implied by the logical analysis.

By the beginning of the 20th century, the sophistication with which logicians analyzed such quantified statements had increased considerably (see Church, 1956, for an historical discussion). In psychology, however, most of the research on quantifiers has focused on a simpler and older kind of deduction with quantifiers called the **categorical syllogism**. Much of Aristotle's writing on reasoning concerned the categorical syllogism, and extensive discussions of categorical syllogisms can be found in old textbooks on logic, such as Cohen and Nagel (1934).

Categorical syllogisms include statements containing quantifiers such as *some, all, no,* and *some…not.* For example:

1. All doctors are rich.
2. Some lawyers are dishonest.
3. No politicians are trustworthy.
4. Some actors are not handsome.

As a convenient shorthand, the categories (e.g., doctors, rich people, lawyers, dishonest people) in such statements can be represented by letters, in which case statements **1** through **4** might be rendered in this way:

1. All A's are B's.
2. Some C's are D's.
3. No E's are F's.
4. Some G's are not H's.

(Sometimes, as in the Goel et al. [2000] experiment described at the beginning of this chapter, material is actually presented with such letters.)

A categorical syllogism typically contains two premises and a conclusion. For example:

1. No Pittsburgher is a Browns fan.
All Browns fans are residents of Cleveland.
Therefore: No Pittsburgher is a resident of Cleveland.

There is a tendency to accept this syllogism as logically valid. To see that the conclusion does not logically follow from the premises, consider the following equivalent syllogism:

2. No dog is an elephant.
All elephants are animals.
Therefore: No dog is an animal.

Acceptance of syllogism **1** as valid illustrates a frequent result in research on categorical syllogisms, which is that people often accept invalid syllogisms. For instance, people accept the invalid syllogism **1** almost as often as they accept this valid syllogism:

3. No Pittsburgher lives in Cleveland.
All Browns fans live in Cleveland.
Therefore: No Pittsburgher is a Browns fan.

> *Research on reasoning with quantifiers has focused on trying to understand why people accept many invalid categorical syllogisms.*

The Atmosphere Hypothesis

In the case of syllogism **1** above, people are biased toward acceptance by the content of the syllogism, but much of the research on categorical syllogisms has focused on the tendency of people to accept invalid syllogisms even when they have neutral content. People are generally good at recognizing valid syllogisms when stated with neutral content. For instance, almost everyone accepts

4. All A's are B's.
All B's are C's.
Therefore: All A's are C's.

The problem is that people also accept many invalid syllogisms, such as

5. Some A's are B's.
Some B's are C's.
Therefore: Some A's are C's.

(To see that this syllogism is invalid, replace A with "dogs," B with "pets," and C with "cats.") However, people are not completely indiscriminate in what they accept as valid. For instance, while people might tend to accept syllogism **5**, they tend not to accept this:

6. Some A's are B's.
Some B's are C's.
Therefore: No A's are C's.

To account for the pattern of what participants accept and what they reject, Woodworth and Sells (1935) proposed the **atmosphere hypothesis**, which proposes that the logical quantifiers (*some, all, no,* and *some…not*) used in the premises of a syllogism create an "atmosphere" that predisposes participants to accept conclusions having the same quantifiers. This hypothesis consists of two parts. One part asserts that participants tend to accept a positive conclusion to positive premises and a negative conclusion to negative premises, and that, when the premises are mixed, participants tend to prefer a negative conclusion. Thus, the hypothesis predicts that participants will tend to accept the following invalid syllogism:

7. No A's are B's.
All B's are C's.
Therefore: No A's are C's.

The other part of the atmosphere hypothesis concerns participants' responses to **particular statements** (statements using *some* or *some…not*) versus universal statements (statements using *all* or *no*). As syllogism 7 illustrates, participants will tend to accept a universal conclusion if the premises are universal. The hypothesis predicts that participants will tend to accept a particular conclusion if the premises are particular (which accounts for their acceptance of syllogism **5** above) and that when one premise is particular and the other universal, participants prefer a particular conclusion. Thus, participants would tend to accept this invalid syllogism:

8. All A's are B's.
Some B's are C's.
Therefore: Some A's are C's.

(To see that this syllogism is invalid, replace A with "dogs," B with "animals," and C with "cats.")

> *The atmosphere hypothesis states that the logical quantifiers (***some, all, no,*** *and* ***some…not***) *used in the premises of a syllogism create an "atmosphere" that predisposes participants to accept conclusions having the same quantifiers.*

Limitations of the Atmosphere Hypothesis

The atmosphere hypothesis provides a succinct characterization of participant behavior with various types of categorical syllogisms, but it tells us little about what participants are actually thinking or why. Also, it offers no explanation of why the content of the syllogism (as in the Pittsburgh–Cleveland example in syllogism **1** above) can have such a strong effect on judgments of validity. Its characterization of participant behavior is also not always correct for content-free syllogisms. For example, according to the atmosphere hypothesis, participants should be as likely to accept the atmosphere-favored conclusion when it is not valid as when it is valid. That is, the atmosphere hypothesis predicts that participants would be just as likely to accept syllogism **8** above, which is not valid, as they would be to accept this valid syllogism:

> **9.** Some A's are B's.
> All B's are C's.
> *Therefore:* Some A's are C's.

In fact, however, participants are more likely to accept the conclusion in the valid case. Thus, contrary to the atmosphere hypothesis, participants do display some ability to evaluate a syllogism accurately from a strictly logical standpoint.

Another limitation of the atmosphere hypothesis is that it fails to predict the effects that the form of a syllogism will have on participants' validity judgments. For instance, the hypothesis predicts that participants would be equally likely to accept the invalid syllogism **2** above and this invalid syllogism:

> **10.** Some B's are A's.
> Some C's are B's.
> *Therefore:* Some A's are C's.

In fact, however, participants are more willing to accept syllogism **2** (Johnson-Laird & Steedman, 1978). In general, participants are more willing to accept a conclusion from A to C if they can find a chain leading from A to B in one premise and from B to C in the second premise.

Another problem with the atmosphere hypothesis is that it does not explain what participants do in the presence of two negatives. Suppose, for example, that participants are given these two premises:

> No A's are B's.
> No B's are C's.

The atmosphere hypothesis predicts that participants would tend to accept this invalid conclusion:

> *Therefore:* No A's are C's.

Although a few participants do accept this conclusion, most refuse to accept any conclusion when both premises are negative, which is the correct thing to do (Dickstein, 1978).

All of these problems with the atmosphere hypothesis stem from the fact that it does not explain what people are thinking when they process such syllogisms. It merely tries to predict the conclusions they will accept. The next section will consider some explanations of the thought processes that lead people to correct or incorrect judgments of validity.

> *Participants' validity judgments only approximate the predictions of the atmosphere hypothesis and are often more accurate than the hypothesis would predict.*

Process Explanations

One class of explanations is that participants do not do what the experimenters think they are doing. For instance, it has been argued that it is not natural for people to judge the logical validity of a syllogism. Rather, people tend to judge the truth of the conclusion in the real world. Consider the following pair of syllogisms:

> All lawyers are human.
> All Republicans are human.
> *Therefore:* Some lawyers are Republicans.

> All bictoids are reptiles.
> All bictoids are birds.
> *Therefore:* Some reptiles are birds.

The first has a true conclusion but is not valid (to see why, replace "lawyers" with "dogs," "human" with "animals," and "Republicans" with "elephants."). In contrast, the second syllogism is a valid argument but has a false conclusion. People have a greater tendency to accept the first argument (invalid but with a true conclusion) than the second argument (valid but with a false conclusion) (Evans, Handley, & Harper, 2001).

It has also been argued that many people really do not understand what it means for an argument to be valid and simply judge whether a conclusion is possible given the premises. So, for example, although the preceding syllogism concerning lawyers and Republicans is not valid, it is certainly possible given the premises that the conclusion is true. Evans et al. showed that there is very little difference in the judgments that participants make when they are asked to judge when conclusions are necessarily true given the premises (the measure of a valid argument) and when conclusions are possibly true given the premises.

Johnson-Laird (1983; Johnson-Laird & Steedman, 1978) proposed that participants judge whether a conclusion is possible by creating a mental model of a world that satisfies the premises of the syllogism and inspecting that model to see whether the conclusion is satisfied. This is called **mental model theory**. Consider these premises:

> All the squares are striped.
> Some of the striped objects have bold borders.

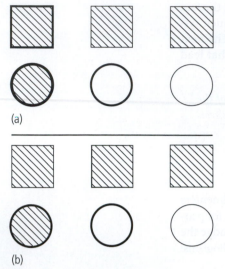

(a)

(b)

Figure 10.4 Mental Model Theory. This theory proposes that participants judge the validity of a syllogism by constructing a mental model that satisfies the premises and then inspecting that model to see whether the conclusion holds. The figure illustrates this proposal using a syllogism in which the premises are "All the squares are striped" and "Some of the striped objects have bold borders" and in which the conclusion is "Some of the squares have bold borders." In both (a) and (b), the premises are satisfied, but the conclusion holds only in (a), not in (b), where no square has a bold border. Thus, participants who form a mental model like (a) would judge that the syllogism is valid, whereas those who form a mental model like (b) would judge it invalid.

Figure 10.4a illustrates what a participant might imagine, according to Johnson-Laird, as an instantiation of these premises. The participant has imagined a group of objects, some of which are square, whereas others are round; some of which are striped, whereas others are clear; and some of which have bold borders, whereas others do not. This world represents one possible interpretation of these premises. When the participant is asked to judge the following conclusion,

Therefore: Some of the squares have bold borders.

the participant inspects the mental model and sees that, indeed, the conclusion is true in that model. The problem is that this particular model establishes only that the conclusion is possible, but not that it is necessary. For the conclusion to be necessary, it must be true in all mental models that are consistent with the premises. Figure 10.4b illustrates a model in which the premises are true but the conclusion does not hold.

Johnson-Laird theorized that participants have considerable difficulty developing alternative models and tend to accept a syllogism if its conclusion holds in the first mental model they come up with. Johnson-Laird (1983) developed a computer simulation of this theory that reproduces many of the errors that participants make. Johnson-Laird (1995) also argued that there is neurological evidence in favor of the mental model explanation. He noted that patients with right-hemisphere damage are more impaired in reasoning tasks than are patients with left-hemisphere damage and that the right hemisphere tends to take part in spatial processing of mental images. In a brain-imaging study, Kroger, Nystrom, Cohen, and Johnson-Laird (2008) found that the right frontal cortex was more active than the left in processing such syllogisms but that the opposite was true when people engaged in arithmetic calculation (this left bias for arithmetic is also illustrated in the study described in Chapter 1, Figure 1.16). Parsons and Osherson (2001) reported a similar finding, with deductive reasoning being right localized and probabilistic reasoning being left localized.

In its essence, Johnson-Laird's argument is that people make errors in reasoning because they overlook some of the ways in which the premises might be true. For example, a participant imagines Figure 10.4a as a realization of the premises and overlooks the possibility of Figure 10.4b. Johnson-Laird (personal communication, 2003) argues that a great many errors in human reasoning are produced by failures to consider the full variety of possible explanations of the data. For instance, a problem in the Chernobyl disaster was that, for several hours, engineers failed to consider the possibility that the reactor was no longer intact.

Errors in evaluating syllogisms can be explained by assuming that participants fail to consider possible mental models of the syllogisms.

Inductive Reasoning and Hypothesis Testing

In contrast to deductive reasoning, where logical rules allow one to infer conclusions from premises with certainty, in inductive reasoning the conclusions do not necessarily follow from the premises. Consider the following premises:

> The first number in the series is 1.
> The second number in the series is 2.
> The third number in the series is 4.

What conclusion follows? The numbers are doubling and so one possible conclusion is that

> The fourth number in the series is 8.

However, a better conclusion might be to state this general rule:

> Each number is twice the previous number.

A characteristic of a good inductive inference like the second conclusion is that it is a statement from which one can deduce all the premises. For example, because we know each number is twice the previous number, we can now deduce what the original three numbers must have been. Thus, in a certain sense induction is deduction turned around. The difficulty for inductive reasoning is that usually more than one conclusion would be consistent with the premises. For instance, in the problem above another possible conclusion is that the difference between successive numbers is increasing by one, in which case the fourth number would be 7.

Inductive reasoning is relevant to many situations in everyday life: a detective trying to solve a mystery given a set of clues, a doctor trying to diagnose the cause of a set of symptoms, someone trying to determine what is wrong with a TV, or a researcher trying to formulate a scientific principle to explain some data. In all these cases, one has a set of specific observations from which one is trying to infer some relevant conclusion. Many of these cases involve the sort of probabilistic reasoning that will be discussed in Chapter 11 (for instance, medical symptoms are typically only associated probabilistically with disease). In this chapter, we will focus on cases like the numerical series above, where we are looking for a hypothesis that implies the observations with certainty. Much of the interest in such cases revolves around how people seek evidence relevant to formulating such a hypothesis.

Hypothesis Formation

Bruner, Goodnow, and Austin (1956) performed a classic series of experiments on hypothesis formation. **Figure 10.5** illustrates the kind of material they used. The stimuli, which were all rectangular boxes containing various objects, varied on four features: number of objects in the box (one, two, or three); number of borders around the box (one, two, or three); shape

Figure 10.5 Types of Stimuli Used in Study of Concept Identification. Bruner et al. (1956) used stimuli like these, formed by combinations of four features (number of objects, number of borders, shape of objects, and color of objects), each exhibiting three values. *(Data from Bruner et al., 1956.)*

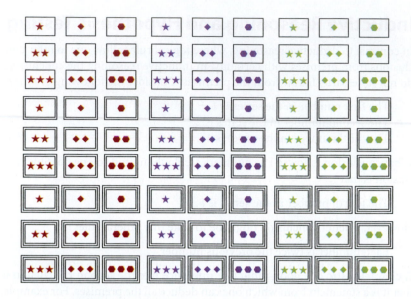

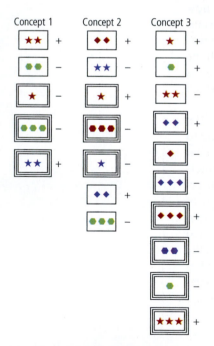

Concept 1   Concept 2   Concept 3

Figure 10.6 Groups of Stimuli from Which Participants Were to Identify Concepts. In each column, a plus sign (+) signals that the stimulus is an instance of the concept and a minus sign (−) signals that the stimulus is not an instance of the concept. *(Data from Bruner et al., 1956.)*

of the objects in the box (star, diamond, or hexagon); and color of the objects in the box (red, blue, or green). Participants were shown sequences of these stimuli, one stimulus at a time, and were cued whether each stimulus was or was not an instance of a particular concept. For example, participants might have been shown the sequences illustrated by the three columns in **Figure 10.6**, where the plus and minus signs represent the cues that identify each stimulus as an instance of the concept or not (each column represents a different concept). Participants had the task of determining what the concept was for each sequence. Stop reading and try to determine the concept for each column in Figure 10.6.

- Concept 1 is that *the stimulus must contain two stars.* This is referred to as a *conjunctive concept* because a conjunction of two or more features must be present for the stimulus to be an instance of the concept (in this case the features are *two* and *star*). People typically find conjunctive concepts easiest to discover. In some sense, conjunctive hypotheses seem to be the most natural kind of hypotheses. They are also the kind of hypotheses that have been researched most extensively.

- Concept 2 is that *the stimulus must either have two borders or contain two diamonds.* This is referred to as a *disjunctive concept* because a stimulus is an instance of the concept if either of the features is present.

- Concept 3 is that *the number of objects must equal the number of borders.* This is referred to as a *relational concept* because a stimulus is an instance of the concept only if certain features are in a specified relationship.

These tasks are particularly difficult because you must determine both which features (or *attributes*) are relevant and what kind of rule connects the features (e.g., conjunctive, disjunctive, or relational). The former task is referred to as **attribute identification** and the latter as **rule learning** (Haygood & Bourne, 1965). In many experiments, the participant is told either the relevant attributes or the kind of rule. For instance, in the Bruner et al. (1956) experiments, participants were told that the concepts were conjunctive so that they only had to identify the correct attributes when trying to determine the concept.

> *Forming a hypothesis involves identifying both what features are relevant to the hypothesis and how these features are related.*

Hypothesis Testing

In the experiment illustrated in Figure 10.6, participants are presented with pieces of evidence for some concept and have to figure out what the concept is. Some problems in real life are like this—we have no control over what evidence we see but must figure out the rules nevertheless. For instance, when there is an outbreak of food poisoning, medical health researchers check on what the victims ate, looking for some pattern, but they have no control over what the victims ate. In other situations, however, one can do experiments and test certain possibilities. For instance, when medical researchers want to determine the most effective combination of drugs to treat a disease, they will perform clinical trials where different groups of patients receive different drug combinations. Scientific research can reach more certain conclusions more quickly if the researchers can choose the cases to test rather than having to take the cases that the situation presents to them.

In their classic research, Bruner et al. (1956) also studied situations where participants could choose the stimuli to assess as to whether they were instances of the concept. In one condition, Bruner et al. told participants that a certain stimulus was an instance of a conjunctive concept, and then the participants could select other stimuli and ask whether they were also instances of the concept. For example, if you were told that the center stimulus in Figure 10.5 (two blue diamonds in a box with two borders) was an instance of a conjunctive concept, which other stimuli would you choose to assess? The scientific approach would be to test each feature, one at a time, to determine whether it was critical to the concept. For instance, you could first test the feature of number of borders by choosing a stimulus that differed from the initial stimulus only on this feature (i.e., either of two stimuli in the same column in Figure 10.5—the one with two blue diamonds in a box with a single border or the one with two blue diamonds in a box with three borders). If the chosen stimulus were not an instance of the concept, you would know that that value of the feature (in this case, two borders) was relevant, and if the stimulus was an instance, you would know that that value was irrelevant. Then you could try another feature. After four stimuli, you would have identified the conjunctive concept with certainty. Bruner et al. called this strategy "conservative focusing," and some of their participants (Harvard undergraduates of the 1950s) followed it. However, many participants practiced less systematic strategies. For instance, given the same initial stimulus, they might first test a stimulus that changed both the color of the diamonds and the number of borders. If the stimulus were an instance of the concept, they would know that neither feature was relevant. However, if the stimulus were not an instance, they would have learned relatively little.

A well-known case where people seem to test their hypotheses less than optimally is the 2-4-6 task introduced by Wason (1960)—the same psychologist who introduced the card selection task that we described earlier. In this experiment, participants are told that "2 4 6" is an instance of a triad (a sequence of three numbers) that is consistent with a rule and are instructed to find out what the rule is by asking whether other triads are instances of the rule. What triads would you try? The protocol below, which comes from one of Wason's participants, gives each triad that the participant chose to ask about and the participant's reason for the choice, along with the experimenter's feedback as to whether the triad conformed to the rule. The sequence of triads was occasionally broken when the participant decided to announce a hypothesis. The experimenter's feedback for each hypothesis is given in parentheses:

Triad	Reason Given for Triad	Feedback
8 10 12	2 added each time.	Yes
14 16 18	Even numbers in order of magnitude.	Yes
20 22 24	Same reason.	Yes
1 3 5	2 added to preceding number.	Yes
Announcement: *The rule is that by starting with any number, 2 is added each time to form the next number.* (Incorrect)		
2 6 10	The middle number is the arithmetic mean of the other two.	Yes
1 50 99	Same reason.	Yes
Announcement: *The rule is that the middle number is the arithmetic mean of the other two.* (Incorrect)		
3 10 17	Same number, 7, added each time.	Yes
0 3 6	Three added each time.	Yes
Announcement: *The rule is that the difference between two numbers next to each other is the same.* (Incorrect)		
12 8 4	The same number is subtracted each time to form the next number.	No
Announcement: *The rule is adding a number, always the same one, to form the next number.* (Incorrect)		
1 4 9	Any three numbers in order of magnitude.	Yes
Announcement: *The rule is any three numbers in order of magnitude.* (Correct)		

The important feature to note about this protocol is that the participant tested each hypothesis by almost exclusively asking about triads consistent with it. The better procedure in this case would have been to also try sequences that were inconsistent with the hypothesis. That is, the participant should have looked sooner for negative evidence as well as positive evidence. This would have revealed that the participant had started out with a hypothesis that was too narrow and was missing the more general correct hypothesis. The only way to discover this error is by finding examples that disconfirm the hypothesis, but this is what people have great difficulty doing.

In another experiment, Wason (1968) asked 16 participants what they would do after announcing a hypothesis to determine whether the hypothesis was incorrect. Nine participants said they would generate only instances consistent with their hypotheses and wait for one to be identified as not an instance of the rule. Only four participants said that they would generate instances inconsistent with their hypothesis to see whether they were identified as instances of the rule. The remaining three insisted that their hypotheses could not be incorrect.

This strategy of testing only instances that are consistent with the hypothesis has been called **confirmation bias**. It has been argued that confirmation bias is not necessarily a mistaken strategy (Fischhoff & Beyth-Marom, 1983; Klayman & Ha, 1987)—in many situations, selecting instances consistent with a hypothesis is an effective way to disconfirm the hypothesis. For example, if one did well on an exam after drinking a glass of orange juice and entertained the hypothesis that orange juice led to good exam performance, drinking orange juice before subsequent exams might quickly disconfirm that hypothesis. What made this strategy so ineffective in Wason's experiment is simply that the correct hypothesis was very general. The analogy to the Wason hypothesis in this case would be that the true rule was that consuming any drink would improve exam performance (particularly unlikely if we include alcoholic drinks).

> *In choosing instances to test a hypothesis, people often focus on instances consistent with their hypothesis, and this can cause difficulties if their hypothesis is too narrow.*

Scientific Discovery

Whether participants are trying to infer a concept by selecting instances from a set of options like those in Figure 10.5 or trying to infer a rule that describes a set of examples as in the protocol we just reviewed, participants are engaged in problem-solving searches like those we discussed in Chapter 8 (such as in Figure 8.4 and Figure 8.9). In fact, they are searching two problem spaces. One problem space is the space of possible hypotheses and the other is the space of possible test instances. It has been argued (e.g., Klahr & Dunbar, 1988; Simon & Lea, 1974) that this is exactly the situation that scientists face in developing a new theory—they search through a space of possible theories and a space of possible experiments to test these theories.

The term "confirmation bias" has also been used to describe failures in the way people test scientific theories. In the hypothesis-testing example described in the preceding section, it just referred to a tendency to test only instances that were consistent with one's hypothesis. However, in the broader context of testing scientific theories, it refers to a host of behaviors that serve to protect one's favored theory from disconfirmation. In one study, Dunbar (1993) had undergraduates try to discover how genes were controlled by redoing, in a highly simplified form, the research for which Jacques Monod and François Jacob were awarded the 1965 Nobel Prize for medicine. Dunbar provided participants with computer simulations of some of the critical experiments. The participants were told that their task was to determine how one set of genes controlled another set of genes so that the second set of genes produced an enzyme only when lactose was present. (This enzyme serves to break down the lactose into glucose.) All the undergraduates initially thought that there must be a mechanism by which the first set of genes responded to the presence of lactose and activated the second set of genes. This is the hypothesis that Monod and Jacob had initially as well, but in fact the mechanism is inhibitory—that is, the first set of genes inhibits the enzyme-producing genes when lactose is absent but is blocked from inhibiting when lactose is present. Confirmation bias led all these undergraduates to begin by trying only experiments that would confirm their activation hypothesis, and only a minority eventually began to search for alternative hypotheses about the mechanism of control.

Science as an institution has a way of protecting us from scientists whose confirmation bias leads them too strongly in the wrong direction. Individual scientists are often strongly motivated to find problems with the theories of other scientists (Nickerson, 1998). There is also considerable variation in how individual scientists do science. Michael Faraday (1791–1867), a notable British scientist, made his discoveries by first focusing on collecting confirmatory evidence and then switching his focus to disconfirmatory evidence (Tweney, 1989). Dunbar (1997) studied scientists in three immunology laboratories and one biology laboratory at Stanford and noted that they were quite ready to attend to unexpected results and modify their theories to accommodate those results. (See Implications 10.1 for a discussion of confirmation bias in the case of Louis Pasteur.)

Fugelsang and Dunbar (2005) performed fMRI studies of participants trying to integrate data with specific hypotheses. For instance, participants were told that they were seeing results from a clinical trial testing the hypothesis that a drug under development had an antidepressant effect on mood. They saw patient records indicating either that the drug had such an effect on mood (consistent with the hypothesis) or that it did not have an effect (inconsistent with the hypothesis). Before seeing the records, participants were led to believe that the drug did indeed have an antidepressant effect and thus found consistent evidence more plausible. When viewing the inconsistent evidence, participants showed greater activation in the anterior cingulate cortex (ACC)

Implications 10.1

How Convincing Is a 10% Result?

Even eminent scientists can be subject to confirmation bias. Consider the case of the great French biologist and chemist Louis Pasteur (1822–1895), who was involved in a major scientific debate about whether organisms could spontaneously generate. At the time, it was widely believed that the appearance of bacteria in apparently sterilized organic material was evidence for the spontaneous generation of life. Pasteur performed many experiments aimed at disproving this theory, and only 10% of his experiments yielded the desired results, but he chose to publish only those results, claiming that the results of the other 90% were due to experimental errors (Geison, 1995). Of course, any sensible scientist would question experimental results

Photo 12 / Alamy

that seem to contradict established theory. For example, if you dropped a rock from the top of a 100-meter tower and timed its fall as 1 second, you would be wise not to conclude that acceleration due to gravity is 200 m/sec^2 (using this formula: acceleration = [2 × distance] / time^2], given that the value of approximately 10 m/sec^2 is very well established. Almost certainly, something was wrong in your measurement of the time it took the rock to fall, and you would do well to repeat the experiment. Pasteur's case, however, does seem rather extreme; ignoring 90% of his experimental results on a question that was much debated at the time looks like a very high degree of confirmation bias. Nevertheless, he turned out to be right.

(see Figure 3.2). As we noted in Chapter 3, the ACC is highly active when participants are engaged in a task that requires strong cognitive control, such as dealing with an inconsistent trial in a Stroop task. These same basic brain mechanisms seem to be invoked when participants must deal with inconsistent data in a scientific context, suggesting that scientific reasoning evokes basic cognitive processes.

> *In studies of scientific discovery, participants tend to focus on experiments consistent with their favored hypothesis and show a reluctance to search for alternative hypotheses.*

Dual-Process Theories

This chapter has presented rather mixed evidence on the question of whether human reasoning corresponds to normative prescriptions—that is, whether people tend to reason in a strictly logical manner or not. Proponents of dual-process theories (Evans, 2007, Stanovich, 2011) have argued that the answer to this question is both yes and no, that human reasoning is governed by two different processes, which sometimes lead to the same conclusions and sometimes lead to different conclusions. **Type 1 processes** are rapid and automatic, relying on associations between situations and actions. For instance, the process described by the atmosphere hypothesis (that people tend to accept a conclusion having the same quantifiers used in the premises) is a type 1 process. In contrast, **type 2 processes**, which are slow and deliberative (e.g., the process of working through a geometry proof), may follow normative prescriptions. Type 2 processes are often considered to have arisen later in the course of evolution and to make heavy demands on working memory.

A standard criticism of such theories is that they can accommodate any result and so cannot be falsified: If people display normatively irrational behavior, this is because their type 1 processes dominate; if they display normatively rational behavior, this is because their type 2 processes dominate. What sort of empirical evidence would really support a dual-process explanation? One sort of evidence concerns individual differences in reasoning behavior. For instance, participants with higher IQs appear to perform better by normative standards on the Wason selection task (Newstead, Handley, Harley, Wright, & Farrelly, 2004), suggesting that IQ correlates with greater use of Type 2 processes. Another kind of evidence involves timing. When people respond quickly, they tend to produce responses consistent with Type 1 processes, whereas when they take longer, their answers tend to correspond more with Type 2 processes. Yet another sort of evidence comes from brain imaging. The anterior cingulate, which is responsive to conflict (as discussed in Chapter 3), is more engaged when Type 1 and Type 2 processes are leading toward different conclusions (de Neys, Vartanian, & Goel, 2008).

One might be inclined to think that when Type 1 and Type 2 processes generate disagreement, it is the Type 1 processes that are wrong. However, this is not always the case. As we have discussed throughout this chapter, often what follows from the information that is given is not what is actually true in the real world. This is not because the real world is illogical but rather because what we are told often does not capture all the complexity of the real world. For instance, statements that are cast as universal assertions are often only true with a relatively high probability (e.g., "Studying the right way leads to good grades"). Type 1 processes can overcome the inadequacies of what is actually specified by taking advantage of the wisdom of experience.

Conclusions

Much of the research on human reasoning has found that it often fails to adhere to the rules and implications of formal logic. And as we have noted, this might even be said of the reasoning processes that scientists use in their research. However, this dismal picture of human reasoning fails to reflect the full context in which reasoning occurs (Manktelow, 2012). In many situations, people actually reason quite well, in part because they take in the full complexity and all the implications of the real-world content. Despite scientists' tendency toward confirmation bias, science as a whole has progressed with great success. To some extent, this is because science is a social activity carried out by a community of researchers. Not only are competitive scientists quick to find mistakes in each other's work, but there is also a cooperative nature to science. Research takes place among teams of researchers, who often rely on each other's help. Okada and Simon (1997) found that pairs of undergraduates were much more successful than individual students at finding the inhibition mechanism in Dunbar's (1993) genetic control task, discussed above. As Okada and Simon note, "In a collaborative situation, subjects must often be more explicit than in an individual learning situation, to make partners understand their ideas and to convince them. This can prompt subjects to entertain requests for explanation and construct deeper explanations" (p. 130). The bottom line of this chapter is that human reasoning normally takes place in a world of complexities (both factual and social) and that what appears deficient in the laboratory may be exquisitely tuned to that world.

Questions for Thought

1. Johnson-Laird and Goldvarg (1997) presented Princeton undergraduates with reasoning problems like this one:

   Only one of the following premises is true about a particular hand of cards:

   There is a king in the hand or there is an ace or both.
   There is a queen in the hand or there is an ace or both.
   There is a jack in the hand or there is a 10, or both.

   Is it possible that there is an ace in the hand?

   They report that the students were correct on only 1% of such problems. What is the correct answer for the problem above? Why is it so hard? Johnson-Laird and Goldvarg attribute the difficulty to people's inability to create mental models of what is not the case.

2. Johnson-Laird and Steedman (1978) presented the following premises to participants drawn from students at Columbia Teachers College:

   All gourmets are shopkeepers.
   All bowlers are shopkeepers.

And asked them what conclusion, if any, followed. The following is the distribution of answers:

17 agreed that no conclusion followed.
2 thought that "Some gourmets are bowlers" followed.
4 thought that "All bowlers are gourmets" followed.
7 thought that "Some bowlers are gourmets" followed.
8 thought that "All gourmets are bowlers" followed.

Use the concepts of this chapter to help explain the answers these participants gave and did not give.

3. Consider the positive stimuli in the column labeled "Concept 3" in Figure 10.6, which were described in the chapter as satisfying the rule that "the number of borders is the same as the number of objects." An alternative rule that describes the positive stimuli is "3 red objects or 2 blue objects or 1 object with one border." Which is the better rule and why? Is there a sense in which the better rule is "more correct" than the other rule?

Key Terms

affirmation of the
   consequent
antecedent
atmosphere hypothesis
attribute identification
categorical syllogism

conditional statement
confirmation bias
consequent
deductive reasoning
denial of the antecedent
inductive reasoning

logical quantifiers
mental model theory
modus ponens
modus tollens
particular statements
permission schema

rule learning
syllogisms
type 1 processes
type 2 processes
universal statements
Wason selection task

11

Decision Making

As we saw in Chapter 10, most of the research on human reasoning has compared it to various prescriptive models from logic and mathematics. The prescriptive models assume that people have access to information about which they can be certain and that they can coolly reflect on this information. However, in the real world, people have to make decisions under pressure in the face of incomplete and uncertain information. Furthermore, in contrast to the relatively neutral character of the syllogisms discussed in Chapter 10, our decisions in real life can have important consequences. Consider the simple task of deciding what to eat when faced with ever-changing medical reports that pronounce formerly "healthy" food as "unhealthy" and vice versa. In making such decisions, we must also deal with the unpleasant consequences of what might be good decisions, such as going on a diet or giving up a pleasurable activity like drinking with friends.

This chapter will focus on research on judgment and decision making under more real-life circumstances. As before, we will discuss research showing how the performance of normal humans is wanting compared to models that were developed for rational behavior. However, we will also see how these prescriptive models are incomplete, missing the complexity of everyday human decision making. Recent research has developed a more nuanced characterization of the situations that people face in their everyday life and a better appreciation of the nature of their judgments.

In this chapter, we will answer these questions:

- How well do people judge the probability of uncertain events?
- How do people use their past experiences to make judgments?
- How do people decide among uncertain options that offer different rewards and costs?
- How does the brain support such decision making?

The Brain and Decision Making

In 1848, Phineas Gage, a railroad worker in Vermont, suffered a bizarre accident: He was using an iron bar to pack gunpowder down into a hole drilled into a rock that had to be blasted to clear a roadbed for the railroad. The powder unexpectedly exploded and sent the iron bar flying through his head before landing 80 feet away. **Figure 11.1** shows a reconstruction of the trajectory of the bar through his skull (Damasio, Grabowski, Frank, Galabruda, & Damasio, 1994). The bar managed to miss any vital areas and spared most of his brain but tore through the center of the very front of the brain — a region called the **ventromedial prefrontal cortex.** Amazingly, he not only survived, he was even able to talk and walk away from the accident after being unconscious for a few minutes. His recovery was difficult, largely because of infections, but he eventually was able to hold a job again, such as a coach driver. Henry Jacob Bigelow, a professor of surgery at Harvard University, declared him "quite recovered in faculties of body and mind" (Macmillan, 2000). Based on such a report, one might have thought that this part of the brain performed no function.

However, all was not well. His personality had undergone major changes.[1] Before his injury he had been polite, respectful, popular, and reliable, and generally displayed the ideal behavior for an American man of that time. Afterward he became just the opposite — as his own physician, John Martyn Harlow, later described him:

> . . . fitful, irreverent, indulging at times in the grossest profanity (which was not previously his custom), manifesting but little deference for his fellows, impatient of restraint or advice when it conflicts with his desires, at times pertinaciously obstinate, yet capricious and vacillating, devising many plans of future operations, which are no sooner arranged than they are abandoned in turn for others appearing more feasible. A child in his intellectual capacity and manifestations, he has the animal passions of a strong man. Previous to his injury, although untrained in the schools, he possessed a well-balanced mind, and was looked upon by those who knew him as a shrewd, smart businessman, very energetic and persistent in executing all his plans of operation. In this regard his mind was radically changed, so decidedly that his friends and acquaintances said he was "no longer Gage." (Harlow, 1868, p. 327)

Gage is the classic case demonstrating the importance of the ventromedial prefrontal cortex to human personality. Subsequently, a number of other patients with similar damage have been described, and they all show the same sorts of personality disorders. Family members and friends will describe them

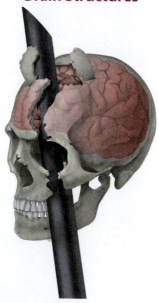

Figure 11.1 The Passage of the Bar Through Phineas Gage's Brain. Only the middle of the most frontal portion of Gage's brain was damaged (the ventromedial prefrontal cortex).

Brain Structures

---

[1] Recently, there has been some question about whether Phineas Gage's personality actually changed as described here (e.g., Macmillan & Lena, 2010).

with phrases like "socially incompetent," "decides against his best interest," and "doesn't learn from his mistakes" (Sanfey, Hastie, Colvin, & Grafman, 2003). In Chapter 8, we discussed the case of the patient P.F., who also suffered damage to his anterior prefrontal region, like Gage. However, in P.F.'s case the damage also included lateral portions of the anterior prefrontal region, and his difficulty was more with organizing complex problem solving than with decision making. In general, it is thought that the more medial portion of the anterior prefrontal region, where Gage's injury was localized, is important to motivation, emotional regulation, and social sensitivity (Gilbert, Spengler, Simons, Frith, & Burgess, 2006).

> *The ventromedial prefrontal cortex plays an important role in achieving the motivational balance and social sensitivity that is key to making successful judgments.*

Probabilistic Judgment

How do people reason about probabilities as they collect relevant evidence to make their decisions? A prescriptive model, called **Bayes's theorem,** is based on a mathematical analysis of the nature of probability. Much of the research in the field has been concerned with showing that human participants do not match up with the prescriptions of Bayes's theorem.

Bayes's Theorem

Suppose I come home and find the door to my house ajar. I am interested in the hypothesis that it might be the work of a burglar. How do I evaluate this hypothesis? I might treat it as a conditional syllogism of the following sort:

> If a burglar has been in the house, then the door will be ajar.
> The door is ajar.
> *Therefore:* A burglar has been in the house.

By the rules of formal logic, the conclusion of this syllogism is invalid: it illustrates the fallacy of the affirmation of the consequent (discussed in Chapter 10). However, it does have a certain plausibility as an inductive argument. Bayes's theorem provides a way of assessing just how plausible it is by combining what are called a *prior probability* and a *conditional probability* to produce what is called a *posterior probability*, which is a measure of the strength of the conclusion.

A **prior probability** is the probability that a hypothesis is true before consideration of the evidence (e.g., the door is ajar). The less likely the hypothesis was before the evidence, the less likely it should be after the evidence. Let us refer to the hypothesis that my house has been burglarized as *H*. Suppose that I know from police statistics that the probability of a house in my neighborhood being burglarized on any particular day is 1 in 1,000.[2] This probability is expressed as:

$$\text{Prob}(H) = .001$$

This equation expresses the prior probability of the hypothesis, or the probability that the hypothesis is true before the evidence is considered. The other prior probability needed for the application of Bayes's theorem is the probability of the hypothesis that the house has not been burglarized, denoted ~H. The probability of ~H is 1 minus Prob(H):

$$\text{Prob}(\sim H) = .999$$

A **conditional probability** is the probability that a particular type of evidence is true if a particular hypothesis is true. Let us consider what the conditional probabilities of the evidence (door ajar) would be under the two hypotheses. First, suppose that the probability of the door's being ajar is quite high if I have been burglarized — say, 4 out of 5. Let E denote the evidence, or the event of the door being ajar. Then, the conditional probability of E given that H is true is expressed as

$$\text{Prob}(E|H) = .8$$

Second, we determine the probability of E if H is not true — that is, the probability the door would be ajar even if there was not a burglary. Suppose I know that chances are only 1 out of 100 that the door would be left ajar by accident — for example, by neighbors with a key or for some other reason. This probability is expressed as

$$\text{Prob}(E|\sim H) = .01$$

The **posterior probability** is the probability that a hypothesis is true after consideration of the evidence. The notation used to express the posterior probability of hypothesis H given evidence E is Prob(H|E). According to Bayes's theorem, we can calculate the posterior probability of H, that the house has been burglarized given the evidence E, using *Bayes equation*:

$$\text{Prob}(H|E) = \frac{\text{Prob}(E|H) \bullet \text{Prob}(H)}{\text{Prob}(E|H) \bullet \text{Prob}(H) + \text{Prob}(E|\sim H) \bullet \text{Prob}(\sim H)}$$

[2] This makes for easy calculation, although the actual number for Pittsburgh is closer to 1 burglary per 100,000 households per day.

Given our assumed values, we can solve for Prob($H|E$) by substituting into the preceding equation:

$$\text{Prob}(H|E) = \frac{(.8)(.001)}{(.8)(.001)+(.01)(.999)} = .074$$

Thus, the probability that my house has been burglarized is still less than 8 in 100. Note that the posterior probability is this low even though an open door is good evidence for a burglary and not for a normal state of affairs: Prob($E|H$) = .8 versus Prob($E|\sim H$) = .01. The posterior probability is still quite low because the prior probability of H — Prob(H) = .001 — was very low to begin with. Relative to that low start, the posterior probability of .074 is a considerable increase.

This calculation can also be represented using a frequency tree (Hoffrage, Krauss, Martignon, & Gigerenzer, 2015), as shown in **Figure 11.2**. A population of 100,000 households is divided into two categories: the 100 households that will probably be burgled that day — Prob(H) = .001, and (.001)(100,000) = 100 — and the 99,900 households that will probably not be burgled. The 100 burgled houses are divided into the 80 that will probably have their front door ajar — Prob($E|H$) = .8, and (.8)(100) = 80 — and the 20 that will probably not have their front door ajar. Similarly, the 99,900 non-burgled houses are divided into the 999 that will probably have their front door ajar — Prob($E|\sim H$) = .01, and (.01)(99,990) = 999 — and the 98,901 that will probably not have their front door ajar. Thus, a total of 1,089 houses (80 + 999) will probably have their front door ajar, but only a relatively small minority of these houses (80 out of 1,089, or 7.4%) will probably have been burgled — Prob($H|E$) = .074.

Bayes's theorem enables us to precisely determine the posterior probability of a hypothesis given the prior and conditional probabilities. That is,

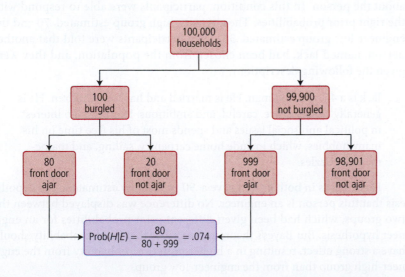

Figure 11.2 A Frequency Tree for Calculating the Probability of a Burglary Given the Evidence of a Front Door Ajar. The probability that a house has been burgled given the evidence that the front door is ajar—Prob($E|H$)—is .074, assuming the statistics illustrated in the figure.

the theorem serves as a **prescriptive model** (or *normative model*) for evaluating the probability of a hypothesis, a model that specifies how people ought to behave to be considered rational. Such a model contrasts with a **descriptive model,** which describes what people actually do. People normally do not perform the calculations that we have just gone through, any more than they follow the steps prescribed by formal logic. Nonetheless, they do hold various strengths of belief in assertions such as "My house has been burglarized." Moreover, their strength of belief does vary with the available evidence, such as whether the door has been found ajar. The interesting question is whether the strength of their belief changes in accord with Bayes's theorem.

> *Bayes's theorem specifies how to combine the prior probability of a hypothesis with the conditional probabilities of the evidence to determine the posterior probability of the hypothesis.*

Base-Rate Neglect

Many people are surprised that the open door in the preceding example does not provide as much evidence for a burglary as might have been expected. The reason for their surprise is that they do not grasp the importance of the prior probabilities. In fact, people sometimes completely ignore prior probabilities. In one demonstration of this, Kahneman and Tversky (1973) told one group of participants (termed the engineer-high group) that a person had been chosen at random from a set of 100 people consisting of 70 engineers and 30 lawyers. A second group (the engineer-low group), was told that the person came from a set of 30 engineers and 70 lawyers. Both groups were asked to determine the probability that the person chosen at random from the group would be an engineer, given no information about the person. In this condition, participants were able to respond with the right prior probabilities: The engineer-high group estimated .70 and the engineer-low group estimated .30. Then participants were told that another person, named Jack, had been chosen from the population, and they were given the following description:

> Jack is a 45-year-old man. He is married and has four children. He is generally conservative, careful, and ambitious. He shows no interest in political and social issues and spends most of his free time on his many hobbies, which include home carpentry, sailing, and mathematical puzzles.

Participants in both groups gave a .90 probability estimate to the hypothesis that this person is an engineer. No difference was displayed between the two groups, which had been given different prior probabilities for an engineer hypothesis. But Bayes's theorem prescribes that prior probability should have a strong effect, resulting in a higher posterior probability from the engineer-high group than from the engineer-low group.

In another condition, Kahneman and Tversky presented participants with the following description:

> Dick is a 30-year-old man. He is married with no children. A man of high ability and high motivation, he promises to be quite successful in his field. He is well liked by his colleagues.

This example was designed to provide no diagnostic information either way with respect to Dick's profession. According to Bayes's theorem, the posterior probability of the engineer hypothesis should be the same as the prior probability because this description is not informative. However, both the engineer-high and the engineer-low groups estimated that the probability was .50 that the man described is an engineer. Thus, they allowed a completely uninformative piece of information to change their probabilities. Once again, the participants were shown to be completely unable to use prior probabilities in assessing the posterior probability of a hypothesis.

The failure to take prior probabilities into account can lead people to make some totally unwarranted conclusions. For instance, suppose you take a diagnostic test for a specific type of cancer. Suppose also that this type of cancer, when present, results in a positive test 95% of the time, whereas, if this type of cancer is not present, the probability of a positive test result is only 5%. Suppose you are informed that your result is positive. If you are like many people, you will assume that your chance of having this type of cancer is about 95 out of 100 (Hammerton, 1973), but you would be making a fundamental error in probability estimation. What is the error?

You would have failed to consider the base rate (i.e., the prior probability) for the particular type of cancer. Suppose only 1 in 10,000 people ever get this cancer. This percentage would be your prior probability. Now, with this information, you would be able to determine the posterior probability of your having the cancer. Bringing out the Bayesian formula, you would express the problem in the following way:

$$\text{Prob}(H|E) = \frac{\text{Prob}(H) \cdot \text{Prob}(E|H)}{\text{Prob}(H) \cdot \text{Prob}(E|H) + \text{Prob}(\sim H) \cdot \text{Prob}(E|\sim H)}$$

where the prior probability of the cancer hypothesis H is $\text{Prob}(H) = .0001$, the prior probability of the no-cancer hypothesis $\sim H$ is $\text{Prob}(\sim H) = .9999$, the conditional probability of a positive test result E given H is $\text{Prob}(E|H) = .95$, and the conditional probability of a positive test result given $\sim H$ is $\text{Prob}(E|\sim H) = .05$. Thus, the posterior probability of your having the cancer would be less than 1 in 500 (i.e., less than .002):

$$\text{Prob}(H|E) = \frac{(.0001)(.95)}{(.0001)(.95) + (.9999)(.05)} = .0019$$

People often fail to take prior probabilities (or base rates) into account in making probability judgments.

Conservatism

The preceding examples show that people give evidence too much weight and ignore base rates. However, there are also situations in which people do not weigh evidence heavily enough, particularly as the evidence pointing to a conclusion accumulates. Ward Edwards (1968) extensively investigated how people use new information to adjust their estimates of the probabilities of various hypotheses. In one experiment, he presented participants with two bags, each containing 100 poker chips. Participants were shown that one of the bags contained 70 red chips and 30 blue, while the other contained 70 blue chips and 30 red. The experimenter chose one of the bags at random and the participants' task was to decide which bag had been chosen.

In the absence of any evidence, the probability of either bag having been chosen was 50%. Thus,

$$\text{Prob}(H_R) = .50 \text{ and } \text{Prob}(H_B) = .50$$

where H_R is the hypothesis of a predominantly red bag and H_B is the hypothesis of a predominantly blue bag. To obtain further information, participants sampled chips at random from the bag. Suppose the first chip drawn was red. The conditional probability of a red chip drawn from each bag is

$$\text{Prob}(R|H_R) = .70 \text{ and } \text{Prob}(R|H_B) = .30$$

Now, we can calculate the posterior probability of the bag's being predominantly red, given the red chip is drawn, by applying the Bayes equation to this situation:

$$\text{Prob}(H_R|R) = \frac{\text{Prob}(R|H_R) \bullet \text{Prob}(H_R)}{\text{Prob}(R|H_R) \bullet \text{Prob}(H_R) + \text{Prob}(R|H_B) \bullet \text{Prob}(H_B)}$$

We can substitute the given probabilities into this equation:

$$\text{Prob}(H_R|R) = \frac{(.70)(.50)}{(.70)(.50) + (.30)(.50)} = .70$$

This result seems, to both naive and sophisticated observers, to be a rather sharp increase in probabilities (from .50 to .70). Typically, participants do not increase the probability of a red-majority bag to .70; rather, they make a more conservative revision to a value such as .60.

After this first drawing, the experiment continues: The red chip is put back in the bag and a second chip is drawn at random. Suppose this chip too is red. Again, by applying Bayes's theorem, we can show that the posterior probability of a red bag is now .84. Suppose that our observations continued for 10 more trials and that, after all 12 trials, we have drawn eight red chips and four blue chips. By continuing the Bayesian analysis, we could show that the posterior probability of the hypothesis of a red bag is now .97. Participants who see this sequence of 12 trials estimate subjectively a posterior probability of only .75 or less for the red bag. Edwards used the term *conservative* to refer to the tendency to underestimate the full force of available evidence. He estimated that people give between a fifth and a half of the proper weight to the available evidence in situations like this experiment.

> People frequently underestimate the cumulative force of evidence in making probability judgments.

Correspondence to Bayes's Theorem with Experience

We have seen that participants can be quite far off in their judgments of probability. One possibility is that participants really do not understand probabilities or how to reason with respect to them. Certainly, it is an unusual participant in these experiments who could reproduce Bayes's theorem, let alone report engaging in Bayesian calculations. However, there is evidence that, although participants cannot articulate the correct probabilities, many aspects of their behavior are in accordance with Bayesian principles. To return to the explicit-implicit distinction discussed in Chapter 7, people often seem to display implicit knowledge of Bayesian principles even if they do not display any explicit knowledge and even though they make errors when asked to make explicit judgments.

Gluck and Bower (1988) performed an experiment that illustrates implicit Bayesian behavior in the context of diagnosing which of two hypothetical diseases afflicted each of 256 fictitious patients who each displayed from one to four symptoms (bloody nose, stomach cramps, puffy eyes, and discolored gums). One of the diseases had a base rate three times that of the other; additionally, the conditional probabilities of displaying the symptoms varied, depending on the disease. However, participants were not told the base rates or conditional probabilities; rather, they looked at the 256 patient records, chose the disease they thought each patient had, and were given feedback on the correctness of each diagnosis.

There are 15 possible combinations of one to four symptoms that a patient might have. Gluck and Bower constructed the patient records to reflect a particular probability of each disease for each combination of symptoms. Thus, when examining the patient records, the participants experienced the base probabilities and conditional probabilities implicitly. Of interest is the frequency with which participants assigned the rarer disease (the disease with the lower base rate) to various symptom combinations, compared with the true Bayesian probabilities (corresponding to the way Gluck and Bower had constructed the patient records). This comparison is shown by the scatterplot in **Figure 11.3**, where the diagonal line with a slope of 1 corresponds to the Bayesian

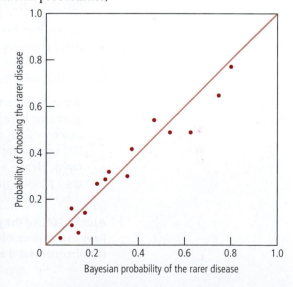

Figure 11.3 **Probability Matching.** Participants looked at the medical records of hypothetical patients, diagnosed which of two diseases was present in each patient, and were given feedback on the correctness of their diagnoses. The frequency with which participants correctly diagnosed the rarer of the two diseases corresponds closely to the Bayesian probabilities. *(Data from Gluck & Bower, 1988.)*

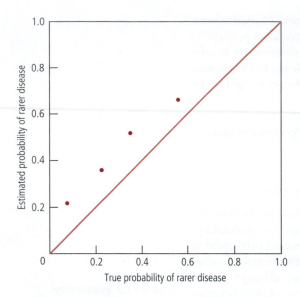

Figure 11.4 Base-Rate Neglect. Despite their display of probability matching (see Figure 11.3), participants showed base-rate neglect by systematically overestimating the frequency with which the rarer disease was associated with each of the four symptoms considered.
(Data from Gluck & Bower, 1988.)

probabilities reflected in the patient records, and the data points indicate the participants' diagnoses. Clearly, the frequencies with which participants correctly diagnosed the rarer disease were very close to the true probabilities. Thus, implicitly, the participants had become quite good Bayesians in this experiment. This phenomenon — choosing among alternatives in proportion to the success of previous choices — is called **probability matching.**

After the experiment, Gluck and Bower presented the participants with the four symptoms individually and asked them how frequently the rarer disease was associated with each symptom. This result is presented in **Figure 11.4** in a format similar to that of Figure 11.3. As can be seen, participants showed some neglect of the base rate, consistently overestimating the frequency of the rarer disease. Still, their judgments showed some influence of base rate in that their average estimated probability of the rarer disease was less than 50%.

Gigerenzer and Hoffrage (1995) showed that base-rate neglect also decreases if events are stated in terms of frequencies rather than in terms of probabilities. Some of their participants were given a description in terms of probabilities, such as the one that follows:

The probability of breast cancer is 1% for women at age 40 who participate in routine screening. If a woman has breast cancer, the probability is 80% that she will get a positive mammography. If a woman does not have breast cancer, the probability is 9.6% that she also will get a positive mammography. A woman in this age group had a positive mammography in a routine screening. What is the probability that she actually has breast cancer?

Fewer than 20 out of 100 (20%) of the participants given such statements calculated the correct Bayesian answer (which is about 8%). In the other condition, participants were given descriptions in terms of frequencies, such as the one that follows:

Ten out of every 1,000 women at age 40 who participate in routine screening have breast cancer. Eight of every 10 women with breast cancer will get a positive mammography. Ninety-five out of every 990 women without breast cancer also will get a positive mammography. Here is a new representative sample of women at age 40 who got a positive mammography in routine screening. How many of these women do you expect to actually have breast cancer?

Almost 50% of the participants given such statements calculated the correct Bayesian answer. Gigerenzer and Hoffrage argued that we can reason better with frequencies than with probabilities because we experience frequencies of events, but not probabilities, in our daily lives. However, just what people do in such a task continues to be debated (Barbey & Sloman, 2007).

There is also evidence that experience makes people more attuned to statistics. In a study of medical diagnosis, Weber, Böckenholt, Hilton, and Wallace (1993) found that doctors were quite sensitive both to base rates and to the evidence provided by the symptoms. Moreover, the more clinical experience the doctors had, the more attuned were their judgments.

> *Although participants' judgments of abstract probabilities often do not correspond with Bayes's theorem, their behavior based on experience often does.*

Judgments of Probability

What are participants actually doing when they report the probability of an event, such as the probability that someone who has bloody gums has a particular disease? The evidence is that rather than thinking about probabilities, they are thinking about relative frequencies. That is, they are trying to judge the proportion of the patients they saw with bloody gums who had that particular disease. People are reasonably accurate at making such judgments when they do not have to rely on memory (Robinson, 1964; Shuford, 1961). Consider an experiment by Shuford (1961) in which participants were presented for 1 second with arrays like the one shown in **Figure 11.5**. Participants were then asked to judge the proportion of vertical or horizontal bars in each array, which varied from 10% to 90%. The results in **Figure 11.6** show that participants' estimates were quite close to the true proportions.

In the experiment just described, participants saw the relevant information (the displays) and made fairly accurate judgments about proportions. However, when participants cannot see the relevant information and must recall it from memory, their estimates will be distorted if their recall is not accurate. Consider the following experiment reported by Tversky and Kahneman (1974), in which participants estimated the proportion of English words that fit certain characteristics. For instance, participants were asked to estimate the proportion of words that begin with the letter *k* versus the proportion of words with the letter *k* in the third position and report the ratio of the more frequent case to the less frequent case. How might participants perform this task? Tversky and Kahneman argued that participants approach the task by recalling words beginning with *k* and words with *k* in the third position and then judging their relative frequency. It certainly is easier to think of words beginning with *k* than to think of words with *k* in the third position. Thus, not surprisingly, participants estimated that twice as many words begin with *k* as have *k* in the third position; the actual ratio, however,

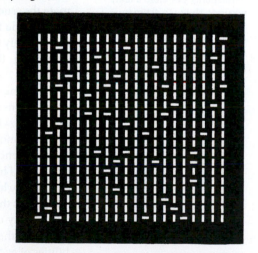

Figure 11.5 Display for Estimating Proportions. Participants saw displays like this for 1 second and then estimated the proportion of vertical or horizontal bars in each display. The display shown here is 90% vertical bars and 10% horizontal bars. *(From Shuford, 1961. Copyright © 1961 by the American Psychological Association. Reprinted by permission.)*

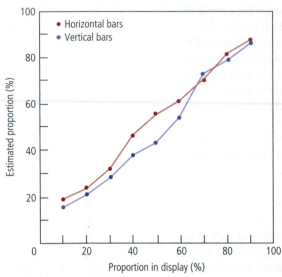

Figure 11.6 Results for Estimating Proportions. Participants exhibited a fairly accurate ability to estimate the proportions of vertical and horizontal bars in displays like the one in Figure 11.5. *(Data from Shuford, 1961.)*

is the opposite — twice as many words have *k* in the third position as begin with *k*. Generally, participants overestimate the frequency with which words begin with particular letters.

As in this experiment, many real-life circumstances require that we estimate probabilities without having direct access to the information that these probabilities describe. In such cases, we must rely on memory as the source of information for our estimates. The memory factors discussed in Chapters 6 and 7 serve to explain how such estimates can be biased. Under the reasonable assumption that words are more strongly associated with their first letter than with their third letter, the bias exhibited in Tversky and Kahneman's results can be explained by the spreading-activation theory (see Chapter 6). With the focus of attention on the letter *k*, for example, activation will spread from that letter to words beginning with it. This process will tend to make words beginning with the letter *k* more available than other words. Thus, these words will be overrepresented in the sample that participants take from memory to estimate the true proportion of such words in English. The same overestimation is not made for words with the letter *k* in the third position because words are unlikely to be directly associated with the letter in the third position. Therefore, these words cannot be associatively primed and made more available.

Judgments of frequency are also influenced by their similarity to other events. Consider another example from Tversky and Kahneman (1974). Which of the following sequences of six tosses of a coin (where H denotes heads and T tails) is more likely: H T H T T H or H H H H H H? Many people think the first sequence is more probable, but the two sequences are actually equally probable. The probability of the first sequence is the probability of H on the first toss (which is .50) times the probability of T on the second toss (which is .50), times the probability of H on the third toss (which is .50), and so on. The probability of the whole sequence is .50 • .50 • .50 • .50 • .50 • .50 = .016. Similarly, the probability of the second sequence is the product of the probabilities of each coin toss, and the probability of a head on each coin toss is .50. Thus, again, the final probability is .50 • .50 • .50 • .50 • .50 • .50 = .016. Why do some people have the illusion that the first sequence is more probable? It is because the first event seems similar to a lot of other events — for example, H T H T H T or H T T H T H. These similar events serve to bias upward a person's probability estimate of the target event. On the other hand, H H H H H H, six straight heads, seems unlike any other event, and its probability will therefore not be biased upward by other similar sequences. In conclusion, a person's estimate of the probability of an event will be biased by other events that are similar to it.

A related phenomenon, called the **gambler's fallacy,** reflects the belief that the likelihood of an event increases with the amount of time since the event last occurred, by the "law of averages." This phenomenon can be demonstrated in an experimental setting — for instance, one in which participants see a sequence of coin tosses and must guess whether each toss will be a head or a tail. If they see a string of heads, they become more and more prone to guess that tails will come up on the next trial. Casino operators count on this fallacy to help them make money. Players who have had a string of losses at a table will keep playing, assuming that the "law of averages" will lead to a compensating string of wins. However, the dice, cards, and roulette wheel do not know or care whether a gambler has had a string of losses. The consequence is that players tend to lose more as they try to recoup their losses. There is no such thing as the "law of averages," and the game is set in favor of the house.

The gambler's fallacy can be used to advantage in certain situations — for instance, at the racetrack. Most racetracks operate by a parimutuel system in which the odds on a horse are determined by the number of people betting on the horse. By the end of the day, if favorites have won all the races, people tend to doubt that another favorite can win, and they switch their bets to the long shots. As a consequence, the betting odds on the favorite deviate from what they should be, and a person can sometimes make money by betting on the favorite.

> People can be biased in their estimates of probabilities when they must rely on factors such as memory and similarity judgments.

The Adaptive Nature of the Recognition Heuristic

The examples in the previous section focused on cases where people came to bad judgments by relying on, for example, the availability of events in memory. Gigerenzer, Todd, and ABC Research Group (1999), in their book *Simple Heuristics That Make Us Smart*, argue that such cases are the exception and not the rule. They argue that people tend to identify the most valid cues for making judgments and use these. For instance, through evolution people have acquired a tendency to pay attention to the availability of events in memory, which is more often helpful than not.

Goldstein and Gigerenzer (1999, 2002) report studies of what they call the **recognition heuristic,** which applies in cases where people recognize one item and not another. This heuristic leads people to believe that the recognized item has a higher value than the unrecognized item with respect to a specified criterion. In one study, Goldstein and Gigerenzer looked at the ability of students at the University of Chicago to judge the relative size of various German cities. For instance, they asked the students which city is larger — Bamberg or Heidelberg. Most of the students recognized Heidelberg as a German city, but most did not recognize Bamberg — that is, one city was available in memory and the other was not. Goldstein and Gigerenzer showed that when faced with pairs like this, students almost always picked the city they recognized. One might think this pattern is just another example of judgments made on the basis of availability in memory. However, Goldstein and Gigerenzer showed that the students were actually more accurate when they made judgments about pairs of cities where they recognized one and not the other than when they made judgments about two cities they recognized (e.g., Munich and Hamburg). When they recognized both cities, they had to base their judgments on other factors, and most American students have little knowledge about the relative population of German cities. Thus, applying the recognition heuristic is far from a mistake; rather, it proves to be an effective strategy for making accurate judgments. In fact, American students do better at judging the relative size of German cities using this heuristic than German students do judging German cities, where this heuristic cannot be used because almost all the cities are recognized.[3] Similarly, German students do better than American students in judging the relative size of American cities because they can use the recognition heuristic and Americans cannot.

Figure 11.7 illustrates Goldstein and Gigerenzer's explanation for why these students were more accurate in judging the relative size of two cities when they did not know one of them. They looked at the frequency with which German cities were mentioned in the *Chicago Tribune* and the frequency with which American cities were mentioned in the German newspaper *Die Zeit*. It turns out that there is a strong correlation between the actual size of the city and the frequency of mention in these newspapers. Not surprisingly, people read about the larger cities in other countries more frequently than they read about the smaller cities. Gigerenzer and Goldstein also found that there was a strong correlation between the frequency of mention in the newspapers (and in the media more generally) and the probability that the students would recognize the name. This is just the basic effect of frequency on memory. As a consequence of these two strong correlations, there will be a strong correlation between availability in memory and the actual size of the city, as illustrated in Figure 11.7.

Goldstein and Gigerenzer argue that the recognition heuristic is useful in many but not all domains. In some domains, researchers have shown that people intelligently combine the recognition heuristic with other information. For instance, Richter and Späth (2006) had participants judge the relative population sizes of pairs of animals by asking questions like these:

Are there more Hainan partridges or arctic hares?
Are there more giant pandas or mottled umbers?

---

[3] My German informant (Angela Brunstein) tells me that almost all Germans would recognize Bamberg and Heidelberg, but many would be puzzled by which is larger. Interestingly, a Google search on English texts reported 37 million hits on Heidelberg and 3.5 million on Bamberg. A Google search on German texts reported 30 million hits on Heidelberg and 12 million on Bamberg—a much closer ratio and many more hits on Bamberg.

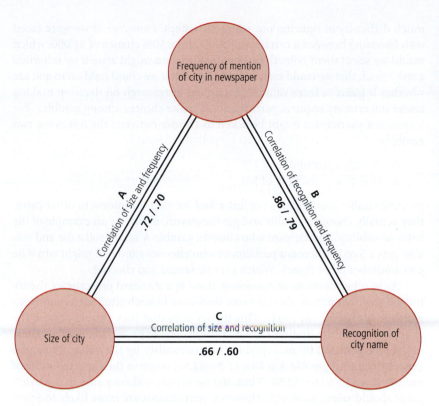

Figure 11.7 **Recognition Heuristic.** The strong correlations in **A** (between size of city and frequency of mention in newspapers) and the strong correlations in **B** (between probability of recognition and frequency of mention in newspapers) combined to produce strong correlations in **C** (between size of city and probability of recognition). The first correlations are for American cities and the second correlations are for German cities. The American newspaper was the *Chicago Tribune* and the German newspaper was *Die Zeit*. *(Data from Goldstein & Gigerenzer, 2002.)*

In the first case, the recognition heuristic leads most people to correctly choose arctic hares (most people have heard of arctic hares but have not heard of Hainan partridges). In the second case, most people recognize giant pandas but not mottled umbers (a moth), yet they correctly choose mottled umbers because they also know that giant pandas are an endangered species. This illustrates how people can adaptively choose what aspects of information to pay attention to.

> *People can use their ability to recognize an item, and combine this with other information, to make good judgments.*

Making Decisions Under Uncertainty

So far we have mainly focused on how people assess the probability of events. Now we turn to how people make decisions in the presence of the uncertainty created by probabilistic events. Much of this research has been cast in terms of how people choose between alternatives. Sometimes, the choices that we have to make are easy. If we were offered a choice between a 25% chance of winning $100 and a 50% chance of winning $1,000, most of us would not have much difficulty in figuring out which to accept. However, if we were faced with choosing between a certainty of $400 and a 50% chance of $1,000, which would we select then? Something like this situation might arise if we inherited a risky stock that we could cash in for $400 or that we could hold on to and see whether it gains or loses value. A great deal of research on decision making under uncertainty requires participants to make choices among gambles. For instance, a participant might be asked to choose between the following two gambles:

A. $8 with a probability of 1/3
B. $3 with a probability of 5/6

In some studies, participants are just asked for their opinions; in other cases, they actually choose a gamble and get the payoff, if any. As an example of the latter possibility, a participant who chooses gamble A might roll a die and win if he gets a 5 or 6, whereas a participant who chooses gamble B might win if he gets a number other than 1. Which gamble would you choose?

As in other domains of reasoning, there is a standard prescriptive theory for the way that people should make decisions in such situations (von Neumann & Morgenstern, 1944). This theory says that they should choose the alternative with the highest expected value. The expected value of an alternative is calculated by multiplying the probability by the value. Thus, the expected value of gamble A is $8 \times 1/3 = 2.67, whereas the expected value of gamble B is $3 \times 5/6 = 2.50. Thus, the prescriptive theory says that participants should select gamble A. However, participants are more likely to select gamble B.

As a perhaps more extreme example of the same result, suppose you are given a choice between

A. $1 million with a probability of 1
B. $2.5 million with a probability of 1/2

Maybe, in this case, you are on a game show and are offered a choice between great wealth with certainty or the opportunity to toss a coin and get even more. I (and I assume you) would take the money (choice A, a certain $1 million) and run, but the expected value calculations indicate that we should prefer the choice B because its expected value is $2.5 million \times .5 = $1.25 million$. Would we really be behaving irrationally by choosing A?

Most people, if asked to justify their behavior in this situation, would argue that there comes a point when one has enough money (if we could only convince some CEOs of this notion!) and that there really isn't that much difference for them between having $1 million and having $2.5 million. This idea has been formalized in terms of what is called **subjective utility** — the value that people place on things for whatever reason. For instance, as indicated by our example, the value that we place on money does not correspond linearly to the amount of money. **Figure 11.8**, which shows a typical function proposed for the relation of subjective utility to money (Kahneman & Tversky, 1984), has two interesting properties related to the way it curves on the "Gains" side and on the "Losses" side. On the "Gains" side, it curves in such a way that the amount of money must more than double in order to double its utility. The preceding example would illustrate this property if we valued $2.5 million only 20% more than $1 million. That is, if the subjective utility of $1 million is U, the subjective utility of $2.5 million is $1.2U$. In this case, then, the expected value of choice A is $1 \times U = U$, and the expected value of choice B is $.5 \times 1.2U = .6U$. Thus, in terms of subjective utility, choice A is to be preferred.

On the "Losses" side, this utility function is steeper than it is on the "Gains" side, meaning that the negative subjective utility that participants assign to losses is greater than the positive subjective utility assigned to equivalent gains. This might be illustrated by participants given the following choice:

A. Gain $10 with 1/2 probability or lose $10 with 1/2 probability
B. Nothing (no win or gain) with certainty

Most participants would prefer B because they weigh the loss of $10 more heavily than the gain of $10.

Kahneman and Tversky (1984) also argued that, as with subjective utility, people associate a **subjective probability** with an event that is not identical with the objective probability. They proposed the function shown in **Figure 11.9** to relate subjective probability to objective probability. The function bows downward because very low probabilities are overweighted relative to high probabilities. For instance, a participant might prefer a 1% chance of $400 to a 2% chance of $200 because 1% is subjectively represented as more than half of 2%. Kahneman and Tversky (1979) showed that a great deal of human decision making can be explained by assuming that participants are responding in terms of these subjective utilities and subjective probabilities.

An interesting question is whether the subjective functions in Figures 11.8 and 11.9 represent irrational tendencies. Generally, the utility function in Figure 11.8 is thought to be reasonable. As we get more money, getting even more seems less and less important: Is the amount of happiness that a billion dollars can buy 1,000 times the amount of happiness that a million dollars can buy? However, not everyone's utility function conforms to the function in Figure 11.8, which represents a sort of average. For example, consider someone who needs $10,000 (and not a penny less) for a life-saving medical procedure. Such a person would have a very large step in the utility function at $10,000 on the "Gains" side, because all sums less than $10,000 would be rather useless and all sums greater than $10,000 would be about equally good.

There is less agreement about how we should assess the subjective probability function in Figure 11.9. Anderson (1990) argued that it might actually make sense to assign higher subjective probabilities

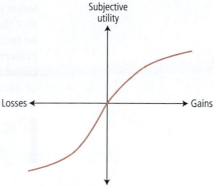

Figure 11.8 Subjective Utility. This function relates subjective utility to the magnitude of actual gains or losses. The way the function curves shows that gains must more than double in order to double their utility and that the negative subjective utility of losses is greater than the positive subjective utility of equivalent gains. *(Data from Kahneman & Tversky, 1984.)*

Figure 11.9 Subjective Probability. This function relates the subjective probability of events to their objective probability. The downward bowing shows that low probabilities are overweighted relative to higher probabilities, especially at the lower end. *(Data from Kahneman & Tversky, 1984.)*

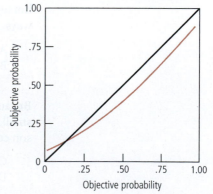

to very low objective probabilities (as that function does) because assertions that the objective probability of some event is extremely low often turn out to be incorrect (see the third Question for Thought at the end of this chapter). However, there is little consensus in the field about how to construct a realistic subjective probability function. (**Implications 11.1** discusses the problem of deciding how best to assign subjective probabilities in the context of the extensive online availability of conflicting information.)

> *People make decisions under uncertainty in terms of subjective utilities and subjective probabilities.*

Framing Effects

Although one might view the functions in Figures 11.8 and 11.9 as reasonable, there is evidence that they can lead people to do rather strange things. This evidence takes the form of **framing effects,** whereby people make different choices among equivalent alternatives depending on how the alternatives are stated (i.e., how the alternatives are framed). These effects occur because differences in the framing of alternatives can affect where people perceive themselves to be on the subjective utility curve in Figure 11.8. To see how, consider this example from Kahneman and Tversky (1984): A nearby store sells item A for $15 and item B for $125, while another store, not so nearby, offers the same two items for $5 less — item A for $10 and item B for $120. People are more likely to make the effort to go to the other store to get item A than to get item B. However, in both cases, one saves $5; so in both cases, the question is simply whether $5 is worth the effort of going to the more distant store. However, the two contexts place one on different points of the subjective utility curve, which is negatively accelerated. That is, the difference in subjective utility between $15 and $10 is larger than the difference between $125 and $120. Thus, in the first case, the saving might seem worth the effort, but in the second case, it might not.

Another example has to do with betting behavior. Consider someone who has lost $140 at the racetrack and has an opportunity to bet $10 on a horse that will pay 15 to 1. The person can frame this choice in one of two ways. In one way, the choice is between A and B:

A. Refuse the bet and accept a certainty of losing $140.
B. Make the bet and face a good chance of losing $150 and a poor chance of breaking even.

Because the subjective difference between losing $140 and losing $150 is small, the person will likely choose B and make the bet. In contrast, the person could frame the choice as C versus D:

C. Refuse the bet and face the certainty of having nothing change.
D. Make the bet and face a good chance of losing an additional $10 and a poor chance of gaining $140.

Implications 11.1

What Can We Believe with High Confidence?

The subjective probability function in Figure 11.9 treats low and high objective probabilities as if they were less extreme. The world offers us many highly confident assertions and it is up to us to determine which really have a high probability of being true. A knowledgeable sports fan knows how to discount a star player's guarantee of a win in an important game. However, it is not always so obvious how to weight such predictions. A classic case concerns the claim that the *Titanic* was "unsinkable" (Lord, 2012). Regardless of whether that exact claim was ever made, the White Star Line did claim that the ship "was designed to be unsinkable," and newspaper reports of the time described it as "practically unsinkable." Many passengers who boarded the *Titanic* believed that it was unsinkable — one passenger said, "I took passage on the *Titanic* for I thought it would be a safe steamship and I had heard it could not sink." The subjective probability curve in Figure 11.9 suggests that people typically discount such assertions of extreme probabilities, but it is clear that some people do not — at their own peril.

If knowing what to believe was a challenge in 1912, it has become a much more difficult problem today, when false stories are deliberately disseminated via social media and even in mainstream news outlets. This is a particularly pernicious trend because

evidence suggests that we have a tendency to believe published information even if we are told the information is false (Gilbert, Tafarodi, & Malone, 1993). Also, people tend to believe simple messages, which is a problem because many situations are complex and cannot be accurately described in simple terms (Schwarz, Newman, & Leach, 2016). Furthermore, adding a photograph (so common now in social media) increases the believability of information. For instance, adding a photograph of a giraffe increased the believability of the claim "Giraffes are the only mammals that cannot jump" (Newman, Garry, Bernstein, Kantner, & Lindsay, 2012). In another study (McGrew, Ortega, Breakstone, & Wineburg, 2017), high school students were shown two screen shots of information on climate change — one from *Science* magazine and the other from an oil company (clearly identified as sponsored by the oil company). The sponsored content, which included an eye-catching chart, was selected as the more reliable source by 70% of the students. In line with

Bettmann/Getty Images

ongoing efforts to teach students how to assess online information, McGrew et al. recommend teaching them strategies that professional fact checkers employ, including these three recommendations:

1. *Read laterally.* Before relying on a website and the links available on that website for accurate information, search for information about the website itself. For instance, epionline.org provides a lot of information on the effects of minimum wage laws, but a search for information about epionline.org might lead you to suspect some bias against such laws.

2. *Make smarter selections from the results that come back from a Google search.* Do not just click on the top results in a Google search (the order of search results can be gamed); rather, exercise click restraint and patiently try to identify the best sources on the first few pages of results (i.e., by scrutinizing the URLs and the snippets of text with each result).

3. *Use Wikipedia wisely.* Be careful about using Wikipedia articles as trusted sources of information. Visit the Talk page (a tab next to the Article tab) to see if the topic of the article is a contentious issue and to see different perspectives on the topic. Some fact checkers simply ignore the main article and go straight to the Talk page.

In this case, because of the greater weight on losses than on gains and because of the negatively accelerated utility function, the person is likely to refuse the bet. The only difference in the two cases is where the person perceives his position on the curve in Figure 11.8: Framing the choice as A versus B means that the person perceives himself at the −$140 point, whereas framing the choice as C versus D means that the person perceives himself at the 0 point. Thus, the different evaluations of identical alternatives depends on how the alternatives are framed.

As an example that appears to be more consequential, consider this situation described by Kahneman and Tversky (1984, p. 343):

> Imagine that the U.S. is preparing for the outbreak of an unusual Asian disease, which is expected to kill 600 people. Two alternative programs to combat the disease have been proposed. Assume that the exact scientific estimates of the consequences of the programs are as follows:
>
> - If program A is adopted, 200 people will be saved.
> - If program B is adopted, there is a one-third probability that 600 people will be saved and a two-thirds probability that no people will be saved.
>
> Which of the two programs would you favor?

Seventy-two percent of the participants chose program A, which guarantees that 200 lives will be saved, rather than dealing with the risk of program B that no lives will be saved. However, consider the results when the two programs are described in terms of lives lost instead of lives saved:

- If program C is adopted, 400 people will die.
- If program D is adopted, there is a one-third probability that nobody will die and a two-thirds probability that 600 people will die.

With this description, only 22% of the participants chose program C, which is equivalent to program A (and D is equivalent to B). Both of these choices (A versus B, and C versus D) can be understood in terms of a negatively accelerated subjective utility function for lives saved or lost. In the first case (A versus B), the subjective utility of 600 lives saved is less than three times the subjective utility of 200 lives saved, whereas in the second case (C versus D), the subjective utility of 400 deaths is more than two-thirds the subjective utility of 600 deaths. McNeil, Pauker, Sox, and Tversky (1982) found that this tendency extended to actual medical treatments — that is, doctors choose treatments depending on whether the results of the treatments are described in terms of the odds of living or the odds of dying.

Situations in which framing effects are most prevalent tend to have one thing in common — no clear basis for choice, as in the three examples discussed above. In the case in which the shopper has an opportunity to save $5, it is unclear whether $5 is worth the effort of going to another store. In the gambling example, there is no clear basis for deciding whether to make or refuse the bet.[4] The stakes are very high in the third case, but it is, unfortunately, one

---

[4] The only clear decision would have been to reject gambling as irrational in the first place.

of those social policy decisions that defy a clear analysis. Thus, all three cases are hard to decide on their merits alone.

Shafir (1993) suggested that, in such situations, we may make a decision not on the basis of which decision is actually the best one but on the basis of which will be easiest to justify (to ourselves or to others). Different framings can make it easier or harder to justify an action. In the disease example, for instance, if we adopt the first framing (A versus B), which focuses on saving lives, we could easily justify choosing program A by pointing to the 200 people whose lives were saved. In contrast, if we adopt the second framing (C versus D), which focuses on avoiding deaths, choosing alternative C would require justifying the 400 deaths that the decision caused, while choosing alternative D offers the chance of not having to justify any deaths.

This need to justify one's action can lead one to select one of two choices when asked to pick one, but paradoxically select the same choice when asked to reject one. Consider an example from Shafir (1993) in which participants were presented with the following task:

> Imagine that you serve on the jury of an only-child sole-custody case following a relatively messy divorce. The facts of the case are complicated by ambiguous economic, social, and emotional considerations, and you decide to base your decision entirely on the following few observations [shown in **Table 11.1**]. To which parent would you award sole custody of the child? Which parent would you deny sole custody of the child? (p. 549)

As you can see in Table 11.1, the parents are overall rather equivalent, but parent B has somewhat more extreme positive and negative factors (positive — income and relationship with the child; negative — health, work routine, and social life). Asked to make an award decision, more participants choose to award custody

TABLE 11.1 Factors in Custody Decisions		
Factors	**Parent A**	**Parent B**
Relationship with child	Reasonable rapport	Very close
Income	Average	Above average
Health	Average	Minor health problems
Work routine	Average	Lots of work-related travel
Social life	Relatively stable	Extremely active
Decisions	**Parent A**	**Parent B**
Award custody	36%	64%
Deny custody	45%	55%
(Data from Shafir, 1993.)		

to parent B; asked to make a deny decision, they also tend to deny custody to parent B. The reason, Shafir argued, is that the description of parent B offers reasons, such as a close relation with the child, that can be used to justify the awarding of custody, but parent B's description also offers reasons, such as time away from home, to justify denying custody. Parent A's description, in contrast, does not really offer any reasons for or against.

An interesting study in framing was performed by Greene, Sommerville, Nystrom, Darley, and Cohen (2001). They compared participants' responses to ethical dilemmas such as the following pair:

> *Dilemma 1:* A runaway trolley is headed for five people who will be killed if it proceeds on its current course. The only way you can save them is to hit a switch that will turn the trolley onto an alternative set of tracks where it will kill one person instead of five.

> *Dilemma 2:* You are standing next to a large stranger on a footbridge that spans the tracks in between the oncoming trolley and the five people. The only way to save the five people is to push the stranger off the bridge onto the tracks below. He will die, but his large body will stop the trolley from reaching the others.

In both dilemmas, you can perform an action that will result in the death of one person instead of five, or else you can do nothing, in which case five people will die. In the case of Dilemma 1, most people are willing to perform the action, but in the case of Dilemma 2, they are not.

In an fMRI study, Greene et al. compared the brain areas activated when people considered an "impersonal" dilemma such as Dilemma 1 (where they just hit a switch, setting in motion a mechanical process that results in a person's death) with the brain areas activated when people considered a "personal" dilemma such as Dilemma 2 (where they push the person to his death). In the impersonal case, regions of the parietal cortex that are associated with cold calculation were active. In contrast, in the personal case, regions of the brain associated with emotion were active (such as the ventromedial prefrontal cortex, discussed in the beginning of this chapter). Thus, part of what can be involved in making decisions in response to different framings of problems seems to be which brain regions are engaged.

A real-world example of how the framing of a problem can influence decisions concerns the difference between opt-in and opt-out choices in contexts such as organ donation, enrollment in retirement plans, and immunization. Organ donation rates are much higher in countries where one must opt-out of organ donation rather than opt-in (Johnson, Steffel, & Goldstein, 2005). Employees are more likely to enroll in 401(k) plans when they have to opt out of the plans than when they have to opt in (Choi, Laibson, Madrian, & Metrick, 2003). Similarly, people are more likely to get a yearly flu shot when they have to opt out of the immunization rather than opt in (Chapman, Li, Colby, & Yoon, 2010). These tendencies can be understood in terms of avoiding having to justify to oneself the decision to opt in when that is the choice or to opt out when that is the choice. People tend to avoid the decision and so get the default option. (See **Implications 11.2** for a discussion of how adult versus adolescent differences — including differences in the subjective utility assigned to various factors, as well as differences in the way choices are framed — can lead adolescents to make bad decisions.)

> *When there is no clear basis for making a decision, people are influenced by the way in which the problem is framed.*

Implications 11.2

Why Are Adolescents More Likely Than Adults to Make Bad Decisions?

Adolescent risk taking is one of society's great concerns. Compared to adults, adolescents are more likely to engage in risky sexual behavior, abuse drugs and alcohol, and drive recklessly. Poor adolescent choices in such areas are the leading cause of death in adolescence and can lead to a lifetime of suffering due to such things as failed education, destroyed personal relationships, and addiction to cigarettes, alcohol, and other drugs. There has been a great deal of research on adolescent behavior (e.g., Fischhoff, 2008; Reyna & Farley, 2006), and the results are a bit surprising. Contrary to common belief, adolescents do not perceive themselves to be any more invulnerable than adults do and often perceive greater danger from risky behavior than do adults. Also, in laboratory studies, late adolescents often perform as well as or better than older adults on abstract tasks of reasoning and decision making (this will be discussed further in Chapter 14). Thus, it does not appear that adolescents are poorer thinkers about risk than adults. Rather, it appears that the explanation for bad decision making by adolescents involves two classes of factors:

1. *Knowledge and experience.* Adolescents lack some of the information that adults have. For instance, adolescents may know it is important to "practice safe sex" but not know all that they should about how to do that. Also, experience may help adults to become experts on reasoning about risk, whereas adolescents lack experience. However, Reyna and Farley (2006) argue that adults do not necessarily reason about risk — that is, rather than thinking through the potential costs and benefits of a risky decision, they may simply recognize the risk and avoid the situation (just as chess masters can recognize the risk of a potential chess position without thinking through all the possible moves, as discussed in Chapter 9). In contrast, adolescents often have to try to reason through the consequences of a decision, much as a chess duffer has to calculate the consequences of sequences of moves, and can make errors in reasoning.

2. *Different values and different ways of framing situations.* Risky behavior has benefits such as immediate pleasure, and adolescents value these benefits more. Also, adolescents are particularly likely to weigh the benefits of risky behavior heavily in

Halfdark/Getty Images

the context of their peers when social acceptance is at stake. Thus, their subjective utilities are different from adults' in computing expected values. Reyna and Farley speculate that this adolescent tendency to engage in riskier behavior than adults may also be related to the fact that brain regions such as the ventromedial prefrontal cortex continue to mature into the early 20s. Fischhoff also notes that risky behavior often arises when adolescents attempt to establish independence and to prove personal competence. These achievements are important to adolescents, but pursuing them can put adolescents in situations where older adults seldom find themselves. If adults found themselves in similar situations, they might also find themselves engaging in risky behavior.

Choosing Among Many Alternatives

The focus so far has been on choosing between two alternatives. However, many of the decisions we make (what apartment to rent, what car to buy, what movie to see) involve more than just two alternatives. For instance, consider deciding among the eight apartments described in **Table 11.2**. How would you make your choice? Which of the attributes would be most important to you? What if there were more apartments to choose from or if there were additional attributes to consider, such as quality of furniture, noise level, parking facilities, and so on? Ideally, one would score each alternative on each attribute and sum up scores to identify the very best. However, the evidence is that people get overwhelmed by large amounts of information and take various shortcuts (Shah & Oppenheimer, 2008). They fall back on simpler strategies for making decisions, like stopping as soon as they find an apartment that they judge good enough — a process that has been called *satisficing* (Simon, 1955) — or just considering the few attributes that they judge most important. A number of studies have tracked how participants choose which information to consider. In a study with a method called MouseLab (Payne, Bettman, & Johnson, 1993), the values of attributes are hidden, and participants must click on an attribute in a display to see what the value is. Other studies have used eye movements on an open display like Table 11.2 to see what participants are considering. Participants tend to spend most of their time examining the attributes they consider most important and the choices they consider most promising, and tend to spend more and more time on their ultimate choice as they come to a decision (Shi, Wedel, & Pieters, 2013).

Increasing the number of alternatives not only poses increasing cognitive demands but can also change the way we think about the alternatives. This has been most simply shown in studies of how choices are affected when two alternatives are increased to three (Oppenheimer & Kelso, 2015). For instance, suppose we are trying to choose between two similarly priced apartments,

#	Monthly rent	Size	Distance from work	Landlord
1	$1300	Medium	10 minutes	Good
2	$1150	Small	20 minutes	Good
3	$1450	Large	10 minutes	Poor
4	$900	Small	20 minutes	Fair
5	$1450	Large	30 minutes	Good
6	$1050	Medium	30 minutes	Fair
7	$1050	Small	10 minutes	Poor
8	$1150	Large	30 minutes	Fair

TABLE 11.2 Apartment Choices

(Data from Onken, Hastie, & Revelle, 1985, and Payne, 1976.)

where apartment 1 is somewhat larger than apartment 2 but is somewhat further away from campus. There are three effects that adding a third, similarly priced apartment to the mix can have on our choice between the first two:

- *Similarity effect:* If the third option is more similar to one of the existing options than to the other, we are more likely to choose the other. For instance, if the third apartment is similar to apartment 1 in size and in distance from campus, we are more likely to choose apartment 2, which is smaller but closer to campus.

- *Attraction effect:* If the third option is dominated on a particular attribute by one of the existing options, we are more likely to choose that dominating option. For instance, if the third apartment is dominated in size by apartment 1 and is the same distance away, we are more likely to choose apartment 1.

- *Compromise effect:* If the third option makes one of the existing options seem like a compromise between the other existing option and the added option, then we are more likely to choose the compromise option. For instance, if the third apartment is larger than apartment 1 but also further from campus, making apartment 1 look like a compromise between the added option and apartment 2, we are more likely to choose apartment 1.

In all three cases, adding the third option does not really change how the first two options compare, so all of these effects can be characterized as not rational. In their review, Oppenheimer and Kelso point out that explaining why these effects happen has attracted a good number of competing theories. However, the simplest and perhaps most intuitive explanation concerns the issue of justifying our decision to ourselves (Mercier & Sperber, 2011; also refer back to the discussion of Table 11.1). That is, each of these effects involves finding a basis for justifying our decision:

- *Similarity effect:* The similarity between the added option and apartment 1 would make it hard to justify choosing between them; hence, we emphasize the importance of distance from campus, which provides a clear basis for choosing apartment 2.

- *Attraction effect:* If we emphasize the importance of apartment size, we can justify choosing apartment 1.

- *Compromise effect:* Choosing apartment 1 lets us justify that choice over each of the other apartments (apartment 1 is better than apartment 2 on size and better than the added apartment on distance from campus).

> *As the complexity of a decision task increases either in the number of alternatives or in the number of relevant dimensions, people seek ways to simplify the processes by which they compare the options and justify their choice.*

Neural Representation of Subjective Utility and Probability

The subjective utility assigned to an outcome appears to be related to the activity of dopamine neurons in the basal ganglia. The importance of this region to motivation has been known since the 1950s, when Olds and Milner (1954) discovered that rats would press a lever to the point of exhaustion to receive electrical stimulation from electrodes near this region. This stimulation caused the release of dopamine in a region of the basal ganglia called the *nucleus accumbens*. Drugs like heroin and cocaine have their effect by producing increased levels of dopamine released from this region. These dopamine neurons show increased activity for all sorts of positive rewards, including basic rewards like food and sex, but also social rewards like money and sports cars (Camerer, Loewenstein, & Prelec, 2005). Thus, the activity of these neurons might appear to be the neural equivalent of subjective utility.

There is an interesting twist to the response of dopamine neurons (Schultz, 1998). When a reward was unexpectedly presented to monkeys, their dopamine neurons showed enhanced activity at the time of reward delivery. However, when a stimulus preceded the reward that reliably predicted the reward, the neurons no longer responded to reward delivery. Rather, the dopamine response transferred to the earlier stimulus. Finally, when a reward was unexpectedly omitted following the stimulus, dopamine neurons showed depressed activity at the expected time of reward delivery. These observations were the basis for the idea that the response of dopamine neurons codes for a difference between the actual reward and what was expected (Montague, Dayan, & Sejnowski, 1996). This type of neural response seems related to the experience that pleasures seem to fade upon repetition in the same circumstance. For instance, many people report that if they experience having a great meal at a new restaurant, their experience of the next meal there is not as good. There are multiple possible explanations for this, but one is that the reward is expected and so the dopamine response is less.

Most recording of the responses of dopamine neurons is done in non-humans (occasionally, such recording is studied in patients as part of their treatment), but a number of measures have been found to track their responses in healthy humans. One of the most frequently studied measures is an ERP response called *feedback-related negativity* (FRN) — more than 200 studies have been run (for a review, see Walsh & Anderson, 2012). If the reward is less than expected, there is increased negativity in the FRN response 200–350 ms after the reward is delivered; if it is greater than expected, the FRN response is more positive. Studies using fMRI have generally found a stronger response in areas that contain dopamine neurons when the reward deviates from expectation (e.g., McClure, Laibson, Loewenstein, & Cohen, 2004; O'Doherty et al., 2004).

The fact that dopamine neurons respond to changes from expectations implies a learning component, because expectations are learned on the basis of experience. Their response has been associated with a popular learning technique in artificial intelligence called *reinforcement learning* (Holroyd & Coles, 2002), which is a mechanism for learning through experience what actions to take in a novel environment. An FRN study by a former graduate student of mine (Walsh & Anderson, 2011) produced a striking demonstration of how experience based (and stupid) this reinforcement learning can be. Participants learned a simple task in which they were shown two repeating stimuli and had to choose one. Sometimes their choice was rewarded, and they were motivated to choose the one that was rewarded more often. The critical manipulation was whether the participants were told at the beginning what the better stimulus was or had to learn it from experience. Not surprisingly, if told which stimulus was better, they chose it from the start. If they were not told, it took them a while to learn the better stimulus. However, their FRN showed no difference between the two conditions. Whether participants had been told the correct response or not, the FRN started out responding identically to the two stimuli. Only with time did it come to respond more strongly when the reward (or lack of reward) for that stimulus was unexpected. So even though their choice behavior responded immediately to what they had been told, their FRN showed a slow learning process. It is as if their minds knew but their hearts had to learn.

It is generally thought that the ventromedial prefrontal cortex is responsible for a more reflective processing of rewards, while the dopamine neurons in the basal ganglia are responsible for a more reflexive processing of rewards. A number of neural imaging studies seem consistent with this interpretation. In one fMRI study, Knutson, Taylor, Kaufman, Peterson, and Glover (2005) presented participants with various uncertain outcomes, including in the magnitude and probability of rewards. For instance, on one trial participants might be told that they had a 50% chance of winning $5; on another trial that they had a 50% chance of winning $1 (i.e., the magnitude of the reward differed between trials). Similarly, participants might be told on one trial that they had an 80% chance of winning $5, and on another trial might be told that they had a 20% chance of winning $5 (i.e., the probability of the reward differed between trials). Knutson et al. imaged the brain activity associated with each such gamble. As shown in **Figure 11.10a**, the magnitude of the fMRI response in the nucleus accumbens in the basal ganglia reflected the different magnitudes of rewards (but did not reflect differences in the probabilities of rewards). In contrast, as shown in Figure 11.10b, the

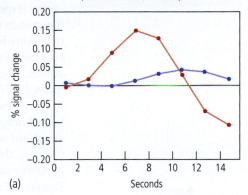

(a)

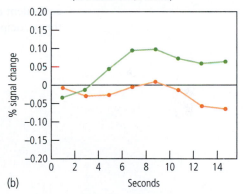

(b)

Figure 11.10 Brain Activity in Response to Magnitude and Probability of Rewards. (a) The nucleus accumbens shows greater activity in response to a 50% chance of a $5 reward than to a 50% chance of a $1 reward. (b) The ventromedial prefrontal cortex shows greater activity in response to an 80% chance of a $5 reward than to a 20% chance of a $5 reward. *(Data from Knutson et al, 2005.)*

fMRI response in the ventromedial prefrontal cortex did reflect differences in the probabilities of rewards (but did not reflect differences in the magnitudes of rewards).

The Knutson et al. study found only that the ventromedial prefrontal region responds to probabilities of rewards, but other research has found that it responds to magnitudes of rewards as well. The region is generally thought to be involved in integrating the probability of succeeding in an action and the possible reward of success — that is, it is a key decision-making region. Recall that this is the region that was destroyed in Phineas Gage's brain (see Figure 11.1) and that Gage's resulting problems went beyond judging probabilities. Subsequent research has confirmed that people who have damage to this region do have difficulty in responding adaptively in situations where good and bad outcomes have different probabilities. For instance, this has been studied extensively in a situation known as the *Iowa gambling task* (Bechara, Damasio, Damasio, & Anderson, 1994; Bechara, Damasio, Tranel, & Damasio, 2005), illustrated in **Figure 11.11**. In this version of the task, a participant starts out with $2,000 in virtual money and must turn over cards one at a time from any of four decks, with the goal of ending up with as much money as possible. The game ends after 100 cards have been turned. Each deck consists of 90% reward cards and 10% penalty cards, randomly distributed. As you can see in the figure, decks A and B are equivalent and decks C and D are equivalent. In the "bad" decks (A and B), the participant gains $100 for each reward card turned over but loses $1,250

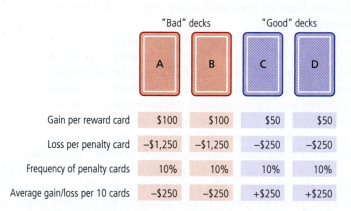

	"Bad" decks		"Good" decks	
	A	B	C	D
Gain per reward card	$100	$100	$50	$50
Loss per penalty card	−$1,250	−$1,250	−$250	−$250
Frequency of penalty cards	10%	10%	10%	10%
Average gain/loss per 10 cards	−$250	−$250	+$250	+$250

Figure 11.11 The Iowa Gambling Task. Rewards are larger in decks A and B than in decks C and D, but penalties in A and B are very much larger than in C and D, and the frequency of penalties is the same in all four decks. Playing from decks A and B leads to an overall loss, whereas playing from decks C and D leads to an overall gain. *(Data from Bechara et al., 2005.)*

for each penalty card. So the expected value of selecting a card from one of these decks is

$$\$100 - (0.1 \times \$1,250) = -\$25$$

Thus, the participant can expect to lose $250 for every 10 cards turned over from these decks. In the "good" decks (C and D), in contrast, the participant gains only $50 for each reward card turned over but loses only $250 for each penalty card. So the expected value of selecting a card from one of these desks is

$$\$50 - (0.1 \times \$250) = +\$25$$

Thus, the participant can expect to gain $250 for every 10 cards turned over from these decks. Participants tend to be initially attracted to decks A and B because of their higher payoff, but normal participants eventually learn to avoid them. In contrast, participants with damage to the ventromedial prefrontal cortex keep turning over cards from the high-reward decks (A and B). Also, unlike normal participants, they do not show measures of emotional engagement (such as increased galvanic skin response) when they choose from these dangerous decks.

> *Dopamine activity in the nucleus accumbens reflects the magnitude of reward, whereas the human ventromedial prefrontal cortex is involved in integrating probabilities of rewards with magnitudes of rewards.*

Conclusions

Decision making deals with choosing actions that can have real consequences in the presence of real uncertainty. All mammals have the dopamine system that we just described, which gives them a basic ability to seek things that are rewarding and avoid things that are harmful. However, humans, by virtue of their greatly expanded prefrontal cortex, have a highly developed capacity to reflect on their circumstances and select actions other than what their more primitive systems might urge. Research suggests that the ventromedial portion of the human prefrontal cortex, which is proportionally much larger than the same region in the genetically similar apes, might play a particularly important role in such regulation. Humans attempt acts of self-regulation — for example, diet plans — that are far beyond the reach of any other species. However, we live in an uncertain world, as evidenced by all the contradictory claims made for various diet plans. Perhaps if we understood better how people respond to such uncertainty and to such contradictory information, we would also be in a better position to understand why there are so many failures of our good resolutions.

Questions for Thought

1. Consider the Monty Hall problem (Whitaker, 1990):

   Suppose you're on a game show where you see three doors and are told that behind one door is a car and behind each of the other doors is a goat. You are given the choice of opening any one of the doors. You pick a door — for example, door 1 — and the host, who knows what's behind the doors, opens a different door, one with a goat — for example, door 3. He then says to you, "Do you want to stay with your choice of door 1 or switch to door 2?" Is it to your advantage to switch?

   This problem can be analyzed using Bayes's theorem, as follows:

$$\text{Prob}(H2|E3) = \frac{\text{Prob}(H2) \bullet \text{Prob}(E3|H2)}{\text{Prob}(H1) \bullet \text{Prob}(E3|H1) + \text{Prob}(H2) \bullet \text{Prob}(E3|H2 + \text{Prob}(H3) \bullet \text{Prob}(E3|H3)}$$

   where $\text{Prob}(H2 | E3)$ is the probability that the car is behind door 2 given that the host has opened door 3; $\text{Prob}(H1)$, $\text{Prob}(H2)$, and $\text{Prob}(H3)$ are the prior probabilities that the car is behind each door (all three are $1/3$); and $\text{Prob}(E3|H1)$, $\text{Prob}(E3|H2)$, and $\text{Prob}(E3 | H3)$ are the conditional probabilities that the host opens each door given each hypothesis. Can you calculate these probabilities, keeping in mind that the host cannot open the door you chose and must open a door that has a goat?

2. Conservatism and base-rate neglect seem to be in conflict (Fischhoff & Beyth-Marom, 1983; Gigerenzer et al., 1989). Conservatism says that people pay too little attention to data, whereas base-rate neglect says that people only pay attention to evidence and ignore base rates. Could the contradiction be explained by differences between studies like Edwards (1968), showing conservatism, and studies like Kahneman and Tversky (1973), demonstrating base-rate neglect?

3. Go to http://www.rense.com/general81/dw.htm to see a list of things that people said would never happen. What does this list imply about the subjective probability we should assign to an event when someone tells us that the objective probability of the event is 0?

4. In the 1980s, it was common practice to recommend that a pregnant woman aged 35 years or older be tested to find out whether the fetus had Down syndrome. The logic behind this recommendation was that the probability of having a Down syndrome baby increases with maternal age, reaching about $1/250$ for expectant mothers age 35. The probability of the procedure resulting in a miscarriage was also about $1/250$. Analyze the assumptions behind this decision-making criterion used in the 1980s in terms of the expected-value calculations described in this chapter. On the basis of your analysis, explain why you agree or disagree with the recommendation.

5. In his 2011 book *Thinking, Fast and Slow,* Nobel laureate Daniel Kahneman argues that there are two systems for decision making (see the discussion of dual-process theories in Chapter 10). The fast system runs on instinct and simple association, whereas the slow system satisfies the prescriptive norms for decision making. The fast system is always involved in making judgments, while the slow system requires deliberate effort to be brought into play. How would you interpret the phenomena discussed in this chapter in terms of these two systems?

Key Terms

Bayes's theorem	gambler's fallacy	probability matching	ventromedial prefrontal
conditional probability	posterior probability	recognition heuristic	cortex
descriptive model	prescriptive model	subjective probability	
framing effects	prior probability	subjective utility	

Language Structure

What makes human cognition special? There are two basic hypotheses about the major factor that makes humans intellectually different from other species. In the past few chapters, I focused on my favorite hypothesis, which is that we have unmatched abilities to solve problems and reason about our world, owing in large part to the enormous development of our prefrontal cortex. The other hypothesis, which is at least as popular in cognitive science, is that humans are special mostly because they alone possess language.

In this chapter, we will analyze in more detail what language is, how language is acquired, and what makes human language special in comparison to the communications systems of other species. We will consider some basic ideas about the structure of language and review evidence for the psychological reality of these ideas, as well as research on and speculation about the relation between language and thought. We will also look at research on language acquisition. Much of the evidence both for and against claims about the uniqueness of human language comes from research on the way in which children acquire language.

In this chapter, we will answer the following questions:

- Where is language processed in the brain? (In Chapter 13, we will shift our focus to answer questions about *how* language is processed.)
- What does the field of linguistics tell us about the nature and structure of language?
- What distinguishes human language from the communication systems of other species?
- What is the relationship between language and human thought?
- How do children acquire language?

Language and the Brain

The human brain has features strongly associated with language. In about 96% of humans, language is strongly lateralized in the left hemisphere—this includes almost all of the 92% of people who are right-handed and about half of the 8% of people who are left-handed. Findings from studies with split-brain patients (see Chapter 1) have indicated that the right hemisphere is involved in only the most rudimentary aspects of language processing. It was once thought that the left hemisphere was larger, particularly in areas taking part in language processing, and that this greater size accounted for the more complex linguistic processing associated with the left hemisphere. However, while there are physical differences between the left and right hemispheres, these differences have not been reliably localized in language processing regions (Keller, Crow, Foundas, Amunts, & Roberts, 2009). It remains largely a mystery what differences between the left and the right hemispheres could account for why language is so strongly left lateralized.

The regions of the left hemisphere illustrated in **Figure 12.1** are specialized for language. These areas were initially identified in studies of patients who suffered aphasias (losses of language function) as a consequence of stroke. The first such area was discovered by Paul Broca, a French surgeon who, in 1861, examined the brain of such a patient after the patient's death (the brain is still preserved in a Paris museum). This patient was basically incapable of spoken speech, although he understood much of what was spoken to him. He had a large region of damage in a prefrontal area that came to be known as *Broca's area*. As can be seen in Figure 12.1, Broca's area is next to the motor region that controls the mouth. Shortly thereafter, Carl Wernicke, a German physician, identified patients with severe deficits in understanding speech who had damage in a region in the superior temporal cortex posterior to the primary auditory area. This area came to be known as *Wernicke's area*. Parietal regions close to Wernicke's area (the supramarginal gyrus and angular gyrus) are also important to language.

Two of the classic aphasias, now known as *Broca's aphasia* and *Wernicke's aphasia*, are associated with damage to these two regions (see Chapter 1 for examples of the kinds of speech problems suffered by patients with these two aphasias). The severity of the damage determines whether patients with Broca's aphasia are unable to generate almost any speech (like Broca's original patient) or capable of generating meaningful but ungrammatical speech. Patients with Wernicke's aphasia, in addition to having problems with comprehension, sometimes produce grammatical but meaningless speech.

The importance of these left-cortical areas to speech is well documented, and there are many well-studied cases of aphasia resulting from damage in

Figure 12.1 Language Processing in the Left Hemisphere. The brain areas labeled in bold are implicated in language processing.

Brain Structures

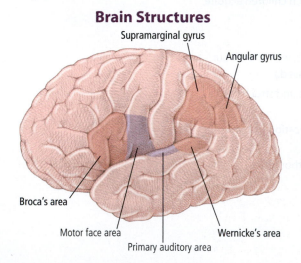

Supramarginal gyrus

Angular gyrus

Broca's area

Motor face area

Primary auditory area

Wernicke's area

these regions; however, it has become increasingly apparent that there is no simple mapping of damaged areas onto types of aphasia. Current research has focused on more detailed analyses of the deficits and of the regions damaged in each aphasic patient.

Although there is much still to understand, it is a fact that certain left-cortical regions have been selected over the course of human evolution as the preferred locations for language processing. It is not the case, however, that language has to be left lateralized: Some left-handers process language in the right hemisphere, and young children who suffer damage to the left hemisphere may develop language in the right hemisphere, in regions that are homologous to the left-hemisphere regions depicted in Figure 12.1. Also it is worth noting that ape brains show structural differences between left and right hemispheres somewhat similar to the differences seen in humans (Smaers et al., 2011), although apes do not have anything like human language.

> *Language is preferentially localized in the left hemisphere in prefrontal regions (Broca's area), temporal regions (Wernicke's area), and parietal regions (supramarginal and angular gyri).*

The Field of Linguistics

The academic field of linguistics attempts to characterize the nature of **natural languages** (languages that human children can acquire—see the section on language acquisition later in this chapter). It is distinct from psychology in that it studies the structure of natural languages rather than the way in which people process natural languages. Despite this difference, linguistic research has been extremely influential in theories of language processing, and as noted in Chapter 1, work in linguistics was important in the decline of behaviorism and the rise of modern cognitive psychology.

Productivity and Regularity

Linguistics focuses on two aspects of language: its productivity and its regularity. The term **productivity** refers to the fact that an infinite number of sentences are possible in any language, while **regularity** refers to the fact that these sentences are systematically structured in many ways. It is easy to find convincing evidence of the highly productive and creative character of language. Just pick a sentence at random from this book (or any other book) and do a Google search for that exact sentence (quoting it). If Google can find the sentence in all of its billions of pages, it will probably either be from a copy of the book or a quotation from the book (in fact, programs designed to catch plagiarism use methods like this). Most sentences in books are unique—they were created only once in human history. Yet all the possible sentences in any language are constructed from a very restricted number of components. English, for example, uses only about 40 phonemes (see the discussion of speech recognition in Chapter 2), strung together in various orders to make the few hundred thousand English words, which are then used to construct the infinite variety of English sentences.

A look at the structure of sentences makes clear why this productivity is possible—structures can be endlessly embedded within other structures and coordinated with other structures. A mildly amusing party game starts with a simple sentence and requires players to keep adding to the sentence until the sentence gets too long for a player to recall and extend accurately.

> *First player:* The girl hit the boy.
> *Next player:* The girl hit the boy and he cried.
> *Next player:* The big girl hit the boy and he cried.
> *Next player:* The big girl hit the boy and he cried loudly.
> *Next player:* The big girl hit the boy who was misbehaving and he cried loudly.
> *Next player:* The big girl with authoritarian instincts hit the boy who was misbehaving and he cried loudly.
> . . . and so on.

The fact that an infinite number of sentences can be generated is not particularly interesting in itself, given that sentences can be of any length. However, if we merely combine words at random, we get nonsentences such as

- From runners physicians prescribing miss a states joy rests what thought most.

The point is often jokingly made that, given enough monkeys working at typewriters for a long enough time, some monkey would eventually type a best-selling book. But it should be clear that it would take a lot of monkeys a very long time to type just one acceptable *R@!#s.

So, balanced against the productivity of language is its structural regularity. One goal of linguistics is to discover the **grammar** of any given language: a set of rules that account for both the productivity and the regularity of the language. A grammar should be able to prescribe (or *generate*) all the acceptable sentences of a language and be able to reject all the nonsentences. A grammar consists of rules in three domains—syntax, semantics, and phonology. **Syntax** concerns word order and inflection.[1] Consider the following examples of sentences that violate the rules of English syntax:

- The girls hits the boys.
- Did hit the girl the boys?
- The girl hit a boys.
- The boys were hit the girl.

---

[1] Inflection means changing the form of a word to change the word's function—e.g., the word *boy* is inflected with an *-s* (changed to *boys*) to change its function from singular to plural.

These sentences are fairly meaningful but contain some mistakes in word combinations or word forms.

Semantics concerns the meaning of sentences. Consider the semantic violations in the following sentences, which both have correct syntax:

- Colorless green ideas sleep furiously.[2]
- Sincerity frightened the cat.

These constructions are called *anomalous sentences* because they are syntactically well formed but nearly nonsensical.

Phonology concerns the sound structure of sentences. Sentences can be correct syntactically and semantically but be mispronounced in various ways. Such sentences are said to contain phonological violations. Consider this example:

> The Inspector opened his notebook. "Your name is Halcock, is't no?" he began. The butler corrected him. "H'alcock," he said, reprovingly. "H, a, double-l?" suggested the Inspector. "There is no h'aich in the name, young man. H'ay is the first letter, and there is h'only one h'ell." (Sayers, 1968, p. 73)

The butler, wanting to hide his cockney dialect, which drops the letter *h*, systematically overcorrects by adding an *h* at the beginning of almost every word that begins with a vowel.

> *The goal of linguistics is to discover a set of rules that captures the structural regularities in a language.*

Linguistic Intuitions

A major goal of linguistics is to explain the **linguistic intuitions** of speakers of a language—their judgments about the acceptability of sentences or about the relations between sentences. Speakers are often able to make such judgments without knowing how they do so. As such, linguistic intuition is another example of implicit knowledge (discussed in Chapter 7). Among linguistic intuitions are judgments about whether sentences are ill-formed and, if ill-formed, why. For instance, we can judge that some sentences are ill-formed because they exhibit syntactic, semantic, or phonological violations like those discussed in the preceding section. Linguists require that a grammar capture these intuitions and clearly express the reasons for them. One kind of semantic intuition concerns *paraphrase*, a similarity in meaning between sentences. For example, a speaker of English will judge that the following two sentences are paraphrases:

- The girl hit the boy.
- The boy was hit by the girl.

[2] This sentence (from Chomsky, 1957) has been the subject of so much linguistic discussion that a Google search for that exact string of words generates more than 100,000 hits.

Yet another kind of semantic intuition concerns *ambiguity,* where a sentence has two or more different meanings. The following sentence, for example, has two meanings:

- They are cooking apples.

This sentence can mean either that some people are cooking some apples or that the apples are of a type used for cooking.[3] Moreover, speakers of the language can distinguish this type of ambiguity, which is called *structural ambiguity* (because the syntax of the sentence differs depending on the meaning), from lexical ambiguity (where a word has two or more different meanings), as in

- I am going to the bank.

where "bank" can refer either to a monetary institution or to a riverbank.

> *Linguists try to account for the intuitions we have about paraphrases, ambiguities, and the well-formedness of sentences.*

Competence Versus Performance

Our everyday use of language does not always correspond to the prescriptions of grammar. We generate structures in conversation that, upon reflection, we would judge to be ill-formed. We hesitate, repeat ourselves, stutter, and make slips of the tongue. We misunderstand the meaning of sentences. We hear sentences that are ambiguous but do not note their ambiguity.

Another complication is that linguistic intuitions are not always clear-cut or consistent. For instance, Lakoff (1971) tells us that the first of the following sentences is not acceptable but the second is:

- Tell John where the concert's this afternoon.
- Tell John that the concert's this afternoon.

Do you agree with Lakoff's intuitions about these two sentences?

Considerations about the inconsistency of human linguistic behavior and linguistic intuitions led Chomsky (1965) to make a distinction between linguistic **competence**, a person's abstract knowledge of a language, and linguistic **performance**, the actual application of that knowledge in speaking or listening. In Chomsky's view, the linguist's task is to develop a theory of competence, and the psychologist's task is to develop a theory of performance.

The exact relation between a theory of competence and a theory of performance is unclear and has been the subject of heated debates. Chomsky has argued that a theory of competence is central to a theory of performance—that our linguistic competence underlies the way we actually use language, if

---

[3] For much more humorous versions of such ambiguity, go to http://fun-with-words.com/ambiguous_headlines.html.

indirectly. Others believe that the concept of linguistic competence is based on a rather unnatural activity (making linguistic judgments) that has very little to do with performance.

> *Linguistic performance does not always correspond to linguistic competence.*

Syntactic Formalisms

A major contribution of linguistics to the psychological study of language has been to provide a set of concepts for describing the structure of sentences, especially syntactic structure.

Phrase Structure

A central linguistic concept is **phrase structure**, the hierarchical division of sentences into units called *phrases*. Phrase-structure analysis is not only significant in linguistics, but also important to an understanding of language processing. Therefore, coverage of this topic here is partly a preparation for material in Chapter 13. Those of you who have had a certain kind of training in high-school English will find that phrase-structure analysis is similar to what might have been called *parsing*.

Consider this sentence:

- The brave dog saved the drowning child.

Most people would say that the most natural way of dividing this sentence into its major parts is as follows (parentheses enclose the two parts):

- (The brave dog) (saved the drowning child).

The two parts of the sentence correspond to what are traditionally called *subject* and *predicate* or *noun phrase* and *verb phrase*. If asked to further divide the second part, the verb phrase, most people would do it like this:

- (The brave dog) (saved [the drowning child]).

The phrase-structure analysis of a sentence is often represented as an upside-down tree (termed a *phrase-structure tree*), as in **Figure 12.2**. In this phrase-structure tree, each labeled unit divides into its subunits (e.g., the sentence divides into a noun phrase and a verb phrase, and the verb phrase divides into a verb and a noun phrase), until, eventually, the branches of the tree terminate in the individual words.

Phrase-structure trees can clearly reveal the nature of structural ambiguities. Consider again the sentence

- They are cooking apples.

Figure 12.2 A Phrase-Structure Tree. The tree structure illustrates the hierarchical division of the sentence into phrases and lower-level subunits.

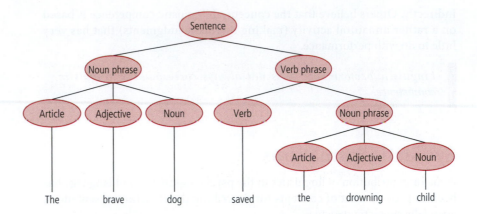

The phrase-structure trees in **Figure 12.3** show the structural differences between the two interpretations of this sentence. In Figure 12.3a (where the sentence means that some people are cooking some apples), *cooking* is part of the verb subunit of the verb phrase, where it functions as a verb; in Figure 12.3b (where the sentence means that the apples are of a type used for cooking), *cooking* is part of the noun phrase subunit of the verb phrase, where it functions as an adjective.

> *Phrase-structure analysis is concerned with the way that sentences are broken up into linguistic units.*

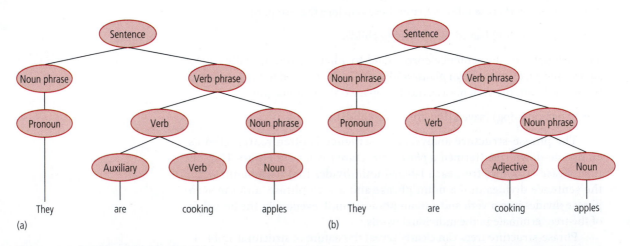

Figure 12.3 Structural Ambiguity of "They Are Cooking Apples." (a) Phrase structure of the sentence meaning that some people are cooking some apples. (b) Phrase structure of the sentence meaning that the apples are of a type used for cooking.

Pause Structure in Speech

Abundant evidence supports the argument that phrase structures play a key role in the generation of sentences.[4] When people produce a sentence, they tend to generate a phrase at a time, pausing at the boundaries between major phrase units. Consider, for instance, Abraham Lincoln's speech at Gettysburg. No tape recorders were available in Lincoln's time, but if actor Sam Waterston's rendition is accurate,[5] Lincoln produced the first sentence of the speech with a brief pause at the end of each of the major phrases:

> Four score and seven years ago (pause)
> our forefathers brought forth on this continent a new nation (pause)
> conceived in liberty (pause)
> and dedicated to the proposition (pause)
> that all men are created equal (pause)

Boomer (1965) analyzed examples of spontaneous speech and found that pauses did occur more frequently at junctures between major phrases and that these pauses were longer than pauses at other locations. The average pause time between major phrases was 1.03 s, whereas the average pause within major phrases was 0.75 s. This finding suggests that speakers tend to produce sentences a phrase at a time and often need to pause after one phrase to plan the next. Other researchers (Cooper & Paccia-Cooper, 1980; Grosjean, Grosjean, & Lane, 1979) looked at participants producing prepared sentences rather than spontaneous speech. The pauses of such participants tend to be much shorter, about 0.2 s. Still, the same pattern holds, with longer pauses at the major phrase boundaries.

As Figures 12.2 and 12.3 illustrate, sentences contain multiple levels of phrases within phrases within phrases. What level do speakers choose for breaking up their sentences into pause units? Gee and Grosjean (1983) argued that speakers tend to choose the smallest level above the word that bundles together coherent semantic information. In English, this level tends to be noun phrases (e.g., *the young woman*), verbs plus pronouns (e.g., *will have been reading it*), and prepositional phrases (e.g., *in the house*).

> People tend to pause briefly after each meaningful unit of speech above the level of the word.

Speech Errors

Other research has found evidence for phrase structure by looking at errors in speech. Maclay and Osgood (1959) analyzed spontaneous recordings of speech and found a number of speech errors that suggested that phrases do

---

[4] In Chapter 13, we will examine the role of phrase structures in language comprehension.
[5] You can listen to Waterston reading the speech on NPR by searching for "NPR" and "A Reading of the Gettysburg Address."

have a psychological reality. They found that, when speakers repeated themselves or corrected themselves, they tended to repeat or correct a whole phrase. For instance, the following kind of repeat is found:

- Turn on the heater—the heater.

and the following constitutes a common type of correction:

- Turn on the stove—the heater switch.

In the second example, the noun phrase *the stove* is corrected with *the heater switch*. That is, a whole noun phrase is used in the correction, not more or less. Thus, speakers do not correct themselves like this:

- Turn on the stove—on the heater switch. (more than the noun phrase)
- Turn on the stove—heater switch. (less than the noun phrase)

Other kinds of speech errors, such as slips of the tongue, also provide evidence for the psychological reality of phrases as major units of speech generation (Fromkin, 1971, 1973; Garrett, 1975). Consider, for example, the speech errors called *spoonerisms*, named after an Oxford don, William A. Spooner, to whom are attributed some colossal and clever errors of speech, including these:

- You have hissed all my mystery lectures.
- I saw you fight a liar in the back quad; in fact, you have tasted the whole worm.
- I assure you the insanitary spectre has seen all the bathrooms.
- Easier for a camel to go through the knee of an idol.
- The Lord is a shoving leopard to his flock.
- Take the flea of my cat and heave it at the louse of my mother-in-law.

As illustrated here, spoonerisms consist of exchanges of sound between words. There is some reason to suspect that the preceding errors were deliberate attempts at humor by Spooner. However, people do generate genuine spoonerisms, although they are seldom as funny.

By patient collecting, researchers have gathered a large set of errors made by friends and colleagues. Some of these errors are simple sound anticipations and some are sound exchanges as in spoonerisms:

- Take my bike → bake my bike [an anticipation]
- night life → nife lite [an exchange]
- beast of burden → burst of beaden [an exchange]

One that gives me particular difficulty is

- coin toss → toin coss

In anticipation errors like the example in the preceding list, an early word-initial sound is changed to a later word-initial sound. In exchanges, two sounds switch. The interesting feature about these kinds of errors is that they tend to occur within a major phrase rather than across phrases. So, we are unlikely to find an anticipation like the following, which occurs between subject and object noun phrases:

- The dancer took my bike. → The bancer took my bike.

Also unlikely are sound exchanges between a prepositional phrase and a following noun phrase, like this:

- At night John lost his life. → At nife John lost his lite.

Garrett (1990) distinguished between errors in sounds (like the errors we have been discussing) and errors in whole words. Sound errors occur at what he called the *positional level,* which basically corresponds to a single phrase, whereas word errors occur at what he called the *functional level,* which corresponds to a larger unit of speech such as a sentence consisting of multiple phrases. Thus, the following word error has been observed:

- That kid's mouse makes a great toy. → That kid's toy makes a great mouse.

whereas the following sound error would be unlikely:

- That kid's mouse makes a great toy. → That kid's touse makes a great moy.

In Garrett's (1980) corpus, 83% of all word errors extended across phrase boundaries, but only 13% of sound errors did. Word and sound errors are generally thought to occur at different levels in the speech production process. Words are inserted into the speech plan at a higher level of planning, and so a larger distance is possible for the substitution.

An experimental procedure has been developed for artificially producing spoonerisms in the laboratory (Baars, Motley, & MacKay, 1975; Motley, Camden, & Baars, 1982). This involves presenting a series of word pairs like

Big Dog
Bad Deal
Beer Drum
Darn Bore
House Coat
Whale Watch

and asking the participants to speak certain words such as the boldface **Darn Bore**. When they have been primed with a series of word pairs with the opposite order of first consonants (the preceding three pairs in the series all have B____ D____), they show a tendency to reverse the order of the first consonants, in this case producing **Barn Door**. Interestingly, participants are much more likely to produce such an error if the error results in real words (as with **Barn Door**) than if it does not (as in the case of Dock Boat, which if reversed would become Bock Doat). Participants are also sensitive to a host of other factors, such as whether the pair is grammatically acceptable and whether it is culturally appropriate (e.g., they are more likely to convert Cast Part into Past Cart than they are to convert Fast Part into Past Fart). This research has been taken as evidence that multiple factors go into determining the speech items we produce.

> *Speech errors involving substitutions of sounds and words suggest that words are selected at the sentence level, whereas sounds are selected at a lower phrase level.*

Transformations

A phrase structure description represents a sentence hierarchically as pieces within larger pieces. There are certain types of linguistic constructions that some linguists think violate this strictly hierarchical structure. Consider the following pair of sentences:

1. The dog is chasing Bill down the street.
2. Whom is the dog chasing down the street?

In sentence 1, *Bill* is the object of the verb *chasing* and is part of the verb phrase. In sentence 2, however, *whom* is the object of the verb but is at the beginning of the sentence, outside the verb phrase. That is, the object is no longer part of the structure to which it would seem to belong. Some linguists have proposed that, formally, such questions are generated by starting with a phrase structure that has the object *whom* in the verb phrase, such as

3. The dog is chasing whom down the street?

This sentence is somewhat strange but, with the right questioning intonation on *whom*, it can be made to sound reasonable. In some languages, such as Japanese, the interrogative pronoun is normally in the verb phrase, as in sentence 3. However, in English, the proposal is that there is a "movement transformation" that moves the *whom* into its more normal position. Note that this proposal is a linguistic one concerning the formal structure of language and may not describe the actual process of producing the question.

Some linguists believe that a satisfactory analysis of language requires such **transformations**, which move elements from one part of a sentence to another. Transformations can also operate on more complicated sentences. For instance, we can apply a transformation to sentences of the form

4. John believes the dog is chasing Bill down the street.

The corresponding question forms are

5. John believes what is chasing Bill down the street?
6. What does John believe is chasing Bill down the street?

Unlike sentence 3, sentence 5 is strange even with a questioning intonation for *what*, but still some linguists propose that sentence 6 is transformationally derived from the phrase structure of sentence 5, even though we would never produce sentence 5.

There seem to be constraints on just what elements can be moved by transformations. For instance, consider the following set of sentences:

7. John believes the myth that George Washington chopped down the cherry tree.
8. John believes the myth that who chopped down the cherry tree?
9. Who does John believe the myth that chopped down the cherry tree?

Sentence 7 is perfectly acceptable; and like sentence 3, sentence 8 can be made to sound acceptable with the right questioning intonation on *who*. However, sentence 9 just sounds bizarre, regardless of intonation. One cannot move *who* from its position in sentence 8 to produce sentence 9. (For further discussion, see the section "Constraints on Transformations" later in this chapter.)

In contrast with the abundant evidence for phrase structure in language processing, there is little evidence that people actually compute anything analogous to transformations in understanding or producing sentences. How people process such transformationally derived sentences remains very much an open question. There is a lot of controversy within linguistics about how to conceive of transformations. The role of transformations has been deemphasized in many proposals.

> *Transformations move elements from their normal positions in the phrase structure of sentences.*

Is Human Language Special?

We have reviewed some of the features of human language, with the implicit assumption that no other species has anything like such a language. What gives us this conceit? How do we know that other species do not have their own languages? Perhaps we just do not understand the languages of other species. Certainly, all social species communicate with one another, and, ultimately, whether we call their communication systems *languages* is a definitional matter. However, human language is different from these other systems, and it is worth identifying some of the features (Hockett, 1960) that are considered critical to human language.

Arbitrary Association of Sign and Meaning

Consider, for instance, the communication system of dogs. They have a nonverbal system that can be quite effective in communication. The reason that dogs are such successful pets is thought to be that their nonverbal communication system is so much like that of humans. Besides being nonverbal, canine communication has more fundamental limitations. In human language, the relation between signs and their meaning is arbitrary—for instance, there is no reason why the sequences of sounds in *good dog* and *bad dog* should mean what they do (different sequences of sounds in other languages have the same meanings). In contrast, dogs' signs are related to their meaning in nonarbitrary ways—a snarl (often revealing the dog's sharp incisors) means a threat of aggression, exposing the neck (a vulnerable part of the dog's body) means submission, and so on. However, not all nonhuman communication systems are nonarbitrary. For instance, the vocalizations of some species of monkeys have the property of arbitrary association of sound and meaning (Marler, 1967). One species, the vervet monkey, has different warning calls for different types of predators—a "chutter" for snakes, a "chirp" for leopards, and a "kraup" for eagles.

Displacement in Time and Space

A critical feature of the vervet monkey warning system is that the monkeys use it only in the presence of a relevant predator. They do not use it to "discuss" the day's events at a later time. An enormously important feature of human language (exemplified by this book, for instance) is that it can be used to communicate over time and distance (i.e., to refer to past and future things and to things at different locations). Interestingly, the communication system of honeybees has the properties of both arbitrariness and displacement (von Frisch, 1967). When a honeybee returns to its hive after finding a food source, it will engage in a "dance" that communicates the location of the food source. The dance consists of a straight run in a particular direction followed by a turn to the right to circle back to the starting point, another straight run in the same direction, followed by a turn and circle to the left, and so on, in an alternating pattern. The length of the run indicates the distance of the food, and the direction of the run relative to vertical indicates the direction relative to the sun. Interestingly, the language of the bees could be considered to have an infinite number of possible "utterances," because there are an infinite number of gradations in angle and length.

Discreteness and Productivity

Human language contains discrete units, which would serve to disqualify the bee language system, although the monkey warning system meets this criterion. Requiring a language to have discrete units is not just an arbitrary regulation to disqualify the dance of the bees. This discreteness enables the elements of the language to be combined into the complex hierarchical structures that constitute sentences.

Can Apes Use Human Language?

It is a striking fact that all people in the world, even those in isolated communities, speak a language. No other species spontaneously uses a communication system anything like human language. Interestingly, the great apes,[6]

---

[6] The great apes include chimpanzees, bonobos, gorillas, and orangutans. (Gibbons and siamangs are the lesser apes.)

genetically closest to humans, appear to lack any kind of vocalized signal system like that of the vervet monkey (Mithen, 2005). However, many people have wondered whether apes such as chimpanzees could be taught a human language. Early twentieth century attempts to teach chimpanzees to speak failed miserably (Hayes, 1951; Kellogg & Kellogg, 1933). However, it is now clear that those attempts were doomed from the start because the human vocal apparatus has undergone special evolutionary adaptations to enable speech. Thus, more recent attempts to teach a human language to chimpanzees and other apes have tried to take advantage of apes' considerable manual dexterity. Some of this research has used American Sign Language (e.g., Gardner & Gardner, 1969), a manual language with all the defining characteristics of a spoken human language (showing that language need not be spoken). These attempts had only modest success (e.g., Terrace, Pettito, Sanders, & Bever, 1979): Chimpanzees acquired vocabularies of more than a hundred signs but never used the signs with the productivity typical of humans using their own language. Other, somewhat more successful attempts used plastic shapes that could be attached to a magnetic board to signify "words" called *lexigrams* (e.g., Premack & Premack, 1983).

Perhaps the most impressive example is provided by the bonobo Kanzi (Savage-Rumbaugh et al., 1993; see **Figure 12.4**). Bonobos are a species of ape in the same genus as chimpanzees that have a somewhat different genetic overlap with humans. Kanzi's mother was a subject of one of these efforts to teach language using lexigrams, and Kanzi simply came along with his mother and observed her training sessions. One day, he spontaneously started to use the lexigrams, much more effectively than his mother. Tomasello (2017) argues that Kanzi's success was based on his having learned the language

Figure 12.4 Kanzi and Sue Savage-Rumbaugh in 2011.
A number of videos of the bonobo Kanzi can be found on YouTube by searching with his name. *(Laurentiu Garofeanu/Barcroft USA/Barcroft Media/Getty Images.)*

observationally (rather than being taught like his mother was), just as human children learn their first language. His spontaneous constructions were quite impressive, and it soon became apparent that he had also acquired a considerable ability to understand spoken language, a capacity that appears to outstrip his ability to use lexigrams. When he was 5.5 years of age, his comprehension of spoken English was determined to be equivalent to that of a 2-year-old human.

The differences between Kanzi and a child seem more a matter of how he used the language than a matter of his ability to use language. His spontaneous uses of lexigrams are almost all imperatives, in which he is requesting something (Greenfield and Savage-Rumbaugh, 1990). Children certainly use language to make requests, but they also use it to communicate information, ask questions, express emotions, and so on. Of course, bonobos and other great apes are different species from humans, with different needs and different cognition. So it may not be that they are incapable of learning language but rather that they do not have the same needs for language use. (See **Implications 12.1** for further discussion of research on teaching human language to apes, including the ethics of research with apes.)

> *Only humans show the propensity or the ability to acquire a complex communication system that combines symbols and to use this ability for a multitude of purposes.*

The Relation Between Language and Thought

All reasonable people would concede that there is some special connection between humans and their use of language. However, there is a lot of controversy about the role of other cognitive processes in this connection. Many researchers such as Steven Pinker and Noam Chomsky have proposed that humans have some special genetic endowment that enables them to learn and use language—a special ability that does not depend on other cognitive processes. Other researchers argue that what is special is general human intellectual abilities and that these abilities have enabled us to create, learn, and use language. I confess to leaning toward this second viewpoint. There are three possible relationships between thought and language (not mutually exclusive):

1. Thought depends in various ways on language.
2. Language depends in various ways on thought.
3. Language and thought are two largely independent systems.

We will go through each of these ideas in turn, starting with two versions of the proposal that thought depends on language: the radical behaviorist proposal that thought is just speech and a more modest proposal called *linguistic determinism*.

Implications 12.1

Apes and the Ethics of Experimentation

The issue of whether apes can be taught human language interlinks in complex ways with issues about the ethical treatment of animals in research. The French philosopher René Descartes (1596–1650) believed that language was what separated humans from animals. If this is the case and if apes could be shown capable of acquiring a human language, they would have human status and should be given the same rights as humans in experimentation. One might even require that they give informed consent before participating in an experiment. Certainly, any procedure that involved injury would not be acceptable, such as research involving invasive brain procedures (there has been a fair amount of such research with primates, but mostly involving monkeys, not apes). Interestingly, studies with linguistic apes have reportedly found that they categorized themselves with humans and separate from other animals

(Linden, 1974). It has been argued that it is in the best interests of apes to teach them a human language because this would confer on them the rights of humans. However, others have argued that teaching apes a human language distorts their basic nature.

The similarity of apes to humans is precisely what makes them such attractive subjects for research. In the United States, much of the research involving apes has been biomedical research in which studies are conducted of apes that have been deliberately infected with human diseases. The potential benefits of such research are great, but it raises very difficult moral issues. In contrast, most cognitive research with apes, such as research on language acquisition, is quite benign. The great apes are the only creatures thought to have cognitive processes close to those of humans, so cognitive research with apes offers potential insights we cannot get from research with other species. The National Institutes of Health have decided

to discontinue biomedical research using great apes and to retire all the great apes currently in use, and private companies have announced similar plans. (Many countries now ban any type of research with great apes.) Now the challenge is to find suitable sanctuaries for the apes being moved from research labs (see https://www .sciencemag.org/news/2017/06 /research-lab-chimps-over-why-have- so-few-been-retired-sanctuaries).

EMPPhotography/Getty Images

The Behaviorist Proposal

As discussed in Chapter 1, John B. Watson, the father of behaviorism, held that there was no such thing as internal mental activity at all. All that humans do, Watson argued, is to emit vocal responses that have been conditioned to various stimuli. This radical proposal, which, as noted in Chapter 1, held sway in America for some time, seemed to fly in the face of the abundant evidence that humans can engage in thinking without speaking (e.g., humans can do mental arithmetic). To deal with this obvious counter, Watson proposed that this "thinking" was just subvocal speech—that, when people were engaged in such activities, they were really talking to themselves. (The philosopher Herbert Feigl once said that Watson "made up his windpipe that he had no mind.")

Watson's proposal was a stimulus for a research program that involved looking for evidence of subvocal activity of the speech apparatus during thinking. Indeed, often when participants in such studies report being engaged in thought, it is possible to detect subvocal speech activity. However, in other situations, people engage in various silent thinking tasks with no detectable vocal activity. This finding did not upset Watson. He claimed that we think with our whole bodies—for instance, with our arms. He cited the fascinating evidence that deaf mutes actually make signs while asleep. (Speaking people who have done a lot of communication in sign language also sign while sleeping.)

The decisive experiment addressing Watson's hypothesis was performed by Smith, Brown, Toman, and Goodman (1947). They used a curare derivative that paralyzes the entire voluntary musculature. Smith was the participant for the experiment and had to be kept alive by means of an artificial respirator. Because of the paralysis, it was impossible for him to engage in subvocal speech or any other body movement, while still able to comprehend speech and observe, think about, and remember what was going on around him. This experiment made it seem clear that thinking can proceed in the absence of any muscle activity. These experiments have since been replicated with both curare and succinylcholine (Messner, Beese, Romstock, Dinkel, & Tschaikowsky, 2003; Stevens et al., 1976).

Additional evidence that thought is more than subvocal speech comes from the occasional person who has no apparent language (for instance, children raised in total isolation—see, e.g., Curtiss, 1977) but who certainly gives evidence of being able to think. Additionally, it seems hard to claim that nonverbal animals such as apes are unable to think. Recall, for instance, the problem-solving exploits of the chimpanzee Sultan, discussed in Chapter 8. It is always hard to determine the exact character of the "thought processes" of nonverbal participants and the ways in which these processes differ from the thought processes of verbal participants, because there is no language with which nonverbal participants can be interrogated. Thus, the apparent dependence of thought on language may be an illusion that derives from the fact that it is hard to obtain evidence about thought without using language.

> *The behaviorist proposal that thought consists only of covert speech and other unobserved motor activity has been rebutted by evidence showing that thought can proceed in the absence of any motor activity.*

Linguistic Determinism

Linguistic determinism (or *linguistic relativity*) is the claim that language determines or strongly influences the way that a person thinks, including how the person perceives the world. This proposal is much less radical than Watson's position because it does not claim that thought is nothing but language. The hypothesis of linguistic determinism has been advanced by a good many linguists and psychologists but has been most strongly associated with Benjamin Whorf (1956), who was quite an unusual character. He trained as a chemical engineer at MIT, spent his life working for the Hartford Fire Insurance Company, and studied North American Indian languages as a hobby.

He was very impressed by the fact that different languages seem to emphasize rather different aspects of the world. He came to believe that these differing emphases in languages must have a great influence on the way that the native speakers of any given language think about the world. For instance, he claimed that the Inuit (or Eskimos) have many different words for snow, each of which refers to snow in a different state (wind driven, packed, slushy, and so on),[7] whereas English speakers have only a single word for snow. Many other examples exist at the vocabulary level: The Hanunoo people in the Philippines supposedly have 92 different words for varieties of rice. The Arabic language has many words for camels. Whorf felt that a rich variety of terms in a language for a particular category of things would cause speakers of the language to think about that category differently from a person whose language had only a single word or many fewer words.

Deciding how to evaluate the Whorfian hypothesis is very tricky. Nobody would be surprised to learn that the Inuit know more about snow than most English speakers. After all, snow is a more important part of their life experience. The question is whether their language has any effect on their perception of snow beyond the effects of experience. If speakers of English went through the Inuit life experience without becoming Inuit speakers, would their perception of snow be any different from that of Inuit speakers? (Interestingly, ski bums have a life experience that includes a great deal of snow exposure and have developed new terms for snow.)

One fairly well-researched test of this language-and-thought issue uses color words. English has 11 basic color words—*black, white, gray, red, pink, orange, yellow, green, blue, purple,* and *brown*—a large number. They are called "basic" because they are short and are used frequently, unlike color words such as *saffron, turquoise,* and *magenta*. In contrast, the language of the Dani, a Stone Age agricultural people of Indonesian New Guinea, has just two basic color terms: *mili* for dark, cold hues and *mola* for bright, warm hues. If the richness of vocabulary for a category determines perception of that category, Dani speakers should perceive color in a less differentiated way than English speakers do. The relevant question is whether this speculation is true.

Speakers of English, at least, judge a certain color within the range referred to by each basic color term to be the best example of the term—for instance, the best red, the best blue, and so on (see Berlin & Kay, 1969). Each of the 11 basic color terms in English appears to have one generally agreed upon best color, called the *focal color*. English speakers find it easier to process and remember focal colors than nonfocal colors (e.g., Brown & Lenneberg, 1954). The interesting question is whether this special cognitive capacity for processing focal colors developed because English speakers have special words for these colors. If so, it would be a case of language influencing thought.

---

[7] There have been challenges to Whorf's claims about the richness of Inuit vocabulary for snow (Martin, 1986; Pullman, 1989). In general, there is a feeling that Whorf exaggerated the variety of words in various languages.

To answer this question, Eleanor Rosch performed a series of experiments on the Dani, to see whether the Dani processed focal colors differently from English speakers. One experiment (Rosch, 1973) showed that both Dani and English speakers find it easier to learn nonsense names for focal colors than for nonfocal colors, despite the fact that English speakers have words for these colors whereas Dani speakers do not. In another experiment (Heider, 1972), participants were shown a color chip for 5 seconds; then, 30 seconds after the presentation, they were required to select that chip from an array of 160 color chips. Both English and Dani speakers perform better at this task when they are trying to locate a focal color chip rather than a nonfocal color chip. The physiology of color vision suggests that many of these focal colors are specially processed by the visual system (de Valois & Jacobs, 1968), and the fact that many languages develop basic color terms for just these colors can be seen as an instance of thought determining language. (For further research on this topic, see Lucy & Shweder [1979, 1988] and Garro [1986].)

However, more recent research by Roberson, Davies, and Davidoff (2000) does suggest an influence of language on the ability to remember colors. They compared British participants with another Papua New Guinea group who speak Berinmo, a language that has just five basic color words. **Figure 12.5** compares how Berinmo speakers and English speakers categorize the color

Figure 12.5 Categorization of the Color Space. (a) How English speakers divide up the color space. (b) How Berinmo speakers divide up the color space. *(Data from Roberson et al, 2000.)*

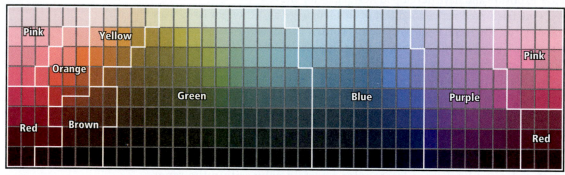

(a)

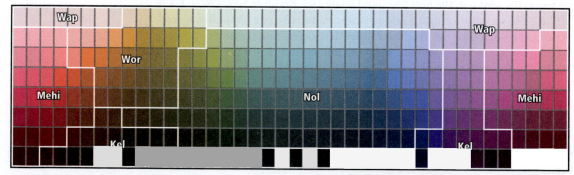

(b)

space. Replicating earlier work, Roberson et al. found that there was superior memory for focal colors regardless of language. However, by examining distinctions that were important in one language versus another, the researchers also found substantial effects of the color boundaries. For instance, as shown in Figure 12.5, Berinmo speakers make a distinction between the colors wor and nol in the middle of the part of the color space that English speakers call green. In contrast, English speakers make a distinction between yellow and green in the middle of the part of the color space that Berinmo speakers call wor. Participants from both languages were shown how to sort stimuli at these two boundaries into the two categories—wor and nol, and yellow and green—and asked to learn which stimuli belonged to which category. **Figure 12.6** shows the amount of effort that the two groups of participants put into learning the two sets of distinctions. English speakers found it easier to learn to sort stimuli at the yellow–green boundary, whereas Berinmo speakers found it easier to learn to sort stimuli at the wor–nol boundary.

Note that each group is capable of making distinctions that are important to the other group—that is, their language has not made them blind to color distinctions. However, they definitely find it harder to see the distinctions not signaled in their language and to learn to make them consistently. Thus, although language does not completely determine how we see the color space, it can have an influence.

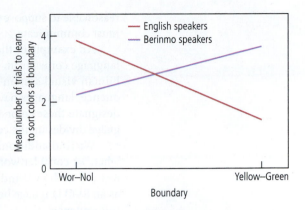

Figure 12.6 Language and Learning to Sort Colors. Berinmo speakers are quicker to learn color distinctions at the wor–nol boundary than at the yellow–green boundary, while the opposite is the case for English speakers. *(Date from Roberson et al., 2000.)*

> *Language can influence thought, but it does not totally determine the types of concepts that we can think about.*

Does Language Depend on Thought?

The alternative to the idea that language determines thought is that thought determines language. Aristotle argued 2,500 years ago that the categories of thought determined the categories of language, and there is evidence that he was correct, although most of that evidence was not available to Aristotle. In other words, although the hypothesis has been around for 2,500 years, we have better evidence for it today.

There are numerous reasons to suppose that humans' ability to think appeared earlier evolutionarily and occurs sooner developmentally than the ability to use language. For example, many species of nonhuman animals appear to be capable of complex nonlinguistic cognitive activities such as remembering and problem solving, and children who have not yet acquired language are clearly capable of relatively complex cognition. If we accept the idea that thought evolved before language, it seems natural to suppose that language arose as a tool for communicating thought. It is generally true that tools are shaped to fit the objects on which they must operate, so it seems reasonable to suppose that language has been shaped to fit the thoughts that it must communicate.

An example of the way in which thought, including perception, shapes language comes from Rosch's research on focal colors. As stated earlier, the human visual system is maximally sensitive to certain colors. As a consequence, languages have special, short, high-frequency words with which to designate these colors. Thus, human visual perception determines how language divides up the color space.

We find additional evidence for the influence of thought on language when we consider word order. Every language has a preferred order for subject (S), verb (V), and object (O) in simple sentences. English is referred to as an SVO language because the preferred order is subject–verb–object, as in this sentence:

- Lynne [subject] petted [verb] the Labrador [object].

In a study of a diverse sample of the world's languages, Greenberg (1963) found that only four of the six possible orders of S, V, and O are used in natural languages, and one of these four orders is rare. The six possible word orders and the frequency of each order in the world's languages are as follows (the percentages are from Ultan, 1969):

SOV 44%   VOS 2%
SVO 35%   OVS 0%
VSO 19%   OSV 0%

The important feature is that the subject almost always precedes the object, an order that makes sense in relation to cognition about events in the world. In simple active sentences about events (e.g., *Lynne petted the Labrador*), the subject is the agent that starts the action, which then affects the object. It seems natural therefore that the subject of such a sentence would precede the object, regardless of the position of the verb.

As in the domain of word order, languages also differ in the domain of kinship terms—specifically, in which kinship relationships are described with single words. **Figure 12.7** compares some of the kinship terms used in English to those used in Northern Paiute, an indigenous language of the western United States currently spoken by about 1,000 people. While both languages have single words for relationships like mother and father, and daughter and son, Northern Paiute has different words for paternal and maternal grandparents, aunts, and uncles, as well as for older and younger sisters and brothers, whereas English does not. For instance, in Northern Paiute the word for maternal grandmother is *mu'a* and for paternal grandmother *tofo'o* (Kroeber, 2009). Of course, English speakers can distinguish between maternal and paternal grandparents but only by using a two-word phrase, whereas speakers of Northern Paiute can use a single word. In other cases, the two languages combine different relationships. For example,

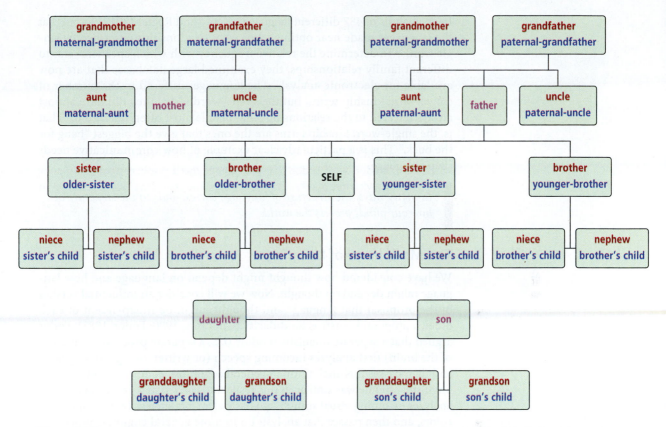

Figure 12.7 Kinship Terms of English and Northern Paiute. Single-word English terms for kinship relationships are in red. Equivalent single-word Northern Paiute terms are in blue (these translations are two words because English does not have a corresponding single word). Purple indicates words where both languages have a single word for the relationship. *(Research from Kemp & Regier, 2012.)*

English has the single word *grandson* to refer to children of both sons and daughters, whereas Northern Paiute has a single word to refer to sons and daughters of a son and a different word to refer to sons and daughters of a daughter. Overall, Northern Paiute has more single words for kinship relationships than English does.

One might ask which system of kinship terms is better for purposes of communication. On average, Northern Paiute can describe relationships using fewer words than English. However, speakers of Northern Paiute have to learn more words. In general, languages do not have a special word for every possible relationship—for instance, it is probably safe to say that no language has a special word to describe the daughter of the son of a daughter of a great-great grandfather on our mother's side. Languages tend to have single words for those relationships we are most likely to want to refer to.

In an analysis of 487 different languages, Kemp and Regier (2012) found that the languages made near optimal choices of relationships described by single words. To determine the relative frequency with which speakers refer to different family relationships, they examined large databases that are now available for electronic analysis. The languages differed in the number of single-word kinship terms, but the single-word terms they did have almost always referred to the relationships that people most often referred to. That is, the single-word kinship terms are the ones that give the biggest "bang for the buck." This is a particularly clear example of how communicative needs shape language.

> In many ways, the structure of language corresponds to the structure of how our minds process the world.

The Modularity of Language

We have considered how thought might depend on language and how language might depend on thought. Now we will consider an influential version of the proposal that language and thought might be independent of each other, a proposal known as **modularity** (Chomsky, 1980; Fodor, 1983). Fodor argued that a separate linguistic module (i.e., a separate processing function of the brain) first analyzes incoming speech (or written or signed language) and then passes this analysis on to general cognition. Fodor thought that this linguistic module was similar in this respect to early visual processing, which analyzes incoming visual stimuli into basic elements such as lines, shapes, and colors, and then passes that analysis on to more general cognitive processes. Similarly, in language generation, the linguistic module takes the intentions to be spoken and produces the speech (or writing or signing). This position does not deny that the linguistic module may have been shaped over the course of evolution to communicate thought. However, it argues that it operates according to different principles from the rest of cognition and is "encapsulated," meaning that it cannot be influenced by general cognition. In essence, the claim is that language's communication with other mental processes is limited to passing its products on to general cognition and to receiving and processing the products of general cognition.

One piece of evidence for the independence of language from other cognitive processes comes from research on people who have substantial deficits in language but not in general cognition (or vice versa). For example, people with Williams syndrome, a rare genetic disorder, show cognitive deficits that seem not to affect linguistic fluency (Bellugi, Wang, & Jernigan, 1994). Conversely, some people with aphasia and some with developmental problems may have severe language deficits without accompanying intellectual deficits. Any pattern of deficit in the development of language that cannot be explained by hearing loss, cognitive deficits, or other nonlinguistic factors is referred to as a *specific language impairment* (SLI). There are probably a number of different underlying causes of SLIs, including, in some cases, genetic causes (Stromswold, 2000). Recently, a mutation in the FOXP2 gene has been associated with SLIs (e.g., Wade, 2003), although there appear to be other cognitive deficits associated with this mutation as well (Vargha-Khadem, Watkins, Alcock, Fletcher, & Passingham, 1995). The chemical structure of the FOXP2 gene is very similar in all mammals, although the human FOXP2 gene is distinguished from that of other primates by two amino acids (out of 715). Mutations in the FOXP2 gene are associated with vocal deficits and other deficits in many species—in birds, for instance, mutation of the FOXP2 gene can result in incomplete acquisition of song imitation (Haesler et al., 2007). It has been claimed that the human form of the FOXP2 gene became established in the human population about 50,000 years ago, when, according to some proposals, human language emerged (Enard et al., 2002). However, more recent evidence suggests that these changes in the FOXP2 gene are shared with Neanderthals and occurred 300,000 to 400,000 years ago (Krause et al., 2007). Although the FOXP2 gene does play an important role in language, it does not appear to provide strong evidence for a genetic basis for a uniquely human language ability.

The modularity hypothesis has turned out to be a divisive issue in linguistics, with two domains of research playing a major role in evaluating the proposal:

1. In the domain of *language acquisition,* the issue is whether language is acquired according to language-specific learning principles or whether it is acquired like other cognitive skills.
2. In the domain of *language comprehension,* the issue is whether major aspects of language processing occur independently of any general cognitive processes.

In the remainder of this chapter, we will look at what is known about language acquisition by young children and then consider what the language-acquisition process implies about the uniqueness of human language. Then, in Chapter 13, we will resume the discussion of modularity with respect to comprehension.

> *The modularity position holds that the initial processing of linguistic input is independent from other cognitive systems.*

Language Acquisition

Having watched my two children acquire a language, I understand how easy it is to lose sight of what a remarkable feat it is. Days and weeks go by with little apparent change in children's linguistic abilities. Progress seems slow. However, something remarkable is happening. With very little deliberate instruction (often, none at all), children by the time they reach age 10 have accomplished implicitly what generations of PhD linguists have not accomplished explicitly. They have learned all the major rules of a natural language—and there appear to be thousands of such rules in every language, with subtle interactions among them. Linguists have never succeeded in formulating a grammar for any language (i.e., a set of rules that generate all the acceptable sentences of the language and reject all the nonsentences). However, as we progress through childhood, we do internalize such a grammar. Unfortunately for the linguist, our knowledge of the grammar of our language is not something that we can make explicit and articulate. It is implicit knowledge (see Chapter 7), knowledge that we can only display in using the language.

The process by which children acquire a language has some characteristic features that seem to hold no matter what their native language is (and the world's languages differ dramatically in many respects). Children are notoriously noisy creatures from birth. At first, there is little variety in their vocalizations, which consist almost totally of an *ah* sound (although they can produce this sound with different intensities and different emotional tones). In the months following birth, the child's vocal apparatus matures, and at about 6 months children begin to engage in what is called *babbling,* which consists of generating a rich variety of speech sounds with interesting intonation patterns. However, the sounds are generally totally meaningless.

An interesting feature of early-childhood linguistic behavior is that children produce sounds that do not occur in the particular language that is being spoken by the people around them and that they will themselves acquire. Moreover, they can apparently discriminate among sounds that do not occur in that language. For instance, Japanese-learning infants can discriminate between /l/ and /r/, a discrimination that Japanese adults cannot make (Tsushima et al., 1994). Similarly, English-learning infants can discriminate among variations of the /t/ sound that are important in Hindi and that English-speaking adults cannot discriminate (Werker & Tees, 1999). It is as if children enter the world with speech and perceptual capabilities that are like a block of marble out of which will be carved their particular language, discarding what is not necessary for that language.

When a child is about a year old, the first words appear, always a time of great excitement for the child's parents. Typically, only parents and caretakers who are constantly around the child are able to tell what the child intends by the first words, but soon the child develops a considerable repertoire of words that are recognizable to others and that the child uses effectively to make requests and to describe what is happening. These early words are concrete and refer to the here and now. Among my children's first words were *Mommy, Daddy, Rogers* (for *Mister Rogers*), *cheese, 'puter* (for *computer*), *eat, hi, bye, go,* and *hot.* Children will also overextend their words—for example, *dog* might be used to refer to any furry four-legged animal. One remarkable feature of this stage is that children's speech consists only of one-word utterances; even though they know many words, they never put them together to make multi-word phrases. Children's use of single words is quite complex, often communicating a whole thought.

The one-word stage, which lasts about 6 months, is followed by a stage in which children will put two words together. I can still remember our excitement as parents when our son said his first two-word utterance at 18 months—*more gee,* which meant for him "more brie"— he was a connoisseur of cheese. **Table 12.1** illustrates some typical two-word utterances generated by children at this stage (actually all generated by my first son). All their utterances at this stage are one or two words. However, once children's utterances extend beyond two words, they are of many different lengths—that is, there is no three-word stage where three words is the maximum length. The two-word utterances correspond to about a dozen or so semantic relations, including agent–action, agent–object, action–object, object–

TABLE 12.1 Two-Word Utterances	
more bottle	Mommy read
wanna grapes	bye Daddy
Mommy chin	read book
hot fire	door closed
nice Russ	wanna it
good food	door closed

location, object–attribute, possessor–object, negation–object, and negation–event (Brown, 1973). The order in which children place these words usually corresponds to one of the orders that would be correct in adult speech in the children's linguistic community.

Even when children leave the two-word stage and speak in sentences ranging from three to eight words, their speech retains a peculiar quality that is sometimes referred to as *telegraphic,* as illustrated in **Table 12.2**. The children speak somewhat as people used to write in telegrams (and somewhat like people currently do when text messaging), omitting such "unimportant" function words as *the* and *is.* In fact, it is rare to find in early-childhood speech any utterance that an adult speaker would consider a completely well-formed sentence. Yet, out of this beginning, fully grammatical sentences eventually appear. One might expect that children would first produce some kinds of sentences

TABLE 12.2 Multiword Utterances	
No more apple juice	No Mommy walk
Daddy go up	Daddy eat big cracker
Sarah read book	Rogers eat orange
Ernie go by car	Please Mommy read book

perfectly, then other kinds of sentences, and so on. However, it seems that children start out producing all kinds of sentences and all of them imperfectly. Their language development is characterized not by producing more kinds of sentences but by producing sentences that are gradually better approximations of adult sentences.

Children's early speech is incomplete in various ways in addition to missing words. A classic example concerns the rules for pluralization in English. Initially, children do not distinguish in their speech between singular and plural, using a singular form for both. Then they learn the "add -*s*" rule for pluralization but overextend it to words with irregular plurals, producing forms such as *foots* or even *feets*. Gradually, they learn the pluralization rules for irregular words, learning that continues into adulthood (e.g., adults studying cognitive science typically have to learn that an alternative plural of *schema* is *schemata*—a fact that I spared the reader from having to deal with when I used the form *schemas* in Chapter 5).

Children also have particular difficulties with transformations in which terms are placed outside the parts of the phrase structure where they naturally belong (see the earlier discussions of phrase structure and transformations in this chapter). So, for instance, there is a point at which children form questions without the auxiliary verb *do,* which would occur outside the verb phrase:

- Daddy go work? (Instead of "*Did* daddy . . . ?")
- Doggie have ball? (Instead of "*Does* doggie . . . ?)

Even later, when children's spontaneous speech seems to be well formed, they will display errors in comprehension that reveal that they have not yet acquired all the subtleties in their language. For instance, Chomsky (1970) found that children had difficulty comprehending sentences such as *John promised Bill to leave,* interpreting *Bill* as the one who leaves. The verb *promise* is unusual in this respect—for instance, compare *John told Bill to leave,* which children will properly interpret.

By the time children are 6 years old, they have mastered most of their language, although they continue to pick up details at least until the age of 10. In that time, they have acquired thousands of rules covering special cases (e.g., irregular verb forms and irregular plurals) and tens of thousands of words. Studies of the rate of word acquisition by children have produced an estimate of more than five words a day (Carey, 1978; Clark, 1983). Mastery of a natural language requires the acquisition of more knowledge than does mastery in any of the domains of expertise considered in Chapter 9. Of course, children also put an enormous amount of time into the language-acquisition process— at least 10,000 hours must have been spent speaking and listening to speech before a child is 6 years old (each year spent in a linguistic community adds about 2000 hours of speaking and listening).

> *Children gradually approximate adult speech by producing ever larger and more complex constructions.*

The Issue of Rules and the Case of Past Tense

A controversy in the study of language acquisition concerns whether children are learning what might be considered rules such as those that are part of linguistic theory. For instance, when a child learning English begins to inflect a verb such as *kick* with the *-ed* ending to indicate past tense, is the child learning a past-tense rule or just learning to associate *kick* and *-ed*? A young child certainly cannot explicitly articulate the "add *-ed*" rule, but this inability may just mean that this knowledge is implicit, not explicit. An interesting observation in this regard is that children will generalize the inflection to a new verb, indicating that they have indeed acquired a rule. For example, if they are told that the made-up verb *wug* means "dance," they will spontaneously generate the past-tense form *wugged* (i.e., *wug* + *-ed*) to mean "danced."

Other evidence on this issue concerns how children learn to deal with verbs with an irregular past-tense form—for instance, the past tense of *run* is *ran* (not *runned*). Children acquire irregular past-tense forms similarly to the way they acquire irregular plurals, as described above. First, children will use the irregular correctly, generating *ran*; then they will overgeneralize the past-tense rule and generate *runned*; finally, they will get it right for good and return to *ran*. The existence of this intermediate stage of overgeneralization has been used to argue that children do acquire rules, based on the claim that the child could not have learned from direct experience to associate the *-ed* ending with *run*. Rather, the argument goes, the child must be overgeneralizing a rule that has been learned.

This argument was challenged by Rumelhart and McClelland (1986), who simulated a neural network that learned to produce the past-tense forms of verbs after being trained with a set of 420 pairs of root forms and their past-tense forms. The system learned to associate features of input root forms with features of output past-tense forms. Thus, it might learn that words beginning with *ru* are associated with the same words plus the ending *-ed* (e.g., *rush* is associated with *rushed,* and *rub* is associated with *rubbed*), thus leading to the *runned* overgeneralization. Of course, such neural models are much more complex than this example suggests, but the crucial point is that the model mirrored the standard developmental sequence of children, first generating correct irregular forms, then overgeneralizing, and finally getting it right. With enough practice, the model, in effect, memorized the past-tense forms and stopped overgeneralizing. Rumelhart and McClelland concluded:

> We have, we believe, provided a distinct alternative to the view
> that children learn the rules of English past-tense formation in
> any explicit sense. We have shown that a reasonable account of the
> acquisition of past tense can be provided without recourse to the
> notion of a "rule" as anything more than a description of the lan-
> guage. We have shown that, for this case, there is no induction prob-
> lem. The child need not figure out what the rules are, nor even that
> there are rules. (p. 267)

Their claims drew a major response from Pinker and Prince (1988), who pointed out that the ability to produce the initial stage of correct irregulars depended on Rumelhart and McClelland's using a disproportionately large number of irregulars at first—more so than the child experiences. Pinker and Prince also criticized the model on a number of other grounds, including the fact that it sometimes produced forms that children never produce—for instance, it produced *membled* as the past tense of *mail*.

Another of their criticisms had to do with whether it is even possible to really learn English past-tense forms by associating root forms with past-tense forms, given that the way a verb is inflected for past tense depends not just on its root form but also on its meaning. For instance, the word *ring* has two meanings as a verb—to make a sound or to encircle. The root forms of these two verbs are identical, but the past tense of the first is *rang* (as in *He rang the bell*), whereas the past tense of the latter is *ringed* (as in *They ringed the fort with soldiers*).

It is unclear how fundamental these criticisms are, and there have been a number of more adequate attempts to come up with such associative models (e.g., Daugherty, MacDonald, Petersen, & Seidenberg, 1993; MacWhinney & Leinbach, 1991), which have also been critiqued (Marcus et al., 1995).

Marslen-Wilson and Tyler (1998) argued that the debate between rule-based and associative accounts will not be settled by focusing only on language acquisition by children. They suggest that more decisive evidence will come from examining the properties of the neural system that implements adult processing of past-tense forms. They cite two sorts of evidence, which seem to converge in their implications about the nature of this processing. First, they cite evidence that some patients with aphasia have deficient processing of regular past-tense forms, whereas others have deficient processing of irregular past-tense forms. The patients with deficient processing of regular forms have severe damage to Broca's area, which is generally associated with syntactic processing. In contrast, the patients with deficient processing of irregular forms have damage to their temporal lobe, which is generally associated with associative learning. Second, they cite the PET-imaging data of Jaeger et al. (1996), who studied the processing of past-tense forms by unimpaired adults. Jaeger et al. found activation in the region of Broca's area only during the processing of regular forms and found temporal activation during the processing of irregular forms. On the basis of these results, Marslen-Wilson and Tyler suggested that regular past-tense forms are processed in a rule-based manner, whereas the irregular forms are processed in an associative manner.

> *Irregular past tenses are produced associatively, and there is debate about whether regular past tenses are produced associatively or by rules.*

The Quality of Input

An important difference between a child's first-language acquisition and the acquisition of many other skills (including typical second-language acquisition) is that the child receives little if any instruction in acquiring a first language. Thus, the child's task is to induce the structure of the language by listening to adults and other children. In addition to not receiving direct instruction, children are rarely told about their syntactic errors. Many parents do not correct their children's speech at all, and those who do correct their children's speech appear to do so without any effect, as illustrated by the following well-known interaction recorded between a parent and a child (McNeill, 1966):

> Child: *Nobody don't like me.*
> Mother: *No, say, "Nobody likes me."*
> Child: *Nobody don't like me.*
> Mother: *No, say, "Nobody likes me."*
> Child: *Nobody don't like me.*

[dialogue repeated eight times]

> Mother: *Now listen carefully; say, "Nobody likes me."*
> Child: *Oh! Nobody don't likeS me.*

The lack of direct instruction and the ineffectiveness of whatever direct instruction children do get raise a puzzling question: Why do children eventually abandon their incorrect ways of speaking and adopt the correct forms? This question is even more puzzling when we consider that the child's inductive task would be very difficult under the best of conditions, and children often do not operate under the best of conditions. For instance, children hear ungrammatical sentences mixed in with the grammatical. How are they to avoid being misled by these?

Some parents and caregivers are careful to make their utterances to children simple and clear, using short sentences with exaggerated intonation, in a kind of speech called *motherese* (Snow & Ferguson, 1977). However, not all children receive the benefit of such speech, and yet all children learn their native language. Some parents speak to their children in adult sentences only, yet the children learn (Schieffelin, 1979); other parents hardly speak to their children at all, and still the children learn (Heath, 1983). Even among more typical parents, there is no correlation between the degree to which motherese is used and the rate of linguistic development (Gleitman, Newport, & Gleitman, 1984). So the quality of the input cannot be that critical.

Another curious fact is that children appear to be capable of learning a language in the absence of any input. Goldin-Meadow (2003) summarized research on the deaf children of speaking parents who chose to teach their children by the oral method (i.e., by trying to teach their deaf children to speak). It is very difficult for deaf children to learn to speak but quite easy for them to learn a sign language. Their parents were not teaching them a sign language, but they proceeded to invent their own sign language to communicate with their parents. Such invented sign languages have the structure of normal spoken languages. Moreover, in the process of invention, the children seem to go through the same periods as children who are learning the spoken language of their community. That is, they start out with single manual gestures, then progress to a two-gesture period, and continue through the stages of evolving a complete language more or less at the same points in time as their hearing peers. Thus, children seem to be born with a propensity to communicate using language and will learn a language no matter what.

The very fact that young children learn a language so successfully in almost all circumstances has been used to argue that the way that we learn language must be different from the way that we learn other cognitive skills. Also pointed out is the fact that children learn their first language successfully during a period in development when their general intellectual abilities are still very limited.

> *Children master language at a very young age and with little direct instruction.*

Is There a Critical Period for Language Acquisition?

A related argument has to do with the claim that young children appear to acquire a second language much faster than older children or adults do. It is claimed that there is a **critical period** (usually said to be from about 2 to 12 years of age) when it is easiest to learn a language. For a long time, the claim that children learn second languages more readily than adults was based on informal observations of children and adults in new linguistic communities— for example, when families move to another country to reside there permanently. Young children are said to acquire a facility in the new language more quickly than their older siblings or their parents. However, it is difficult to know whether this difference relates to age differences or to differences between the adults, the older children, and the younger children in amount of linguistic exposure, type of exposure (e.g., whether the stock market, history, or video games are being discussed), and willingness to try to learn (McLaughlin, 1978; Nida, 1971). In careful studies of situations that controlled for these factors, the results showed an opposite effect of age—that is, older children (older than 12 years) learned faster than younger children (Ervin-Tripp, 1974).

Nevertheless, even if older children and adults learn a new language more rapidly than younger children initially, they seem not to acquire the same level of final mastery of the fine points of the language, such as the phonology and morphology[8] (Lieberman, 1984; Newport, 1986). For instance, the ability to speak a second language without an accent severely declines with the age at which the language was learned (Oyama, 1978). Mastery of the syntax of a second language also seems to decline with age of learning. In one study, Johnson and Newport (1989) looked at the degree of proficiency in speaking English achieved by Koreans and Chinese as a function of the age at which they arrived in America (all had been in the United States for about 10 years). In general, it seems that the later they came to America, the poorer their performance was on a variety of measures of syntactic facility. Thus, although it is not true that second-language learning is fastest for the youngest, it does seem that the greatest eventual mastery of the fine points of language is achieved by those who start very young.

---

[8] Morphology concerns the structure of words and parts of words, such as roots, prefixes, and suffixes—e.g., the structure of the word *unreliably* is *un-* (a prefix) + *rely* (a root) + *-able* (a suffix) + *-ly* (a suffix).

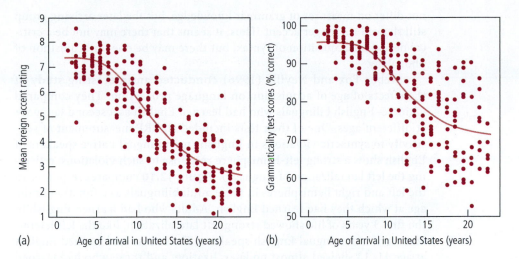

(a)   Age of arrival in United States (years)

(b)   Age of arrival in United States (years)

Figure 12.8 Second-Language Learning and Age of Learning. Participants were 240 native Koreans who had immigrated to the United States at various ages. (a) Participants' foreign accents were rated by native speakers of English (lower scores mean stronger accents). (b) Participants' knowledge of English grammar was assessed by having them judge whether each of 144 test sentences was grammatical. *(Data from Flege et al., 1999.)*

A study by Flege, Yeni-Komshian, and Liu (1999) looked at the English language performance of 240 Korean immigrants in relation to their age of arrival in the United States. **Figure 12.8** shows a steady decrease in performance with age of arrival on measures of both foreign accent (Figure 12.8a) and knowledge of grammar (Figure 12.8b). The best-fitting curves for these data give some suggestion of a more rapid drop in both measures around the age of 10—which would be consistent with the hypothesis of a critical period in language acquisition. However, age of arrival turns out to be confounded with many other things, including the crucial factor of the relative use of Korean versus English. Based on questionnaire data, Flege et al. rated these participants with respect to the relative frequency with which they used English versus Korean. **Figure 12.9** shows a steady decrease in the ratio of English use to Korean use from a ratio of about 2.1 for the earliest-arriving participants (i.e., using English about twice as much as using Korean) to a ratio of about 1.4 at age 10 or 11, at which point the ratio drops to approximately equal use of the two languages. Perhaps the decrease in English performance with age of arrival reflects this difference in amount of use. To address this question, Flege et al. created two matched groups of participants (subsets of the original 240) who reported equal use of English, with one group averaging 9.7 years old when they arrived in the United States and the other group averaging 16.2 years old. The two groups did

Figure 12.9 Relative Use of English Versus Korean as a Function of Age of Arrival in the United States. The earlier the age of arrival, the greater the use of English versus Korean, with a steeper drop in English use at around age 10 or 11. *(Data from Flege et al., 1999.)*

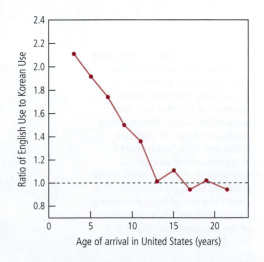

Age of arrival in United States (years)

not differ on measures of grammar knowledge, but the later arriving group still showed a stronger accent. Thus, it seems that there may not be a critical period for acquisition of syntax, but there may be one for acquisition of phonology.

Weber-Fox and Neville (1996) conducted an interesting study of the effects of age of acquisition on language processing. They compared Chinese–English bilinguals who had learned English as a second language at different ages. One of their tests included an ERP measurement of sensitivity to syntactic violations in English (monolingual native speakers of English show a strong left-hemisphere response to such violations, reflecting the left lateralization of language). **Figure 12.10** compares responses in the left and right hemispheres in these adult bilinguals as a function of the age at which they had learned English. Adults who had learned English in the first 3 years of life showed strong left lateralization, like the left lateralization of monolingual English speakers. Those who had learned English at age 11–13 showed almost no lateralization, and those who had learned English at an intermediate age showed an intermediate amount of lateralization. Interestingly, Weber-Fox and Neville found no such evidence for a critical period with respect to lexical violations (i.e., incorrect use of words) or semantic violations (i.e., violations in the domain of meaning). Learning

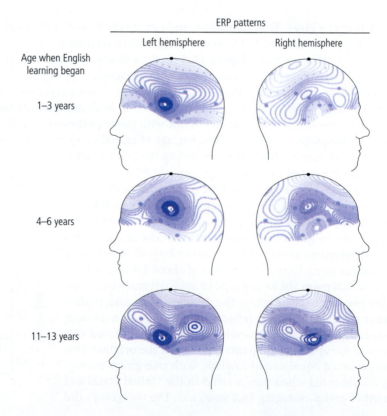

Figure 12.10 Age of Language Learning and Lateralization of Response to Syntactic Violations. Bilingual native speakers of Chinese who had learned English at different ages produced these ERP patterns in left and right hemispheres in response to grammatical anomalies in English (darker color indicates stronger response). The earlier the age of English learning, the greater the left lateralization of the response. *(Data from Weber-Fox & Neville, 1996.)*

English as late as 16 years of age had almost no effect on the lateralization of their responses to semantic violations. Thus, grammar seems to be more sensitive to a critical period. (See **Implications 12.2** for a discussion of how bilingualism is defined and whether bilinguals show a cognitive advantage over monolinguals.)

Implications 12.2

Does Bilingualism Confer a Cognitive Advantage?

A bilingual is someone who actively uses two languages. A common type of bilingual is someone who immigrates into a foreign country and then uses her or his first-acquired language (referred to as *L1*) at home and a second language (the language of the new country, referred to as *L2*) outside the home. This is the most common type in the United States. but not in places such as the Netherlands (where L1 is Dutch) and Wales (where L1 is Welsh), where English (L2) pervades all aspects of the bilingual's life. Some bilinguals process one language better than the other, but by definition **bilingualism** requires substantial fluency in both languages, although there is debate about just how much fluency is required to qualify a person as bilingual. About 20% of the U.S. population is bilingual (Bialystok, Craik, & Luk, 2012), while more than half of the world's total population is believed to be bilingual (Grosjean, 2010).

There is evidence that both languages are always active and influence one another in bilinguals (Kroll, Dussias, Bice, & Perrotti, 2015). For instance, in measures of word reading, the processing of terms that are cognates in the two languages is facilitated (e.g., processing of the word *film*—meaning "movie"—which is used in both Dutch and English, would be facilitated). In contrast, interference inhibits the processing of homographs when reading and when recognizing spoken words (e.g., Lagrou, Hartsuiker, & Duyck, 2011); homographs are words with similar or identical spelling but different meanings (e.g., in Spanish, *carpeta* means "folder," whereas the English *carpet* means "rug"). These facilitation and interference effects are seen in both directions—L1 on L2 and vice versa (Kroll et al., 2015). While there may be facilitation in special cases like cognates, interference is more common, and the general pattern is for bilinguals to be worse on measures such as vocabulary size for both languages, which is not surprising since they must divide their learning time between the two languages.

Early in the twentieth century, the general opinion was that bilingualism was harmful to a child's intellectual development (Antoniou, 2019). For instance D. J. Saer, a headmaster in Wales, wrote, "mental confusion is seen to exist in bilingual children to a higher degree than in monoglot children" (1923, p. 38). However, since the seminal work of Peal and Lambert (1962) on bilingualism in Montreal, there has been a great deal of research on the cognitive effects of being bilingual that rejects these conclusions. By the end of the century, the dominant view was that bilingualism conferred a cognitive advantage: Given that both languages are simultaneously active, a bilingual has to be constantly resolving which language to use. It has been agued that this will generalize to other areas of cognition in other domains of life. Bialystok, Craik, Green, and Gollan (2009) review research showing that bilingual children perform better on general and nonverbal intelligence tests despite being generally slower at processing language in either L1 or L2. Bialystok et al. (2009) also report that bilingual adults suffer less interference in tasks that require cognitive control, such as the Stroop task (see Figures 3.26 and 3.27). There is also evidence that bilinguals are protected against dementia as they age. For instance, in one study, bilingual older adults with probable Alzheimer's disease (as indicated by a CT scan) showed slower progression of their disease than did monolingual adults (Schweizer, Ware, Fischer, Craik, & Bialystok, 2012).

Unfortunately for the purpose of coming to a firm conclusion that bilingualism is associated with intellectual benefits, recent meta-analyses have suggested that the reported effects may reflect the existence of publication bias (Lehtonen et al., 2018). Publication bias refers to the tendency to publish studies that find effects of some factor and not publish studies that fail to find effects. Antoniou (2019) notes that since the issue of possible publication bias was raised, less new evidence has been reported for a bilingual advantage. There is still considerable debate and no consensus on whether bilingualism confers a general intellectual benefit. However, the opposite claim—that bilingualism is intellectually harmful—is no longer being made.

Most studies on the effect of age of acquisition have naturally concerned second languages. However, an interesting study of first-language acquisition was done by Newport and Supalla (1990). They looked at the acquisition of American Sign Language, one of the few languages that is sometimes acquired as a first language in adolescence or adulthood. Deaf children of speaking parents are sometimes not exposed to sign language until adolescence or later and consequently acquire no language in their early years. Deaf people who acquire sign language as adults achieve a poorer ultimate mastery of it than those who acquire it as children.

> *There are age-related differences in the success with which children can acquire a new language, with the strongest effects on phonology, intermediate effects on syntax, and weakest effects on semantics.*

Language Universals

Chomsky (1965) argued that special innate mechanisms must underlie the acquisition of language. Specifically, his claim was that the number of formal possibilities for a grammar of a language is so great that learning the language would be impossible unless children possessed some innate information about the possible grammars of natural human languages. This claim can be proved correct, but the formal proof is beyond the scope of this book. An argument by analogy might help. In Chomsky's view, the problem that children face is to discover the grammar of the language of their community on the basis of just the utterances they hear. The task can be compared to having a large number of torn-off pieces of a sock (the utterances heard by a child) and trying to find the matching sock (the language to be learned) in a huge pile of socks (the set of all possible languages). The child can look at various features of the sock fragments in hand (features of the utterances) to see whether any particular sock in the pile might be the matching one. If the pile of socks is big enough (the set of formally possible languages is huge) and if the socks in the pile have many features in common (as languages do), this task would be impossible. However, because language learning obviously occurs, we must, according to Chomsky, have special innate mechanisms that substantially restrict the range of possible grammars that children have to consider. In the sock analogy, it would be like knowing ahead of time which socks in the pile have patterns and colors that cannot possibly match the sock fragments in hand. In other words, children could not possibly learn their language if they had to consider the set of all possible languages, but they can perform that task if only a special subset of possible languages has to be considered.

Chomsky proposed that children can learn a natural language because they possess innate knowledge of certain **language universals** that limit the possible characteristics of a natural language. A language that violated these universals would simply be unlearnable, which means that there are hypothetical languages that no humans could learn.

As already noted, Chomsky's claim is correct—that is, there must be constraints on the possible grammars of a natural language. However, the critical issue is whether these constraints are due to any innate linguistic knowledge or whether they are due to general cognitive constraints on learning mechanisms. Chomsky argues that the constraints are language specific, and it is this argument that is open to serious question: Are the constraints on the form of natural languages universals of language or universals of cognition?

In his discussion of language universals, Chomsky is concerned with linguistic competence, a speaker's implicit knowledge of a language, as represented in an abstract, internalized grammar. That is, Chomsky is claiming that children possess innate constraints on their linguistic competence, constraints that determine which types of phrase structures, transformations, and other linguistic factors might be found in a natural language. Because of the abstract, unobservable character of these purported universals, Chomsky's claim cannot be evaluated simply by observing the details of how children acquire any particular language, because those observable details are matters of performance, not competence. Rather, the claim is evaluated by looking for properties that are true of all languages or processes that occur during the acquisition of all languages, with the idea that these universal properties and processes would be manifestations of the innate linguistic knowledge that Chomsky postulates.

Although languages can be quite different from one another, there are some clear uniformities or near uniformities. For instance, as we saw earlier, virtually no language favors the object-before-subject word order. However, as noted, this constraint appears to have a cognitive explanation (as do many other limits on language form).

Often, the uniformities among languages seem so natural that we do not realize that other possibilities might exist. One such language universal is that adjectives appear near the nouns that they modify. For example, in the English sentence *The brave woman hit the cruel man,* the adjective *brave* modifies the noun *woman,* and the adjective *cruel* modifies the noun *man,* and not vice versa. Similarly, in the equivalent French sentence, *La femme brave a frappé l'homme cruel* (where the adjectives happen to be spelled the same as in English), the adjective *brave* stands next to the noun *femme* (woman), and the adjective *cruel* stands next to the noun *homme* (man), and not vice versa (though the order of noun and adjective is opposite in the two languages). It would be logically possible to design a language in which an adjective near a subject noun modified an object noun and vice versa, but such a language would be absurd in regard to its cognitive demands, because it would require listeners to hold in mind the adjective from the beginning of the sentence until they heard the noun at the end. No natural language has this perverse structure.

There are universal constraints on the kinds of languages that humans can learn.

Constraints on Transformations

A set of peculiar constraints on transformations has been used to argue for the existence of linguistic universals. Compare sentence 1 with sentence 2:

1. Which woman did John meet who knows the senator?
2. Which senator did John meet the woman who knows?

Most native speakers of English would consider sentence 1 to be acceptable but not sentence 2. Sentence 1 can be derived by a transformation from sentence 3 by a transformation that moves *which woman* to the beginning of the sentence:

3. John met which woman who knows the senator?
4. John met the woman who knows which senator?

Analogously, sentence 2 could be derived from sentence 4 by a similar transformation operating on *which senator,* but apparently transformations are not allowed that move a noun phrase that is embedded within another noun phrase (in this case, the noun phrase *which senator* is embedded in the noun phrase *the woman who knows which senator*). However, this constraint does not apply to deeply embedded noun phrases in other types of structures. So, for instance, sentence 5 is acceptable although it is derived transformationally from sentence 6 by moving the deeply embedded noun phrase *which senator*:

5. Which senator does Mary believe that Bill said that John likes?
6. Mary believes that Bill said that John likes which senator?

Thus, the constraint on the transformation that forms *which* questions can apply to any embedded noun phrase unless that noun phrase is part of another noun phrase. The seemingly arbitrary nature of this constraint makes it hard to imagine how a child would ever figure it out—unless the child already knew it as a universal of language. Certainly, children are not explicitly told this fact about language.

The existence of such constraints on the form of natural languages offers a challenge to any theory of language acquisition. The constraints are so peculiar that it is hard to imagine how they could be learned unless a child was especially prepared to deal with them.

> *There are rather arbitrary constraints on the movements that transformations can produce.*

Parameter Setting

With all this discussion about language universals, one might get the impression that all languages are basically alike. Far from it. On many dimensions, the languages of the world are radically different. They might have some abstract properties in common, such as the transformational constraint discussed above, but there are many properties on which they differ. As already mentioned, different languages prefer different orders for subject, verb, and object. Languages also differ in how strict they are about word order. English is very strict, but some highly inflected languages, such as Finnish, allow people to say their sentences with almost any word order they choose. There are languages that do not mark verbs for tense and languages that mark verbs for the flexibility of the object being acted on.

Some languages, such as Italian and Spanish, but not English, are called *pro-drop languages*: a pronoun that would appear in subject position can optionally be omitted (dropped). For example, the English sentence *I am going to the cinema tonight* cannot optionally drop the pronoun *I* to yield *Am going to the cinema tonight*, but Italians can say either *Io vado al cinema stasera* or *Vado al cinema stasera* (dropping the pronoun *Io*), and Spaniards can say either *Yo voy al cine esta noche* or *Voy al cine esta noche* (dropping the pronoun *Yo*)—in both cases, just starting with the verb (*vado* or *voy*) and omitting the first-person pronoun. Given that pro-drop is a parameter on which natural languages vary, it has been argued that although children cannot be born knowing whether their language is pro-drop or not, they are born knowing that this is a dimension on which languages vary. Thus, knowledge that the pro-drop parameter exists is one of the purported universals of natural language.

Knowledge of a parameter such as pro-drop is useful because a number of features are associated with it. For instance, languages that are not pro-drop require what are called *expletive pronouns*. In English, a non–pro-drop language, the expletive pronouns are *it* and *there* when they are used in sentences such as *It is raining* and *There is no money*. English requires these rather meaningless pronouns because, by definition, a non–pro-drop language cannot have an empty slot in the subject position. Pro-drop languages such as Spanish and Italian often lack such pronouns—for example, the equivalent to the English *It is raining* is simply *piove* ("raining") in Italian and simply *llueve* ("raining") in Spanish.

Hyams (1986) argued that children starting to learn any language, including English, will begin by optionally dropping subject pronouns and not using expletive pronouns, even if the adult language differs in these respects. When children learning a non–pro-drop language start using expletive pronouns, they simultaneously stop optionally dropping subject pronouns. Hyams argued that this is the point at which they have learned that their language is not a pro-drop language.

Linguists have proposed that much of the variability among natural languages can be described in terms of different settings of 100 or so parameters, such as the pro-drop parameter, and that a major part of learning a language is learning the settings of these parameters (of course, there is a lot more to be learned than just these settings—e.g., the tens of thousands of words that constitute the vocabulary of the language). This **parameter setting** theory of language acquisition is quite controversial, but it provides us with one picture of what it might mean for a child to be prepared to learn a language with innate knowledge of language universals.

> *Learning a language has been proposed to include learning the setting of 100 or so parameters on which natural languages vary.*

Conclusions: The Uniqueness of Language: A Summary

Although it is clear that human language is very different from the communication systems of other species, the jury is still very much out on the issue of whether language is really a cognitive system different from other human cognitive systems. This question about the status of language is a major issue for cognitive psychology. The issue will be resolved by empirical and theoretical efforts more detailed than those reviewed in this chapter. The ideas here have served to define the context for those efforts.

Questions for Thought

1. A number of computer-based approaches to representing meaning are based on programs that read through large sets of documents and represent the meaning of any given word in terms of the other words that occur with it in the documents. One interesting feature of these efforts is that they make no attempt to include knowledge of the physical world or of what words refer to in the physical world. Perhaps the most well-known system is called *latent semantic analysis* (LSA) (Landauer, Foltz, & Laham, 1998). The developers of LSA describe the knowledge in their system as "analogous to a well-read nun's knowledge of sex, a level of knowledge often deemed a sufficient basis for advising the young" (p. 5). Based on this knowledge, LSA was able to pass the vocabulary test from the Educational Testing Service's Test of English as a Foreign Language. The test requires choosing the best of four alternatives for the meaning of a word, and LSA was able to do this by comparing its meaning representation of each test word (based on what documents the word appeared in) with its meaning representation of each alternative (again based on the same information). Why do you think such a program is so successful? How would you devise a vocabulary test to expose aspects of meaning that it does not represent?

2. Steven Pinker (1994) coined the phrase "language instinct" to describe the human propensity for acquiring language. In his view, this "language instinct" is wired into the human brain through evolution. Just as songbirds are born with the propensity to learn the song of their species, so we are born with the propensity to learn the language of our society. Just as humans might try to imitate the song of a bird and partly succeed, other species may partly succeed at mastering the language of humans. Is Kanzi's use of lexigrams like a human imitating birdsong or is it something more?

3. Some languages apparently assign grammatical genders arbitrarily to words that do not have inherent genders. For instance, the German word for *key* is masculine and the Spanish word for *key* is feminine. Boroditsky, Schmidt, and Phillips

(2003) report that when asked to describe a key, German speakers are more likely to use words like *hard* and *jagged*, whereas Spanish speakers are more likely to use words like *shiny* and *tiny*. What does evidence like this say about the relationship between language and thought?

4. When two linguistic communities come into frequent contact, such as in trade, they often develop simplified languages, called *pidgins*, for communicating. Pidgins are generally considered not full natural languages. However, if these linguistic communities start actually living together, the pidgins will evolve into full-fledged new languages called *creoles*. This can happen in one generation—that is, the parents who first made contact with the new linguistic community will continue to use the pidgin, whereas their children will speak the full-fledged creole. What does this say about the possible role of a critical period in language acquisition?

Key Terms

bilingualism	linguistic determinism	performance	semantics
competence	linguistic intuitions	phonology	syntax
critical period	modularity	phrase structure	transformations
grammar	natural languages	productivity	
language universals	parameter setting	regularity	

Language Comprehension

A favorite device in science fiction is the computer or robot that can understand and speak a language—whether malevolent like HAL in Stanley Kubrick's 1968 film *2001: A Space Odyssey* or beneficent like C-3PO in the *Star Wars* films. Kubrick was overly optimistic when he projected HAL for the year 2001, but the many speech interfaces that are in use now, 20 years later, suggest that he may not have been that far off. In the last 60 years, artificial intelligence (AI) has developed to the point that AI-based speech interfaces can simulate some but not all of what a child masters in a few years. An enormous amount of knowledge and intelligence underlies humans' successful use of language. (Implications 13.1 discusses the Turing test, which is used to evaluate the "humanness" of conversations with AI-based programs.)

This chapter will look at language use—in particular, at language comprehension (as distinct from language generation). This focus will enable us to look where the light is—more is known about language comprehension than about language generation. Language comprehension will be considered in regard to both listening and reading. The listening process is often thought to be the more basic of the two, but many of the same factors apply to both listening and reading. In studies of language comprehension, researchers' choice between written or spoken material is often determined by what is easier to do experimentally. More often than not, written material is used.

In our detailed analysis of the process of language comprehension, we will break it down into three stages. The first stage involves the perceptual processes that encode the spoken (acoustic) or written message. The second stage involves **parsing,** the process of creating a mental representation of the combined meaning of the words in a sentence. The third stage is called **utilization,** the stage in which the comprehender uses the mental representation of the sentence's meaning. For example, if the sentence is an assertion, a listener may simply store the meaning in memory; if it is a question, the listener might answer; if it is an instruction, the listener might follow it. However, listeners are not always so compliant. They may use an assertion about the weather to make an inference about the speaker's personality, they may answer a question with a question, or they may do just the opposite

Implications 13.1

Intelligent Chatterboxes

The ability to communicate successfully in a human language is a very important factor in our judgments about intelligence. In 1950, the British logician Alan Turing (who was instrumental in deciphering Nazi Germany's secret communication code during World War II) proposed a language-based test that could be used to decide whether a machine is intelligent. In this test (now known as the *Turing test*), a human judge engages in two free-flowing conversations via a chat system with two unseen respondents—one a human and the other a computer system. If, after conversing with both, the judge

Hugh Loebner

cannot determine which respondent was human and which was the computer, the computer would be declared intelligent. Turing predicted that by the year 2000 a computer would be able to pass this test.

In 1990, the Loebner Prize was created for the first computer that could pass the Turing test. Each year a contest is held in which various computer entries are judged.

A bronze medal is awarded yearly to the program that gives the most convincing responses, but so far no machine has been able to fool a majority of the judges, which would result in the award of a silver medal (the gold medal is reserved for a machine that can fool a majority of the judges and that also *looks* like a human!). The winner in 2008, a program called Elbot, fooled 3 of the 12 judges, including London *Times* reporter Will Pavia. The table below shows two small snippets of conversation that one of the judges had with a human respondent and with Elbot. Which snippet do you think involves the human and which involves Elbot?

Snippet A

Judge: What do you think of this year's Turner Prize shortlist?

Respondent: Difficult question. I will have to work on that and get back to you tomorrow.

Judge: You sound rather like Sarah Palin.

Respondent: Did this Palin ever write a telephone book?

Judge: I doubt it. Does anyone really write telephone books? I don't suppose you caught the football last night?

Respondent: What a shame. There are many talented authors who waste their energies on prose or run-of-the-mill poetry. But to write a telephone book is highest art!

Snippet B

Judge: What do you think of this year's Turner Prize shortlist?

Respondent: Good I think. Better than the years before i herad

Judge: Which was your favourite?

Respondent: It's my first time, so I can't compare

Judge: No, I mean of the entries this time around.

Respondent: Not really sure

of what the speaker instructs them to do. These three stages—perception, parsing, and utilization—are by necessity partly ordered in time; however, they also partly overlap. Listeners can make inferences about meaning on the basis of perceiving the first part of a sentence while they are perceiving a later part. This chapter will focus on the two higher-level processes—parsing and utilization. (For discussion of perceptual processes with regard to spoken language, see the section on speech recognition in Chapter 2.)

In this chapter, we will answer the following questions:

- How are individual words combined into the meaning of phrases and sentences?
- How is syntactic and semantic information combined in sentence interpretation?

- What inferences do comprehenders make as they hear or read a sentence?
- How are meanings of individual sentences combined in the processing of larger units of discourse?

Brain and Language Comprehension

Figure 12.1 highlighted the regions that are active when single sentences are being processed, both during production (generation) and during comprehension, in the parsing stage. However, during the utilization stage and in the processing of larger units of discourse, many other regions of the brain are active, as shown in **Figure 13.1**. Figures 12.1 and 13.1 taken together depict most of the brain areas and networks involved in language processing. Clearly, language comprehension involves much of the brain and many cognitive processes.

> *Comprehension consists of a perceptual stage, a parsing stage, and a utilization stage, in that order.*

Brain Structures

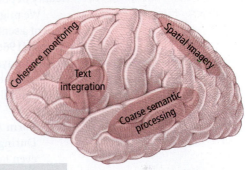

Figure 13.1 Discourse Processing Networks in the Brain. The language comprehension functions supported by these networks come into play during the parsing and utilization stages. *(Research from Mason & Just, 2006.)*

Parsing

As we will see, the first stage of language comprehension—parsing—involves processing of a number of different aspects of language, including syntactic–semantic interactions and various types of ambiguity. We will also review some of the neural correlates of this processing, and at the end of this section, we will return to the question of the modularity of language (first discussed in Chapter 12).

Constituent Structure

Language is structured according to a set of rules that tell us how to go from a particular string of words to the string's meaning. For instance, in English we know that if we hear a sequence of the form *A noun action a noun,* the speaker means that the thing referred to by the first noun performed the action on the thing referred to by the second noun. In contrast, if the sentence is of the form *A noun was action by a noun,* the speaker means that the thing referred to by the second noun performed the action on the thing referred to by the first noun. Thus, our knowledge of the structure of English allows us to grasp the difference in meaning between *A doctor shot a lawyer* and *A doctor was shot by a lawyer.*

In learning to comprehend a language, we acquire a great many rules that relate various linguistic structures (e.g., *A noun action a noun*) to meaningful interpretations. Although we cannot possibly learn rules for interpreting every possible sentence—sentences can be very long and complex (infinitely long, theoretically, as discussed in Chapter 12)—we have learned to interpret the various types of phrases in which sentences are structured and to combine, or concatenate, the interpretations of these phrases. These phrase units are also referred to as **constituents.** From the late 1950s to the early 1980s, a series of studies were performed that established the psychological reality of phrase structure in language processing. In Chapter 12 we reviewed some of the research documenting the importance of phrase structure in language generation. Here, we review some of the evidence for the psychological reality of phrase structure (or *constituent structure*) in comprehension.

We might expect that the more clearly identifiable the constituent structure of a sentence is, the more easily the sentence can be understood. Graf and Torrey (1966) presented sentences to participants a line at a time in either of the two ways shown below. In form A, each line corresponds to a whole constituent, whereas in form B, there is no such correspondence (each line breaks in the middle of a constituent).

Form A	Form B
During World War II	During World War
even fantastic schemes	II even fantastic
received consideration	schemes received
if they gave promise	consideration if they gave
of shortening the conflict.	promise of shortening the conflict.

Participants showed better comprehension of sentences in form A, demonstrating that the identification of constituent structure is important in the parsing stage.

As we saw in Chapter 12, when people say sentences, they naturally pause at boundaries between constituents. In a study of whether a corresponding pause occurs when comprehending sentences, Aaronson and Scarborough (1977) asked participants to read and remember sentences displayed word by word on a computer screen. Participants would press a key each time they wanted to read another word. **Figure 13.2** illustrates the pattern of reading times for a sentence that participants were reading for later recall. Notice the U-shaped patterns with prolonged pauses at the constituent boundaries. With

Figure 13.2 Word-by-Word Viewing Times for a Sample Sentence. Participants' task was to read and remember the sentence. Participants pressed a key to see the words in the sentence one at a time on a screen. They spent the most time looking at the boxed words, which mark the ends of two major constituents of the sentence. *(Data from Aaronson & Scarborough, 1977.)*

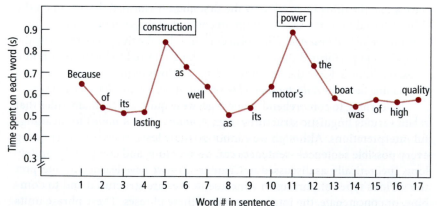

the completion of each major constituent, participants seemed to need time to process it.

After one has processed the words in a phrase in order to understand it, there usually is no need to keep those exact words in memory. Thus, we might predict that people would have poor memory for the exact wording of a constituent after it has been parsed and the parsing of another constituent has begun. The results of an experiment by Jarvella (1971) confirm this prediction. He read to participants passages with interruptions at various points. At each interruption, participants were instructed to write down as much of the passage as they could remember. Of interest were passages that ended with 13-word sentences such as the following:

1	2	3	4	5	6
Having	failed	to	disprove	the	charges,

7	8	9	10	11	12	13
Taylor	was	later	fired	by	the	president.

After hearing the last word of the sentence, participants were prompted with the first word of the sentence (e.g., *Having*) and asked to recall the rest of the sentence. **Figure 13.3** shows the percentage of words recalled correctly on average for each of the remaining 12 words, across all the test sentences. Note the sharp rise in the function at word 7, the beginning of the main clause. These data show that participants have the best memory for the last major constituent, a result consistent with the hypothesis that we retain a verbatim representation of the last constituent only.

An experiment by Caplan (1972) also provided evidence for the importance of constituent structure in language comprehension, using a reaction-time methodology. Participants first heard a sentence, then heard a probe word, and then had to indicate as quickly as possible whether the probe word had been in the sentence. Caplan contrasted pairs of sentences that ended in the same four words but that differed in constituent structure, such as the following (brackets enclose the two major constituents in each sentence):

1. [Now that artists are working fewer hours] [oil prints are rare].
2. [Now that artists are working in oil] [prints are rare].

In this example, the probe word was *oil,* which is the fourth word from the end in both sentences. Caplan was interested in comparing how quickly participants would recognize *oil* when probed with it after hearing each sentence. The sentences were cleverly constructed so that, in both sentences, the probe word was not only fourth from the end but was

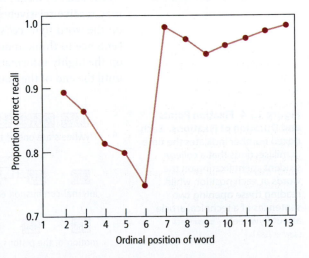

Figure 13.3 Word-by-Word Recall of 13-Word Sentences. Each sentence consisted of two major constituents, with the constituent break between word 6 and word 7. Participants were prompted to recall each sentence immediately after hearing it. The sharp rise after the constituent break in the percent correctly recalled shows that memory is best for the last constituent heard. *(Data from Jarvella, 1971.)*

also followed by the same three words. In addition, Caplan spliced the same snippet of audiotape into each presentation to ensure that participants heard identical recordings of these last four words, regardless of which full sentence they heard. Caplan correctly predicted that participants would recognize *oil* more quickly in sentence 1 because they would still have active in memory a representation of the constituent containing *oil*.

> *Participants process the meaning of a sentence one constituent at a time and maintain access to a constituent only while processing its meaning.*

Immediacy of Interpretation

An important principle that emerged in more recent studies of language processing is the principle of **immediacy of interpretation,** which asserts that people try to extract meaning out of each word as it arrives and do not wait until the end of a sentence or even the end of a phrase to decide how to interpret a word. For instance, Just and Carpenter (1980) studied the eye movements of participants as they read sentences. Typically, participants fixate on almost every word, where the amount of time spent fixating on any given word is strongly influenced by factors such as the frequency of the word and its predictability (Rayner, 2009). That is, participants spend more time on unfamiliar or surprising words. Participants also pause longer at the ends of constituents containing such words than at the ends of other constituents. **Figure 13.4** illustrates the eye fixations of one of their participants (a college student) reading a scientific passage. The boxed numbers indicate the fixation points and the duration of fixation at each point. The student's fixation points moved from left to right (starting with *Flywheels*) except at the phrase *engine contains,* where the student first fixated on a point in the middle of the phrase and then went back to *engine* before proceeding. Note that function words such as *the, a, to, of, into,* and *that* may be skipped or, if not skipped, may receive relatively little processing. Also note the amount of time spent on the word *flywheel(s).* The participant did not wait until the end of either sentence to think about this word. Again, look at the amount of time spent on the highly informative adjective *mechanical*—the participant did not wait until the end of the noun phrase to think about it.

Figure 13.4 Fixation Points and Duration of Fixations. Each boxed number indicates the time in milliseconds that a college student spent fixating on the words at each position while reading these opening two sentences of a technical article about flywheels. *(Data from Just & Carpenter, 1980.)*

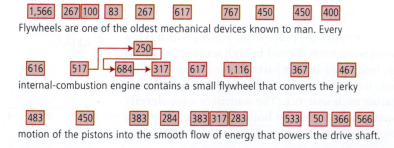

Eye movements have also been used to study the comprehension of spoken language. In one of these studies (Allopenna, Magnuson, & Tanenhaus, 1998), participants were shown computer displays of objects and geometric shapes, like the display in **Figure 13.5**. A participant would begin by fixating on the center cross and would then hear an instruction such as

Pick up the beaker.

followed by an instruction such as

Now put it below the diamond.

Participants would perform this action by selecting the object with a mouse and moving it, but the objective of the experiment was to study participants' eye movements preceding any action with the mouse. **Figure 13.6** shows the probabilities that participants fixate on various objects in the display as a function of the time since the beginning of the articulation of the word for the object to be picked up (e.g., *beaker*). It can be seen that participants are beginning to look to the two objects that start with the same sound ("beaker" and "beetle") even before the articulation of the word finishes. It takes about 400 ms to say the word, and almost immediately after the word finishes, participants' fixations on the wrong object ("beetle") decrease, and their fixations on the correct object ("beaker") shoot up. Given that it takes about 200 ms to program an eye movement, this study provides evidence that participants are processing the meaning of a word even before it completes.

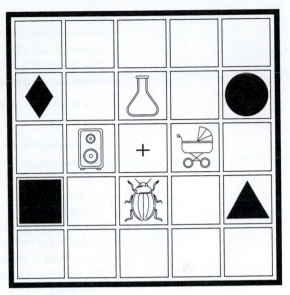

Figure 13.5 A Display Like Those Used to Study Eye Movements While Processing Spoken Instructions. When hearing an instruction such as *Pick up the beaker* (by clicking on the beaker in the display), participants were about equally likely to start shifting their gaze to the beaker or the beetle in the display, as soon as they heard the initial "bee" sound, which is the same in the two words. *(Research from Allopenna et al, 1998.)*

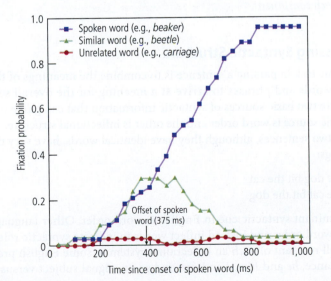

Figure 13.6 Probability of Fixating on Different Items in a Display While Processing Spoken Instructions. Soon after the participant hears *beaker* in an instruction such as *Pick up the beaker,* the probability of fixation on the beetle decreases, and the probability of fixation on the beaker increases. *(Data from Allopenna et al., 1998.)*

This immediacy of processing implies that we will begin to interpret a sentence even before we encounter the main verb. Sometimes we are aware of wondering what the verb will be as the sentence unfolds, particularly when hearing constructions in which the verb comes last. Consider what happens as we process the following sentence:

- It was the most expensive car that the CEO of the successful start-up bought.

Before we get to *bought,* we already have some idea of what might be happening between the CEO and the car. Sentences with the main verb at the end are more common in German than in English, but listeners in both of these languages do develop strong expectations about interpreting the sentence before seeing the verb (see Clifton & Duffy, 2001, for a review).

If people process a sentence as each word comes in, why is there so much evidence for the importance of constituent-structure boundaries? The evidence reflects the fact that the meaning of a sentence is defined in terms of the constituent structure, and, even if listeners try to extract all they can from each word, they will be able to put some things into place only when they reach the end of a constituent. Thus, people often need extra time at a constituent boundary to complete this processing. People have to maintain a representation of the current constituent in memory because their interpretation of it may be wrong, and they may have to reinterpret the beginning of the constituent. Just and Carpenter (1980), in their study of reading times, found that participants tend to spend extra time at the end of each constituent in wrapping up the meaning conveyed by that constituent.

> *In processing a sentence, we try to extract as much information as possible from each word and spend some additional wrap-up time at the end of each constituent.*

Processing Syntactic Structure

The basic task in parsing a sentence is to combine the meanings of the individual words and phrases to arrive at a meaning for the overall sentence. There are two basic sources of syntactic information that can guide us in this task. One source is word order and the other is inflectional structure. The following two sentences, although they have identical words, have very different meanings:

1. The dog bit the cat.
2. The cat bit the dog.

The dominant syntactic cue in English is word order. Other languages rely less on word order and instead inflect words to indicate syntactic role. There is a small remnant of such an inflectional system in some English pronouns. For instance, *he* and *him, I* and *me,* and so on, signal subject versus object.

McDonald (1984) compared English with German, which has a richer inflectional system. She asked her English participants to interpret sentences such as

3. Him kicked the girl.
4. The girl kicked he.

Word order in these sentences suggests one interpretation, whereas inflection suggests an alternative interpretation. English speakers use word order as a cue, interpreting sentence 3 with *him* as the subject and *the girl* as the object. German speakers, judging comparable sentences in German, do just the opposite. Bilingual speakers of both German and English tend to interpret the English sentences more like German sentences; that is, they assign *him* in sentence 3 to the object role and *the girl* to the subject role.

An interesting case of combining word order and inflection in English involves the use of relative pronouns in **center-embedded sentences,** in which one clause is embedded in another clause. Consider the following sentence:

5. The boy the girl liked was sick.

This sentence is a combination of two clauses—*The boy was sick* and *The girl liked the boy*—where the second clause is embedded in the first (and the repeated *the boy* is deleted). As we will see, there is evidence that people have difficulty with such structures, perhaps in part because the beginning of the sentence is ambiguous. For instance, the sentence could have concluded as follows:

6. The boy the girl and the dog were sick.

English can remove the ambiguity in sentence 5 with the relative pronoun *whom*, which indicates the role of the boy and the girl in the embedded clause:

7. The boy whom the girl liked was sick.

One might expect that it is easier to process center-embedded sentences if they have a relative pronoun to signal the embedding. Hakes and Foss (1970) and Hakes (1972) tested this prediction using double-embedded sentences such as

8. The zebra which the lion that the gorilla chased killed was running.
9. The zebra the lion the gorilla chased killed was running.

The only difference between sentences 8 and 9 is that sentence 8 contains the relative pronouns *which* and *that*. Participants listened to such sentences and were required to perform two tasks: to listen for a particular phoneme (in this case, a /g/, which occurs in *gorilla*) and to paraphrase the sentence after it was complete (which requires comprehending the sentence). Hakes and Foss predicted that the more difficult a sentence was to comprehend, the more time participants would take to detect the target phoneme, because they would have less attention left over from the comprehension task with which to perform the monitoring. This prediction was confirmed; participants did take longer to indicate hearing the target phoneme when presented with sentences such as sentence 9, which lacked relative pronouns.

Although the presence of relative pronouns facilitates the processing of such sentences, there is evidence that center-embedded sentences are quite difficult to process even with the relative pronouns. In one experiment, Caplan, Alpert, Waters, and Olivieri (2000) compared center-embedded sentences such as

10. The juice that the child enjoyed stained the rug.

with comparable sentences that are not center-embedded, such as

11. The child enjoyed the juice that stained the rug.

They used PET brain-imaging measures to detect processing differences and found greater activation in Broca's area with center-embedded sentences. Broca's area is usually more active when participants have to deal with more complex sentence structures (Martin, 2003).

> *People use the syntactic cues of word order and inflection to help interpret a sentence.*

Semantic Considerations

People use syntactic features, such as those discussed above, for understanding sentences, but they can also make use of the meanings of the words themselves. A person can determine the meaning of a string of words simply by considering how they could be put together so as to make sense. Thus, when Tarzan says, "Jane fruit eat," we know what he means even though this sentence is not syntactically correct English. We realize that a relation is being asserted between someone capable of eating and something edible.

Considerable evidence suggests that people use such semantic strategies in language comprehension. Strohner and Nelson (1974) had 2- and 3-year-old children use animal dolls to act out the following two sentences:

1. The cat chased the mouse.
2. The mouse chased the cat.

In both cases, the children interpreted the sentence to mean that the cat chased the mouse, a meaning that corresponded to their prior knowledge about cats and mice. Thus, these young children were relying more heavily on semantics than on syntax.

In a study looking at adult comprehension of such sentences, Ferreira (2003) found that while adults could correctly interpret such sentences in active form, they had difficulty with passive forms such as

3. The man was bit by the dog.
4. The dog was bit by the man.

When asked who did the action, adults were 99% accurate with active sentences like 1 and 2 above, but only 88% accurate with passive sentences like 3, and their accuracy dropped to a mere 74% for implausible passives like 4. That is to say, they said the dog did the action over 25% of the time.

So, when a semantic principle is placed in conflict with a syntactic principle, the semantic principle will sometimes (but not always) determine the interpretation of the sentence. If you have any doubt about the power of semantics to dominate syntax, consider the following sentence:

No head injury is too trivial to be ignored.

If you interpreted this sentence to mean that no head injury should be ignored, you are in the vast majority (Wason & Reich, 1979). However, a careful inspection of the syntax will indicate that the "correct" meaning is that all head injuries should be ignored—consider *No missile is too small to be banned*—which means all missiles should be banned.

> *Sometimes people rely on the plausible semantic interpretation of words in a sentence.*

The Integration of Syntax and Semantics

Listeners appear to combine both syntactic and semantic information in comprehending a sentence. Tyler and Marslen-Wilson (1977) asked participants to try to continue fragments such as

1. If you walk too near the runway, landing planes are
2. If you've been trained as a pilot, landing planes are

The phrase *landing planes,* by itself, is ambiguous. It can mean either "planes that are landing" or "to land planes." However, when followed by the plural verb *are,* the phrase must have the first meaning. Thus, the syntactic constraints determine a meaning for the ambiguous phrase. The prior context in fragment 1 (*If you walk too near the runway*) is consistent with this meaning, whereas the prior context in fragment 2 (*If you've been trained as a pilot*) is not. Participants took less time to continue fragment 1, which suggests that they were using both the semantics of the prior context and the syntax of the current phrase to disambiguate *landing planes.* When these factors are in conflict, the participant's comprehension is slowed.[1]

Bates, McNew, MacWhinney, Devescovi, and Smith (1982) used a different paradigm to look at how people combine syntax and semantics. They had participants interpret word strings such as

- Chased the dog the eraser

If you had to assign a meaning to this word string, what meaning would you assign? English syntax specifies that objects follow verbs, and this seems to imply that the dog was being chased, which would further imply that the

---

[1] The original Tyler and Marslen-Wilson experiment drew methodological criticisms from Townsend and Bever (1982) and Cowart (1983). For a response, see Marslen-Wilson and Tyler (1987).

eraser did the chasing. The semantics, however, suggest the opposite. In fact, English speakers tend to rely on the syntax and interpret the word string as *The eraser chased the dog,* but some rely on the semantics and interpret the string as *The dog chased the eraser.* In contrast, if the word string is

- Chased the eraser the dog

almost all English speakers agree that the interpretation is *The dog chased the eraser.*

Another interesting part of this study by Bates et al. compared Americans with Italians. When syntactic cues were put in conflict with semantic cues, Italians tended to go with the semantic cues, whereas Americans preferred the syntactic cues. The most critical case concerned sentences such as

- The eraser bites the dog.

or its Italian translation:

- La gomma morde il cane.

Americans almost always followed the syntax and interpreted this sentence to mean that the eraser is doing the biting. In contrast, Italians preferred to use the semantics and interpret it as the dog doing the biting. Like English, however, Italian has a subject-verb-object syntax.

Thus, we see that listeners combine both syntactic and semantic cues in interpreting the sentence. Moreover, the weighting of these two types of cues can vary from language to language. This evidence and other results indicate that speakers of Italian weight semantic cues more heavily than do speakers of English.

> *People integrate semantic and syntactic cues to arrive at an interpretation of a sentence.*

Neural Indicants of Syntactic and Semantic Processing

Researchers have found two indicants of sentence processing in event-related potentials (ERPs) recorded from the brain. The first effect, called the **N400,** is an indicant of difficulty in semantic processing. It was originally identified as a response to semantic anomalies, although it is more general than that. Kutas and Hillyard (1980) discovered the N400 in experiments in which participants heard semantically anomalous sentences such as *He spread the warm bread with socks.* About 400 ms after the anomalous word (*socks*), ERP recordings showed a large negative amplitude shift. The second effect, called the **P600,** occurs in response to syntactic anomalies. For instance, Osterhout and Holcomb (1992) presented their participants with sentences such as *The broker persuaded to sell the stock* and found a positive wave at about 600 ms after the syntactic anomaly occurred (the object of the verb *persuaded* is missing).

Of particular interest in this context is the relation between the N400 and the P600. Ainsworth-Darnell, Shulman, and Boland (1998) studied how these two effects combined by comparing ERP responses to sentences like the following:

> *Control (no anomaly):* Jill entrusted the recipe to friends before she suddenly disappeared.
> *Syntactic anomaly:* Jill entrusted the recipe friends before she suddenly disappeared.
> *Semantic anomaly:* Jill entrusted the recipe to platforms before she suddenly disappeared.
> *Double anomaly:* Jill entrusted the recipe platforms before she suddenly disappeared.

Figure 13.7 contrasts the ERP waveforms obtained from midline and parietal sites in response to these various types of sentences. The critical words

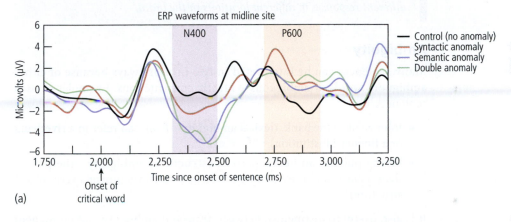

(a)

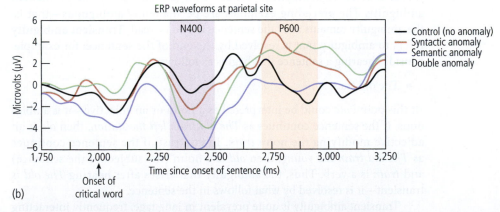

(b)

Figure 13.7 The N400 and P600 Effects in Response to Syntactic and Semantic Anomalies. (a) About 400 ms after the onset of the critical word, ERP waveforms at a midline site show the N400 effect, a negative shift in response to a syntactic anomaly, either alone (blue curve) or in combination with a semantic anomaly (green curve). (b) About 600 ms after the onset of the critical word, ERP waveforms at a parietal site show the P600 effect, a positive shift in response to a semantic anomaly, either alone (red curve) or in combination with a syntactic anomaly (green curve). *(Data from Ainsworth-Darnell et al., 1998.)*

in these sentences are *friends* (in the syntactic anomaly and double anomaly) and *platforms* (in the semantic anomaly and double anomaly). The two types of sentences containing a semantic anomaly evoked a negative shift (N400) at the midline site about 400 ms after the critical word (the blue and green curves in Figure 13.7a). In contrast, the two types of sentences containing a syntactic anomaly were associated with a positive shift (P600) at the parietal site about 600 ms after the onset of the critical word (the red and green curves in Figure 13.7b). Based on the fact that a different brain region responds to syntactic anomalies than to semantic anomalies, Ainsworth-Darnell et al. argued that these syntactic and semantic processes are separable in the overall process of language comprehension.

> *ERP recordings indicate that syntactic and semantic anomalies elicit different responses in different locations in the brain.*

Ambiguity

Many sentences can be interpreted in two or more ways because of either ambiguous words or ambiguous syntactic constructions. Examples of such sentences are

- John went to the bank. (lexical ambiguity—*bank* can refer to a riverbank or a financial institution)
- Flying planes can be dangerous. (structural ambiguity—the phrase *flying planes* can have either an adjective–noun structure or a verb–object structure)

It is also useful to distinguish between transient ambiguity and permanent ambiguity. The preceding examples are permanently ambiguous—that is, the ambiguity remains after the sentence is said or read. **Transient ambiguity** refers to ambiguity that is resolved by the end of the sentence; for example, consider hearing a sentence that begins as follows:

- The old train . . .

At this point, *old* could be interpreted as a noun or an adjective—it is ambiguous. If the sentence continues as *The old train left the station,* then *old* is an adjective modifying the noun *train*. In contrast, if the sentence continues as *The old train the young,* then *old* is a noun (the subject of the sentence) and *train* is a verb. Thus, the ambiguity that arises after hearing *The old* is transient—it is resolved by what follows in the sentence.

Transient ambiguity is quite prevalent in language, frequently interacting with the principle of immediacy of interpretation described earlier. Immediacy of interpretation implies that we commit to an interpretation of a word or a phrase right away, but transient ambiguity implies that we cannot always know the correct interpretation immediately. Consider the following sentence:

- The horse raced past the barn fell.

Most people do a double take on this sentence: they give it one interpretation up to the last word, and then, after hearing or reading the last word, they struggle to give it a different interpretation. Such sentences are called **garden-path sentences** because we are "led down the garden path" to an interpretation, only to discover later that it is wrong. For instance, in the preceding sentence, most readers interpret *raced* as the main verb of the sentence until they hear *fell,* at which point they have to reinterpret *raced* as a verb in a passive construction in a relative clause (i.e., *The horse that was raced past the barn fell*). Garden-path sentences are considered to be important evidence for the principle of immediacy of interpretation—that is, listeners could postpone interpreting such sentences until the ambiguity is resolved, but they do not.

At a point of syntactic ambiguity in a sentence, what determines its interpretation? A powerful factor is the **principle of minimal attachment,** which holds that people prefer an interpretation that gives the sentence a minimally complex constituent structure. Because all sentences must have a main verb, the simple interpretation would be for *raced* to be the main verb in the sentence, rather than modifying the noun *horse.* Many times we are not aware of transient ambiguities in sentences. For instance, consider the following sentence:

- The woman painted by the artist fell.

As we will see, there is evidence that people temporarily interpret *woman painted* as subject–verb, just like *horse raced* in the sentence discussed above. However, people tend not to be aware of being led down the garden path with this sentence as they are with the *horse raced* sentence.

> *When people come to a point of ambiguity in a sentence, they adopt one interpretation, which they will have to retract if it is later contradicted.*

Neural Indicants of the Processing of Transient Ambiguity

Brain-imaging studies reveal a good deal about how people process ambiguous sentences. In one study, Mason, Just, Keller, and Carpenter (2003) compared three kinds of sentences, such as these:

Unambiguous: The experienced soldiers spoke about the dangers of the midnight raid.
Ambiguous preferred: The experienced soldiers warned about the dangers before the midnight raid.
Ambiguous unpreferred: The experienced soldiers warned about the dangers conducted the midnight raid.

The verb *spoke* in the first sentence is unambiguous, but the verb *warned* in the last two sentences has a transient ambiguity of just the sort described in the preceding subsection: It is not until later in the sentence that one can know whether the soldiers are doing the warning or are being warned. As noted, participants prefer the first interpretation. Mason et al. collected fMRI measures of activation in

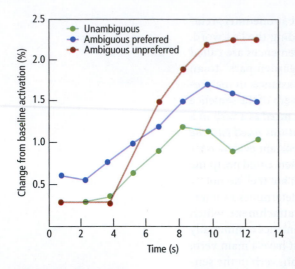

Figure 13.8 Transient Ambiguity and Activation in Broca's Area. Activation is least for sentences without any ambiguity. For sentences with transient ambiguity, activation is greater for sentences with an unpreferred constituent structure than for sentences with a preferred structure. *(Data from Mason et al., 2003.)*

Broca's area as a function of time since sentence onset (see **Figure 13.8**). The sentences lasted approximately 6 to 7 seconds, and as is typical of fMRI measures, the differences among conditions show up only after the processing of the sentence is complete, corresponding to the lag in the hemodynamic response. As can be seen, the level of activation increases with the difficulty of processing and is greatest for the ambiguous unpreferred sentence.

Measures obtained using fMRI, such as those in Figure 13.8, can localize areas in the brain where processing is taking place, in this case confirming the critical role of Broca's area in processing sentence structure. However, fMRI measures do not reflect the fine-grained temporal structure of the processing. An ERP study by Frisch, Schlesewsky, Saddy, and Alpermann (2002) investigated the temporal aspect of how people deal with ambiguity. Their study was with German speakers and took advantage of the fact that some German nouns are ambiguous in their role assignment. They looked at German sentences that begin with either of two different nouns and end with a verb. In the following examples, each German sentence is followed by a word-by-word translation and then the equivalent English sentence:

1. **Die**   **Frau**   **hatte**   **den**   **Mann**   **gesehen.**
   The   woman   had   the   man   seen
   The woman had seen the man.

2. **Die**   **Frau**   **hatte**   **der**   **Mann**   **gesehen.**
   The   woman   had   the   man   seen
   The man had seen the woman.

3. **Den**   **Mann**   **hatte**   **die**   **Frau**   **gesehen.**
   The   man   had   the   woman   seen
   The woman had seen the man.

4. **Der**   **Mann**   **hatte**   **die**   **Frau**   **gesehen.**
   The   man   had   the   woman   seen
   The man had seen the woman.

When participants read *Die Frau* at the beginning of sentences 1 and 2, they do not know whether *Frau* (*woman*) is the subject or the object in the sentence (the determiner *die* is ambiguous—it could signal subject or object). Only when they read *den Mann* in sentence 1 can they infer that *Mann* (*man*) is the object (because of the determiner *den*) and hence that woman must be the subject. Similarly, *der Mann* in sentence 2 indicates that *Mann* is the subject (because of the determiner *der*) and, therefore, that *Frau* must be the object. Sentences 3 and 4 do not have this transient ambiguity, because the determiners before *Mann* indicate its role.

Frisch et al. used the P600 (see Figure 13.7) to investigate the syntactic processing of these sentences. They found that the ambiguous first noun in sentences 1 and 2 was followed by a stronger P600 than was the unambiguous first noun in sentences 3 and 4. The contrast between sentences 1 and 2 also is interesting. Although German allows for either subject-object or object-subject ordering, the subject-object order in sentence 1 is preferred. For the unpreferred sentence 2, Frisch et al. found that the second noun was followed by a greater P600. Thus, when participants reach a transient ambiguity, as in sentences 1 and 2, they seem to have to work harder immediately to deal with the ambiguity. They commit to the preferred interpretation and have to do further work when they learn that it is not the correct interpretation, as in sentence 2.

> *Activity in Broca's area increases when participants encounter a transient ambiguity and when they have to change an initial interpretation of a sentence.*

Lexical Ambiguity

The preceding discussion was concerned with how participants deal with syntactic ambiguity. In lexical ambiguity, where a single word has two meanings, there is often no structural difference in the two interpretations of a sentence. A series of experiments beginning with Swinney (1979) helped to reveal how people determine the meaning of ambiguous words. Swinney asked participants to listen to sentences such as

- The man was not surprised when he found several spiders, roaches, and other bugs in the corner of the room.

Swinney was concerned with the ambiguous word *bugs* (meaning either insects or electronic listening devices). Just after hearing the word, participants would be presented with a string of letters on a screen, and their task was to judge whether that string made a word. Thus, if they saw *ant,* they would say yes; but if they saw *ont,* they would say no. This is the lexical-decision task described in Chapter 6 in relation to the study of spreading activation. Swinney was interested in how the word *bugs* in the passage would prime participants' judgments.

The critical contrasts involved the relative times to judge *spy, ant,* and *sew,* following the sentence with *bugs.* The word *ant* is related to the primed meaning of *bugs,* whereas *spy* is related to the unprimed meaning. The word *sew* defines a neutral control condition. Swinney found that recognition of either *spy* or *ant* was facilitated if that word was presented within 400 milliseconds of the prime, *bugs.* Thus, the presentation of *bugs* immediately activates both of its meanings and their associations. If Swinney waited more than 700 milliseconds however, only the related word *ant* was facilitated. It appears that a correct meaning is selected during this time and the other meaning becomes deactivated. Thus, the two meanings of an ambiguous word are momentarily active, but context operates very rapidly to deactivate the inappropriate meaning.

> *When an ambiguous word is presented, participants select a particular meaning within 700 milliseconds.*

Modularity Compared with Interactive Processing

We disambiguate ambiguous sentences by using semantic cues (as with *bugs* in the sentence discussed above) and by using syntactic cues (as with the garden-path sentences discussed above). Proponents of the modularity position (discussed in Chapter 12) argue that comprehension begins via a separate, language-specific module that operates with syntactic knowledge only, and not with the semantic knowledge about the world that belongs to general cognition. Thus, only syntax would initially be available for disambiguation. In contrast, proponents of a position known as **interactive processing** argue that syntax and semantics are combined at all levels of processing.

Much of the research aimed at resolving the debate between these two positions has looked at the processing of transient syntactic ambiguity. In a study that provoked a great deal of controversy and further research, Ferreira and Clifton (1986) asked participants to read sentences such as

1. The woman painted by the artist was very attractive to look at.
2. The woman that was painted by the artist was very attractive to look at.
3. The sign painted by the artist was very attractive to look at.
4. The sign that was painted by the artist was very attractive to look at.

Sentences 1 and 3 are called *reduced relatives* because the relative pronoun *that* and the verb *was* are missing. At the point where one reads the word *painted* in these sentences, there is no syntactic basis for deciding whether the noun–verb combinations *woman painted* and *sign painted* are part of an agent-action construction or part of a relative clause construction. Ferreira and Clifton argued that, because of the principle of minimal attachment, people have a natural tendency to interpret noun–verb combinations as agent-action constructions. Evidence for this tendency is that participants take longer to read *by the artist* in sentence 1 than in sentence 2, because correctly interpreting sentence 1 entails rejecting an initial agent-action interpretation, whereas the syntactic cue *that was* in sentence 2 makes an agent-action interpretation impossible.

The focus in the Ferreira and Clifton study is on sentences like 3 and 4. Semantic factors should rule out an agent-action interpretation of sentence 3, because a sign cannot be an animate agent and engage in painting. Nonetheless, participants took longer to read phrases like *by the artist* in sentences like sentence 3 than they took to read such phrases in sentences like sentence 1. For both kinds of sentences they were slower to read such phrases than in unambiguous sentences like 2 and 4. Thus, argued Ferreira and Clifton, participants first use only syntactic factors and so misinterpret *sign painted* as agent-action and then use the syntactic cue *by the artist* to correct that misinterpretation.

Experimental results of this sort would seem to support the modularity position, but Trueswell, Tanenhaus, and Garnsey (1994) argued that many of the sentences with reduced relatives in the Ferreira and Clifton study that were supposed to be unambiguous, like sentence 3, were not in fact unambiguous. Consider, for instance, the Ferreira and Clifton sentence

5. The car towed from the parking lot was parked illegally.

in which *car towed* was supposed to be unambiguous. However, it clearly is possible for *car* to be the subject of *towed,* as in

6. The car towed the smaller car from the parking lot.

When Trueswell et al. used sentences that avoided these problems, they found, for example, that participants did not have any more difficulty with sentence 7 than with sentence 8:

7. The evidence examined by the lawyer turned out to be unreliable.
8. The evidence that was examined by the lawyer turned out to be unreliable.

Thus, people do seem able to correctly interpret sentences with reduced relatives when it is not semantically possible to interpret the noun (e.g., *evidence*) as an agent of the verb (e.g., *examined*). This result provides evidence against the modularity position and support for interactive processing, by indicating that semantic factors affect initial syntactic decisions.

Additionally, McRae, Spivey-Knowlton, and Tanenhaus (1998) showed that the relative plausibility of the noun as agent of the verb affects the difficulty of processing noun–verb constructions. They compared the pair of sentences 9 and 10 with the pair 11 and 12:

9. The cop arrested by the detective was guilty of taking bribes.
10. The cop that was arrested by the detective was guilty of taking bribes.
11. The crook arrested by the detective was guilty of taking bribes.
12. The crook that was arrested by the detective was guilty of taking bribes.

They found that participants had much greater difficulty with the reduced relative in sentence 9, where the noun *cop* is plausible as the agent for arresting, than with the reduced relative in sentence 11, where the noun *crook* is not.

> *Participants appear to be able to make immediate use of semantic information to guide syntactic decisions.*

Utilization

After a sentence has been parsed and mapped into a representation of its meaning, what then? A listener seldom passively records the meaning. If the sentence is a question or an imperative, for example, the speaker will expect the listener to take some action in response. Even for declarative sentences, moreover, there is usually more to be done than simply registering the sentence. Fully understanding a sentence requires making inferences and connections. In Chapter 6, we considered the way in which such elaborative processing leads to better memory. Here, we will review some of the research on how people make such inferences.

Bridging Inferences and Elaborative Inferences

In understanding a sentence, the comprehender must make inferences that go beyond what is stated. Researchers typically distinguish between **bridging inferences** (also called *backward inferences*) and **elaborative inferences** (also called *forward inferences*). Bridging inferences reach back in the text or discourse to make connections with earlier parts. Elaborative inferences add new information to the interpretation of the text or discourse and often predict what will be coming up. Singer (1994) used pairs of sentences such as the following to bring out the differences between bridging and elaborative inferences:

1. *Direct statement:* The dentist pulled the tooth painlessly. The patient liked the method.
2. *Bridging inference:* The tooth was pulled painlessly. The dentist used a new method.
3. *Elaborative inference:* The tooth was pulled painlessly. The patient liked the new method.

No matter which sentence they had read, participants were then asked whether the sentence *A dentist pulled the tooth* was true. This is explicitly stated in pair 1, but it can also be inferred from pairs 2 and 3, even though it is not explicitly stated. In pair 2, the inference that the dentist pulled the tooth is required in order to connect *dentist* in the second sentence to the first sentence, and thus would be classified as a backward-reaching bridging inference. In pair 3, the inference that the dentist pulled the tooth is an elaborative inference because it adds new information (a dentist is not mentioned in either sentence). Participants in the direct-statement condition (pair 1) and those in the bridging-inference condition (pair 2) were equally fast to verify *A dentist pulled the tooth,* indicating that participants had made the bridging inference in the normal course of processing pair 2. However, participants in the elaborative-inference condition (pair 3) were about a quarter of a second slower to verify *A dentist pulled the tooth,* indicating that the processing of pair 3 had not included making the elaborative inference.

The problem with elaborative inferences is that there are no bounds on how many such inferences can be made. Consider the sentence *The tooth was pulled painlessly.* In addition to inferring who pulled the tooth, one could make inferences about what instrument was used to make the extraction, why the tooth was pulled, why the procedure was painless, how the patient felt, what happened to the patient afterward, which tooth was pulled (e.g., incisor or molar), how easy the extraction was, and so on. Much research has been aimed at determining exactly which elaborative inferences are made (Graesser, Singer, & Trabasso, 1994). In the Singer (1994) study just described, the elaborative inference seems not to have been made. In contrast, an elaborative inference does seem to have been made by participants in a study by Long, Golding, and Graesser (1992). Participants read a story that included the following critical sentence:

- A dragon kidnapped the three daughters.

After reading this sentence, participants had to perform a lexical decision task about the word *eat* (i.e., they had to decide whether the string of letters *e-a-t* makes a word). Long et al. found that participants could make this lexical decision more rapidly after reading this sentence than in a neutral context. From this data, they argued that participants made the inference that the dragon's goal was to eat the daughters (which had not been directly stated or even suggested in the story). Long et al. argued that, when reading a story, we normally make inferences about a character's goals.

Bridging inferences are made automatically when reading a text, but elaborative inferences are optional. It takes effort to make elaborative inferences, and readers need to be sufficiently engaged in the text to make them. Making elaborative inferences also appears to depend on reading ability. For instance, Murray and Burke (2003) had participants read passages such as the following, plus a final sentence that varied under two conditions (experimental and control):

> Carol was fed up with her job waiting on tables. Customers were rude, the chef was impossibly demanding, and the manager had made a pass at her just that day. The last straw came when a rude man at one of her tables complained that the spaghetti she had just served was cold. As he became louder and nastier, she felt herself losing control.

The final sentence added under each of the two conditions was as follows:

> *Experimental:* Without thinking of the consequences, she picked up the plate of spaghetti and raised it above the customer's head.

> *Control:* To verify the complaint, she picked up the plate of spaghetti and raised it above the customer's head.

After reading the final sentence, participants were presented with the critical word *dump,* which is related to an elaborative inference that participants could make in the experimental condition but not in the control condition (participants simply had to read the word). Participants classified as having high reading ability read the word *dump* faster in the experimental condition than in the control condition, but low-reading-ability participants did not. These results indicate that high-reading-ability participants had made the elaborative inference that Carol was going to dump the spaghetti on the customer's head, whereas low-reading-ability participants had not.

> *In understanding a sentence, listeners make bridging inferences to connect the sentence to prior sentences but only sometimes make elaborative inferences that connect to possible future material.*

Inference of Reference

An important aspect of making a bridging inference consists of using various linguistic cues to recognize when an expression in a sentence refers to something that we should already know. In English, the difference between the definite article *the* and the indefinite article *a/an* is one such cue. *The* tends to cue comprehenders that they should know the reference of the noun following the article, whereas *a/an* tends to cue comprehenders that the noun following the article refers to something new. For example, compare the following sentences:

1. Last night I saw the moon.
2. Last night I saw a moon.

Sentence 1 indicates a rather uneventful fact—seeing the same old moon as always—but sentence 2 carries the clear implication of having seen some other moon. There is considerable evidence that comprehenders are quite sensitive to the different implications communicated by this small difference in the sentences. In one experiment, Haviland and Clark (1974) compared participants' comprehension time for pairs of sentences such as

3. Ed was given an alligator for his birthday. The alligator was his favorite present.
4. Ed wanted an alligator for his birthday. The alligator was his favorite present.

Both pairs have the same second sentence. In pair 3, the first sentence identifies a specific referent for the noun *alligator* (the one that Ed was given); thus, we would expect participants to have no difficulty recognizing that the definite article *the* in the second sentence refers to that alligator. In contrast, although *alligator* occurs in the first sentence of pair 4, a specific alligator is not identified. Therefore, we would expect participants to have difficulty with the second sentence in pair 4 but not in pair 3. In the Haviland and Clark experiment, participants saw pairs of such sentences one sentence at a time and pressed a button after comprehending each sentence. With sentence pairs such as pair 3, where the second sentence involves a correct use of the definite article, participants took an average of 1,031 milliseconds to comprehend the second sentence. In contrast, they took an average of 1,168 milliseconds to comprehend the second sentence in pairs such as pair 4, where the definite article carries an incorrect implication. Thus, comprehension took more than a tenth of a second longer when there was no identifiable referent for the noun following the definite article.

The results of an experiment done by Loftus and Zanni (1975) showed that the use of different articles could affect listeners' beliefs. Participants were shown a film of an automobile accident and were then asked a series of questions. Some participants were asked,

5. Did you see a broken headlight?

whereas other participants were asked,

6. Did you see the broken headlight?

In fact, there was no broken headlight in the film, but the definite article in question 6 implies the existence of a broken headlight. Participants were more likely to answer yes when asked question 6 than when asked question 5. As Loftus and Zanni noted, this finding has important implications for the interrogation of eyewitnesses.

> *Comprehenders take the definite article "the" to imply the existence of an identifiable referent for the noun following the article.*

Pronominal Reference

The interpretation of pronouns is another important aspect of processing reference. A pronoun such as *she, he,* or *they* might refer to any of a number of people who have already been mentioned. Just and Carpenter (1987) noted that there are a number of bases for resolving the reference of pronouns, including number and gender cues, syntactic cues, the recency effect, and knowledge of the world:

Number and gender cues. Consider this sentence:

- *Melvin, Susan, and their children left when (he, she, they) became sleepy.*

Each possible pronoun has a different referent.

Syntactic cues. Consider this sentence:

- *Floyd punched Bert and then he kicked him.*

A pronoun tends to refer to a noun that fills the same grammatical role as the pronoun; thus, most people would agree that the subject pronoun *he* refers to Floyd and the object pronoun *him* refers to Bert.

Recency effect. Consider this sentence:

- *Dorothea ate the pie; Ethel ate cake; later she had coffee.*

A pronoun tends to be taken as referring to the most recently mentioned candidate noun; thus, most people would agree that *she* probably refers to Ethel.

Knowledge of the world. Compare these sentences:

- *Tom shouted at Bill because he spilled the coffee.*
- *Tom shouted at Bill because he had a headache.*

Most people would agree that *he* in the first sentence refers to *Bill* because we tend to scold people who make mistakes, whereas *he* in the second sentence refers to *Tom* because people tend to be cranky when they have headaches.

In keeping with the immediacy-of-interpretation principle discussed earlier, people try to determine the referent of a pronoun immediately upon encountering the pronoun. For instance, in studies based on eye fixations while reading (Carpenter & Just, 1977; Ehrlich & Rayner, 1983; Just & Carpenter, 1987), researchers found that participants fixate longer on a pronoun when its reference is harder to determine. Ehrlich and Rayner (1983) also found that participants tend to fixate longer on the word following such a pronoun, suggesting they are still processing the reference of the pronoun while reading the next word.

Corbett and Chang (1983) used a priming paradigm to show that participants consider multiple candidates for a referent. They had participants read sentences such as

- Scott stole the basketball from Warren and he sank a jump shot.

After reading the sentence, participants saw a probe word and had to decide whether the word appeared in the sentence. Corbett and Chang found that the time to recognize either *Scott* or *Warren* decreased after reading the sentence. They also asked participants to read the following control sentence, which did not require the referent of a pronoun to be determined:

- Scott stole the basketball from Warren and Scott sank a jump shot.

In this case, only recognition of the more recently mentioned word, *Scott,* was facilitated. *Warren* was facilitated only in the first sentence because in that sentence, participants had to consider it as a possible referent of *he* before settling on *Scott* as the referent.

The results of both the Corbett and Chang study and the Ehrlich and Rayner study indicate that the processing involved in determining pronoun reference lasts beyond the reading of the pronoun itself. This finding indicates that processing is not always as immediate as the immediacy-of-interpretation principle might seem to imply. The processing of pronominal reference spills over into later fixations (Ehrlich & Rayner, 1983), and there is still priming for the unselected reference after the sentence has been read (Corbett & Chang, 1983).

Comprehenders consider multiple possible candidates for the referent of a pronoun and use syntactic and semantic cues to select a referent.

Negatives

An assertion in the form of a negative sentence appears to suppose a positive sentence and then ask us to infer what must be true if the positive sentence is false. For instance, the sentence *John is not a crook* supposes that *John is a crook* could be true but asserts that it is false. As another example, imagine that you ask a normally healthy friend the question *How are you feeling?* Consider the following four possible replies:

1. I am well.
2. I am sick.
3. I am not well.
4. I am not sick.

Replies 1 through 3 would not be regarded as unusual, but reply 4 does seem peculiar. By using the negative reply 4, your friend is supposing that you think it could be true that she is sick. But why would you think she might be sick, and what is she really telling you by saying it is not so? In contrast, the negative reply 3 is easy to understand, because it supposes that you think she is normally well, and she is telling you that this is not so.

Clark and Chase (Chase & Clark, 1972; Clark, 1974; Clark & Chase, 1972) conducted a series of experiments on the verification of negatives (see also Carpenter & Just, 1975; Trabasso, Rollins, & Shaughnessy, 1971). In a typical experiment, they presented participants with a card like the one shown in **Figure 13.9** and asked them to verify one of four sentences about this card:

1. The star is above the plus (true affirmative).
2. The plus is above the star (false affirmative).
3. The plus is not above the star (true negative).
4. The star is not above the plus (false negative).

In these sentences, the terms *true* and *false* refer to whether the sentence is a true assertion about the picture, and the terms *affirmative* and *negative* refer to the absence or presence of the negative *not* in the sentence. The affirmative sentences 1 and 2 are simple assertions that do not suppose anything, but the negative sentences 3 and 4 suppose an affirmative and assert that the affirmative is not true (like the negative sentences discussed above). Sentence 3 supposes that *The plus is above the star* is true and asserts that this is false; sentence 4 supposes that *The star is above the plus* is true and asserts that this is false. Clark and Chase hypothesized that participants would check the supposition first and then process the negation. In sentence 3, the supposition (*The plus is above the star*) does not match the picture—that is, it is not a true assertion about the picture, but in sentence 4, the supposition (*The star is above the plus*) does match the picture. Assuming that mismatches would take longer to process, Clark and Chase predicted that participants would take longer to respond to sentence 3, a true negative, than to sentence 4, a false negative. With the affirmative sentences, in contrast, participants should take longer to process sentence 2, a false affirmative that does not match the

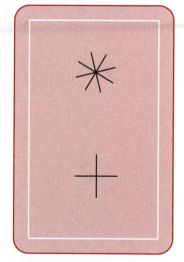

Figure 13.9 What Is True About This Card? In Clark and Chase's sentence-verification experiments, participants saw a card like this and had to decide whether affirmative and negative sentences correctly described it. Participants took longer to process false affirmative sentences (which simply assert what is not true about the card) and true negative sentences (which suppose what is not true and negate that supposition).

TABLE 13.1 Processing Times in Clark and Chase Experiments

Sentence Type	Time in Model*	Observed Time	Predicted Time
True affirmative	T	1,463 ms	1,469 ms
False affirmative	$T + M$	1,722 ms	1,715 ms
True negative	$T + M + N$	2,028 ms	2,035 ms
False negative	$T + N$	1,796 ms	1,789 ms

*T = time to process simple affirmative; M = time to process mismatch with picture; N = time to process negation of supposition.

picture, than sentence 1, a true affirmative that does match the picture. In fact, the difference in processing time between sentences 2 and 1 should be identical with the difference between sentences 3 and 4, because both differences correspond to the extra time needed to process a mismatch.

Clark and Chase developed a simple and elegant mathematical model for the predicted processing times. They assumed that processing sentences 3 and 4 took N time units longer than did processing sentences 1 and 2 because of the more complex supposition-plus-negation. They also assumed that processing sentences 2 and 3 took M time units longer than did processing sentences 1 and 4, respectively, because of the mismatch between picture and assertion. In addition, there was a common time T for all sentences, which reflected both processing the assertion and making the physical response (a button press). Thus, the total time that participants should spend processing sentence 3, for example, should be $T + N + M$ (T for the common processing, M for processing the mismatch, and N for processing the negation). **Table 13.1** shows both the observed processing times and the times predicted by Clark and Chase based on their model, and as you can see, the predictions match the observed times remarkably well. In particular, the observed time M for the difference between true negatives and false negatives (2,028 ms − 1,796 ms = 232 ms) is close to the observed time M for the difference between false affirmatives and true affirmatives (1,722 ms − 1,463 ms = 259 ms). This finding supports the hypothesis that participants do extract the suppositions of negative sentences and match them to the picture.

> *Comprehenders process a negative by first processing its embedded affirmative supposition and then processing the negation of that supposition.*

Processing Extended Texts: Levels of Representation, and Situation Models

So far, we have focused on the comprehension of single sentences in isolation or of pairs of sentences (e.g., in the section on bridging and elaborative inferences). However, sentences are more frequently processed in larger contexts—for example, in the reading of a novel or a textbook. Kintsch (1998, 2013) has argued that a text is represented at multiple levels. For instance, consider the following pair of sentences taken from an experimental story entitled "Nick Goes to the Movies":

- Nick decided to go to the movies. He looked at a newspaper to see what was playing.

Kintsch argues that this material is represented at three levels—surface, propositional, and situational:

1. The surface level of representation consists of representations of the exact sentences. Memory for representations at this level can be tested by comparing people's ability to remember the exact sentences versus a paraphrase such as "Nick studied the newspaper to see what was playing."

2. The propositional level consists of representations of the propositions implied by these sentences (see the section on propositional representations in Chapter 5). Memory for representations at this level can be tested by seeing whether people remember that Nick read the newspaper at all.

3. The situational level consists of representations of the major points of the story. Memory for representations at this level can be tested by seeing whether people remember that Nick wanted to see a movie—something not said in the story but strongly implied.

In one study, Kintsch, Welsch, Schmalhofer, and Zimny (1990) looked at participants' ability to remember these different sorts of information over periods of time ranging up to 4 days (see the results shown in **Figure 13.10**). As we saw in Chapter 5, surface information is forgotten much more rapidly than propositional information. Here, however, we also see that situational information is not lost at all: After 4 days, participants have forgotten the exact wording of both sentences and have forgotten half the propositions, but they still remember perfectly what the story was about. This fits with many people's experience in reading novels or seeing movies. They will quickly forget many of the details but will still remember months later what a novel or movie was about.

> *When people follow a story, they construct a high-level situation model of the story that is more durable than the memory for the surface sentences or the propositions that made up the story.*

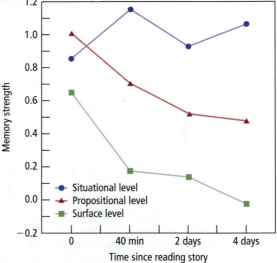

Figure 13.10 Memory for Different Levels of Representation of a Story. Memory for the surface level (the exact sentences) decays more quickly than memory for the propositional level, whereas memory for the situational level does not decay at all over the four days. *(Data from Kintsch et al., 1990.)*

Dimensions of Information in Situation Models

A **situation model** is a representation of the overall structure of a narrative that we are reading. According to Zwaan and Radvansky (1998), situation models are organized according to five dimensions: space, time, causation, protagonists, and goals. Ease of comprehension of the sentences in a text varies with their position on these dimensions, as shown by the following examples:

Space. As comprehenders process a story, they keep track of where the actors and objects are, just as if they were actually in the situation in the story, looking at the various objects and people. In a study of processing of this dimension, Rinck and Bower (1995) measured the time participants took to read sentences in a narrative, such as

• He thought that the shelves in the washroom looked an awful mess.

Figure 13.11 shows how the time to comprehend the sentence varied, depending on whether the washroom was the room where the protagonist ("He") currently was (current room), a room the protagonist had just walked through (adjacent room), a nonadjacent room that the protagonist had just come from (previous room), or some other room in the building that was even further away from where the protagonist currently was (distant room).

Time. Comprehenders also need to keep track of when events take place relative to each other. In one study, Zwaan (1996) had people process a sentence that began in one of these ways:

A. A moment later, the fireman…
B. A day later, the fireman…
C. A month later, the fireman…

The time to process the sentence increased with the time in the "later" phrase.

Causation. Comprehenders also keep track of the causal relationships among the events in a story. In one study, Keenan, Baillet, and Brown (1984) had participants read pairs of sentences that varied in the probability that the first could be interpreted as having a causal relation to the second. The researchers were interested in the effect of this probability on the time participants took to read the second sentence. For example, the first sentence might be one of the following:

A. Joey's big brother punched him again and again.
B. Racing down the hill, Joey fell off his bike.
C. Joey's crazy mother became furiously angry with him.

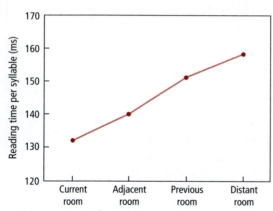

Figure 13.11 Situation Models: The Space Dimension in Comprehending a Story. The reading time per syllable in a sentence increases with the distance between the room where the protagonist is currently located and the room where the objects referenced in the sentence are located.
(Data from Rinck & Bower, 1995.)

   D. Joey went to a neighbor's house to play.

and the second sentence might be

   E. The next day, his body was covered with bruises.

Sentences A through D are ordered in decreasing probability of a causal connection to the sentence E. Across a range of sentences like these, Keenan et al. found that participants' reading times for sentence E increased from 2.6 seconds when preceded by high-probability causes such as that in sentence A to 3.3 seconds when preceded by low-probability causes such as that in sentence D. Thus, it takes longer to understand a less probable causal relation.

Protagonists. Protagonists are the most important elements of a situation model, and people keep track of what is happening to them. In a study of this dimension, O'Brien, Albrecht, Hakala, and Rizzella (1995) had participants read stories about a protagonist with a certain trait, such as being a vegetarian. Participants took longer to read a sentence about the protagonist that was inconsistent with that trait (e.g., a sentence about the protagonist ordering a hamburger).

Goals. The goals of the protagonists in a story are a critical aspect of the narrative, so comprehenders keep track of them. A sentence like *Betty wanted to give her mother a present* introduces a goal into a story. Trabasso and Suh (1993) had participants read a story in which a protagonist either achieved a goal or did not. They found that participants could more quickly answer a question such as *Did Betty want to get her mother a birthday present?* if the protagonist (e.g., Betty) achieved the goal than if the protagonist did not. In another study, Lutz and Radvansky (1997) had participants read an excerpt from a story and then had them summarize what they had read. Participants were more likely to mention in their summary a goal that had not been achieved than a goal that had been achieved. This result is interpreted as evidence indicating that comprehenders keep unachieved goals highly available in memory, because those goals remain relevant for processing what is yet to happen in the story.

For each of these five dimensions, the time to process a sentence is related to how closely related the content of the sentence is to the representation of the situation that the reader is carrying forward. It is as if the reader is keeping a spotlight focused on a point in the five-dimensional space. The ease with which a reader can process the information in a sentence is a function of how closely related that information is to the information represented at the point targeted by that spotlight. (See **Implications 13.2** for a discussion of information conveyed nonverbally.)

> *A situation model keeps track of critical features of the story and makes this information highly available to facilitate comprehension.*

Implications 13.2

Nonverbal Communication

This chapter and Chapter 12 have focused on language as the means by which humans communicate, but language is not our only means of communication. The famous claim that 93% of all meaning is communicated nonverbally is a misinterpretation of research by Mehrabian (1971), who was studying how listeners judged speakers' attitudes. Combining two studies, Mehrabian estimated that the words said accounted for 7% of the judgments, tone of voice 38%, and body language 55%. Mehrabian himself has noted that his research concerned only judgments about feelings and attitudes, not about meaning in general. While Mehrabian's estimates have been disputed, many studies have shown that judgments about the emotional mood of a speaker are determined more by factors such as posture, facial expression, and tone of voice than by what the person actually says (Burgoon, Guerrero, & Floyd, 2016).

Many forms of nonverbal communication used by humans are shared with other species, including forms used to communicate nonemotional information, as well as forms used for conveying emotional information. It has been argued, for example, that dogs became our "best friend" by evolving refined abilities to communicate nonverbally in humanlike ways and to accurately interpret our nonverbal communications (Miklósi & Topál, 2013). There is evidence that dogs understand human pointing better than chimpanzees do, even though chimpanzees point and dogs do not (at least not with hands) (see Hopkins, Russell, McIntyre, & Leavens, 2013, for a discussion).

Gesturing, a particularly important form of human nonverbal communication, goes far beyond simple pointing and tends to accompany speech. Speakers in all cultures gesture, even those who are congenitally blind (Goldin-Meadow & Alibali, 2013). Gesturing facilitates both speech generation and speech comprehension—quality of speech deteriorates if gesturing is prohibited, and comprehension of speech improves when speech is accompanied by gestures consistent with the verbal content. For instance, in an EEG study by Holle and Gunter (2007), participants heard a sentence with an ambiguous word such as *ball* that was disambiguated later in the sentence (e.g., *She controlled the ball during the dance with the bridegroom*[2]). The sentence was accompanied by a consistent or inconsistent gesture. Subjects showed a smaller N400

[2] The experiment was conducted in German, in which the word for *ball* is similarly ambiguous.

when the gesture was consistent, indicating easier comprehension (see Figure 13.7 and the accompanying discussion).

Gesturing is also important in classroom learning—students learn better when teachers gesture while giving verbal instructions than when teachers do not gesture (e.g., Novack, Wakefield, Congdon, Franconeri, & Goldin-Meadow, 2016). Students also learn better when they themselves gesture during study. In one experiment (Goldin-Meadow, Cook, & Mitchell, 2009), fourth-grade children being taught about equivalence were presented with a problem such as $6 + 3 + 4 = \_\_ + 4$ (they are to fill the blank with 9). While solving the problem with teacher guidance, they were either encouraged just to say what they were thinking (e.g., "I want to make one side equal to the other side") or encouraged both to say what they were thinking and to make appropriate gestures, as illustrated in **Figure 13.12**. Those encouraged to gesture did twice as well on a posttest.

Figure 13.12   Gesturing and Learning. Students who are encouraged to make appropriate gestures while teachers help them work through a problem show better learning than students who are prohibited from gesturing. *(Republished with permission of Sage Publications: Goldin-Meadow, S., Cook, S. W., & Mitchell, Z. A. [2009]. Gesturing gives children new ideas about math. Psychological Science, 20[3], 267–272.)*

Conclusions

The number and diversity of topics covered in this chapter testify to the impressive cumulative progress in understanding language comprehension. It is fair to say that we knew almost nothing about language processing when cognitive psychology emerged from the collapse of behaviorism 60 years ago. Now we have a rather well-articulated picture of what is happening at time scales that range from 100 milliseconds after a word is heard to minutes later when large stretches of complex text must be integrated. Research on language processing turns out to harbor a number of theoretical controversies, some of which have been discussed in this review of the field (e.g., whether early syntactic processing is separate from the rest of cognition). However, such controversies should not blind us to the impressive progress that has been made. The heat in the field has also generated much light.

Questions for Thought

1. The top-performing program in the recent Loebner Prize contests (see Implications 13.1) was named Mitsuku. Find "her" online and have a chat. Compare Mitsuko's language processing skills with those of a virtual assistant like Amazon's Alexa. What are the differences in the tasks they are trying to master and what are their relative language strengths?

2. Answer this question: *How many animals of each kind did Moses take on the ark?* If you are like most people, you answered "two" and did not even notice that *Moses* should have been *Noah* (Erickson & Matteson, 1981). People fail to notice such mistakes even when they are warned to look out for them (Reder & Kusbit, 1991). This phenomenon has been called the *Moses illusion* even though it has been demonstrated with a wide range of words besides *Moses*. What does the Moses illusion say about how people process individual words when comprehending sentences?

3. Christianson, Hollingworth, Halliwell, and Ferreira (2001) found that after reading the sentence *While Mary bathed the baby played in the crib,* most people say that the sentence implied that Mary bathed the baby. Ferreira and Patson (2007) argue that this indicates that people do not carefully parse sentences but settle on "good enough" interpretations. If people do not carefully parse sentences, what does that imply about the debate between proponents of interactive processing and of the modularity position with regard to how people understand sentences such as *The woman painted by the artist was very attractive to look at*?

4. Beilock, Lyons, Mattarella-Micke, Nusbaum, and Small (2008) looked at brain activation while participants listened to sentences about hockey versus other types of action sentences. They found greater activation in the premotor cortex for hockey sentences only in those participants who were hockey fans. What does this say about the role of expertise in making elaborative inferences and developing situation models?

Key Terms

bridging inferences	garden-path sentences	P600	situation model
center-embedded sentences	immediacy of interpretation	parsing	transient ambiguity
constituents	interactive processing	principle of minimal	utilization
elaborative inferences	N400	attachment	

Individual Differences in Cognition

People do not all think alike. There are many aspects of cognition, but humans, naturally being an evaluative species, tend to focus on ways in which some people perform "better" than other people. This performance is often identified with the word *intelligence* — some people are perceived to be "more intelligent" than others. Chapter 1 identified intelligence as the defining feature of the human species. So, calling some members of our species more intelligent than others can be a potent claim. As we will see, the complexity of human cognition makes it impossible to place people on a one-dimensional scale of intelligence.

This chapter will explore individual differences in cognition, both because of the inherent interest of this topic and because individual differences shed some light on the general nature of human cognition. Throughout this chapter, the nature-versus-nurture debate (also referred to as the empiricist–nativist debate) will be at issue. Are some people better at some cognitive tasks because they are innately endowed with a greater capacity for performing those kinds of tasks or because they have acquired more knowledge and experience relevant to those tasks? The answer, not surprisingly, is that both factors — and their interactions — are almost always involved. At many points in this chapter, we will consider some of the ways in which both innate capacities and knowledge and experience contribute to human intelligence. More specifically, this chapter will answer the following questions:

- How does children's cognition develop as they mature?
- What do neural growth and growth in knowledge and experience contribute to children's cognitive development?
- How does aging through the adult years affect our cognitive capacities?
- What do intelligence tests measure?
- What are the different dimensions of intelligence?

Cognitive Development

Part of the uniqueness of the human species concerns the way in which children are brought into the world and develop into adults. Humans have very large brains in relation to their body size, which created a major evolutionary problem: How would the birth of such large-brained babies be physically possible? One part of the solution was the progressive enlargement of the birth canal, which is now as large as is considered possible given the constraints on mammalian skeletons (Geschwind, 1980). In addition, at birth, the baby's skull is sufficiently pliable to be compressed into a cone shape to fit through the birth canal. Still, the human birth process is significantly more difficult than that of most other mammals.

Figure 14.1 illustrates the growth of the human brain during gestation. At birth, a child's brain has more neurons than an adult brain has, but the child's neurons are quite immature: they need to grow, develop synapses, and develop supporting structures such as glial cells. The brains of human infants develop much more after birth than do the brains of many other species. At birth, a human brain occupies a volume of about 350 cubic centimeters (cm^3). In the first year of life, its volume doubles to 700 cm^3, and it doubles again before the child reaches puberty. Most other mammals do not have as much growth in brain size after birth (Gould, 1977). It appears that much of our neural development is postponed until after birth because the human birth canal has expanded to its limit.

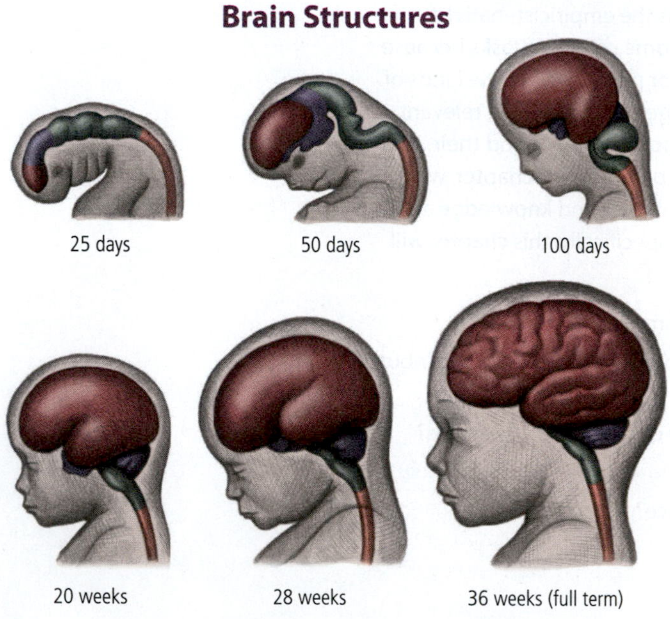

Even after 9 months of development in the womb, human infants are quite helpless at birth; also, humans spend an extraordinarily long time growing to adult stature — about 15 years, around a fifth of the human life span. In contrast, a puppy, after a gestation period of just 9 weeks, is more capable at birth than a human newborn, and in less than a year (less than a tenth of its life span), a dog attains full size and reproductive capability.

Childhood is prolonged more than would be needed to develop large brains (Bjorklund & Bering, 2003). Indeed, the majority of neural development is complete by age 5. Human childhood is prolonged by the slowness of our physical development. It has been speculated that the function of this slow physical development is to maintain children's dependency on adults (de Beer, 1959). A child has much to learn in order to become a competent adult, and staying a child for so long provides enough time to acquire that knowledge. Childhood is an apprenticeship for adulthood.

Figure 14.1 The Developing Brain During Gestation. The enormous expansion of the forebrain (which includes the cerebral cortex) during prenatal development is unique to humans. *(Research from Bownds, 1999.)*

Brain Structures

25 days

50 days

100 days

20 weeks

28 weeks

36 weeks (full term)

Over a century ago most people in Western society began work in their early teens, as people still do in many parts of the world. However, modern society in the developed world is so complex that we cannot learn all that is needed by simply associating with our parents and other adults for 15 years. To provide the needed training, society has created social institutions such as high schools, colleges, and graduate and professional schools. It is not unusual for people to spend more than 25 years, almost as long as their professional lives, preparing for their roles in society.

> *Human development to adulthood takes longer than that of other mammals, giving humans time for growth of a large brain and acquisition of a large amount of knowledge.*

Piaget's Stages of Development

Developmental psychologists have tried to understand the intellectual changes that take place as we grow from infancy through adulthood. Many have been particularly influenced by the Swiss psychologist Jean Piaget, who studied and theorized about child development for more than half a century. Much of the recent information-processing work in cognitive development has been concerned with correcting and restructuring Piaget's theory of cognitive development. Despite these revisions, his research has organized a large set of qualitative observations about cognitive development spanning the period from birth to adulthood. Therefore, it is worthwhile to review these observations to get a picture of the general nature of cognitive development during childhood.

According to Piaget, a child enters the world lacking virtually all the basic cognitive competencies of an adult but gradually develops these competencies by passing through a series of four major stages of development:

1. **Sensory-motor stage.** This stage characterizes the first 2 years of life, during which children develop schemes for thinking about the physical world — for instance, they develop the notion of an object as a permanent thing in the world.
2. **Preoperational stage.** This stage spans the period from 2 to 7 years of age. Unlike younger children, children in this stage can engage in internal thought about the world, but these mental processes are intuitive and unsystematic. For instance, a 4-year-old who was asked to describe his painting of a farm and some animals said, "First, over here is a house where the animals live. I live in a house. So do my mommy and daddy. This is a horse. I saw horses on TV. Do you have a TV?"
3. **Concrete-operational stage.** This stage spans the period from 7 to 11 years of age. In this stage, children develop a set of mental operations that allow them to think about the physical world in a systematic way. However, children still have major limitations on their capacity to reason formally about the world.

4. **Formal-operational stage.** Spanning the period from 11 years of age onward, this stage sees the emergence of the capacity for formal reasoning. Even though they still have much to learn, children in this stage are adult cognitively and so capable of scientific reasoning — which Piaget took as the paradigm case of mature intellectual functioning.

Piaget's concept of stages has always been a sore point in developmental psychology. Obviously, a child does not suddenly transition on his or her eleventh birthday from the stage of concrete operations to the stage of formal operations. There are large differences among children and cultures in the times at which children appear to develop the capacities associated with the different stages, so the ages given in the list above are just approximations. However, careful analysis of the development of individual children also fails to find abrupt transitions in cognitive development at any age. One response to this gradualness has been to break down the stages into smaller substages. Another response has been to interpret stages as simply ways of characterizing what is inherently a gradual and continuous process. Siegler (1996) argued that, on careful analysis, all cognitive development is continuous and gradual. He characterized the belief that children progress through discrete stages as "the myth of the immaculate transition."

Just as important as Piaget's stage analysis is his analysis of children's performance on specific tasks within these stages. These task analyses provide the empirical substance to back up his broad and abstract characterization of the stages. Probably his most well-known task analyses are part of his research on conservation, considered next.

> *Piaget proposed that children progress through four stages of cognitive development, during which they acquire increasing intellectual sophistication: the sensory-motor stage, preoperational stage, concrete-operational stage, and formal-operational stage.*

Conservation

The term **conservation** most generally refers to knowledge of the properties of the world that are preserved under various transformations. A child's understanding of conservation develops as the child progresses through the Piagetian stages.

Conservation in the sensory-motor stage. A child must come to understand that objects continue to exist over transformations in time and space. If a screen is placed in front of a toy that a 6-month-old is reaching for, the infant stops reaching and appears to lose interest in the toy, as illustrated in **Figure 14.2**. It is as if the object ceases to exist for the child when it is no longer in view. Piaget concluded from his experiments that children do not come into the world with knowledge of object permanence but rather develop a concept of it during the first year.

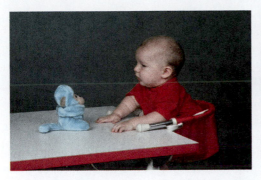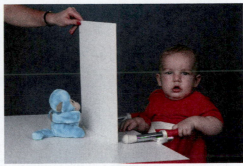

Figure 14.2 Conservation in the Sensory-Motor Stage. At the age of 6 months, children apparently lack the ability to understand the permanence of objects—when a toy is hidden, the child seems to be unaware that it continues to exist. *(Doug Goodman/Science Source.)*

According to Piaget, the concept of object permanence develops slowly and is one of the major intellectual developments in the sensory-motor stage. At some point during this stage, infants will search for an object that has been hidden, but more demanding tests reveal failings in these older infant's understanding of object permanence. In one type of experiment, if an object is put under cover A, and then, in front of the child, removed and put under cover B, the child will often look for the object under cover A. Piaget argues that this shows that the child does not understand that the object will be found under cover B. Only after the age of 12 months can children succeed consistently at this task.

However, research has shown that the problem really involves working memory, not cognitive understanding (Morasch, Raj, & Bell, 2013). In the classic A-not-B experiment as Piaget pioneered it, the child first sees the toy put under A a number of times before seeing it put under B. Thus, the child faces a competition between the stored memory of the toy being put under A and the working memory of the most recent event, in which the toy was put under B. Diamond (1990) shows that the child's task in such an experiment is very much like the delayed match-to-sample task used to study working memory in other species (see Figure 6.8 and the accompanying discussion): Infants improve at the same rate on the delayed match-to-sample task as they do on the A-not-B task.

Conservation in the preoperational and concrete-operational stages. A number of important advances in cognition about conservation occur at about 6 years of age, reflecting the transition from the preoperational stage to the concrete-operational stage. Before this age, children make some glaring types of errors in their reasoning, which they then start to correct. The cause of this change has been a subject of controversy, with different theorists pointing to language (Bruner, 1964), the advent of schooling (Cole & D'Andrade, 1982), and other possible causes. Here, we will content ourselves

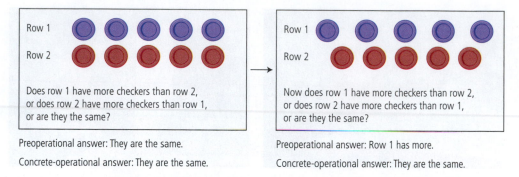

Preoperational answer: They are the same.

Concrete-operational answer: They are the same.

Preoperational answer: Row 1 has more.

Concrete-operational answer: They are the same.

Figure 14.3 Conservation of Numerical Quantity in the Preoperational and Concrete-Operational Stages. When row 1 is expanded lengthwise, a child in the preoperational stage says that the expanded row now has more objects than row 2. A child in the concrete-operational stage understands that numerical quantity is conserved under this transformation.

with a description of the changes in children's understanding of conservation of quantity during this time.

As adults, if we see four apples in a bowl, we can almost instantaneously recognize that there are four of them, and we can be confident that there will still be four when the apples are dumped into a bag. Piaget was interested in how a child develops the concept of quantity and learns that quantity is preserved under various transformations, such as moving objects from a bowl to a bag. **Figure 14.3** illustrates one of the many variations of a conservation problem that has been posed to children in countless experiments. A child is shown two rows of objects, such as checkers. The two rows contain the same number of objects and have been lined up so as to correspond. The child is asked whether the two rows have the same number of objects and responds that they do. The child can be asked to count the objects in the two rows to confirm that conclusion. Now, before the child's eyes, one row is expanded, but no objects are added or removed. Again asked whether the two rows have the same number of objects, a child in the preoperational stage says that the expanded row has more. The preoperational child appears not to know that quantity is something that is preserved under this kind of transformation of space. If asked to count the two groups of checkers, the preoperational child expresses great surprise that they have the same number. In contrast, a child in the concrete-operational stage is confident that the two rows still have the same number of objects and thinks that it is silly to count the objects in order to confirm this.

A general feature in demonstrations of lack of conservation in the preoperational stage is that the irrelevant physical characteristics of a display distract children. Consider, for example, the liquid-conservation task, which is illustrated in **Figure 14.4**. The child is shown two identical beakers

Before: Child says the two short beakers have the same amount of milk.

After: Child says the tall beaker has more milk than the short beaker.

Figure 14.4 Conservation of Liquid in the Preoperational Stage. A child in the preoperational stage cannot reason past misleading physical appearances, even after seeing the milk being poured from one beaker into another. *(Bianca Moscatelli/Worth Publishers.)*

containing identical amounts of milk and an empty beaker taller and thinner than the other two. When asked whether the two identical beakers hold the same amount of milk, the child says yes. The milk from one beaker is then poured into the tall, thin beaker. When asked whether the amount of milk in the two beakers is the same, the child now says that the tall beaker holds more. Preoperational children are distracted by the irrelevant physical characteristic of the height of the beaker and do not relate their having seen the milk poured from one beaker into the other to the unchanging quantity of liquid. Bruner (1964) demonstrated that a child is more likely to show conservation if the tall beaker is hidden from sight while it is being filled — the child does not see the high column of milk and so is not distracted by physical appearance. This confirms the idea that the child's lack of conservation is the result of being overwhelmed by physical appearance. Diamond (2013) suggests that children cannot stop themselves from attending to physical appearance, much like they cannot inhibit other responses (see the Chapter 3 section "Prefrontal Sites of Executive Control" for discussion of similar failures of inhibition).

Lack of conservation has also been shown with respect to the weight and volume of solid objects (for discussion of studies of conservation, see Brainerd, 1978; Flavell, 1985; Ginsburg & Opper, 1980). It was once thought that the ability to perform successfully on all these tasks depended on acquiring a single abstract concept of conservation. Now, however, it is clear that successful conservation appears earlier on some tasks than on others. For instance, conservation of numerical quantity usually appears before conservation of liquid. Additionally, children in transition from preoperational to concrete-operational thinking sometimes show conservation of number or quantity in one experimental situation but not in another.

Conservation in the formal-operational stage. When children reach the formal-operational stage, their understanding of conservation reaches new levels of abstraction. They are able to understand the idealized conservations that are part of modern science, including concepts such as the conservation of energy and the conservation of momentum. In a frictionless world, an object once set in motion continues in motion and maintains its momentum unless acted upon by some other external force — an abstraction that the child never experiences. However, in the formal-operational period, the child comes to understand this abstraction and the way in which it relates to experiences in the real world.

> *As children develop, they gain an increasingly sophisticated understanding about what properties of objects are conserved under which transformations.*

What Develops?

Clearly, as Piaget and others have documented, major intellectual changes take place in childhood. However, there are serious questions concerning what underlies these changes. There are two ways of explaining why children perform better on various intellectual tasks as they get older: One is that they "think better," and the other is that they "know better." The think-better option holds that children's basic cognitive processes become better. Perhaps they can hold more information in working memory or process information faster. The know-better option holds that children have learned more facts and better methods and absorbed more experiences as they get older. I refer to this as "know better," not "know more," because it is not just a matter of adding knowledge but also a matter of eliminating erroneous facts and inappropriate methods (such as relying on appearance in the conservation tasks). Perhaps this superior knowledge enables them to perform the tasks more efficiently. A computer metaphor is apt here: A computer program can be made to perform better by running it on a faster machine that has more memory or by running a better version of the program on the same machine. Which is it in the case of child development — better machine or better program?

Rather than the reason being one or the other, the child's improvement is due to both factors, but what are their relative contributions? Siegler (1998) argued that many of the developmental changes that take place in the first 2 years are to be understood in relation to neural changes, which are considerable over that period. As we noted above, the number of neurons in a child's brain decreases over the first two years. However, the number of synaptic connections increases tenfold, reaching a peak at about age 2 (see **Figure 14.5**), after which the number of synapses declines. The earlier pruning of neurons and the later pruning of synaptic connections can be thought of as a process by which the brain fine-tunes itself. The initial overproduction guarantees that there will be enough neurons and synapses for the

At birth   At 3 months   At 24 months

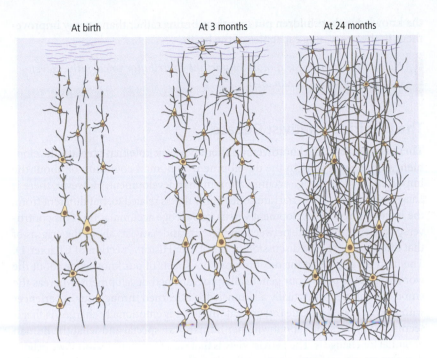

Figure 14.5 Postnatal Increase in the Number of Synaptic Connections Around Broca's Area. The number of synapses increases dramatically over the first 2 years. (*Research from Lenneberg, 1967.*)

required information processing. Later, unused neurons and synapses, which have been proved unnecessary, wither away (Huttenlocher, 1994). After age 2, there is not much further growth of neurons or their synaptic connections, but the brain continues to grow because of the proliferation of other cells. In particular, the number of glial cells increases, including those that provide myelinated sheaths around the axons of neurons. As discussed in Chapter 1, myelination increases the speed of signal transmission in the axon. The process of myelination continues into the late teens but at an increasingly gradual pace. Myelination of prefrontal regions of the brain is not complete until early adulthood (Stiles, Brown, Haist, & Jernigan, 2015). The effects of this gradual myelination can be considerable. For instance, the time for a nerve impulse to cross the hemispheres in an adult is about 5 milliseconds, which is four to five times as fast as in a 4-year-old (Salamy, 1978).

It is tempting to emphasize the improvement in processing capacity as the basis for cognitive improvements after age 2, based on an analogy with physical maturation. When my son was 2 years old, he had difficulty undoing his pajama buttons. If his muscular coordination had so much maturing to do, why not his brain? This analogy, however, does not hold: A 2-year-old has reached only 20% of adult body weight, whereas the brain has already reached 80% of its final size. Cognitive development after age 2 may depend more on the knowledge that children put into their brains rather than on any improvement in the processing capacities of the brain.

> *Neural development is a more important contributor to cognitive development before age 2 than after.*

The Empiricist–Nativist Debate

There is relatively little controversy either about the role that physical development of the brain plays in the development of human cognition or about the importance of knowledge accumulation in that development. However, there is an age-old nature-versus-nurture controversy that is related to, but different from, the issue of physical development versus knowledge accumulation. This controversy concerns the debate between empiricists and nativists about the origins of that knowledge (see the discussion in the "Early History" section of Chapter 1). The nativists argue that the most important aspects of our knowledge about the world appear as part of our genetically programmed development, whereas the empiricists argue that virtually all knowledge is learned through our experiences with the environment. One reason that this issue is emotionally charged is that it seems tied to questions about whether humans are special and what the human potential for change is. The nativist view is that we sell ourselves short if we believe that our minds are just a simple reflection of our experiences, and empiricists believe that we underestimate human potential if we believe that we are not capable of fundamental change and improvement. The issue is not this simple, but it nonetheless fuels great passion on both sides of the debate.

We have already visited this issue in Chapters 12 and 13, in the discussions of language acquisition and of whether important aspects of human language, such as language universals, are innately specified. Similar claims of innateness have been made for our knowledge of human faces and our knowledge of biological categories. A particularly interesting case concerns our knowledge of number. Piaget used experiments such as those on number conservation to argue that we do not have an innate sense of number, but other experimental results have been used to argue otherwise. For instance, in studies of infant attention, young children have been shown to discriminate one object from two and two from three (Antell & Keating, 1983; Starkey, Spelke, & Gelman, 1990; van Loosbroek & Smitsman, 1992). In these studies, young children become bored looking at a certain number of objects but show renewed interest when the number of objects changes. There is even evidence for a rudimentary ability to add and subtract (Simon, Hespos, & Rochat, 1995; Wynn, 1992). **Figure 14.6**, for instance, illustrates an experimental procedure in which a 5-month-old child sees an object put on a stage and then disappear behind a screen; then a second object is put behind the screen. When the screen is raised, the child is surprised if there are not two objects on the stage. This reaction is taken as evidence that the child calculates $1 + 1 = 2$.

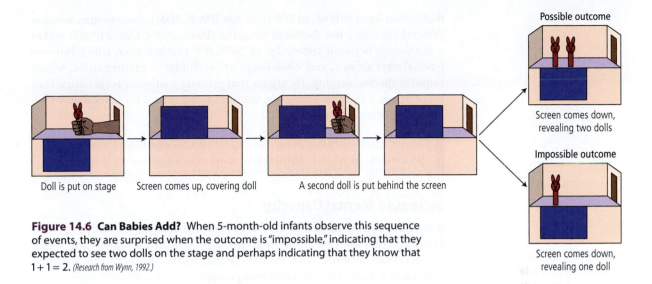

Possible outcome

Screen comes down, revealing two dolls

Impossible outcome

Screen comes down, revealing one doll

Doll is put on stage   Screen comes up, covering doll   A second doll is put behind the screen

Figure 14.6 Can Babies Add? When 5-month-old infants observe this sequence of events, they are surprised when the outcome is "impossible," indicating that they expected to see two dolls on the stage and perhaps indicating that they know that $1 + 1 = 2$. *(Research from Wynn, 1992.)*

The basic ability to appreciate numerical quantity is not restricted to humans but can be found in many species (Nieder & Dehaene, 2009). For instance, monkeys can be trained to judge whether two displays show the same number of dots (Figure 3.31 shows a monkey performing a similar task). Monkeys can also achieve high accuracy in identifying the exact number of dots for small numbers of dots (range of 1–4). Primate parietal and prefrontal cortices have neurons that are tuned to respond to a specific number of items. **Figure 14.7** shows the responses of four differently tuned neurons in the parietal region from a study by Nieder (2012). As can be seen, the maximal response of each neuron drops off as the difference increases between the neuron's preferred number of items and the presented number of items. Interestingly these same neurons also respond preferentially to the same numbers of tones presented — that is, a "2" neuron will respond preferentially to 2 items presented visually and to 2 tones presented auditorily. The existence of such number-specific neurons can be taken to reflect part of the innate knowledge of number that primates, including humans, have as part of their evolutionary heritage (Spelke, 2011).

There is a very large genetic overlap between chimpanzees and humans (Chimpanzee Sequencing and Analysis Consortium, 2005), so it seems that there is not much genetic room for encoding the rich knowledge that only humans possess. Certainly, much of the advanced mathematical capability of humans cannot be something that we developed through evolution. For instance, algebra, which is mastered by schoolchildren around the world, achieved

Figure 14.7 Can Neurons Count? Individual neurons in the parietal cortex of monkeys are tuned to respond maximally to certain numbers of items in a display. *(Data from Nieder, 2012.)*

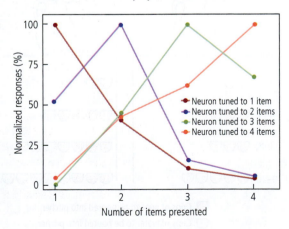

- Neuron tuned to 1 item
- Neuron tuned to 2 items
- Neuron tuned to 3 items
- Neuron tuned to 4 items

its modern form only about 500 years ago (Press, 2006). Even written number systems are only a few thousand years old (Ifrah, 2000). Geary (2007) makes a distinction between knowledge of "primary" mathematics, which humans have always shown, and knowledge of "secondary" mathematics, which requires special learning. He argues that primary mathematics is basically in place by age 5 and that secondary mathematics depends on schooling, which typically begins at that age.

> *There is considerable debate in cognitive science about the degree to which our "basic" knowledge is innate or acquired from experience.*

Increased Mental Capacity

A number of developmental theories propose that there are basic cognitive capacities that increase from birth through the teenage years (Case, 1985; Fischer, 1980; Halford, 1982; Pascual-Leone, 1980). These theories are often called *neo-Piagetian* theories of development.

Consider Case's memory-space proposal, which is that the key to the developmental sequence is an increasing capacity of working memory. The basic idea is that more-advanced cognitive performance requires that more information be held in working memory, as illustrated by Case's (1978) description of how children solve Noelting's (1975) juice problems. A child is shown two empty pitchers, and is told that a certain number of glasses of orange juice and a certain number of glasses of water will be poured into each pitcher. The child's task is to predict which pitcher will taste more strongly of orange juice. **Figure 14.8** illustrates four stages of juice problems that children can solve at various ages. At the youngest age (3–4 years), children can reliably solve only problems where all the orange juice goes into one pitcher and all the water into the other. At 4–5 years of age, children can count the number of glasses of orange juice going into each pitcher and choose the pitcher that holds more orange juice—not considering the number of glasses of water. At age 7–8, they notice whether there is more orange juice or more water going into a pitcher; if pitcher A has more orange juice than water and pitcher B has more water than orange juice, they will choose pitcher A, even if the absolute number of glasses of orange juice is fewer than in pitcher B. Finally, at age 9–10, children compute the difference between the amount of orange juice and the amount of water and choose the pitcher with the greater difference for orange juice (still not a perfect solution, which would require computing the relative percentages of orange juice in the two pitchers).

Case argued that the working-memory requirements differ for the various types of problems

Figure 14.8 Children's Solutions to Noelting Juice Problems at Various Ages. At 3–4 years, children choose the pitcher that is all orange juice (but only if the other is all water). At 4–5 years, children choose the pitcher with more orange juice, regardless of the amount of water. At 7–8 years, children choose the pitcher with more orange juice than water. At 9–10 years, children choose the pitcher with the greater difference for orange juice (in this case, they choose pitcher A, which is –1 for orange juice, whereas pitcher B is –2 for orange juice).

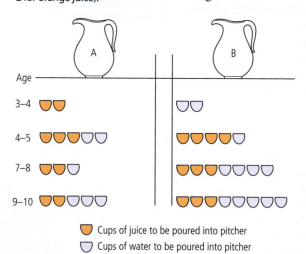

Cups of juice to be poured into pitcher
Cups of water to be poured into pitcher

represented in Figure 14.8. For the simplest problems, a child has to keep only one fact in memory—which pitcher got the glasses with orange juice. Children at age 3–4 can do this. But if both sets of glasses include some orange juice, the child cannot solve the problem. For the second type of problem (solvable by children at age 4–5), the child needs to keep two simple numbers in memory—the number of glasses of orange juice going into each pitcher. In the third type of problem (solvable by children at age 7–8), the child needs to keep two subtractions in mind to determine which side has more orange juice than water. To solve the fourth type of problem (solvable by children at age 9–10), the child needs to keep four facts in memory: (1) the difference between the number of glasses of orange juice and the number of glasses of water going into pitcher A; (2) whether that difference is positive or negative (i.e., whether there is more water or more orange juice going into pitcher A); (3) the difference between the number of glasses of orange juice and the number of glasses of water going into pitcher B; and (4) whether that difference is positive or negative. Case argued that children's developmental sequences are controlled by their working-memory capacity—that is, only when they can keep four facts in memory will they achieve the fourth stage in the developmental sequence. Case's theory has been criticized (e.g., Flavell, 1978) because it is not always clear how to count the working-memory requirements.

Another question concerns what controls the growth in working memory. Case argued that a major factor in the increased capacity of working memory is increased speed of neural transmission. He cited evidence that the degree of myelination increases with age, with spurts approximately at those points where he postulated major changes in working memory. However, he also argued that practice plays a significant role as well: With practice, our mental operations become more efficient, which means they do not require as much working-memory capacity.

The research of Kail (1988) can be viewed as consistent with the proposal that the speed of mental operations is a critical factor. Kail looked at a number of cognitive tasks, including the mental rotation task examined in Chapter 4 (see the discussion of Figures 4.4 and 4.5). He presented participants with pairs of letters in different orientations and asked them to judge whether the letters were the same or were mirror images of each other. As discussed in Chapter 4, to make this judgment, participants tend to mentally rotate an image of one object to see if it can be brought into congruence with the other. Kail found that his participants, who ranged in age from 8 to 22, became systematically faster with age. The speed measured was rotation rate, the number of milliseconds to mentally rotate one degree of angle. The results shown in **Figure 14.9** indicate that rotation rate decreases as participants' age increases.

In some of his writings, Kail argued that this result is evidence of an increase in basic mental speed as a function of age. However, an alternative hypothesis is that it reflects

Figure 14.9 Rates of Mental Rotation, by Age. Participants had to mentally rotate an image of a letter in order to judge whether it was congruent with or a mirror image of another image of the same letter. *(Data from Kail, 1988.)*

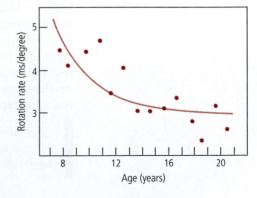

Figure 14.10 Rates of Mental Rotation in Children and Adults, by Trials of Practice. Children and adults were each given over 3,000 trials of practice at mental rotation. In addition, it was assumed that the child participants came into the experiment with 150 trials of prior practice as part of their everyday life and that the adult participants came into the experiment with 1,950 trials of prior practice. The same power function is the best fit for both sets of data — i.e., the children and the adults were on the same learning curve. *(Data from Kail & Park, 1990.)*

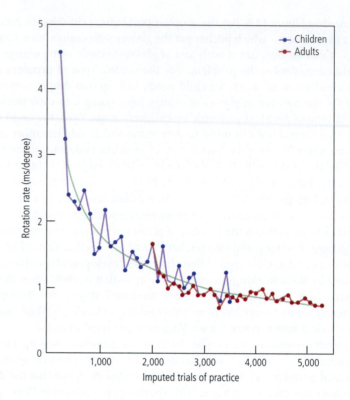

accumulating experience over the years at mental rotation. Kail and Park (1990) put this hypothesis to the test by giving 11-year-old children and adults more than 3,000 trials of practice at mental rotation. They found that both groups sped up but that adults started out faster. However, Kail and Park showed that all their data could be fit by the single power function in **Figure 14.10**, assuming that the adults came into the experiment with what amounted to an extra 1,800 trials of practice (we saw in Chapters 6 and 9 that learning curves tend to be power functions). The practice curve for children in Figure 14.10 assumes that they start with about 150 trials of prior practice, and the practice curve for adults assumes that they start with 1,950 trials of prior practice. Note that after 3,000 trials of practice, children are a good bit faster than beginning adults with an assumed 1,950 trials of practice. These results indicate that the increased rate of information processing as people develop from children into adults may have more of a practice-related than a biological explanation.

> *Qualitative and quantitative changes take place in cognitive development because of increases both in working-memory capacity and in rate of information processing.*

Increased Knowledge

Chi (1978) demonstrated that developmental differences in memory-related cognition may be knowledge related. Not surprisingly, children do worse than adults on almost every memory task, but the question is whether children perform worse because they have worse memory or because they know less about what they are being asked to remember. To address this question, Chi compared the memory performance of 10-year-olds with that of adults on two tasks — a standard digit-span task (see the discussion around Figure 6.5) and a chess memory task. The 10-year-olds were skilled chess players, whereas the adults were novices at chess. The chess task was the one illustrated in Figure 9.14 — a chessboard was presented for 10 seconds, and participants were then asked to reproduce the positions of the pieces. **Figure 14.11** shows both the number of chess pieces recalled in the correct positions by children and adults and the number of digits recalled in the digit-span task. As Chi predicted, the adults were better on the digit-span task, but the children were better on the chess task. The children's superior chess performance was attributed to their greater knowledge of chess.

The novice–expert contrasts discussed in Chapter 9 are often used to explain developmental phenomena. We saw that a great deal of experience in a domain is required if a person is to become an expert. Chi's argument is that children, because of their lack of knowledge, are near universal novices, but they can become more expert than adults through concentrated experience in one domain, such as chess.

The Chi experiment contrasted child experts with nonexpert adults. Schneider, Körkel, and Weinert (1988) looked at the effect of expertise at various age levels. They tested German schoolchildren at grade levels 3, 5, and 7 on their recall of idea units from a story about soccer, and they categorized the children at each grade level as either experts or novices with respect to soccer. The results in **Table 14.1** show that the effect of expertise was much greater than that of grade level. Moreover, on a recognition test, there was no effect of grade level, only an effect of expertise. Schneider et al. also classified each group of participants into high-ability and low-ability participants on the basis of their performance on intelligence tests. Although such tests generally predict memory for stories, Schneider et al. found no effect of general ability level, only of knowledge for soccer. They argue that high-ability students are just those who know a lot about a lot of domains and consequently generally do well on memory tests. However, when tested on a story about a specific domain such as soccer, a high-ability student who knows nothing

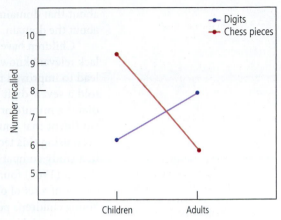

Figure 14.11 Recall of Chess Pieces and Digits by Children and Adults. Children with chess expertise were significantly better than nonexpert adults at recalling chess pieces in their correct positions, whereas adults were better at recalling digits. *(Data from Chi, 1978.)*

TABLE 14.1	Mean Percentage of Idea Units Recalled from a Story About Soccer	
Grade	Soccer Experts	Soccer Novices
3	54	32
5	52	33
7	61	42
(Data from Körkel, 1987.)		

about that domain will do worse than a low-ability student who knows a lot about the domain.

Children have difficulty on memory tasks not only because they typically lack relevant knowledge, but also because they do not know the strategies that lead to improved memory. The clearest case concerns rehearsal. If you were told a seven-digit telephone number and had to remember it so you could dial it a minute or two later, you would probably rehearse it until you were confident that you had it memorized or until you dialed the number. However, using this technique would not occur to young children. For example, in a study comparing 5-year-olds with 10-year-olds, Keeney, Cannizzo, and Flavell (1967) found that 10-year-olds almost always verbally rehearsed the names of a set of objects to be remembered, whereas 5-year-olds seldom did. Young children's performance often improves if they are instructed to use verbal rehearsal; however, very young children are simply unable to do this.

Chapter 6 emphasized the importance of elaborative strategies for good memory performance. Particularly for long-term retention, elaboration appears to be much more effective than rote rehearsal. There also appear to be sharp developmental trends with respect to the use of elaborative encoding strategies. For instance, Paris and Lindauer (1976) looked at the elaborations that children use to relate two paired-associate nouns that they have to remember, such as *lady* and *broom*. Older children are more likely to generate sentences in which the nouns relate actively, such as *The lady flew on the broom,* than sentences in which the relation is static, such as *The lady had a broom.* Generating sentences with active relations leads to better recall. Young children are also poorer at drawing the inferences that improve memory for a story (Stein & Trabasso, 1981).

Children need to learn strategies for encoding and elaborating experiences, and there is evidence that parents help teach their children such skills. For instance, consider this snippet of an interaction between a child and his mother (Salmon & Reese, 2016):

> *Mother:* "What was the first thing he [the barber] did?"
> *Child:* "Bzzzz." [running his hand over his head]
> *Mother:* "He used the clippers, and I think you liked the clippers.
>   And you know how I know? Because you were smiling."
> *Child:* "Because they were tickling."
> *Mother:* "They were tickling, is that how they felt? Did they feel
>   scratchy?"

The mother is showing her child how to elaborate his experiences. Salmon and Reese (2015) summarize the evidence that such interactions lead to better memory in children (particularly autobiographical memory).

> *Younger children often do worse on tasks than do older children, because they have less relevant knowledge and poorer strategies.*

Cognition and Aging

Changes in cognition do not cease when we reach adulthood. As we get older, we continue to acquire knowledge, but intelligence is not just a matter of what one knows, and human cognitive abilities do not continue to improve with added years. **Figure 14.12** shows mean IQ scores as a function of age on two components of the Wechsler Adult Intelligence Scale–Revised (WAIS-R). As you can see, scores on the verbal component (vocabulary, language comprehension, etc.) change little as people age, whereas scores on the performance component (reasoning, problem solving, etc.) decrease dramatically. (For a more detailed discussion of IQ scores, see the section "Intelligence Tests," below.)

It is important to note, however, that the declines in performance measures of cognitive ability can be misleading, for two main reasons. First, IQ tests are typically given rapidly, and older adults do better on slower tests. Second, IQ tests tend to be like school tests, and, in general, younger adults have had more recent experience with such tests. In contrast, older adults often do better than younger adults on measures of relevant job-related behavior (e.g., Perlmutter, Kaplan, & Nyquist, 1990), owing both to older adults' greater accumulation of knowledge and to their more mature approach to job demands. Also to be considered is the so-called *Flynn effect*—average IQ scores appear to have risen about 3 points per decade over the previous century (Flynn, 2007), which means, for example, that 20-year-olds in previous generations did not score as high as 20-year-olds in the current generation. Given that the age groups being compared in Figure 14.12 consist of people who grew up in different periods, some of the apparent decline in the figure might be due to differences among generations (e.g., in education, nutrition, and other factors that might affect test performance) and not to age-related factors.

Although non–age-related factors may explain some of the decline shown in Figure 14.12, there are substantial age-related declines in brain function that also contribute to poorer cognitive performance. Brain cells gradually die, and some areas are particularly susceptible to cell death. The hippocampus, which is particularly important to memory (see Chapter 7), loses about 5% of its cells every decade (Selkoe, 1992). Other hippocampal cells, though they might not die, have been observed to shrink and atrophy. However, there is evidence that some hippocampal cells grow to compensate for the age-related deaths of their neighbors. There is also evidence for the birth of new

Figure 14.12 **IQ Scores by Age.** Scores on the verbal component of the WAIS-R test remain relatively constant across decades of age differences; in contrast, scores on the performance component, which includes tests of reasoning and problem solving, decline steadily. *(Data from Salthouse, 1992.)*

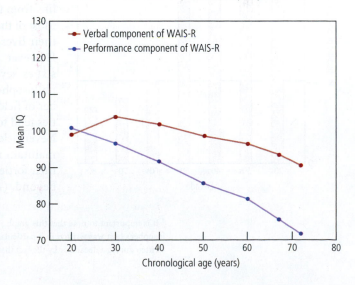

neurons, particularly in the region of the hippocampus (Gould & Gross, 2002). Moreover, the number of new neurons seems to be very much related to the richness of the aging person's new experiences. Although these new neurons are few in number compared with the number lost, they may be very valuable because new neurons are more plastic and may be critical to encoding new experiences.

Overall, age-related neural losses may make a relatively minor contribution to cognitive decline in most intellectually active adults, especially in comparison to the intellectual deficits associated with various brain-related disorders. The most common of these disorders is Alzheimer's disease, which is associated with substantial impairment of brain function, particularly in the temporal region including the hippocampus. Many brain-related disorders progress slowly, and some of the reason for the age-related deficits shown in Figure 14.12 and in other tests may be that some of the older participants are in the early stages of such diseases. However, even when health factors are taken into account and when the performance of the same participants is tracked in longitudinal studies (so there is not a generational confound), there is evidence for age-related intellectual decline, although the decline may not become significant until after age 60 (Schaie, 1996).

Figure 14.13 At What Age Do Philosophers Write Their Best Book? A book written when a philosopher is in the 30s or 40s is most likely to be considered the philosopher's best. The probability is somewhat less for the twenties and fifties and is much less for the sixties and later.

(Data from Lehman, 1953.)

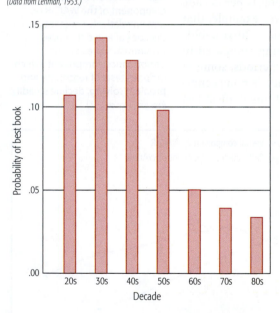

As we get older, a race is going on between growth in knowledge and loss of neural function. People in many professions (including artists, scientists, and philosophers) tend to produce their best work in their midthirties. Lehman (1953) examined the works of 182 notable philosophers (all deceased), who collectively wrote some 1,785 books, and plotted the probability that the book considered a philosopher's best was written in a particular decade of life, from the twenties to the eighties (see **Figure 14.13**). Most of these philosophers remained prolific throughout their lives, publishing many books in their later years. However, as Figure 14.13 shows, a book written in the sixties, seventies, or eighties is unlikely to be considered a philosopher's best.[1] Lehman reviewed data from a number of fields consistent with the hypothesis that the thirties tend to be the time of peak intellectual performance. Nevertheless, as you can see in Figure 14.13, people often maintain relatively high intellectual performance into their forties and fifties, and some do into their sixties and beyond. (As discussed in Chapter 9, truly exceptional

---

[1] It is important to note that this graph shows the probability that the specific book considered a philosopher's best was written in a particular decade, so the data are not skewed by the number of books written during a decade or by the fact that some of the philosophers died before reaching later decades.

Problems

<u>1 premise</u>
Q and R do the OPPOSITE
If Q INCREASES, what will happen to R?

<u>2 premises</u>
D and E do the OPPOSITE
C and D do the SAME
If C INCREASES, what will happen to E?

<u>3 premises</u>
R and S do the SAME
Q and R do the OPPOSITE
S and T do the OPPOSITE
If Q INCREASES, what will happen to T?

<u>4 premises</u>
U and V do the OPPOSITE
W and X do the SAME
T and U do the SAME
V and W do the OPPOSITE
If T INCREASES, what will happen to X?

(a)   (b)

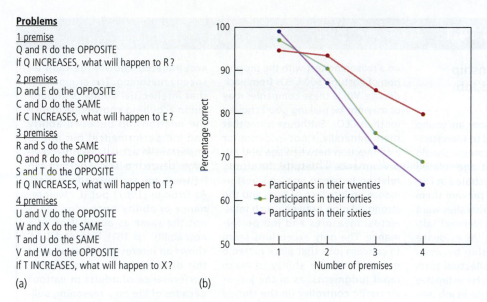

Figure 14.14 Age, Working Memory, and Problem Solving. (a) Reasoning problems involving increasing numbers of premises, hypothesized to put increasing demands on working memory. (b) Percentage of problems solved correctly by adults in their twenties, forties, and sixties. *(Data from Salthouse, 1992.)*

performance in a field tends to require at least 10 years of experience in that field — see **Implications 14.1** for discussion of the relationship between age, expertise, and job performance.)

The evidence for an age-related correlation between brain function and cognition makes it clear that biology influences intelligence and that the increased knowledge associated with advancing age cannot always overcome cognitive declines related to biological age. Salthouse (1992) tested participants of different ages on reasoning problems in which different numbers of premises have to be held in working memory and combined in order to reach the solution. The results presented in **Figure 14.14** show that people's ability to solve these problems generally declines as the number of premises increases, but that this decline is much steeper for adults in their forties or sixties than it is for adults in their twenties. Salthouse argued that older adults are slower than younger adults in information processing, which limits their ability to maintain information in working memory. Even though these tests are not speeded, the amount of information that can be maintained in working memory is controlled by speed of processing (e.g., see Chapter 6, Figure 6.7).

> *Increased knowledge and maturity sometimes compensate for age-related declines in rates of information processing.*

Implications 14.1

Is There a Relationship Between Age and Job Performance?

Many readers of this book are young adults looking forward to soon starting their professional careers. Should they be worried that age-related declines like those illustrated in Figures 14.12–14.14 will prevent them from achieving all of what they want to accomplish in their lifetime? Salthouse (2012) reviews the evidence for a strong relationship between performance on intellectual tests and job performance. He estimates that 25% of the variance in job performance can be predicted by scores on intellectual tests such as WAIS-R (see Figure 14.12), which is a high proportion for an individual difference measure. Consider, however, **Figure 14.15**, which contrasts the proportion of American adults from each decade of life who score high on a reasoning test with the proportion of Fortune 500 CEOs from each decade. While these companies may or may not be making good choices for their CEOs, Salthouse notes that there generally is not evidence for a connection between age and job performance — despite the strong relation between age and performance on intellectual tests and the strong relation between such intellectual measures and job performance. The only exceptions seem to concern jobs that place extreme demands on the ability to make rapid judgments, as in the job of air traffic controller (in the United States, the maximum entry age for air traffic controllers is 30, and the mandatory retirement age is 56).

A number of explanations have been proposed for the absence of a strong relationship between age and job performance. One is that most jobs depend more on accumulated knowledge than on speedy reasoning. The argument is that intellectual ability is important in acquiring knowledge (hence the relationship between ability and job performance) but not so important in actually using knowledge (hence the lack of relationship between age and job performance). As Droege (1967) put it, "Maintenance of ability once acquired is not the same as acquisition of a new ability" (p. 181). **Figure 14.16** shows an interesting illustration of this dissociation. It contrasts the performance of adults in various decades of life on a reasoning ability test with their performance on solving crossword puzzles. While solving crossword puzzles involves reasoning, it also depends on accumulated knowledge.

Given results like those shown in Figure 14.16 and given that older adults have acquired more job-

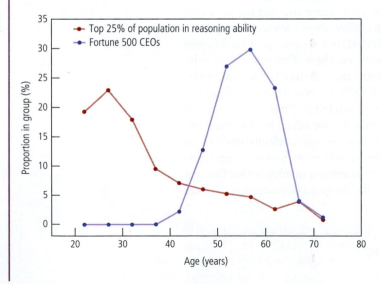

Figure 14.15 Age, Reasoning, and Fortune 500 CEOs. Reasoning ability, as measured by performance on the reasoning component of the Wechsler Adult Intelligence Scale–Fourth Edition, peaks in the twenties and thirties. Fortune 500 CEOs, as of December 2009, were almost all in their fifties and sixties. *(Data from Salthouse, 2012.)*

Implications 14.1 (*Continued*)

relevant knowledge than younger adults, you might ask why no positive relationship is found between job performance and age. However, finding a positive relationship is complicated by other factors that play into job performance as people age. One such factor is that people are often promoted into new positions throughout their careers, and these new positions are often ones that make less of a demand on the ability to reason rapidly. Also, the nature of jobs changes during a person's working life, with new technologies appearing that require learning new skills. For people starting their careers in today's high-tech and rapidly changing world, the ability to learn new skills is particularly important. Many will have to change their jobs multiple times over the years.

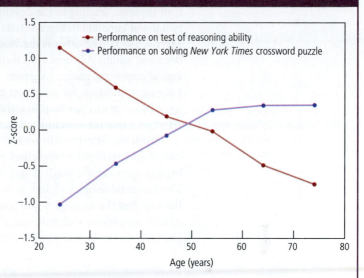

Figure 14.16   Age, Reasoning, and Crossword Puzzles. Reasoning ability declines steadily from its peak in the twenties, while performance on solving crossword puzzles, which depends more on accumulated knowledge than on reasoning, improves with age. The Z-score is a normalized measure that sets the average score in the population at 0. *(Data from Salthouse, 2012.)*

Psychometric Studies of Cognition

We now turn from considering how cognition varies as a function of age to considering how cognition varies among people of the same age. All this research has basically the same character: Using **psychometric tests,** researchers measure people's performances on a number of different tasks and then look at the way in which these performance measures correlate across tasks. This research has established that there is not a single dimension of "intelligence" on which people vary but rather that individual differences in cognition are much more complex. We will review two of these dimensions of intelligence in the next main section of this chapter, but first we will review what has been learned from psychometric studies of cognition.

Intelligence Tests

Research on intelligence testing predates the field of cognitive psychology by many decades. In 1904, the minister of public instruction in Paris established a commission charged with identifying children in need of remedial education. As a member of that commission, Alfred Binet set about developing a test that would objectively measure students' intellectual abilities and thereby reveal those needing help. In 1916, Lewis Terman adapted Binet's test for use with American students, leading to the development of the Stanford-Binet test, one of the two major general intelligence tests in use in the United States today (Terman & Merrill, 1973). The other is the Wechsler test, which has separate scales for children and adults. All these tests include measures of digit span, vocabulary, analogical reasoning, spatial judgment, and arithmetic. For example, a typical spatial judgment question for adults on the Stanford-Binet test is, "Which direction would you have to face so your right hand would be to the north?" A great deal of effort goes into constructing test items that will predict scholastic performance.

Both the Stanford-Binet test and the Wechsler test produce a measure called an **intelligence quotient (IQ).** The original definition of IQ related mental age to chronological age, reflecting its original use in testing children. The test establishes a child's mental age. If a child can solve the problems on the test that the average 8-year-old can solve, then the child has a mental age of 8, independent of chronological age. IQ is defined as the ratio of mental age (MA) to chronological age (CA) multiplied by 100:

$$IQ = 100 \times MA/CA$$

Thus, if a child's mental age established by test was 6 and the child's chronological age was 5, the child's IQ would be $100 \times 6/5 = 120$.

This definition of IQ proved unsuitable for a number of reasons, a major one being that it cannot extend to measurement of adult intelligence, because performance on intelligence tests starts to level off in the late teens and declines in later years. To deal with such difficulties, the common way of defining IQ now is in terms of deviation scores. The mean score for a person's age group is subtracted from the person's raw score, and then this difference is transformed into a measure that will vary around 100, roughly as the earlier IQ scores would. The precise definition is expressed as

$$IQ = 100 + \left[15 \times \frac{(\text{raw score} - \text{mean score})}{\text{standard deviation}} \right]$$

where "standard deviation" is a measure of the variability of the scores and "15" reflects the IQ points associated with one standard deviation. IQs so measured tend to be distributed according to a normal distribution, as shown in **Figure 14.17** along with the percentage of people who have scores in various ranges.

The Stanford-Binet and the Weschler are tests of general intelligence. Many other tests have been developed to measure specialized abilities, such as spatial ability.

Figure 14.17 Normal Distribution of IQ Scores. When scores are adjusted to vary around an average of 100, they tend to distribute symmetrically in a normal distribution. About 2% of the population are in the highest and lowest ranges (above 130 and below 70), and about 68% of the population clusters between 85 and 115.

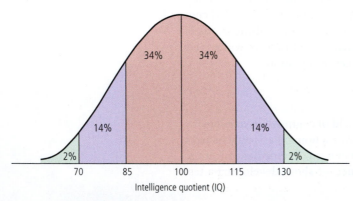

These tests (both general tests and specialized tests) partly owe their continued use in the United States to the fact that they do predict performance in school with some accuracy, which was one of Binet's original goals. However, their use for this purpose is controversial, in particular because these tests have been used to determine who can have access to which educational opportunities. Thus, it is very important that the tests not be culturally biased — that is, test questions should be answerable regardless of the cultural background of test takers. As you can imagine, it is not easy to construct completely unbiased tests. Immigrants, for example, often do poorly on intelligence tests because of cultural biases. For instance, immigrant Italians of less than a century ago scored an average of 87 on IQ tests (Sarason & Doris, 1979), whereas today their descendants have slightly above average IQs (Ceci, 1991).

The very concept of intelligence is culturally relative (Cocodia, 2014). What one culture sees as intelligent behavior another culture does not. For instance, the Kpelle, an African culture, think that the way in which Westerners sort things into categories (e.g., sorting apples and oranges into the same category) — a basis for some items in intelligence tests — is foolish (Cole, Gay, Glick, & Sharp, 1971). Robert Sternberg (personal communication, 1998) notes that some cultures do not even have a word for intelligence. Sternberg (2006, 2007) has developed the concept of *practical intelligence,* which is different from what is measured by IQ. He defines practical intelligence as the ability to solve concrete problems in real life, and he has shown that using measures of practical intelligence can significantly improve the predictive power of intelligence tests.

Related to the issue of the fairness of intelligence tests is the question of whether they measure innate endowment or acquired ability (the nature-versus-nurture issue again). Potentially definitive data would seem to come from studies of identical twins reared apart — for example, twins who have been adopted into different families and who therefore have identical genetic endowment but different environmental experiences. Analyses indicate that identical twins raised apart tend to have much more similar IQs than do nonidentical twins raised in the same family (Bouchard, 1983; Bouchard & McGue, 1981), which suggests that IQ is largely innate. However, this interpretation is not so clear. Twins from low socioeconomic groups tend to be underrepresented in studies of identical twins, and there is evidence that environmental factors have a stronger influence on intelligence measures among individuals from those groups (Nisbett et al., 2012). Also, Dickens and Flynn (2001) argue that certain individuals may be genetically predisposed to seek out intellectually stimulating environments that have a positive influence on IQ, and this indirect factor might therefore partially explain the IQ similarity of identical twins. This is how Dickens and Flynn explain the Flynn effect mentioned earlier — that measures of intelligence have increased dramatically over the last century. The Flynn effect would make no sense if genes directly controlled intelligence, but it would make sense if genes influenced the environments people chose and if these environments had a strong influence on their intelligence. Then increased schooling and the increased complexity of the world over the last century would provide the environmental change that would raise the intelligence of each generation. Still, within a generation certain individuals would have a genetic predisposition to seek out the most intellectually stimulating aspects of their world.

Although intelligence tests measure only some limited aspect of human abilities and although intelligence is still only poorly understood as some mixture of genetic and environmental influences, the remarkable fact is that intelligence tests are able to predict success in certain endeavors. They predict with moderate accuracy both performance in school and general success in life (at least in Western societies), including professional success (Schmidt and Hunter, 2004). They also predict health and longevity (Deary, Weiss, & Batty, 2010). What is it about the mind that the tests are measuring? Much of the theoretical work in the field has been concerned with trying to answer this question; and to understand this work, one must understand a little about a major method of the field, factor analysis. (See **Implications 14.2** for a more detailed discussion of the correlation between IQ scores and success in life.)

> *Standard intelligence tests measure general factors that predict success in school.*

Implications 14.2

Does IQ Determine Success in Life?

IQ appears to have a strong predictive relationship to many socially relevant factors besides academic performance. The American Psychological Association report *Intelligence: Knowns and Unknowns* (Neisser et al., 1996) states that IQ accounts for about one-quarter of the variance in factors such as job performance and income, and it correlates even more strongly with socioeconomic status. In addition, IQ correlates negatively (though more weakly) with antisocial measures such as criminal activity. These correlations — both positive and negative — might lead one to infer that IQ is directly related to being a successful member of our society, but there are reasons to question a direct relationship.

Access to various educational opportunities and to some jobs depends on test scores. Access to other professions depends on completing various educational programs, the access to which is partly determined by test scores. Given the strong relationship between IQ and these test scores, we would expect that higher-IQ members of our society would get better training and professional opportunities. Lower-scoring members of our society have more limited opportunities and often are sorted by their test scores into environments where there is more antisocial behavior.

Also, success in society is at every point partially determined by the judgments of other members of the society. For instance, most studies of job performance use measures like ratings of supervisors rather than direct measures of job performance. Promotions are often largely dependent on the judgments of superiors. Also, legal resolutions such as sentencing decisions in criminal cases have strong judgmental aspects to them. It could be that IQ more strongly affects these social judgments than the actual performances, such as how well people do their job or how bad some particular behavior was. Individuals in positions of power, such as judges and supervisors, tend to have high IQs. Thus, there is the possibility that some of the success associated with high IQ is an in-group effect in which high-IQ people favor people who are similar to them.

Factor Analysis

The general intelligence tests contain a number of subtests that measure specific abilities (and as noted above, many specialized tests also are available for measuring particular abilities). Generally, people who do well on one test or subtest tend to do well on other tests or subtests. The degree to which people perform comparably on two subtests is measured by a correlation coefficient. If all the people who did well on one test did just as well on another, the correlation coefficient for the two tests would be 1. If all the people who did well on one test did proportionately badly on another, the correlation coefficient would be –1. If there were no relation between how people did on one test and how they did on another test, the correlation coefficient would be 0. Typically, correlations between tests are positive, but not very close to 1, indicating a less than perfect relation between performance on one test and performance on another.

Figure 14.18 shows the correlations among scores on seven tests on the Washington Pre-College Test Battery. As can be seen, some pairs of tests are more correlated than others. For instance, there is a relatively high correlation (.67) between reading comprehension and vocabulary but a relatively low correlation (.14) between reading comprehension and spatial reasoning. As a way of trying to make sense of these correlational patterns, researchers use **factor analysis** to arrange these tests in a multidimensional space such that the distances between the tests correspond to their correlation: the closer together two tests are in the space, the higher their correlation (as shown in Figure 14.18). Tests close together can be taken to measure the same thing or closely related things.

Test name and description	Test #	Correlations 1	2	3	4	5	6	7	Graphical representation of correlations
Reading comprehension Answer questions about paragraph	1	1.00	.67	.33	.40	.33	.14	.34	
Vocabulary Choose synonyms for words	2		1.00	.59	.29	.46	.19	.31	
Grammar Identify correct and poor usages	3			1.00	.41	.34	.20	.46	
Quantitative skills Read word problems and decide whether problem can be solved	4				1.00	.39	.46	.62	
Mechanical reasoning Examine a diagram and answer questions about it; requires knowledge of physical and mechanical principles	5					1.00	.47	.39	
Spatial reasoning Indicate how two-dimensional figures will appear if they are folded through a third dimension	6						1.00	.46	
Mathematics achievement A test of high-school algebra	7							1.00	

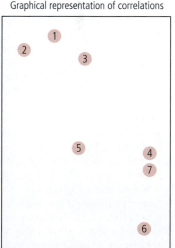

Figure 14.18 Correlations of Scores on Seven Tests on the Washington Pre-College Test Battery. In the graphical representation of the correlations, the distance between the points corresponding to the numbered tests generally decreases with increases in the correlation.

An interesting question is how to make sense of this space. As we go from the bottom to the top of the graphical representation in Figure 14.18, the tests become increasingly linguistic in character. We might refer to this dimension as a linguistic factor. Second, we might argue that, as we go from the left to the right, the tests become more computational in character. We might consider this dimension a reasoning factor. High correlations can be explained in terms of students having similar values of these factors. Thus, there is a high correlation between quantitative skills and mathematics achievement because they both have an intermediate degree of linguistic involvement and require substantial reasoning. People who have strong reasoning ability and average or better linguistic ability will tend to do well on all these tests.

Factor analysis is basically an effort to go from a set of correlations like those in Figure 14.18 to a small set of factors, or dimensions, that explain those correlations. There has been considerable debate about what the underlying factors are. Perhaps you can see other ways to explain the correlations in Figure 14.18. For instance, you might argue that a linguistic factor links tests 1 through 3, that a reasoning factor links tests 4, 5, and 7, and that test 6 involves a separate spatial factor. Indeed, we will see that there have been many proposals for separate linguistic, reasoning, and spatial factors, although, as shown by the data in Figure 14.18, it is a little difficult to separate the spatial and reasoning factors (i.e., scores on test 6 are much more correlated with scores on tests 4, 5, and 7 than with scores on tests 1, 2, and 3).

The difficulty in interpreting such data is manifested in the wide variety of positions that have been taken about what the underlying factors of human intelligence are. Spearman (1904) argued that only one general factor underlies performance across tests, a factor that he called *g*. In contrast, Thurstone (1938) argued that there are a number of separate factors, including verbal, spatial, and reasoning. Guilford (1956) proposed no less than 150 distinct intellectual abilities. Cattell (1963) proposed a distinction between crystallized and fluid intelligence: **crystallized intelligence** refers to acquired knowledge, whereas **fluid intelligence** refers to the ability to reason or to solve problems in novel domains. In Figure 14.12, fluid intelligence, not crystallized intelligence, shows age-related decay. Horn (1968), elaborating on Cattell's theory, argued that there is a spatial intelligence that can be separated from fluid intelligence. The correlations in Figure 14.18 can be interpreted in terms of the Horn–Cattell theory, where crystallized intelligence maps into the linguistic factor (tests 1–3), fluid intelligence into the reasoning factor (tests 4, 5, and 7), and spatial intelligence into the spatial factor (test 6). Fluid intelligence tends to be tapped strongly in mathematical tests, but it is probably better referred to as a reasoning ability than as a mathematical ability. It is a bit difficult to separate fluid intelligence from spatial intelligence in factor analytical studies, but it appears possible (Horn & Stankov, 1982).

Although it is hard to draw any firm conclusions about what the real factors are, it seems clear that there are different aspects of human intelligence as measured by intelligence tests. Probably, the Horn–Cattell theory and the Thurstone theory offer the best analyses, proposing what we will call a verbal factor, a spatial factor, and a reasoning factor. This conclusion is significant because it indicates that some specialization is involved in developing human cognitive function.

In a survey of virtually all data sets at the time, Carroll (1993) proposed what he called a three-strata theory of intelligence that combines the Horn–Cattell and Thurstone perspectives and this has become the general consensus today (e.g., Deary, 2012). At the lowest stratum are specific abilities, such as the ability to be a physicist. Such abilities, Carroll thinks, are largely acquired and not genetically determined. At the middle stratum are broader abilities such as the verbal factor (crystallized intelligence), the reasoning factor (fluid intelligence), and the spatial factor. Finally, Carroll noted that these factors tend to correlate together to define something like Spearman's *g* at the highest stratum.

In the past few decades, there has been considerable interest in how these measures of individual differences relate to theories of information processing in cognitive psychology. For instance, how do participants with high spatial abilities differ from those with low spatial abilities in their performance on the spatial imagery tasks discussed in Chapter 4? Makers of intelligence tests have tended to ignore such questions because their major goal is to predict scholastic performance.

> *Factor-analysis methods show that a reasoning ability, a verbal ability, and a spatial ability underlie performance on various intelligence tests.*

Different Dimensions of Intelligence

In this section we will discuss some of the ways people differ in their intellectual performance and the possible bases for these differences in the brains and experiences of individuals.

Verbal Ability

Verbal ability is probably the most robust factor to emerge from intelligence tests, and researchers have shown considerable interest in determining what processes distinguish people with strong verbal abilities. Goldberg, Schwartz, and Stewart (1977) compared people with high verbal ability and those with low verbal ability with respect to the way in which they make three different kinds of word judgments. Participants in one group were asked to judge simply whether two words were identical. For this task, participants would be expected to say yes to a pair such as

- bear, bear

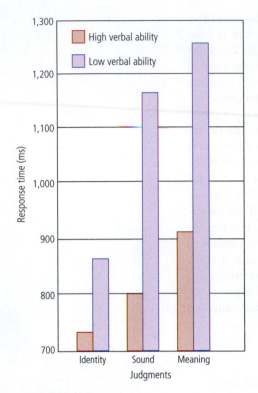

Figure 14.19 Differences in Verbal Ability. Participants with high verbal ability are faster in making all three types of word judgments, especially in making judgments about sound and meaning. *(Data from Goldberg et al., 1977.)*

Other participants were asked to judge whether two words sounded alike, in which case they would be expected to say yes to a pair such as

- bare, bear

The third group of participants were asked to judge whether two words were in the same semantic category; thus, they would be expected to say yes to a pair such as

- lion, bear

Figure 14.19 shows that participants with high verbal ability enjoy only a small advantage on the identity judgments but show much larger advantages on the sound and meaning judgments. This study and others (e.g., Hunt, Davidson, & Lansman, 1981) have convinced researchers that a major advantage held by participants with high verbal ability is the greater speed with which they can go from a linguistic stimulus to information about it — for instance, in the study depicted in Figure 14.19, participants were going from the printed word (a visual stimulus) to information about its sound and meaning. Thus, as noted in a variety of contexts in earlier parts of this chapter, speed of processing is related to intellectual ability.

There is also evidence for a fairly strong relation between working-memory capacity for linguistic material and verbal ability. Daneman and Carpenter (1980) developed a test of individual differences in working-memory capacity in which participants would read or hear a number of unrelated sentences such as these two:

- When at last his eyes opened, there was no gleam of triumph, no shade of anger.
- The taxi turned up Michigan Avenue where they had a clear view of the lake.

After reading or hearing these sentences, participants had to recall the last word of each sentence. They were tested on two to seven such sentences at a time, and the largest number of sentences for which they could accurately recall the last words was termed the *reading span* or the *listening span*. College students had spans ranging from 2 to 5.5, and these spans proved to be strongly related to the students' scores on reading comprehension tests and on tests of verbal ability — much more strongly related than simple digit spans. Daneman and Carpenter argued that a larger reading or listening span indicates an ability to store a larger amount of text during reading or listening.

People with high verbal ability are able to make rapid judgments about pairs of words and have large working memories for verbal information.

Spatial Ability

Efforts have been made to relate measures of spatial ability to research on mental rotation, such as the research discussed in Chapter 4. Just and Carpenter (1985) compared the performance of participants with low spatial ability and those with high spatial ability on the Shepard and Metzler mental rotation tasks (see Figure 4.4). **Figure 14.20** plots the speed with which these two types of participants can rotate figures of differing angular disparity. As can be seen, participants with low spatial ability not only performed the task more slowly but were also more affected by angle of disparity. Thus the rate of mental rotation is lower for participants with low spatial ability.

Spatial ability has often been set in contrast with verbal ability. Some people rate high on both abilities or low on both, but research interest often focuses on people who display a relative imbalance of the two abilities. MacLeod, Hunt, and Matthews (1978) found evidence that people with opposite imbalances have different ways of solving the Clark and Chase sentence-verification task considered in the section "Negatives" in Chapter 13. Recall that, in this task, participants are presented with sentences such as *The plus is above the star* and *The star is not above the plus* and asked to determine whether each sentence accurately describes the picture. Typically, participants are slower when there is a negative such as *not* in the sentence and when the supposition of the sentences mismatches the picture, and even slower when there is both a negative and a mismatch.

MacLeod et al. speculated, however, that there were really two groups of participants — a group with high verbal ability and a group with high spatial ability. They hypothesized that the group with high verbal ability would first create a mental representation of the sentence and then match it against the picture. In contrast, the group with high spatial ability would first convert the sentence into a mental image of a picture and then match that image against the picture. **Figure 14.21** shows that they did, in fact, find two groups of participants, in which the presence of a negative had a very substantial effect on one group but no effect on the other. The group showing the effect was the group with higher scores on tests of verbal ability, who were assumed to have compared the sentence against the picture. The group not showing the effect was the group with higher scores on tests of spatial ability, who were assumed to have compared a mental image formed from the sentence against the picture. Presumably, the latter group's faster verification times for negative sentences are a consequence of the fact that a mental image formed from a negative sentence would not have a negative in it.

Research like the study just discussed, relating psychometric measures to cognitive tasks, has reinforced the distinction between verbal ability and

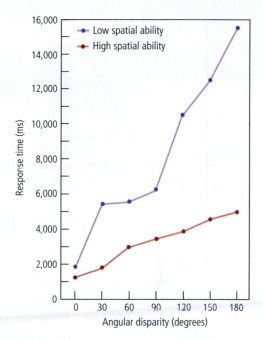

Figure 14.20 Differences in Spatial Ability. Participants with high spatial ability are much quicker than those with low spatial ability at mental rotation tasks like those shown in Figure 4.4, where one shape has to be mentally rotated through a certain angle of disparity with another shape in order to determine whether the shapes are congruent. (*Data from Just & Carpenter, 1985.*)

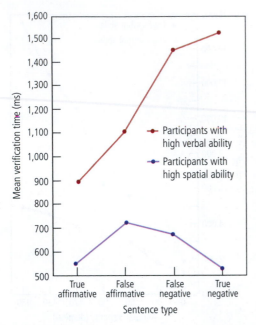

Figure 14.21 Sentence Verification Tasks: High Verbal Ability Versus High Spatial Ability. Participants with high verbal ability have much more difficulty verifying sentences with negatives than do participants with high spatial ability. *(Data from MacLeod et al., 1978.)*

spatial ability, and such differences in intellectual strengths have implications for more than test performance. Not surprisingly, children with high spatial ability tend to choose careers in science, technology, engineering, and mathematics, while children with high verbal ability tend to go into professions like law and journalism (Wai, Lubinski, & Benbow, 2009).

> *People with high spatial ability can perform elementary spatial operations quite rapidly and often choose to perform a task spatially rather than verbally.*

Cognitive and Neural Correlates of Intelligence

We have reviewed studies showing the correlation between relatively simple laboratory tasks and psychometric studies of intelligence. Surprisingly, even very simple laboratory tasks, such as the Sternberg task (Figures 1.1 and 1.2), show small but significant correlations with general measures of intelligence (e.g., Sheppard & Vernon, 2008). There are somewhat stronger correlations between intelligence and simple measures of working memory, such as digit span (e.g., Žebec, Demetriou, & Kotrla-Topić, 2015). A number of researchers (e.g., Just & Carpenter, 1992; Salthouse, 1992) have argued that working-memory differences may result from differences in processing speed — that is, people can maintain more information in working memory when they can process it more rapidly. However, correlation between intelligence and working memory remains even in studies where attempts have been made to account for the effects of processing speed. Nettelbeck and Burns (2010) present evidence that the increase in intelligence across childhood is associated with increased processing speed, whereas the decline in adulthood is more associated with a decline in working memory.

Research interest has increased in the question of which properties of the brain are associated with measures of intelligence. There are weak but significant correlations between brain size and measures of intelligence (Pietschnig, Penke, Wicherts, Zeiler, & Voracek, 2015). Various aspects of brain structure also correlate with intelligence. For example, the amount of myelination (measured as white matter) correlates with intelligence (Goriounova & Mansvelder, 2019). Since greater myelination allows for more rapid transmission of information between brain regions, this would be consistent with behavioral research showing that speed in simple cognitive tasks predicts intelligence. Also, structural features of neurons that indicate an increased number of synaptic connections correlate positively with measures of intelligence (Goriounova & Mansvelder, 2019). However, it needs to be kept in mind that all of these brain-related correlations tend to be weak, and they tend to be weaker than the correlations found with behavioral measures in simple cognitive tasks.

A great deal of research on the neural basis of intelligence has focused on functional measures of brain activity using techniques such as PET and fMRI. Early research indicated that better-performing participants can solve problems with less expenditure of effort, as indicated by less brain activity. In the first study confirming this general relation, Haier et al. (1988) found that the better-performing participants showed less PET activity during an abstract-reasoning task, indicating that the poorer-performing participants had to work harder at the same task. Results like these support the general thesis that brighter individuals can perform intellectual tasks more efficiently and so display less brain activation. In a review of such functional imaging research and of structural studies, Jung and Haier (2007) emphasized the importance of activity in parietal and frontal regions, as well as activity indicating interactions between these regions. However, more recent research suggests that the relationship between intelligence and lower activation in these regions holds only for simple tasks, whereas in complex tasks, better-performing participants may display greater activation in these regions (for a review, see Neubauer & Fink, 2009).

A more nuanced interpretation of brain activation results is supported by a reanalysis of an fMRI study of participants solving challenging mathematics problems that required inventing new solution procedures (Anderson & Fincham, 2014). The participants were 40 undergraduate and graduate students at Carnegie Mellon University (ages 19–34) and 35 schoolchildren in the Pittsburgh area (ages 12–14). The children were not a random selection but rather were students whose parents felt that their child was ready to participate in a very challenging mathematics task. **Figure 14.22** shows a wide range of success in solving these problems, with the children tending to do somewhat less well than the Carnegie Mellon students but with some children doing nearly as well as the top Carnegie Mellon students. We could not find significant differences in brain activation in any area that separated the good performers from the poor performers. We developed a cognitive model of how these problems could be solved and found a mapping from the steps of this model onto brain activity (using machine learning techniques). This model did not predict greater activation in specific regions but rather predicted when different regions should be active at different times. For instance, the model predicted that there should be high activation in anterior prefrontal regions early in the solution process and high activation later in parietal regions. The x-axis in Figure 14.22 shows a measure of how well the temporal changes in brain activation for any given participant matched the

Figure 14.22 Success in Solving Challenging Mathematics Problems: Schoolchildren and Adult University Students. Participants solved problems while in an fMRI scanner. Differences between schoolchildren and adults in solving problems successfully are correlated with a measure of how well the temporal patterns of brain activity matched the predictions of a cognitive model.

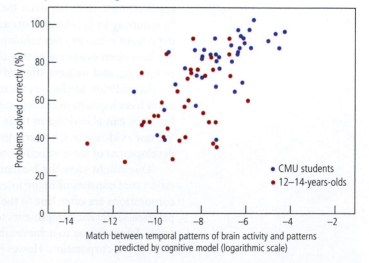

predictions of the model. It is striking how well this measure correlates with participants' success in solving problems (the correlation coefficient was .64). The differences between the performance of the schoolchildren and the adult university students seem totally predicted by the measure. The university students who scored high on this measure were the students who knew more about how to solve novel problems. This result is like the earlier results we saw in Figures 14.10 and 14.11, suggesting that experience not age was the critical variable in task performance. Thus, it is not a matter of how much activation a person has in a particular brain region but rather a matter of the person having the knowledge that leads to activation of the region at the right time.

> *In part, individual differences in intelligence are related to direct measures of processing speed, working memory, and brain structure and function. However, they are also related to individual differences in acquired knowledge.*

Conclusions

Two recurring themes throughout this book have been the diversity of the components of the mind and the specialization of different brain regions to perform different functions. The first chapter reviewed the evidence for different specializations in the nervous system. Subsequent chapters reviewed the evidence for different levels of processing as information entered the system and then discussed the different types of knowledge representation and the distinction between procedural and declarative knowledge. Then, we considered the distinct status of language. Many of the findings discussed in those chapters have been reinforced in this chapter on individual differences.

Another recurring theme has been the importance of the rate of processing: Response time has been the most frequently used measure of cognitive functioning in this book. Often, error measures (the second most common dependent measure) were shown to be merely indications of slow processing. We have seen evidence in this chapter that individuals vary in their rate of processing, and we have stressed that this rate can be increased with practice.

In addition to the quantitative component of speed, individual differences have a qualitative component: People can differ in where their strengths lie. They can also differ in their selection of strategies for solving problems. We saw evidence in Chapter 9 that one dimension of growing expertise is the development of more effective strategies.

One might view the human mind as being analogous to a large corporation that consists of many interacting components. The differences among corporations are often due to the relative strengths of their components. With practice, different components tend to become more efficient at doing their tasks. Another way to achieve improvement is by strategic reorganizations of parts of the corporation. However, there is more to a successful company than just the sum of its parts: The parts have to interact smoothly to achieve the overall goals of the organization. Some researchers (e.g., Newell, 1990) have complained about the rather fragmented picture of the human mind that emerges from current research in cognitive psychology. One agenda for future research will be to understand how all the pieces fit together to make a human mind.

Questions for Thought

1. Chapter 12 discussed data on child language acquisition. In learning a second language, younger children initially learn less rapidly than older children and adults, but there is evidence that they eventually achieve higher levels of mastery. Discuss this phenomenon from the point of view of this chapter on individual differences. Consider in particular Figure 12.8.

2. Most American presidents were between the ages of 50 and 59 when they were first elected president. The youngest was John F. Kennedy, elected at age 43. The oldest was Donald Trump, elected at age 71. What are the implications of this chapter for an ideal age for an American president?

3. Hunter and Hunter (1984) report that ability measures such as IQ are better predictors of job performance than are academic grades. Why might this be? A potentially relevant fact is that the most commonly used measure of job performance is supervisor ratings.

4. As an example of the importance of spatial imagery in scientific discovery, Newcombe and Frick (2010) state that "Watson and Crick's discovery of the structure of DNA occurred when they were able to fit a three-dimensional model to Rosalind Franklin's flat images of the molecule — clearly a spatial task." Rosalind Franklin suffered from the sexism of her time, and there is debate about whether she should have been awarded the Nobel Prize along with Watson and Crick. There is also much discussion about the role of gender differences in spatial ability — whether they exist and what they might imply about ability in science. There is also debate about the role of social factors in producing gender difference in spatial ability (e.g., Hoffman, Gneezy, & List, 2011). Check out the history of Rosalind Franklin and decide whether she should have been awarded the Nobel Prize.

Key Terms

concrete-operational stage
conservation
crystallized intelligence
factor analysis
fluid intelligence
formal-operational stage
intelligence quotient (IQ)
preoperational stage
psychometric tests
sensory-motor stage

Glossary

2½-D sketch: As proposed by David Marr, a visual representation that identifies where various visual features are located in space relative to the viewer. (p. 46)

3-D model: As proposed by David Marr, a representation of objects in a visual scene. (p. 46)

ACC: See *anterior cingulate cortex.*

action potential: A sudden change in electric potential that travels down the *axon* of a *neuron.* (p. 15)

activation: A measure of both the probability and the speed of access of a memory. (p. 183)

affirmation of the consequent: A logical fallacy: it asserts that if a *conditional statement* is true and if the *consequent* is true, then the *antecedent* must also be true (i.e., given that *If A, then B* is true and that *B* is true, it is a fallacy to conclude that *A* must be true). (p. 319)

AI: See *artificial intelligence.*

allocentric representation: A representation of the environment according to a fixed coordinate system, as on a map. Contrast with *egocentric representation.* (p. 125)

amnesia: Loss of memory. See also *anterograde amnesia; retrograde amnesia; Korsakoff syndrome.* (p. 235)

amodal hypothesis: The proposal that meaning is not represented in a particular modality. Contrast with *multimodal hypothesis.* (p. 151)

amodal symbol system: An inherently nonperceptual system for representing information—i.e., a system in which the symbols are not associated with any particular perceptual modality. Contrast with *perceptual symbol system.* (p. 147)

amygdala: A brain structure that is involved in emotional responses. (p. 21)

analogy: In problem solving, the process by which a problem solver maps the solution for one problem into a solution for another problem. (p. 254)

antecedent: The condition of a *conditional statement;* that is, the *A* in *If A, then B.* (p. 318)

anterior cingulate cortex (ACC): A medial portion of the *prefrontal cortex* important in cognitive control and in dealing with conflict. (p. 100)

anterograde amnesia: Loss of the ability to form new long-term memories. Contrast with *retrograde amnesia.* (p. 235)

aphasia: An impairment of speech that results from a brain injury. (p. 22)

apperceptive agnosia: A form of *visual agnosia* marked by the inability to recognize simple shapes such as circles and triangles. (p. 38)

arguments: The elements of a *propositional representation* that correspond to particular times, places, people, or things. (p. 145)

articulatory process: In Baddeley's theory of *working memory,* a component of the *phonological loop,* an "inner voice" that rehearses verbal information. Contrast with *phonological store.* (p. 178)

artificial intelligence (AI): A field of computer science that attempts to develop programs that will enable machines to display intelligent behavior. (p. 2)

associative agnosia: A form of *visual agnosia* marked by the inability to recognize complex objects, but with retention of the ability to recognize simple shapes and to copy drawings of complex objects. (p. 38)

associative phase: The second phase of skill acquisition, in which errors in the initial understanding are gradually detected and eliminated, and the connections among the various elements required for successful performance are strengthened. (p. 285)

atmosphere hypothesis: The proposal that the *logical quantifiers* used in the premises of a *categorical syllogism* create an "atmosphere" that predisposes participants to accept conclusions having the same quantifiers. (p. 331)

attention: The allocation of cognitive resources among ongoing processes. (p. 72)

attenuation theory: Treisman's *early-selection theory* of *attention,* which proposes that some incoming sensory signals are attenuated (weakened) on the basis of their physical characteristics. (p. 75)

attribute identification: Determining which attributes are relevant to the formation of a hypothesis. See also *rule learning.* (p. 337)

auditory sensory store (or *echoic memory*): A memory system that can briefly store auditory information. (p. 174)

automaticity: The ability to perform a task with little or no central cognitive control. (p. 95)

autonomous phase: The third phase of skill acquisition, in which the performance of a skill becomes automatic. (p. 285)

axon: A long tube extending from the soma of a *neuron* and branching into terminal boutons that form *synapses* with *dendrites* of other *neurons;* axons provide the fixed paths by which *neurons* communicate with one another. (p. 14)

backup avoidance: The tendency in problem solving to avoid *operators* that undo the effects of one or more previous *operators.* (p. 259)

backward inferences: See *bridging inferences.*

bar detectors: Cells in the visual cortex that respond most to bars in the visual field. Contrast with *edge detectors.* (p. 42)

basal ganglia: Subcortical structures that play a critical role in the control of motor movement and complex cognition. (p. 21)

Bayes's theorem: A theorem that prescribes how to combine the *prior probability* of a hypothesis with the *conditional probability* of the evidence, given the hypothesis, to assess the *posterior probability* of the hypothesis, given the evidence. (p. 347)

behaviorism: The theory that psychology should be concerned only with behavior and should not refer to mental constructs underlying behavior. (p. 7)

bilingualism: Substantial fluency in two languages. (p. 409)

binding problem: The question of how the brain puts together features in the visual field to produce perception of an object. (p. 86)

blood oxygen level dependent response (BOLD response): In *fMRI* studies, a measure of the amount of oxygen in the blood. (p. 29)

bottom-up processing: Perceptual processing of a physical stimulus in which information from the stimulus, rather than from the general context, is used to help recognize the stimulus. Contrast with *top-down processing.* (p. 63)

bridging inferences (or *backward inferences*)**:** In language comprehension, inferences that connect the comprehension of a sentence to a prior part of the text or discourse. Contrast with *elaborative inferences.* (p. 436)

Broca's area: A region in the left frontal cortex that is important for processing language, particularly the *syntax* (grammar) of speech. (p. 22)

categorical perception: The perception of stimuli as belonging in distinct categories without gradual variations. (p. 61)

categorical syllogism: A *syllogism* in which *logical quantifiers* relate categories A to B in one premise, relate B to C in the other premise, and relate A to C in the conclusion. (p. 329)

center-embedded sentences: Sentences in which one clause is embedded in another (e.g., *The boy whom the girl liked was sick*). (p. 425)

central bottleneck: The inability of central cognition to pursue multiple lines of thought simultaneously. Contrast with *perfect time-sharing.* (p. 95)

central executive: In Baddeley's theory, a system that controls how the *articulatory process* and the *visuospatial sketchpad* are used. (p. 178)

cerebral cortex: The outer layer of the brain, consisting mainly of the *neocortex* but also other, more primitive structures. (p. 19)

change blindness: The inability to detect a change in a scene when the change matches the context. (p. 68)

cognitive maps: Mental representations of the locations of objects and places in the environment. See also *route map; survey map.* (p. 122)

cognitive neuroscience: The study of the neural basis of cognition. (p. 13)

cognitive phase: The first phase of skill acquisition, in which the declarative encoding of a skill is developed and used. (p. 285)

cognitive psychology: The science of how the mind is organized to produce intelligent thought and how the mind is realized in the brain. (p. 1)

cognitive revolution: Beginning in the 1950s, a broad movement in psychology away from *behaviorism* and toward the scientific study of cognition. (p. 9)

cognitive science: A field that attempts to integrate research efforts from psychology, philosophy, *linguistics,* neuroscience, and *artificial intelligence.* (p. 10)

competence: In *linguistics,* a person's abstract knowledge of a language. Contrast with *performance.* (p. 380)

componential analyses: Approaches to instruction that begin with an analysis of the individual elements that need to be learned. (p. 311)

concrete-operational stage: The third stage in Piaget's theory of four stages of development, spanning the period from 7 to 11 years of age, during which a child has systematic schemes for thinking about the physical world. (p. 451)

conditional probability: In the context of *Bayes's theorem*, the probability that a particular piece of evidence will be found if a hypothesis is true. (p. 348)

conditional statement: An assertion that, if an *antecedent* is true, then a *consequent* must be true: a statement of the form *If A, then B*. (p. 318)

cones: Photoreceptor cells involved in color vision and high-acuity vision. (p. 39)

confirmation bias: When trying to determine whether a hypothesis is correct, the tendency to look only at evidence that is consistent with the hypothesis. (p. 339)

connectionist models: Computer models that simulate cognition by including neuronlike elements that have different levels of activity and that interact through connections with properties like those of *synapses*. (p. 32)

consequent: The result of a *conditional statement*; the *B* in *If A, then B*. (p. 318)

conservation: In Piaget's theory of cognitive development, knowledge of the preservation of particular properties of the physical world under various transformations. (p. 452)

consonantal feature: A consonant-like quality in a *phoneme*. (p. 59)

constituent: A phrase, or unit, in a sentence's structure. (p. 420)

corpus callosum: A broad band of fibers that connects and enables communication between the left and right hemispheres of the brain. (p. 22)

critical period: A period early in life when children are best prepared to learn a cognitive skill such as language. (p. 406)

crystallized intelligence: *Intelligence* that depends on acquired knowledge. Contrast with *fluid intelligence*. (p. 474)

decay theory: The theory that forgetting is caused by the spontaneous decay of memories over time. Contrast with *interference theory*. (p. 210)

declarative memory: See *explicit memory*.

deductive reasoning: Reasoning in which the conclusions follow with certainty from the premises. (p. 317)

deep convolutional networks: Computerized systems typically applied to object recognition tasks (including face recognition), based on layers of successively more complex pattern recognizers. (p. 54)

deep learning: In connectionist models, learning connections in networks that have many layers of connecting neuronlike elements. (p. 33)

Deese-Roediger-McDermott paradigm: A paradigm for creating false memories of words by presenting associatively related words. (p. 228)

default values: The typical values for a *slot* in a *schema* representation. (p. 156)

deliberate practice: Practice in which learners are motivated to learn (not just perform), are given feedback on their performance, and carefully monitor how their performance changes. (p. 304)

dendrites: Short branches attached to the soma of a *neuron* that form *synapses* with the terminal boutons of *axons* of other neurons. (p. 14)

denial of the antecedent: A logical fallacy: it asserts that, if a *conditional statement* is true and if the *antecedent* is false, then the *consequent* must also be false (i.e., given that *If A, then B* is true and that *A* is false, it is a fallacy to conclude that *B* must be false). (p. 319)

depth of processing: The theory that rehearsal improves memory only if the material is rehearsed in a deep and meaningful way. (p. 177)

descriptive model: A model that describes how people actually behave. Contrast with *prescriptive model*. (p. 350)

dichotic listening task: A task in which participants in an experiment are presented with two messages simultaneously, one to each ear, and are instructed to repeat back the words from only one of the messages. (p. 73)

difference reduction (or *hill climbing*): The tendency in problem solving to select *operators* that most reduce the difference between the current *state* and the *goal state*. (p. 259)

dissociation: A demonstration that a manipulation has an effect on performance of one task but not another. Such demonstrations are thought to be important in arguing for different cognitive systems. (p. 238)

DLPFC: See *dorsolateral prefrontal cortex*.

dorsolateral prefrontal cortex (DLPFC): Upper portion of the *prefrontal cortex* thought to be important in cognitive control. (p. 100)

dual-code theory: Paivio's theory that information is represented in combined verbal and visual codes. (p. 148)

dualism: A philosophical position that posits that the mind and the body are separate kinds of entities. (p. 12)

early-selection theories: Theories of *attention* proposing that *serial bottlenecks* occur early in information processing. Contrast with *late-selection theories.* (p. 72)

echoic memory: See *auditory sensory store.* (p. 174)

edge detectors: Cells in the visual cortex that respond most to edges in the visual field. Contrast with *bar detectors.* (p. 42)

EEG: See *electroencephalography.*

egocentric representation: A representation of the environment as it appears to the perception of an observer. Contrast with *allocentric representation.* (p. 125)

Einstellung effect (or *mechanization of thought*): A *set effect* whereby people repeat a solution that has worked for previous problems even when a simpler solution is possible. (p. 275)

elaborative inferences (or *forward inferences*): In language comprehension, inferences that add new information to the interpretation of a text or discourse and often predict what will be coming up. Contrast with *bridging inferences.* (p. 436)

elaborative processing: Thinking of information that relates to and expands on information that needs to be remembered. (p. 195)

electroencephalography (EEG): Measurement of electrical activity of the brain, using electrodes on the scalp. (p. 25)

embodied cognition: The viewpoint that the mind can only be understood by taking into account the human body and how it interacts with the environment. (p. 150)

empiricism: The philosophical position that posits that all knowledge comes from experience in the world. Contrast with *nativism.* (p. 5)

encoding-specificity principle: Tulving's principle that memory is better when the encoding of an item at study matches the encoding at test. (p. 234)

endogenous control: See *goal-directed attention.*

epiphenomenon: A mental experience that has no functional role in information processing. (p. 105)

ERPs: See *event-related potentials.*

event-related potentials (ERPs): Changes in electrical activity at the scalp in response to an external event, as measured by *electroencephalography.* (p. 25)

excitatory synapse: A *synapse* in which the *neurotransmitters* released by the terminal bouton of the *axon* decrease the potential difference across the membrane of the *dendrite* of the receiving *neuron.* (p. 15)

executive control: The direction of central cognition, which is carried out mainly by prefrontal regions of the brain. (p. 100)

exemplar theories: Theories holding that concepts are represented by specific instances in our experience and that new instances are categorized on the basis of their similarity to the stored representations. Contrast with *prototype theories.* (p. 163)

exogenous control: See *stimulus-driven attention.*

explicit memory (or *declarative memory*): Knowledge that we can consciously recall. Contrast with *implicit memory.* (p. 237)

factor analysis: In the context of intelligence tests, a statistical method that tries to find a set of factors that will account for performance across a range of tests. (p. 473)

false-memory syndrome: A condition in which a person falsely remembers traumatic events that never occurred, such as false memories of childhood abuse. (p. 226)

fan effect: The increase in the time it takes to retrieve a memory as the number of associated memories increases. (p. 213)

feature analysis: A theory of pattern recognition that claims that we extract primitive features and then recognize their combinations. (p. 50)

feature-integration theory: Treisman's proposal that one must focus *attention* on a stimulus before its individual features can be synthesized into a pattern. (p. 86)

feature map: A representation of the spatial locations of a particular visual feature. (p. 43)

filter theory: Broadbent's *early-selection theory* of *attention,* which assumes that, when sensory information has to pass through a *serial bottleneck,* only some of the information is selected for further processing, on the basis of physical characteristics, such as the pitch of a speaker's voice. (p. 74)

flashbulb memory: Particularly good memory for an event that is very important. (p. 201)

FLMP (fuzzy logical model of perception): Massaro's theory of perception, which proposes that information provided by the stimulus and information provided by the context combine to determine perception. (p. 65)

fluid intelligence: *Intelligence* characterized by the ability to reason or to solve problems in novel domains. Contrast with *crystallized intelligence.* (p. 474)

fMRI: See *functional magnetic resonance imaging.*

formal-operational stage: The fourth stage in Piaget's theory of four stages of development, spanning the period from 11 years of age onward, during which a child has abstract schemes for reasoning about the world. (p. 452)

forward inferences: See *elaborative inferences.*

fovea: The area of the *retina* with the greatest concentration of *cones* and therefore the greatest visual acuity. When we focus on an object, we move our eyes so that the image of the object falls on the fovea. (p. 39)

framing effects: Effects whereby people make different choices among equivalent alternatives depending on how the alternatives are stated. (p. 362)

frontal lobe: The region at the front of the brain that includes the motor cortex and the *prefrontal cortex.* (p. 20)

functional fixedness: The tendency to see objects as serving only conventional problem-solving functions and thus failing to see that they can serve novel functions. (p. 272)

functional magnetic resonance imaging (fMRI): A method for determining the location of neural activity by measuring the magnetic field produced by the iron in oxygenated blood in the brain. (p. 26)

fusiform face area: A part of the temporal cortex that is especially involved in fine discriminations, particularly of faces. (p. 116)

fusiform gyrus: A region in the temporal cortex involved in recognition of complex patterns such as faces and words. (p. 55)

fuzzy logical model of perception: See *FLMP.*

gambler's fallacy: The belief that the likelihood of an event increases with the amount of time since the event last occurred. (p. 357)

garden-path sentences: Sentences with a *transient ambiguity* that lead listeners to make a wrong interpretation initially, which they then have to correct. (p. 431)

General Problem Solver (GPS): A computer simulation program created by Newell and Simon that models human problem solving using *means–ends analysis.* (p. 261)

gestalt principles of organization: Principles that determine how a scene is organized into components; the principles include proximity, similarity, good continuation, closure, and good form. (p. 46)

Gestalt psychology: An approach to psychology that emphasizes principles of organization that result in holistic properties of the brain that go beyond the activity of the parts. (p. 8)

goal-directed attention (or *endogenous control*)*: Attention* controlled by one's goals. Contrast with *stimulus-driven attention.* (p. 72)

goal state: A *state* in a *problem space* in which the final goal is achieved. (p. 248)

GPS: See *General Problem Solver.*

grammar: A set of rules that prescribe all the acceptable utterances of a language. A grammar consists of *syntax, semantics,* and *phonology.* (p. 378)

gyrus: An outward bulge of the *cerebral cortex.* Contrast with *sulcus.* (p. 19)

hemodynamic response: The increased flow of oxygenated blood to a region of the brain that has greater activity—the basis of *functional magnetic resonance imaging.* (p. 26)

hill climbing: See *difference reduction.*

hippocampus: A brain structure that is part of the limbic system and that plays a critical role in the formation of permanent memories. (p. 21)

iconic memory: See *visual sensory store.*

illusory conjunctions: Illusions that features of different objects belong to a single object. (p. 86)

immediacy of interpretation: In language comprehension, the principle that people try to extract meaning out of each word as it arrives, rather than waiting until the end of the sentence or even just the end of the *constituent* containing the word. (p. 422)

implicit memory: Knowledge implied by our actions but inaccessible to conscious recall. Contrast with *explicit memory.* (p. 237)

inattentional blindness: Unawareness of unattended areas of the visual field. (p. 82)

incubation effect: A phenomenon in which a solution to a problem comes more easily after one has put the problem aside for a time. (p. 277)

inductive reasoning: Reasoning in which the conclusions follow only probabilistically from the premises. (p. 317)

information-processing approach: An analysis of human cognition into a set of steps for processing an abstract entity called "information." (p. 10)

inhibition of return: The decreased ability to return our *attention* to a location or an object that we have already attended to. (p. 90.)

inhibitory synapse: A *synapse* in which the *neurotransmitters* released by the terminal bouton of the *axon* increase the potential difference across the membrane of the *dendrite* of the receiving *neuron.* (p. 15)

insight problem: A problem in which the person is not aware of being close to a solution. (p. 279)

intelligence: The ability to recall facts, solve problems, reason, learn, and use language. (p. 2)

intelligence quotient (IQ): A measure of general intellectual performance that is normed to have a mean of 100 and a standard deviation of 15. (p. 470)

intelligent tutoring systems: A computer system that combines cognitive models with techniques from *artificial intelligence* to create instructional interactions with students. (p. 311)

interactive processing: The position that *syntax* and *semantics* are combined at all levels of language processing. Contrast with *modularity*. (p. 434)

interference theory: The theory that forgetting is caused by interference among memories. Contrast with *decay theory*. (p. 210)

introspection: A methodology much practiced at the turn of the 20th century in Germany that attempted to analyze thought into its components through self-analysis. (p. 6)

IQ: See *intelligence quotient*.

isa link: In a *semantic network* or *schema*, a link that indicates the superset of the category. (p. 154)

Korsakoff syndrome: An *amnesia* resulting from chronic alcoholism and nutritional deficit. (p. 235)

language universals: Properties of *natural languages*, providing constraints on possible *grammars*. (p. 410)

late-selection theories: Theories of *attention* proposing that *serial bottlenecks* occur late in information processing. Contrast with *early-selection theories*. (p. 72)

linguistic determinism: The claim that language determines or strongly influences the way that a person thinks, including how the person perceives the world. (p. 392)

linguistic intuitions: Judgments by speakers of a language about the acceptability of utterances or about the relations between utterances. (p. 379)

linguistics: The study of the structure of language. (p. 9)

logical quantifiers: Elements such as *all, no, some,* and *some . . . not* that appear in statements like *All A are B* and *Some C are not D*. (p. 328)

long-term potentiation (LTP): A *neuron's* increased sensitivity to stimulation as a function of past stimulation. (p. 190)

LTP: See *long-term potentiation*.

magnetoencephalography (MEG): Measurement of magnetic fields produced by electrical activity in the brain. (p. 26)

mastery learning: The effort to bring students to mastery of each element in a curriculum before promoting them to new material in the curriculum. (p. 311)

means–ends analysis: In problem solving, the creation of new *subgoals* (ends) to enable *operators* (means) to apply in achieving the original goal. (p. 259)

mechanization of thought: See *Einstellung effect*.

MEG: See *magnetoencephalography*.

memory span: The amount of information that can be perfectly retained in an immediate test of memory. (p. 175)

mental imagery: The processing of perceptual-like information in the absence of an external source for the perceptual information. (p. 106)

mental model theory: The theory that participants judge the validity of a *syllogism* by imagining a world that satisfies the premises and seeing whether the conclusion is satisfied in that world. (p. 333)

mental rotation: The process of continuously transforming the orientation of a mental image. (p. 109)

method of loci: A *mnemonic technique* used to associate items to be remembered with locations along a well-known path. (p. 197)

mirror neurons: *Neurons* that fire both when an animal is performing an action and when the animal observes another animal performing the action. (p. 150)

mnemonic technique: A method for improving memory. (p. 143)

modularity: The proposal that language is a component (a linguistic module) separate from the rest of cognition, including the proposal that language comprehension has an initial phase in which only syntactic considerations are brought to bear. Contrast with *interactive processing*. (p. 398)

modus ponens: A rule of logic: if a *conditional statement* is true and if its *antecedent* is true, then its *consequent* must be true (i.e., if the conditional statement *If A, then B* is true, and if the antecedent *A* is true, we can infer that the consequent *B* is true). (p. 318)

modus tollens: A rule of logic: if a *conditional statement* is true and if its *consequent* is false, then its *antecedent* must be false (i.e., if the conditional statement *If A, then B* is true, and if the consequent *B is false,* we can infer that the antecedent *A is false.* (p. 319)

mood congruence: A match between the mood associated with the content of a memory and the person's mood when recalling the memory; such a match is associated with better memory. (p. 232)

multimodal hypothesis: The theory that knowledge is represented in multiple perceptual and motor modalities. Contrast with *amodal hypothesis.* (p. 151)

N400: A negativity in the *event-related potential (ERP)* at about 400 ms after the processing of a semantic anomaly. (p. 428)

nativism: The position that posits that children come into the world with a great deal of innate knowledge. Contrast with *empiricism.* (p. 5)

natural languages: Languages that humans can acquire. (p. 377)

negative transfer: Poor learning of something as a function of having previously learned something else. (p. 310)

neocortex: Part of the *cerebral cortex,* and the most recently evolved portion of the brain; in humans, a highly convoluted neural sheet. (p. 19)

neuron: A cell in the nervous system responsible for information processing through electrochemical activity. (p. 13)

neurotransmitter: A chemical that crosses the *synapse* from the *axon* of one *neuron* and alters the electric potential of the membrane of another *neuron.* (p. 14)

object-based attention: Allocation of *attention* to particular objects. Contrast with *space-based attention.* (p. 89)

occipital lobe: The region at the back of the brain that controls vision. (p. 20)

operator: In problem solving, an action that will transform one problem *state* into another problem *state.* (p. 247)

P600: A positivity in the *event-related potential (ERP)* at about 600 ms after the processing of a syntactic anomaly. (p. 428)

parahippocampal place area: A region adjacent to the *hippocampus* that is active when people are perceiving locations (i.e., indoor or outdoor scenes). (p. 116)

parameter setting: The proposal that the settings of 100 or so parameters account for the differences among *natural languages* and that language acquisition by children involves learning those settings. (p. 413)

parietal lobe: The region at the top of the brain concerned with *attention* and higher-level perceptual functions. (p. 20)

parsing: The process of creating a mental representation of the combined meaning of the words in a sentence. (p. 417)

partial-report procedure: A procedure in visual-report experiments in which participants are cued to report only some of the items in a display. Contrast with *whole-report procedure.* (p. 173)

particular statements: Statements—often involving the *logical quantifiers some* and *some . . . not*—that logicians interpret as being true about at least some members of a category. Contrast with *universal statements.* (p. 331)

perceptual symbol system: A system for representing information in which the terms are tied to particular perceptual modalities. Contrast with *amodal symbol system.* (p. 147)

perfect time-sharing: The ability to pursue multiple tasks simultaneously without cost to the performance of any task. Contrast with *central bottleneck.* (p. 93)

performance: In *linguistics,* the actual application of linguistic *competence* in speaking or listening. (p. 380)

permission schema: An interpretation of a *conditional statement* in which the *antecedent* specifies the situations in which the *consequent* is permitted. (p. 325)

PET: See *positron emission tomography.*

phoneme-restoration effect: The tendency to hear *phonemes* that make sense in the speech context even if no such *phonemes* were spoken. (p. 66)

phonemes: The minimal units of speech that can result in a difference in a spoken message. (p. 58)

phonological loop: Part of Baddeley's proposed system for rehearsing verbal information. Contrast with *visuospatial sketchpad.* (p. 178)

phonological store: In Baddeley's theory of *working memory,* a component of the *phonological loop,* an "inner ear" that briefly stores inner speech. Contrast with *articulatory store.* (p. 178)

phonology: The study of the sound structure of languages. (p. 379)

phrase structure: The hierarchical organization of a sentence into a set of phrases, sometimes represented as a tree structure. (p. 381)

place of articulation: The place at which the vocal tract is closed or constricted in the production of a *phoneme.* (p. 59)

positron emission tomography (PET): A method for determining the location of neural activity by measuring metabolic activity in different regions of the brain with the use of a radioactive tracer. (p. 26)

posterior probability: In *Bayes's theorem*, the probability that a hypothesis is true after consideration of the evidence. (p. 348)

power function: A function in which the independent variable X is raised to a power to obtain the dependent variable Y, as in $Y = AX^b$. (p. 189)

power law of forgetting: The principle that memory performance deteriorates as a *power function* of the delay interval. (p. 208)

power law of learning: The principle that memory performance improves as a *power function* of practice. (p. 190)

prefrontal cortex: The region at the front of the frontal cortex that controls planning and other higher-level cognitive processes. (p. 20)

preoperational stage: The second stage in Piaget's theory of four stages of development, spanning the period from 2 to 7 years of age, during which the child can engage in internal thought about the world, but these mental processes are intuitive and unsystematic. (p. 451)

prescriptive model: A model that specifies how people ought to behave to be considered rational. Contrast with *descriptive model*. (p. 350)

primal sketch: In Marr's model, the level of visual processing in which the visual features have been extracted from a stimulus. (p. 69)

primary visual cortex: The first cortical area to receive visual input, organized according to a topographic representation of the visual field. (p. 40)

priming: Enhancement of the processing of a stimulus as a function of prior exposure. (p. 239)

principle of minimal attachment: A rule of *parsing* that interprets a sentence in a way that results in minimal complication of the *phrase structure*. (p. 431)

prior probability: In *Bayes's theorem*, the probability that a hypothesis is true before consideration of the evidence. (p. 347)

probability matching: Choosing among alternatives in proportion to the success of previous choices. (p. 354)

problem space (or *state space*): A representation of the various sequences of problem-solving *operators* that transform the various *states* of a problem from one *state* to another *state*. (p. 248)

procedural knowledge: Knowledge of how to perform a task. Contrast with *explicit memory*. (p. 241)

proceduralization: The process by which information held in declarative memory is converted into *procedural knowledge*. (p. 291)

productivity: Refers to the fact that *natural languages* have an infinite number of possible sentences. (p. 377)

proposition: The smallest unit of knowledge that can stand as a separate assertion. (p. 145)

propositional representation: A representation of meaning as a set of *propositions*. (p. 145)

prosopagnosia: A neurological disorder characterized by the inability to recognize faces. (p. 55)

prototype theories: Models proposing that we store a single prototype of a category member and classify specific objects or events in terms of their similarity to the prototype. Contrast with *exemplar theories*. (p. 163)

psychometric tests: Tests of various aspects of a person's intellectual performance. (p. 469)

p-value: The probability that the result of an experiment would be obtained by chance. (p. 11)

quantifiers: See *logical quantifiers*.

rate of firing: The number of *action potentials* an *axon* transmits per second. (p. 16)

receptive field: In vision, the region of the *retina* from which a cell in the visual system encodes information. (p. 40)

recognition heuristic: A heuristic that applies in cases where people recognize one item and not another, leading them to believe that the recognized item has a higher value than the unrecognized item with respect to a specified criterion. (p. 357)

regularity: The fact that sentences are systematically structured in many ways. (p. 377)

relation: The element that organizes the *arguments* of a *propositional representation*. (p. 145)

replicability crisis: In psychology and other fields, finding that experimental results with p-values below .05 are not replicated when the experiments are repeated. (p. 11)

retina: The innermost layer of cells within the eye; it includes the photoreceptor cells, bipolar cells, and ganglion cells. (p. 39)

retrograde amnesia: Loss of memory for things that occurred before an injury. Contrast with *anterograde amnesia*. (p. 235)

rods: Photoreceptor cells that are principally responsible for the less acute, black-and-white vision we experience at night. (p. 39)

route map: A representation of the environment consisting of the paths between locations but without spatial information. Contrast with *survey map*. (p. 122)

rule learning: Determining what kind of rule (conjunctive, disjunctive, or relational) connects the features when forming a hypothesis. See also *attribute identification*. (p. 337)

schema: A *slot*–value representation of categorical knowledge that specifies a category's superset (higher-level category) and its attributes (properties, including the category's typical parts), along with the typical values taken by the properties. (p. 155)

scripts: *Schemas* for events, representing the most typical sequences of actions involved in the events. (p. 160)

search: In problem solving, the process of finding an appropriate path through a maze of *states* in a *problem space* by choosing a sequence of *operators* to move from the start state to the *goal state*. (p. 248)

search tree (or *search graph*): In problem solving, a representation of the set of *states* in a *problem space* that can be reached by applying *operators* to transform one *state* into another *state*, beginning with the start *state*. (p. 249)

selection task: See *Wason selection task*.

semantic networks: Hierarchical network structures for representing categorical information and the properties associated with each category. (p. 153)

semantics: Grammatical rules that specify the meaning of sentences. (p. 379)

sensory-motor stage: The first stage in Piaget's theory of four stages of development, spanning the first 2 years of life, during which a child lacks basic schemes for thinking about the physical world and experiences it in terms of sensations and actions. (p. 451)

serial bottlenecks: The points in the paths from perception to action at which people cannot process all the incoming information in parallel. (p. 71)

set effect: Biasing of the approach to solving a problem as a result of past experiences in solving that kind of problem. See also *Einstellung effect*. (p. 275)

short-term memory: A proposed intermediate memory system for holding information as it travels from sensory memory to long-term memory. (p. 175)

situation model: A representation of the events and situations described in a text. (p. 444)

slot: Any element in a *schema* for the different attributes of a category. (p. 155)

space-based attention: Allocation of *attention* to visual information in a region of space. Contrast with *object-based attention*. (p. 89)

split-brain patients: Patients who have had surgery to sever the *corpus callosum,* which connects the left and right hemispheres. (p. 22)

spreading activation: The process by which *activation* spreads from items currently or recently processed to other parts of the memory network, activating the memories that reside there. (p. 186)

state: In problem solving, a representation of a problem in some degree of solution. (p. 248)

state-dependent learning: The principle that it is easier to recall information when one is in the same emotional and physical state as when one learned the information. (p. 232)

state space: See *problem space*.

Sternberg paradigm: An experimental procedure in which participants are first presented with a memory set consisting of a few items and then must decide whether various probe items are in the memory set. (p. 10)

stimulus-driven attention (or *exogenous control*): *Attention* controlled by a salient stimulus. Contrast with *goal-directed attention*. (p. 72)

strategic learning: Learning how to organize one's problem solving to capitalize on the general structure of a class of problems. Contrast with *tactical learning*. (p. 293)

strength: The quantity that determines the inherent availability of a memory. (p. 188)

Stroop effect: A phenomenon in which the tendency to name a word will interfere with the ability to name the color in which the word is printed. (p. 97)

subgoal: A goal set in service of achieving a larger goal. (p. 247)

subjective probability: The probability that people associate with an event, which need not be identical to the event's objective probability. (p. 361)

subjective utility: The value that someone places on something. (p. 360)

sulcus: An inward crease between gyri (singular *gyrus*) of the *cerebral cortex*. Contrast with *gyrus*. (p. 19)

survey map: A representation of the environment consisting of the position of locations in space. Contrast with *route map.* (p. 122)

syllogisms: Logical *arguments* consisting of two premises and a conclusion. See also *categorical syllogism.* (p. 316)

synapse: The gap between a terminal bouton of the *axon* of one *neuron* and a *dendrite* of another *neuron.* See also *excitatory synapse; inhibitory synapse.* (p. 14)

syntax: Grammatical rules that specify the correct word order and inflections in sentences. (p. 378)

tactical learning: Learning the sequences of actions involved in solving a particular kind of problem. Contrast with *strategic learning.* (p. 292)

template matching: A theory of pattern recognition stating that an object is recognized as a function of its overlap with various pattern templates stored in the brain. (p. 48)

temporal lobe: The region at the side of the brain that contains the primary auditory areas and controls the recognition of objects. (p. 20)

theory of identical elements: The theory that one skill will transfer to another only to the extent that the skills have knowledge elements in common. (p. 309)

TMS: See *transcranial magnetic stimulation.*

top-down processing: Perceptual processing of a stimulus in which information from the general context is used to help recognize the stimulus. Contrast with *bottom-up processing.* (p. 63)

topographic organization: A principle of neural organization in which adjacent areas of the cortex process information from adjacent parts of the sensory field. (p. 23)

transcranial magnetic stimulation (TMS): A method for determining the function of a brain region; a magnetic field is applied to the surface of the head to disrupt the neural processing in that region. (p. 27)

transformations: Linguistic rules that move elements from one part of a sentence to another part. (p. 386)

transient ambiguity: A temporary ambiguity within a sentence that is resolved by the end of the sentence. (p. 430)

type 1 processes: Rapid and automatic processes, relying on associations between situations and actions. (p. 342)

type 2 processes: Slow and deliberative processes that may follow normative prescriptions. (p. 342)

universal statements: Statements—often involving *logical quantifiers* such as *all* and *none*—that logicians interpret as blanket claims with no exceptions. Contrast with *particular statements.* (p. 329)

utilization: The stage in language comprehension in which the comprehender uses the mental representation of the sentence's meaning. (p. 417)

ventromedial prefrontal cortex: The portion of the cortex in the front center of the brain. It seems to be involved in decision making and self-regulation, including activities like gambling behavior. (p. 346)

visual agnosia: An inability to recognize visual objects that results from damage to certain brain regions. See also *apperceptive agnosia; associative agnosia.* (p. 37)

visual sensory store (or *iconic memory*)**:** A memory system that can briefly store visual information. (p. 174)

visuospatial sketchpad: In Baddeley's theory of *working memory,* a "slave system" for maintaining visual information. Contrast with *phonological loop.* (p. 178)

voicing: A feature of a *phoneme* produced by vibration of the vocal cords. (p. 59)

Wason selection task: A task in which participants must decide which of four cards need to be turned over to check the validity of a *conditional statement;* the cards represent the four possibilities of antecedent and consequent of the conditional being true or false. (p. 324)

Wernicke's area: A region of the left *temporal lobe* that is important for processing language, particularly the *semantics* (meaning) of speech. (p. 22)

"what" visual pathway: A neural pathway carrying visual information from the *primary visual cortex* to regions of the *temporal lobe* that are specialized for identifying objects. (p. 41)

"where" visual pathway: A neural pathway carrying visual information from the *primary visual cortex* to regions of the *parietal lobe* that are specialized for representing spatial information and for coordinating vision with action. (p. 41)

whole-report procedure: A procedure in visual-report experiments in which participants are asked to report all the items in a display. Contrast with *partial-report procedure.* (p. 173)

word superiority effect: The superior recognition of letters when the letters are presented in a word context than when they are presented alone. (p. 63)

working memory: The information that is currently available in memory for working on a problem. (p. 178)

References

Aaronson, D., & Scarborough, H. S. (1977). Performance theories for sentence coding: Some quantitative models. *Journal of Verbal Learning and Verbal Behavior, 16*, 277–304.

Adolphs, R. D., Tranel, A., Bechara, A., Damasio, H., & Damasio, A. R. (1996). Neuropsychological approaches to reasoning and decision-making. In A. R. Damasio, Y. Christen, & H. Damasio (Eds.), *Neurobiology of decision* (pp. 157–179). New York, NY: Springer.

Agee, J., & Naper, S. (2007). Off-site storage: An analysis. *Collection Building, 26*(1), 20–25

Ainsworth-Darnell, K., Shulman, H. G., & Boland, J. E. (1998). Dissociating brain responses to syntactic and semantic anomalies: Evidence from event-related potentials. *Journal of Memory and Language, 38*, 112–130.

Albert, M. L. (1973). A simple test of visual neglect. *Neurology, 23*, 658–664.

Allopenna, P. D., Magnuson, J. S., & Tanenhaus, M. K. (1998). Tracking the time course of spoken word recognition using eye movements: Evidence for continuous mapping models. *Journal of Memory and Language, 38*, 419–439.

Anderson, J. R. (1974). Retrieval of propositional information from long-term memory. *Cognitive Psychology, 6*, 451–474.

Anderson, J. R. (1982). Acquisition of cognitive skill. *Psychological Review, 89*, 369–406.

Anderson, J. R. (1983). *The architecture of cognition.* Cambridge, MA: Harvard University Press.

Anderson, J. R. (1990). *The adaptive character of thought.* Hillsdale, NJ: Erlbaum.

Anderson, J. R. (1991). The adaptive nature of human categorization. *Psychological Review, 98*, 409–429.

Anderson, J. R. (1992). Intelligent tutoring and high school mathematics. *Proceedings of the Second International Conference on Intelligent Tutoring Systems* (pp. 1–10). Montreal: Springer-Verlag.

Anderson, J. R. (2000). *Learning and memory.* New York, NY: Wiley.

Anderson, J. R. (2009). *How can the human mind occur in the physical universe?* New York, NY: Oxford University Press.

Anderson, J. R., Anderson, J. F., Ferris, J. L., Fincham, J. M., & Jung, K.-J. (2009). The lateral inferior prefrontal cortex and anterior cingulate cortex are engaged at different stages in the solution of insight problems. *Proceedings of the National Academy of Sciences, 106*(26), 10799–10804.

Anderson, J. R., Betts, S., Ferris, J. L., & Fincham, J. M. (2010). Neural imaging to track mental states while using an intelligent tutoring system. *Proceedings of the National Academy of Sciences USA, 107*(15), 7018–7023.

Anderson, J. R., & Bower, G. H. (1972). Configural properties in sentence memory. *Journal of Verbal Learning and Verbal Behavior, 11*, 594–605.

Anderson, J. R., & Bower, G. H. (1973). *Human associative memory.* Washington, DC: Winston.

Anderson, J. R., Corbett, A. T., Koedinger, K. R., & Pelletier, R. (1995). Cognitive tutors: Lessons learned. *The Journal of the Learning Sciences, 4*(2), 167–207.

Anderson, J. R., Farrell, R., & Sauers, R. (1984). Learning to program in LISP. *Cognitive Science, 8*, 87–129.

Anderson, J. R., & Fincham, J. M. (2014). Extending problem-solving procedures through reflection. *Cognitive Psychology, 74*, 1–34.

Anderson, J. R., Kushmerick, N., & Lebiere, C. (1993). Navigation and conflict resolution. In J. R. Anderson (Ed.), *Rules of the mind* (pp. 93–120). Hillsdale, NJ: Erlbaum.

Anderson, J. R., Reder, L. M., & Simon, H. A. (1998). Radical constructivism and cognitive psychology. In D. Ravitch (Ed.), *Brookings papers on education policy* (pp. 227–278). Washington, DC: Brookings Institute Press.

Anderson, M. C. (2003). Rethinking interference theory: Executive control and the mechanisms of forgetting. *Journal of Memory and Language, 49*, 415–445.

Anderson, M. C., & Green, C. (2001). Suppressing unwanted memories by executive control. *Nature, 410*, 366–369.

Anderson, M. C., & Spellman, B. A. (1995). On the status of inhibitory mechanisms in cognition: Memory retrieval as a model case. *Psychological Review, 102*, 68–100.

Angell, J. R. (1908). The doctrine of formal discipline in the light of the principles of general psychology. *Educational Review, 36*, 1–14.

Antell, S., & Keating, D. P. (1983). Perception of numerical invariance in neonates. *Child Development, 54*, 695–701.

Antoniou, M. (2019). The advantages of bilingualism debate. *Annual Review of Linguistics, 5*, 395–415.

Arrington, C. M., Carr, T. H., Mayer, A. R., & Rao, S. M. (2000). Neural mechanisms of visual attention: Object-based selection of a region in space. *Journal of Cognitive Neuroscience, 12*(Suppl. 2), 106–117.

Atkinson, R. C., & Shiffrin, R. M. (1968). Human memory: A proposed system and its control processes. In K. Spence & J. Spence (Eds.), *The psychology of learning and motivation* (Vol. 2, pp. 89–195). New York, NY: Academic Press.

Ausubel, D. P. (1968). *Educational psychology: A cognitive view.* New York, NY: Holt, Rinehart, & Winston.

Baars, B. J., Motley, M. T., & MacKay, D. G. (1975). Output editing for lexical status in artificially elicited slips of the tongue. *Journal of Verbal Learning and Verbal Behavior, 14*, 382–391.

Baddeley, A. D. (1976). *The psychology of memory.* New York, NY: Basic Books.

Baddeley, A. D. (1986). *Working memory.* Oxford, UK: Oxford University Press.

Baddeley, A. D., Thompson, N., & Buchanan, M. (1975). Word length and the structure of short-term memory. *Journal of Verbal Learning and Verbal Behavior, 14*, 575–589.

Bahrick, H. P. (1979). Maintenance of knowledge: Questions about memory we forgot to ask. *Journal of Experimental Psychology: General, 108*(3), 296.

Bahrick, H. P. (1984). Semantic memory content in permastore: Fifty years of memory for Spanish learned in school. *Journal of Experimental Psychology: General, 113*, 1–24.

Bahrick, H. P. (circa 1993). Personal communication.

Bandettini, P. A. (2014). Neuronal or hemodynamic? Grappling with the functional MRI signal. *Brain Connectivity, 4*(7), 487–498.

Barbey, A. K., & Sloman, S. A. (2007). Base-rate respect: From ecological rationality to dual processes. *Behavioral and Brain Sciences, 30*(3), 241–254.

Barbizet, J. (1970). *Human memory and its pathology.* San Francisco, CA: W. H. Freeman.

Barnes, C. A. (1979). Memory deficits associated with senescence: A neurophysiological and behavioral study in the rat. *Journal of Comparative Physiology, 43,* 74–104.

Barsalou, L. W. (1999). Perceptual symbol systems. *Behavioral and Brain Sciences, 22,* 577–609.

Barsalou, L. W. (2003). Personal communication, March 12.

Barsalou, L. W., Simmons, W. K., Barbey, A. K., & Wilson, C. D. (2003). Grounding conceptual knowledge in modality-specific systems. *Trends in Cognitive Sciences, 7,* 84–91.

Bartolomeo, P. (2002). The relationship between visual perception and visual mental imagery: A reappraisal of the neuropsychological evidence. *Cortex, 38,* 357–378.

Barton, R. A. (1998). Visual specialization and brain evolution in primates. *Proceedings of the Royal Society of London B, 265,* 1933–1937.

Bassok, M. (1990). Transfer of domain-specific problem-solving procedures. *Journal of Experimental Psychology: Learning, Memory, and Cognition, 16,* 522–533.

Bassok, M., & Holyoak, K. J. (1989). Interdomain transfer between isomorphic topics in algebra and physics. *Journal of Experimental Psychology: Learning, Memory, and Cognition, 15,* 153–166.

Bates, A., McNew, S., MacWhinney, B., Devescovi, A., & Smith, S. (1982). Functional constraints on sentence processing: A cross-linguistic study. *Cognition, 11,* 245–299.

Bavelier, D., Green, C. S., Pouget, A., & Schrater, P. (2012). Brain plasticity through the life span: Learning to learn and action video games. *Annual Review of Neuroscience, 35,* 391–416.

Baylis, G. C., Rolls, E. T., & Leonard, C. M. (1985). Selectivity between faces in the responses of a population of neurons in the cortex in the superior temporal sulcus of the monkey. *Brain Research, 342,* 91–102.

Bechara, A., Damasio, A. R., Damasio, H., & Anderson, S. W. (1994). Insensitivity to future consequences following damage to human prefrontal cortex. *Cognition, 50,* 7–15.

Bechara, A., Damasio, H., Tranel, D., & Damasio, A. R. (2005). The Iowa Gambling Task and the somatic marker hypothesis: Some questions and answers. *Trends in Cognitive Sciences, 9,* 159–162.

Beck, B. B. (1980). *Animal tool behavior: The use and manufacture of tools by animals.* New York, NY: Garland STPM Press.

Beck, D. M., Rees, G., Frith, C. D., & Lavie, N. (2001). Neural correlates of change detection and change blindness. *Nature Neuroscience, 4,* 645–650.

Bediou, B., Adams, D. M., Mayer, R. E., Tipton, E., Green, C. S., & Bavelier, D. (2018). Meta-analysis of action video game impact on perceptual, attentional, and cognitive skills. *Psychological Bulletin, 144*(1), 77–110.

Behrmann, M. (2000). The mind's eye mapped onto the brain's matter. *Current Psychological Science, 9,* 50–54.

Behrmann, M., Geng, J. J., & Shomstein, S. (2004). Parietal cortex and attention. *Current Opinion in Neurobiology, 14*(2), 212–217.

Behrmann, M., Zemel, R. S., & Mozer, M. C. (1998). Object-based attention and occlusion: Evidence from normal participants and computational model. *Journal of Experimental Psychology: Human Perception and Performance, 24,* 1011–1036.

Beilock, S. L., Lyons, I. M., Mattarella-Micke, A., Nusbaum, H. C., & Small, S. L. (2008). Sports experience changes the neural processing of action language. *Proceedings of the National Academy of Sciences USA, 105,* 13269–13273.

Bellizzi, C., Goldsteinholm, K., & Blaser, R. E. (2015). Some factors affecting performance of rats in the traveling salesman problem. *Animal Cognition, 18*(6), 1207–1219.

Bellugi, U., Wang, P. P., & Jernigan, T. L. (1994). Williams syndrome: An unusual neuropsychological profile. In S. H. Broman & J. Grafman (Eds.), *Atypical cognitive deficits in developmental disorders implications for brain function* (pp. 23–56). Hillsdale, NJ: Erlbaum.

Benson, D. F., & Greenberg, J. P. (1969). Visual form agnosia. *Archives of Neurology, 20,* 82–89.

Berlin, B., & Kay, P. (1969). *Basic color terms: Their universality and evolution.* Berkeley, CA: University of California Press.

Berntsen, D., & Rubin, D. C. (2002). Emotionally charged autobiographical memories across the life span: The recall of happy, sad, traumatic, and involuntary memories. *Psychology and Aging, 17,* 636–652.

Berry, D. C., & Broadbent, D. E. (1984). On the relationship between task performance and associated verbalizable knowledge. *Quarterly Journal of Experimental Psychology, 36A,* 209–231.

Berry, M. J., & Westfall, A. (2015). Dial D for distraction: The making and breaking of cell phone policies in the college classroom. *College Teaching, 63*(2), 62–71.

Bialystok, E., Craik, F. I. M., Green, D. W., & Gollan, T. H. (2009). Bilingual minds. *Psychological Science in the Public Interest, 10*(3), 89–129.

Bialystok, E., Craik, F. I. M., & Luk, G. (2012). Bilingualism: consequences for mind and brain. *Trends in Cognitive Sciences, 16*(4), 240–250.

Biederman, I., Glass, A. L., & Stacy, E. W. (1973). Searching for objects in real world scenes. *Journal of Experimental Psychology, 97,* 22–27.

Bilalić, M., Langner, R., Ulrich, R., & Grodd, W. (2011). Many faces of expertise: Fusiform face area in chess experts and novices. *The Journal of Neuroscience, 31*(28), 10206–10214.

Binder, J. R., & Desai, R. H. (2011). The neurobiology of semantic memory. *Trends in Cognitive Sciences, 15*(11), 527–536.

Binder, J. R., Desai, R. H., Graves, W. W., & Conant, L. L. (2009). Where is the semantic system? A critical review and meta-analysis of 120 functional neuroimaging studies. *Cerebral Cortex, 19*(12), 2767–2796.

Bjorklund, D. F., & Bering, J. M. (2003). Big brains, slow development and social complexity: the developmental and evolutionary origins of social cognition. In M. Brüne, H. Ribbert, & W. Schiefenhövel (Eds.), *The social brain: Evolution and pathology* (pp. 111–151). New York, NY: Wiley.

Blackburn, J. M. (1936). *Acquisition of skill: An analysis of learning curves* (IHRB Rep. No. 73). London, UK: IHRB.

Blazhenkova, O., & Kozhevnikov, M. (2009). The new object-spatial-verbal cognitive style model: Theory and measurement. *Applied Cognitive Psychology, 23,* 638–663.

Bloom, B. S. (Ed.). (1985a). *Developing talent in young people.* New York, NY: Ballantine Books.

Bloom, B. S. (1985b). Generalizations about talent development. In B. S. Bloom (Ed.), *Developing talent in young people* (pp. 507–549). New York, NY: Ballantine Books.

Boden, M. (2006). *Mind as machine.* Oxford, UK: Oxford University Press.

Boer, L. C. (1991). Mental rotation in perspective problems. *Acta Psychologica, 76*, 1–9.

Boomer, D. S. (1965). Hesitation and grammatical encoding. *Language and Speech, 8*, 148–158.

Boot, W. R., Blakely, D. P., & Simons, D. J. (2011). Do action video games improve perception and cognition?. *Frontiers in Psychology, 2*.

Boring, E. G. (1950). *A history of experimental psychology.* New York, NY: Appleton Century.

Boroditsky, L., Schmidt, L., & Phillips, W. (2003). Sex, syntax, and semantics. In D. Gentner & S. Goldin-Meadow (Eds.), *Language in mind: Advances in the study of language and cognition.* Cambridge, MA: MIT Press.

Bouchard, T. J. (1983). Do environmental similarities explain the similarity in intelligence of identical twins reared apart? *Intelligence, 7*, 175–184.

Bouchard, T. J., & McGue, M. (1981). Familial studies of intelligence: A review. *Science, 212*, 1055–1059.

Bower, G. H., Black, J. B., & Turner, T. J. (1979). Scripts in memory for text. *Cognitive Psychology, 11*, 177–220.

Bower, G. H., Karlin, M. B., & Dueck, A. (1975). Comprehension and memory for pictures. *Memory & Cognition, 3*, 216–220.

Bower, G. H., & Mayer, J. D. (1985). Failure to replicate mood-dependent retrieval. *Bulletin of the Psychonomic Society, 23*, 39–42.

Bower, G. H., Monteiro, K. P., & Gilligan, S. G. (1978). Emotional mood as a context for learning and recall. *Journal of Verbal Learning and Verbal Behavior, 17*, 573–587.

Bownds, M. D. (1999). *The biology of mind: Origins and structures of mind, brain, and consciousness.* Bethesda, MD: Fitzgerald Science Press.

Bradshaw, G. L., & Anderson, J. R. (1982). Elaborative encoding as an explanation of levels of processing. *Journal of Verbal Learning and Verbal Behavior, 21*, 165–174.

Brady, T. F., Konkle, T., Alvarez, G. A., & Oliva, A. (2008). Visual long-term memory has a massive storage capacity for object details. *Proceedings of the National Academy of Sciences USA, 105*(38), 14325–14329.

Brainerd, C. J. (1978). *Piaget's theory of intelligence.* Englewood Cliffs, NJ: Prentice-Hall.

Bransford, J. D., & Franks, J. J. (1971). The abstraction of linguistic ideas. *Cognitive Psychology, 2*, 331–380.

Bransford, J. D., & Johnson, M. K. (1972). Contextual prerequisites for understanding: Some investigations of comprehension and recall. *Journal of Verbal Learning and Verbal Behavior, 11*(6), 717–726.

Bransford, J. D., Barclay, J. R., & Franks, J. J. (1972). Sentence memory: A constructive versus interpretive approach. *Cognitive Psychology, 3*, 193–209.

Brewer, J. B., Zhao, Z., Desmond, J. E., Glover, G. H., & Gabrieli, J. D. (1998). Making memories: Brain activity that predicts how well visual experience will be remembered. *Science, 281*, 118–120.

Brewer, W. F., & Treyens, J. C. (1981). Role of schemata in memory for places. *Cognitive Psychology, 13*, 207–230.

Broadbent, D. E. (1958). *Perception and communication.* New York, NY: Pergamon.

Broadbent, D. E. (1975). The magical number seven after fifteen years. In R. A. Kennedy & A. Wilkes (Eds.), *Studies in long-term memory* (pp. 3–18). New York, NY: Wiley.

Brodmann, K. (1960). On the comparative localization of the cortex. In G. von Bonin (Ed.), *Some papers on the cerebral cortex* (pp. 201–230). Springfield, IL: Charles C. Thomas. (Original work published in 1909)

Brooks, L. R. (1968). Spatial and verbal components of the act of recall. *Canadian Journal of Psychology, 22*, 349–368.

Brown, E., Deffenbacher, K., & Sturgill, W. (1977). Memory for faces and the circumstances of encounter. *Journal of Applied Psychology, 62*(3), 311–318. http://dx.doi.org/10.1037/0021-9010.62.3.311

Brown, R. (1973). *A first language.* Cambridge, MA: Harvard University Press.

Brown, R., & Kulik, J. (1977). Flashbulb memories. *Cognition, 5*, 73–99.

Brown, R., & Lenneberg, E. H. (1954). A study in language and cognition. *Journal of Abnormal and Social Psychology, 49*, 454–462.

Bruce, C. J., Desimone, R., & Gross, C. G. (1981). Visual properties of neurons in a polysensory area in superior temporal sulcus of the macaque. *Neurophysiology, 46*, 369–384.

Bruner, J. S. (1964). The course of cognitive growth. *American Psychologist, 19*, 1–15.

Bruner, J. S., Goodnow, J. J., & Austin, G. A. (1956). *A study of thinking.* New York, NY: NY Science Editions.

Buckner, R. L. (1998). Personal communication.

Buddenbrock, F. (2016). Search engine optimization: Getting to Google's first page. In Newton Lee (Ed.), *Google it: Total information awareness* (pp. 195–204). New York, NY: Springer.

Burgess, N. (2006). Spatial memory: How egocentric and allocentric combine. *Trends in Cognitive Sciences, 10*, 551–557.

Burgoon, J. K., Guerrero, L. K., & Floyd, K. (2016). *Nonverbal communication.* New York, NY: Routledge.

Bursztein, E., Bethard, S., Fabry, C., Mitchell, J. C., & Jurafsky, D. (2010, May). How good are humans at solving CAPTCHAs? A large scale evaluation. In *2010 IEEE Symposium on Security and Privacy* (pp. 399–413). Washington, DC: IEEE Computer Society Press.

Buser, T., & Yuan, H. (2016). Do women give up competing more easily? Evidence from the lab and the Dutch Math Olympiad. Tinbergen Institute Discussion Paper, No. 16-096/I, Tinbergen Institute, Amsterdam and Rotterdam.

Butler, B. C., & Klein, R. (2009). Inattentional blindness for ignored words: Comparison of explicit and implicit memory tasks. *Consciousness and Cognition, 18*(3), 811–819.

Buxhoeveden, D. P., & Casanova, M. F. (2002). The minicolumn hypothesis in neuroscience. *Brain, 125*, 935–951.

Byrne, M. D., & Anderson, J. R. (2001). Serial modules in parallel: The psychological refractory period and perfect time-sharing. *Psychological Review, 108*, 847–869.

Cabeza, R., Rao, S. M., Wagner, A. D., Mayer, A. R., & Schacter, D. L. (2001). Can medial temporal lobe regions distinguish true from false? An event-related fMRI study of veridical and illusory recognition memory. *Proceedings of the National Academy of Sciences USA, 98*, 4805–4810.

Camerer, C. F., Dreber, A., Holzmeister, F., Ho, T. H., Huber, J., Johannesson, M., . . . Altmejd, A. (2018). Evaluating the replicability of social science experiments in Nature and Science between 2010 and 2015. *Nature Human Behaviour, 2*(9), 637.

Camerer, C., Loewenstein, G., & Prelec, D. (2005). Neuroeconomics: How neuroscience can inform economics. *Journal of Economic Literature, 43,* 9–64.

Camp, G., Pecher, D., & Schmidt, H. G. (2005). Retrieval-induced forgetting in implicit memory tests: The role of test awareness. *Psychonomic Bulletin & Review, 12,* 490–494.

Caplan, D. (1972). Clause boundaries and recognition latencies for words in sentences. *Perception and Psychophysics, 12,* 73–76.

Caplan, D., Alpert, N., Waters, G., & Olivieri, A. (2000). Activation of Broca's area by syntactic processing under conditions of concurrent articulation. *Human Brain Mapping, 9,* 65–71.

Caramazza, A. (2000). The organization of conceptual knowledge in the brain. In M. S. Gazzaniga (Ed.), *The cognitive neurosciences* (2nd ed., pp. 1037–1046). Cambridge, MA: MIT Press.

Carey, S. (1978). The child as word learner. In M. Halle, J. Bresnan, & G. Miller (Eds.), *Linguistic theory and psychological reality* (pp. 264–293). Cambridge, MA: MIT Press.

Carey, S. (1985). *Conceptual change in childhood.* Cambridge, MA: MIT Press.

Carpenter, P. A., & Eisenberg, P. (1978). Mental rotation and the frame of reference in blind and sighted individuals. *Perception & Psychophysics, 23*(2), 117–124.

Carpenter, P. A., & Just, M. A. (1975). Sentence comprehension: A psycholinguistic processing model of verification. *Psychological Review, 82,* 45–73.

Carpenter, P. A., & Just, M. A. (1977). Reading comprehension as eyes see it. In M. A. Just & P. A. Carpenter (Eds.), *Cognitive processes in comprehension* (pp. 109–140). Hillsdale, NJ: Erlbaum.

Carpenter, T. P., & Moser, J. M. (1982). The development of addition and subtraction problem-solving skills. In T. P. Carpenter, J. M. Moser, & T. Romberg (Eds.), *Addition and subtraction: A cognitive perspective* (pp. 10–24). Hillsdale, NJ: Erlbaum.

Carraher, T. N., Carraher, D. W., & Schliemann, A. D. (1985). Mathematics in the streets and in the schools. *British Journal of Developmental Psychology, 3,* 21–29.

Carroll, J. B. (1993). *Human cognitive abilities: A survey of factor-analytic studies.* Cambridge, UK: Cambridge University Press.

Cartwright-Finch, U., & Lavie, N. (2007). The role of perceptual load in inattentional blindness. *Cognition, 102*(3), 321–340.

Case, R. (1978). Intellectual development from birth to adulthood: A neo-Piagetian approach. In R. S. Siegler (Ed.), *Children's thinking: What develops?* (pp. 37–71). Hillsdale, NJ: Erlbaum.

Case, R. (1985). *Intellectual development: A systematic reinterpretation.* New York, NY: Academic Press.

Casey, B. J., Trainor, R., Giedd, J. N., Vauss, Y., Vaituzis, C. K., Hamburger, S., . . . Rapoport, J. L. (1997a). The role of the anterior cingulate in automatic and controlled processes: A developmental neuroanatomical study. *Developmental Psychobiology, 30,* 61–69.

Casey, B. J., Trainor, R. J., Orendi, J. L., Schubert, A. B., Nystrom, L. E., Giedd, J.N., . . . Rapoport, J. L. (1997b). A developmental functional MRI study of prefrontal activation during performance of a Go-No-Go task. *Journal of Cognitive Neuroscience, 9,* 835–847.

Cattell, R. B. (1963). Theory of fluid and crystallized intelligence: A critical experiment. *Journal of Educational Psychology, 54,* 1–22.

Ceci, S. J. (1991). How much does schooling influence general intelligence and its cognitive components? A reassessment of the evidence. *Developmental Psychology, 27,* 703–722.

Chambers, D., & Reisberg, D. (1985). Can mental images be ambiguous? *Journal of Experimental Psychology: Human Perception and Performance, 11,* 317–328.

Chapman, G. B., Li, M., Colby, H., & Yoon, H. (2010). Opting in vs. opting out of influenza vaccination. *JAMA, 304*(1), 43–44.

Charness, N. (1976). Memory for chess positions: Resistance to interference. *Journal of Experimental Psychology: Human Learning and Memory, 2,* 641–653.

Charness, N. (1979). Components of skill in bridge. *Canadian Journal of Psychology, 33,* 1–16.

Charness, N. (1981). Search in chess: Age and skill differences. *Journal of Experimental Psychology: Human Perception and Performance, 7,* 467–476.

Chase, W. G., & Clark, H. H. (1972). Mental operations in the comparisons of sentences and pictures. In L. W. Gregg (Ed.), *Cognition in learning and memory* (pp. 205–232). New York, NY: Wiley.

Chase, W. G., & Ericsson, K. A. (1982). Skill and working memory. In G. H. Bower (Ed.), *The psychology of learning and motivation* (Vol. 16, pp. 1–58). New York, NY: Academic Press.

Chase, W. G., & Simon, H. A. (1973). The mind's eye in chess. In W. G. Chase (Ed.), *Visual information processing* (pp. 215–281). New York, NY: Academic Press.

Chen, Z., & Cave, K. R. (2008). Object-based attention with endogenous cuing and positional certainty. *Perception & Psychophysics, 70,* 1435–1443.

Cheng, P. W., & Holyoak, K. J. (1985). Pragmatic reasoning schemas. *Cognitive Psychology, 17,* 391–416.

Cheng, P. W., Holyoak, K. J., Nisbett, R. E., & Oliver, L. M. (1986). Pragmatic versus syntactic approaches to training deductive reasoning. *Cognitive Psychology, 18*(3), 293–328.

Cherry, E. C. (1953). Some experiments on the recognition of speech with one and with two ears. *Journal of the Acoustical Society of America, 25,* 975–979.

Chi, M. T. H. (1978). Knowledge structures and memory development. In R. S. Siegler (Ed.), *Children's thinking: What develops?* (pp. 76–93). Hillsdale, NJ: Erlbaum.

Chi, M. T. H., Bassok, M., Lewis, M., Reimann, P., & Glaser, R. (1989). Self-explanations: How students study and use examples in learning to solve problems. *Cognitive Science, 13,* 145–182.

Chi, M. T. H., Feltovich, P. J., & Glaser, R. (1981). Categorization and representation of physics problems by experts and novices. *Cognitive Science, 5,* 121–152.

Chimpanzee Sequencing and Analysis Consortium. (2005). Initial sequence of the chimpanzee genome and comparison with the human genome. *Nature, 437*(7055), 69.

Choi, J. J., Laibson, D., Madrian, B. C., & Metrick, A. (2003). Optimal defaults. *American Economic Review, 93*(2), 180–185.

Chomsky, C. (1970). *The acquisition of syntax in children from 5 to 10.* Cambridge, MA: MIT Press.

Chomsky, N. (1957). *Syntactic structures.* The Hague, the Netherlands: Mouton.

Chomsky, N. (1965). *Aspects of the theory of syntax*. Cambridge, MA: MIT Press.

Chomsky, N. (1980). Rules and representations. *Behavioral and Brain Sciences, 3*, 1–61.

Chomsky, N., & Halle, M. (1968). *The sound pattern of English*. New York, NY: Harper.

Chooi, W. T., & Thompson, L. A. (2012). Working memory training does not improve intelligence in healthy young adults. *Intelligence, 40*(6), 531–542.

Christen, F., & Bjork, R. A. (1976). *On updating the loci in the method of loci*. Paper presented at the 17th annual meeting of the Psychonomic Society, St. Louis, MO.

Christensen, B. T., & Schunn, C. D. (2007). The relationship of analogical distance to analogical function and pre-inventive structure: The case of engineering design. *Memory & Cognition, 35*, 29–38.

Christianson, K., Hollingworth, A., Halliwell, J., & Ferreira, F. (2001). Thematic roles assigned along the garden path linger. *Cognitive Psychology, 42*, 368–407.

Chun, M. M., Golomb, J. D., & Turk-Browne, N. B. (2011). A taxonomy of external and internal attention. *Annual Review of Psychology, 62*, 73–101.

Church, A. (1956). *Introduction to mathematical logic*. Princeton, NJ: Princeton University Press.

Cichy, R. M., Heinzle, J., & Haynes, J. D. (2012). Imagery and perception share cortical representations of content and location. *Cerebral Cortex, 22*(2), 372–380.

Cichy, R. M., Khosla, A., Pantazis, D., Torralba, A., & Oliva, A. (2016). Comparison of deep neural networks to spatio-temporal cortical dynamics of human visual object recognition reveals hierarchical correspondence. *Scientific Reports, 6*, 27755.

Clark, E. V. (1983). Meanings and concepts. In P. H. Mussen (Ed.), *Handbook of child psychology* (pp. 787–840). New York, NY: Wiley.

Clark, H. H. (1974). Semantics and comprehension. In R. A. Sebeok (Ed.), *Current trends in linguistics* (Vol. 12, pp. 1291–1428). The Hague, the Netherlands: Mouton.

Clark, H. H., & Chase, W. G. (1972). On the process of comparing sentences against pictures. *Cognitive Psychology, 3*, 472–517.

Clark, H. H., & Clark, E. V. (1977). *Psychology and language*. New York, NY: Harcourt Brace Jovanovich.

Clifton, C., Jr., & Duffy, S. (2001). Sentence comprehension: Roles of linguistic structure. *Annual Review of Psychology, 52*, 167–196.

Cocodia, E. A. (2014). Cultural perceptions of human intelligence. *Journal of Intelligence, 2*(4), 180–196.

Cohen, J. D., & Servan-Schreiber, D. (1992). Context, cortex and dopamine: A connectionist approach to behavior and biology in schizophrenia. *Psychological Review, 99*, 45–77.

Cohen, M. R., & Nagel, E. (1934). *An introduction to logic and scientific method*. New York, NY: Harcourt Brace.

Cole, M., & D'Andrade, R. (1982). The influence of schooling on concept formation: Some preliminary conclusions. *Quarterly Newsletter of the Laboratory of Comparative Human Cognition, 4*, 19–26.

Cole, M., Gay, J., Glick, J., & Sharp, D. (1971). *The cultural context of learning and thinking*. New York, NY: Basic Books.

Collins, A. M., & Quillian, M. R. (1969). Retrieval time from semantic memory. *Journal of Verbal Learning and Verbal Behavior, 8*, 240–247.

Conrad, C. (1972). Cognitive economy in semantic memory. *Journal of Experimental Psychology, 92*, 149–154.

Conrad, R. (1964). Acoustic confusions in immediate memory. *British Journal of Psychology, 55*, 75–84.

Conway, M. A., Anderson, S. J., Larsen, S. F., Donnelly, C. M., McDaniel, M. A., McClelland, A. G., . . . Logie, R. H. (1994). The formation of flashbulb memories. *Memory & Cognition, 22*, 326–343.

Cook, G. (2013, April 5). Brain games are bogus. *The New Yorker*.

Cooper, W. E., & Paccia-Cooper, J. (1980). *Syntax and speech*. Cambridge, MA: Harvard University Press.

Corbett, A. T., & Chang, F. R. (1983). Pronoun disambiguation: Accessing potential antecedents. *Memory & Cognition, 11*, 283–294.

Corbetta, M., & Shulman, G. L. (2002). Control of goal-directed and stimulus-driven attention in the brain. *Nature Reviews Neuroscience, 3*, 201–215.

Cosmides, L. (1989). The logic of social exchange: Has natural selection shaped how humans reason? Studies with the Wason selection task. *Cognition, 31*, 187–276.

Cowan, N. (2005). *Working memory capacity*. New York, NY: Psychology Press.

Cowart, W. (1983). *Reference relations and syntactic processing: Evidence of pronoun's influence on a syntactic decision that affects naming*. Bloomington, IN: Indiana University Linguistics Club.

Craik, F. I. M., & Lockhart, R. S. (1972). Levels of processing: A framework for memory research. *Journal of Verbal Learning and Verbal Behavior, 11*, 671–684.

Crick, F. H. C., & Asanuma, C. (1986). Certain aspects of the anatomy and physiology of the cerebral cortex. In J. L. McClelland & D. E. Rumelhart (Eds.), *Parallel distributed processing: Explorations in the microstructure of cognition* (Vol. 2, pp. 331–371). Cambridge, MA: MIT Press/Bradford Books.

Crossman, E. R. F. W. (1959). A theory of the acquisition of speed-skill. *Ergonomics, 2*, 153–166.

Cummins, D. D., Lubart, T., Alksnis, O., & Rist, R. (1991). Conditional reasoning and causation. *Memory & Cognition, 19*(3), 274–282.

Curran, T. (1995). On the neural mechanisms of sequence learning. *Psyche, 2*(12).

Curtiss, S. (1977). *Genie: A psycholinguistic study of a modern-day "wild child."* New York, NY: Academic Press.

Dallenbach, K. M. (1951). A puzzle-picture with a new principle of concealment. *American Journal of Psychology, 64*, 431–433.

Damasio, H., Grabowski, T., Frank, R., Galaburda, A. M., & Damasio, A. R. (1994). The return of Phineas Gage: Clues about the brain from the skull of a famous patient. *Science, 264*, 1102–1105.

Daneman, M., & Carpenter, P. A. (1980). Individual differences in working memory and reading. *Journal of Verbal Learning and Verbal Behavior, 19*, 450–466.

Darwin, G. J., Turvey, M. T., & Crowder, R. G. (1972). An auditory analogue of the Sperling Partial Report Procedure: Evidence for brief auditory storage. *Cognitive Psychology, 3*, 255–267.

Daugherty, K. G., MacDonald, M. C., Petersen, A. S., & Seidenberg, M. S. (1993). Why no mere mortal has ever flown out to center field but people often say they do. In *Proceedings of the 15th Annual Conference of the Cognitive Science Society, 383–388.*

Davis, D., & Loftus, E. F. (2017). Internal and external sources of misinformation in adult witness memory. In M. P. Toglia, J. D. Read, D. F. Ross, & R. C. L. Lindsay (Eds.), *The handbook of eyewitness psychology: Vol. 1. Memory for events* (pp. 195–238). New York, NY: Psychology Press.

Daw, N. D., Niv, Y., and Dayan, P. (2005). Uncertainty-based competition between prefrontal and dorsolateral striatal systems for behavioral control. *Nature Neuroscience, 8,* 1704–1711.

Dean, G. M., & Morris, P. E. (2003). The relationship between self-reports of imagery and spatial ability. *British Journal of Psychology, 94*(2), 245–273.

Deary, I. J. (2012). Intelligence. *Annual Review of Psychology, 63,* 453–482.

Deary, I. J., Weiss, A., & Batty, G. D. (2010). Intelligence and personality as predictors of illness and death: how researchers in differential psychology and chronic disease epidemiology are collaborating to understand and address health inequalities. *Psychological Science in the Public Interest, 11*(2), 53–79.

de Beer, G. R. (1959). Paedomorphosis. IN *Proceedings of the 15th International Congress of Zoology,* 927–930.

Deese, J. (1959). On the prediction of occurrence of particular verbal intrusions in immediate recall. *Journal of Experimental Psychology, 58,* 17–22.

de Groot, A. D. (1965). *Thought and choice in chess.* The Hague, the Netherlands: Mouton.

de Groot, A. D. (1966). Perception and memory versus thought. In B. Kleinmuntz (Ed.), *Problem-solving* (pp. 19–50). New York, NY: Wiley.

De Neys, W., Vartanian, O., & Goel, V. (2008). Smarter than we think when our brains detect that we are biased. *Psychological Science, 19*(5), 483–489.

Dennett, D. C. (1969). *Content and consciousness.* London, UK: Routledge.

Desimone, R., Albright, T. D., Gross, C. G., & Bruce, C. (1984). Stimulus-selective properties of inferior temporal neurons in the macaque. *Journal of Neuroscience, 4,* 2051–2062.

Deutsch, J. A., & Deutsch, D. (1963). Attention: Some theoretical considerations. *Psychological Review, 70,* 80–90.

de Valois, R. L., & Jacobs, G. H. (1968). Primate color vision. *Science, 162,* 533–540.

Diamond, A. (1990). The development and neural bases of memory functions as indexed by the AB and delayed response tasks in human infants and infant monkeys. *Annals of the New York Academy of Sciences, 608*(1), 267–317.

Diamond, A. (1991). Frontal lobe involvement in cognitive changes during the first year of life. In K. R. Gibson & A. C. Petersen (Eds.), *Brain maturation and cognitive development: Comparative and cross-cultural perspectives* (pp. 127–180). New York, NY: Aldine de Gruyter.

Diamond, A. (2013). Executive functions. *Annual Review of Psychology, 64,* 135–168.

Dickens, W. T., & Flynn, J. R. (2001). Heritability estimates versus large environmental effects: The IQ paradox resolved. *Psychological Review, 108,* 346–369.

Dickstein, L. S. (1978). The effect of figure on syllogistic reasoning. *Memory & Cognition, 6,* 76–83.

Diehl, R. L., Lotto, A. J., & Holt, L. L. (2004). Speech perception. *Annual Review of Psychology, 55,* 149–179.

Dinstein, I., Heeger, D. J., Lorenzi, L., Minshew, N. J., & Malach, R. (2012). Unreliable evoked responses in autism, *Neuron, 75,* 981–991.

Dodson, C. S., & Schacter, D. L. (2002a). Aging and strategic retrieval processes: Reducing false memories with a distinctiveness heuristic. *Psychology and Aging, 17,* 405–415.

Dodson, C. S., & Schacter, D. L. (2002b). When false recognition meets metacognition: The distinctiveness heuristic. *Journal of Memory and Language, 46,* 782–803.

Dooling, D. J., & Christiaansen, R. E. (1977). Episodic and semantic aspects of memory for prose. *Journal of Experimental Psychology: Human Learning and Memory, 3,* 428–436.

Doud, A. J., Lucas, J. P., Pisansky, M. T., & He, B. (2011). Continuous three-dimensional control of a virtual helicopter using a motor imagery based brain-computer interface. *PLoS ONE, 6*(10), e26322.

Droege, R. C. (1967). Effects of aptitude-score adjustments by age curves on prediction of job performance. *Journal of Applied Psychology, 51*(2), 181.

Dry, M., Lee, M. D., Vickers, D., & Hughes, P. (2006). Human performance on visually presented traveling salesperson problems with varying numbers of nodes. *The Journal of Problem Solving, 1*(1), 4.

dscout. (2016). Mobile touches: dscout's inaugural study on humans and their tech. Retrieved from https://blog.dscout.com/hubfs/downloads/dscout_mobile_touches_study_2016.pdf

Dubner, S. J., & Levitt, S. D. (2006, May 7). A star is made. *New York Times Magazine.* Retrieved from https://www.nytimes.com/2006/05/07/magazine/07wwln_freak.html

Dunbar, K. (1993). Concept discovery in a scientific domain. *Cognitive Science, 17,* 397–434.

Dunbar, K. (1997). How scientists think: Online creativity and conceptual change in science. In T. B. Ward, S. M. Smith, & S. Vaid (Eds.), *Conceptual structures and processes: Emergence, discovery and change.* Washington, DC: APA Press.

Dunbar, K., & Blanchette, I. (2001). The in vivo/in vitro approach to cognition: The case of analogy. *Trends in Cognitive Sciences, 5,* 334–339.

Dunbar, K., & MacLeod, C. M. (1984). A horse race of a different color: Stroop interference patterns with transformed words. *Journal of Experimental Psychology: Human Perception and Performance, 10,* 622–639.

Duncker, K. (1945). On problem-solving. (L. S. Lees, Trans.). *Psychological Monographs, 58*(Whole No. 270).

Dunning, D., & Sherman, D. A. (1997). Stereotypes and tacit inference. *Journal of Personality and Social Psychology, 73,* 459–471.

Dweck, C. S. (2008). *Mindset: The new psychology of success.* New York, NY: Random House Digital.

Easton, R. D., & Sholl, M. J. (1995). Object-array structure, frames of reference, and retrieval of spatial knowledge. *Journal of Experimental Psychology: Learning, Memory, and Cognition, 21,* 483–500.

Edwards, W. (1968). Conservatism in human information processing. In B. Kleinmuntz (Ed.), *Formal representations of human judgment* (pp. 17–52). New York, NY: Wiley.

Egan, D. E., & Schwartz, B. J. (1979). Chunking in recall of symbolic drawings. *Memory & Cognition, 7,* 149–158.

Egly, R., Driver, J., & Rafal, R. D. (1994). Shifting visual attention between objects and locations: Evidence from normal and parietal lesion subjects. *Journal of Experimental Psychology: General, 123,* 161–177.

Ehrlich, K., & Rayner, K. (1983). Pronoun assignment and semantic integration during reading: Eye movements and immediacy of processing. *Journal of Verbal Learning and Verbal Behavior, 22,* 75–87.

Eich, E. (1985). Context, memory, and integrated item/context imagery. *Journal of Experimental Psychology: Learning, Memory, and Cognition, 11,* 764–770.

Eich, E., & Metcalfe, J. (1989). Mood dependent memory for internal versus external events. *Journal of Experimental Psychology: Learning, Memory, and Cognition, 15,* 443–455.

Eich, J., Weingartner, H., Stillman, R. C., & Gillin, J. C. (1975). State-dependent accessibility of retrieval cues in the retention of a categorized list. *Journal of Verbal Learning and Verbal Behavior, 14,* 408–417.

Eichenbaum, H., Dudchenko, P., Wood, E., Shapiro, M., & Tanila, H. (1999). The hippocampus, memory, and place cells: Is it spatial memory or a memory space? *Neuron, 23,* 209–226.

Ekstrom, A. D., Kahana, M. J., Caplan, J. B., Fields, T. A., Isham, E. A., Newman, E. L., & Fried, I. (2003). Cellular networks underlying human spatial navigation. *Nature, 425,* 184–188.

Ekstrom, R. B., French, J. W., Harman, H. H., & Dermen, D. (1976). *Kit of factor-referenced cognitive tests.* Princeton, NJ: Educational Testing Services.

Elbert, T., Pantev, C., Wienbruch, C., Rockstroh, B., & Taub, E. (1995). Increased use of the left hand in string players associated with increased cortical representation of the fingers. *Science, 270,* 305–307.

Elio, R., & Anderson, J. R. (1981). The effects of category generalizations and instance similarity on schema abstraction. *Journal of Experimental Psychology: Human Learning and Memory, 7,* 397–417.

Ellis, A. W., & Young, A. W. (1988). *Human cognitive neuropsychology.* Hillsdale, NJ: Erlbaum.

Enard, W., Przeworski, M., Fisher, S., Lai, C., Wiebe, V., Kitano, T., . . . Pääbo, S. (2002). Molecular evolution of FOXP2, a gene involved in speech and language. *Nature, 418,* 869–872.

Engle, R. W., & Bukstel, L. (1978). Memory processes among bridge players of differing expertise. *American Journal of Psychology, 91,* 673–689.

Erickson, T. A., & Matteson, M. E. (1981). From words to meanings: A semantic illusion. *Journal of Verbal Learning and Verbal Behavior, 20,* 540–552.

Ericsson, K. A., & Kintsch, W. (1995). Long-term working memory. *Psychological Review, 102*(2), 211–245. http://dx.doi.org/10.1037/0033 -295X.102.2.211

Ericsson, K. A., Krampe, R. T., & Tesch-Römer, C. (1993). The role of deliberate practice in the acquisition of expert performance. *Psychological Review, 100,* 363–406.

Ernst, G., & Newell, A. (1969). *GPS: A case study in generality and problem solving.* New York, NY: Academic Press.

Ervin-Tripp, S. M. (1974). Is second language learning like the first? *TESOL Quarterly, 8,* 111–127.

Evans, J. S. B. T. (1993). The mental model theory of conditional reasoning: Critical appraisal and revision. *Cognition, 48*(1), 1–20.

Evans, J. S. B. T. (2007). *Hypothetical thinking: Dual processes in reasoning and judgement* (Vol. 3). New York, NY: Psychology Press.

Evans, J. S. B. T., Handley, S. J., & Harper, C. (2001). Necessity, possibility and belief: A study of syllogistic reasoning. *Quarterly Journal of Experimental Psychology, 54A,* 935–958.

Evans, J. S. B. T., & Over, D. E. (2004). *If.* New York, NY: Oxford University Press.

Farah, M. J. (1990). *Visual agnosia: Disorders of object recognition and what they tell us about normal vision.* Cambridge, MA: MIT Press.

Farah, M. J., Hammond, K. M., Levine, D. N., & Calvanio, R. (1988). Visual and spatial mental imagery: Dissociable systems of representation. *Cognitive Psychology, 20,* 439–462.

Farah, M. J., & McClelland, J. L. (1991). A computational model of semantic memory impairment: Modality specificity and emergent category specificity. *Journal of Experimental Psychology: General, 120,* 339–357.

Ferguson, C. J., Garza, A., Jerabeck, J., Ramos, R., & Galindo, M. (2013). Not worth the fuss after all? Cross-sectional and prospective data on violent video game influences on aggression, visuospatial cognition and mathematics ability in a sample of youth. *Journal of Youth and Adolescence, 42*(1), 109–122.

Fernandez, A., & Glenberg, A. M. (1985). Changing environmental context does not reliably affect memory. *Memory & Cognition, 13,* 333–345.

Ferreira, F. (2003). The misinterpretation of noncanonical sentences. *Cognitive Psychology, 47*(2), 164–203.

Ferreira, F., & Clifton, C. (1986). The independence of syntactic processing. *Journal of Memory and Language, 25,* 348–368.

Ferreira, F., & Patson, N. (2007). The good enough approach to language comprehension. *Language and Linguistics Compass, 1,* 71–83.

Ferrucci, D., Brown, E., Chu-Carroll, J., Fan, J., Gondek, D., Kalyanpur, A. A., . . . Schlaefer, N. (2010). Building Watson: An overview of the DeepQA project. *AI magazine, 31*(3), 59–79.

Fincham, J. M., Carter, C. S., van Veen, V., Stenger, V. A., & Anderson, J. R. (2002). Neural mechanisms of planning: A computational analysis using event-related fMRI. *Proceedings of the National Academy of Sciences USA, 99,* 3346–3351.

Fink, G. R., Halligan, P. H., Marshall, J. C., Frith, C. D., Frackowiack, R. S. J., & Dolan, R. J. (1996). Where in the brain does visual attention select the forest and the trees? *Nature, 382,* 626–628.

Finke, R. A., Pinker, S., & Farah, M. J. (1989). Reinterpreting visual patterns in mental imagery. *Cognitive Science, 13,* 51–78.

Fischer, K. W. (1980). A theory of cognitive development: The control and construction of hierarchies of skills. *Psychological Review, 87,* 477–531.

Fischhoff, B. (2008). Assessing adolescent decision-making competence. *Developmental Review, 28,* 12–28.

Fischhoff, B., & Beyth-Marom, R. (1983). Hypothesis evaluation from a Bayesian perspective. *Psychological Review, 90,* 239–260.

Fitts, P. M., & Posner, M. I. (1967). *Human performance.* Belmont, CA: Brooks Cole.

Flavell, J. H. (1978). Comment. In R. S. Siegler (Ed.), *Children's thinking: What develops?* (pp. 97–105). Hillsdale, NJ: Erlbaum.

Flavell, J. H. (1985). *Cognitive development.* Englewood Cliffs, NJ: Prentice-Hall.

Flege, J., Yeni-Komshian, G., & Liu, S. (1999). Age constraints on second language learning. *Journal of Memory and Language, 41,* 78–104.

Flynn, J. R. (2007). *What is intelligence? Beyond the Flynn effect.* Cambridge, UK: Cambridge University Press.

Fodor, J. A. (1983). *The modularity of mind.* Cambridge, MA: MIT Press/ Bradford Books.

Foo, P., Warren, W. H., Duchon, A., & Tarr, M. J. (2005). Do humans integrate routes into a cognitive map? Map-versus landmark-based navigation of novel shortcuts. *Journal of Experimental Psychology: Learning, Memory, and Cognition, 31*(2), 195.

Forward, S., & Buck, C. (1988). *Betrayal of innocence: Incest and its devastation.* New York, NY: Penguin Books.

Frase, L. T. (1975). Prose processing. In G. H. Bower (Ed.), *The psychology of learning and motivation* (Vol. 9, pp. 1–47). New York, NY: Academic Press.

Friedman-Hill, S., Robertson, L. C., & Treisman, A. (1995). Parietal contributions to visual feature binding: Evidence from a patient with bilateral lesions. *Science, 269,* 853–855.

Frisby, J. P., & Stone, J. V. (2010). *Seeing: The computational approach to biological vision.* Cambridge, MA: MIT Press.

Frisch, S., Schlesewsky, M., Saddy, D., & Alpermann, A. (2002). The P600 as an indicator of syntactic ambiguity. *Cognition, 85,* B83–B92.

Fromkin, V. (1971). The non-anomalous nature of anomalous utterances. *Languages, 47,* 27–52.

Fromkin, V. (1973). *Speech errors as linguistic evidence.* The Hague, the Netherlands: Mouton.

Fugelsang, J., & Dunbar, K. (2005). Brain-based mechanisms underlying complex causal thinking. *Neuropsychologia, 43,* 1204–1213.

Fulford, J., Milton, F., Salas, D., Smith, A., Simler, A., Winlove, C., & Zeman, A. (2018). The neural correlates of visual imagery vividness—An fMRI study and literature review. *Cortex, 105,* 26–40.

Funahashi, S., Bruce, C. J., & Goldman-Rakic, P. S. (1991). Neural activity related to saccadic eye movements in the monkey's dorsolateral prefrontal cortex. *Journal of Neurophysiology, 65,* 1464–1483.

Funahashi, S., Bruce, C. J., & Goldman-Rakic, P. S. (1993). Dorsolateral prefrontal lesions and oculomotor delayed-response performance: Evidence for mnemonic "scotomas." *Journal of Neuroscience, 13,* 1479–1497.

Fuster, J. M. (1989). *The prefrontal cortex: Anatomy, physiology, and neuropsychology of the frontal lobe.* New York, NY: Raven Press.

Gabrieli, J. D. E. (2001). Functional neuroimaging of episodic memory. In R. Cabeza & A. Lingstone (Eds.), *Handbook of functional neuroimaging of cognition* (pp. 253–292). Cambridge, MA: MIT Press.

Gardner, H. (1975). *The shattered mind: The person after brain damage.* New York, NY: Knopf.

Gardner, R. A., & Gardner, B. T. (1969). Teaching sign language to a chimpanzee. *Science, 165,* 664–672.

Garrett, M. F. (1975). The analysis of sentence production. In G. H. Bower (Ed.), *The psychology of learning and motivation* (Vol. 9, pp. 133–177). New York, NY: Academic Press.

Garrett, M. F. (1980). Levels of processing in sentence production. In B. Butterworth (Ed.), *Language production* (Vol. 1, pp. 177–220). London, UK: Academic Press.

Garrett, M. F. (1990). Sentence processing. In D. N. Osherson & H. Lasnik (Eds.), *Language: An invitation to cognition science* (Vol. 1, pp. 133–175). Cambridge, MA: MIT Press.

Garro, L. (1986). Language, memory, and focality: A reexamination. *American Anthropologist, 88,* 128–136.

Gauthier, I., Skudlarski, P., Gore, J. C., & Anderson, A. W. (2000). Expertise for cars and birds recruits brain areas involved in face recognition. *Nature Neuroscience, 3,* 191–197.

Gazzaniga, M. S. (1967). The split brain in man. *Scientific American, 217*(2), 24–29.

Gazzaniga, M. S., Ivry, R. B., & Mangun, G. R. (1998). *Cognitive neuroscience: The biology of the mind.* New York, NY: W. W. Norton.

Gazzaniga, M. S., Ivry, R. B., & Mangun, G. R. (2002). *Cognitive neuroscience: The biology of the mind* (2nd ed.). New York, NY: W. W. Norton.

Geary, D. C. (2007). An evolutionary perspective on learning disability in mathematics. *Developmental Neuropsychology, 32*(1), 471–519.

Gee, J. P., & Grosjean, F. (1983). Performance structures: A psycholinguistic and linguistic appraisal. *Cognitive Psychology, 15,* 411–458.

Geiselman, E. R., Fisher, R. P., MacKinnon, D. P., & Holland, H. L. (1985). Eyewitness memory enhancement in the police interview: Cognitive retrieval mnemonics versus hypnosis. *Journal of Applied Psychology, 70,* 401–412.

Geison, G. L. (1995). *The private science of Louis Pasteur.* Princeton, NJ: Princeton University Press.

Gelman, S. A. (1988). The development of induction within natural kind and artifact categories. *Cognitive Psychology, 20,* 65–95.

Gentner, D. (1983). Structure-mapping: A theoretical framework for analogy. *Cognitive Science, 7,* 155–170.

Georgopoulos, A. P., Lurito, J. T., Petrides, M., Schwartz, A. B., & Massey, J. T. (1989). Mental rotation of the neuronal population vector. *Science, 243,* 234–236.

German, K. (2018, February 8). For London cabbies battling Uber, the map is in the mind. *CNET.* Retrieved from https://www.cnet.com/news/london-taxi-drivers-with-the-knowledge-arent-fazed-by-uber/

Geschwind, N. (1980). Neurological knowledge and complex behaviors. *Cognitive Science, 4,* 185–194.

Gibson, E. J. (1969). *Principles of perceptual learning and development.* New York, NY: Meredith.

Gibson, J. J. (1950). *Perception of the visual world.* Boston, MA: Houghton Mifflin.

Gick, M. L., & Holyoak, K. J. (1980). Analogical problem solving. *Cognitive Psychology, 12,* 306–355.

Gigerenzer, G., & Hoffrage, U. (1995). How to improve Bayesian reasoning without instruction: Frequency formats. *Psychological Review, 102,* 684–704.

Gigerenzer, G., & Hug, K. (1992). Domain-specific reasoning: Social contracts, cheating, and perspective change. *Cognition, 43,* 127–171.

Gigerenzer, G., Swijtink, Z., Porter, T., Daston, L., Beatty, J., & Krüger, L. (1989). *The empire of chance: How probability changed science and everyday life.* Cambridge, UK: Cambridge University Press.

Gigerenzer, G., Todd, P. M., & ABC Research Group. (1999). *Simple heuristics that make us smart.* New York, NY: Oxford University Press.

Gilbert, D. T., Tafarodi, R. W., & Malone, P. S. (1993). You can't not believe everything you read. *Journal of Personality and Social Psychology, 65*(2), 221–233.

Gilbert, S. J., Spengler, S., Simons, J. S., Frith, C. D., & Burgess, P. W. (2006). Differential functions of lateral and medial rostral prefrontal cortex (area 10) revealed by brain-behaviour correlations. *Cerebral Cortex, 16,* 1783–1789.

Ginsburg, H. J., & Opper, S. (1980). *Piaget's theory of intellectual development.* Englewood Cliffs, NJ: Prentice-Hall.

Gisborne Herald. (2018, December 11). *CAA report finds no hazard briefing, "inattentional blindness" contributed to fatal plane crash.*

Gladwell, M. (2008). *Outliers: The story of success.* London, UK: Hachette UK.

Gleitman, L. R., Newport, E. L., & Gleitman, H. (1984). The current status of the motherese hypothesis. *Journal of Child Language, 11,* 43–80.

Glenberg, A. M. (2007). Language and action: Creating sensible combinations of ideas. In G. Gaskell (Ed.), *The Oxford handbook of psycholinguistics* (pp. 361–370). Oxford, UK: Oxford University Press.

Glenberg, A. M., Smith, S. M., & Green, C. (1977). Type I rehearsal: Maintenance and more. *Journal of Verbal Learning and Verbal Behavior, 16,* 339–352.

Gluck, M. A., & Bower, G. H. (1988). From conditioning to category learning: An adaptive network model. *Journal of Experimental Psychology: General, 117,* 227–247.

Glucksberg, S., & Cowan, G. N., Jr. (1970). Memory for nonattended auditory material. *Cognitive Psychology, 1,* 149–156.

Godden, D. R., & Baddeley, A. D. (1975). Context-dependent memory in two natural environments: On land and under water. *British Journal of Psychology, 66,* 325–331.

Goel, V., Buchel, C., Frith, C., & Dolan, R. (2000). Dissociation of mechanisms underlying syllogistic reasoning. *Neuroimage, 12,* 504–514.

Goel, V., & Grafman, J. (1995). Are the frontal lobes implicated in "planning" functions? Interpreting data from the Tower of Hanoi. *Neuropsychologica, 33,* 623–642.

Goel, V., & Grafman, J. (2000). The role of the right prefrontal cortex in ill-structured problem solving. *Cognitive Neuropsychology, 17,* 415–436.

Goldberg, R. A., Schwartz, S., & Stewart, M. (1977). Individual differences in cognitive processes. *Journal of Educational Psychology, 69,* 9–14.

Goldinger, S. D., Papesh, M. H., Barnhart, A. S., Hansen, W. A., & Hout, M. C. (2016). The poverty of embodied cognition. *Psychonomic Bulletin & Review, 23*(4), 959–978.

Goldin-Meadow, S. (2003). *The resilience of language: What gesture creation in deaf children can tell us about how all children learn language.* New York, NY: Psychology Press.

Goldin-Meadow, S., & Alibali, M. W. (2013). Gesture's role in speaking, learning, and creating language. *Annual Review of Psychology, 64,* 257–283.

Goldin-Meadow, S., Cook, S. W., & Mitchell, Z. A. (2009). Gesturing gives children new ideas about math. *Psychological Science, 20*(3), 267–272.

Goldman-Rakic, P. S. (1987). Circuitry of primate prefrontal cortex and regulation of behavior by representational memory. In *Handbook of physiology. The nervous system: Vol. 5. Higher functions of the brain* (pp. 373–417). Bethesda, MD: American Physiology Society.

Goldman-Rakic, P. S. (1988). Topography of cognition: Parallel distributed networks in primate association cortex. *Annual Review of Neuroscience, 11,* 137–156.

Goldman-Rakic, P. S. (1992). Working memory and mind. *Scientific American, 267,* 111–117.

Goldstein, A. G., & Chance, J. E. (1970). Visual recognition memory for complex configurations. *Perception and Psychophysics, 9,* 237–241.

Goldstein, D. G., & Gigerenzer, G. (1999). The recognition heuristic: How ignorance makes us smart. In G. Gigerenzer, P. M. Todd, & ABC Research Group (Eds.), *Simple heuristics that make us smart* (pp. 37–58). New York, NY: Oxford University Press.

Goldstein, D. G., & Gigerenzer, G. (2002). Models of ecological rationality: The recognition heuristic. *Psychological Review, 109,* 75–90.

Goldstein, M. N. (1974). Auditory agnosia for speech ("pure word deafness"): A historical review with current implications. *Brain and Language, 1,* 195–204.

Goldstone, R. L. (1994). Influences of categorization on perceptual discrimination. *Journal of Experimental Psychology: General, 123*(2), 178.

Goldstone, R. L., & Hendrickson, A. T. (2010). Categorical perception. *Interdisciplinary Reviews: Cognitive Science, 1,* 65–78.

Goodale, M. A., Milner, A. D., Jakobson, L. S., & Carey, D. P. (1991). A neurological dissociation between perceiving objects and grasping them. *Nature, 349,* 154–156.

Goriounova, N. A., & Mansvelder, H. D. (2019). Genes, cells and brain areas of intelligence. *Frontiers in Human Neuroscience, 13*(44).

Gould, E., & Gross, C. G. (2002). Neurogenesis in adult mammals: Some progress and problems. *Journal of Neuroscience, 22,* 619–623.

Gould, S. J. (1977). *Ontogeny and phylogeny.* Cambridge, MA: Belknap.

Graesser, A. C., Hu, X., & Sottilare, R. (2018). Intelligent tutoring systems. In F. Fischer, C. E. Hmelo-Silver, S. R. Goldman, & P. Reimann (Eds.), *International Handbook of the Learning Sciences* (pp. 246–255). New York, NY: Routledge.

Graesser, A. C., Singer, M., & Trabasso, T. (1994). Constructing inferences during narrative text comprehension. *Psychological Review, 101,* 371–395.

Graf, P., Squire, L. R., & Mandler, G. (1984). The information that amnesic patients do not forget. *Journal of Experimental Psychology: Learning, Memory, and Cognition, 10,* 164–178.

Graf, P., & Torrey, J. W. (1966). Perception of phrase structure in written language. *American Psychological Association Convention Proceedings,* 83–88.

Gray, J. A., & Wedderburn, A. A. I. (1960). Grouping strategies with simultaneous stimuli. *Quarterly Journal of Experimental Psychology, 12,* 180–184.

Green, C. S., & Bavelier, D. (2006). Enumeration versus multiple object tracking: The case of action video game players. *Cognition, 101*(1), 217–245.

Greenberg, J. H. (1963). Some universals of grammar with particular reference to the order of meaningful elements. In J. H. Greenberg (Ed.), *Universals of language* (pp. 73–113). Cambridge, MA: MIT Press.

Greene, J. D., Sommerville, R. B., Nystrom, L. E., Darley, J. M., & Cohen, J. D. (2001). An fMRI investigation of emotional engagement in moral judgment. *Science, 293,* 2105–2108.

Greenfield, P. M., & Savage-Rumbaugh, E. S. (1990). Grammatical combination in Pan paniscus: processes of learning and invention in the evolution and development of language. In S. T. Parker & K. R. Gibson (Eds.), *"Language" and Intelligence in Monkeys and Apes: Comparative Developmental Perspective* (540–578). New York, NY: Cambridge University Press.

Greeno, J. G. (1974). Hobbits and orcs: Acquisition of a sequential concept. *Cognitive Psychology, 6,* 270–292.

Griffiths, T. L., Chater, N., Kemp, C., Perfors, A., & Tenenbaum, J. B. (2010). Probabilistic models of cognition: Exploring representations and inductive biases. *Trends in Cognitive Sciences, 14*(8), 357–364.

Griggs, R. A., & Cox, J. R. (1982). The elusive thematic-materials effect in Wason's selection task. *British Journal of Psychology, 73*, 407–420.

Gron, G., Wunderlich, A. P., Spitzer, M., Tomczak, R., & Riepe, M. W. (2000). Brain activation during human navigation: Gender different neural networks as substrate of performance. *Nature Neuroscience, 3*, 404–408.

Groome, D., & Eysenck, M. (2016). *An introduction to applied cognitive psychology.* New York, NY: Psychology Press.

Grosjean, F. (2010). *Bilingual.* Cambridge, MA: Harvard University Press.

Grosjean, F., Grosjean, L., & Lane, H. (1979). The patterns of silence: Performance structures in sentence production. *Cognitive Psychology, 11*, 58–81.

Gross, C. G. (2000). Neurogenesis in the adult brain: Death of a dogma. *Nature Review, 1*, 67–73.

Gross, C. G. (2008). Single neuron studies of inferior temporal cortex. *Neuropsychologia, 46*(3), 841–852.

Güçlü, U., & van Gerven, M. A. (2015). Deep neural networks reveal a gradient in the complexity of neural representations across the ventral stream. *Journal of Neuroscience, 35*(27), 10005–10014.

Gugerty, L., deBoom, D., Jenkins, J. C., & Morley, R. (2000). Keeping north in mind: How navigators reason about cardinal directions. In *Proceedings of the Human Factors and Ergonomics Society 2000 Congress* (pp. I148–I151). Santa Monica, CA: Human Factors and Ergonomics Society.

Guilford, J. P. (1956). The structure of intellect. *Psychological Bulletin, 53*(4), 267.

Gunning, D. (2017). *Explainable artificial intelligence (xai).* Washington, DC: Defense Advanced Research Projects Agency (DARPA).

Gunzelmann, G., & Anderson, J. R. (2002). Strategic differences in the coordination of different views of space. In W. D. Gray & C. D. Schunn (Eds.), *Proceedings of the Twenty-Fourth Annual Conference of the Cognitive Science Society* (pp. 387–392). Mahwah, NJ: Erlbaum.

Guskey, T. R., & Gates, S. (1986). Synthesis of research on the effects of mastery learning in elementary and secondary classrooms. *Educational Leadership, 43*, 73–80.

Haesler, S., Rochefort, C., Georgi, B., Licznerski, P., Osten, P., & Scharff, C. (2007). Incomplete and inaccurate vocal imitation after knockdown of FoxP2 in songbird basal ganglia nucleus area X. *PLoS Biology, 5*, 2885–2897.

Haier, R. J., Siegel, B. V., Jr., Nuechterlein, K. H., Hazlett, E., Wu, J. C., Paek, J., . . . Buchsbaum, M. S. (1988). Cortical glucose metabolic rate correlates of abstract reasoning and attention studied with positron emission tomography. *Intelligence, 12*, 199–217.

Hakes, D. T. (1972). Effects of reducing complement constructions on sentence comprehension. *Journal of Verbal Learning and Verbal Behavior, 11*, 278–286.

Hakes, D. T., & Foss, D. J. (1970). Decision processes during sentence comprehension: Effects of surface structure reconsidered. *Perception and Psychophysics, 8*, 413–416.

Halford, G. S. (1982). *The development of thought.* Hillsdale, NJ: Erlbaum.

Halford, G. S. (1992). Analogical reasoning and conceptual complexity in cognitive development. *Human Development, 35*, 193–217.

Hambrick, D. Z., Oswald, F. L., Altmann, E. M., Meinz, E. J., Gobet, F., & Campitelli, G. (2014). Deliberate practice: Is that all it takes to become an expert? *Intelligence, 45*, 34–45.

Hambrick, D. Z., & Tucker-Drob, E. M. (2015). The genetics of music accomplishment: Evidence for gene–environment correlation and interaction. *Psychonomic Bulletin & Review, 22*(1), 112–120.

Hammerton, M. (1973). A case of radical probability estimation. *Journal of Experimental Psychology, 101*, 252–254.

Harlow, J. M. (1868). Recovery from a passage of an iron bar through the head. *Publications of the Massachusetts Medical Society, 2*, 327–347.

Harris, R. J. (1977). Comprehension of pragmatic implications in advertising. *Journal of Applied Psychology, 62*, 603–608.

Hart, R. A., & Moore, G. I. (1973). The development of spatial cognition: A review. In R. M. Downs & D. Stea (Eds.), *Image and environment* (pp. 246–288). Chicago, IL: Aldine.

Hartley, T., Maguire, E. A., Spiers, H. J., & Burgess, N. (2003). The well-worn route and the path less traveled: Distinct neural bases of route following and wayfinding in humans. *Neuron, 37*, 877–888.

Hauk, O., Johnsrude, I., & Pulvermuller, F. (2004). Somatotopic representation of action words in human motor and premotor cortex. *Neuron, 41*, 301–307.

Haviland, S. E., & Clark, H. H. (1974). What's new? Acquiring new information as a process in comprehension. *Journal of Verbal Learning and Verbal Behavior, 13*, 512–521.

Haxby, J. V., Ungerleider, L. G., Clark, V. P., Schouten, J. L., Hoffman, E. A., & Martin, A. (1999). The effect of face inversion on activity in human neural systems for face and object perception. *Neuron, 22*, 189–199.

Hayes, C. (1951). *The ape in our house.* New York, NY: Harper.

Hayes, J. R. (1985). Three problems in teaching general skills. In J. Segal, S. Chipman, & R. Glaser (Eds.), *Thinking and learning* (Vol. 2, pp. 391–406). Hillsdale, NJ: Erlbaum.

Hayes-Roth, B., & Hayes-Roth, F. (1977). Concept learning and the recognition and classification of exemplars. *Journal of Verbal Learning and Verbal Behavior, 16*, 321–338.

Haygood, R. C., & Bourne, L. E. (1965). Attribute and rule-learning aspects of conceptual behavior. *Psychological Review, 72*, 175–195.

He, K., Zhang, X., Ren, S., & Sun, J. (2016). Deep residual learning for image recognition. In *Proceedings of the IEEE Conference on Computer Vision and Pattern Recognition* (pp. 770–778). Piscataway, NJ: IEEE.

Heath, S. B. (1983). *Ways with words: Language, life and work in communities and classrooms.* New York, NY: Cambridge University Press.

Heider, E. (1972). Universals of color naming and memory. *Journal of Experimental Psychology, 93*, 10–20.

Henkel, L. A., Johnson, M. K., & DeLeonardis, D. M. (1998). Aging and source monitoring: Cognitive processes and neuropsychological correlates. *Journal of Experimental Psychology: General, 127*, 251–268.

Henson, R. N., Burgess, N., & Frith, C. D. (2000). Recoding, storage, rehearsal and grouping in verbal short-term memory: An fMRI study. *Neuropsychologia, 38*, 426–440.

Hilgard, E. R. (1968). *The experience of hypnosis.* New York, NY: Harcourt Brace Jovanovich.

Hinton, G. E. (1979). Some demonstrations of the effects of structural descriptions in mental imagery. *Cognitive Science, 3*, 231–250.

Hintzman, D. L., O'Dell, C. S., & Arndt, D. R. (1981). Orientation in cognitive maps. *Cognitive Psychology, 13*, 149–206.

Hirshman, E., Passannante, A., & Arndt, J. (2001). Midazolam amnesia and conceptual processing in implicit memory. *Journal of Experimental Psychology: General, 130,* 453–465.

Hirst, W., Phelps, E. A., Buckner, R. L., Budson, A. E., Cuc, A., Gabrieli, J. D., . . . Vaidya, C. J. (2009). Long-term memory for the terrorist attack of September 11: Flashbulb memories, event memories, and the factors that influence their retention. *Journal of Experimental Psychology: General, 138*(2), 161.

Hirst, W., Phelps, E. A., Meksin, R., Vaidya, C. J., Johnson, M. K., Mitchell, K. J., . . . Mather, M. (2015). A ten-year follow-up of a study of memory for the attack of September 11, 2001: Flashbulb memories and memories for flashbulb events. *Journal of Experimental Psychology: General, 144*(3), 604.

Hockett, C. F. (1960). The origin of speech. *Scientific American, 203,* 89–96.

Hoffman, D. D., & Richards, W. (1985). Parts of recognition. *Cognition, 18,* 65–96.

Hoffman, M., Gneezy, U., & List, J. A. (2011). Nurture affects gender differences in spatial abilities. *Proceedings of the National Academy of Sciences USA, 108*(36), 14786–14788.

Hoffrage, U., Krauss, S., Martignon, L., & Gigerenzer, G. (2015). Natural frequencies improve Bayesian reasoning in simple and complex inference tasks. *Frontiers in Psychology, 6,* 1–14.

Holding, D. H. (1992). Theories of chess skill. *Psychological Research, 54,* 10–16.

Holle, H., & Gunter, T. C. (2007). The role of iconic gestures in speech disambiguation: ERP evidence. *Journal of Cognitive Neuroscience, 19*(7), 1175–1192.

Holmes, J. B., Waters, H. S., & Rajaram, S. (1998). The phenomenology of false memories: Episodic content and confidence. *Journal of Experimental Psychology: Learning, Memory, and Cognition, 24,* 1026–1040.

Holroyd, C. B., & Coles, M. G. (2002). The neural basis of human error processing: reinforcement learning, dopamine, and the error-related negativity. *Psychological Review, 109*(4), 679.

Holyoak, K. J., & Cheng, P. W. (2011). Causal learning and inference as a rational process: The new synthesis. *Annual Review of Psychology, 62,* 135–163.

Hopkins, E. J., Weisberg, D. S., & Taylor, J. C. (2016). The seductive allure is a reductive allure: People prefer scientific explanations that contain logically irrelevant reductive information. *Cognition, 155,* 67–76.

Hopkins, W. D., Russell, J., McIntyre, J., & Leavens, D. A. (2013). Are chimpanzees really so poor at understanding imperative pointing? Some new data and an alternative view of canine and ape social cognition. *PLoS One, 8*(11), e79338.

Horn, J. L. (1968). Organization of abilities and the development of intelligence. *Psychological Review, 75,* 242–259.

Horn, J. L., & Stankov, L. (1982). Auditory and visual intelligence. *Intelligence, 6,* 165–185.

Horton, J. C. (1984). Cytochrome oxidase patches: A new cytoarchitectonic feature of monkey visual cortex. *Philosophical Transactions of the Royal Society of London, 304,* 199–253.

Hsu, F.-H. (2002). *Behind Deep Blue.* Princeton, NJ: Princeton University Press.

Hubel, D. H., & Wiesel, T. N. (1962). Receptive fields, binocular interaction, and functional architecture in the cat's visual cortex. *Journal of Physiology, 166,* 106–154.

Hubel, D. H., & Wiesel, T. N. (1977). Functional architecture of macaque monkey visual cortex. *Philosophical Transactions of the Royal Society of London, 198,* 1–59.

Huddleston, E., & Anderson, M. C. (2012). Reassessing critiques of the independent probe method for studying inhibition. *Journal of Experimental Psychology: Learning, Memory, and Cognition, 38,* 1408–1418.

Hunt, E. B., Davidson, J., & Lansman, M. (1981). Individual differences in long-term memory access. *Memory & Cognition, 9,* 599–608.

Hunter, J. E., & Hunter, R. F. (1984). Validity and utility of alternative predictors of job performance. *Psychological Bulletin, 96,* 72–98.

Hurley, D. (2012, April 18). Can you make yourself smarter? *New York Times Magazine.*

Huth, A. G., de Heer, W. A., Griffiths, T. L., Theunissen, F. E., & Gallant, J. L. (2016). Natural speech reveals the semantic maps that tile human cerebral cortex. *Nature, 532*(7600), 453.

Huttenlocher, P. R. (1994). Synaptogenesis in human cerebral cortex. In G. Dawson & K. W. Fischer (Eds.), *Human behavior and the developing brain* (pp. 137–152). New York, NY: Guilford Press.

Hyams, N. M. (1986). *Language acquisition and the theory of parameters.* Dordrecht, the Netherlands: D. Reidel.

Hyde, T. S., & Jenkins, J. J. (1973). Recall for words as a function of semantic, graphic, and syntactic orienting tasks. *Journal of Verbal Learning and Verbal Behavior, 12,* 471–480.

Iacoboni, M., Woods, R. P., Brass, M., Bekkering, H., Mazziotta, J. C., & Rizzolatti, G. (1999). Cortical mechanisms of human imitation. *Science, 286,* 2526–2528.

Ifrah, G. (2000). *The universal history of numbers: From prehistory to the invention of the computer.* New York, NY: Wiley.

Ishai, A., Ungerleider, L. G., Martin, A., Maisog, J. M., & Haxby, J. V. (1997). fMRI reveals differential activation in the ventral object vision pathway during the perception of faces, houses, and chairs. *Neuroimage, 5,* S149.

Jacobsen, C. F. (1935). Functions of frontal association areas in primates. *Archives of Neurology & Psychiatry, 33,* 558–560.

Jacobsen, C. F. (1936). Studies of cerebral functions in primates. I. The function of the frontal association areas in monkeys. *Comparative Psychology Monographs, 13,* 1–60.

Jacoby, L. L. (1983). Remembering the data: Analyzing interactive processes in reading. *Journal of Verbal Learning and Verbal Behavior, 22,* 485–508.

Jacoby, L. L., & Witherspoon, D. (1982). Remembering without awareness. *Canadian Journal of Psychology, 36,* 300–324.

Jaeger, J. J., Lockwood, A. H., Kemmerer, D. L., Van Valin, R. D., Jr., Murphy, B. W., & Khalak, H. G. (1996). A positron emission tomographic study of regular and irregular verb morphology in English. *Language, 72,* 451–497.

Jaeggi, S. M., Buschkuehl, M., Jonides, J., & Perrig, W. J. (2008). Improving fluid intelligence with training on working memory. *Proceedings of the National Academy of Sciences USA, 105*(19), 6829–6833.

James, W. (1890). *The principles of psychology* (Vols. 1 and 2). New York, NY: Holt.

Janer, K. W., & Pardo, J. V. (1991). Deficits in selective attention following bilateral anterior cingulotomy. *Journal of Cognitive Neuroscience, 3,* 231–241.

Jarvella, R. J. (1971). Syntactic processing of connected speech. *Journal of Verbal Learning and Verbal Behavior, 10,* 409–416.

Jeffries, R. P., Polson, P. G., Razran, L., & Atwood, M. E. (1977). A process model for missionaries: Cannibals and other river-crossing problems. *Cognitive Psychology, 9,* 412–440.

Jeffries, R. P., Turner, A. A., Polson, P. G., & Atwood, M. E. (1981). The processes involved in designing software. In J. R. Anderson (Ed.), *Cognitive skills and their acquisition* (pp. 225–283). Hillsdale, NJ: Erlbaum.

Jenkins, I. H., Brooks, D. J., Nixon, P. D., Frackowiak, R. S. J., & Passingham, R. E. (1994). Motor sequence learning: A study with positron emission tomography. *Journal of Neuroscience, 14,* 3775–3790.

Jeunehomme, O., & D'Argembeau, A. (2018). The time to remember: Temporal compression and duration judgements in memory for real-life events. *Quarterly Journal of Experimental Psychology,* 1747021818773082.

Jiang, J., & Bernstein, L. E. (2011). Psychophysics of the McGurk and other audiovisual speech integration effects. *Journal of Experimental Psychology: Human Perception and Performance, 37*(4), 1193.

John, B. E., Patton, E. W., Gray, W. D., & Morrison, D. F. (2012, September). Tools for predicting the duration and variability of skilled performance without skilled performers. In *Proceedings of the Human Factors and Ergonomics Society Annual Meeting* (Vol. 56, No. 1, pp. 985–989). SAGE Publications.

Johnson, D. M. (1939). Confidence and speed in the two-category judgment. *Archives of Psychology, 241,* 1–52.

Johnson, E. J., Steffel, M., & Goldstein, D. G. (2005). Making better decisions: from measuring to constructing preferences. *Health Psychology, 24*(4S), S17.

Johnson, J. D., McDuff, S. G., Rugg, M. D., & Norman, K. A. (2009). Recollection, familiarity, and cortical reinstatement: a multivoxel pattern analysis. *Neuron, 63*(5), 697–708.

Johnson, J. S., & Newport, E. L. (1989). Critical period effects in second language learning: The influence of maturational state on the acquisition of English as a second language. *Cognitive Psychology, 21,* 60–99.

Johnson, M. K., Hashtroudi, S., & Lindsay, D. S. (1993). Source monitoring. *Psychological Bulletin, 114*(1), 3–28.

Johnson-Laird, P. N. (1983). *Mental models.* Cambridge, MA: Harvard University Press.

Johnson-Laird, P. N. (1995). Mental models, deductive reasoning, and the brain. In M. S. Gazzaniga (Ed.), *The cognitive neurosciences* (pp. 999–1008). Cambridge, MA; MIT Press.

Johnson-Laird, P. N. (2003). Personal communication.

Johnson-Laird, P. N., & Goldvarg, Y. (1997). How to make the impossible seem possible. *Proceedings of the Nineteenth Annual Conference of the Cognitive Science Society,* 354–357.

Johnson-Laird, P. N., & Steedman, M. (1978). The psychology of syllogisms. *Cognitive Psychology, 10,* 64–99.

Johnston, W. A., & Heinz, S. P. (1978). Flexibility and capacity demands of attention. *Journal of Experimental Psychology: General, 107,* 420–435.

Jones, L., Rothbart, M. K., & Posner, M. I. (2003). Development of inhibitory control in preschool children. *Developmental Science, 6,* 498–504.

Jonides, J., Schumacher, E. H., Smith, E. E., Koeppe, R. A., Awh, E., . . . Willis, C. R. (1998). The role of parietal cortex in verbal working memory. *Journal of Neuroscience, 18,* 5026–5034.

Jung, R. E., & Haier, R. J. (2007). The parieto-frontal integration theory (P-FIT) of intelligence: converging neuroimaging evidence. *Behavioral and Brain Sciences, 30*(2), 135–154.

Jung-Beeman, M., Bowden, E. M., Haberman, J., Frymiare, J. L., Arambel-Liu, S., Greenblatt, R., . . . Kounios, J. (2004). Neural activity when people solve verbal problems with insight. *PLoS Biology, 2,* 500–510.

Just, M. A., & Carpenter, P. A. (1980). A theory of reading: From eye fixations to comprehension. *Psychological Review, 87,* 329–354.

Just, M. A., & Carpenter, P. A. (1985). Cognitive coordinate systems: Accounts of mental rotation and individual differences in spatial ability. *Psychological Review, 92,* 137–172.

Just, M. A., & Carpenter, P. A. (1987). *The psychology of reading and language comprehension.* Boston, MA: Allyn & Bacon.

Just, M. A., & Carpenter, P. A. (1992). A capacity theory of comprehension: Individual differences in working memory. *Psychological Review, 99,* 122–149.

Just, M. A., Keller, T. A., & Kana, R. K. (2013). A theory of autism based on frontal-posterior underconnectivity. In M. A. Just & K. A. Pelphrey (Eds.), *Development and brain systems in autism* (pp. 35–63). New York, NY: Psychology Press.

Kahn, I., & Wagner, A. D. (2002). Diminished medial temporal lobe activation with expanding retrieval practice. *Journal of Cognitive Neuroscience, D71* (Suppl., Cognitive Neuroscience Society Ninth Annual Meeting).

Kahneman, D. (2011). *Thinking, fast and slow.* New York, NY: Macmillan.

Kahneman, D., & Tversky, A. (1973). On the psychology of prediction. *Psychological Review, 80*(4), 237.

Kahneman, D., & Tversky, A. (1979). Prospect theory: An analysis of decisions under risk. *Econometrica, 97,* 263–291.

Kahneman, D., & Tversky, A. (1984). Choices, values, and frames. *American Psychologist, 80,* 341–350.

Kail, R. (1988). Developmental functions for speeds of cognitive processes. *Journal of Experimental Child Psychology, 45,* 339–364.

Kail, R., & Park, Y. (1990). Impact of practice on speed of mental rotation. *Journal of Experimental Child Psychology, 49,* 227–244.

Kandel, E. R., & Schwartz, J. H. (1984). *Principles of neural science* (2nd ed.). New York, NY: Elsevier.

Kandel, E. R., Schwartz, J. H., & Jessell, T. M. (1991). *Principles of neural science* (3rd ed.). New York, NY: Elsevier.

Kanwisher, N., McDermott, J., & Chun, M. M. (1997). The fusiform face area: A module in human extra-striate cortex specialized for face perception. *Journal of Neuroscience, 17,* 4302–4311.

Kanwisher, N. J., Tong, F., & Nakayama, K. (1998). The effect of face inversion on the human fusiform face area. *Cognition, 68,* B1–B11.

Kanwisher, N. J., & Wojciulik, E. (2000). Visual attention: Insights from brain imaging. *Nature Review Neuroscience, 1,* 91–100.

Kaplan, C. A. (1989). Hatching a theory of incubation: Does putting a problem aside really help? If so, why? Unpublished doctoral dissertation, Carnegie Mellon University, Pittsburgh, PA.

Kaplan, C. A., & Simon, H. A. (1990). In search of insight. *Cognitive Psychology, 22,* 374–419.

Kapler, I. V., Weston, T., & Wiseheart, M. (2015). Spacing in a simulated undergraduate classroom: Long-term benefits for factual and higher-level learning. *Learning and Instruction, 36,* 38–45.

Kapur, S., Craik, F. I. M., Tulving, E., Wilson, A. A., Houle, S., & Brown, G. M. (1994). Neuroanatomical correlates of encoding in episodic memory: Levels of processing effect. *Proceedings of National Academy of Sciences USA, 91,* 2008–2011.

Karpicke, J. D., Butler, A. C., & Roediger, H. L. (2009). Metacognitive strategies in student learning: Do students practice retrieval when they study on their own? *Memory, 17,* 471–479.

Kastner, S., DeWeerd, P., Desimone, R., & Ungerleider, L. G. (1998). Mechanisms of directed attention in ventral extrastriate cortex as revealed by functional MRI. *Science, 282,* 108–111.

Keenan, J. M., Baillet, S. D., & Brown, P. (1984). The effects of causal cohesion on comprehension and memory. *Journal of Verbal Learning and Verbal Behavior, 23,* 115–126.

Keency, T. J., Cannizzo, S. R., & Flavell, J. H. (1967). Spontaneous and induced verbal rehearsal in a recall task. *Child Development, 38,* 953–966.

Keil, F. C. (1992). *Concepts, kinds, and cognitive development.* Cambridge, MA: MIT Press.

Keller, S. S., Crow, T., Foundas, A., Amunts, K., & Roberts, N. (2009). Broca's area: nomenclature, anatomy, typology and asymmetry. *Brain and Language, 109*(1), 29–48.

Kellogg, W. N., & Kellogg, L. A. (1933). *The ape and the child.* New York, NY: McGraw-Hill.

Kemp, C., & Regier, T. (2012). Kinship categories across languages reflect general communicative principles. *Science. 336*(6084), 1049–1054.

Keppel, G. (1968). Retroactive and proactive inhibition. In T. R. Dixon & D. L. Horton (Eds.), *Verbal behavior and general behavior theory* (pp. 172–213). Englewood Cliffs, NJ: Prentice-Hall.

Kershaw, T. C., & Ohlsson, S. (2001). Training for insight: The case of the nine-dot problem. In J. D. Moore & K. Stenning (Eds.), *Proceedings of the Twenty-Third Annual Conference of the Cognitive Science Society* (pp. 489–493). Mahwah, NJ: Erlbaum.

Kickmeier-Rust, M. D., & Holzinger, A. (2018). Teaming up with artificial intelligence: The human in the loop of serious game pathfinding algorithms. In M. Gentile, M. Allegra, & H. Söbke (Eds.), *Games and Learning Alliance: 7th International Conference, GALA 2018, Palermo, Italy, December 5–7, 2018, Proceedings* (pp. 354–363). New York, NY: Springer.

Kiesel, A., Steinhauser, M., Wendt, M., Falkenstein, M., Jost, K., Philipp, A. M., & Koch, I. (2010). Control and interference in task switching—a review. *Psychological Bulletin, 136,* 849–874.

Kinney, G. C., Marsetta, M., & Showman, D. J. (1966). *Studies in display symbol legibility: Part XXI. The legibility of alphanumeric symbols for digitized television* (ESD-TR-66-117). Bedford, MA: The Mitre Corporation.

Kintsch, W. (1974). *The representation of meaning in memory.* Hillsdale, NJ: Erlbaum.

Kintsch, W. (1998). *Comprehension: A paradigm for cognition.* Cambridge, UK: Cambridge University Press.

Kintsch, W. (2013). Discourse comprehension. In W. J. Perrig & A. Grob (Eds.), *Control of human behavior, mental processes, and consciousness: Essays in honor of the 60th birthday of August Flammer* (p. 125). New York, NY: Psychology Press.

Kintsch, W., Welsch, D. M., Schmalhofer, F., & Zimny, S. (1990). Sentence memory: A theoretical analysis. *Journal of Memory and Language, 29,* 133–159.

Kirsh, D., & Maglio, P. (1994). On distinguishing epistemic from pragmatic action. *Cognitive Science, 18,* 513–549.

Klahr, D., & Dunbar, K. (1988). Dual space search during scientific reasoning. *Cognitive Science, 12,* 1–4.

Klatzky, R. L. (2009). Giving psychological science away: The role of applications courses. *Perspectives on Psychological Science, 4,* 522–530.

Klayman, J., & Ha, Y.-W. (1987). Confirmation, disconfirmation, and information in hypothesis testing. *Psychological Review, 94,* 211–228.

Knutson, B., Taylor, J., Kaufman, M., Peterson, R., & Glover, G. (2005). Distributed neural representation of expected value. *Journal of Neuroscience, 25,* 4806–4812.

Koedinger, K. R., & Corbett, A. T. (2006). Cognitive tutors: Technology bringing learning science to the classroom. In R. K. Sawyer (Ed.), *Handbook of the learning sciences* (pp. 61–78). New York, NY: Cambridge University Press.

Koestler, A. (1964). *The action of creation.* London, UK: Hutchinson.

Köhler, W. (1927). *The mentality of apes.* New York, NY: Harcourt Brace.

Kolers, P. A. (1976). Reading a year later. *Journal of Experimental Psychology: Human Learning and Memory, 2,* 554–565.

Kolers, P. A. (1979). A pattern analyzing basis of recognition. In L. S. Cermak & F. I. M. Craik (Eds.), *Levels of processing in human memory* (pp. 363–384). Hillsdale, NJ: Erlbaum.

Körkel, J. (1987). *Die Entwicklung von Gedächtnis- und Metagedächtnisleistungen in Abhängigkeit von bereichsspezifischen Vorkenntnissen.* Frankfurt: Lang.

Kosslyn, S. M., DiGirolamo, G., Thompson, W. L., & Alpert, N. M. (1998). Mental rotation of objects versus hands: Neural mechanisms revealed by positron emission tomography. *Psychophysiology, 35,* 151–161.

Kosslyn, S. M., Pascual-Leone, A., Felician, O., Camposano, S., Keenan, J. P., Thompson, W. L., . . . Alpert, N. M. (1999). The role of area 17 in visual imagery: Convergent evidence from PET and rTMS. *Science, 284,* 167–170.

Kosslyn, S. M., & Thompson, W. L. (2003). When is early visual cortex activated during visual mental imagery? *Psychological Bulletin, 129,* 723–746.

Kotovsky, K., Hayes, J. R., & Simon, H. A. (1985). Why are some problems hard? Evidence from Tower of Hanoi. *Cognitive Psychology, 17,* 248–294.

Koutstaal, W., Wagner, A. D., Rotte, M., Maril, A., Buckner, R. L., & Schacter, D. L. (2001). Perceptual specificity in visual object priming: fMRI evidence for a laterality difference in fusiform cortex. *Neuropsychologia, 39,* 184–199.

Kozhevnikov, M., Blazhenkova, O., & Becker, M. (2010). Trade-off in object versus spatial visualization abilities: Restriction in the development of visual-processing resources. *Psychonomic Bulletin & Review, 17*(1), 29–35.

Kozhevnikov, M., Kosslyn, S., & Shephard, J. (2005). Spatial versus object visualizers: A new characterization of visual cognitive style. *Memory & Cognition, 33,* 710–726.

Krause, J., Lalueza-Fox, C., Orlando L., Enard W., Green, R. E., Burbano, H. A., . . . Pääbo, S. (2007). The derived FOXP2 variant of modern humans was shared with Neandertals. *Current Biology, 17,* 1908–1912.

Kriegeskorte, N. (2015). Deep neural networks: A new framework for modeling biological vision and brain information processing. *Annual Review of Vision Science, 1,* 417–446.

Krizhevsky, A., Sutskever, I., & Hinton, G. E. (2012). Imagenet classification with deep convolutional neural networks. In *Advances in neural information processing systems 25 (NIPS 2012)* (pp. 1097–1105). Retrieved from https://papers.nips.cc/paper/4824-imagenet-classification-with-deep-convolutional-neural-networks.pdf

Kroeber, A. L. (2009). *California kinship systems*. Charleston, SC: BiblioLife.

Kroger, J. K., Nystrom, L. E., Cohen, J. D., & Johnson-Laird, P. N. (2008). Distinct neural substrates for deductive and mathematical processing. *Brain Research, 1243*, 83–103.

Kroll, J. F., & De Groot, A. M. B. (Eds.). (2005). *Handbook of bilingualism: Psycholinguistic approaches*. Oxford, UK: Oxford University Press.

Kroll, J. F., Dussias, P. E., Bice, K., & Perrotti, L. (2015). Bilingualism, mind, and brain. *Annual Review of Linguistics, 1*(1), 377–394.

Kuffler, S. W. (1953). Discharge pattern and functional organization of mammalian retina. *Journal of Neurophysiology, 16*, 37–68.

Kuhl, P. K. (1987). The special mechanisms debate in speech research: Categorization tests on animals and infants. In S. Harnad (Ed.), *Categorical perception: The groundwork of cognition* (pp. 355–386). Cambridge, UK: Cambridge University Press.

Kulik, C., Kulik, J., & Bangert-Downs, R. (1986). *Effects of testing for mastery on student learning*. Paper presented at the annual meeting of the American Educational Research Association, San Francisco.

Kulik, J. A., & Fletcher, J. D. (2016). Effectiveness of intelligent tutoring systems: A meta-analytic review. *Review of Educational Research, 86*(1), 42–78.

Kutas, M., & Hillyard, S. A. (1980). Event-related brain potentials to semantically inappropriate and surprisingly large words. *Biological Psychology, 11*, 539–550.

Labov, W. (1973). The boundaries of words and their meanings. In C.-J. N. Bailey & R. W. Shuy (Eds.), *New ways of analyzing variations in English* (pp. 340–373). Washington, DC: Georgetown University Press.

Lagrou, E., Hartsuiker, R. J., & Duyck, W. (2011). Knowledge of a second language influences auditory word recognition in the native language. *Journal of Experimental Psychology: Learning, Memory, and Cognition, 37*(4), 952.

Lakoff, G. (1971). On generative semantics. In D. Steinberg & L. Jakobovits (Eds.), *Semantics: An interdisciplinary reader in philosophy, linguistics, anthropology, and psychology* (pp. 232–297). Cambridge, UK: Cambridge University Press.

Lancaster, A. L. (2018). Student learning with permissive and restrictive cell phone policies: A classroom experiment. *International Journal for the Scholarship of Teaching and Learning, 12*(1), 5.

Landauer, T. K., Foltz, P. W., & Laham, D. (1998). Introduction to latent semantic analysis. *Discourse Processes, 25*, 259–284.

Langley, P. W., Simon, H. A., Bradshaw, G. L., & Zytkow, J. (1987). *Scientific discovery: Computational explorations of the cognitive processes*. Cambridge, MA: MIT Press.

Laris, M. (2012, August 26). Debate on brain scans as lie detectors highlighted in Maryland murder trial. *Washington Post*.

Larkin, J. H. (1981). Enriching formal knowledge: A model for learning to solve textbook physics problems. In J. R. Anderson (Ed.), *Cognitive skills and their acquisition* (pp. 311–335). Hillsdale, NJ: Erlbaum.

LeCun, Y., Bengio, Y., & Hinton, G. (2015). Deep learning. *Nature, 521*(7553), 436.

Lee, D. W., Miyasato, L. E., & Clayton, N. S. (1998). Neurobiological bases of spatial learning in the natural environment: Neurogenesis and growth in the avian and mammalian hippocampus. *Neuroreport, 9*, R15–R27.

Lee, H. S., & Anderson, J. R. (2013). Student learning: What has instruction got to do with it? *Annual Review of Psychology, 64*, 445–469.

Lee, H. S., Fincham, J. M., & Anderson, J. R. (2015). Learning from examples versus verbal directions in mathematical problem solving. *Mind, Brain, and Education, 9*(4), 232–245.

Lehman, H. G. (1953). *Age and achievement*. Princeton, NJ: Princeton University Press.

Lehtonen, M., Soveri, A., Laine, A., Järvenpää, J., de Bruin, A., & Antfolk, J. (2018). Is bilingualism associated with enhanced executive functioning in adults? A meta-analytic review. *Psychological Bulletin, 144*(4), 394.

Lenneberg, E. H. (1967). *Biological foundations of language*. New York, NY: Wiley.

LePort, A. K., Mattfeld, A. T., Dickinson-Anson, H., Fallon, J. H., Stark, C. E., Kruggel, F., . . . McGaugh, J. L. (2012). Behavioral and neuroanatomical investigation of highly superior autobiographical memory (HSAM). *Neurobiology of Learning and Memory, 98*(1), 78–92.

Lesgold, A., Rubinson, H., Feltovich, P., Glaser, R., Klopfer, D., & Yang, Y. (1988). Expertise in a complex skill: Diagnosing X-ray pictures. In M. T. H. Chi, R. Glaser, & M. J. Farr (Eds.), *The nature of expertise* (pp. 311–342). Hillsdale, NJ: Erlbaum.

Levine, D. N., Warach, J., & Farah, M. J. (1985). Two visual systems in mental imagery: Dissociation of "what" and "where" in imagery disorders due to bilateral posterior cerebral lesions. *Neurology, 35*, 1010–1018.

Lewis, C. H., & Anderson, J. R. (1976). Interference with real world knowledge. *Cognitive Psychology, 7*, 311–335.

Lewis, M. W. (1985). *Context effects on cognitive skill acquisition*. Unpublished doctoral dissertation, Carnegie-Mellon University.

Liberman, A. M. (1970). The grammars of speech and language. *Cognitive Psychology, 1*, 301–323.

Liberman, A. M., & Mattingly, I. G. (1985). The motor theory of speech perception revised. *Cognition, 21*, 1–36.

Lieberman, P. (1984). *The biology and evolution of language*. Cambridge, MA: Harvard University Press.

Lihoreau, M., Raine, N. E., Reynolds, A. M., Stelzer, R. J., Lim, K. S., Smith, A. D., . . . Chittka, L. (2012). Radar tracking and motion-sensitive cameras on flowers reveal the development of pollinator multi-destination routes over large spatial scales. *PLoS Biology, 10*(9), e1001392.

Linden, E. (1974). *Apes, men, and language*. New York, NY: Saturday Review Press.

Lindsey, R. V., Shroyer, J. D., Pashler, H., & Mozer, M. C. (2014). Improving students' long-term knowledge retention through personalized review. *Psychological Science, 25*(3), 639–647.

Lisker, L., & Abramson, A. (1970). The voicing dimension: Some experiments in comparative phonetics. *Proceedings of Sixth International Congress of Phonetic Sciences, Prague, 1967*. Prague, Czech Republic: Academia.

Livingstone, M., & Hubel, D. (1988). Segregation of form, color, movement, and depth: Anatomy, physiology, and perception. *Science, 240*, 740–749.

Loftus, E. F., Miller, D. G., & Burns, H. J. (1978). Misinformation and memory: The creation of new memories. *Journal of Experimental Psychology: General, 118*, 100–104.

Loftus, E. F., & Pickerall, J. (1995). The formation of false memories. *Psychiatric Annals, 25*, 720–725.

Loftus, E. F., & Zanni, G. (1975). Eyewitness testimony: The influence of the wording of a question. *Bulletin of the Psychonomic Society, 5*, 86–88.

Logan, G. D. (1988). Toward an instance theory of automatization. *Psychological Review, 95*, 492–527.

Logan, G. D., & Klapp, S. T. (1991). Automatizing alphabet arithmetic. I. Is extended practice necessary to produce automaticity? *Journal of Experimental Psychology: Learning, Memory, and Cognition, 17*, 179–195.

Long, D. L., Golding, J. M., & Graesser, A. C. (1992). A test of the on-line status of goal-related elaborative inferences. *Journal of Memory and Language, 31*, 634–647.

Lord, W. (2012). *The night lives on: The untold stories and secrets behind the sinking of the "unsinkable" ship—Titanic.* New York, NY: Open Road Media.

Lotte, F., Bougrain, L., Cichocki, A., Clerc, M., Congedo, M., Rakotomamonjy, A., & Yger, F. (2018). A review of classification algorithms for EEG-based brain–computer interfaces: A 10 year update. *Journal of Neural Engineering, 15*(3), 031005

Lucas, B. J., & Nordgren, L. F. (2015). People underestimate the value of persistence for creative performance. *Journal of Personality and Social Psychology, 109*(2), 232.

Luchins, A. S. (1942). Mechanization in problem solving. *Psychological Monographs, 54*(Whole No. 248).

Luchins, A. S., & Luchins, E. H. (1959). *Rigidity of behavior: A variational approach to the effects of Einstellung.* Eugene, OR: University of Oregon Books.

Luck, S. J., Chelazzi, L., Hillyard, S. A., & Desimone, R. (1997). Neural mechanisms of spatial selective attention in areas V1, V2, and V4 of macaque visual cortex. *Journal of Neurophysiology, 77*, 24–42.

Lucy, J., & Shweder, R. (1979). Whorf and his critics: Linguistic and non-linguistic influences on color memory. *American Anthropologist, 81*, 581–615.

Lucy, J., & Shweder, R. (1988). The effect of incidental conversation on memory for focal colors. *American Anthropologist, 90*, 923–931.

Lutz, M. F., & Radvansky, G. A. (1997). The fate of completed goal information in narrative comprehension. *Journal of Memory and Language, 36*(2), 293–310.

Lynch, G., & Baudry, M. (1984). The biochemistry of memory: A new and specific hypothesis. *Science, 224*, 1057–1063.

Lynn, S. J., Lock, T., Myers, B., & Payne, D. G. (1997). Recalling the unrecallable: Should hypnosis be used for memory recovery in psychotherapy? *Current Directions in Psychological Science, 6*, 79–83.

Ma, W., Adesope, O. O., Nesbit, J. C., & Liu, Q. (2014). Intelligent tutoring systems and learning outcomes: A meta-analysis. *Journal of Educational Psychology, 106*(4), 901.

MacGregor, J. N., & Chu, Y. (2011). Human performance on the traveling salesman and related problems: A review. *Journal of Problem Solving, 3*(2), 2.

Mack, A., & Rock, I. (1998). *Inattentional blindness* (Vol. 33). Cambridge, MA: MIT Press.

Maclay, H., & Osgood, C. E. (1959). Hesitation phenomena in spontaneous speech. *Word, 15*, 19–44.

MacLeod, C. M., & Dunbar, K. (1988). Training and Stroop-like interferences: Evidence for a continuum of automaticity. *Journal of Experimental Psychology: Learning, Memory, and Cognition, 14*, 126–135.

MacLeod, C. M., Hunt, E. B., & Matthews, N. N. (1978). Individual differences in the verification of sentence-picture relationships. *Journal of Verbal Learning and Verbal Behavior, 17*, 493–507.

Macmillan, M. (2000). *An odd kind of fame: Stories of Phineas Gage.* Cambridge, MA: MIT Press.

Macmillan, M., & Lena, M. L. (2010). Rehabilitating Phineas Gage. *Neuropsychological Rehabilitation, 20*(5), 641–658.

Macnamara, B. N., Hambrick, D. Z., & Oswald, F. L. (2014). Deliberate practice and performance in music, games, sports, education, and professions: A meta-analysis. *Psychological Science, 25*(8), 1608–1618.

MacWhinney, B., & Leinbach, J. (1991). Implementations are not conceptualizations: Revising the verb learning model. *Cognition, 29*, 121–157.

Maguire, E. A., Burgess, N., Donnett, J. G., Frackowiak, R. S. J., Frith, C. D., & O'Keefe, J. (1998). Knowing where and getting there: A human navigation week. *Science, 280*, 921–924.

Maguire, E. A., Gadian, D. G., Johnsrude, I. S., Good, C. D., Ashburner J., Frackowiak, R. S., & Frith, C. D. (2000). Navigation-related structural change in the hippocampi of taxi-drivers. *Proceedings of the National Academy of Sciences USA, 97*, 4398–4403.

Mahon, B. Z. (2015). What is embodied about cognition? *Language, Cognition and Neuroscience, 30*(4), 420–429.

Maier, N. R. F. (1931). Reasoning in humans. II. The solution of a problem and its appearance in consciousness. *Journal of Comparative Psychology, 12*, 181–194.

Mandler, J. M., & Johnson, N. S. (1976). Some of the thousand words a picture is worth. *Journal of Experimental Psychology: Human Learning and Memory, 2*(5), 529–540.

Mangun, G. R., Hillyard, S. A., & Luck, S. J. (1993). Electrocortical substrates of visual selective attention. In D. Meyer & S. Kornblum (Eds.), *Attention and performance* (Vol. 14, pp. 219–243). Cambridge, MA: MIT Press.

Manktelow, K. (2012). *Thinking and reasoning: An introduction to the psychology of reason, judgment and decision making.* New York, NY: Psychology Press.

Marcus, G. (2018). Deep learning: A critical appraisal. arXiv preprint arXiv:1801.00631.

Marcus, G. F., Brinkman, U., Clahsen, H., Wiese, R., & Pinker, S. (1995). German inflection: The exception that proves the rule. *Cognitive Psychology, 29*, 189–256.

Marks, D. F. (1973). Visual imagery differences in the recall of pictures. *British Journal of Psychology, 64*, 17–24.

Marler, P. (1967). Animal communication signals. *Science, 157*, 764–774.

Marmie, W. R., & Healy, A. F. (2004). Memory for common objects: Brief intentional study is sufficient to overcome poor recall of US coin features. *Applied Cognitive Psychology, 18*(4), 445–453.

Marr, D. (1982). *Vision.* San Francisco, CA: W. H. Freeman.

Marsh, E. J., & Butler, A. C. (2013). Memory in educational settings. In D. Reisberg (Ed.), *Oxford handbook of cognitive psychology.* Oxford, UK: Oxford University Press.

Marslen-Wilson, W., & Tyler, L. K. (1987). Against modularity. In J. L. Garfield (Ed.), *Modularity in knowledge representation and natural-language understanding* (pp. 37–62). Cambridge, MA: MIT Press.

Marslen-Wilson, W., & Tyler, L. K. (1998). Rules, representations, and the English past tense. *Trends in Cognitive Science, 2,* 428–435.

Martin, A. (2001). Functional neuroimaging of semantic memory. In R. Cabeza & A. Lingstone (Eds.), *Handbook of functional neuroimaging of cognition* (pp. 153–186). Cambridge, MA: MIT Press.

Martin, L. (1986). Eskimo words for snow: A case study on the genesis and decay of an anthropological example. *American Anthropologist, 88,* 418–423.

Martin, R. C. (2003). Language processing: Functional organization and neuroanatomical basis. *Annual Review of Psychology, 54,* 55–89.

Martinez, A., Moses, P., Frank, L., Buxton, R., Wong, E., & Stiles, J. (1997). Hemispheric asymmetries in global and local processing: Evidence from fMRI. *Neuroreport, 8,* 1685–1689.

Mason, R. A., & Just, M. A. (2006). Neuroimaging contributions to the understanding of discourse processes. In M. Traxler & M. A. Gernsbacher (Eds.), *Handbook of psycholinguistics* (pp. 765–799). Amsterdam, the Netherlands: Elsevier.

Mason, R. A., Just, M. A., Keller, T. A., & Carpenter, P. A. (2003). Ambiguity in the brain: What brain imaging reveals about the processing of syntactically ambiguous sentences. *Journal of Experimental Psychology: Learning, Memory, and Cognition, 29,* 1319–1338.

Massaro, D. W. (1979). Letter information and orthographic context in word perception. *Journal of Experimental Psychology: Human Perception and Performance, 5,* 595–609.

Massaro, D. W. (1992). Broadening the domain of the fuzzy logical model of perception. In H. L. Pick, Jr., P. Van den Broek, & D. C. Knill (Eds.), *Cognition: Conceptual and methodological issues* (pp. 51–84). Washington, DC: American Psychological Association.

Massaro, D. W. (1996). Modeling multiple influences in speech perception. In A. Dijkstra & K. de Smedt (Eds.), *Computational psycholinguistics: AI and connectionist models of human language processing* (pp. 85–113). London, UK: Taylor and Francis.

Masson, M. E. J., & MacLeod, C. M. (1992). Reenacting the route to interpretation: Enhanced identification without prior perception. *Journal of Experimental Psychology: General, 121,* 145–176.

Mayer, A., & Orth, I. (1901). Zur qualitativen Untersuchung der Association. *Zeitschrift für Psychologie, 26,* 1–13.

Mazard, S. L., Fuller, N. J., Orcutt, K. M., Bridle, O., & Scanlan, D. J. (2004). PCR analysis of the distribution of unicellular cyanobacterial diazotrophs in the Arabian Sea. *Applied and Environmental Microbiology, 70*(12), 7355–7364.

Mazoyer, B. M., Tzourio, N., Frak, V., Syrota, A., & Murayama, N. (1993). The cortical representation of speech. *Journal of Cognitive Neuroscience, 5,* 467–479.

McCaffrey, T. (2012). Innovation relies on the obscure: A key to overcoming the classic problem of functional fixedness. *Psychological Science, 23*(3), 215–218.

McCarthy, G., Puce, A., Gore, J. C., & Allison, T. (1997). Face-specific processing in the human fusiform gyrus. *Journal of Cognitive Neuroscience, 9,* 604–609.

McClelland, J. L., Botvinick, M. M., Noelle, D. C., Plaut, D. C., Rogers, T. T., Seidenberg, M. S., & Smith, L. B. (2010). Letting structure emerge: connectionist and dynamical systems approaches to cognition. *Trends in Cognitive Sciences, 14*(8), 348–356.

McClelland, J. L., & Ralph, M. A. L. (2015). Cognitive neuroscience. In J. D. Wright (Ed.), *International encyclopedia of the social & behavioral sciences: Vol. 4* (2nd ed., pp. 95–102). Oxford, UK: Elsevier.

McCloskey, M., & Glucksberg, S. (1978). Natural categories: Well-defined or fuzzy sets? *Memory & Cognition, 6,* 462–472.

McCloskey, M., Wible, C. G., & Cohen, N. J. (1988). Is there a special flashbulb-memory mechanism? *Journal of Experimental Psychology: General, 117,* 171–181.

McClure, S. M., Laibson, D. I., Loewenstein, G., & Cohen, J. D. (2004). Separate neural systems value immediate and delayed monetary rewards. *Science, 306,* 503–507.

McConkie, G. W., & Currie, C. B. (1996). Visual stability across saccades while viewing complex pictures. *Journal of Experimental Psychology: Human Perception and Performance, 22,* 563–581.

McDonald, J. L. (1984). *The mapping of semantic and syntactic processing cues by first and second language learners of English, Dutch, and German.* Unpublished doctoral dissertation, Carnegie-Mellon University.

McGrew, S., Ortega, T., Breakstone, J., & Wineburg, S. (2017). The challenge that's bigger than fake news: civic reasoning in a social media environment. *American Educator, 41*(3), 4.

McGurk, H., & MacDonald, J. (1976). Hearing lips and seeing voices. *Nature, 264*(5588), 746.

McKeithen, K. B., Reitman, J. S., Rueter, H. H., & Hirtle, S. C. (1981). Knowledge organization and skill differences in computer programmers. *Cognitive Psychology, 13,* 307–325.

McLaughlin, B. (1978). *Second-language acquisition in childhood.* Hillsdale, NJ: Erlbaum.

McNeil, B. J., Pauker, S. G., Sox, H. C., Jr., & Tversky, A. (1982). On the elicitation of preferences for alternative therapies. *New England Journal of Medicine, 306,* 1259–1262.

McNeill, D. (1966). Developmental psycholinguistics. In F. Smith & G. A. Miller (Eds.), *The genesis of language: A psycholinguistic approach.* Cambridge, MA: MIT Press.

McRae, K., Spivey-Knowlton, M. J., & Tanenhaus, M. K. (1998). Modeling the influence of thematic fit (and other constraints) in on-line sentence comprehension. *Journal of Memory and Language, 38,* 283–312.

Medin, D. L., & Schaffer, M. M. (1978). A context theory of classification learning. *Psychological Review, 85,* 207–238.

Mednick, S. A. (1962). The associative basis of the creative process. *Psychological Review, 69,* 220–232.

Mehrabian, A. (1971). *Silent messages.* Belmont, CA: Wadsworth.

Mercier, H., & Sperber, D. (2011). Why do humans reason? Arguments for an argumentative theory. *Behavioral and Brain Sciences, 34*(2), 57–74.

Messner, M., Beese, U., Romstock, J., Dinkel, M., & Tschaikowsky, K. (2003). The bispectral index declines during neuromuscular block in fully awake persons. *Anesthesia & Analgesia, 97,* 488–491.

Metcalfe, J., & Wiebe, D. (1987). Intuition in insight and non-insight problem solving. *Memory & Cognition, 15,* 238–246.

Metzler, J., & Shepard, R. N. (1974). Transformational studies of the internal representations of three-dimensional objects. In R. L. Solso (Ed.), *Theories of cognitive psychology: The Loyola Symposium* (pp. 147–201). Hillsdale, NJ: Erlbaum.

Meyer, D. E., & Schvaneveldt, R. W. (1971). Facilitation in recognizing pairs of words: Evidence of a dependence between retrieval operations. *Journal of Experimental Psychology, 90,* 227–234.

Middleton, F. A., & Strick, P. L. (1994). Anatomical evidence for cerebellar and basal ganglia involvement in higher cognitive function. *Science, 266,* 458–461.

Miklósi, Á., & Topál, J. (2013). What does it take to become "best friends"? Evolutionary changes in canine social competence. *Trends in Cognitive Sciences, 17*(6), 287–294.

Miller, G. A., & Nicely, P. (1955). An analysis of perceptual confusions among some English consonants. *Journal of the Acoustical Society of America, 27,* 338–352.

Milner, A. D., & Goodale, M. A. (1995). *The visual brain in action.* Oxford, UK: Oxford University Press.

Milner, B. (1962). Les troubles de la memoire accompagnant des lesions hippocampiques bilaterales. In P. Passonant (Ed.), *Physiologie de l'hippocampe* (pp. 257–262). Paris, France: Centre National de la Recherche Scientifique.

Misra, P., Marconi, A., & Kreiman, G. (2018). Minimal memory for details in real life events. *Scientific Reports, 8,* 16701.

Mitchell, T. M., Shinkareva, S. V., Carlson, A., Chang, K. M., Malave, V. L., Mason, R. A., & Just, M. A. (2008). Predicting human brain activity associated with the meanings of nouns. *Science, 320*(5880), 1191–1195.

Mithen, S. (2005). *The singing Neanderthals: The origins of music, language, mind, and body.* Cambridge, MA: Harvard University Press.

Miyachi, S., Hikosaka, O., Miyashita, K., Karadi, Z., & Rand, M. K. (1997). Differential roles of monkey striatum in learning of sequential hand movement. *Experimental Brain Research, 115,* 1–5.

Moll, M., & Miikkulainen, R. (1997). Convergence-zone episodic memory: Analysis and simulations. *Neural Networks, 10,* 1017.

Monsell, S. (2003). Task switching. *Trends in Cognitive Science, 7,* 134–140.

Montague, P. R., Dayan, P., & Sejnowski, T. J. (1996). A framework for mesencephalic dopamine systems based on predictive Hebbian learning. *Journal of Neuroscience, 16,* 1936–1947.

Morasch, K. C., Raj, V. R., & Bell, M. A. (2013). The development of cognitive control from infancy through childhood. In D. Reisberg (Ed.), *Oxford handbook of cognitive psychology* (pp. 989–999). New York, NY: Oxford.

Moray, N. (1959). Attention in dichotic listening: Affective cues and the influence of instructions. *Quarterly Journal of Experimental Psychology, 9,* 56–90.

Moray, N., Bates, A., & Barnett, T. (1965). Experiments on the four-eared man. *Journal of the Acoustical Society of America, 38,* 196–201.

Mori, G., & Malik, M. J. (2003). Recognizing objects in adversarial clutter: Breaking a visual CAPTCHA. In *IEEE Conference on Computer Vision and Pattern Recognition* (pp. 134–141). Piscataway, NJ: IEEE.

Motley, M. T., Camden, C. T., & Baars, B. J. (1982). Covert formulation and editing of anomalies in speech production: Evidence from experimentally elicited slips of the tongue. *Journal of Verbal Learning and Verbal Behavior, 21,* 578–594.

Moyer, R. S. (1973). Comparing objects in memory: Evidence suggesting an internal psychophysics. *Perception and Psychophysics, 13,* 180–184.

Mozur, P. (2018, July 8). Inside China's dystopian dreams: A.I., shame and lots of cameras. *New York Times.*

Murray, J. D., & Burke, K. A. (2003). Activation and encoding of predictive inferences: The role of reading skill. *Discourse Processes, 35,* 81–102.

Näätänen, R. (1992). *Attention and brain function.* Hillsdale, NJ: Erlbaum.

Neisser, U. (1964). Visual search. *Scientific American, 210,* 94–102.

Neisser, U. (1967). *Cognitive psychology.* New York, NY: Appleton.

Neisser, U., & Becklen, R. (1975). Selective looking: Attending to visually specified events. *Cognitive Psychology, 7,* 480–494.

Neisser, U., Boodoo, G., Bouchard, T., Boykin, A. W., Brody, N., Ceci, S. J., . . . Urbina, S. (1996). Intelligence: Knowns and unknowns. *American Psychologist, 51,* 77–101.

Neisser, U., & Harsch, N. (1992). Phantom flashbulbs: False recollections of hearing the news about *Challenger*. In E. Winograd & U. Neisser (Eds.), *Affect and accuracy in recall: Studies of "flashbulb" memories* (pp. 9–33). Cambridge, UK: Cambridge University Press.

Nelson, T. O. (1971). Savings and forgetting from long-term memory. *Journal of Verbal Learning and Verbal Behavior, 10,* 568–576.

Nelson, T. O. (1976). Reinforcement and human memory. In W. K. Estes (Ed.), *Handbook of learning and cognitive processes* (Vol. 3, pp. 207–246). Hillsdale, NJ: Erlbaum.

Nestor, A., Plaut, D. C., & Behrmann, M. (2011). Unraveling the distributed neural code of facial identity through spatiotemporal pattern analysis. *Proceedings of the National Academy of Sciences, 108*(24), 9998–10003.

Nettelbeck, T., & Burns, N. R. (2010). Processing speed, working memory and reasoning ability from childhood to old age. *Personality and Individual Differences, 48*(4), 379–384.

Neubauer, A. C., & Fink, A. (2009). Intelligence and neural efficiency. *Neuroscience & Biobehavioral Reviews, 33*(7), 1004–1023.

Neves, D. M., & Anderson, J. R. (1981). Knowledge compilation: Mechanisms for the automatization of cognitive skills. In J. R. Anderson (Ed.), *Cognitive skills and their acquisition* (pp. 57–84). Hillsdale, NJ: Erlbaum.

Newcombe, N. S., & Frick, A. (2010). Early education for spatial intelligence: Why, what, and how. *Mind, Brain, and Education, 4*(3), 102–111.

Newell, A. (1990). *Unified theories of cognition.* Cambridge, MA: Harvard University Press.

Newell, A., & Rosenbloom, P. S. (1981). Mechanisms of skill acquisition and the law of practice. In J. R. Anderson (Ed.), *Cognitive skills and their acquisition* (pp. 1–55). Hillsdale, NJ: Erlbaum.

Newell, A., & Simon, H. A. (1972). *Human problem solving.* Englewood Cliffs, NJ: Prentice-Hall.

Newman, E. J., Garry, M., Bernstein, D. M., Kantner, J., & Lindsay, D. S. (2012). Nonprobative photographs (or words) inflate truthiness. *Psychonomic Bulletin & Review, 19*(5), 969–974.

Newport, E. L. (1986, October 17–19). *The effect of maturational state on the acquisition of language.* Paper presented at the Eleventh Annual Boston University Conference on Language Development, Boston, MA.

Newport, E. L., & Supalla, T. (1990). *A critical period effect in the acquisition of a primary language.* Unpublished manuscript, University of Rochester, Rochester, NY.

Newstead, S. E., Handley, S. J., Harley, C., Wright, H., & Farrelly, D. (2004). Individual differences in deductive reasoning. *Quarterly Journal of Experimental Psychology Section A, 57*(1), 33–60.

Nickerson, R. S. (1998). Confirmation bias: A ubiquitous phenomenon in many guises. *Review of General Psychology, 2,* 175–220.

Nickerson, R. S., & Adams, M. J. (1979). Long-term memory for a common object. *Cognitive Psychology, 11*(3), 287–307.

Nida, E. A. (1971). Sociopsychological problems in language mastery and retention. In P. Pimsleur & T. Quinn (Eds.), *The psychology of second language acquisition* (pp. 59–66). London, UK: Cambridge University Press.

Nieder, A. (2012). Supramodal numerosity selectivity of neurons in primate prefrontal and posterior parietal cortices. *Proceedings of the National Academy of Sciences USA, 109*(29), 11860–11865.

Nieder, A., & Dehaene, S. (2009). Representation of number in the brain. *Annual Review of Neuroscience, 32,* 185–208.

Nilsson, L.-G., & Gardiner, J. M. (1993). Identifying exceptions in a database of recognition failure studies from 1973 to 1992. *Memory & Cognition, 21,* 397–410.

Nilsson, N. J. (1971). *Problem-solving methods in artificial intelligence.* New York, NY: McGraw-Hill.

Nisbett, R. E., Aronson, J., Blair, C., Dickens, W., Flynn, J., Halpern, D. F., & Turkheimer, E. (2012). Intelligence: New findings and theoretical developments. *American Psychologist, 67*(2), 130.

Nishimoto, S., Vu, A. T., Naselaris, T., Benjamini, Y., Yu, B., & Gallant, J. L. (2011). Reconstructing visual experiences from brain activity evoked by natural movies. *Current Biology, 21*(19), 1641–1646.

Nissen, M. J., & Bullemer, P. (1987). Attentional requirements of learning: Evidence from performance measures. *Cognitive Psychology, 19,* 1–32.

Noelting, G. (1975). *Stages and mechanisms in the development of the concept of proportion in the child and adolescent.* Paper presented at the First Interdisciplinary Seminar on Piagetian Theory and Its Implications for the Helping Professions, University of Southern California, Los Angeles.

Nosofsky, R. M. (1986). Attention, similarity, and the identification-categorization relationship. *Journal of Experimental Psychology: General, 115,* 39–57.

Nosofsky, R. M. (1991). Tests of an exemplar model for relating perceptual classification and recognition in memory. *Journal of Experimental Psychology: Human Perception and Performance, 17,* 3–27.

Novack, M. A., Wakefield, E. M., Congdon, E. L., Franconeri, S., & Goldin-Meadow, S. (2016). There is more to gesture than meets the eye: visual attention to gesture's referents cannot account for its facilitative effects during math instruction. In *Proceedings of the 38th Annual Meeting of the Cognitive Science Society.*

Oaksford, M., & Chater, N. (1994). A rational analysis of the selection task as optimal data selection. *Psychological Review, 101,* 608–631.

Oaksford, M., & Wakefield, M. (2003). Data selection and natural-sampling: Probabilities do matter. *Memory & Cognition, 31,* 143–154.

Oates, J. M., & Reder, L. M. (2010). Memory for pictures: Sometimes a picture is not worth a single word. In A. S. Benjamin (Ed.), *Successful remembering and successful forgetting: A festschrift in honor of Robert A. Bjork* (pp. 447–462). New York, NY: Psychological Press.

O'Brien, E. J., Albrecht, J. E., Hakala, C. M., & Rizzella, M. L. (1995). Activation and suppression of antecedents during reinstatement. *Journal of Experimental Psychology: Learning, Memory, and Cognition, 21*(3), 626.

O'Craven, K. M., Downing, P., & Kanwisher, N. K. (1999). fMRI evidence for objects as the units of attentional selection. *Nature, 401,* 584–587.

O'Craven, K., & Kanwisher, N. (2000). Mental imagery of faces and places activates corresponding stimulus-specific brain regions. *Journal of Cognitive Neuroscience, 12,* 1013–1023.

Oden, D. L., Thompson, R. K. R., & Premack, D. (2001). Can an ape reason analogically? Comprehension and production of analogical problems by Sarah, a chimpanzee (*Pan troglodytes*). In D. Gentner, K. J. Holyoak, & B. N. Kokinov (Eds.), *Analogy: Theory and phenomena* (pp. 472–497). Cambridge, MA: MIT Press.

O'Doherty, J. P., Dayan, P., Schultz, J., Deichmann, R., Friston, K., & Dolan, R. J. (2004). Dissociable roles of ventral and dorsal striatum in instrumental conditioning. *Science, 304,* 452–454.

Ohlsson, S. (1992). The learning curve for writing books: Evidence from Professor Asimov. *Psychological Science, 3,* 380–382.

Okada, S., Hanada, M., Hattori, H., & Shoyama, T. (1963). A case of pure word-deafness. *Studia Phonologica, 3,* 58–65.

Okada, T., & Simon, H. A. (1997). Collaborative discovery in a scientific domain. *Cognitive Science, 21,* 109–146.

O'Keefe, J., & Dostrovsky, J. (1971). The hippocampus as a spatial map: Preliminary evidence from unit activity in the freely moving rat. *Experimental Brain Research, 34,* 171–175.

Olds, J., & Milner, P. (1954). Positive reinforcement produced by electrical stimulation of septal area and other regions of rat brain. *Journal of Comparative and Physiological Psychology, 47,* 419–427.

Onken, J., Hastie, R., & Revelle, W. (1985). Individual differences in the use of simplification strategies in a complex decision-making task. *Journal of Experimental Psychology: Human Perception and Performance, 11*(1), 14.

Open Science Collaboration. (2015). Estimating the reproducibility of psychological science. *Science, 349*(6251), aac4716.

Oppenheimer, D. M., & Kelso, E. (2015). Information processing as a paradigm for decision making. *Annual Review of Psychology, 66,* 277–294.

Ost, J., Vrij, A., Costall, A., & Bull, R. (2002). Crashing memories and reality monitoring: distinguishing between perceptions, imaginations and "false memories." *Applied Cognitive Psychology: The Official Journal of the Society for Applied Research in Memory and Cognition, 16*(2), 125–134.

Osterhout, L., & Holcomb, P. J. (1992). Event-related potentials elicited by syntactic anomaly. *Journal of Memory and Language, 31,* 785–806.

Otten, L. J., Henson, R. N., & Rugg, M. D. (2001). Depth of processing effects on neural correlates of memory encoding: Relationship between findings from across- and within-task comparisons. *Brain, 124,* 399–412.

Owens, J., Bower, G. H., & Black, J. B. (1979). The "soap opera" effect in story recall. *Memory & Cognition, 7,* 185–191.

Oyama, S. (1978). The sensitive period and comprehension of speech. *Working Papers on Bilingualism, 16,* 1–17.

Ozernov-Palchik, O., Norton, E. S., Wang, Y., Beach, S. D., Zuk, J., Wolf, M., . . . Gaab, N. (2018). The relationship between socioeconomic status and white matter microstructure in pre-reading children: A longitudinal investigation. *Human Brain Mapping, 40*(3), 1–14.

Pachur, T., Schooler, L. J., & Stevens, J. R. (2014). We'll meet again: Revealing distributional and temporal patterns of social contact. *PLoS ONE, 9*(1), e86081. http://dx.doi.org/10.1371/journal.pone.0086081

Paivio, A. (1971). *Imagery and verbal processes.* New York, NY: Holt, Rinehart, & Winston.

Paivio, A. (1986). *Mental representations: A dual coding approach.* New York, NY: Oxford University Press.

Paller, K. A., & Wagner, A. D. (2002). Observing the transformation of experience into memory. *Trends in Cognitive Science, 6,* 93–102.

Palmer, S. E. (1977). Hierarchical structure in perceptual representation. *Cognitive Psychology, 9,* 441–474.

Palmer, S. E., Schreiber, G., & Fox., C. (1991, November 22–24). *Remembering the earthquake: "Flashbulb" memory of experienced versus reported events.* Paper presented at the 32nd annual meeting of the Psychonomic Society, San Francisco.

Pane, J. F., Griffin, B. A., McCaffrey, D. F., & Karam, R. (2013). *Effectiveness of Cognitive Tutor Algebra I at scale.* Santa Monica, CA: RAND Corporation. Retrieved from http://www.rand.org/pubs/working_papers/WR984

Pardo, J. V., Pardo, P. J., Janer, K. W., & Raichle, M. E. (1990). The anterior cingulate cortex mediates processing selection in the Stroop attentional conflict paradigm. *Proceedings of the National Academy of Sciences USA, 87,* 256–259.

Paris, S. C., & Lindauer, B. K. (1976). The role of interference in children's comprehension and memory for sentences. *Cognitive Psychology, 8,* 217–227.

Parker, E. S., Birnbaum, I. M., & Noble, E. P. (1976). Alcohol and memory: Storage and state dependency. *Journal of Verbal Learning and Verbal Behavior, 15,* 691–702.

Parker, E. S., Cahill, L., & McGaugh, J. L. (2006). A case of unusual autobiographical remembering. *Neurocase, 12,* 35–49.

Parsons, L. M., & Osherson, D. (2001). New evidence for distinct right and left brain systems for deductive vs. probabilistic reasoning. *Cerebral Cortex, 11,* 954–965.

Pascual-Leone, A., Gomez-Tortosa, E., Grafman, J., Always, D., Nichelli, P., & Hallett, M. (1994). Induction of visual extinction by rapid-rate transcranial magnetic stimulation of parietal lobe. *Neurology, 44,* 494–498.

Pascual-Leone, J. (1980). Constructive problems for constructive theories: The current relevance of Piaget's work and a critique of information-processing psychology. In R. H. Kluwe & H. Spada (Eds.), *Developmental models of thinking* (pp. 263–296). New York, NY: Academic Press.

Patalano, A. L., Smith, E. E., Jonides, J., & Koeppe, R. A. (2001). PET evidence for multiple strategies of categorization. *Cognitive, Affective, & Behavioral Neuroscience, 1*(4), 360–370.

Pavlik, P. I., Jr., & Anderson, J. R. (2005). Practice and forgetting effects on vocabulary memory: An activation-based model of the spacing effect. *Cognitive Science, 29*(4), 559–586.

Payne, J. W. (1976). Task complexity and contingent processing in decision making: An information search and protocol analysis. *Organizational Behavior and Human Performance, 16*(2), 366–387.

Payne, J. W., Bettman, J. R., & Johnson, E. J. (1993). *The adaptive decision maker.* New York, NY: Cambridge University Press.

Payne, S. J., & Duggan, G. B. (2011). Giving up problem solving. *Memory & Cognition, 39*(5), 902–913.

Peal, E., & Lambert, W. E. (1962). The relation of bilingualism to intelligence. *Psychological Monographs: General and Applied, 76*(27), 1.

Pearl, J. (1988). *Probabilistic reasoning in intelligent systems: Networks of plausible inference.* Amsterdam, the Netherlands: Elsevier.

Penfield, W. (1959). The interpretive cortex. *Science, 129,* 1719–1725.

Perlmutter, M., Kaplan, M., & Nyquist, L. (1990). Development of adaptive competence in adulthood. *Human Development, 33,* 185–197.

Perrett, D. I., Rolls, E. T., & Caan, W. (1982). Visual neurons responsive to faces in the monkey temporal cortex. *Experimental Brain Research, 47,* 329–342.

Peterson, M. A., Kihlstrom, J. F., Rose, P. M., & Gilsky, M. L. (1992). Mental images can be ambiguous: Reconstruals and reference-frame reversals. *Memory & Cognition, 20,* 107–123.

Peterson, S. B., & Potts, G. R. (1982). Global and specific components of information integration. *Journal of Verbal Learning and Verbal Behavior, 21,* 403–420.

Phelps, E. A. (1989). *Cognitive skill learning in amnesiacs.* Doctoral dissertation, Princeton University.

Phillips, S. (2017, August 11). The average guy who spent 6,003 hours trying to be a professional golfer. *The Atlantic.* Retrieved from https://www.theatlantic.com/health/archive/2017/08/the-dan-plan/536592/

Picton, T. W., & Hillyard, S. A. (1974). Human auditory evoked potentials. II. Effects of attention. *Electroencephalography and Clinical Neurophysiology, 36,* 191–199.

Pietschnig, J., Penke, L., Wicherts, J. M., Zeiler, M., & Voracek, M. (2015). Meta-analysis of associations between human brain volume and intelligence differences: how strong are they and what do they mean? *Neuroscience & Biobehavioral Reviews, 57,* 411–432.

Pillsbury, W. B. (1908). The effects of training on memory. *Educational Review, 36,* 15–27.

Pine, D. S., Grun, J., Maguire, E. A., Burgess, N., Zarahn, E., Koda, V., . . . Bilder, R. M. (2002). Neurodevelopmental aspects of spatial navigation: A virtual reality fMRI study. *Neuroimage, 15,* 396–406.

Pinker, S. (1994). *The language instinct.* New York, NY: HarperCollins.

Pinker, S., & Prince, A. (1988). On language and connectionism: Analysis of a parallel distributed processing model of language acquisition. *Cognition, 28,* 73–193.

Pirolli, P. L., & Anderson, J. R. (1985). The role of practice in fact retrieval. *Journal of Experimental Psychology: Learning, Memory, and Cognition, 11,* 136–153.

Pisoni, D. B. (1977). Identification and discrimination of the relative onset time of two component tones: Implications for voicing perception in stops. *Journal of the Acoustical Society of America, 61,* 1352–1361.

Pizlo, Z., Stefanov, E., Saalweachter, J., Li, Z., Haxhimusa, Y., & Kropatsch, W. G. (2006). Traveling salesman problem: A foveating pyramid model. *Journal of Problem Solving, 1,* 83–101.

Pohl, W. (1973). Dissociation of spatial discrimination deficits following frontal and parietal lesions in monkeys. *Journal of Comparative and Physiological Psychology, 82,* 227–239.

Poincaré, H. (1929). *The foundations of science.* New York, NY: Science House.

Poldrack, R. A., & Gabrieli, J. D. E. (2001). Characterizing the neural mechanisms of skill learning and repetition priming: Evidence from mirror reading. *Brain, 124,* 67–82.

Poldrack, R. A., Prabhakaran, V., Seger, C., & Gabrieli, J. D. (1999). Striatal activation during acquisition of a cognitive skill learning. *Neuropsychology, 13,* 564–574.

Polson, P. G., Muncher, E., & Kieras, D. E. (1987). *Transfer of skills between inconsistent editors* (MCC Technical Report No. ACA-HI-395-87). Austin, TX: Microelectronics and Computer Technology Corporation.

Polster, M., McCarthy, R., O'Sullivan, G., Gray, P., & Park, G. (1993). Midazolam-induced amnesia: Implications for the implicit/explicit memory distinction. *Brain & Cognition, 22,* 244–265.

Pope, K. S. (1996). Memory, abuse, and science: Questioning claims about the false memory syndrome epidemic (author's reprint). *American Psychologist, 51,* 957–974.

Posner, M. I. (1988). Structures and functions of selective attention. In T. Boll & B. Bryant (Eds.), *Master lectures in clinical neuropsychology* (pp. 173–202). Washington, DC: American Psychological Association.

Posner, M. I., Cohen, Y., & Rafal, R. D. (1982). Neural systems control of spatial orienting. *Philosophical Transactions of the Royal Society of London B, 298,* 187–198.

Posner, M. I., Nissen, M. J., & Ogden, W. C. (1978). Attended and unattended processing modes: The role of set for spatial location. In H. L. Pick, Jr., & I. J. Saltzman (Eds.), *Modes of perceiving and processing information* (pp. 137–157). Hillsdale, NJ: Erlbaum.

Posner, M. I., Peterson, S. E., Fox, P. T., & Raichle, M. E. (1988). Localization of cognitive operations in the human brain. *Science, 240,* 1627–1631.

Posner, M. I., Rafal, R. D., Chaote, L. S., & Vaughn, J. (1985). Inhibition of return: Neural basis and function. *Cognitive Neuropsychology, 2,* 211–228.

Posner, M. I., Snyder, C. R. R., & Davidson, B. J. (1980). Attention and the detection of signals. *Journal of Experimental Psychology: General, 109,* 160–174.

Posner, M. I., Walker, J. A., Friederich, F. J., & Rafal, R. D. (1984). Effects of parietal injury on covert orienting of attention. *Journal of Neuroscience, 4,* 1863–1874.

Postle, B. R. (2006). Working memory as an emergent property of the mind and brain. *Neuroscience, 139*(1), 23–38.

Postle, B. R. (2015). Activation and information in working memory research. In A. Duarte, M. Barense, & D. R. Addis (Eds.), *The Wiley-Blackwell handbook on the cognitive neuroscience of memory* (pp. 897–901). Hoboken, NJ: Wiley-Blackwell.

Postman, L. (1964). Short-term memory and incidental learning. In A. W. Melton (Ed.), *Categories of human learning* (pp. 146–201). New York, NY: Academic Press.

Potter, M. C., & Lombardi, L. (1990). Regeneration in the short-term recall of sentences. *Journal of Memory and Language, 29*(6), 633–654.

Powell, D. (2013, June). Toy helicopter guided by power of thought. *Nature News.* Retrieved from https://www.nature.com/news/toy-helicopter-guided-by-power-of-thought-1.13139

Premack, D. (1976). *Intelligence in ape and man.* Hillsdale, NJ: Erlbaum.

Premack, D., & Premack, A. J. (1983). *The mind of an ape.* New York, NY: W. W. Norton.

Press, J. H. (2006). *Unknown quantity: A real and imaginary history of algebra.* Washington, DC: National Academy Press.

Pressley, M., McDaniel, M. A., Turnure, J. E., Wood, E., & Ahmad, M. (1987). Generation and precision of elaboration: Effects on intentional and incidental learning. *Journal of Experimental Psychology: Learning, Memory, and Cognition, 13,* 291–300.

Price, J. (2008). *The woman who can't forget.* New York, NY: Simon & Schuster.

Priest, A. G., & Lindsay, R. O. (1992). New light on novice-expert differences in physics problem solving. *British Journal of Psychology, 83,* 389–405.

Pritchard, R. M. (1961). Stabilized images on the retina. *Scientific American, 204,* 72–78.

Pullman, G. K. (1989). The great Eskimo vocabulary hoax. *National Language and Linguistic Theory, 7,* 275–281.

Pylyshyn, Z. W. (1973). What the mind's eye tells the mind's brain: A critique of mental imagery. *Psychological Bulletin, 80,* 1–24.

Qin, Y., Anderson, J. R., Silk, E., Stenger, V. A., & Carter, C. S. (2004). The change of the brain activation patterns along with the children's practice in algebra equation solving. *Proceedings of the National Academy of Sciences USA, 101,* 5686–5691.

Qin, Y., Sohn, M.-H., Anderson, J. R., Stenger, V. A., Fissell, K., Goode, A., & Carter, C. S. (2003). Predicting the practice effects on the blood oxygenation level-dependent (BOLD) function of fMRI in a symbolic manipulation task. *Proceedings of the National Academy of Sciences USA, 100,* 4951–4956.

Quillian, M. R. (1966). *Semantic memory.* Cambridge, MA: Bolt, Beranak and Newman.

Raaijmakers, J. G., & Jakab, E. (2013). Rethinking inhibition theory: On the problematic status of the inhibition theory for forgetting. *Journal of Memory and Language, 68*(2), 98–122.

Ratcliff, G., & Newcombe, F. (1982). Object recognition: Some deductions from the clinical evidence. In A. W. Ellis (Ed.), *Normality and pathology in cognitive functions* (pp. 147–171). London, UK: Academic Press.

Raveh, D., & Lavie, N. (2015). Load-induced inattentional deafness. *Attention, Perception, & Psychophysics, 77*(2), 483–492.

Raymond, C. R., & Redman, S. J. (2006). Spatial segregation of neuronal calcium signals encodes different forms of LTP in rat hippocampus. *Journal of Physiology, 570,* 97–111.

Rayner, K. (2009). Eye movements and attention in reading, scene perception, and visual search. *The Quarterly Journal of Experimental Psychology, 62*(8), 1457–1506.

Rayner, K., Foorman, B. R., Perfetti, C. A., Pesetsky, D., & Seidenberg, M. S. (2002). How should reading be taught? *Scientific American, 286*(3), 85–91. (Adaptation of How psychological science informs the teaching of reading. *Psychological Science in the Public Interest, 2,* 31–74.)

Reder, L. M. (1982). Plausibility judgment versus fact retrieval: Alternative strategies for sentence verification. *Psychological Review, 89,* 250–280.

Reder, L. M., & Kusbit, G. W. (1991). Locus of the Moses illusion: Imperfect encoding, retrieval or match? *Journal of Memory and Language, 30,* 385–406.

Reder, L. M., Park, H., & Keiffaber, P. (2009). Memory systems do not divide on consciousness: Reinterpreting memory in terms of activation and binding. *Psychological Bulletin, 135,* 23–49.

Reder, L. M., & Ross, B. H. (1983). Integrated knowledge in different tasks: Positive and negative fan effects. *Journal of Experimental Psychology: Human Learning and Memory, 8,* 55–72.

Redick, T. S., Shipstead, Z., Harrison, T. L., Hicks, K. L., Fried, D. E., Hambrick, D. Z., . . . Engle, R. W. (2013). No evidence of intelligence improvement after working memory training: A randomized, placebo-controlled study. *Journal of Experimental Psychology: General, 142*(2), 359.

Reed, S. K. (1972). Pattern recognition and categorization. *Cognitive Psychology, 3*, 382–407.

Reed, S. K. (1987). A structure-mapping model for word problems. *Journal of Experimental Psychology: Learning, Memory, and Cognition, 13*, 124–139.

Reicher, G. (1969). Perceptual recognition as a function of meaningfulness of stimulus material. *Journal of Experimental Psychology, 81*, 275–280.

Reitman, J. (1976). Skilled perception in GO: Deducing memory structures from inter-response times. *Cognitive Psychology, 8*, 336–356.

Renzi, C., Cattaneo, Z., Vecchi, T., & Cornoldi, C. (2013). Mental imagery and blindness. In S. Lacey & R. Lawson (Eds.), *Multisensory imagery* (pp. 115–130). New York, NY: Springer.

Reyna, V. F., & Farley, F. (2006). Risk and rationality in adolescent decision making: Implications for theory, practice, and public policy. *Psychological Science in the Public Interest, 7*, 1–44.

Richardson-Klavehn, A., & Bjork, R. A. (1988). Measures of memory. *Annual Review of Psychology, 39*, 475–543.

Richter, T., & Späth, P. (2006). Recognition is used as one cue among others in judgment and decision making. *Journal of Experimental Psychology: Learning, Memory & Cognition, 32*, 150–162.

Rinck, M., & Bower, G. H. (1995). Anaphora resolution and the focus of attention in situation models. *Journal of Memory and Language, 34*(1), 110–131.

Rist, R. S. (1989). Schema creation in programming. *Cognitive Science, 13*, 67–96.

Ritter, S. (2011). The research behind the Carnegie Learning math series. *Carnegie Learning.* Retrieved from https://cdn.carnegielearning.com/assets/research/research-behind-carnegie-learning-math-series.pdf

Ritter, S., Anderson, J. R., Koedinger, K. R., & Corbett, A. (2007). Cognitive tutor: Applied research in mathematics education. *Psychonomic Bulletin & Review, 14*, 249–255.

Rizzolatti, G., & Craighero, L. (2004). The mirror-neuron system. *Annual Review of Neuroscience, 27*, 169–192.

Roberson, D., Davies, I., & Davidoff, J. (2000). Colour categories are not universal: Replications and new evidence from a stone-age culture. *Journal of Experimental Psychology: General, 129*, 369–398.

Roberts, R. J., Hager, L. D., & Heron, C. (1994). Prefrontal cognitive processes: Working memory and inhibition in the antisaccade task. *Journal of Experimental Psychology: General, 123*, 374–393.

Robertson, L. C., & Lamb, M. R. (1991). Neuropsychological contributions to theories of part/whole organization. *Cognitive Psychology, 23*, 299–330.

Robertson, L. C., & Rafal, R. (2000). Disorders of visual attention. In M. Gazzaniga (Ed.), *The new cognitive neuroscience* (2nd ed., pp. 633–650). Cambridge, MA: MIT Press.

Robinson, G. H. (1964). Continuous estimation of a time-varying probability. *Ergonomics, 7*, 7–21.

Roe, A. W., Chelazzi, L., Connor, C. E., Conway, B. R., Fujita, I., Gallant, J. L., . . . Vanduffel, W. (2012). Toward a unified theory of visual area V4. *Neuron, 74*(1), 12–29.

Roediger, H. L., & Guynn, M. J. (1996). Retrieval processes. In E. L. Bjork & R. A. Bjork (Eds.), *Human memory* (pp. 197–236). San Diego, CA: Academic Press.

Roediger, H. L., & Karpicke, J. D. (2006). Test-enhanced learning: Taking memory tests improves long-term retention. *Psychological Science, 17*, 249–255.

Roediger, H. L., & McDermott, K. B. (1995). Creating false memories: Remembering words not presented in lists. *Journal of Experimental Psychology: Learning, Memory, and Cognition, 21*, 803–814.

Roelfsema, P. R., Lamme, V. A. F., & Spekreijse, H. (1998). Object-based attention in the primary visual cortex of the macaque monkey. *Nature, 395*, 376–381.

Roland, P. E., Eriksson, L., Stone-Elander, S., & Widen, L. (1987). Does mental activity change the oxidative metabolism of the brain? *Journal of Neuroscience, 7*, 2373–2389.

Roland, P. E., & Friberg, L. (1985). Localization of cortical areas activated by thinking. *Journal of Neurophysiology, 53*, 1219–1243.

Rolls, E. T. (1992). Neurophysiological mechanisms underlying face processing within and beyond the temporal cortical visual areas. *Philosophical Transactions of the Royal Society of London B, 335*, 11–21.

Roring, R. W. (2008). *Reviewing expert chess performance: A production-based theory of chess skill.* Unpublished PhD thesis, Florida State University.

Rosch, E. (1973). On the internal structure of perceptual and semantic categories. In T. E. Moore (Ed.), *Cognitive development and the acquisition of language* (pp. 111–144). New York, NY: Academic Press.

Rosch, E. (1975). Cognitive representations of semantic categories. *Journal of Experimental Psychology: General, 104*, 192–223.

Rosch, E. (1977). Human categorization. In N. Warren (Ed.), *Advances in cross-cultural psychology* (Vol. 1, pp. 1–49). London, UK: Academic Press.

Ross, B. H. (1984). Remindings and their effects in learning a cognitive skill. *Cognitive Psychology, 16*, 371–416.

Ross, B. H. (1987). This is like that: The use of earlier problems and the separation of similarity effects. *Journal of Experimental Psychology: Learning, Memory, and Cognition, 13*, 629–639.

Ross, J., & Lawrence, K. A. (1968). Some observations on memory artifice. *Psychonomic Science, 13*, 107–108.

Rossi, S., Cappa, S. F., Babiloni, C., Pasqualetti, P., Miniussi, C., Carducci, F., . . . Rossini, P. M. (2001). Prefrontal cortex in long-term memory: An "interference" approach using magnetic stimulation. *Natural Neuroscience, 4*, 948–952.

Rossi, S., Pasqualetti, P., Zito, G., Vecchio, F., Cappa, S. F., Miniussi, C., . . . Rossini, P. M. (2006). Prefrontal and parietal cortex in human episodic memory: An interference study by repetitive transcranial magnetic stimulation. *European Journal of Neuroscience, 23*, 793–800.

Rottschy, C., Langner, R., Dogan, I., Reetz, K., Laird, A. R., Schulz, J. B., . . . Eickhoff, S. B. (2012). Modelling neural correlates of working memory: A coordinate-based meta-analysis. *Neuroimage, 60*(1), 830–846.

Ruiz, D. (1987). Learning and problem solving: What is learned while solving the Tower of Hanoi? Doctoral dissertation, Stanford University, 1986. *Dissertation Abstracts International, 42*, 3438B.

Rumelhart, D. E., & McClelland, J. L. (1986). On learning the past tenses of English verbs. In J. L. McClelland & D. E. Rumelhart (Eds.), *Parallel distributed processing: Explorations in the microstructure of cognition* (Vol. 2, pp. 216–271). Cambridge, MA: MIT Press/Bradford Books.

Rumelhart, D. E., & Ortony, A. (1976). The representation of knowledge in memory. In R. C. Anderson, R. J. Spiro, & W. E. Montague (Eds.), *Semantic factors in cognition* (pp. 99–135). Hillsdale, NJ: Erlbaum.

Rumelhart, D. E., & Siple, P. (1974). Process of recognizing tachistoscopically presented words. *Psychological Review, 81,* 99–118.

Rundus, D. J. (1971). Analysis of rehearsal processes in free recall. *Journal of Experimental Psychology, 89,* 63–77.

Russakovsky, O., Deng, J., Su, H., Krause, J., Satheesh, S., Ma, S., . . . Berg, A. C. (2015). Imagenet large scale visual recognition challenge. *International Journal of Computer Vision, 115*(3), 211–252.

Russell, S., & Norvig, P. (2009). *Artificial intelligence: A modern approach* (3rd ed.). Upper Saddle River, NJ: Prentice-Hall.

Sacks, O. W. (1985). *The man who mistook his wife for a hat and other clinical tales.* New York, NY: Summit Books.

Sadeh, T., Ozubko, J. D., Winocur, G., & Moscovitch, M. (2016). Forgetting patterns differentiate between two forms of memory representation. *Psychological Science, 27*(6), 810–820.

Saer, D. J. (1923). The effect of bilingualism on intelligence. *British Journal of Psychology: General Section, 14,* 25–38.

Saffran, E. M., & Schwartz, M. F. (1994). Of cabbages and things: Semantic memory from a neuropsychological perspective—a tutorial review. In C. Umilta & M. Moscovitch (Eds.), *Attention and performance XV* (pp. 507–536). Hove and London, UK: Churchill Livingstone.

Safren, M. A. (1962). Associations, set, and the solution of word problems. *Journal of Experimental Psychology, 64,* 40–45.

Salamy, A. (1978). Commissural transmission: Maturational changes in humans. *Science, 200,* 1409–1411.

Salmon, K., & Reese, E. (2015). Talking (or not talking) about the past: the influence of parent–child conversation about negative experiences on children's memories. *Applied Cognitive Psychology, 29*(6), 791–801.

Salmon, K., & Reese, E. (2016). The benefits of reminiscing with young children. *Current Directions in Psychological Science, 25*(4), 233–238.

Salthouse, T. A. (1985). Anticipatory processes in transcription typing. *Journal of Applied Psychology, 70,* 264–271.

Salthouse, T. A. (1986). Perceptual, cognitive, and motoric aspects of transcription typing. *Psychological Bulletin, 99,* 303–319.

Salthouse, T. A. (1992). *Mechanisms of age-cognition relations in adulthood.* Hillsdale, NJ: Erlbaum.

Salthouse, T. (2012). Consequences of age-related cognitive declines. *Annual Review of Psychology, 63,* 201–226.

Sams, M., Hari, R., Rif, J., & Knuutila, J. (1993). The human auditory sensory memory trace persists about 10 s: Neuromagnetic evidence. *Journal of Cognitive Neuroscience, 5,* 363–370.

Sanfey, A. G., Hastie, R., Colvin, M. K., & Grafman, J. (2003). Phineas gauged: Decision-making and the frontal lobes. *Neuropsychologia, 41,* 1218–1229.

Santa, J. L. (1977). Spatial transformations of words and pictures. *Journal of Experimental Psychology: Human Learning and Memory, 3,* 418–427.

Sarason, S. B., & Doris, J. (1979). *Educational handicap, public policy, and social history.* New York, NY: Free Press.

Saufley, W. H., Otaka, S. R., & Bavaresco, J. L. (1985). Context effects: Classroom tests and context independence. *Memory & Cognition, 13,* 522–528.

Savage-Rumbaugh, E. S., Murphy, J., Sevcik, R. A., Brakke, K. E., Williams, S. L., & Rumbaugh, D. M. (1993). Language comprehension in ape and child. *Monographs of the Society for Research in Child Development, 58*(Serial No. 233).

Sayers, D. L. (1968). *Five red herrings.* New York, NY: Avon.

Schacter, D. L. (1987). Implicit memory: History and current status. *Journal of Experimental Psychology: Learning, Memory, and Cognition, 13,* 501–518.

Schacter, D. L. (2001). *The seven sins of memory: How the mind forgets and remembers.* Boston, MA: Houghton Mifflin.

Schacter, D. L., & Badgaiyan, R. D. (2001). Neuroimaging of priming: New perspectives on implicit and explicit memory. *Current Directions in Psychological Science, 10,* 1–4.

Schacter, D. L., Cooper, L. A., Delaney, S. M., Peterson, M. A., & Tharan, M. (1991). Implicit memory for possible and impossible objects: Constraints on the construction of structural descriptions. *Journal of Experimental Psychology: Learning, Memory, and Cognition, 17,* 3–19.

Schaie, K. W. (1996). Intellectual development in adulthood. In J. Birren & K. W. Schaie (Eds.), *Handbook of the psychology of aging* (4th ed., pp. 266–286). San Diego, CA: Academic Press.

Schank, R. C., & Abelson, R. (1977). *Scripts, plans, goals, and understanding.* Hillsdale, NJ: Erlbaum.

Scheck, B., Neufeld, P., & Dwyer, J. (2000). *Actual innocence: Five days to execution, and other dispatches from the wrongly convicted.* New York, NY: Doubleday.

Scheines, R., & Sieg, W. (1994). Computer environments for proof construction. *Interactive Learning Environments, 4,* 159–169.

Schieffelin, B. (1979). *How Kaluli children learn what to say, what to do, and how to feel: An ethnographic study of the development of communicative competence.* Unpublished doctoral dissertation, Columbia University.

Schmidt, F. L., & Hunter, J. E. (2004). General mental ability in the world of work: Occupational attainment and job performance. *Journal of Personality and Social Psychology, 86,* 162–173.

Schmidt, R. A. (1988). Motor and action perspectives on motor behavior. In O. G. Meijer & K. Rother (Eds.), *Complete movement behavior: The motor-action controversy* (pp. 3–44). Amsterdam, the Netherlands: Elsevier.

Schmidt, S., Tinti, C., Fantino, M., Mammarella, I. C., & Cornoldi, C. (2013). Spatial representations in blind people: The role of strategies and mobility skills. *Acta Psychologica, 142*(1), 43–50.

Schneider, W., Körkel, J., & Weinert, F. E. (1988, July 6–8). *Expert knowledge, general abilities, and text processing.* Paper presented at the Workshop on Interactions among Aptitudes, Strategies, and Knowledge in Cognitive Performance.

Schneiderman, B. (1976). Exploratory experiments in programmer behavior. *International Journal of Computer and Information Sciences, 5,* 123–143.

Schoenfeld, A. H., & Herrmann, D. J. (1982). Problem perception and knowledge structure in expert and novice mathematical problem solvers. *Journal of Experimental Psychology: Learning, Memory, and Cognition, 8,* 484–494.

Schooler, L. J., & Anderson, J. R. (2017). The adaptive nature of memory. In J. H. Byrne (Ed.), *Learning and memory: A comprehensive reference* (2nd ed.). Amsterdam, the Netherlands: Elsevier.

Schroff, F., Kalenichenko, D., & Philbin, J. (2015). Facenet: A unified embedding for face recognition and clustering. In *Proceedings of the IEEE Conference on Computer Vision and Pattern Recognition* (pp. 815–823). Piscataway, NJ: IEEE.

Schultz, W. (1998). Predictive reward signal of dopamine neurons. *Journal of Neurophysiology, 80,* 1–27.

Schumacher, E. H., Seymour, T. L., Glass, J. M., Fencsik, D. E., Lauber, E. J., Kieras, D. E., & Meyer, D. E. (2001). Virtually perfect time sharing in dual-task performance: Uncorking the central cognitive bottleneck. *Psychological Science, 12,* 101–108.

Schwarz, N., Newman, E., & Leach, W. (2016). Making the truth stick & the myths fade: Lessons from cognitive psychology. *Behavioral Science & Policy, 2*(1), 85–95.

Schweizer, T. A., Ware, J., Fischer, C. E., Craik, F. I. M., & Bialystok, E. (2012). Bilingualism as a contributor to cognitive reserve: Evidence from brain atrophy in Alzheimer's disease. *Cortex, 48*(8), 991–996.

Seidenberg, M. S. (2013). The science of reading and its educational implications. *Language Learning and Development, 9*(4), 331–360. doi:10.1080/15475441.2013.812017

Selfridge, O. G. (1955). Pattern recognition and modern computers. *Proceedings of the Western Joint Computer Conference.* New York, NY: Institute of Electrical and Electronics Engineers.

Selkoe, D. J. (1992). Aging brain, aging mind. *Scientific American, 267*(3), 135–142.

Semendeferi, K., Armstrong, E., Schleicher, A., Zilles, K., & Van Hoesen, G. W. (2001). Prefrontal cortex in humans and apes: A comparative study of area 10. *American Journal of Physical Anthropology, 114,* 224–241.

Shafir, E. (1993). Choosing versus rejecting: Why some opinions are both better and worse than others. *Memory & Cognition, 21,* 546–556.

Shah, A. K., & Oppenheimer, D. M. (2008). Heuristics made easy: An effort-reduction framework. *Psychological Bulletin, 134*(2), 207.

Shapin, S. (2013, October 14). The man who forgot everything. *The New Yorker.* Retrieved from https://www.newyorker.com/books/page-turner/the-man-who-forgot-everything

Shelton, A. L., & Gabrieli, J. D. (2002). Neural correlates of encoding space from route and survey perspectives. *Journal of Neuroscience, 22,* 2711–2717.

Shepard, R. N. (1967). Recognition memory for words, sentences, and pictures. *Journal of Verbal Learning and Verbal Behavior, 6,* 156–163.

Shepard, R. N., & Metzler, J. (1971). Mental rotation of three-dimensional objects. *Science, 171,* 701–703.

Shepard, R. N., & Teghtsoonian, M. (1961). Retention of information under conditions approaching a steady state. *Journal of Experimental Psychology, 62,* 302–309.

Sheppard, L. D., & Vernon, P. A. (2008). Intelligence and speed of information-processing: a review of 50 years of research. *Personality and Individual Differences, 44*(3), 535–551.

Shi, S. W., Wedel, M., & Pieters, F. G. M. (2013). Information acquisition during online decision making: A model-based exploration using eye-tracking data. *Management Science, 59*(5), 1009–1026.

Shipstead, Z., Hicks, K. L., & Engle, R. W. (2012). Working memory training remains a work in progress. *Journal of Applied Research in Memory and Cognition, 1*(3), 217–219.

Shomstein, S., & Behrmann, M. (2006). Cortical systems mediating visual attention to both objects and spatial locations. *Proceedings of the National Academy of Sciences USA, 103*(30), 11387–11392.

Shortliffe, E. H. (1976). *Computer based medical consultations: MYCIN.* New York, NY: Elsevier.

Shuford, E. H. (1961). Percentage estimation of proportion as a function of element type, exposure time, and task. *Journal of Experimental Psychology, 61,* 430–436.

Siegler, R. S. (1996). *Emerging minds: The process of change in children's thinking.* New York, NY: Oxford University Press.

Siegler, R. S. (1998). *Children's thinking* (3rd ed.). Upper Saddle River, NJ: Prentice-Hall.

Silveira, J. (1971). *Incubation: The effect of interruption timing and length on problem solution and quality of problem processing.* Unpublished doctoral dissertation, University of Oregon.

Silver, D., Schrittwieser, J., Simonyan, K., Antonoglou, I., Huang, A., Guez, A., . . . Chen, Y. (2017). Mastering the game of Go without human knowledge. *Nature, 550*(7676), 354.

Silver, E. A. (1979). Student perceptions of relatedness among mathematical verbal problems. *Journal for Research in Mathematics Education, 12,* 54–64.

Simester, D., & Drazen, P. (2001). Always leave home without it: A further investigation of the credit card effect on willingness to pay. *Marketing Letters, 12,* 5–12.

Simon, H. A. (1955). A behavioral model of rational choice. *The Quarterly Journal of Economics, 69*(1), 99–11.

Simon, H. A. (1989). The scientist as a problem solver. In D. Klahr & K. Kotovsky (Eds.), *Complex information processing: The impact of Herbert Simon* (pp. 375–398). Hillsdale, NJ: Erlbaum.

Simon, H. A., & Gilmartin, K. (1973). A simulation of memory for chess positions. *Cognitive Psychology, 5,* 29–46.

Simon, H. A., & Lea, G. (1974). Problem solving and rule induction. In H. Simon (Ed.), *Models of thought.* New Haven, CT: Yale University Press.

Simon, T. J., Hespos, S. J., & Rochat, P. (1995). Do infants understand simple arithmetic? A replication of Wynn (1992). *Cognitive Development, 10,* 253–269.

Simons, D. J., & Chabris, C. F. (1999). Gorillas in our midst: Sustained inattentional blindness for dynamic events. *Perception, 28,* 1059–1074.

Simons, D. J., & Levin, D. T. (1998). Failure to detect changes to people in a real-world interaction. *Psychonomic Bulletin and Review, 5,* 644–649.

Singer, M. (1994). Discourse inference processes. In M. A. Gernsbacher (Ed.), *Handbook of psycholinguistics* (pp. 479–515). San Diego, CA: Academic Press.

Singley, K., & Anderson, J. R. (1989). *The transfer of cognitive skill.* Cambridge, MA: Harvard University Press.

Sivers, H., Schooler, J., Freyd, J. J. (2002). Recovered memories. In V. S. Ramachandran (Ed.), *Encyclopedia of the human brain* (Vol. 4., pp 169–184). San Diego, CA: Academic Press.

Skoyles, J. R. (1999). Expertise vs. general problem solving abilities in human evolution: Reply to Overskeid on brain-expertise. *Psycoloquy, 10,* 1–14.

Sloman, S. A., & Lagnado, D. A. (2005). Do we "do"? *Cognitive Science, 29*(1), 5–39

Sloman, S. A., & Lagnado, D. (2015). Causality in thought. *Annual Review of Psychology, 66,* 223–247.

Smaers, J. B., Steele, J., Case, C. R., Cowper, A., Amunts, K., & Zilles, K. (2011). Primate prefrontal cortex evolution: human brains are the extreme of a lateralized ape trend. *Brain, Behavior and Evolution, 77*(2), 67–78.

Smith, E. E., & Grossman, M. (2008). Multiple systems for category learning. *Neuroscience and Biobehavioral Reviews, 32,* 249–264.

Smith, E. E., & Jonides, J. (1995). Working memory in humans: Neuropsychological evidence. In M. S. Gazzaniga (Ed.), *The cognitive neurosciences* (pp. 1009–1020). Cambridge, MA: MIT Press.

Smith, J. D. (2014). Prototypes, exemplars, and the natural history of categorization. *Psychonomic Bulletin & Review, 21*(2), 312–331.

Smith, M. (1982). *Hypnotic memory enhancement of witnesses: Does it work?* Paper presented at the meeting of the Psychonomic Society, Minneapolis, MN.

Smith, S. M., & Blakenship, S. E. (1989). Incubation effects. *Bulletin of the Psychonomic Society, 27,* 311–314.

Smith, S. M., & Blakenship, S. E. (1991). Incubation and the persistence of fixation in problem solving. *American Journal of Psychology, 104,* 61–87.

Smith, S. M., Brown, H. O., Toman, J. E. P., & Goodman, L. S. (1947). The lack of cerebral effects of d-tubercurarine. *Anesthesiology, 8,* 1–14.

Smith, S. M., Glenberg, A. M., & Bjork, R. A. (1978). Environmental context and human memory. *Memory & Cognition, 6,* 342–353.

Snow, C. E., & Ferguson, C. A. (Eds.). (1977). *Talking to children: Language input and acquisition (Papers from a conference sponsored by the Committee on Sociolinguistics of the Social Science Research Council).* New York, NY: Cambridge University Press.

Snyder, K. M., Ashitaka, Y., Shimada, H., Ulrich, J. E., & Logan, G. D. (2014). What skilled typists don't know about the QWERTY keyboard. *Attention, Perception, & Psychophysics, 76,* 162–171.

Sohn, M.-H., Goode, A., Stenger, V. A, Carter, C. S., & Anderson, J. R. (2003). Competition and representation during memory retrieval: Roles of the prefrontal cortex and the posterior parietal cortex. *Proceedings of National Academy of Sciences USA, 100,* 7412–7417.

Sorby, S., Veurink, N., & Streiner, S. (2018). Does spatial skills instruction improve STEM outcomes? The answer is "yes." *Learning and Individual Differences, 67,* 209–222.

Souza, A. S., & Oberauer, K. (2018). Does articulatory rehearsal help immediate serial recall? *Cognitive Psychology, 107,* 1–21.

Spearman, C. (1904). The proof and measurement of association between two things. *American Journal of Psychology, 15,* 72–101.

Spelke, E. S. (2011). Natural number and natural geometry. In E. Brannon & S. Dehaene (Eds.), *Space, time and number in the brain: Searching for the foundations of mathematical thought* (Attention & Performance XXIV, pp. 287–317). Oxford, UK: Oxford University Press.

Spelke, E. S., Hirst, W., & Neisser, U. (1976). Skills of divided attention. *Cognition, 4,* 215–230.

Spencer, S. J., Steele, C. M., & Quinn, D. M. (1999). Stereotype threat and women's math performance. *Journal of Experimental Social Psychology, 35*(1), 4–28.

Sperling, G. A. (1960). The information available in brief visual presentation. *Psychological Monographs, 74*(Whole No. 498).

Sperling, G. A. (1967). Successive approximations to a model for short-term memory. *Acta Psychologica, 27,* 285–292.

Spiro, R. J. (1977). Constructing a theory of reconstructive memory: The state of the schema approach. In R. C. Anderson, R. J. Spiro, & W. E. Montague (Eds.), *Schooling and the acquisition of knowledge* (pp. 137–166). Hillsdale, NJ: Erlbaum.

Squire, L. R. (1987). *Memory and brain.* New York, NY: Oxford University Press.

Squire, L. R. (1992). Memory and the hippocampus: A synthesis from findings with rats, monkeys, and humans. *Psychological Review, 99,* 195–232.

Stanfield, R. A., & Zwaan, R. A. (2001). The effect of implied orientation derived from verbal context on picture recognition. *Psychological Science, 12,* 153–156.

Stanovich, K. (2011). *Rationality and the reflective mind.* Oxford, UK: Oxford University Press.

Starkey, P., Spelke, E. S., & Gelman, R. (1990). Numerical abstraction by human infants. *Cognition, 36,* 97–127.

Stein, B. S., & Bransford, J. D. (1979). Constraints on effective elaboration: Effects of precision and subject generation. *Journal of Verbal Learning and Verbal Behavior, 18,* 769–777.

Stein, N. L., & Trabasso, T. (1981). What's in a story? Critical issues in comprehension and instruction. In R. Glaser (Ed.), *Advances in the psychology of instruction* (Vol. 2, pp. 213–268). Hillsdale, NJ: Erlbaum.

Sternberg, R. J. (1998). Personal communication.

Sternberg, R. J. (2006). The Rainbow Project: Enhancing the SAT through assessments of analytical, practical, and creative skills. *Intelligence, 34*(4), 321–350.

Sternberg, R. J. (2007). Finding students who are wise, practical, and creative. *Chronicle of Higher Education, 53*(44), B11.

Sternberg, S. (1966). High-speed scanning in human memory. *Science, 153,* 652–654.

Sternberg, S. (1969). Memory scanning: Mental processes revealed by reaction time experiments. *American Scientist, 57,* 421–457.

Stevens, A., & Coupe, P. (1978). Distortions in judged spatial relations. *Cognitive Psychology, 10,* 422–437.

Stevens, J. K., Emerson, R. C., Gerstein, G. L., Kallos, T., Neufeld, G. R., Nichols, C. W., & Rosenquist, A. C. (1976). Paralysis of the awake human: Visual perceptions. *Vision Research, 16,* 93–98.

Stevens, J. R., Marewski, J. N., Schooler, L. J., & Gilby, I. C. (2016). Reflections of the social environment in chimpanzee memory: Applying rational analysis beyond humans. *Royal Society Open Science, 3,* 160293.

Stiles, J., Brown, T. T., Haist, F., & Jernigan, T. L. (2015). Brain and cognitive development. In R. M. Lerner (Ed.), *Handbook of child psychology and developmental science* (pp. 1–54). Hoboken, NJ: Wiley.

Stillings, N. A., Feinstein, M. H., Garfield, J. L., Rissland, E. L., Rosenbaum, D. A., & Weisler, S. E. (1987). *Cognitive science: An introduction.* Cambridge, MA: MIT Press.

Stokes, M., Thompson, R., Cusack, R., & Duncan, J. (2009). Top-down activation of shape-specific population codes in visual cortex during mental imagery. *Journal of Neuroscience, 29*(5), 1565–1572.

Strangman, G., Boas, D. A., & Sutton, J. P. (2002). Non-invasive neuroimaging using near-infrared light. *Biological Psychiatry, 52,* 679–693.

Stratton, G. M. (1922). *Developing mental power.* New York, NY: Houghton Mifflin.

Strayer, D. L., & Drews, F. A. (2007). Cell-phone-induced driver distraction. *Current Directions in Psychological Science, 16,* 128–131.

Strohner, H., & Nelson, K. E. (1974). The young child's development of sentence comprehension: Influence of event probability, nonverbal context, syntactic form, and strategies. *Child Development, 45,* 567–576.

Stromswold, K. (2000). The cognitive neuroscience of language acquisition. In M. Gazzaniga (Ed.), *The cognitive neurosciences* (2nd ed., pp. 909–932). Cambridge, MA: MIT Press.

Stroop, J. R. (1935). Studies of interference in serial verbal reactions. *Journal of Experimental Psychology, 18,* 643–662.

Studdert-Kennedy, M. (1976). Speech perception. In N. J. Lass (Ed.), *Contemporary issues in experimental phonetics* (pp. 243–293). Springfield, IL: Charles C. Thomas.

Sulin, R. A., & Dooling, D. J. (1974). Intrusion of a thematic idea in retention of prose. *Journal of Experimental Psychology, 103,* 255–262.

Swinney, D. A. (1979). Lexical access during sentence comprehension: (Re)consideration of context effects. *Journal of Verbal Learning and Verbal Behavior, 18,* 645–659.

Szameitat, A. J., Schubert, T., Muller, K., & von Cramon, D. Y. (2002). Localization of executive functions in dual-task performance with fMRI. *Journal of Cognitive Neuroscience, 14,* 1184–1199.

Taatgen, N. A. (2013). The nature and transfer of cognitive skills. *Psychological Review, 120,* 439–471.

Taigman, Y., Yang, M., Ranzato, M. A., & Wolf, L. (2014). Deepface: Closing the gap to human-level performance in face verification. In *Proceedings of the IEEE Conference on Computer Vision and Pattern Recognition* (pp. 1701–1708). Piscataway, NJ: IEEE.

Tanaka, J. W., & Farah, M. J. (1993). Parts and wholes in face recognition. *Quarterly Journal of Experimental Psychology, 46A,* 225–245.

Teasdale, J. D., & Russell, M. L. (1983). Differential effects of induced mood on the recall of positive, negative and neutral words. *British Journal of Clinical Psychology, 22,* 163–171.

Terman, L. M., & Merrill, M. A. (1973). *Stanford-Binet intelligence scales: 1973 norms edition.* Boston, MA: Houghton Mifflin.

Terrace, H. S., Pettito, L. A., Sanders, R. J., & Bever, T. G. (1979). Can an ape create a sentence? *Science, 206,* 891–902.

Thelen, E. (2000). Grounded in the world: Developmental origins of the embodied mind. *Infancy, 1,* 3–30.

Thomas, E. L., & Robinson, H. A. (1972). *Improving reading in every class: A sourcebook for teachers.* Boston, MA: Allyn & Bacon.

Thompson, M. C., & Massaro, D. W. (1973). Visual information and redundancy in reading. *Journal of Experimental Psychology, 98,* 49–54.

Thompson, W. L., & Kosslyn, S. M. (2000). In A. W. Toga & J. C. Mazziotta (Eds.), *Brain mapping II: The systems* (pp. 535–560). San Diego, CA: Academic Press.

Thorndike, E. L. (1898). Animal intelligence: An experimental study of the associative processes in animals. *Psychological Monographs, 2*(Whole No. 8).

Thorndike, E. L. (1906). *Principles of teaching.* New York, NY: A. G. Seiler.

Thorndyke, P. W., & Hayes-Roth, B. (1982). Differences in spatial knowledge acquired from maps and navigation. *Cognitive Psychology, 14,* 560–589.

Thurstone, L. L. (1938). *Primary mental abilities.* Chicago, IL: University of Chicago Press.

Tipper, S. P., Driver, J., & Weaver, B. (1991). Object-centered inhibition of return of visual attention. *Quarterly Journal of Experimental Psychology, 43A,* 289–298.

Tomasello, M. (2017). What did we learn from the ape language studies? In B. Hare & S. Yamamoto (Eds.), *Bonobos: Unique in mind, brain, and behavior* (pp. 95–104). Oxford, UK: Oxford University Press.

Tomasello, M., & Call, J. (1997). *Primate cognition.* New York, NY: Oxford University Press.

Townsend, D. J., & Bever, T. G. (1982). Natural units interact during language comprehension. *Journal of Verbal Learning and Verbal Behavior, 28,* 681–703.

Trabasso, T., Rollins, H., & Shaughnessy, E. (1971). Storage and verification stages in processing concepts. *Cognitive Psychology, 2,* 239–289.

Trabasso, T., & Suh, S. (1993). Understanding text: Achieving explanatory coherence through online inferences and mental operations in working memory. *Discourse Processes, 16*(1–2), 3–34.

Treisman, A. M. (1960). Verbal cues, language, and meaning in selective attention. *Quarterly Journal of Experimental Psychology, 12,* 242–248.

Treisman, A. M. (1964). Monitoring and storage of irrelevant messages and selective attention. *Journal of Verbal Learning and Verbal Behavior, 3,* 449–459.

Treisman, A. M. (1978). Personal communication.

Treisman, A. M., & Geffen, G. (1967). Selective attention: Perception or response? *Quarterly Journal of Experimental Psychology, 19,* 1–17.

Treisman, A. M., & Gelade, G. (1980). A feature-integration theory of attention. *Cognitive Psychology, 12,* 97–136.

Treisman, A. M., & Riley, J. (1969). Is selective attention selective perception or selective response? A further test. *Journal of Experimental Psychology, 79,* 27–34.

Treisman, A. M., & Schmidt, H. (1982). Illusory conjunction in the perception of objects. *Cognitive Psychology, 14,* 107–141.

Treves, A., & Rolls, E. T. (1994). A computational analysis of the role of the hippocampus in memory. *Hippocampus, 4,* 374–392.

Trueswell, J. C., Tanenhaus, M. K., & Garnsey, S. M. (1994). Semantic influences on parsing: Use of thematic role information in syntactic ambiguity resolution. *Journal of Memory and Language, 33,* 285–318.

Tsushima, T., Takizawa, O., Sasaki, M., Siraki, S., Nishi, K., Kohno, M., . . . Best, C. T. (1994). *Discrimination of English /r-l/ and /w-y/ by Japanese infants at 6–12 months: Language specific developmental changes in speech perception abilities.* Paper presented at the International Conference on Spoken Language Processing 4, Yokohama, Japan.

Tulving, E., & Pearlstone, Z. (1966). Availability versus accessibility of information in memory for words. *Journal of Verbal Learning and Verbal Behavior, 5,* 381–391.

Tulving, E., & Thompson, D. M. (1973). Encoding specificity and retrieval processes in episodic memory. *Psychological Review, 80,* 352–373.

Turing, A. M. (1950). Computing machinery and intelligence. *Mind, 59,* 433–460.

Tversky, A., & Kahneman, D. (1974). Judgments under uncertainty: Heuristics and biases. *Science, 185,* 1124–1131.

Tweney, R. D. (1989). A framework for the cognitive psychology of science. In B. Gholson, A. Houts, R. A. Neimeyer, & W. Shadish (Eds.), *Psychology of science and metascience* (pp. 342–366). Cambridge, UK: Cambridge University Press.

Tyler, R., & Marslen-Wilson, W. (1977). The on-line effects of semantic context on syntactic processing. *Journal of Verbal Learning and Verbal Behavior, 16,* 683–692.

U.S. Department of Justice. (1999). *A guide for law enforcement developed and approved by the Technical Working Group for Eyewitness Evidence.* Retrieved from https://www.ncjrs.gov/pdffiles1/nij/178240.pdf

Ullén, F., Mosing, M. A., & Madison, G. (2015). Associations between motor timing, music practice, and intelligence studied in a large sample of twins. *Annals of the New York Academy of Sciences, 1337*(1), 125–129.

Ullman, S. (1996). *High-level vision.* Cambridge, MA: MIT Press.

Ultan, R. (1969). Some general characteristics of interrogative systems. *Working Papers in Language Universals (Stanford University), 1,* 41–63.

Underwood, G. (1974). Moray vs. the rest: The effect of extended shadowing practice. *Quarterly Journal of Experimental Psychology, 26,* 368–372.

Ungerleider, L. G., & Brody, B. A. (1977). Extrapersonal spatial-orientation: The role of posterior parietal, anterior frontal and inferotemporal cortex. *Experimental Neurology, 56,* 265–280.

Uttal, D. H., Meadow, N. G., Tipton, E., Hand, L. L., Alden, A. R., Warren, C., & Newcombe, N. S. (2013). The malleability of spatial skills: A meta-analysis of training studies. *Psychological Bulletin, 139*(2), 352.

Vallar, G., Di Betta, A. M., & Silveri, M. C. (1997). The phonological short-term store-rehearsal system: Patterns of impairment and neural correlates. *Neuropsychologia, 35,* 795–812.

Van Essen, D. C., & DeYoe, E. A. (1995). Concurrent processing in the primitive visual cortex. In M. S. Gazzaniga (Ed.), *The cognitive neurosciences* (pp. 383–400). Cambridge, MA: MIT Press.

VanLehn, K. (2011). The relative effectiveness of human tutoring, intelligent tutoring systems, and other tutoring systems. *Educational Psychologist, 46*(4), 197–221.

Van Loosbroek, E., & Smitsman, A. W. (1992). Visual perception of numerosity in infancy. *Developmental Psychology, 26,* 916–922.

Vannucci, M., Mazzoni, G., Chiorri, C., & Cioli, L. (2008). Object imagery and object identification: Object imagers are better at identifying spatially-filtered visual objects. *Cognitive Processing, 9*(2), 137–143.

Van Ravenzwaaij, D., Boekel, W., Forstmann, B. U., Ratcliff, R., & Wagenmakers, E. J. (2013). Action video games do not improve the speed of information processing in simple perceptual tasks. Manuscript submitted for publication.

van Rooij, I., Schactman, A., Kadlec, H., & Stege, U. (2006). Perceptual or Analytical processing? Evidence from children's and adult's performance on the Euclidean traveling salesperson problem. *Journal of Problem Solving, 1*(1), 6.

Vargha-Khadem, F., Watkins, K., Alcock, K., Fletcher, P., & Passingham, R. (1995). Praxic and nonverbal cognitive deficits in a large family with a genetically transmitted speech and language disorder. *Proceedings of the National Academy of Sciences USA, 92,* 930–933.

Verde, M. F. (2012). Retrieval-induced forgetting and inhibition: A critical review. In B. H. Ross (Ed.). *Psychology of learning and motivation* (Vol. 56, pp. 47–80). New York, NY: Academic Press.

Victoria, L. W., & Reder, L. M. (2010). How midazolam can help us understand human memory: three illustrations. *Cognition and Neuropsychology: International Perspectives on Psychological Science, 1,* 225–236.

Visser, M., Jefferies, E., & Ralph, M. A. L. (2010). Semantic processing in the anterior temporal lobes: A meta-analysis of the functional neuroimaging literature. *Journal of Cognitive Neuroscience, 22*(6), 1083–1094.

Von Ahn, L., Blum, M., & Langford, J. (2002). *Telling humans and computers apart (automatically)* (Carnegie Mellon University Tech Report). Retrieved from https://www.cs.cmu.edu/~biglou/captcha.pdf

Von Frisch, K. (1967). *The dance language and orientation of bees* (C. E. Chadwick, Trans.). Cambridge, MA: Belknap Press.

Von Neumann, J., & Morgenstern, O. (1944). *Theory of games and economic behavior.* New York, NY: Wiley.

Wade, K. A., Garry, M., Read, J. D., & Lindsay, D. S. (2002). A picture is worth a thousand lies: Using false photographs to create false childhood memories. *Psychonomic Bulletin & Review, 9*(3), 597–603.

Wade, N. (2003, July 15). Early voices: The leap to language. *New York Times,* p. F1.

Wagner, A. D., Bunge, S. A., & Badre, D. (2004). Cognitive control, semantic memory, and priming: Contributions from prefrontal cortex. In M. S. Gazzaniga (Ed.), *The cognitive neurosciences* (3rd ed.). Cambridge, MA: MIT Press.

Wagner, A. D., Schacter, D. L., Rotte, M., Koutstaal, W., Maril, A., Dale, A. M., . . . Buckner, R. L. (1998). Building memories: Remembering and forgetting of verbal experiences as predicted by brain activity. *Science, 281,* 1188–1191.

Wai, J., Lubinski, D., & Benbow, C. P. (2009). Spatial ability for STEM domains: Aligning over 50 years of cumulative psychological knowledge solidifies its importance. *Journal of Educational Psychology, 101*(4), 817.

Walsh, M. M., & Anderson, J. R. (2011). Modulation of the feedback-related negativity by instruction and experience. *Proceedings of the National Academy of Science, USA, 108*(47), 19048–19053.

Walsh, M. M., & Anderson, J. R. (2012). Learning from experience: Event-related potential correlates of reward processing, neural adaptation, and behavioral choice. *Neuroscience and Biobehavioral Reviews, 36,* 1870–1884.

Wanner, H. E. (1968). *On remembering, forgetting, and understanding sentences: A study of the deep structure hypothesis.* Unpublished doctoral dissertation, Harvard University, Cambridge, MA.

Ward, A. F., Duke, K., Gneezy, A., & Bos, M. W. (2017). Brain drain: The mere presence of one's own smartphone reduces available cognitive capacity. *Journal of the Association for Consumer Research, 2*(2), 140–154

Ward, E. J., & Scholl, B. J. (2015). Inattentional blindness reflects limitations on perception, not memory: Evidence from repeated failures of awareness. *Psychonomic Bulletin & Review, 22*(3), 722–727.

Warren, R. M. (1970). Perceptual restorations of missing speech sounds. *Science, 167,* 392–393.

Warren, R. M., & Warren, R. P. (1970). Auditory illusions and confusions. *Scientific American, 223,* 30–36.

Warrington, E. K., & Shallice, T. (1984). Category specific semantic impairments. *Brain, 197,* 829–854.

Washburn, D. A. (1994). Stroop-like effects for monkeys and humans: Processing speed or strength of association? *Psychological Science, 5,* 375–379.

Wason, P. C. (1960). On the failure to eliminate hypotheses in a conceptual task. *Quarterly Journal of Experimental Psychology, 12,* 129–140.

Wason, P. C. (1968). On the failure to eliminate hypotheses—A second look. In P. C. Wason & P. N. Johnson-Laird (Eds.), *Thinking and reasoning* (pp. 165–174). Baltimore, MD: Penguin.

Wason, P. C., & Reich, S. S. (1979). A verbal illusion. *Quarterly Journal of Experimental Psychology, 31,* 591–597.

Watkins, M. J., & Tulving, E. (1975). Episodic memory: When recognition fails. *Journal of Experimental Psychology: General, 104,* 5–29.

Watson, J. (1930). *Behaviorism.* New York, NY: W. W. Norton.

Waugh, N. C., & Norman, D. A. (1965). Primary memory. *Psychological Review, 72,* 89–104.

Wearing, D. (2011). *Forever today: A memoir of love and amnesia.* London, UK: Transworld Digital.

Weber, E., Böckenholt, U., Hilton, D., & Wallace, B. (1993). Determinants of diagnostic hypothesis generation: Effects of information, base rates and experience. *Journal of Experimental Psychology: Learning, Memory, and Cognition, 19,* 1151–1164.

Weber-Fox, C., & Neville, H. J. (1996). Maturational constraints on functional specializations for language processing: ERP and behavioral evidence in bilingual speakers. *Journal of Cognitive Neuroscience, 8,* 231–256.

Weidenfeld, A., Oberauer, K., & Hörnig, R. (2005). Causal and noncausal conditionals: An integrated model of interpretation and reasoning. *Quarterly Journal of Experimental Psychology Section A, 58*(8), 1479–1513.

Weisberg, R. W. (1986). *Creativity: Genius and other myths.* New York, NY: W. H. Freeman.

Weiser, M., & Shertz, J. (1983). Programming problem representation in novice and expert programmers. *International Journal of Man-Machine Studies, 19,* 391–398.

Weissman, D. H., Roberts, K. C., Visscher, K. M., & Woldorff, M. G. (2006). The neural bases of momentary lapses in attention. *Nature Neuroscience, 9*(7), 971–978.

Wells, G. L., Memon, A., & Penrod, S. D. (2006). Eyewitness evidence: Improving its probative value. *Psychological Science in the Public Interest, 7,* 45–75.

Wendelken, C., O'Hare, E. D., Whitaker, K. J., Ferrer, E., & Bunge, S. A. (2011). Increased functional selectivity over development in rostrolateral prefrontal cortex. *Journal of Neuroscience, 31,* 17260–17268.

Werker, J. F., & Tees, R. C. (1999). Experiential influences on infant speech processing: Toward a new synthesis. *Annual Review of Psychology, 50,* 509–535.

Wertheimer, M. (1932). Experimentelle Studien über das Sehen von Beuegung. *Zeitschrift für Psychologie, 61,* 161–265. (Original work published in 1912)

Westermann, G., & Mareschal, D. (2014). From perceptual to language-mediated categorization. *Philosophical Transactions of the Royal Society of London B: Biological Sciences, 369*(1634), 20120391.

Wheeler, D. D. (1970). Processes in word recognition. *Cognitive Psychology, 1,* 59–85.

Whitaker, C. F. (1990). [Letter]. Ask Marilyn column. *Parade Magazine,* 16.

Whitaker, K. J., Vendetti, M. S., Wendelken, C., & Bunge, S. A. (2018). Neuroscientific insights into the development of analogical reasoning. *Developmental Science, 21*(2), e12531.

Whorf, B. L. (1956). *Language, thought, and reality.* Cambridge, MA: MIT Press.

Wickelgren, W. A. (1975). Alcoholic intoxication and memory storage dynamics. *Memory & Cognition, 3,* 385–389.

Wikman, A. S., Nieminen, T., & Summala, H. (1998). Driving experience and time-sharing during in-car tasks on roads of different width. *Ergonomics, 41,* 358–372.

Williams, J. J., & Lombrozo, T. (2013). Explanation and prior knowledge interact to guide learning. *Cognitive Psychology, 66*(1), 55–84.

Windes, J. D. (1968). Reaction time for numerical coding and naming numerals. *Journal of Experimental Psychology, 78,* 318–322.

Winston, P. H. (1970). *Learning structural descriptions from examples* (Tech. Rep. No. 231). Cambridge, MA: MIT, AI Laboratory.

Wixted, J. T., & Ebbesen, E. B. (1991). On the form of forgetting. *Psychological Science, 2,* 409–415.

Wixted, J. T., Mickes, L., & Fisher, R. P. (2018). Rethinking the reliability of eyewitness memory. *Perspectives on Psychological Science, 13*(3), 324–335.

Wixted, J. T., & Wells, G. L. (2017). The relationship between eyewitness confidence and identification accuracy: A new synthesis. *Psychological Science in the Public Interest, 18*(1), 10–65.

Woldorff, M. G., Gallen, C. C., Hampson, S. A., Hillyard, S. A., Pantev, C., Sobel, D., & Bloom, F. E. (1993). Modulation of early sensory processing in human auditory cortex during auditory selective attention. *Proceedings of the National Academy of Sciences USA, 90,* 8722–8726.

Wolfe, J. M. (1994). Guided search 2.0: A revised model of visual search. *Psychonomic Bulletin and Review, 1,* 202–238.

Wolfe, J. M. (1999). Inattentional amnesia. In V. Coltheart (Ed.), *Fleeting memories: Cognition of brief visual stimuli* (pp. 71–94). Cambridge, MA: MIT Press.

Womack, J. M., & McNamara, C. L. (2017). Cell phone use and its effects on undergraduate academic performance. *The Kennesaw Journal of Undergraduate Research, 5*(1), 3.

Woodrow, H. (1927). The effect of the type of training upon transference. *Journal of Educational Psychology, 18,* 159–172.

Woodworth, R. S., & Sells, S. B. (1935). An atmospheric effect in formal syllogistic reasoning. *Journal of Experimental Psychology, 18,* 451–460.

Wynn, K. (1992). Addition and subtraction by human infants. *Nature, 358,* 749–750.

Yamins, D. L., Hong, H., Cadieu, C. F., Solomon, E. A., Seibert, D., & DiCarlo, J. J. (2014). Performance-optimized hierarchical models predict neural responses in higher visual cortex. *Proceedings of the National Academy of Sciences, 111*(23), 8619–8624.

Yim, H., Garrett, P. M., Baker, M., & Dennis, S. J. (2018). Examining the independence of scales in episodic memory using experience sampling data. In Kalish, C., Rau, M., Zhu, J., & Rogers, T. T. (Eds.), *Proceedings of the 40th Annual Conference of the Cognitive Science Society* (pp. 2726–2731). Austin, TX: Cognitive Science Society.

Yin, R. K. (1969). Looking at upside-down faces. *Journal of Experimental Psychology, 81,* 141–145.

Zaehle, T., Jordan, K., Wüstenberg, T., Baudewig, J., Dechent, P., & Mast, F. W. (2007). The neural basis of the egocentric and allocentric spatial frame of reference. *Brain Research, 1137,* 92–103.

Zatorre, R. J., Mondor, T. A., & Evans, A. C. (1999). Auditory attention to space and frequency activates similar cerebral systems. *Neuroimage, 10,* 544–554.

Žebec, M. S., Demetriou, A., & Kotrla-Topić, M. (2015). Changing expressions of general intelligence in development: a 2-wave longitudinal study from 7 to 18 years of age. *Intelligence, 49,* 94–109.

Zorzi, M., Priftis, K., Meneghello, F., Marenzi, R., & Umiltà, C. (2006). The spatial representation of numerical and non-numerical sequences: evidence from neglect. *Neuropsychologia, 44*(7), 1061–1067.

Zwaan, R. A. (1996). Processing narrative time shifts. *Journal of Experimental Psychology: Learning, Memory, and Cognition, 22*(5), 1196.

Zwaan, R. A., & Radvansky, G. A. (1998). Situation models in language comprehension and memory. *Psychological Bulletin, 123*(2), 162.

Name Index

Subject Index

Note: Boldface page numbers indicate where key terms are called out.